St. Louis Community College

Forest Park
Florissant Valley
Meramec

Instructional Resources
St. Louis, Missouri

Working with Young Children

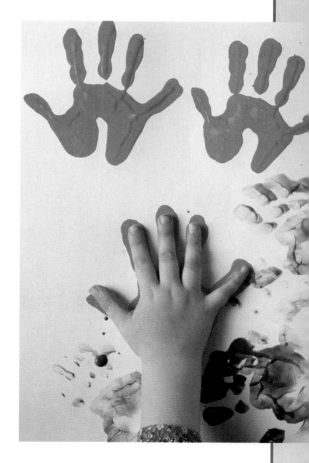

Dr. Judy Herr

Associate Dean, College of Human Development
University of Wisconsin—Stout
Menomonie, Wisconsin

Publisher
The Goodheart-Willcox Company, Inc.
Tinley Park, Illinois

Copyright 1998

by

The Goodheart-Willcox Company, Inc.

Previous Editions Copyright 1994, 1990

All rights reserved. No part of this book may be reproduced,
stored in a retrieval system, or transmitted in any form or by
any means, electronic, mechanical, photocopying, recording,
or otherwise, without the prior written permission of The
Goodheart-Willcox Company, Inc. Manufactured in the United
States of America.

Library of Congress Catalog Card Number 97-8351
International Standard Book Number 1-56637-387-5

1 2 3 4 5 6 7 8 9 10   98   01 00 99 98 97

Library of Congress Cataloging-in-Publication Data

Herr, Judy.
    Working with young children / Judy Herr.
        p.   cm.
    Includes index.
    ISBN 1-56637-387-5
    1. Child care services--United States. 2. Child care workers--
United States. 3. Early childhood education--United States.
I. Title.
HQ778.7.U6H47   1998
305.23'07--dc21   97-8351
                                                          CIP

Cover photo: Charles Thatcher/Tony Stone Images©

Introduction

Working with Young Children is designed to help you prepare for a career in child care. It teaches practical ways to guide children through a variety of daily experiences in safe, educational ways.

Success in working with children begins by understanding children. This book starts with an overview of the physical, intellectual, social, and emotional characteristics of young children. Using this information will help you plan for and react to children with confidence that your actions are developmentally appropriate.

Once you understand children, you are ready to develop and build your guidance skills. This text teaches you practical techniques for guiding children as you establish rules and handle daily routines. It also gives helpful suggestions for dealing with guidance problems.

An important part of child care involves creating a safe, healthy learning environment. As you read this text, you will learn techniques for keeping children safe, healthy, and nourished. In addition, you will learn to provide experiences that build children's enthusiasm for learning.

Working with Young Children prepares you for other important aspects of child care. These include planning developmentally appropriate curriculum and developing strategies for involving parents in child care programs. The book also prepares you to handle special concerns related to infants, toddlers, and children with special needs. Finally, the book prepares you to launch a career in child care, helping you explore the types of programs and refine your job hunting skills.

About the Author

The quality of this textbook reflects Judy Herr's intense dedication to early childhood education, with over 24 years of experience in the field. Judy previously supervised and administered seven children's programs at the University of Wisconsin-Stout, where she is currently Associate Dean of the College of Human Development. In addition, she serves as the program director for early childhood education.

Judy has published several books, manuals, and articles on early childhood education. Her articles have been printed in such noted journals as *Young Children, Journal of Family and Consumer Sciences, Early Childhood News,* and *Texas Child Care Quarterly.*

Judy has been a guest speaker at local, regional, national, and international conferences. She is active in several professional associations including the National Association for the Education of Young Children and the National Association of Early Childhood Teacher Educators. Judy has received many awards, including the Shirley Dean Award for Distinguished Service to the Midwestern Association for the Education of Young Children. Recently, Judy participated in the prestigious Management Development Program at Harvard University.

Contents

Part 4 Learning Experiences for Children

Part 5 Other People You Will Meet

Part 1

The Children and You

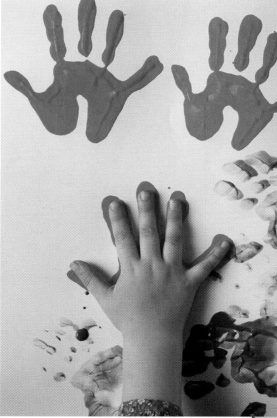

Who you are and what you know affects your ability to work with young children. In this part, you will explore current career opportunities in the early childhood field. You will also examine the responsibilities and characteristics of successful early childhood teachers. Various types of early childhood programs will be described.

This part will help you understand the characteristics of children at different ages. It will give you an overview of their physical, cognitive, social, and emotional development. You will learn how to change your teaching skills to fit the developmental needs and interests of children at different ages.

One of the best ways to learn about children is to observe them. Techniques for objectively observing and recording children's behavior will be described in this part.

Working with young children is challenging, but rewarding.
Do you have the characteristics needed to have
a successful career in child care?

Chapter 1

You: Working with Young Children

After studying this chapter, you will be able to

- explain how social and economic changes will increase the need for child care services.
- describe career opportunities in the early childhood field.
- describe the CDA Credential.
- list responsibilities of the early childhood teacher.
- explain how certain personal characteristics can help early childhood teachers care for and educate young children.

Terms to Know

early childhood

nanny

au pair

licensing specialist

entrepreneur

Child Development Associate (CDA) Credential

Mary takes care of infants, 1-1. Suzie, who has been a preschool teacher for two years, has taken a position as a center director. Her friend Marko is the parent coordinator in a local Head Start center, while Tom, who was another classmate, is a parent educator. Two other classmates,

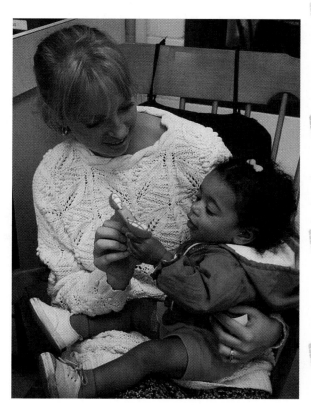

1-1 Taking care of infants is one of many job opportunities for people who study early childhood.

Sung Jee and Sally, recently opened a children's clothing store. Each of these individuals studied early childhood. These are just a few of the many challenging and rewarding career opportunities within the early childhood field.

Already you may be asking yourself, "What is early childhood?" **Early childhood** covers the period from birth up to nine years of age. During this period of time, growth is very rapid. The child develops a sense of self as well as language, social, problem-solving, and motor skills. These accomplishments are an important foundation for later learning.

People who are considering careers in the field of early childhood often have at least three main questions. First, they want to know whether there will be a need for people trained in early childhood. They also want to know about the job responsibilities of early childhood educators. In addition, they ask about the personal characteristics needed to be successful in this field.

This chapter reviews social and economic changes that will continue to create a need for child care teachers. It also gives an overview of teachers' responsibilities and characteristics of successful teachers.

Social and Economic Changes

The social and economic changes in society will continue to create a need for more child care services. These changes occur in the family, employers' attitudes, educators' attitudes, and in job opportunities.

Changes in Families

Families no longer fit the traditional model—a mother as homemaker and a father as breadwinner. The traditional family structure exists only in a small percentage of families. An even smaller percentage is expected in the future. Several trends support this prediction.

- Women are becoming more highly educated.
- Married couples are having fewer children.
- Women with preschool children are returning to the labor force in increasing numbers. Today it is estimated 14.6 million preschool children have work-

ing mothers. This represents a growth of 88 percent over the past 18 years.
- Women are working for economic reasons.
- Many working women are widowed, divorced, single, separated, or married to men earning a salary that is too low to support the family.

The number of single parents is continuing to rise. In the last decade alone, they have doubled in number. Child care services are needed by many of these families.

In the next decade, the under-five population is expected to increase. Consequently, there will be an increasing need for early childhood teachers.

Changes in Employers' Attitudes

Corporate or employer-sponsored child care is expected to grow. This growth will present many employment opportunities for early childhood professionals. The United States Chamber of Commerce has reported that many companies are exploring various forms of child care assistance as optional employee benefits.

By providing some type of child care benefit, companies have reported tangible payoffs. Included are positive effects on recruitment, morale, and productivity. Turnover and absenteeism are reduced. Other positive results are better public relations, tax benefits, ease of scheduling, and improved quality of the workforce.

In addition to the on-site model of child care, other means of providing child care assistance are being offered. Included may be a referral service for locating quality child care. Lists of child care providers, maps, and brochures may be provided to parents. This type of service respects the employee's right to choose a suitable arrangement.

Some corporations may even hire early childhood specialists to provide sick child care. This model provides short-term home health care for sick children. The average child experiences ten days of illness each year. As a result, many parents are forced to stay home from work. This model has been designed to help reduce the parents' stress, guilt, and worry that occur when inappropriate child care is provided. See 1-2.

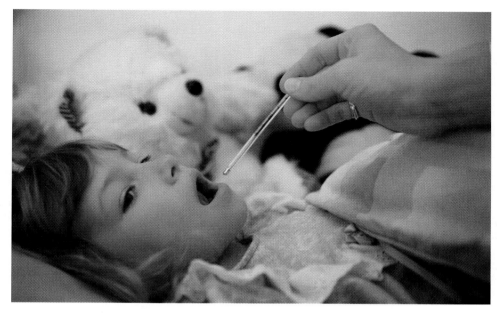

1-2 Parents can concentrate on their work when they feel sure that their sick children are getting proper care.

Intergenerational care is another service being provided by some corporations. This model is often called dependent care. It provides services for the elderly as well as young children.

Changes in Education Attitudes

Working parents are becoming more aware of their children's developmental needs. They are looking for quality environments that will promote their children's growth and development. As a result, many of today's working parents are selecting licensed child care centers. This represents a change. In the 1960's, just one of 20 children of working parents were attending a child care center. Today, nearly one in three children of working parents are attending a child care center.

Full-day kindergartens are increasing in numbers. There is a continuing movement toward full-day kindergartens for five-year-olds throughout the nation. This, in turn, will create a need for more certified teachers and aides. Some school districts are introducing kindergarten programs for four-year-old children, as well as preschool programs for special needs children.

Child care advocates are working toward greater allocation of public educational resources for early childhood. Their purpose is to remedy some current problems in education for young children. Many four-year-olds already attend a preschool program. They may be enrolled in a government subsidized program, such as Head Start, for low income families. They may also be enrolled in programs supported by middle- and upper-class families.

Job Opportunities in Early Childhood

Never have there been more job opportunities in early childhood. Early childhood programs occur in a wide variety of settings. Schools, homes, centers, businesses, parks, and churches are examples. As a result, you, as an early childhood specialist, may find yourself choosing from among a number of job alternatives. Nannies, au pairs, kindergarten teachers, child care teachers and directors, and licensing specialists all will be needed. In addition, you may find other possibilities in business settings. See 1-3.

Job Possibilities	
• Aide in the public school system • Au Pair • Author of children's books • Beautician for children • Children's art instructor • Children's book salesperson • Children's clothing designer • Children's clothing salesperson • Children's dance instructor • Children's furniture salesperson • Children's librarian • Children's photographer • Children's shoe salesperson • Children's ski instructor • Children's swimming instructor • Children's toy designer • Director of preschool or Head Start center	• Editor of children's magazines • Entertainer for parties • Family child care provider • Foster parent • Head Start teacher • Licensing specialist • Nanny • Parent educator • Preschool teacher • Recreation director • Religious education director • Referral specialist for corporate child care • School-age child care instructor • School supply salesperson • Sick child care specialist for corporate child care • Toy salesperson

1-3 A variety of job opportunities exist in the field of early childhood.

Nannies and Au Pairs

There is currently a great demand for trained nannies and au pairs. A **nanny** provides care in a child's home. Depending on the parents' needs, some nannies may live in the child's home. They receive meals and housing as part of their wages. Other nannies have their own homes or apartments, depending on the parents' needs.

The dual-career family has contributed to the increasing demand for nannies. One employment service reported that it received over 50 requests for nannies per day. Due to a lack of trained personnel, the placement officers were able to place only 50 nannies in an entire year. Since many nannies have come from other countries, tighter immigration controls have decreased the supply of nannies in the United States. This has created new opportunities for nannies who are trained in the United States.

An **au pair** (oh pare) is a person from a foreign country who lives with a family and performs tasks similar to a nanny. In exchange for room, board, and transportation, the au pair provides child care and may do some housework.

Kindergarten Teachers

Although kindergarten attendance is not required in all states, the opportunity is provided.

Thus kindergarten teachers are needed in public as well as private schools. Even many child care centers hire kindergarten teachers. These centers provide an all-day kindergarten program for children of working parents.

Child Care Teachers and Directors

With the number of children attending child care centers growing, the need for educated, qualified professionals is also growing. By 2005, the U.S. Bureau of Labor Statistics is predicting there will be 611,000 job openings for early childhood educators. Usually the teacher is responsible for planning curriculum and teaching children. The director's responsibilities are broader. Marketing the program, recruiting children, hiring and supervising staff, and managing the budget are all included. Building maintenance is also the responsibility of the director in some centers.

Family Child Care Home

Family child care homes provide child care for children ranging in age from six weeks to 12 years. This type of care allows a child care provider to operate a program within his or her own home. Parents may be attracted to this type of program because of the longer hours of operation and homelike atmosphere. Likewise, child care providers may prefer this arrangement because they can also care for their own children.

Licensing Specialists

Due to the rapid increase in child care centers, the number of licensing positions are expanding. The **licensing specialist** is usually employed by the state. The role of this person is to protect and promote the health, safety, and welfare of children attending the center.

Licensing specialists generally make regularly scheduled on-site visits to assigned centers. During each visit, the licensing specialist observes to see that the center is following state licensing guidelines. They may check the number of children in the center, the adult-child ratio, the size of the facility, the food service, and the curriculum provided. Building safety, health practices, educational preparation of staff, and physical space are monitored, also.

Other Job Opportunities

Many other job opportunities exist for you as an early childhood specialist. With this background, you are prepared to hold a variety of positions. You may choose a business-related career. You may open a children's toy or clothing store. Because they understand curriculum needs, some early childhood teachers sell school supplies for book and stationery companies. Others work as authors of children's books or as aides in the public school system.

You may start a company related to child care. An **entrepreneur** is a person who starts his or her own business. For example, in a larger city you could start a company that specializes in providing substitute staff for child care centers. When a center needs personnel to cover for a staff member who is on vacation, at a conference, or ill, the administrator could contact you. Your responsibility would be to furnish a substitute teacher, cook, janitor, or secretary.

The job responsibilities of a parent educator may also appeal to you. In this position, you would work with parents to help them learn parenting skills, 1-4. You might work days, evenings, or weekends. You could design written materials or produce visuals to help parents

1-4 Parent educators present information that will help parents improve their child care skills.

better understand their roles and the nature of young children. Since education is no longer a place but a process, you may even produce materials to be shared on the World Wide Web.

Knowledge of child growth and development is necessary for the community recreation leader. Children's furniture salespersons will also find a background in this field valuable. They can share children's growth rates and safety needs with parents while they select furniture for their children. Indeed, the demand for workers educated in early childhood exceeds the current supply.

Education and Training Needed to Work with Young Children

As you can see, there are many job opportunities for people who are interested in working with young children, or in related careers. What education and training is required for these jobs?

A few entry-level positions require little training or experience. For instance, a person with only a high school education might work as a teacher's aide or playground supervisor. A teacher's aide would assist the teacher, helping the children with their snacks or supervising their play activities.

Most child care jobs require that a person have additional training and education beyond high school. A first step for many is to obtain the **Child Development Associate (CDA) Credential.** Those who have this national credential have taken postsecondary courses in child care education and have demonstrated their ability to work with young children. The six CDA Competency Goals identify the skills needed by early childhood professionals. These goals are divided into 13 functional areas, which describe major tasks caregivers must accomplish to satisfy the competency goals. To be eligible for this credential, a person must be eighteen years of age and have a high school diploma. In addition, the candidate must have a minimum number of hours of child care experience and have taken courses in child care education.

Most of the jobs described in this chapter require at least a two-year associate's degree in child development or a related area. Some states are requiring that early childhood teachers have a CDA Credential to be licensed. The credential is not required, however, if the teacher has an associate or bachelor's degree in Early Childhood Education, Child Development, or a closely related field. A bachelor's degree usually requires a minimum of four years of college. Directors of child care programs generally need a bachelor's degree.

Each state establishes its own qualifications for staff who work in licensed child care centers. There is no uniform standard established by the federal government. The qualifications will depend upon the job you are seeking and the state in which you plan to work. It is important that you know the minimum qualifications required in your state. You can contact the local agency that licenses child care centers to find out what those standards are.

The Teacher's Responsibilities

Many employment opportunities exist in early childhood. The majority, however, will be as teachers or teacher's aides. These professionals are needed for child care centers, preschools, Head Start programs, and in early childhood programs in public and private schools. Because of this need, the contents of this book will focus on the knowledge and skills needed for teaching young children.

Your responsibilities as an early childhood teacher will be complex and demanding. You will have both direct and indirect influences on children. Directly, you will interact with children. Indirectly, you will influence children through the arrangement of space and activities. As an early childhood teacher, you will serve a dual role. Often you will play both the teacher and parent-educator role. Usually, the younger the child, the more support you need to provide to the parent in the transition from home to center. The parent may also seek advice on such aspects of child development as toilet training, biting, and thumbsucking.

You will also need to be a friend, colleague, counselor, janitor, nurse, decorator, safety expert, and even a cook on some days. Not all of your tasks will be pleasant. Sometimes your work may be unpleasant, such as changing messy diapers and cleaning up after a sick child. Noses have to be wiped and messes, such as spilled milk, dumped paint, or a leaky sensory table, must be cleaned up.

Challenging and rewarding are two words that can best describe the responsibilities of an early childhood teacher. You will be challenged planning developmentally appropriate curriculum, designing class materials, and coping with behavior problems in the classroom. At times you may become discouraged, particularly when behavioral changes are slow. Once the changes occur, however, the rewards are well worth the time and effort. Early childhood teachers usually feel useful, needed, and important, 1-5. Working with young children is an act of hope for a better future. Equally important, teachers usually feel loved by the children. For these reasons, most early childhood teachers thoroughly enjoy their profession.

To Know How Children Grow and Develop

Teachers need to know what children are like. Regardless of your position, you will need

1-5 Love from children helps make teaching in early childhood a rewarding career.

a thorough understanding of child growth and development. You will need to understand the abilities and interests of children at particular ages. This understanding will help you prepare inviting and developmentally appropriate environments for young children. Likewise, it will help you design educational experiences that promote children's growth in knowledge, skills, and self-confidence. Moreover, knowing the principles of child development will assist you in developing curriculum that is challenging and interesting without being difficult or discouraging.

Understanding children's behavior will help you work effectively with individuals and groups of children. You will learn that children behave the way they do because their behavior brings them pleasure. That is, what happens to the child after he acts determines whether this behavior will be continued. A child who throws a temper tantrum to get a second turn on a bike (and gets a second turn) will usually repeat this behavior. Thus, you teach children to behave the way they do. Most of what they learn, they will learn from other people and you.

Working with young children, you will notice differences in behavior. Children can learn

to be friendly, and they can learn to be aggressive. As a teacher, you will be responsible for teaching children to interact positively. Thus, you will teach them to be cooperative and skillful in getting along with others. To do this, you will need to learn and use developmentally appropriate guidance and group management techniques.

To Plan a Developmentally Appropriate Curriculum

Teachers are responsible for planning a developmentally appropriate curriculum. Quality programs focus on the "whole child." Physical, social, cognitive, and emotional development are all emphasized. Such programs can provide long-term, positive differences in the lives of young children.

Physical development is stressed in a quality early childhood curriculum. Young children develop a variety of skills through physical experiences that are a foundation for later learning. Coordination, stamina, flexibility, strength, and sensory awareness are all included. See 1-6.

1-6 Curriculum should include activities that help improve muscle strength and coordination.

Social development is another important aspect of a quality curriculum. Young children must learn to interact positively with other children and adults. Likewise, they need to learn to adapt to the expectations that are established in the center.

Young children need to acquire information to be able to understand and function in the world. As a result, cognitive development is an important area of the child's development. Thus, problem solving through hands-on activities will be an important part of the children's learning.

Emotional development is also an important element of a developmentally appropriate curriculum. Young children need to understand themselves. Feelings need to be understood in order to develop self-awareness and self-knowledge. Children need help in learning to recognize, label, and accept their feelings. They need to learn to assert their rights in culturally accepted ways without hurting others.

Your curriculum will need to be designed for the children. A broad knowledge of all the curriculum areas outlined in this book is important. You will find that an understanding of science, math, music, social studies, art, dramatic play, and storytelling will influence what you do with children.

To Prepare the Environment

A large part of the teaching process involves preparing an inviting and stimulating learning environment. Learning is an active process whereby children gain knowledge and develop new skills. The environment that you provide must encourage children to independently experiment, explore, and manipulate, 1-7. Interaction with materials is an important learning vehicle.

As a teacher, you will need to provide a variety of materials. These materials will encourage children to engage in positive social activities. They also will promote physical, social, cognitive, and emotional development. Lack of variety or quantity can lead to lags in development. For instance, if there are not enough interesting materials, children may fight over the few that they enjoy. Chapters have been included in this book to teach you how to arrange space and select toys, equipment, and supplies.

1-7 It is up to you as a teacher to make learning an active process.

To Communicate Effectively

To be an effective teacher, you need to have good communication skills. These skills are important for ease in expressing ideas and gaining trust with children, their families, and your peers. Not only will you need to relate to the children, but you will also need to relate to their parents. Most preschool child care teachers have daily contact with the children's parents or guardians. Thus, information is usually exchanged on a continuous basis. Early childhood teachers must also be able to form meaningful relationships with their colleagues. To provide a quality educational program for young children, all staff must work cooperatively. This requires open communication with others.

To Get Along with Coworkers

An important part of any job is getting along with your coworkers. Staff in early childhood programs need to work as a team, 1-8. To be a team member, you will need to help make your coworkers feel important. Everyone enjoys feeling important and valued.

To work well with a staff, you need to provide support to your coworkers through actions

1-8 When staff members take and give suggestions on curriculum, they are able to give children the best care possible.

and words. Empathize with them by recognizing and reflecting their feelings. Share ideas with them. Tell them when they have planned interesting activities. Praise them for meaningful interactions with the children. Furthermore, accept their style of caregiving.

To Manage Time Wisely

Rarely does an early childhood teacher have time to do everything he or she wants to do. Thus, time management skills are important. Time management skills help teachers work smarter, not harder. They help you organize your time, set priorities, and distinguish between important and urgent matters.

No matter what you accomplish, there is always more that could be done. You might want to make one more bulletin board, write a letter to a parent, or develop new materials. Time management skills will help you make choices and use your time wisely.

To Continue to Learn

Professional development is an ongoing process, 1-9. A teacher never finishes learning. In order to keep up with happenings in the field,

1-9 Reading is an important part of continuing education for early childhood teachers.

you need to be a committed, lifelong learner. Conferences, in-service training, course work, journals, study groups, and books all help teachers learn more about their field. In addition, participating in one or more professional organizations is essential to learning new developments in the field.

The National Association for the Education of Young Children was founded in 1926 to improve professional practice and preparation. With over 100,000 members, it is the primary organization for the early childhood field. This organization has state and local affiliates. Membership services include annual state and national conferences. The organization also develops and distributes a journal and other professional publications. Reading these materials will keep you informed of teaching trends, issues, research, legislation, upcoming conferences, and new publications including children's books.

Career advancement often requires experience and more education. After completing an associate degree in early childhood, many students enroll in bachelor's degree programs. After this, some continue in a graduate degree program.

Characteristics of Successful Teachers

Working with young children requires a special kind of person. As an early childhood teacher, you will need to build on your own strengths and develop your own style. Each teacher is different. Some teachers are outgoing and lively. Other teachers may be reserved and naturally quiet. Both styles can be effective. Simply copying the style of another teacher will not necessarily make you a successful teacher. You must develop a style that best suits your personality. When your style suits your personality, you will feel more comfortable working with children and adults. You will also find more enjoyment in your profession.

Although teachers may use very different styles, successful teachers tend to have some common characteristics. See 1-10. These traits help teachers deal effectively with the day-to-day situations that are naturally part of their work.

Characteristics of a Successful Teacher

- Has a positive attitude.
- Is fond of children.
- Relates easily and spontaneously to others.
- Is a patient, confident, and caring individual.
- Is a positive, happy individual.
- Is dependable and reliable.
- Makes friends easily.
- Possesses a sense of humor.
- Is flexible and adapts well to the requirements of others.
- Is compassionate, accepting children's strong emotions such as anger, love, and wonder.
- Takes initiative in the classroom.
- Has knowledge in curriculum, child growth and development, and child guidance.
- Keeps abreast of changes in the field by reading, attending conferences, seminars, and courses.
- Desires continuous learning.
- Enjoys challenge and problem solving.
- Can juggle several activities at one time.
- Feels rewarded by progress even if it is minimal.
- Provides interesting materials.

1-10 Teachers who have these characteristics tend to have high success in teaching and caring for young children.

Fondness for Children

The most important trait of an early childhood teacher is fondness for children. The rapport established with each child will reflect the program's success. Every child needs to be understood and accepted. Each child's family background, interests, and desires also need to be respected.

As an early childhood teacher, you will need to notice and show love for each child with whom you work. You need to be kind, firm, and understanding with each child. These actions do not just affect how children feel about themselves. They show children how they should treat each other. As part of their social development, young children need to be taught that people and feelings are important.

Feeling loved, safe, and emotionally secure helps children develop intellectually and emotionally, 1-11. As you show children that they are important, children have confidence in themselves. They are more willing to try new activities.

Patience

Effective teachers are also patient, allowing children time to explore, solve problems, and create. Young children often need extra time to complete tasks. Children also need the opportunity to repeat tasks. Much of a child's learning occurs as the result of repetition.

Children are naturally curious and may constantly repeat simple questions. Children do not always remember everything they have been told. Repeating information and reminding children of rules may seem tedious at times. When these situations are handled patiently, however, teachers help children grow and learn while building their self-esteem.

Compassion

Compassionate teachers are able to accept others without prejudice. Being compassionate requires self-knowledge and self-acceptance. It involves accepting any emotion from others such as grief, joy, fear, love, or even hate.

A compassionate teacher does not simply observe a child's feelings. He or she takes part in the feelings of a child and reacts accordingly. The teacher is sensitive to both positive and negative feelings.

Teachers show compassion by praising and complimenting children for their successes. They also avoid actions that make children feel worthless, such as punishment and shaming.

1-11 Children who feel loved are more receptive to learning.

Compassionate teachers work to help children understand the feelings of other children and motivate children to respect each other.

Confidence

Having confidence in your abilities helps you relax in the classroom. Teachers who are relaxed and natural tend to be more successful with children. Children, especially the younger ones, can become easily excited. By remaining calm and self-assured, you will have a calming effect on the children.

Your confidence is affected by your ability to make sensible decisions. You need to feel sure that the choices you make are in the best interest of the children. For instance, when it is raining, children should not be taken outside. Children may not always understand such decisions. If you stand by them with confidence, children will accept them.

Sense of Humor

A sense of humor is helpful when working with children. Children enjoy adults who can laugh. Laughter helps children relax and feel content. When children see a teacher with a positive, cheerful attitude, they are more likely to be positive and cheerful. See 1-12.

Keeping a sense of humor also can make your work more enjoyable. Seeing the funny side of children can be a rewarding experience. Seeing the humor in situations can also help you cope with some of the daily stresses of teaching. Of course, you must be careful to laugh with, not at, children.

Commitment

In many ways, the job of an early childhood teacher is anything but easy. Demands on your energy will be high. You will be expected to be an expert in child development, child guidance, and curriculum. Parents will ask your advice on child rearing. Questions such as, When should I begin toilet training? or, What kinds of toys should two-year-olds have? are common.

You will find that meeting the demands of this field requires a serious commitment. To keep up with current developments in the field, you must constantly study. This can be accomplished through reading books and attending seminars, classes, and conferences. Discussions with other teachers are also helpful.

Preparing for daily teaching is also time consuming. To be a successful teacher, you must be prepared. You, as a teacher, must fully understand the purpose of each activity. You also need to be sure that the activities planned for the day

1-12 A teacher who smiles and laughs encourages children to smile and laugh.

1-13 Spending the time needed to plan an effective curriculum takes a strong commitment from a teacher.

address all areas of a child's development. You must also balance the pace of activities so that children are not constantly active or quiet. Providing a developmentally appropriate curriculum that meets children's needs and is inviting takes time and careful thought, 1-13.

Personal Desire

Knowing that you really want to teach young children is important to your success. Although you may have doubts, you need to feel that working with young children is rewarding for you. Hearing children make comments, such as I love you or you're pretty, should boost your self-esteem. Otherwise, you will not feel enthusiastic enough about your work to do a good job.

Questioning a career choice is not unusual. You will discover that even experienced teachers have days when they wonder why they chose this career. These questions are healthy. If they help you determine that you do belong in early childhood education, you will feel more confident and committed to your career choice.

Only you can answer the question, Is teaching really for me? You will need to examine carefully your own interests, feelings, and satisfactions. See 1-14. Studying the chapters in this book can help you. Each chapter contains important concepts. Explore possibilities for applying these concepts to a group of young children.

Working with children will increase your insights. However, provide yourself sufficient time. Until you understand how children grow and develop, how to guide them, and how to develop appropriate curriculum, you might not feel much self-satisfaction. Given time, however, you are bound to discover the real joys and rewards of working with young children.

A Letter to a New Teacher

Dear Teacher:

As you begin working with young children, you will be meeting new challenges and finding new answers. This process will continue throughout your teaching career. Like friendship, you will find being a good teacher is a matter of caring for yourself, the children you teach, their families, and your colleagues.

There will be many exciting and fulfilling days. The children will be experiencing many new discoveries. Many times over they may tell you that you are beautiful or you have a pretty voice.

You will also have discouraging days. Teaching is not an easy job. It is physically and mentally exhausting. At times, the costs may seem to exceed the rewards. Luckily, the majority of the time you will find that teaching is rewarding and personally satisfying.

When you leave the center at night, often you will reflect on the day's happenings. Replaying in your mind something a child said or did is not uncommon. Thinking about your responses is a method of preparing for the next time.

Remember that you will only get out of a career what you invest in it. You must be willing to work overtime if needed and to seek new answers. You must also take advantage of opportunities to improve professionally for the benefit of the children and their families.

Try learning as much as you can about child development, child guidance, and curriculum. Talking to your colleagues, reading professional journals, and attending conferences are several methods. Taking additional course work and obtaining advanced degrees will also help strengthen your understanding of young children and improve your competence. Chances are, if you are actively involved, you will never lose your love of teaching.

1-14 Deciding whether you want to be an early childhood teacher is an important step in having a successful career.

Summary

Many social and economic changes are creating new opportunities in child care. With fewer traditional families and more dual-career families, the demand for quality child care services is growing. Employers are becoming more willing to offer child care benefits for their employees. Child care advocates are working to expand the availability of early childhood programs. New job opportunities are being created and expanded. Most jobs in child care require a CDA Credential, a two-year associate's degree, or a bachelor's degree. Qualifications vary from state to state.

Most employment opportunities in early childhood are as teachers or assistant teachers. The main focus of this book is to prepare you for a career as an early childhood teacher.

Teachers have many important responsibilities. They must understand principles of child growth and development. Teachers develop curriculum and create classroom environments that meet children's developmental needs. They need to communicate effectively and get along with their coworkers. Teachers must manage their time wisely. They need to constantly update and expand their knowledge in the early childhood field.

A successful teacher develops a style that works well for him or her. However, most successful teachers have many traits in common. These teachers are fond of children, patient, and compassionate. They have confidence in their abilities and know how to keep a sense of humor. They are committed to teaching young children. They have a strong desire to be with and guide children. Successful teachers find their work a rewarding and joyous experience. Viewing professional development as an on-going process, they take advantage of opportunities to improve their professional growth.

Review and Reflect

1. _____ covers the period from birth up to nine years of age.

2. True or false. Social and economic changes have created a need for more child care services.

3. Why do companies provide child care?

4. _____ or _____ provide care for children in parents' homes.

5. A _____ is responsible for enforcing state child care rules and regulations.

6. Give two job opportunities in which education in early childhood is helpful. Explain how a background in early childhood is helpful in those jobs.

7. Describe the CDA Credential.

8. How does the environment affect a child's development?

9. In teaching, _____ skills are needed to work smarter, not harder.

10. What is the name of the primary professional organization for teachers of young children?

11. True or false. People who are naturally quiet and reserved cannot be effective early childhood teachers.

12. Give two common characteristics of successful early childhood teachers and explain why these characteristics are helpful.

Apply and Explore

1. Look through the want-ad section of a newspaper. Write down jobs listed in which early childhood training would be helpful.

2. Take a survey of early childhood teachers. Ask them to share the advantages and disadvantages of teaching. Share your findings with the class.

3. Review the qualities of a successful teacher given in chart 1-10. Make a list of qualities from the chart that you possess.

4. Design a bulletin board displaying characteristics of successful teachers.

5. Survey parents of young children to find out what qualities they value in teachers.

6. Write a one-page paper on why you want to teach children.

Chapter 2

Types of Early Childhood Programs

After studying this chapter, you will be able to

- list and describe the various types of early childhood programs available to parents and their children.

- explain the advantages and disadvantages of each type of program.

- name the three types of center sponsorship.

- explain steps a parent may take in choosing quality child care.

- list the components of center accreditation.

Terms to Know

family child care

custodial care

child care centers

Montessori approach

Head Start

school-age child care programs

checking-in services

parent cooperatives

laboratory schools

accredited

Why should children attend early childhood programs? Many parents cite one or two reasons for placing their children in these learning programs.

Studies show that children develop quickly during the first five years. They grow cognitively, socially, emotionally, and physically. In order to take advantage of this growth period, many parents enroll their children in early childhood programs. In these programs, children can learn and take part in active learning activities that will advance their growth, 2-1.

2-1 A challenging environment can help children develop cognitively, emotionally, socially, and physically.

Many parents of young children are employed. These parents provide for their children's health and safety by enrolling them in programs. This arrangement allows children to learn and grow as they receive care.

Distinct differences exist among the many types of early childhood programs. Some provide flexible services for just part of the day. Others provide full-day care, including meals and a scheduled nap time. Some centers focus on children's physical and social growth while others focus on cognitive growth. Other differences are in terms of size, facilities, staff qualifications, parent involvement, ownership, and fees. Some centers operate for profit, while others are nonprofit.

Some types of programs are more common than others. However, all of them serve a very important purpose by meeting the needs of young children.

Family Child Care

The most common type of child care in the United States is called **family child care**. In this type of program, child care is provided in a private home. Most states require these homes be licensed. This, however, is rather difficult to enforce. Some caregivers are not aware of licensing. Others ignore licensing rules.

Program

Programs provided in family child care settings reflect state rules and the skills of the caregivers. The focus in some homes is on **custodial care**. With this type of care, the environment is kept safe and healthy for young children. Meals are usually provided.

In a home where the caregiver has received early childhood training, a developmental curriculum may be planned. This involves planning and equipping the environment to complement the children's developmental needs and interests. For instance, a curriculum for two-year-old children would focus on language and large motor development and social and emotional growth. Ample space would be needed for these children to move around. Developmentally appropriate

puzzles, storybooks, push and pull toys, large blocks, housekeeping equipment, and other toys would also be provided.

Child Care Centers

Facilities that offer full-day children's programs are often called **child care centers** or *day care centers*. This type of program provides a place for child care while parents and or guardians are at work or school. The focus of most child care centers is to provide care and education. The care is designed to meet the child's basic nutrition, health, and safety needs. The educational curriculum emphasizes the whole child including his or her social, emotional, cognitive, and physical needs, 2-2.

Most child care centers open early in the morning and remain open until six or seven o'clock in the evening. Some centers provide care for children 24 hours per day. For parents whose children need care during the evening or early morning hours, this service is most convenient.

2-2 Many parents rely on the skilled staff of child care centers to provide for the basic needs of their children.

Program

The program provided by a child care center depends upon the educational background and skills of the staff. State licensing rules also influence the program. Like family child care, some centers simply provide a safe environment.

Ideally, the program should provide for all developmental needs: physical, cognitive, social, and emotional. The focus should be on the whole child, along with a balance of activities.

Montessori Schools

In the early 1900s, Maria Montessori developed her own method of education. Montessori was the first woman in Italy to receive a degree in medicine. Early in her career, she was an assistant doctor at a clinic that served mentally retarded children.

While working with retarded children, Montessori developed her theory of education. This theory stated that children learn best by being active and doing. Montessori soon learned that these methods could also be used with normal children. This led to the development of a school in Rome's slum district.

Montessori's methods became known all over the world. Because of her success, she was asked to speak in the United States. After her visit, a group of people formed the first Montessori Society. Interest, however, declined for the next 40 years. Then, in the 1950s, there was a rebirth of the Montessori approach. Magazines and television helped make the Montessori method known.

Montessori Approach

In her first schools, Montessori stressed proper diet, cleanliness, and manners. Children also worked with equipment she designed. See 2-3. These materials were self-correcting and required little adult guidance. The materials were organized from simple to complex. As the children worked through the materials, they learned motor and sensory skills, number concepts, and writing skills.

Montessori believed in self-education. The primary goal of the **Montessori approach** was for children to "learn how to learn." This

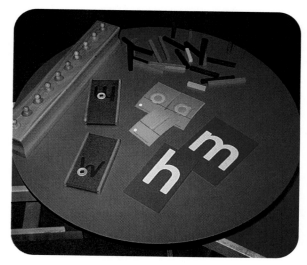

2-3 Materials used in a Montessori school are designed to help children learn with little adult guidance.

approach allowed the child to explore materials that were meant to instruct. Certain materials were given to the child by the teacher in a prescribed sequence. This sequence was related to the child's physical and mental development. Montessori felt that this approach would provide the child freedom within limits.

Independence is stressed in Montessori schools. Children must learn to care for themselves. Teachers provide little help. As a result, children learn to button, zip, tie, and put on coats and boots. These experiences are called *practical life experiences* in the Montessori curriculum.

The purpose of *sensory training* is to help children learn touch, sound, taste, and sight discrimination. One piece of equipment for this training is a set of sandpaper blocks that vary in texture. The children are told to rub their fingers across the blocks. Their goal is to correctly match blocks with like textures. Musical bells with varying tones are used in the same way. Based on tone, children match like tones.

Academics are also stressed in the Montessori program. However, before a child is introduced to these experiences, sensory training must be mastered. Then, to teach letter recognition, sandpaper letters are used. After the teacher introduces a letter, children are encouraged to trace the letter with their fingertips. Numbers are taught in the same manner. When a child demonstrates knowledge of and interest in letters, reading instruction may be started.

Head Start

During the 1960s, the federal government developed a program called Head Start. It is recognized as one of the most successful preschool and family support programs in the country. **Head Start** was designed primarily to meet the social, emotional, physical, and cognitive needs of four- and five-year-old children from low-income families. More recently, Head Start has added limited programs for infants and toddlers.

The first Head Start programs were offered for eight weeks during the summer months. They met with great success and have since been extended to full-year programs. Most of these programs provide half-day care.

Education

The curriculum in a Head Start program is designed to meet the needs of each child. Special considerations are given to cultural and ethnic backgrounds. One goal is to provide the child with a healthy self-concept that will lead to his or her future success in school.

A variety of learning experiences are designed to meet the children's needs. All four areas of development are stressed in these experiences. Staff and parents work as a team to plan curriculum and teach children.

Studies have shown that the Head Start program has been successful. On preschool achievement tests, Head Start children perform equal to or better than their peers. Once they enter school, these children are more likely to be successful.

Nutrition

Many children who take part in Head Start do not receive well-balanced meals at home. Nutrition then is a vital part of the program, 2-4. Federal rules require the center to provide at least one snack and one hot meal every day. Both breakfast and lunch are served in some programs. The goal of this program is to help the children make healthy food choices and develop good eating habits.

2-4 A well-organized, sanitary kitchen is an important link in providing sound nutrition for children.

Health

All children who attend a Head Start program are given a total health plan. Dental, medical, and mental health services are provided. Prior to enrollment, many of these children have never visited a dentist. Children who have not already received childhood immunizations are given them while they are enrolled.

Parental Involvement

Head Start recognizes the parent as the child's primary teacher. Therefore, parental involvement is vital to the program's success. Parents are encouraged to help recruit new children, assist in the center, and take part in policy meetings. Thus, Head Start parents are able to influence administrative decisions.

Kindergarten

In 1837, the first kindergarten was opened by Frederick Froebel in Germany. The kindergarten curriculum stressed play. Froebel believed that self-development took place through creative activities such as play. The children in this kindergarten, like many today, engaged in painting, stringing beads, blockbuilding, and clay modeling. The children also cared for pets, sang songs, and gardened.

The first American kindergarten was opened in Watertown, Wisconsin, in 1856. It was held in the home of Margerenthia Schurz. This mother and teacher had studied under Froebel. Mrs. Schurz first opened the kindergarten for her own children and four of their cousins.

Today, kindergartens are part of most public and many private school systems. They are usually restricted to children who are at least four years old. In the past, these programs usually lasted a half day. Today, however, there are more options.

Schedules

There are three basic scheduling patterns in kindergarten: half-day, full-day, and full-day/alternating day sessions. The half-day session usually runs from two and one-half to three and one-half hours per day. Full-day sessions run from six to eight hours per day. Full-day/alternating day programs vary. Some programs meet every other day. Others require children to attend on Tuesday and Thursday the first week, and on Monday and Friday the next week. Other alternating programs have children attend two full days and one-half day. To illustrate, one group may attend all day on Monday and Wednesday, plus on Friday morning. The other group might attend all day on Tuesday and Thursday, as well as Friday afternoon. For some children, these alternating schedules may be confusing. Studies show that children thrive on predictable schedules.

Goals

Goals for a kindergarten program permit variety. Basic objectives of most kindergarten programs include

- respect for the contributions, property, and rights of other children.
- development of positive feelings about school.
- development of a positive self-concept.
- growth in language, social, and physical skills.
- achievement of problem-solving and cognitive skills.
- growth in creative skills.
- appreciation of objects of beauty.

Similar to preschools, the emphasis in most kindergartens is on the growth of the whole child: physical, emotional, social, and cognitive.

Curriculum

Kindergarten curriculum may vary from school to school. Some schools stress certain preacademic skills, such as learning the names and sounds of alphabet letters. Other programs focus more on social development. These programs are less structured than those that stress preacademics.

Kindergarten teachers, unlike most elementary teachers, have more freedom in planning curriculum. Studies show that in most kindergarten programs, about 50 percent of the day is spent on creative activities. Included are art, woodworking, blockbuilding, storytelling, and music. Free play, self-care, and rest fill the remaining time, 2-5. The teacher provides social studies, mathematics, language, and science activities, as well.

2-5 Free play and creativity are important in kindergarten programs.

School-Age Child Care

School-age child care programs provide care for children before and/or after school. These programs are often sponsored by schools, churches, or child care centers. Children from five to ten years old most often attend, although in some centers you may find eleven- and twelve-year-olds. These children do homework, play games, and take part in other activities.

An alternative to school-age child care programs are checking-in services. **Checking-in services** assign children to caregivers. Caregivers call the children at home to make sure they have arrived home safely from school. Children do not go to the caregivers' homes. These programs have provided a successful option for some families.

Parent Cooperatives

Parent cooperatives are formed and run by parents who wish to take part in their children's preschool experience. Parents prepare a budget, hire teachers, set policies, establish goals for the program, and assist in the classroom.

Cooperatives provide developmental experiences for adults as well as children. Specifically, parents

- obtain guidance in their jobs as parents.
- learn what children are like at different ages and stages.
- gain several free mornings each month.
- become familiar with creative activities, materials, and equipment.
- gain a more objective picture of their child's development.

Due to all of these experiences, many parents have reported feeling a greater sense of self-satisfaction in their parenting roles.

Advantages and Disadvantages

There are many advantages to teaching in a parent cooperative. Since the parents make the administrative decisions, collect fees, and order and repair equipment, the teacher can devote more time to the children and curriculum. Another advantage can be the special relationships that many times develop between parents and teachers.

A major disadvantage of a parent cooperative is the lack of control on the teacher's part. Although the teacher acts as an adviser, parents are usually responsible for making rules. At times, there may be differences of opinion between teacher and parents. For instance, parents may feel that children do not have to help return toys to the storage place. The teacher may feel differently. This can cause problems for many teachers.

Sessions

Parent cooperatives usually operate for two or three hours, two to five days each week. Sometimes these groups are structured by the children's ages. For example, on Tuesday and Thursday mornings, a group of two-year-old children will be scheduled. On Monday, Wednesday, and Friday mornings, three-year-olds may attend. Other centers may prefer to use the "family-type" grouping. In this type of setting, children of mixed ages may all be included in one group.

Fees

Due to the parent's involvement, fees charged at a parent cooperative are often less than at other programs. Costs are reduced by hiring only a head teacher. Parents serve as the classroom aides. Generally, each parent will assist in the classroom several times each month. In addition, parents volunteer to perform many of the service activities. They may clean and maintain the building, prepare snacks, type newsletters, and do some special jobs, such as painting the classroom.

Laboratory Schools

Laboratory schools, or campus schools, are located on a postsecondary or college campus, 2-6. Although they provide excellent programs for children, their primary purpose is to train future teachers and to serve as a study group for research. Most of these schools have a highly qualified staff, a well-planned curriculum, and excellent equipment.

2-6 Laboratory schools generally have highly qualified staffs, well-planned curriculum, and excellent equipment.

High School Child Care Programs

In the last two decades, many high schools have started providing vocational training for child care occupations. Like the laboratory schools, these programs train future child care professionals. Many high schools have their own child care laboratory facilities where students can work with preschool children. The preschool program may operate two or three days a week. Preschool children from the community attend the school.

The high school students plan and present the curriculum under the supervision of a teacher. Some high school students may observe the preschool children while others work directly with the children. The following week, the students who observed the preceding week then work with the preschoolers while the other students observe them.

Sponsorship of Early Childhood Centers

Early childhood centers can be grouped based on sponsorship. Basically, there are three kinds of sponsorship: public, private, and employer-sponsored centers.

Public Sponsorship

Publicly sponsored programs are funded by federal, state, or local governments. Some of these funds come through school districts. Other funds may come through social service agencies.

An example of a publicly sponsored program is Head Start. Most parents pay no fee for their child to attend Head Start. However, a fee is required if their income exceeds the federal guidelines for the program. Most of the expenses for the program are covered through grants received from the federal government. Funding is usually provided on an annual basis.

State funds may help support programs designed for educational purposes. These programs may be housed in a university, college, secondary school, or vocational school. Examples include child care centers, preschool centers, laboratory schools, and high school child care programs.

Publicly funded child care centers, preschools, and laboratory programs may receive several forms of financial support in addition to parental fees. For instance, a publicly funded child care center may also receive funds from the United Way, community donations, and tuition. Additional funding is usually provided through the university's operating budget. Likewise, a laboratory school on a college campus may receive tuition donations or scholarships through alumni groups.

Private Sponsorship

The largest group of privately sponsored programs is the privately owned center. These centers rely on parent fees to cover most of the operating expenses.

A privately sponsored program may be operated by a church, hospital, or charitable organization. Many of these independent child care centers are nonprofit. They may be governed by a voluntary board of community members and operated as a service to the community.

Most private programs are operated by independent owners. Many of these centers are operated by families. Their motivation in operating a center is to provide a service that makes a profit.

National Child Care Chains

Some child care centers are a part of chains operated by large national corporations, although some chains are privately held. Midsize chains typically operate on a regional basis. Often these centers are built and located in large cities and suburban areas. To make a profit in these centers, the enrollment must be high. The chains are managed by a central administration that furnishes the financial backing and sets policy. Curriculum guides may be developed by curriculum specialists hired by the organization and provided to the center staff in each of the locations.

Employer Sponsorship

The number of companies providing their employees with some type of child care assistance is growing. The employer may pay part or all of the costs of the services.

Employers sponsor child care to reduce the conflict between family and work responsibilities. Studies show that there is less employee turnover and absenteeism at companies that provide some form of child care. At such companies, employees have better work attitudes, new employees are attracted, community relations improve, and good publicity is received. Moreover, there are tax incentives for companies who sponsor child care.

Companies can provide child care assistance in several ways, 2-7. The company owned, on-site child care center is one option. Such a center may be located at or near the work site. With this type of program, the company may hire a director to run the program. Other companies

contract with child care chains or firms specializing in child care to operate the center.

There are advantages and disadvantages to an on-site child care facility. One advantage is that parents can spend breaks and lunch hours with their children. In large cities, however, this model may not work. Employees who commute long distances to work may find it difficult to travel with children on public transportation or in car pools.

The off-site center is another option. This model is often used when several companies form a group. Each company may not have enough need for their own child care center. By sharing a facility, the costs and risks are shared by all the companies in the group.

The off-site location may be closer to the parents' homes. Therefore, transportation times are shorter. If space is available, this type of model may also serve other children from the community.

The vendor model allows companies to purchase space in a child care center or several centers. This model is ideal for small companies. It is not as costly as opening a center. There are no costs for start-up, investment in a building, or center administration.

Companies respect parental choice when the voucher model is provided. Parents receive a voucher or coupon worth a certain amount of money from the company. Some companies will pay for all child care costs, while others pay only a portion. This model may be preferred by parents who do not live close to the work site. Thus, it is a useful model for companies in large cities.

One disadvantage of the voucher model is that the money received must be declared as income on tax returns. However, the employee can deduct the cost of child care from federal taxes (and state taxes where allowed).

Child care for ill children is provided by some companies. This benefit can take two forms. A center may provide services for children who are ill and cannot attend school. When this is done, the health department as well as the state licensing agency must be notified. This works best for children who are recovering from an illness, but are not well enough to return to school. The second form allows for a nurse to be sent to a sick child's home to provide care. This allows the parent to go to work.

Types of Employer-Sponsored Child Care Assistance

- Company owned, on-site center.
- Off-site center sponsored by one or more companies.
- Company sponsored, vendor provided centers.
- Vouchers provided by company to subsidize care.
- Sick child care.
- Referral services.

2-7 Companies may assist families with child care in many ways.

Finding a quality child care program within a reasonable distance of the home is a problem for many parents. To assist parents in this process, some companies provide a referral service that matches the parents' needs with centers. The company may hire their own resource specialist or contract a referral agency.

Generally, parents are given a list of community child care centers. Specific information on each center is collected and given to the parents. Included are the center's location, fees, hours of operation, goals, enrollment capacity, policies, curriculum, staff qualifications, and special services. Maps showing the location of the center are often provided to help the parents in the selection process.

Selecting a Child Care Program

Selecting a child care program is important for parents. Studies show that a large percentage of parents choose a program on the advice of a friend. In most cases, the friend has had one or more children attend the program.

Other factors that influence selection of a child care program include cost, location, and type of program provided. Parents whose children will attend an all-day program are influenced more by location. These parents have heavy demands on their time. As a result, programs located in the neighborhood or on a route to work are most convenient.

The type of program provided will most likely influence parents with children in half-day programs. Music, art, and other creative experiences interest some of these parents. Other parents are most interested in a program that stresses the development of the whole child–cognitive, physical, social, and emotional, 2-8.

In addition to talking to friends, parents will seek information about the program in several other ways. Before visiting a center, many parents will call the director to ask questions about the school policies, program, and fees. After this, if they still are interested, they may visit the center.

Visits to a program may take place before, during, or after program hours. More parents visit during program hours. A larger percentage

2-8 Parents choose early childhood programs based on what they want most for their children.

of parents seeking half-day programs visit centers.

Parents will ask many questions related to the program and staff. They usually are interested in the type of program and related activities provided for the children. Questions related to staff experience and background may also be asked. For example, a parent may ask if the staff is trained in early childhood education or child development. Caregivers with a degree in early childhood are more sensitive to children's needs. They also provide more stimulating, child-centered environments.

An example of an information sheet to share with parents is shown in 2-9. This sheet may help them with their selection process.

The Selection Process

Because early childhood programs vary in cost, hours of operation, and program goals, it takes time to select a program that fits individual needs. As a teacher, it is vital that you understand the process parents go through in selecting a program.

The first step many parents take is to talk to other parents. They list all programs that are conveniently located. After this, they may call each center to discuss fees, hours of operation, and whether the center is licensed and accredited.

Selecting Quality Child Care	Yes	No
1. Do the children appear to be happy, active, and secure?		
2. Are all staff members educationally qualified?		
3. Do staff members attend in-service training, professional meetings, and conferences on a regular basis?		
4. Are staff meetings conducted regularly to plan and evaluate program activities?		
5. Do staff members observe and record each child's developmental progress?		
6. Does the curriculum support the children's individual rates of development?		
7. Is the indoor and outdoor environment large enough to support a variety of activities?		
8. Is the environment inviting, warm, and stimulating?		
9. Is equipment provided to promote all four areas of development: physical, cognitive, social, and emotional?		
10. Are safe and sanitary conditions maintained within the building and on the play yard?		
11. Are teacher-child interactions positive?		
12. Are teachers using developmentally appropriate teaching strategies?		
13. Are parents welcome to observe and participate?		
14. Is sufficient equipment available for the number of children attending?		
15. Does the climate in the center "feel" positive?		
16. Is the center accredited by the National Academy of Early Childhood Programs?		

2-9 In order to help ease the burden of choosing child care for their children, you may wish to supply interested parents with this questionnaire.

Parents then may visit those centers that meet family's and children's needs. While at the center, they may talk to the director and teachers.

Programs with high staff turnover may cause suspicion. Directors, teachers, and aides often resign due to low wages or poor working conditions. In either case, high staff turnover often causes morale problems. Remember, too, in order to feel secure, children need consistent, predictable care.

While visiting the center, parents will observe to see if sufficient space is provided for play and personal belongings. There should be at least 35 square feet of free indoor play space and 100 square feet of outdoor play space for each child. In addition, space should be provided for each child to store personal belongings and a change of clothes.

Parents will also observe whether or not enough equipment is provided for the number of children in attendance. There should also be a wide variety.

Group size or the number of children in the room or space is an important factor. Small groups contribute to more positive outcomes. The ratio of children to caregiver is another factor. When the ratio of children to caregiver is low, program quality is more favorable.

To protect their children's health, parents may look for safe, sanitary conditions. The building and grounds should be safe. Electrical outlets should be covered. A smoke alarm and fire extinguisher should be available. An emergency evacuation plan should be posted.

Parents may ask if meals and snacks are provided for the children. If they are provided, menus should be available. The menu should consist of well-balanced and varied meals. The menu should meet children's nutritional requirements.

Parents may also observe the program to see if the staff is patient and responsive to the children. There should be frequent and supportive staff contact with the children. Also, the staff should work together as they perform their duties.

Quality programs follow a well-planned schedule. To see if such a schedule is followed, some parents may wish to observe. They may also ask to see a daily and weekly schedule. They may look for a balance between active and quiet activities. Weather permitting, there should also be a balance of indoor and outdoor activities.

Parents may also study the way children use materials. In a high quality center, teachers encourage children to make their own products.

Parents may observe to see if concern is expressed for the rights of others. Staff should be helping children learn how to take turns, to consider others' feelings, and to stand up for their own when necessary. Angry children should be helped to work through their feelings. All children in the group should be made to feel good about themselves. Parents will be encouraged by children who appear happy, contented, and secure. This is often a sign that the center's program is meeting each child's needs.

Finally, before parents decide whether a center is best for their child, they need to consider whether it meets their needs. Did they feel welcome at the center? Did the director or teacher greet them? Did they receive encouragement to observe? Are the children's experiences in the program shared through a newsletter, conference, or group meeting? Parents' answers to these questions will help determine whether or not they have found the right center for their child.

Center Accreditation

Being **accredited** certifies that a set of standards has been met by a child care center. The National Academy of Early Childhood Programs, a division of NAEYC, administers a voluntary accreditation system. This system has been designed for child care centers and preschools serving children from birth through age five. It is also designed for programs that serve school-age children in before school and after school care.

The purpose of this system is to improve the quality of programs for young children in group care. It assists parents in their search for high quality programs for their children. In addition, it helps assure parents that their children are receiving quality care. Public recognition is the main benefit of achieving accreditation status.

To be eligible for accreditation status, a center must conduct a self-study. The self-study is an evaluation process designed by the National Academy of Early Childhood Programs. The evaluation provides valuable professional development experiences for all involved–directors, staff, and parents. Part of the self-study involves evaluating the 10 component areas identified as goals of quality early childhood programs, 2-10.

A recent study shows that accreditation has improved program quality. Center directors reported the greatest gains in the areas of curriculum, followed by administration, health, and safety. The lowest gains were in staffing, and nutrition and food services. Most directors also reported that accreditation had increased the visibility of their programs.

Ten Component Areas of Quality Early Childhood Programs

- Evaluations
- Curriculum
- Administration
- Health and safety
- Physical environment
- Staff qualification and development
- Staff-children interactions
- Staff-parent interactions
- Staffing
- Nutrition and food services

2-10 A quality early childhood program will meet the developmental needs of children. It also fosters positive interactions between parents, staff, and administrators involved in the program.

Summary

There are many types of early childhood programs. These include family child care, child care centers, Montessori schools, Head Start, kindergartens, school-aged child care programs, parent cooperatives, laboratory schools, and secondary child care programs. Each type of program takes a unique approach to meeting children's physical, cognitive, social, and emotional needs.

Programs may be sponsored in a variety of ways. The type of sponsorship may affect goals and philosophies. Programs may be publicly or privately funded. Chain child care centers can be privately or publicly held. Employer-sponsored programs are designed to reduce some of the burdens of child care for working parents. Employers are using a variety of ways to provide this benefit for their employees.

With the variety of child care programs available, parents consider many factors in choosing the best program for their child. They may begin the selection process by listening to the recommendations of other parents. Some of the other factors that parents consider include the type of program, quality of staff, ratio of children to caregivers, group size, and condition of facilities. As a teacher, you will need to know what parents look for in a program. Then you can strive to make your center the type that parents choose for their children.

Parents may look for programs that have been accredited by NAEYC. Accreditation certifies that a program meets a specific set of standards. Obtaining accreditation involves participation in a self-study, which is designed as an evaluation tool. Center directors, staff, and parents participate in this process. Public recognition is the main benefit of achieving accreditation.

Review and Reflect

1. What is the most common type of child care in the United States?

2. True or false. Child care centers offer full-day programs for young children.

3. Montessori's theory of education stated that children learn best when they are _____.

4. What are "practical life experiences" according to Montessori?

5. Describe the purpose of Head Start.

6. True or false. Nutrition is a vital part of the Head Start program.

7. Name the three basic kindergarten schedules.

8. List five objectives for a kindergarten program.

9. Describe how a checking-in service works for school-age children.

10. _____ are formed and run by parents who wish to take part in their children's preschool experiences.

11. What is the primary purpose of a laboratory school?

12. Publicly sponsored programs are funded by _____.

13. Describe one way employers can provide child care assistance for their employees.

14. A large percentage of parents select a child care center on the advice of _____.

15. Why might a high staff turnover be a concern to parents?

16. Why might parents want to select a child care program that was accredited?

Apply and Explore

1. Visit a family child care home. Ask the provider to outline the daily schedule.

2. Invite a panel of early childhood teachers to speak to your class. Include child care, parent cooperative, kindergarten, and Montessori teachers. Ask them questions about their philosophy, program goals, and curriculum.

3. Visit a Montessori program. Make a list of materials used for practical life experiences, sensory training, and writing and reading.

4. Collect schedules from half-day and full-day child care centers. Discuss similarities and differences.

5. Arrange a visit to a school-age child care program. Ask to review the curriculum.

6. Discuss the advantages and disadvantages of teaching in a parent cooperative.

7. Discuss the value of center accreditation.

Chapter 3

Observing Children: A Tool for Assessment

After studying this chapter you will be able to

- list purposes of assessment.
- contrast initial assessment and ongoing assessment.
- list the factors to consider in choosing a method of assessment.
- list the advantages and disadvantages of various assessment tools.
- compile a list of contents for a child's portfolio.
- summarize guidelines for observing children.

Terms to Know

assessment
developmental norms
anecdotal record
checklist
participation chart
rating scale
portfolio

Young children are fascinating to watch. Just ask any new mother, father, or proud grandparent! A young child's awkward attempts to try new skills or early efforts at conversation can be captivating. Observing children is something everyone enjoys doing.

Observation also serves another purpose. It is one of the oldest and best methods for learning about children. Most of what is known about child growth and development is the result of some form of observation. Many behaviors of children cannot be measured in any other way. A one-year-old, for instance, cannot answer questions orally or in writing, but the child's behavior can be observed, 3-1.

As a student of child development, much of what you will learn about children will come from observing them. You may be asked to observe the children in your school's child care center. At times you may be assigned to observe a specific aspect of a child's behavior or development. You will also be encouraged to observe children informally outside of school.

Jafar, a student majoring in child development, was assigned his first observation. He was amazed at the developmental differences he saw within the group of three- and four-year-olds. Jafar noticed that Ben was constructing an eighteen-piece puzzle. Sitting next to him was Hunter. She was asking the teacher for help in constructing a puzzle that had only four pieces. Standing at the easel, Wyatt was printing the five letters of his name across the top of his art project. Next to him was Wendy. She drew a circle in an upper corner of her work and exclaimed

3-1 Teachers observe largely through their eyes and ears.

with a smile, "That's my name!" Sitting nearby, Tyler needed help using a pair of scissors while Tira was cutting circles out of construction paper.

Each of these children is unique. If you were the teacher in this classroom, how would you plan a curriculum that would meet the needs of each of these children? To begin the process, you would need to gather information. This, too, involves observation. You would need to determine each child's developmental stage. With this information, you could then determine the group's developmental status. The data gathered would provide you with information for planning a curriculum that was sensitive to the needs of the group.

Assessment

Assessment is the process of observing, recording, and documenting children's growth and behavior in order to make decisions about

their education. Information is obtained on children's developmental status, growth, and learning style. Sometimes the terms assessment and evaluation are used interchangeably, but they are two different processes. Assessment is the process of collecting information or data. Observation is one of several means of obtaining information or data as a part of the assessment process. Evaluation is the process of reviewing the information and finding value in it.

Purposes of Assessment

Assessment is important for several reasons. The information collected is used in planning developmentally appropriate curriculum. Assessment keeps the teachers and the curriculum responsive to the needs of the children. It involves the gathering of many pieces of information. This includes information on each child's physical, social, emotional, and cognitive development. Assessment includes information on what the children can do–their needs, strengths, and interests.

During the assessment process, you, as teacher, gain insights into children's learning styles and needs, 3-2. What are their strengths and weaknesses? What does the group know? What are they able to do? What are their interests and dispositions? Finally, what are their needs?

Individual and classroom problems can often be identified through the assessment process. When specific examples of a child's behavior are observed and recorded, behavior patterns become more clear. Answers to behavior problems can more easily be found when the specific behavior is observed and noted.

Classroom problems can be identified through assessment. When a problem arises, plans can be made to remedy the problem. To illustrate, perhaps there have been many instances of pushing and shoving in the dramatic play area. By observing and evaluating, you may realize that the classroom space provided for this activity needs to be expanded. If this is impossible, you may decide to limit the number of children who play in this area at one time to prevent the undesirable behavior.

Assessment also allows you to identify those children who might have special needs.

3-2 During observation, teachers gather information related to a child's strengths, needs, and interests.

Perhaps a child has a hearing or vision impairment. Maybe a child has an emotional or behavior problem that requires counseling. These children can be identified and specialized services obtained.

Through assessment, you will be able to find out where the children are in their development. Information on each child should be recorded at regular intervals. In this way, you can see how each child is progressing in his or her development.

The information gained through assessment can also be useful during parent conferences. Parents want to know how their children are progressing. You will be able to provide them with information on their child's progress. Parents will also be assured that you know and understand their child.

A final purpose for assessment is in evaluating your program. Information obtained through assessment can help your staff determine if your program is effective in meeting its goals.

When to Do Assessments

As a teacher beginning a new year, you will need to do an *initial assessment*. You cannot assume all children of a given age are alike. Developmental differences will exist. Diversity in culture, economic status, and home background will impact each child's development. Therefore, the purpose of an initial assessment is to get a "snapshot" of the entire class. Observing the children is the most common way to gather this information.

You will want to find out as much about the children as possible during your initial assessment. Study the existing folders on each child. Review their home background forms. Read the notes from past parent conferences. If possible, visit each child's home. An alliance with parents is important. Parents can provide you with useful information on a child's learning needs and interests.

In addition to this initial assessment, you will need to do *ongoing assessments* on individual children, as well as the group. A single assessment is not an exact assessment of ability or performance. It is just an indicator.

Ongoing assessment may take more time, but it will also provide more in-depth information. The information gained will be useful in tracking each child's progress and change over time. It should provide evidence of a child's learning and maturation. This information will also be helpful in making decisions for enriching or modifying the curriculum when necessary.

You can gather assessment data during classroom activities. Watch children as they work on art projects and listen to them as they tell stories, 3-3. Observe children as they construct puzzles or build with blocks. Listen in on children's conversations. Discreetly take notes on individual children, especially during free-choice activities. This is when children are most likely to reveal their own personalities and development. These notes will provide important assessment information.

3-3 Teachers can quickly make notes about individual children during classroom activities.

Formal and Informal Observation

Two different methods of observation are used for assessing young children—formal and informal. They differ in how controlled the conditions are for using them. Formal methods include standardized tests and research instruments. As a result of such research, developmental norms for children have been identified. **Developmental norms** are characteristics and behaviors considered normal for children in specific age groups.

Developmental norms will assist you in comparing and noting changes in the growth and development of children in your care, 3-4. They will also help you as you observe young children in preparation for your career working with young children. Examples of developmental norms are included in the Appendix of this book. They are useful tools for assessing children's developmental status. They also form the basis for planning developmentally appropriate curriculum.

While formal observation methods provide important information, they require specialized training for recording data on carefully designed forms. Training is also needed for analyzing and interpreting the data.

3-4 Reviewing developmental norms will help you assess the progress of children in your care.

Preschool teachers usually use informal observation methods to collect data. These methods are easier to use and more appropriate for program planning. They include observing children in the classroom, collecting samples of their work, interviewing parents, and talking with children.

Choosing a Method of Assessment

There are three considerations for choosing a method of assessment. First, the method chosen depends on the type of behavior you want to assess and the amount of detail you need. Another consideration is whether the information needs to be collected for one child or the entire group. Finally, the amount of focused attention required by the observer needs to be considered.

Some methods of assessment will require more of your attention. For example, it is difficult interacting with children when you are in the process of writing an anecdotal record. Checklists, videotapes, and participation charts are easier to use while working with the children.

Usually teachers use a variety of methods for gathering information about the children. Since no one method is the most effective or reveals everything, several methods are used. More complete information is obtained by using several types of assessment. Multiple sources of information also reduces the possibility of error when making evaluations.

Assessment Tools

There are several types of assessment tools that are used in early childhood programs. These include anecdotal records, checklists, participation charts, rating scales, samples of products, photographs, and tapes. Teachers can also interview parents to obtain information.

Anecdotal Records

The simplest form of direct observation is a brief narrative account of a specific incident called an **anecdotal record**. Anecdotal records do not require charts or special settings. They can be recorded in any setting and require no special training. All you need is paper and a writing tool to record what happened in a factual, objective

manner. The observation is open-ended, continuing until everything is witnessed.

The process of recording the incident requires a careful eye and quick pencil to capture all of the details. You will need to note who was involved, what happened, when it happened, and where it occurred. It needs to be done promptly and accurately. Figure 3-5 shows the contents of an anecdotal record.

When you use the narrative form of observation, your eyes and ears act like a video camera. You will be recording pictures of children playing, learning, and interacting. During your observations, you will record how children communicate, both verbally and nonverbally. You will record how they look and what they do. Physical gestures and movements should be noted. You will also detail children's interactions with people and materials.

Anecdotal Records Must Be Objective

During the observation process, it is important to record only objective statements. To be objective, a statement must pass two tests. First, it must describe only observable actions. Thus, generalizations about the motives, attitudes, and feelings of the children are not included. Secondly, the recorded information must be nonevaluative. It should not include an interpretation of why something happened, nor imply that what happened was wrong, right, good, or bad. Labeling should be avoided. No judgments or conclusions should be inferred at this point. The following is an example of a narrative observation:

Contents of Anecdotal Records
• Identifies the child and gives the child's age.
• Includes the date, time of day, and setting.
• Identifies the observer.
• Provides an accurate account of the child's actions and conversations.
• Includes responses of other children and/or adults, if any are involved in the situation.

3-5 Anecdotal records should include the items listed.

Sally arrived at school holding her mother's hand. She slowly walked over to her locker, removed her coat, and hung it on a hook. She turned to her mother and said, "You go to work." Sally's mother hugged her and said, "After work I'll take you to the dentist." Sally looked at her mother and started to cry. She said, "I'm not going to the dentist. I'm staying at school." Sally's mother reached out and hugged Sally. Sally continued crying and hung onto her mother. The teacher walked over to Sally and whispered in her ear. Then the teacher put out her hand and said, "Come and look, Sally. We have a new friend at school today. Jodi brought her new hamster." Sally stopped crying and took the teacher's hand. Together they walked over to see the hamster. Sally's mother watched her for a moment and then left the room.

Notice that only an objective description of the observed behavior is recorded. The statements do not include any of the following: causes, emotions, explanations, feelings, goals, motives, desires, purposes, needs, or wishes.

Interpretation of the Data

Once the narrative data is recorded, a second process begins. This process involves the interpretation of the data. An attempt is made to explain the observed behavior and to give it meaning. Why did the child behave as he or she did? What might have been the child's motives? Did someone or something cause the child to act in this way? This interpretation takes knowledge and skill. It should not be attempted without a thorough understanding of how children grow and develop. The observation itself serves no purpose without the interpretation of behavior to give meaning to the data.

Though an observation may be factual and unbiased, various interpretations are sometimes made. Since no two people are exactly alike, no two people will interpret facts in the exact same way. Each person who interprets a child's behavior may determine different motives for the behavior based on their own personal experiences. Their personal feelings, values, and attitudes may also influence the interpretation of behavior.

To illustrate, an observer wrote the following about Tony:

Tony picked up the pitcher of milk. He moved the pitcher toward his glass. He hit the glass and tipped it over. The milk spilled.

In reviewing the observation of Tony, his behavior might be interpreted in several ways:

- Tony was careless.
- Tony was inexperienced in handling a pitcher.
- Tony wasn't paying attention to what he was doing.
- Tony lacked the strength needed to lift the pitcher.
- Tony lacked the eye-hand coordination necessary to pour from the pitcher.

To decide which interpretation is most accurate, you will need to observe Tony on several occasions over a period of time. You would also need a thorough understanding of how children grow and develop.

Figure 3-6 shows a form for an anecdotal record, although many teachers just use a file card or plain piece of paper. Teachers who record incidents throughout the year have a means of assessing progress. A series of records over time can provide rich details. The records can be extremely valuable in noting progress, strengths, needs, and interests.

Advantages and Disadvantages of Anecdotal Records

There are advantages and disadvantages in using the anecdotal record. An important advantage is that it is the easiest method of use since it requires no special setting or time frame. Anecdotal records can provide a running record over time showing evidence of a child's growth and development. Therefore, teachers who record incidents throughout the year have a means of assessing progress.

There are also disadvantages with using anecdotal records. Because the incident observed is based on the observer's interest, a complete picture may not be provided. Records may not always be accurate. If the observer decides to write down the incident at the end of the day and is poor at recalling details, important information may be missed.

**SUNSHINE CHILD CARE CENTER
ANECDOTAL RECORD**

Child's Name: _____Carrie_____ Date: _10/9/xx_

Child's Age: ____3____ Years ____9____ Months

Setting: _Dramatic Play_ Time: _8:30_ to _8:45_

Observer: _Geneva Peterson_

Incident:

Carrie went directly to the dramatic play area when she arrived at the center. She placed the cash register on a table. After this, she displayed empty food containers on a table. Tony entered the area. He stepped behind the cash register and said, "I want to play with this." Carrie said, "No, it's mine. I had it first." Then using her arm she hit Tony and began pushing him. Tony looked at Carrie, shrugged his shoulders, and walked away. As Tony walked away, a smile came across Carrie's face.

Interpretation:

3-6 You may want to use a form such as this one to record anecdotal events.

Checklists

Another form of assessment is the checklist. **Checklists** are designed to record the presence or absence of specific traits or behaviors. They are easy to use and are especially helpful when many different items need to be observed. They often include lists of specific behaviors to look for while observing. Checklists may be designed for any developmental domain–physical, social, emotional, or cognitive.

Checklists may be developed to survey one child or a group of children. The targeted behaviors are listed in logical order with similar items grouped together. Therefore, you can quickly record the presence or absence of a behavior.

Typically, a check indicates the presence of a behavior.

Checklists require structuring. You may be able to purchase commercially prepared checklists. Most teachers working in child care centers structure their own. A typical checklist for use in observing an individual child is shown in 3-7. The developmental norms found in the Appendix of this book may be adapted as checklists for assessing individual children or groups of children. Figure 3-8 shows a checklist for assessing the gross motor skills of a group of children.

Advantages and Disadvantages of Checklists

One of the advantages of a checklist is that there are no time constraints in collecting the data. The information can be quickly recorded anytime during program hours. In addition, checklists are easy to use, efficient, and can be used in many situations. Data from checklists can be easily analyzed.

A disadvantage, however, of using a checklist is the lack of detailed information. Because of the format, only particular behaviors are

Name: _____Wyatt Anderson_____

Program: _____

Age: ____3____ Years ____6____ Months

Date of Observation: _2/9/xx_

Observer: _Sally Olm_

Fine Motor Skills

	Yes	No
Cuts paper	✓	
Pastes with a finger	✓	
Pours from a pitcher	✓	
Copies a circle from a drawing	✓	
Draws a straight line	✓	
Uses finger to pick up smaller objects	✓	
Draws a person with three parts		✓

3-7 Checklists are efficient to use and require little effort.

Gross Motor Skills Group Assessment Three-Year-Olds						
	Henry	Ed	Jo	Vicki	Cari	Deb
Catches ball with arms extended	✓	✓	✓		✓	
Throws ball underhanded		✓			✓	
Completes forward somersault	✓	✓		✓	✓	✓
Rides tricycle skillfully	✓	✓		✓	✓	✓
Throws ball without losing balance		✓	✓		✓	
Hops on one foot		✓				✓

3-8 You can evaluate the gross motor skills of a group of children using a form such as this one.

noted. Important aspects of behaviors may be missed, such as how a behavior is performed and for how long. Only the presence or absence of a behavior is noted in a checklist.

Participation Chart

A **participation chart** can be developed to gain information on specific aspects of children's behavior. Participation charts have a variety of uses in the classroom. For instance, children's activity preferences during self-selected play can be determined. See 3-9.

Richard O'Grady, an experienced teacher, uses participation charts to record the time each child falls asleep at nap time. He also charts the length of time each child sleeps. He records this information several times a year. After collecting the data, he decides if a change should be made in the scheduled nap time. Likewise, the length of the nap time can be adjusted to reflect the children's needs.

Sometimes teachers find that children's preferences do not match their needs. To illustrate, Randy has weak hand-eye coordination skills. A participation chart shows she spends

Activity Preferences During Self-Selected Play										
	Bryce	Tina	Saul	Ting	Bergetta	Tanya	Hunter	Shawn	Janus	Vida
9:00 - 9:10	b	dp	a	st	m	dp	a	b	st	s
9:10 - 9:20	b	dp	a	st	m	dp	a	b	st	s
9:20 - 9:30	b	dp	m	m	dp	dp	s	b	st	s
9:30 - 9:40	b	st	m	m	dp	dp	b	b	m	a
9:40 - 9:50	b	m	m	m	dp	dp	b	b	m	a
9:50 - 10:00	b	m	s	m	dp	dp	b	b	m	a
a=art; b=blockbuilding; dp=dramatic play; m=manipulatives; s=sensory; sc=science; st=storytelling										

3-9 A participation chart is quick and easy to use, but can give you important information.

most of her time listening to stories and music and watching other children play. To meet Randy's needs, the teacher could introduce her to interesting art activities, puzzles, and other small manipulative learning aids. These materials will help advance Randy's hand-eye coordination skills, which will be necessary for writing and reading.

Rating Scales

Rating scales are used to record the degree to which a quality or trait is present. Rating scales require you to make a judgment about behavior. Where a checklist only indicates the presence or absence of a trait, a rating scale tells how much or how little is present.

Advantages and Disadvantages of Rating Scales

Rating scales are easy to use and require little time to complete. Some scales contain only a numerical range. Others define the behaviors more specifically.

A disadvantage of the rating scale is that only fragments of actions are included. In order to choose a rating, the observer should have a good understanding of the behavior he or she is rating. Figure 3-10 shows a typical rating scale.

Collecting Samples of Children's Products

Collecting samples of children's products is another assessment tool. These products can provide valuable information regarding the child's developmental status. Products collected may include artwork, stories dictated or written, and records of conversations. Over time, these samples can be collected and compared. To illustrate, Chuck could make only random scribbles on paper at the beginning of the year. Figure 3-11 shows an example of his scribbles. When Chuck's teacher asked him to tell her about his work, he explained it. She discovered the sample showed more than Chuck's scribbles. He said, "There is my name. That is how to write it. I wrote my mother's name and my sister's. There is the name of my dog, Smokey." Now he is able to draw a circle. A comparison of the two samples shows that Chuck has demonstrated growth in his hand-eye coordination skills.

A child's products can be stored in a folder or portfolio. Whenever possible, store materials

Social/Emotional Rating Scale

Child: __Jo Ellen__ Date: __4/6/xx__
Age: __4__ Years __1__ Months
Observer: __Mark Zenk__

Behavior	Never	Sometimes	Usually	Always
Shows increased willingness to cooperate			✓	
Is patient and conscientious		✓		
Expresses anger verbally rather than physically				✓
Has strong desire to please		✓		
Is eager to make friends and develop strong friendships			✓	
Respects property rights of others			✓	

3-10 On a rating scale, teachers record the degree to which a quality or trait is present.

3-11 By collecting samples of children's drawings at various times during the year, you can assess their development.

and items in chronological order. This will save you time when evaluating progress or sharing the materials with parents.

Records may be kept in different forms. Samples may be preserved by photographing, sketching, or diagramming children's products. These methods are especially useful for large structures such as block displays and three-dimensional artwork that cannot be stored conveniently.

Videotapes and Audiotapes

Making videotapes and audiotapes are excellent ways to preserve information about a child's developmental status. Tapings may focus on an individual child, a small group of children, or an entire class. Videotapes can be used when both action and speech need to be preserved. Recordings may be made of children telling stories, acting out stories, or explaining their projects. Dramatic play interactions and music experiences can be recorded. By viewing or listening to the tapes, you will be able to note progress in language and speech. The children might also enjoy viewing or listening to the tapes.

Be careful that the presence of the video-camera does not become intrusive. You may want to ask other adults, such as teacher aides or parent volunteers, to assist with the taping. This will allow you to be included in the taping. By reviewing the tape, you can do a self-evaluation of your own interactions with the children.

Portfolios

Materials that you have collected as a part of on-going assessment should be placed in a portfolio for each child. A **portfolio** is a collection of materials that shows a person's abilities, accomplishments, and progress over a period of time. Portfolios that you create for the children in your care summarize each child's abilities. A portfolio includes items that show change over time. It can show where the child has been and where he or she is now.

Depending upon the materials collected, the contents of a portfolio can be stored in a variety of forms. Some teachers prefer three-ring binders. Others prefer to use boxes or large folders to store the portfolio contents.

Contents

A child's portfolio needs to be carefully planned and organized. It should be more than a file of anecdotal records, checklists, and questionnaires. Most teachers include product samples as well. Examples include art projects, audiotapes of conversations, and child-dictated stories. In addition, the portfolios include summaries of parent conferences and parent questionnaires. Figure 3-12 shows the contents of a typical portfolio.

Teachers include samples for each child that reflect unique skills and interests. If Thomas

---

Portfolio Contents

A portfolio may contain . . .
- Teacher observations and other records gathered through assessment.
- Developmental rating scales or checklists.
- Parents' comments and completed questionnaires.
- A dated series of the child's artwork or writing.
- Photographs of the child demonstrating skills or engaged in activities.
- Audiotapes or videotapes of the child speaking, singing, telling stories, etc.
- A list of favorite books, songs, and fingerplays.

3-12 A portfolio contains a wide variety of materials.

built a complex and interesting block structure, his teacher might sketch or photograph it for inclusion in his portfolio. Likewise, teachers may record stories that children dictate to them.

A portfolio should be continually evolving and provide for on-going assessment. It should be a summary of a child's development. Information gained from evaluating the portfolio can guide teachers in designing curriculum, structuring interactions, and setting up the classroom. Parents, too, will gain from reviewing the child's portfolio with the teacher.

By reviewing the portfolios of children in a program, you should be able to identify unique characteristics of each child. For instance, according to Mark's portfolio, he remains in the cooking area until the entire snack is prepared every day. Often he provides the teachers with other methods of preparing the foods. Cory develops elaborate and imaginative buildings in the blockbuilding area. During self-selected play, Maria always chooses the same theme. She dresses as a ballerina in the dramatic play area. Blake is fascinated with the hamster and rabbit. He wants to learn more about different kinds of animals, their eating habits, and behaviors.

Guidelines for Observing Children

During your study of young children, you will observe them in many situations. Whether on the play yard, in a classroom, or on a field trip, your behavior as an observer is important. Whether you are in an outside child care facility or in your school's own laboratory, certain guidelines must be followed.

Whenever you gather data about children, you must use special care. The information you collect must be kept confidential. This is perhaps the most important guideline for you to follow. Though you can discuss a child's behavior in your own classroom, you must refrain from doing so outside that setting. Whenever you are talking, other people are listening. The information you share could be embarrassing or even damaging to a child, parent, or teacher.

To protect confidentiality, your teacher may request that you avoid using a child's name during classroom discussions. First names only are permitted in other classrooms. Both practices

will help protect the real identity of a child. These practices will also prevent information about a particular child from leaving the classroom.

While you are observing, coats, books, and other personal belongings should not be brought into the classroom. Young children are specially curious about purses and bags. Such items may cause an unnecessary distraction. Cosmetics and medications could endanger their safety.

During your observation time, avoid talking to the children, other observers, or the staff. However, it is likely that your presence will spark the curiosity of some of the children. A child may ask you what you are doing. If this happens, answer in a matter-of-fact manner. You might say that you are watching the children play or that you are writing notes on how children play.

One of the best ways to learn about young children is to observe them and to make note of their behavior, 3-13. By sharing your observations with other class members, you will be able to see children as they really are. These records will help you understand children and become a better child care professional.

3-13 By observing children and recording their behavior, you will become a better child care professional.

Summary

Assessment is the process of observing, recording, and documenting children's growth and behavior in order to make decisions about their education. Assessment is important for many reasons, but it is primarily used in planning developmentally appropriate curriculum. An initial assessment is made of all children when they enter a program, but ongoing assessment continues as long as a child remains enrolled in a program.

Most assessment methods involve observing children. Formal observation by researchers has led to the creation of developmental norms. These are characteristics and behaviors considered normal for children in specific age groups. Preschool teachers usually use informal observation methods to collect data.

There are several types of assessment tools that are used in early childhood programs. These include anecdotal records, checklists, participation charts, rating scales, samples of products, photographs, and tape recordings. All of these methods have advantages and disadvantages. Materials that have been collected during the assessment process should be placed in a portfolio for each child.

When observing children, it is important to record only objective statements. Once the narrative data is recorded, the data may be interpreted. This interpretation takes knowledge and skill and requires a thorough understanding of how children grow and develop. Information you collect on children must also be kept confidential. This is perhaps the most important guideline for you to follow.

Review and Reflect

1. List three purposes of assessment.

2. What is the difference between an initial assessment and on-going assessment?

3. Which of the following is considered a formal method of assessment?
    A. checklists
    B. standardized tests
    C. rating scales
    D. anecdotal records

4. List three considerations for choosing a method of assessment.

5. Which of the following are objective statements?
    A. Pours milk.
    B. Rocks the doll.
    C. Gets even.
    D. Feels lonely.

6. Why is the anecdotal record considered the simplest form of direct observation?

7. Which assessment tool would you use to determine the degree to which a quality or trait was present?

8. List one advantage and one disadvantage in using a checklist.

9. What three methods could you choose from to add information on a three-dimensional project to a child's portfolio?

10. List five items that might be included in a child's portfolio.

11. Name three guidelines to keep in mind when observing children.

Apply and Explore

1. Prepare a checklist for a group of children to assess color recognition skills.

2. Using the Appendix, develop a rating scale to assess the motor skills of four-year-olds.

3. Videotape a group of children interacting. Show the tape to classmates. Have each class member write a narrative of what he or she sees. Compare the contents of the narratives.

4. Invite a teacher to visit the class and share how she or he develops and uses portfolios.

5. Develop a participation checklist for the use of outdoor play equipment.

6. Have each student in the class observe a child for 15 minutes and write an anecdotal record of the observation. Compare and discuss the results. Which records contained the most detail? Which records contained only objective statements? Did any of the records contain interpretive statements? If so, what were they?

7. Review the cognitive norms for three-year-old children found in the Appendix. Then construct a rating scale to evaluate six cognitive behaviors. Use the scale to observe a group of children. How could you use the information gained?

Chapter 4

Understanding Children from Birth to Age Two

After studying this chapter, you will be able to

- describe the areas and characteristics of development.

- chart the physical development of children in the first two years after birth.

- describe how children develop cognitively in the first two years after birth.

- explain how children in the first two years after birth develop socially and emotionally.

Terms to Know

development
infant
toddler
preschooler
physical development
gross motor development
fine motor development
cognitive development
social-emotional development

maturation
reflex
motor sequence
object permanence
deferred imitation
telegraphic speech
temperament
attachment
separation anxiety

Studying and understanding child development is an important part of teaching young children. No two children are alike. Children differ in physical, cognitive, social, and emotional growth patterns. They also differ in the ways they respond to play, affection, and other factors in their environment.

Think of the children that you know. Each is different from the others, 4-1. Some may always appear to be happy. Other children's personalities may not seem as pleasant. Some children are active. Still others are typically quiet. You may even find that some children are easier to like. To help all of these children, you need to understand the sequence of their development. Knowledge of child development is essential to guiding young children and planning a developmentally appropriate curriculum.

Child Development

Development refers to change or growth that occurs in a child. By studying child development, you will develop a profile of what children can do at various ages. Understanding growth and development will help you plan appropriate programs for children. For instance, you will learn that two-year-old children like to run. This means that you should provide space for them to move freely. Likewise, you will learn that infants explore through their senses, often mouthing objects. Knowing this, you will need to make sure that all toys for infants are clean and safe.

4-1 Knowledge of child development can help you understand how to work with children who have very different personalities.

Different names are often used to describe young children at different ages. For the first year after birth, a child is called an **infant**. From the first year until the third birthday, children are often called **toddlers**. (The name toddlers was given to this age group because of their awkward style of walking.) The term **preschooler** is often used to describe children ages three to six.

Child development is a relatively recent area of study. Researchers are continually discovering new information on how children grow, develop, and learn about their environment. Therefore, studying the basics of child development should just be the beginning for you. Throughout your career, you will need to update your knowledge of the latest research and trends in the field through seminars, courses, professional articles, and conferences. Professional development is a lifelong process.

Areas of Development

The study of child development is often divided into three main areas. These include physical, cognitive, and social-emotional development. Dividing development into these areas makes it easier to study.

Physical development refers to physical body changes. It occurs in a relatively stable, predictable sequence. Therefore it is orderly, not random. Changes in bone thickness, vision, hearing, and muscles are all included. Changes in size and weight are also part of physical development. See 4-2.

Changes in physical skills, such as crawling, walking, hopping, and writing, are another part of physical development. These skills fall into two main areas of development. **Gross motor development** involves improvement of skills using the large muscles. Such activities as running, skipping, and riding a bike fall into this category. **Fine motor development** involves the small muscles. Grasping, holding, cutting, and

4-2 Changes in height and weight are two of the most obvious signs of physical development.

drawing are some activities requiring fine motor development.

Environmental factors, such as proper nutrition and appropriate toys and activities, also affect what a child can do physically.

Cognitive development, sometimes called intellectual development, refers to mental processes used to gain knowledge. Language, thought, reasoning, and imagination are all included. Identifying colors, and knowing the difference between one and many, are examples of cognitive tasks.

Language and thought are a result of cognitive development. These two skills are closely related. Both are needed for planning, remembering, and problem solving. These skills develop with maturity and experience.

The third area of development is called **social-emotional development**. These two areas are grouped together because they are so interrelated. Learning to relate to others is social development. Emotional development involves refining feelings and expressions of feelings. Trust, fear, confidence, pride, friendship, and humor are all part of social-emotional development. Other emotional traits include fear, timidity, interest, and pleasure. See 4-3. A person's self-concept and self-esteem are also part of this area.

These three developmental areas are interrelated. Development in one area can have a strong effect on development in another area. For instance, both fine motor development and cognitive development are needed to write words. Language, a part of cognitive development, is needed to communicate with others and develop socially and emotionally.

Characteristics of Development

Although each child is different, the basic pattern of development is predictable. Development tends to proceed from the head downward. This is called the *cephalocaudal principle*. According to this principle, the child first gains control of the head, then the arms, then the legs. Therefore, infants gain control of head and face movements within the first two months after birth. In the next few months, they are able to lift themselves up using their arms. By 6 to 12 months of age, infants start to gain leg control and may be able to crawl, stand, or walk.

4-3 Learning to trust and show affection for others is a part of social-emotional development.

Development also proceeds from the center of the body outward according to the *principle of proximodistal development*. This means that the spinal cord develops before outer parts of the body. The child's arms develop before the hands, and the hands and feet develop before the fingers and toes. Finger and toe muscles are the last to develop.

Development depends on maturation. **Maturation** refers to a sequence of biological changes in a child. These changes give children new abilities. Much of maturation depends on changes in the brain and the nervous system. These changes allow children to have improved thinking abilities and motor skills.

Children must mature to a certain point before they can gain some skills, 4-4. For instance, the brain of a four-month-old has not matured enough to allow the child to use language. By two years of age, with help from others, the child will be able to say and understand many words.

4-4 Improved muscle strength and coordination are needed before a child can climb.

The characteristics of development help you understand the order or sequence of development in children. However, each child develops at his or her own rate. You may find children the same age who have developed to different levels in each developmental area. Knowing the patterns of development will help you understand what abilities each child already has gained. It will also help you plan activities that will help the children develop new skills successfully.

Physical Development in the First Two Years

Growth is rapid during the first two years of life. The child's size, shape, senses, and organs change. Some changes are rapid; others are more gradual. With each change, children gain new abilities. Much of the first year of life is spent coordinating motor skills. Through the repetition of motor actions, infants gain physical strength and motor coordination.

As a caregiver, you need to be aware of physical changes in the first two years. Activities, diets, sleep schedules, and safety policies need to be adjusted as children grow. For instance, infants less than four months old do not have enough muscle strength for movement. Typically, these children enjoy being rocked or held for most of the day. They also enjoy sitting in infant seats. However, by twelve months, the infant's large muscles are more developed. At this time, these children need time and space for crawling and walking.

Size and Shape

An infant's weight may change almost daily. The average weight at birth is 7½ pounds. Five months later, the infant will have doubled in weight. By one year, the typical child weighs about 22 pounds–about three times their birth weight. By two years of age, most children weigh almost four times their birth weight.

The infant's length also changes rapidly. The average newborn measures 20 inches. Twelve months later, the infant has usually grown 10 to 12 inches. During the second year of life, most children grow 2 to 6 inches. By 24 months, most children measure 32 to 36 inches in height.

There are weight and height differences between boys and girls by two years of age. At this age, most boys are slightly heavier and taller than girls. Most boys reach about half of their adult height by two years of age. At the same age, girls will have passed their halfway mark by one or two inches.

Reflexes

At birth, the infant's physical abilities are limited to reflexes. A **reflex** is an automatic body response to a stimulus. The person does not control this response. Blinking when something is coming toward your face is an example of a reflex. Some reflexes, such as blinking, continue throughout life. Others appear in infants and disappear after a few weeks or months.

Doctors and others who work with children check reflexes to assess brain and nerve development. When normal reflexes are not present in infants, it may be a sign of brain or nerve damage. If these reflexes continue past the time they should disappear, brain or nerve damage may again be suspected. Professionals often test infants for the reflexes listed in figure 4-5. Infants do not all acquire or lose these reflexes at exactly the same time. The chart shows the age range when each of these reflexes generally disappears.

Rooting Reflex

Some of the infant's reflexes are needed for survival. See 4-6. These include the rooting and sucking reflexes. The rooting reflex causes infants to turn their heads toward anything that brushes their faces. This action helps them find a food source such as a nipple. Once an object is near a healthy infant's lips, the child will immediately start to suck. This reflex helps the child get food and usually disappears by three weeks of age.

Moro Reflex

The Moro reflex is sometimes referred to as the "startle reflex." It occurs when a newborn is startled by a noise or a sudden movement. When this happens, the infant will react by flinging the arms and legs outward and extending the head. Then the infant will quickly draw the arms together, crying loudly. This reflex peaks during the first month and usually disappears after two months.

Palmar Grasp Reflex

The grasp reflex is easy to observe. When you touch the infant's palms, the hands will grip tightly. The grip is tight enough that you can lift

Some Newborn Reflexes	
Reflex	**Age of Disappearance**
Rooting	3 months
Moro	5 to 8 months
Palmar Grasp	3 to 12 months
Babinski	8 to 12 months
Stepping	2 to 3 months

4-5 Continuation of these reflexes after the time they should disappear may be an indication of nerve or brain damage.

4-6 The rooting and sucking reflexes help an infant get food.

the infant into a sitting position. However, do not try this. Since the infant has no control over this response, he or she may let go suddenly. This reflex can also be seen if a rattle or another object is placed across the palm. This reflex disappears after the first three or four months after birth.

Babinski Reflex

The Babinski reflex is present at birth in normal babies who were born at full term. To test for this reflex, stroke the sole of the foot on the outside from the heel to the toe. When you do this, the toes will fan out and curl and the foot twists in. This reflex usually lasts for the first year after birth.

Stepping or Walking Reflex

A stepping or walking reflex can be observed in normal, full-term babies. When an infant is held so that the feet are flat on a surface, the infant will lift one foot after another in a stepping response. This reflex usually disappears two months after birth. This reflex will recur as learned voluntary behavior toward the end of the first year.

Motor Sequence

Motor sequence refers to the order in which a child is able to perform new movements. Each new movement builds upon the previous abilities. Motor sequence depends on the development of the brain and nerves. For this reason, movements tend to develop in areas closest to the brain and spinal cord first.

In the first months after birth, head and trunk control develops. When this occurs, the infant can lift the head from a surface. The infant also can watch a moving object by moving the head from side to side.

By four or five months of age an infant can roll over. Most infants are first able to turn from the stomach to the back. Soon after, the child will be able to roll from back to stomach.

Most infants are able to sit upright in a high chair from four to six months of age. The infant needs to develop strength in the neck and back muscles to accomplish this feat.

Gradually, infants are able to pull themselves into sitting positions. After this, *crawling* is the next skill in the motor sequence. This skill

occurs shortly after the child learns to roll onto the stomach. To crawl, the child pulls with the arms and wiggles the stomach. Some infants may even push with their legs.

Hitching is another movement used by infants. Before they can hitch, infants must be able to sit without support. From this position, they move their arms and legs, sliding their buttocks across the floor.

As the arms and legs strengthen, infants are able to creep. *Creeping* is a movement in which infants support their weight on their hands and knees. See 4-7. They then move their arms and legs to go forward. As arms and legs become stronger, infants are able to stand with help from an adult. Soon after, they are able to stand while supporting themselves with furniture.

With better leg strength and coordination, infants are able to walk when led by an adult. Soon after, they are able to pull themselves up

4-7 Creeping requires stronger leg muscles and better leg control than crawling.

into a standing position. Next, infants are able to stand without any support. Finally, they become true toddlers–able to walk without support or help.

There are stages of development for each skill that involves movement. To illustrate, when progressing toward mature motor skills, children show changes in movement. Picture the child's first attempts at walking. These actions are awkward. At first, it is difficult to maintain an upright posture. Next, there is an unpredictable loss of balance. Short steps are taken and the toes are pointed outward. The child keeps the legs spread to have a wide base of support.

Gradually the walking pattern appears smoother. The step length increases and the arm swinging decreases. The child also brings the legs closer together, decreasing the base of support. See figure 4-8.

Earliest hand movements are reflexive. By three to four months, infants enjoy swiping at objects. At this age, they are still unable to grasp objects because they close their hands too early or too late. By nine months, eye-hand coordination improves and infants can pick up objects.

Infants can begin scribbling with a crayon by about 16 months of age. Simple figures composed of vertical and horizontal lines can be made by

the end of the second year. By two years of age, the child typically is showing a preference for one hand or the other. For some children, hand dominance is not established until age four.

Many other motor skills are gained in the first two years. These skills are listed in the Appendix. The skills listed are norms for each age group. They are considered norms because about half of infants at that age can do the skills. For this reason, you should not worry if a child cannot do every skill listed for his or her age. However, you should seek help for a child who is way behind the norms. For instance, if a 17-month-old cannot roll over, help should be sought.

Cognitive Development in the First Two Years

At birth, most of an infant's movements are the result of reflexes. As infants grow, they begin to learn how to make things happen for themselves. Soon they are able to coordinate the movements needed to grab a bottle and suck milk from it. They also begin to react differently depending on their needs. A baby may spit out a pacifier if he or she is not hungry. However, a hungry baby may be content to suck on the pacifier.

Two main forces–heredity and environment–influence a child's cognitive development. Heredity determines when a child's brain and senses will be mature enough to learn certain skills. Environmental factors also affect learning. Children need opportunities to use their senses and try new things, 4-9. As a caregiver, you need to provide an environment that allows children to develop to their full potential intellectually.

Being able to see, hear, feel, taste, and smell are important to learning. Through these senses, children learn about many objects and concepts. All of the senses develop during the first two years of life. Sight and hearing develop especially quickly.

Birth to Three Months

A newborn's vision is blurry at birth. During the first few weeks after birth, infants appear to focus on objects in the center of their visual field.

Walking Sequence
Immature Stage
• Upright position difficult to maintain
• Rigid appearance
• Loss of balance occurs frequently
• Short steps taken
• Toes turned outward
• Legs spread wide as base of support
• Arms held above waist
Mature Stage
• Upright position and balance maintained
• Step length increases
• Legs closer together, narrow base of support
• Relaxed appearance
• Arms held at side

4-8 Changes in movement cause the walking pattern to gradually become smoother.

4-9 The activities that you provide infants and young toddlers help them develop cognitively.

4-10 Infants prefer faces to most other objects.

Their near vision is better developed than their far vision. They like to look at objects held 8 to 15 inches in front of them.

As their vision improves, infants show preferences for certain objects. Studies show that infants will gaze longer at patterned disks, such as checks and stripes, than at disks of one solid color. Infants seem to prefer bold colors rather than soft pastels. They also pay more attention to faces than to other objects, 4-10. In fact, by two months of age, an infant will gaze longer at a smiling face than at a face with no expression.

As infants grow older, they tend to shift their attention on the face. At one month of age, infants appear to focus on the hairline. By two months, infants show more interest in the eyes. The adult's facial expression is most interesting to a three-month-old child. These changes show that children are giving thought to areas of the face that interest them.

Hearing also develops early in life. From birth, infants will turn their heads toward a source of sound. Newborns are startled by loud noises. They often react to these noises by crying. These same newborns are lulled to sleep by rhythmic sounds such as a lullaby or a heartbeat. They also react to human voices while ignoring other sounds. By three weeks, a newborn can distinguish between the voice of the mother or father and that of a stranger.

During the first three months after birth, infants do not distinguish between themselves and the objects around them. If infants see their hands moving, they do not think of themselves as making this movement. In their thinking, it could easily be someone else's hand.

Children this age start to experiment with reflex actions. Newborns suck everything that touches their lips. They even make sucking motions in their sleep. Gradually, these children adapt such reflexes to objects in their environment. They learn to suck on bottles, pacifiers, and fingers in different ways.

Three to Six Months

During this time, children start to focus on their surroundings. Before this age, a child would just gaze at objects. The infant now begins to examine objects more closely. By six months of age, the child can distinguish between familiar and unfamiliar faces.

Infants also start to learn that they can touch, shake, and hit objects that they see. They notice toys make sounds. Memory, foresight, and self-awareness are all developing. The child learns that hitting the crib gym makes a noise. The infant also learns that his or her own movement caused the noise.

Infants from three to six months of age also start to show judgment. For instance, they prefer the smell and voice of a parent to that of a stranger. As early as three days after birth, infants will respond to noise. Infants in this stage also try to locate noises by turning toward them. The infant will look around to explore sources of sounds such as a doorbell, a dog barking, or an oven timer. Many times, though, they will turn in the wrong direction.

From birth, an infant makes noises. During this stage, vocalizations begin to increase. You will find that children this age make many noises when you hold and play with them.

Infants in this stage also respond in new ways to touch. If you blow on or kiss the baby's stomach, the child may smile or coo in response. Children this age also respond happily to light touches and tickling.

Infants in this stage think with their senses and movements. By four months, an infant will start using a predictable pattern to learn about objects. If you give a child at this stage an object, you will see this pattern. The child will first look at the object. Then he or she will mouth it and try shaking it, 4-11. The child may also try banging the object on the floor. This is the infant's way of learning what the object can do or how it can be used.

Toward the end of this period, body awareness begins to develop. The infant may bite his or her toe while playing. If the child has a tooth, he or she may be surprised by the hurt this causes. This does not stop the child, however, from making the same mistake with other toes or fingers.

4-11 Mouthing is a major way that infants learn about objects.

Six to Nine Months

The concept of **object permanence** begins to develop at this stage. This concept is the understanding that objects continue to exist even if the infant cannot see them. Before this time, anything out of sight was out of mind for the infant. For instance, if a rattle was placed under a blanket, the young infant would not search for it. Now, the child begins to understand that the rattle is still there even though it is covered.

Beginning to understand object permanence shows that these infants are developing memory and goal-oriented thinking. The child will search under a blanket for a rattle that has been covered. This means that the child remembers that the rattle was there. It also means that the child takes actions with the goal of finding the rattle. At this time though, infants give up within a few seconds if they do not find the rattle.

You can test for object permanence by showing the infant an interesting toy. Then cover the toy with a towel or blanket while the child is looking. If the child attempts to uncover the toy, the child shows an understanding of object permanence. This child also shows goal-oriented behavior.

Part of object permanence involves understanding that other people exist all the time. Before this stage, children would simply cry if uncomfortable and stop crying when needs were met. Now, children begin to understand that they can cry as a call to parents or other caregivers. They know that even if a person is not within sight, the person still exists. Their cry will call the person to them.

Crying to call a person is also a sign that infants are learning to communicate. The child learns that making noises can get an adult to understand the child's needs. At this point, the child starts communicating in other ways. When the infant makes a noise, he or she will often listen for a response. If you make a noise in return, the infant will answer back. Usually the infant will listen when spoken to and look up when his or her name is spoken.

Nine to Twelve Months

During this stage, infants become more intentional about their goals. The child has definite ideas about what he or she wants. If confined to a playpen, the child may cry to be taken out. Once out, the child may crawl across the room to get a forbidden object. At the same time, the child may ignore many interesting objects along the way.

These infants also begin to anticipate certain events. A child at this stage may cry when a parent puts on a coat. The infant has learned that when this happens, the parent will leave. When the child sees the parent enter the child care center, he or she may become excited and happy.

Twelve to Eighteen Months

Between twelve and eighteen months, infants' hearing and speech continues to develop. They enjoy playing pat-a-cake and peekaboo games. Children at this stage like trial-and-error problem solving. They experiment with objects to find new ways to use them, 4-12. These might include rolling, tossing, or bouncing. These children express joy when they find that toys can make noise. They begin to understand that the force they use affects the loudness or softness of noise in a toy.

Relationships between cause and effect fascinate these young toddlers. For instance, the child loves to hit water and watch it splash. Children also learn ways to use cause and effect to

4-12 Young toddlers often look for new ways to use objects.

reach goals at this age. For instance, the child may learn that by pulling on a tablecloth, he or she can reach a plate of cookies.

Language is a change of behavior that occurs as a result of experience and maturation. It is also related to the child's environment. In Spain, for instance, children learn to speak Spanish, while children in Italy learn Italian. Language becomes a bigger part of communication at this stage. Before this time, some children may say a few words, such as daddy or mommy. Now, children learn to say many new words. Children's first words usually include objects that move and familiar actions. Included are words such as car, truck, dig, ball, up, down, bye-bye, wet, dirty, and hot. Mostly, children use one or two words to communicate during this stage. They do not yet understand how to combine a series of words to form sentences.

Books become more important to children at this time. A child in this stage will love to sit on your lap and have you read a story. Young toddlers may be able to identify many pictures in simple books. As you point to the pictures, the child may give the names of the objects. Most children at this age can understand even more words than they can say.

Eighteen to Twenty-four Months

As children near their second birthday, there is a change in how they approach their environment. During this stage, children start to think before taking action. They are able to apply what they know about objects to solve problems without as much trial-and-error. For instance, the child may know that standing on a stool in the bathroom helps the child reach the sink. This same child may apply this knowledge to get a cookie on the kitchen counter. Instead of a stool, the child may use a chair or even an open drawer. Children in this stage still tend to think in terms of actions.

Improved thinking skills and motor skills can make caring for toddlers in this stage exhausting. These children want to actively explore everything. They want to find out as much as they can about new places and objects. However, these children are not old enough to understand the dangers that may be involved in exploring. For instance, they may step in an open

drawer to reach something without realizing that the drawer may fall. Therefore, you must continually watch toddlers and try to make sure their environment is as safe as possible.

Pretending starts to be part of a child's world at this stage. A young toddler's pretending is often a form of deferred imitation. **Deferred imitation** is watching another person's behavior and then acting out that behavior later, 4-13. For instance, a father may tuck his child into bed each night and give him or her a kiss on the forehead. At the center the next day, the child may tuck in a doll and give it a kiss on the forehead. Children may also pretend to be animals they have seen, such as dogs.

These children now understand that symbols may represent other real objects. For instance, a younger child might play with a doll by swinging it around and hitting things with it. Now, however, the child will hold the doll like a baby and cover it with a blanket.

4-13 This child is imitating behavior that she has seen at home.

Children are learning more and more words. At first, toddlers only add one to three words to their vocabularies each month. Between 18 to 24 months, however, as many as 10 to 20 new words may be added each month. When their vocabularies reach about 200 words, they begin to combine two words. The term used to describe these two-word phrases is **telegraphic speech**. For instance, the child might say "doggie bark" to let you know that he or she hears a dog barking. Figure 4-14 shows typical two-word phrases used by toddlers during this stage.

Children like to share what they know with you. As you read to them, they may point to objects to tell you what they are. They enjoy pointing to things that you name. For instance, you may say to the child "Touch your nose." Children at this age are quick to respond by pointing to parts of their bodies. Later, you may get them to point to other objects in the room.

Social-Emotional Development in the First Two Years

At birth, infants do not show a wide range of emotions. They seem to be basically comfortable or uncomfortable. To communicate this, they use movements, facial expressions, and sounds. By cooing, they show their comfort or delight. By crying, they show discomfort.

In the first few months of life, you will observe a range of emotions. The most reliable clues are infants' facial expressions. Happiness is shown when the corners of the mouth are pulled back and the cheeks are raised. Between six and nine months, the infant will begin to show fear, anxiety, and anger. Signs of fear are the mouth opened with the corners pulled back, eyes widened, and eyebrows raised. By the end of the second year, children are expressing their emotions in many more ways.

Socially, young children tend to focus on a few adults who are close to them. This is especially true of infants. After the first birthday, children may take more interest in other toddlers, 4-15. However, adults are still most important to children in this age group. As a caregiver, you need to realize that your actions will have a strong effect on children's social-emotional development. These children are ready for relationships. They need to be able to count on caregivers who will respond immediately to their distress signals.

Temperament

Even from birth, children differ in temperament or the ways that they react to their environment. **Temperament** refers to the quality and intensity of emotional reactions. Such factors as passivity, irritability, and activity patterns are part of a child's temperament.

Toddlers Typical Two-Word Phrases
Johnny hit.
Big ball.
Give milk.
My bear.
Hi daddy.
No milk.

4-14 Toddlers often use two-word phrases.

4-15 One-year-olds start to take more interest in their peers.

Passivity relates to how actively involved a child is with his or her surroundings. A passive infant withdraws from a new person or event. An active infant does something in response to a new person or event.

Children also differ in their level of *irritability* or tendency to feel distressed. Some infants cry easily. They may be difficult to comfort, even if you hold them and try to soothe them. There are other infants who rarely cry. These infants do not let changes bother them as much. Caring for these infants is usually easier for adults.

Activity patterns or levels of movement also vary in infants. Some infants can be described as quiet, making few movements. When asleep, these infants may hardly move. Others are constantly moving their arms and legs. These infants may even sleep restlessly.

If you care for infants, you need to adjust to the temperaments of different children. All infants need loving attention. If given patient, tender care, most children will grow to be happy and well-adjusted. This is even true of very irritable infants.

Attachment

Attachment is the strong emotional tie felt between people. Most infants become attached or bonded to a small group of people early in life. They mainly become attached to the people who care for them. Included may be mothers, fathers, caregivers, or older siblings. Young infants learn that when they are hungry, wet, or frightened, they can depend on these people to make them feel better. The quality of attachment depends on the adults.

Several early attachment behaviors are shown by infants. These behaviors show that infants care for and respond to certain people who are important to them. Infants will single these people out for special attention. When approached, the infant may break into a broad, warm smile. Other examples of attachment behaviors are cooing, kicking, gurgling, and laughing. Crying and clinging are also attachment behaviors. These behaviors show that the child is signaling to others.

Attachment begins early in life. Studies show that one-month-old babies show signs of anxiety if they are cared for by an unfamiliar person. These distress signs appear as irregular sleeping or eating patterns.

Separation anxiety is another attachment behavior shown by infants. This happens when a child is unhappy because a familiar caregiver is leaving. The child often cries as a sign of distress. The first signs of separation anxiety appear at about six months of age. The reaction becomes clearer by nine months of age. By 15 months of age, separation anxiety is very strong. After this point, this distress gradually weakens.

As a caregiver, you need to be prepared for the attachment behaviors of children in this age group. Children between 9 and 18 months of age will usually have the most difficulty beginning a child care program. To make the transition easier, you should encourage parents to bring the child's favorite toy or blanket.

As children show separation anxiety, you need to remind yourself not to take the reaction personally. These children are simply fearful because their familiar caregivers are leaving them. They do not know what to expect next, and they are in an unfamiliar surrounding with strange people. As children become more familiar with the center, its people, and its routine, they will show less distress.

Changes Over Time

During the first two years after birth, you will see many changes in children socially and emotionally. As a caregiver, your actions will affect how these children change. Establishing trust is a key factor in social-emotional development. Trust develops when there is predictability. If you meet children needs and encourage them to interact with others, children will learn to trust and care for others. They will feel safe and happy.

Birth to Three Months

At birth, newborns do not have very refined emotions. General excitement and general distress are the only emotions shown. The child may show excitement by looking alert, smiling, or wiggling. Distress is shown by crying. Observing a child in this stage, you may notice that there are no tears when the child cries.

Three to Six Months

By three months, children respond to people with smiles and laughter. They may make happy sounds as adults play with, hold, or feed them. During this stage, infants start to notice and smile at other babies. Crying is still used to show distress. Early in this stage, tears begin to appear. Later, children start to use different cries to signal different types of distress.

Six to Twelve Months

Infants in this stage become actively involved with their caregivers. As adults play with and care for them, these children express happiness, joy, and surprise. They also make sounds in response to the speech of others. Infants in this stage also begin to develop fear. You should not be surprised if a child this age cries at the sight of a stranger. By this age, children have also developed attachment to their caregivers. They may cry and even show anger when their caregivers leave them.

This stage may be the most difficult for the child's parents and for you. Separation anxiety starts to show. As a result, a child may start crying and clinging upon entering the center. When you try taking the child from the parent, the child may attempt to push you away. After the parent leaves, the child may continue to cry. Most children, however, will stop crying within a few minutes. This behavior may continue until 14 to 16 months of age.

Twelve to Twenty-four Months

Early in this stage, children still show separation anxiety. Children in this stage also show anxiety. In other words, they become upset because of something they think will happen in the future. For instance, this child may cling to a parent who will be leaving soon.

These children become more interested in exploring. Although they still fear the unfamiliar, they are curious about new places and objects, 4-16. Children who feel secure are more likely to explore than those who feel unsure of their surroundings. By this age, children start to take more interest in other children. They like to play next to other children, but they do not interact much with them.

Children start to become more aware of their own abilities at this point. This self-awareness is a source of joy and anger for children. Toddlers are proud and happy when they can do things for themselves. However, sometimes they insist on doing things for themselves that they can't do yet. This can cause frustration and anger for the child.

Children who are becoming self-aware also like to say "no." These children like to know that they can make things happen, and they do not always want to do what adults want. Sometimes they may say no to you just to see what will happen. You will need to be kind but firm with these children. You must help them understand that there are rules that must be followed. At the same time, you need to reassure these children that their wants and needs are important.

4-16 Curiosity helps toddlers explore new places and objects.

Summary

Understanding child development will help make you a successful caregiver or early childhood teacher. The study of child development is divided into three main areas—physical, cognitive, and social-emotional development. Growth in the first two years of life is rapid. Physically, children start with many reflexes that are eventually replaced with voluntary movements. As they become bigger and stronger, infants are able to roll over, crawl, creep, and eventually walk.

Cognitive growth shows in children's reactions to the environment. As infants, children will mouth and hit with objects to learn how they work. With growth, children begin to understand how different objects work. They also begin to understand that objects exist even if they are not seen. Children begin to think about how they can reach goals. They also learn to communicate, first by crying, and later by using words.

Each child is born with a temperament that sets the stage for social-emotional development. Young infants tend to show two main emotions—distress and excitement. As infants grow, they become attached to caregivers. They express joy, happiness, surprise, and fear. These children may experience separation anxiety when loved ones leave them. As children grow older, they show interest in other children. They also become interested in their own abilities. These children may often test adults by saying no to rules and suggestions. However, they also take pride in their own achievements. These children still look to adults for love and attention.

Review and Reflect

1. Changes in bone thickness, vision, and hearing are part of _____.

2. True or false. Trust, fear, and pride are part of cognitive development.

3. List and explain three characteristics of development.

4. True or false. Reflex testing can be used to detect whether an infant has brain or nerve damage.

5. Why are infants able to crawl before they are able to creep?

6. If you place a toy car near an infant who is three to six months old, what is the child most likely to do?

   A. Ignore the toy.
   B. Cry.
   C. Put the toy in his or her mouth.
   D. Slide the toy along the floor making car noises.

7. Describe how to test a child for an understanding of object permanence.

8. If a toddler sees his or her mother mowing the lawn one day and then pretends to mow the lawn at the child care center, the toddler is practicing _____.

9. Describe telegraphic speech and provide an example.

10. Describe three factors that affect a child's temperament.

11. True or false. Children do not start to show attachment behaviors until after their first birthday.

12. How would the social-emotional development of a three-month-old differ from that of a one-year-old?

Apply and Explore

1. Visit a child care center serving infants. Observe differences among them.

2. Invite a pediatrician to class to describe the sequences in infant development.

3. Observe a parent playing with or caring for an infant. Record the child's age in months. Write an anecdotal record describing the child's interactions with the parent. Share your observation with the class.

4. Use pictures from magazines or catalogs to make a bulletin board on infant development.

By age three, children begin to form friendships with their peers.

Chapter 5

Understanding Two- and Three-Year-Olds

After studying this chapter, you will be able to

- describe the physical, cognitive, and social-emotional development of two-year-olds.

- explain how three-year-olds develop physically, cognitively, socially, and emotionally.

- relate how the development of two- and three-year-olds will affect your role as a teacher.

Terms to Know

language comprehension

expressive language

egocentrism

gender roles

self-concept

To better understand two- and three-year-olds, you need to develop a mental picture. You need to understand how children in these age groups behave. Generally, two-year-olds are active, demanding, and curious. Three-year-old children tend to be more calm. Generally, they try to please and conform. Understanding these differences will help you plan programs that best meet the needs of each child.

Physical Development of Two-Year-Olds

Two-year-old children continue to grow physically, but the rapid growth that occurred during infancy tapers off. A typical two-year-old will grow two to three inches in height and add about five pounds in weight during the year. Their organs, such as the eyes, stomach, heart, and lungs, become stronger.

The digestive system matures slowly in children. The appetites of two-year-olds vary from day to day. Some days they may be excited about eating at snack time; other days they may reject their snacks. Likewise, what they eat at mealtimes may vary.

The coordination of the two-year-old's body is improving. They are less top heavy and their center of gravity shifts downward. Provided equipment, space, and support, these children can master a variety of gross motor skills, 5-1. They can usually run and jump without falling. The fine motor skills of these children are also improving.

5-1 Two-year-olds have improved muscle strength and coordination.

Gross Motor Development

Improved coordination and body control makes playing with balls great fun for active two-year-olds. They can pick up a ball by bending at the waist. Likewise, they can kick a large ball. These children are usually able to throw a ball without falling.

Two-year-olds have more control in leg and foot muscles than before. They can walk up and down stairs placing both feet on each stair. (Most children this age need to hold on to a rail as they step.) They also are able to stand with both feet on a balance beam. These children have the skill to walk on their toes. From a standing position, they can balance on one foot. Jumping is also possible. They can jump several inches off the floor with both feet. Most children this age can do a standing broad jump of about eight and one-half inches. In addition, most two-year-olds can sit on a riding toy and move it by pushing with their feet.

Fine Motor Development

Two-year-old children are rapidly developing finger dexterity and control. They are able to insert keys into a lock and turn pages in a book one at a time. Most children this age also can string large beads or spools and lace cards, 5-2. They also can hold scissors properly. By two years of age, they can open and close scissors.

Hand preference is fairly developed by this age. Many children will use the same hand for most fine motor activities. However, these children still switch hands for some activities. Alex, for example, draws with his right hand, but eats and throws a ball with his left hand.

You will see children using writing tools at this age. At about 24 months of age, children can scribble. At first, these scribbles look like tangles of lines. By about 30 months, children can draw horizontal lines, vertical lines, and circles. Most children draw by holding the tool, crayon, or pencil, in their fist.

Two-year-olds become skilled at building with blocks. They can build towers of six to seven blocks. They can also use two or more blocks to make a train and push the blocks along.

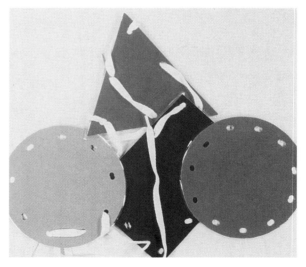

5-2 Having lacing cards like these for two-year-olds help them improve their fine motor skills.

Self-Help Skills

With a little help, two-year-olds can accomplish many self-help skills. At this age, they begin to cooperate in dressing. First, they can undress themselves. They are able to remove simple items of clothing such as socks, shoes, and pants. Snaps can be opened successfully. Next, they begin to dress themselves. At first, this involves pulling on simple garments. Zippers can be zipped and unzipped. By 30 months, most children can unbutton large buttons, close snaps, and put on their socks. However, you will need to help children as they try these skills.

By this age, children can drink from a cup or glass without help. They may spill fairly often, but their drinking skills improve with practice. Two-year-olds are also able to drink using a straw. They can use a spoon to feed themselves, but may revert to eating with their fingers if hurried.

Strides are normally made in toilet training during this time. At two years of age, most children learn to use the toilet or potty chair with reminders. However, accidents are common. Between 24 and 35 months, children seldom have bowel accidents. They may still have problems with wetting for several months. By 33 months, many children can use the toilet without help.

Cognitive Development of Two-Year-Olds

The two-year-old's cognitive development focuses on three main areas. These include language comprehension skills, expressive language skills, and math readiness skills. All of these areas reflect the child's intelligence.

Language Comprehension Skills

A person's understanding of language is called **language comprehension**. Some experts refer to this as receptive or inner language. This form of language is more advanced than expressive language skills in children. For instance, a 20-month-old child may be able to follow directions. However, this child may not be able to say more than a few words.

Language comprehension grows rapidly in two-year-olds. These children can understand and answer routine questions. While reading a story, you may point to a picture and ask "What is that?" The child may respond by saying "Baby." See 5-3.

By 24 months of age, most children can identify at least six body parts. Children can point to these parts on themselves, others, or dolls. They enjoy playing games in which you state "Find your toes" or "Where are your eyes?"

Many other new skills develop around 24 months. Children can comprehend the pronouns *I, my, mine,* and *me.* They also can provide appropriate answers to yes and no questions.

By 30 months of age, other milestones are reached. When asked, children can give you one cookie. They also can follow two-step commands. For instance, you can tell a child "Take off your coat and put it in your locker."

5-3 Two-year-olds will answer questions about pictures in the stories you read them.

These children can also give answers to 44 *where* questions. For instance, you may ask a child "Where is your locker?" or "Where do you wash your hands?"

Understanding the meanings of words continues through the second year. When picking up objects, two-year-olds can tell the difference between soft and heavy. Size concepts are also developing. Children understand such words as *big* and *tall*. Children also start to understand words related to space. These include such words as *on, under, out of, together*, and *away from*.

Expressive Language Skills

Expressive language is the ability to produce language forms. It is a tool that can be used to express a person's thoughts to others. For most two-year-olds, expressive language quickly develops. Like other aspects of development, it follows a sequence. The child's experiences affect the rate and content of expressive language development. Therefore, it is important you provide an environment that stimulates language development.

Speech usually involves simple sentences by two years of age. In the beginning, only two words may be used. "Johnny hurt" or "Tom dog" are examples. Later, the child will begin to put three-word sentences together. Examples include "Tom go home," "I eat corn," or "See my truck." Sentences follow the word order of their native languages.

There are two language strategies that are important when you work with two-year-olds. These are called feeding-in and expansion. *Feeding-in* is a strategy where you provide the child's language. For example, if a child is building with blocks, the teacher might say "You are building with blocks."

Expansion is a strategy used to expand the child's language. Typically this is accomplished by reframing the child's utterance into a sentence. For example, if the child says "car" the teacher might say "This is a blue car." If the child says "wheels" the teacher could say "The car has wheels."

The vocabulary of the average two-year-old is 50 to 200 words. You will notice that children at this age often use words without fully understanding them. You might also observe that girls generally develop language skills faster than boys.

Two-year-olds do not understand how to use grammar to form questions. Instead, they use the tone of their voice. They may ask in a questioning tone "Grandma go?" or "Milk all gone?"

Two-year-olds often make negative sentences. They do this by adding the word *no* to positive sentences. For instance, a child may say "No milk" meaning that he or she does not want any milk. The child may say "Teacher no here" meaning that he or she cannot find the teacher.

Between 27 and 30 months, children may begin to use prepositions. For instance, children may say "Cookies in jar." Around this age, children also begin using plurals. They may request "cookies" or "candies."

Modifiers are also added to the vocabulary. *Some, a lot, all,* and *one* are used as quantifiers. *Mine, his,* and *hers* are used as possessives. *Pretty, new,* and *blue* are some adjectives that might be used as modifiers.

Between 31 and 34 months of age, children may begin adding *ed* to verbs to show past tense. At about the same time, present tense verb helpers appear. These include such terms as *can, are, will,* and *am.*

Math Readiness Skills

Math skills are developed as children interact with others and with objects. When you ask, a child can give you "just one" of something. Children also understand size concepts such as big and small. Awareness of shapes, forms, and colors is also developing during this stage. They begin to sort objects by shape and color.

Social-Emotional Development of Two-Year-Olds

Two-year-olds continue to grow socially and emotionally. At this age, children tend to show many negative attitudes. Children like instant gratification and find it difficult to wait. These qualities make patience an important quality as you work with two-year-olds.

Social Development

At the beginning of this developmental stage, children play next to each other. However, they do not play cooperatively with each other, 5-4. Children in this stage still tend to be more interested in adults. Therefore, they tend to act out adult experiences as they play. These might include driving a car, making a bed, and talking on the phone.

The average two-year-old tends to be possessive. Usually these children do not want to share. There typically is competition for toys. They tend to use body language to let people know how they feel about their possessions.

Two-year-old children can be very physical in their responses. They may push, hit, or shove another child who approaches their toys. Although they have difficulty understanding the concept of sharing, two-year-olds may return a toy that belongs to someone else.

In spite of their negativism and possessiveness, two-year-olds are usually affectionate. They may hug you and hold your hand. Two-year-olds thrive on love and caring from adults. They also enjoy helping you. Whether you are setting the table for lunch or picking up blocks, they are eager to participate.

Emotional Development

These children like to be able to control their surroundings. Because they can't always do that, they tend to get frustrated and angry at times. Trying to do a task that is too hard for them may cause anger, 5-5. Not being allowed to do or have something may stir angry feelings as well. Two-year-olds may have temper tantrums if they do not get their way. They may scream, cry, stamp, or kick. Their anger is not usually at any

5-4 Two-year-olds do not interact much as they play.

5-5 Being able to meet goals quickly is important to two-year-olds. If they do not get instant results, they often become angry.

one person or object; they are simply frustrated. Children this age still have not learned more appropriate ways of expressing anger.

Fears become common at this age. Two-year-olds are often afraid of being hurt or harmed. Many of their fears have to do with their imagination. Two-year-olds don't always separate pretend from reality, so they may be afraid of a monster from a story. A dream may frighten them because they think the characters are real. As a teacher, you need to comfort children when they are afraid. Even imagined fears are real to toddlers.

Love and caring are shown often by these children. They need to receive love and caring in return. Two-year-olds need to know that people still care for them even if they get angry. They also need to know that they can depend on others. To build trust and security, these children need regular routines. For instance, they may need to sit next to the same person or group of people at every meal or snack time.

Teaching Two-Year-Olds

The development of two-year-olds has a strong effect on the way you teach and work with them. You need to be prepared to handle those situations that are typical with these children.

If you were to observe a group of two-year-olds, your first observation might be that they are negative. Two-year-olds often use the word "no." At times, they may even mean "yes" when they say "no." For instance, you may ask "Do you want more milk?" The child may say "no" while extending his or her glass toward you for more milk.

You may find yourself becoming impatient with two-year-old children at times. They always seem to want their own way. Whether you want to read a story or take the children on a field trip, you are bound to find a two-year-old who refuses. The child may refuse to leave his or her present activity or to put on his or her coat. Working with two-year-olds requires gentle, but firm, guidance.

Two-year-olds are very egocentric. **Egocentrism** means that they believe everyone else sees, thinks, and feels like they do. This does not mean they are selfish. They believe that you will think exactly as they do.

Prepare yourself for the dawdling behavior of the typical two-year-old. These children insist on doing things at their own pace. Because of this, routines take longer. When planning a schedule, be aware of this type of behavior. Two-year-olds need plenty of time to move from one activity to the next. Therefore, you will need to be flexible and patient.

Upon entering a classroom of two-year-olds, you will first notice the noise. This is very common. When a child discovers a drum, the child will hit it over and over again. Likewise, they may repeat a new vocal sound many times. If one child starts clapping and stamping his or her feet, the other children may join in. You will need to be prepared for high noise levels and be able to control that noise from time to time.

Curiosity is another trait of two-year-olds. Children of this age enjoy exploring. When new materials are brought into the classroom, the children will carefully inspect them. If you ask them what toy they want, they may have difficulty choosing. Therefore, you should add only a few new items at a time.

Gross motor activity is a favorite of two-year-old children. They delight in movement and are not afraid to try out new equipment. They love to run and chase others. Therefore, adequate supervision is crucial. On field trips, these children like to run ahead. For this reason, you may want to have extra adults on the trips to help supervise.

Two-year-olds like to act out life experiences. They especially like to imitate the activities of adults, 5-6. Therefore, they need a dramatic play corner. Housekeeping equipment, mirrors, dolls, dress-up clothes, toy telephones, trucks, and cars should all be included.

Two-year-olds need some routine in their day. They like to have things done the same way. These children look forward to certain parts of the day, such as story time. Therefore, you need to be careful to follow a similar schedule from day to day. A few changes add interest, but children need to rely on a predictable schedule.

Two-year-olds may also have temper tantrums, but this is normal behavior. It has nothing to do with your skill as a teacher, although you may be embarrassed by a toddler's outburst. What is important is how you handle the tantrum. It is vital that you remain composed.

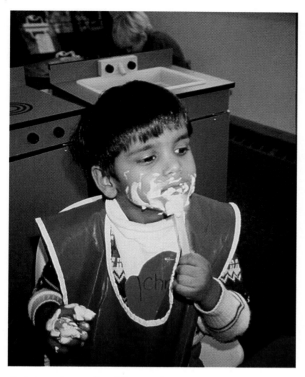

5-6 Teachers should provide many dramatic play materials so two-year-olds can act out such everyday experiences as shaving.

Use a calm voice when speaking to the child. If the child is kicking, you may have to immobilize the child by holding the legs. If the child is a threat to the other children, move the child to another area of the room.

Physical Development of Three-Year-Olds

For three-year-olds, playing is exploring. They are constantly moving, tasting, smelling, and touching. As a result, their body coordination shows great improvement. You will notice that the arms, hands, legs, and feet are all becoming more coordinated. Likewise, their bodies are becoming less top heavy and more streamlined. To stay upright, three-year-olds no longer need to keep their legs spread apart. Their walk appears more natural as their toes point forward and their feet move closer together.

Gross Motor Development

Throwing, jumping, and hopping skills improve as a result of better coordination. The improvement of body coordination is also reflected in the climbing skills of three-year-olds. Now these children can climb and descend stairs easily. In fact, these children can walk up stairs with alternating feet. Their balance is improving.

By 36 months of age, children can catch large balls with their arms. Their catching skill gradually becomes more refined. Eventually, they can catch bouncing balls with their hands. This skill usually emerges toward the end of the third year.

Leg coordination and balancing skills also improve. Three-year-olds can ride and steer tricycles. They can walk heel-to-toe for four steps. They can balance on one foot for up to eight seconds. They can hop on one foot up to three times.

Fine Motor Development

The fine motor skills of three-year-olds continue to develop. Cutting skills become more refined. The two-year-old could only hold and work scissors. However, a three-year-old can use the scissors to cut paper, 5-7. They can cut five-inch squares of paper into two sections. Young three-year-olds can cut across the paper, but they cannot cut along a line. By 42 to 48 months, children can cut along a line straying no more than one-half of an inch away from it.

Three-year-olds have better drawing skills. Making use of their improved fine motor skills, they often reproduce simple shapes as they draw. If you show these children the shape of a cross, they can copy the shape. They also can trace the shape of a diamond. They enjoy drawing faces. The faces usually include the mouth, eyes, nose, and/or ears. These features are not drawn in proportion, but they are usually placed in the correct position on the face. They lack the fine motor coordination needed to create complex figures.

Three-year-olds also enjoy manipulating blocks and puzzles. They can build towers with nine to ten cubes. They also can construct simple puzzles.

5-7 This three-year-old can use scissors to cut paper.

Self-Help Skills

Three-year-olds become increasingly self-sufficient. Daily care routines now require little adult assistance. These children can turn the water faucet on and off as long as they can reach it, 5-8. As a result, they can attend to routines such as washing and drying their hands and face. They also can brush their own teeth.

Three-year-olds become better at dressing themselves. They can now open buckles and put on shoes that do not tie. Three-year-olds need little adult help when their clothing has elastic waists or large button openings. They still are not able to work small buttons and hooks. Three-year-olds have trouble telling the front from the back on clothing, too. They do better with clothing that has a design on the front or a label in the back.

At snack and mealtime, these children are now able to use knives. They can spread butter, jelly, and soft peanut butter on bread. They also can pour liquid from a small pitcher. As a result, these children may enjoy assisting at snack time.

Another step toward independence is mastered at this age. Three-year-olds have almost full

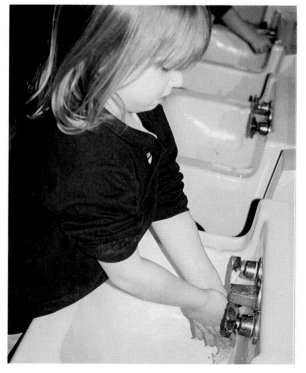

5-8 Being able to turn water on and off increases this three-year-old's ability to help herself.

control over toilet routines. They are even able to get through a night without wetting. This accomplishment is made possible through improved motor control.

Cognitive Development of Three-Year-Olds

By the third birthday, the ability to think matures. Children move away from thinking only in terms of actions. They are able to solve simple problems. For instance, if you place an object under a cup and place nothing under another cup, the child knows which cup the object is under. If you switch the cups while the child is watching, the child still knows where the object is.

Children at this age still do not think logically. They are still egocentric as they have not yet learned to see things from more than one perspective. For instance, they do not realize that something that seems tall to them might actually seem short to an adult. They get confused about time concepts. These children may also become confused about cause and effect. For instance, if a bell rings before each snack is served, children may think the bell causes the snack to appear.

Even though thinking is still flawed, these children learn quickly. Their language comprehension skills, expressive language skills, and math readiness skills continue to improve.

Language Comprehension Skills

Understanding of language continues to grow in three-year-olds. On request, the child can now give you two objects. These children can also remember and follow three-part instructions. For example, you might say "Go to the sink, wash your hands, and dry them with a towel." See 5-9.

Three-year-olds begin to understand the pronouns *you* and *they*. They also understand such words as *who, whose, why,* and *how*. They are able to provide answers to questions based on these words. For instance, you may ask the child "Who lives at the North Pole?" Another question might be "Whose teddy bear is this?" While reading a story you may ask "Why is the girl crying?" These children will be able to answer such questions as "How will your mother bake the pie?"

5-9 Three-year-olds can follow your three-part instructions.

Space concepts become clearer. While moving objects, children will understand your instructions that include such words as *toward, up, top,* and *apart*. Toward the end of the third year, children master more space concepts. They understand such ideas as *around, in front of, in back of,* and *next to*.

Expressive Language Skills

Children's ability to produce language continues to increase. By now, children may use more than 900 words. Three-year-olds also have improved grammar. They may make sentences of four or five words. They may even join sentences together with a conjunction. For instance, the child may say "The bunny died and we don't have it."

Three-year-olds begin to understand the difference between past and present tense. They like to make verbs past tense by adding *ed* to them. These children make statements such as "I talked" or "Daddy walked." However, they do not yet understand that there are exceptions to this rule. They may use such past tense verbs as "runned" and "goed." They may even use the correct form, but still add *ed*. For instance, they may say "ranned" or "wented."

Children start to understand possessive nouns. Three-year-olds may refer to mommy's car, daddy's hammer, and teacher's coat. Negatives are not fully understood by three-year-olds. They understand that such words as *no, not, can't, don't, nothing*, and *never* are negative. However, they use all negative terms when they form negative statements. For instance, a three-year-old may say "Kelsie can't do nothing" or "Jackson can't never go nowhere."

During this stage, children start to use question words, especially *why* and *when*. These children tend to add on the question word to a regular sentence. For instance, they may ask "When Daddy is coming?" or "Why the cloud is moving?"

As these children play, they frequently talk out loud to themselves. For example, three-year-old Jenny is painting at the easel and saying, "Jenny is painting a picture. I need red. Where is the red? Now I need yellow. I need to paint with yellow."

Math Readiness Skills

Three-year-olds continue to learn concepts basic to math. They start to understand the concepts *full, more, less, smaller*, and *empty*. By 42 months of age, most children understand the concept of *largest*. These children like to constantly compare objects, saying one object is bigger or another is smaller.

Counting skills also begin at this stage. If you ask, a three-year-old can give you two objects. These children can also count to three while pointing to corresponding objects. They may be able to recite numbers in order higher than three, but they are not able to count that number of objects.

Children in this age group can distinguish between *one* and *many*. To check for this skill, place one chip on the table. Nearby, place a pile of chips. Ask the child to point to one chip. Repeat the question asking the child to point to many chips. Children who respond correctly have learned the difference between one and many.

Social-Emotional Development of Three-Year-Olds

After the third birthday, children start to grow out of the temper tantrums and contrariness of the two-year-old stage. They become cooperative, happy, and agreeable, 5-10. By this time, children start to learn socially acceptable ways of expressing their feelings. They can use language more effectively to communicate with others. Also, they start to form friendships with their peers.

Social Development

Three-year-olds are eager to help others, especially adults. They like to help with such tasks as passing out crayons and pouring juice. They are learning new ways of showing concern for others. They are learning positive ways to get attention from others. These children are more willing to accept attention from adults and children who are not well-known. They adjust to new people more easily than two-year-olds do.

5-10 Three-year-olds tend to be more content and agreeable than two-year-olds.

By the third birthday, children begin to play with, rather than next to, other children. See 5-11. Although these children interact with each other, their play is not truly organized. For instance, they may play house and each child playing may be the daddy.

Children this age are not as possessive as two-year-olds. They will share with others, but they do not like to share too much. For this reason, three-year-olds usually play with only one or two main friends. These children use language more to communicate with friends. For instance, they may say to a friend "You play with the baby." To another child, they may say "You can't play with us."

Children this age also begin to learn **gender roles**. These are behaviors that are expected of girls or boys. Gender roles are not as clearly defined as they once were, but they are still an important part of learning. Children this age realize that there are physical differences between boys and girls. With the proper role models, they begin to learn how to treat members of the opposite sex with respect.

Emotional Development

Three-year-olds have strong visible emotions. They get excited. They get angry. They get discouraged. However, they are beginning to understand that there are appropriate ways to express these emotions. They realize that adults do not approve of such actions as temper tantrums. Also, they are eager to act in ways that please others. Therefore, these children are developing control over their strong feelings. Instead of striking another child, they may scream "Stop it!"

Unlike two-year-olds, many situations no longer lead to angry outbursts among three-year-olds. Because they have improved coordination, three-year-olds are less likely to become frustrated when they cannot do something. They also have improved language skills. When children can understand why something is happening, they are less likely to get angry. For instance, a child may want a drink just prior to lunch. You can explain, "It's only a few minutes until lunch. You can have a drink then." When the child understands that he or she will have a drink soon, he or she is less likely to get angry.

Three-year-olds are likely to become angry when things do not go their way. However, they begin to direct their anger at objects. For instance, they may be angry at a pitcher if they spill their milk. Children this age are more likely to express their anger in words. They do not hit, stamp, or cry as much as two-year-olds do.

5-11 Although their play is not organized, three-year-olds will play with each other.

The three-year-old is beginning to develop a self-concept. Your **self-concept** is the way you see yourself. A child's self-concept includes a set of beliefs about himself or herself. Ask three-year-olds to tell you about themselves. They will likely provide you with their names, possessions, and physical appearance. As a result, you might hear something like this: "I'm Kelly. I have a dog. I have a brother. I have black hair."

By this stage, children are not as likely to be frightened by objects that they know. For instance, they are not frightened by the noise from a car. However, they are quite fearful of imagined dangers. They may be especially afraid of the dark. These children also become more fearful of pain. They may be scared that a dog will bite them or that they will be hurt during a doctor's visit.

Three-year-olds are affectionate, and they tend to seek affection in return. They may follow, cling to, or help an adult in an effort to get attention, approval, or comfort. Three-year-olds still do not think in terms of the feelings of others.

Children learn to express their own feelings by watching the adults around them. When you express surprise and happiness, they will also show these emotions. Likewise, if you give a hug to comfort someone who is sad, they will imitate your behavior.

Teaching Three-Year-Olds

Three-year-olds are typically happy, sociable, and agreeable. Furthermore, they are very eager to please. As a result, they are likely to accept your suggestions, 5-12. They also adjust easily to new adults, classmates, and situations. For these reasons, you will find that most adults enjoy working with these children.

Three-year-olds enjoy playing. They still like playing alone, but they also enjoy playing in groups of two or three. You can introduce themes to their play. Some themes include treating and healing others. One child will help another who is injured or ill.

The objects that you supply in the classroom will influence a three-year-old's dramatic play. Cooking supplies, tools, phones, and suitcases are popular. These children enjoy pretending to be cooking, making repairs, calling others, and taking trips.

Three-year-old children are becoming increasingly independent. They feel a need to do things for themselves. Signs of independence include such statements as "I can do it" or "Let me do it." These statements are healthy signs that the children are gaining confidence in their abilities.

Some three-year-olds need encouragement to become more independent. They may make such statements as "You do it" or "I can't." When these words are spoken, you need to provide encouragement. These children need to know that you value their independence. They need to feel that they can do things for themselves.

5-12 By the third year, children are more willing to accept and try suggestions from teachers.

Summary

Two-year-olds grow and change in many ways. Their motor skills improve so that they can run, jump, and balance. They also can scribble, drink, and undress. These children are learning to control their elimination.

Two-year-olds are able to understand and say many words. They can answer simple questions and follow simple directions. They are beginning to learn basic math concepts related to size, number, shape, and color.

Socially and emotionally, these children are striving to be independent. They want to do things their own way, and when they can't, they may have temper tantrums. These children still need love and affection from adults.

Three-year-olds grow out of many of the problems of two-year-olds. They have better muscle control and coordination. These children can draw, cut with scissors, and work simple puzzles. They can dress themselves without much help from adults.

The thinking abilities of three-year-olds is improving. These children have a growing understanding and use of language. They have a better understanding of questions and instructions. They are using more complex sentences to communicate. They are beginning to learn grammar rules for past tense. These children are also developing more refined concepts of number and size.

Socially, three-year-olds are beginning to reach out. They seek and favor adults, and they are starting to make friends with other children. These children have strong emotions, but they are learning appropriate ways to express these emotions.

Review and Reflect

1. List three motor skills of two-year-olds.
2. True or false. Most two-year-olds can dress themselves without help from adults.
3. Language comprehension is _____ advanced than expressive language in two-year-olds.
4. Compare the language strategies of expansion and feeding-in.
5. Which sentence is typical of a two-year-old?
    A. "Mommy."
    B. "Mommy go."
    C. "Mommy go and I go too."
    D. "Is Mommy going?"
6. How do most two-year-olds express their anger?
7. When working with two-year-olds, why do you need to allow plenty of time for transitions between activities?
8. True or false. Three-year-olds can climb and descend stairs easily.
9. Describe two self-help skills of three-year-olds.
10. Most three-year-old children can count to _____ while pointing to corresponding objects.
11. Why are three-year-olds less likely to become angry than two-year-olds?

Apply and Explore

1. Visit a local child care center and observe the motor skills of two- and three-year-olds. Use notes from your observations to write a report comparing the motor skills of the two age groups.
2. Design a toy, activity, or teaching aid to help improve the self-help skills of a two- or three-year-old.
3. Invite a child care teacher to discuss the differences in expression of emotions between two-year-olds and three-year-olds.
4. Visit a children's library and find books designed to help young children express their feelings in positive ways. Write a report on one of these books.

Four- and five-year-olds enjoy new experiences and challenges.

Chapter 6

Understanding Four- and Five-Year-Olds

After studying this chapter, you will be able to

- describe the physical, cognitive, and social-emotional development of four- and five-year-olds.
- explain how you as a teacher can plan programs and relate to four- and five-year-olds in developmentally appropriate ways.

Terms to Know

articulation

stuttering

rote counting

Your days with four- and five-year-olds will be filled with fun and challenges. Preschoolers (as four- and five-year-olds are referred to in this chapter) are capable of handling many basic self-help skills. However, to keep growing and learning, they need new experiences and challenges. Preschoolers have many questions about the world around them. Helping them answer these questions can be a rewarding part of teaching.

Physical Development of Four- and Five-Year-Olds

Increased body strength and coordination makes movement great fun for preschoolers, 6-1. Physical skills become easier partly because body proportions are changing. Compared to their total height, toddlers have fairly short legs. But by five and one-half years, most children's legs are about half the length of the body. Their proportions are more similar to adult proportions. This makes running, jumping, and balancing easier for preschoolers.

Preschool children are growing in more than just size. Their bones are becoming harder and stronger. Their permanent teeth are forming beneath their gums. Many children in this age group begin losing their baby teeth. These children need good nutrition to assure that their bones and permanent teeth form properly. Their diets should include foods that are good sources of calcium and vitamin D, such as milk and other dairy products.

6-1 Preschoolers enjoy such large motor activities as climbing.

Gross Motor Development

Four- and five-year olds are using previously acquired skills to perform more complex movements. They improve their skills as their bodies becomes stronger and larger. At four years of age, children can hop on one foot. They also can walk down stairs with alternating feet. Four-year-olds can balance on one foot for about 10 seconds. They can walk backwards, toe-to-heel, for four consecutive steps.

Late in the fourth year, many children may begin learning how to skip. Most five-year-olds have developed this skill. Older four-year-olds may also be riding a bike with training wheels. If they have the opportunity, most children have developed this skill by five years of age. Five-year-olds also can walk forward and backward on a balance beam. See 6-2. They can climb

fences and march to music. They also can jump from table height and land on both feet.

Throwing and catching skills also improve during these years. Most four- and five-year-olds are capable of throwing overhand. As they grow, they are becoming better at using their bodies to direct a ball as they throw. When throwing, they rotate their bodies and shift their weight from the back foot to the front foot, using both hands and visually tracking the ball. These children are also able to catch a ball. A five-year-old is able to keep the hands close to the body until just before catching the ball. As the child's brain matures, there is better coordination of motor and visual systems.

6-2 Improved balance allows this five-year-old to walk forward and backward on a balance beam.

Children this age enjoy working to improve their physical skills. They try to use their skills to the fullest. Sometimes, they may even become reckless. For instance, they may try to ride scooters as fast as they can.

Fine Motor Development

Children's fine motor skills improve rapidly during the preschool years. They find it easier to string beads and work with small game or puzzle pieces. See 6-3. When they build towers from blocks, the towers are straight and tall. By four years, most children can complete a five-piece puzzle. By five years, children can put together puzzles with eight or more pieces. Five-year-olds are also becoming skilled at working clay. They may sculpt simple forms and figures.

Writing and drawing skills also improve quickly. By four years of age, children's drawing forms are more refined. As a result, you will have an easier time recognizing what they are drawing.

6-3 Four-year-olds have an easier time working puzzle pieces than younger children do.

Preschoolers are beginning to recognize letters. They can tell writing from nonwriting. They can also copy a square and print a few letters. Often the letters are printed improperly, though. Letters that are mirror images are especially difficult for preschoolers. For instance, the child may print *b* for *d* or even for *p*. The child may place five or six horizontal lines on an E.

Five-year-olds show marked improvement in controlling a writing tool. They delight in copying triangles and tracing diamond shapes. They are also fairly skilled at staying within the lines when they color. Most five-year-olds enjoy printing their first names. Preschoolers are capable of copying most letters and printing some simple words, but they may still be having problems printing some letters properly. They are beginning to understand that letters and sounds are linked.

Self-Help Skills

Preschoolers become more and more self-sufficient. They are dressing and undressing themselves with very little help. Most of these children are capable of telling the front from the back of clothing. However, you may need to give them reminders from time to time. By four years of age, most children can buckle belts and close zippers. By five years, many children can even button and unbutton fasteners on the backs of garments. They also can put shoes on the correct feet. Some five-year-olds can even tie their own shoelaces.

Self-feeding is easier for preschoolers, too. They enjoy helping with serving. They can use spoons and forks with ease. By four years of age, children are using their forks to cut some large pieces of food. They may even try cutting foods with a knife. Most five-year-olds are able to cut fairly soft foods with knives. Preschoolers are also able to clean up their places after they finish eating.

Preschoolers are also better able to take care of their own hygiene. They become more skilled at handling a toothbrush and brushing their teeth. They also can use a washcloth for wiping their hands and faces. Preschoolers become more skilled at brushing and combing their hair, too.

Cognitive Development of Preschoolers

Children in this age group make many gains in understanding the world around them. They become more skilled in thinking without having to act things out. As a result, they have a better understanding of symbols than younger children. Four- and five-year-olds also have increased language comprehension and expressive language skills. Language is a tool that can help children solve problems mentally.

Four- and five-year-olds now have the language skills to describe what they see and remember. You can test a child's recognition and recall skills. Show the child ten small, familiar toys. Then place the toys in a bag or box. Ask the child what items are in the bag. To recall the items requires the child to create a mental image. Although the child can recognize all ten items, she or he probably will only recall four or five. Children have better recognition than recall skills.

Children start creating their own symbols at this age, 6-4. This is reflected in their play.

6-4 Four- and five-year-olds enjoy adding their own ideas during cooperative play.

Instead of just imitating the actions of adults, preschoolers add their own ideas. For instance, instead of using a bowl for mixing, they may pretend the bowl is a hat. New symbols also appear in art. Before the fourth year, children tend to scribble or just draw simple shapes. Now children make drawings that represent real objects. These drawings are simple and do not always look like what the child really sees. For instance, a hand may have six or even ten fingers. Four-year-olds often make drawings and then name them. By five years, children decide what they want to draw and then draw it.

Understanding symbols is important for developing more advanced cognitive skills. Symbols are a part of learning in language, math, science, social science, and many other areas of education. Therefore, cognitive development during the preschool years helps prepare children for future learning during the school years.

Preschoolers are eager to learn about why things happen around them. They may ask "Why do dogs bark?" or "Why do boats float?" With their endless string of questions, they are trying to make sense of their world. They still have flaws in their thinking, as three-year-olds do. Through asking questions again and again, their thinking becomes more and more logical.

Your curriculum should help promote the children's cognitive growth. As you provide new experiences, the children's vocabularies will grow. They will learn new concepts. For instance, you may show the children a live bunny. These children will explore concepts about the bunny, such as size, color, and method of eating. Children may also learn new vocabulary words as you show the animal. For instance, you might explain that the bunny is "timid." Each new experience helps the children grow intellectually, 6-5.

Language Comprehension Skills

The language comprehension skills of four- and five-year-olds are constantly growing. New words related to space concepts increase their understanding. These include such words as *beside, bottom, backward,* and *forward*. They also understand such words as *down, low, different,* and *thin*. By the fifth year, the words *behind, ahead of, first,* and *last* are added to

6-5 A visit from a resource person can help children's intellectual growth in many ways.

children's understanding. As you instruct children using these words, children will be able to understand and follow directions. For instance, you may tell a child "Place the green block *behind* the blue block."

Children this age become even better at following three-step commands. These children will be able to follow the directions in the order that they are given. For instance, you may tell a child "Pick up the puzzle, put it on the table, and wash your hands." However, if you do not sequence the directions correctly, the child can become confused.

Children have a better understanding of the difference between plural and singular nouns at this age. For instance, you may tell a child to take a sandwich at lunch time. The child understands that he or she is to take only one sandwich. If you tell the child to take cookies, the child knows that he or she can have more than one.

Children start understanding the passive voice at this time. In a *passive voice* sentence, the object of the sentence is placed before the subject. An example of a passive voice sentence would be "The orange was eaten by Brock." Three-year-olds do not usually understand this

word order. They think the sentence means that the orange ate Brock. Four- and five-year-olds understand that Brock ate the orange.

Because many words and phrases have more than one meaning, preschoolers may become confused about some statements. They tend to take literally such comments as "Wanda just flew out the door." See 6-6. You need to be careful about the phrases that you use around these children. For instance, a phrase such as "I'm dying of hunger" may frighten children.

Reading

Most four- and five-year-olds cannot read, but they are developing abilities that lead to reading skills. These abilities are made possible as children begin to understand symbolism. Before children learn to read, they need to understand that a group of letters on paper can symbolize any object, from a ball to an airplane.

Four- and five-year-olds can recognize and name many letters of the alphabet. They also can recognize their own names. Children in this age group enjoy having stories read to them over and over again. As you reread stories, these children may be able to pick out and say words that they

6-6 Preschoolers may have trouble understanding figurative speech.

recognize. The children will also try to guess words that they do not recognize. They tend to look at the first letter of a word and then name any word that begins with that letter. For instance, they may point to the word "ball" and say "baby."

Expressive Language Skills

Preschoolers in this age group become quite talkative. As their vocabularies and grammar skills improve, they enjoy talking to others. See 6-7. At this age, children tend to talk to you rather than have a conversation with you. When you talk about one subject, a child may interrupt to tell you about something entirely unrelated. The child may even make two or three unrelated comments to you in the same conversation. The children can answer your questions. They also listen to answers to their own questions. In later years, these children become better at true two-way communication.

Articulation

Articulation is the ability to speak in clearly pronounced sounds. Articulation improves in many ways at four and five. These preschoolers

6-7 Four- and five-year-olds like to talk with you about their projects.

can make most of the sounds needed to form words. Many children still have trouble making the *ch* sound and the *th* sound in words. Others may have trouble with the *S* sound, causing a lisp.

Some preschoolers also have stuttering problems. **Stuttering** includes repeating sounds or words and pausing for unusually long times while speaking. For most preschoolers, stuttering is a result of thinking faster than they can talk. As children's speech ability catches up to their thinking ability, the stuttering problem tends to disappear.

Vocabulary

Vocabulary grows quickly over these two years. Most four-year-olds have about 1500 words in their vocabularies. Five-year-olds have about 2000. Children do not always have clear ideas of the meanings of all the words they use. They may make up their own meanings to some words.

Preschoolers have mainly concrete nouns and action verbs in their vocabularies. They are beginning to add some modifiers and adjectives. However, words related to ideas or thoughts are still not a big part of their vocabularies. For instance, children this age would be unlikely to use the words *freedom* or *unfair*, unless they were simply imitating the words of adults.

Children this age do imitate phrases that they hear from adults or television. See 6-8. After a meal, a child may say "That was simply delectable!" This child is most likely imitating a statement heard at home or on television. If you ask, the child could not tell you what delectable means. Children might also use such words as *bionic, biodegradable*, and *computer chip*.

Grammar

Children's grammar improves during these years. Children start to learn that there are exceptions to rules for past tense. They use such irregular verbs as *ate, ran*, and *went* properly. These children still put *ed* at the end of these words occasionally.

Children also learn how to properly form questions. The three-year-old would say "Why the sky is blue?" Four- and five-year-olds know to say "Why is the sky blue?"

Some grammar rules still give four- and five-year-olds problems. They especially have

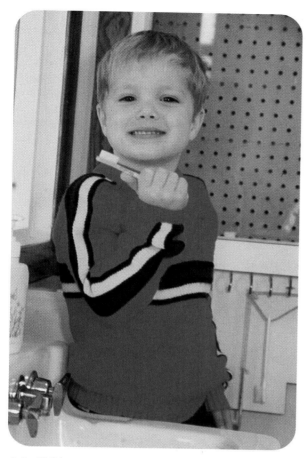

6-8 Children may imitate a phrase from television such as "My teeth feel minty fresh and tingly." These children do not always understand the meaning of the phrase.

trouble using the proper forms of pronouns in sentences. For instance, a child may say "Him and me are going to the zoo." They also have trouble with noun and verb agreement. For instance, a child may say "Tommy don't have a crayon."

Math Skills

Number concepts become easier for children in this age group. Rote counting skills increase quickly. **Rote counting** is reciting numbers in their proper order. This skill is gained by most children before they fully understand that each number represents a certain amount. At four years of age, most children can rote count from one to nine. By the end of the fifth year, most children can rote count to 20. Rote counting skills develop at different rates for children in this age group. Therefore, you need to observe these children to make sure your curriculum fits their skill levels.

True counting, in which an object is counted for each number named, develops more slowly. For instance, a child may try to count ten objects. The child may touch one object and say "one," another and say "two," and another saying "three." However, the child may then point to another object three times in a row, saying "four, five, six." Children in this age group may be able to count three or four objects. However, they have trouble counting more objects.

Children start to recognize numerals in this stage. A four-year-old usually recognizes the numerals 1, 2, 3, 4, and 5. Five-year-olds learn to recognize 6, 7, 8, 9, and 10 as well. By five years of age, many children can dial their own telephone numbers.

Other math skills develop at this age. Children become better at recognizing shapes. About 80 percent of five-year-olds can recognize the square and rectangle shapes. Four- and five-year-olds also understand more terms related to size and number. These include *short, fat, tallest, same size, first*, and *last*.

Children start to understand money concepts in this stage. Most preschoolers can identify a penny, a nickel, and a dime. These children do not yet understand the true value of money, though. If you ask a child this age whether a nickel or a dime is worth more, the child is likely to choose the nickel. Since it is bigger, children think that it is worth more. They do not yet realize that a nickel is worth five pennies and a dime is worth ten.

Time concepts become more clear at this age. The children start to understand the difference between today, tomorrow, and yesterday. However, many time concepts are still confusing for these children. They don't really understand how long an hour or a minute takes. They also get confused because time is described in so many ways. An adult may tell a child that puppet time is at 3:30, at half past three, this afternoon, or in a few hours.

Social-Emotional Development of Preschoolers

Preschoolers continue to be helpful and cooperative, 6-9. With improved language skills, children become more involved with each other. Friendships become more important. They know that a friend is a person who "likes you." Emotions are changing in these children. As they learn and grow, the causes of happiness, fear, anger, and sadness change. And the ways children react to these emotions change.

Social Development

Companionship is important to preschoolers. Friendships, attention, and approval are important as well. However, they are also becoming more independent of adults. They like to play on their own or with other children. They may not always want you or other adults to participate in play. They may still need your help to get materials or settle disputes.

Children this age start to value their friendships with others. They tend to have only a few friends. They also prefer friends of the same sex. Children in this age group become more willing to cooperate as they play with others. They are more likely than younger children to offer a favorite toy to a friend. Many children in this age group choose best friends. They tend to change best friends fairly often, though.

For four-year-olds, over one-third of a child's play is solitary play. However, by age five, play involves more and more interaction and cooperation. Play groups are still small—only two or three children, but children talk to each other more and do more as a group, 6-10.

Children this age accept supervision. They know their own abilities, and they realize that adults have reasons for rules. These children will accept your instructions, and they will ask your permission before doing certain activities.

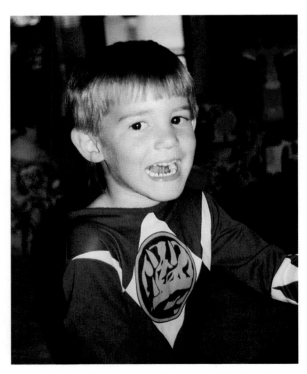

6-9 Four- and five-year-olds are usually cheerful and cooperative.

6-10 Play becomes more cooperative for four- and five-year-olds.

Emotional Development

Four- and five-year-olds begin to realize new ways of showing love and caring. They still understand hugs and other physical signs of affection. They may hug another child who is sad. However, they are starting to realize that helping others is a way of showing love. These children may show love for others by sharing something or helping with a task. They may also seek this sign of love from others. For example, children may ask for help with a task even if they don't need it. These children are looking for assurance that you care.

Children in this age group start to develop a sense of humor. See 6-11. Laughter becomes a way of expressing their happiness. These children do not yet understand most verbal jokes, but they laugh at funny faces or actions. They also laugh at things that they know are unusual. For instance, they may laugh at a dog that says "meow" in a story. These children also need good role models to learn that harm done to others is not funny.

6-11 Children this age enjoy humor.

Fear

Fears are still common, but most only last a few months. Causes of fears change during this stage. These children are still afraid of imagined creatures, such as monsters and ghosts. They may be especially fearful of dreams, because they seem so real. However, they also start to realize that there is a difference between the real and the imagined. This helps children deal with some of these fears. For this reason, you may hear preschoolers state firmly "There's no such thing as dragons." They may ask you repeatedly "Was the story just pretend?"

Other fears may be created by the new knowledge of preschoolers. They are aware of more dangers. However, they do not know enough to fully understand what is and is not dangerous. Their imaginations are vivid. For instance, a child may learn that sharks live in the ocean. This may cause fear of being hurt in the ocean. The child may also become afraid of sharks in rivers, pools, and even bathtubs.

Five-year-olds are also more afraid of being hurt than are younger children. They know of more things that can hurt them. They may be afraid of doctors and dentists. This is because they are aware of pain or injuries associated with these professionals. They may also be afraid of high places and dogs because of prior experiences.

These children sometimes work through fears in play. For instance, a child who is afraid of dogs may pretend to be a fierce dog. A child who is afraid of heights may pretend to be a bird. For these children, play is therapeutic. It helps them act out some of their intense feelings and deal with their fears.

Anger

Like three-year-olds, children in this age group do not have as many causes for anger as toddlers do. However, they can become angry if they are unable to reach their goals. Four- and five-year-old children are more likely to use words and yelling rather than hitting or kicking to express anger. If they do express anger physically, they are more likely to take out their anger on objects or other children. They do not usually respond to adults physically because they know this action is not accepted.

Some preschoolers respond more physically to anger than others. They may become angry more easily than others also. They may use pushing, hitting, or kicking to show anger. They may not have learned better ways of expressing anger from adult role models or they may want attention.

Jealousy

Jealousy may be a problem for some children in this age group. These children are most likely to become jealous of a new brother or sister. They may resent the fact that their parents are spending so much time with a new child. They may fear that their parents do not love them as much.

Jealousy may surface in children in many ways, 6-12. The child may regress to earlier behaviors, such as crying, following adults, and having toileting accidents. The child also may develop physical problems such as stomach aches or nightmares.

6-12 Children who are jealous of a new sibling may become withdrawn or show regressive behaviors at the center.

These children need to be reassured that they are still loved. Sometimes, they may need a little extra attention away from home to make them feel special. Showing these children that their sibling needs help from a "big sister" or "big brother" can make them feel better, too.

Sadness

Four- and five-year-olds start to learn that some situations are sad. They become aware of the concept of death. Their first experiences with death may be the loss of a pet. Preschool children do not understand that death cannot be reversed. As a result, it may take children a while to realize that the pet will not come back to life. However, once they understand this, they often become sad.

Children are not always sure how to express sadness. Children may deal with sadness in play. They may pretend to be the lost pet or to talk to the lost pet. Frequently, they need help from adults to learn that it is okay to cry and to talk about their feelings. They also need adults to model appropriate responses to sadness and to provide clear explanations.

Some children must also deal with the death of a close family member. These children need to have as much explained about the situation as they can understand. They also need help from adults in dealing with the loss and sadness.

Teaching Four- and Five-Year-Olds

Like three-year-olds, four- and five-year-olds tend to be cooperative and helpful. These children are eager to please you, 6-13. If you ask a child to help you, the child feels complimented. These children enjoy feeling needed and important. They may even ask "Can I help you?"

Because these children like to help, you need to carefully select helpers. Choosing the same few helpers time after time can make others feel unimportant. Even children who do not volunteer need to be asked from time to time. These children may be too shy to ask, or they may not feel confident in their abilities to help. By choosing them, you can help build their self-esteem.

6-13 Preschoolers are eager to help you in such ways as caring for pets.

By this age, children become quite talkative. They still enjoy physical play, but they like to spend more time talking. You will enjoy carrying on conversations with these children. These conversations may become a part of learning activities or story time. After you read a story, these children may enjoy retelling the story. They are usually capable of retelling the story in detail and in the proper sequence.

You will notice that children in this age group will imitate your speech. You may hear one child tell another "Christopher, we walk, we don't run, when we are in the hallway." For this reason, you need to be careful of your statements. You should never use words or statements that you would not want the children repeating.

Children are now more content playing with each other. You do not need to function as a playmate as much. However, you will need to handle more disputes among children. These children may have conflicts over group rules. They will look to you for advice on settling these problems. You may also want to add new ideas to play. Preschoolers enjoy playing some simple, organized games that you may lead.

Some children may have imaginary playmates. A child may come to school explaining that Ralph, his playmate, asked to come with him. He may provide space for Ralph on his cot at nap time. He may have conversations with Ralph throughout the day. This kind of play does not necessarily indicate problems. It is simply a way of using the imagination and having fun.

Children in this age group are often proud of their possessions and family members, 6-14. They may like to bring favorite toys to the center. They may also call attention to new shoes or a new jacket. They may beam with pride when their parents visit the center. Children enjoy talking with you and others about their belongings. Asking children questions about something of theirs can help build their self-esteem.

Children in this age group also enjoy working on projects. Their attention spans and goal-setting abilities are improving. Children's ideas for projects may come from play with peers or from adult activities. Such projects as woodworking, cooking, and sculpting clay may be fun for these children. As they get older, they will engage for longer periods of time in these activities. The average time spent in most activities at this age is about seven minutes.

6-14 Preschoolers are proud to have their siblings visit the center.

Summary

The growth of four- and five-year-olds helps them become more independent. These preschoolers become stronger and more coordinated. Their changing body proportions help them improve their balance and motor skills. These children become more skilled at running, jumping, throwing, and catching. They also become better at printing, drawing, working clay, and putting together puzzles. These children also have improved dressing, eating, and hygiene skills.

Four- and five-year-olds' thoughts become more and more adultlike. These children begin to understand and use symbols in play, drawing, and learning. Language skills improve quickly. These children understand and use more words. Their grammar improves also. Much new knowledge helps prepare children for later math learning. These include rote counting and understanding of size and number concepts.

Children become more social with their peers at this age. Their play becomes more cooperative. Children still seek favor and approval from adults. They like to help and talk to adults. Children are learning acceptable ways of expressing their feelings. They are also experiencing feelings for different reasons.

As a teacher, you will enjoy working with four- and five-year-olds. These children can be independent in terms of self-care. They are eager and able to help you, and they enjoy talking with you and learning about new ideas.

Review and Reflect

1. Why is it important to include foods high in calcium and vitamin D in the diets of four- and five-year-olds?

2. True or false. Four- and five-year-olds stand perfectly still when they throw a ball.

3. Describe the writing skills of four- and five-year-olds.

4. Which of the following dressing skills do most five-year-olds have?
   A. They know the front from the back of garments.
   B. They can buckle belts.
   C. They can put shoes on the right feet.
   D. All of the above.

5. At what age do children make drawings and then decide what they are?

6. Describe the reading abilities of four- and five-year-olds.

7. True or false. A four-year-old who uses the word "imitation" probably does *not* know what the word means.

8. Why are time concepts confusing for four- and five-year-olds?

9. True or false. Five-year-olds prefer friends of the opposite sex.

10. Describe a situation that is likely to cause fear in a five-year-old. Explain why this situation would cause fear.

11. Typically, what is the teacher's role in the play of four- and five-year-olds?

Apply and Explore

1. Play catch with a four- or five-year-old. Make sketches or written descriptions of the movements used by the child to catch and to throw. Report your findings to the class.

2. Invite a child care teacher to show the class samples of artwork from four- and five-year-olds. Discuss the types of symbolism used in the artwork.

3. Make a bulletin board based on phrases that might be misinterpreted by four- and five-year-olds. The bulletin board could contain drawings of preschoolers' interpretations of the phrases.

4. Write a research report on recommended ways of helping four- and five-year-olds deal with death.

5. Visit a child care center and observe various ages of children in the playyard. Record their activities and movements. Note the differences in abilities of children of different ages.

Chapter 7

Middle Childhood

After studying this chapter, you will be able to

- describe the physical, cognitive, and social-emotional development of school-age children.
- summarize potential health concerns of middle childhood.
- explain moral development during childhood.

Terms to Know

middle childhood	seriation
farsighted	classification
nearsighted	social comparison
asthma	self-concept
obesity	self-esteem
rehearsal	empathy
operation	compassion
concrete operations	moral development
conservation	morality

Middle childhood refers to the span of years between ages six and twelve. Since this time period begins with the onset of formal schooling, it is often referred to as the *school-age years*.

During middle childhood, children become more self-sufficient and independent. They are interested and involved in many new activities. Peers and teachers play an increasingly important role in their lives. Their circle of friends and acquaintances expands far beyond their own family members. These friendships and school-related activities are taking more and more of their time. As a result, they are learning to adopt new social rules and expectations.

Though developmental changes continue to occur throughout middle childhood, the changes are not as dramatic as they were during infancy and toddlerhood. During the school-age years, the brain undergoes changes that allow more highly developed thinking skills. As a result, the children are becoming better problem solvers. They are also growing in self-knowledge and understanding.

School-age children are beginning the process of entering the adult world and are attending more to their own needs. They are able to get themselves up in the morning, bathe, dress, and eat without any adult assistance. Most families expect more of their school-age children because of their improved skills. Often they assist with cooking, dishwashing, and laundry chores. They are also capable of helping with younger siblings.

Physical Development

Physical development during middle childhood is not as rapid as during the first years of life. Between the ages of six and twelve, children experience steady physical growth, 7-1. There are gradual and consistent increases in weight and height. Heredity and environment account for most differences in physical growth. Health care and nutrition are environmental factors that can affect both weight and height.

During this period, children are interested in their physical growth. They care more about what other people think of them. Thus, their body size, shape, and physical abilities can influence how they feel about themselves.

At the beginning of this stage, children have much better control of their large muscles than their small muscles. During the six-year span, children show continued improvement in skills learned earlier. They show gains in motor skills, agility, and physical strength. These skills are helpful for participation in games and sports.

Height

Boys are usually slightly taller than girls at the beginning of this stage. Until age nine, boys retain this edge. Then the reverse occurs as girls begin to grow more rapidly. At 10 years of age, most girls experience a growth spurt. This growth spurt occurs two years later in boys. At ages 11 and 12, most girls have surpassed boys in height. This difference can be a source of embarrassment for some children.

The typical six-year-old is almost four feet tall. During middle childhood, children usually grow about two to three inches per year. By the age of 12, the average child is about five feet tall. By the end of middle childhood, girls may reach 90 percent of their adult height. At the same time, boys may be about 80 percent of their adult height.

Body proportions change during the school-age years. The upper part of the head grew fast during the first six years of life. Now the arms and legs grow more quickly. Children look less top-heavy now than during the earlier years.

Weight

At age six, the average child weighs about 47 pounds. By age 12, this weight may double. Children gain about five to seven pounds per year during middle childhood.

There are weight differences between girls and boys. From birth through the preschool years, girls usually weigh slightly less than boys. Girls catch up with boys in weight by age 11. By 12 years of age, girls usually weigh about three pounds more than boys.

Large Motor Skills

By watching school-age children on the playground, you can see how their motor skills are improving, 7-2. Physical growth contributes to these changes. Gains in height and weight help with coordination. They possess greater speed and accuracy of movement, with faster reaction times. Movements are more refined and fluid. Moreover, balance has improved.

7-1 Children do not grow as rapidly during middle childhood as they do in the first years of life.

7-2 Motor development continues to improve during the school-age years.

Younger school-age children are constantly practicing and perfecting six skills. These are jumping, balancing, throwing, catching, running, and sequencing foot movements. Their running is faster. With practice, they are more accurate in throwing, catching, and kicking. They can throw balls greater distances.

As they grow older, both boys and girls improve their large motor skills. Even though girls usually surpass boys in height and weight, boys have more physical strength. They have an advantage in muscle mass. As a result, boys may outperform girls in jumping, catching, throwing, and batting. They can usually run faster and for greater distances.

Girls outperform boys in motor skills that require balance, coordination, flexibility, or rhythmic movement. Some examples include playing hopscotch, dancing, and skipping. Girls also have an edge in skills involving the use of the small muscles.

Fine Motor Skills

Children show improvement of their fine motor skills throughout middle childhood. They have better control of the small muscles in their fingers and hands. Their writing is much better since they are using more wrist movement.

Letters and words are more uniform and neater. Moreover, the spacing between letters and words has improved. The improvement of these fine motor skills is also reflected in their drawings, 7-3.

7-3 With better control of the small muscles and hands, children's artwork also improves.

Improved finger dexterity allows school-age children to play musical instruments, such as a piano, guitar, or tonette. Their eye-hand coordination skills are also improving. While grasping tools, they can control the motion and speed. This allows them to learn such skills as sewing and assembling models with small pieces.

Health Concerns

Middle childhood is often one of the healthiest periods for children. The lowest illness rates are for children between five and twelve years of age. Therefore, there are fewer sore throats, upper respiratory diseases, and middle ear infections than during the preschool years. One of the reasons for this reduction is the body's developing immune system, which offers protection against disease. School-age children, however, are not illness free. Many school-age children still have several upper respiratory illnesses each year.

Several chronic illnesses may surface during middle childhood. Ulcers, asthma, and diabetes are examples. In addition, many school-age children develop headaches and acne as they approach adolescence. Some children may develop hearing and vision problems. Lack of exercise is another problem. Others exercise too much, placing their bodies under stress. For these children, overuse can cause sprains, tendinitis (inflammation of a tendon), and even broken bones. A variety of other health problems occur even though most children are at their healthiest.

Hearing

Children's hearing is usually well developed by middle childhood. Awareness of midrange sounds develops first, followed by high range and low range awareness. By 11 years of age, most children have the auditory awareness of adults.

Ear infections can be a health problem. If left untreated, they can cause permanent hearing loss. For most children, the number of ear infections decreases due to structural changes within the body. The eustachian tube, which connects the middle ear to the throat, has changed position. This change helps prevent bacteria and fluids from moving from the mouth to the ear.

Vision

By age six, most children are ready to read. They can see an object with both eyes at the same time. Their ability to focus improves. Many preschool children are somewhat **farsighted**. This means they can see objects in the distance more clearly than those that are close. During the middle years, their close-up vision improves.

Throughout middle childhood, nearsightedness is the most common vision problem. **Nearsightedness** is the ability to see close objects more clearly than those at a distance. The more time children are engaged in reading and close-up work, the greater their chances of becoming nearsighted. With corrective lenses, nearsightedness can be overcome, 7-4. It is estimated that as many as 25 percent of children will need to have their vision corrected by the end of the school years. It is important that children's vision be checked regularly to detect any problems.

7-4 Corrective lenses can overcome most vision problems.

Teeth

During middle childhood, children begin losing their primary or "baby" teeth. First and second graders often have toothless smiles! The first teeth to fall out are the central incisors, which are the lower and upper front teeth, 7-5. By the age of 12, all of the 20 primary teeth will be replaced with permanent teeth. At first, these permanent teeth appear to be out of proportion to the child's face. Gradually the facial bones grow, causing the face to lengthen and the mouth to widen. These changes accommodate the larger, permanent teeth.

Tooth loss can have a psychological effect on some children. They become self-conscious. Calling attention to the change in their appearance may cause them to be uncomfortable.

A common health problem for school-age children is tooth decay. Between four and eight years of age, children are susceptible to cavities. At risk are those children who are in poor health and who have diets high in sugar.

As a teacher, you should promote good dental health. Begin by modeling proper care of your own teeth. Brush your teeth with the children after each meal. Eat a well-balanced diet, and avoid foods high in sugar. Encourage parents to have their children receive regular dental check-ups.

Asthma

You may have children in your program who suffer from asthma attacks. **Asthma** is a respiratory disorder that causes labored breathing, gasping, coughing, and wheezing. It is often an allergic reaction to airborne allergens, infections, certain foods, or other substances. Emotional stress, physical exercise, or fatigue can provoke an attack. When an attack occurs, the bronchial tubes swell, blocking airways and interfering with breathing. Sometimes an asthma attack may be a medical emergency.

If at all possible, asthmatic children need to learn how to prevent attacks. As a teacher, you should remain calm if a child has an asthmatic attack. Help the child to also remain calm. You may be given medicine to administer to the child if an attack occurs.

Obesity

Obesity is becoming a common problem among school-age children. **Obesity** is characterized by excessive bodily fat. A person is considered obese if he or she weighs 20 percent more than other people of the same sex, age, and build. Obesity affects about 25 percent of school-age children.

Being obese can seriously impact a child's emotional health. Obese children are often teased and ridiculed by their peers. They may have fewer friends, and they are often the last to be selected for group projects and teams. As a result, overweight children may have low self-esteem.

Several factors contribute to obesity in children. Some obese children have overweight parents. For them, the tendency to be overweight may be inherited. For other children, environment can be a contributing factor. If the parents

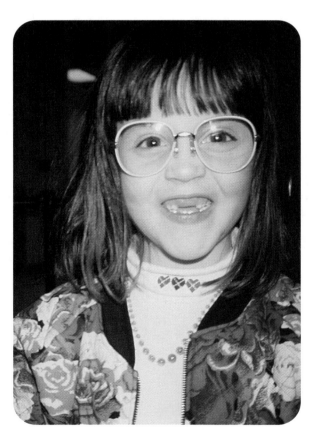

7-5 Hannah's lost teeth are one indication she is entering middle childhood.

and other family members overeat, the children will likely do the same. Still other children overeat due to family stress. Children's eating habits can be affected by abuse, the death of a family member, alcoholism, or divorce. Any of these traumatic events can trigger overeating.

Many children are obese as a result of physical inactivity. They may also watch more television than other children. Studies show that those children who spend more time watching television and playing video games get less physical activity. As a result, they are more likely to be overweight.

Research shows that overweight children often are overweight as adults. Adults who are obese may develop high blood pressure, heart disease, or diabetes. Treating childhood obesity, however, is difficult. Obesity is often a family disorder. Behaviors need to be changed that involve both the child and the parents. Obese children need help in making healthier food choices. They need to learn which foods are lower in fat and calories. They need to be shown how to control the portions they eat. They should be encouraged to exercise more. These children may also need help in overcoming emotional problems.

Cognitive Development

During middle childhood, children begin to think mentally using logic and symbols. They no longer rely only on what they can see or perceive. They begin to use logical thinking instead of perception. In addition, their memory improves and their attention span is longer. They can process and recall information more readily. These improved thinking skills allow them to engage in academic tasks. Their reading, writing, science, and math skills develop continually throughout the school-age years, 7-6.

The desire to achieve is an important influence on cognitive development during middle childhood. Achievement is often related to motivation. Some children have an internal desire to work hard and achieve. Others are motivated by the prospect of rewards or recognition. Whether the desire to succeed comes from within the child or externally, the motivation to do well influences performance.

Attention and Memory

Critical to cognitive development is attention and memory. Memory becomes more controlled

7-6 Children learn to read during middle childhood.

during early childhood. The child's age, motivation, health, and attitude determine the effectiveness of memory. Attention also improves. Children now have the ability to ignore unnecessary information. They are able to focus their attention on the important aspects of a task. They can scan detailed tasks and decide what must be done first. These changes allow thinking skills to become more refined. School-age children are better at processing information. As a result, they are better problem solvers.

To remember information, school-age children often use a technique called rehearsal. **Rehearsal** involves the repetition of information after it is used. The following example will illustrate rehearsal. Bobby is a typical six-year-old. He is able to tell you his address and telephone number. In addition, he knows his grandmother's telephone number and those of several of his friends. His neighbor, Alice, cannot understand how Bobby can remember all of this information at his age.

Bobby uses rehearsal. Bobby usually writes the phone numbers down. While recording the numbers, you can see his lips moving. Then he repeats the numbers many times. His memory is improved by this type of organization and process.

Mental Operations

There are changes in reasoning and thinking during middle childhood. Gradually, school-age children change the way they process information. During the preschool years, children relied totally on what they saw or perceived. Sometimes their perceptions were flawed. Now their perceptions are more accurate because they begin to use logical thinking. An **operation** is defined as the manipulation of ideas based on logic rather than perception. Between seven and eight years of age, children enter the stage of **concrete operations**. This means they use logic, but it is based on what they have experienced or seen.

Because they can now use logic in their mental operations, children learn several new concepts during the middle years. These include the concepts of conservation, seriation, and classification.

Conservation

Children gradually acquire the concept of conservation. **Conservation** means that change in position or shape of substances does not change the quantity. If nothing is added or taken away, the amount stays the same. Such properties as weight, length, mass, and volume do not change. The appearance, however, may change. A child's understanding of the principle of conservation can be tested with liquids, a series of objects, and pliable substances.

To illustrate the conservation of liquids, show a child two identical glasses. Fill each glass with the same amount of liquid. Ask the child if the two glasses have the same amount of liquid, and the child will say that they do. Next, pour the liquid from one glass into a taller, thinner glass. Again ask the child if the two glasses have the same amount of liquid. Until about seven years of age, the child will probably say that the taller glass contains more liquid. Between seven and eight, when children enter the stage of concrete operations, they will say that the amount of liquid has not changed. Their logic has overruled their perception.

You can test a child's understanding of the conservation of length by using a series of identical objects, such as pennies. Place ten pennies in two rows of five each. Place the rows side by side. Ask the child if the number of pennies in each row is the same. The child will agree that the two rows contain the same number of pennies. Next, spread the pennies apart in one of the rows. If the child is at the concrete level of operations, the child will say that the longer row still has the same number of pennies. If the child says that the one row has more pennies, the child is focusing only on the dimension of length. Rather than using logic, the child is relying only on perception.

A child's understanding of the concept of mass can also be tested. Show the child two balls of modeling dough that are the same size and shape. Ask the child if the two balls have the same amount of dough. The child will say yes. Then flatten one ball of modeling dough, and repeat your question. The child who understands conservation will note that the amount of dough is still the same.

Figure 7-7 shows several conservation tasks. It lists the questions to ask children to test their understanding of conservation. Those children who have not reached the stage of concrete operations will respond by saying no. If the children respond by saying yes, they have reached the concrete operations stage.

Seriation

Seriation is the ability to arrange items in an increasing or decreasing order based on weight, volume, or size. Like conservation, seriation typically emerges between the ages of six and eight years of age. To illustrate, you may provide a child with a set of sticks of different lengths. Then ask the child to arrange the sticks from the shortest to the longest. Preschool children will lay the sticks haphazardly. Most school-age children will lay the sticks in an orderly fashion from shortest to longest as requested.

Seriation also can involve sequencing the events in a story. After hearing a story, the child should be able to recall the sequence of events. As a result, the child will be able to retell the story. Likewise, following a recipe involves seriation.

After preparing a simple recipe, the child should be able to recall the preparation steps.

Classification

Simple **classification** is the ability to group objects by common attributes, such as size, color, shape, pattern, or function. The typical preschooler can group objects by one attribute only. For instance, if given a group of different-colored shapes, the preschooler could sort by either color or shape. During the early school-age years, children can mentally handle two aspects of the problem, such as color and shape. For instance, they can sort blue squares into one pile and blue circles into another.

Language

The ability to communicate improves gradually throughout middle childhood. Comparing language development to the preschool years, changes are more subtle. The child's vocabulary doubles between the ages of six and twelve. As they learn to read, they learn many new words each day. Grammar skills improve. They learn sentence structure, using pronouns, plurals, and

Conservation Task		
Present	**Change**	**Ask**
liquid		Is there still the same amount of water in each glass?
number		Are there still the same amount of dimes?
substance		Is there still the same amount of play dough?

7-7　You can determine a child's understanding of conservation by asking these questions.

tense properly. Children during this stage are also moving from using only oral expression to using both oral and written expression.

One form of language play for school-age children is telling riddles and jokes. Cognitive development is linked to humor. Language skills can improve through the use of humor, 7-8.

Social-Emotional Development

School-age children are growing in self-understanding. Their self-concept is forming, which affects their self-esteem. They are experiencing many new emotions, and becoming more aware of the feelings of others.

Social relationships become more complex during middle childhood. By choice, children in this stage are spending less time with their parents and more time with peers. Friendships are becoming more important. The family, however, still plays an important role in supporting the child's development.

Self-Concept

As children enter school, they start to take a closer look at the world around them. They begin to make social comparisons. **Social comparison** is a process where people define themselves in terms of the qualities, skills, and attributes they see in others. Personal strengths and weaknesses are identified as a result of this comparison. A self-concept is formed. **Self-concept** is the view a person has of himself or herself. Though the child's self-concept has been forming since infancy, school-age children are more aware of who they are.

School-age children can describe their strengths and weaknesses in very concrete terms. To illustrate, Luis is seven years old. Recently, his teacher asked him to describe himself. He said, "My name is Luis. I am a boy, and I live in Breckenridge, Colorado. I have brown eyes, black hair, and am tall. My hobbies are biking and skiing. I am good at them. I am not as good using the computer. I swim at the recreation center with my friends. My friends like me. I try to be helpful to them. My teacher says that I am a good speller, so I help my friends with their spelling."

Luis's self-description refers to his sex, physical appearance, and some social comparisons. Luis, like other children his age, has extended the number of people he is looking to

7-8 School-age children begin to develop a sense of humor.

for information. During the preschool years, his references were primarily his family. Now his reference groups include classmates and teachers. The feedback he receives from these individuals influences his self-concept.

Self-Esteem

Self-esteem is the belief that you are worthwhile as a person. While preschool children usually have very high self-esteem, this sometimes changes in middle childhood. To have healthy self-esteem, school-age children need to believe in themselves. By continually evaluating themselves, some children lose their confidence. Subtle messages echoed by adults and peers can promote or undermine self-esteem. Figure 7-9 shows areas in which children evaluate themselves.

As a teacher, you can play an important role in promoting children's self-esteem. A warm, nurturing attitude is important. Avoid making comparisons among children. By avoiding comparisons, you will be helping children develop confidence in their own abilities. Children feel better about themselves.

Accomplishments need to be viewed in relation to a child's efforts and ability. In almost every classroom, there is at least one child who has learned helplessness. These children think, no matter how hard they try, that they cannot be successful. You will spot them immediately. When faced with new experiences or challenges, they give up quickly. Before they make an effort to try, they say "I don't know how" or "I can't do that."

Help children during middle childhood to avoid feelings of helplessness. Encourage them to persist at difficult tasks. Make them believe that with more effort they can overcome failure. Say "I know you can do this if you try harder." Likewise, celebrate when these children do succeed, even in small ways. Provide them with additional feedback on why they were successful.

Understanding Others

With experience and maturity, school-age children make major advances in understanding others. They are developing **empathy**—the ability to understand the feelings of others. At the same time, they are feeling compassion towards others. **Compassion** is being aware of others' distress and wanting to help them, 7-10.

Children's Judgments of Self-Worth Are Based Upon:
Academic Competence
Athletic Competence
Physical Appearance
Behavior
Social Acceptance

7-9 School-age children judge themselves on these factors.

7-10 School-age children are becoming more aware of the feelings of others.

School-age children can describe another person's feelings and personality traits. Prior to this time, children used only physical descriptions of others. For example, when Ben was a preschooler, his grandmother asked him to describe his teacher. He said, "She has brown hair and brown eyes. She wears glasses and she is pretty." When Ben's grandmother asked him to describe his teacher as an eight-year-old, the description went beyond physical traits. He said, "He is really a happy person. He smiles a lot and says things like 'good job.' Sometimes he gets mad, like when Brian is being a jerk. Then he gets angry with him."

Ben has developed the ability to see another's viewpoint. His ability to imagine what his teacher was feeling or thinking is developing. This is an important developmental milestone. Getting along with others throughout life is dependent upon being able to understand another person's point of view. Studies show that children with poor social skills have trouble identifying other people's thoughts and feelings.

Friendships

During the school-age years, friendships take on greater importance. During preschool, a friend was a convenient playmate who shared toys. Now, choosing friends becomes a more selective process. Gender often influences the selection of a friend. Most school-age children choose close friends of the same sex. Children with common interests usually become friends.

These friendships are important to children. A friend is a person who shares important thoughts and feelings. A friend offers companionship and emotional support. Emotional commitment is learned through these early friendships.

Some children seem to be particularly well liked by other children. These children are friendly to others. They also show sensitivity and have good communication skills. During middle childhood, peer acceptance can be influenced by appearance and behavior.

Other children are rejected and avoided by their peers. They are not included in after-school functions or invited to parties. They also tend to be ignored during recess and lunch. These children often lack self-control and act aggressively toward others. They may be disruptive or hostile.

Without friendships, the child does not receive the important benefits of interacting with peers. This can be traumatic for some children. Low self-esteem, the inability to develop social skills, and loneliness are a result. These children often lack confidence in their abilities. They need special help to recognize and overcome their behavior problems.

Peer Group Activities

Peer group activities play an important role in the social development of school-age children. They may join 4-H clubs, church groups, Girl Scouts, or Boy Scouts. In these groups, they learn how to cooperate with others to achieve goals, and they learn rules of group behavior.

Gender Differences

Informal groups are often single sex during the early school-age years. See 7-11. The girls cluster with other girls. The boys, too, prefer other boys. Mixed sex groups may form for talking, eating, or working on projects in the classroom. Boys and girls may enjoy playing kick ball or other games together.

Teasing frequently occurs between boys and girls. Boys love to interrupt the girls play. When this occurs, the girls respond by chasing them away or tattling to adults.

At school, gender often creates boundary differences in play areas and space. Boys tend to control large fixed spaces that are used for team sports. Studies show they control almost ten times more space than girls. Space occupied by girls is usually located closer to the school building.

Activity preferences between girls and boys exist. While girls enjoy jumping rope, playing hopscotch, and doing tricks on the jungle gym, boys prefer competitive sports, such as basketball, football, and baseball.

Girls play involves more taking turns and cooperating with others. Compared to boys, they are often interacting in pairs or small groups. Girls are not as open as boys. They have more select relationships in which they share secrets.

7-11 Friends tend to be of the same sex.

Games with Rules

Can you remember your middle childhood years? Chances are you were enjoying organized games with rules. If you were like most children, during recess you were playing hide-and-seek, red rover, and blind man's bluff. You probably played tag, jump rope, and hopscotch. Basketball, soccer, and softball were played during physical education classes.

These games are important for children's development. They encourage children to take another person's perspective. From this, children learn why rules are important. Children often spend as much time working out the rules for a game as playing the game.

In recent decades, there has been a decrease in the amount of time children spend in child-organized games. More time is being devoted to television, computers, video games, and adult-organized sports. As a result, children are not as physically fit. In addition, they do not have as many opportunities to learn to follow rules.

Team Sports

With improvement in their physical skills, both girls and boys enjoy participating in team sports. Soccer, football, softball, swimming, gymnastics, and basketball are common. The most popular team sport is baseball, 7-12.

7-12 School-age children enjoy participating in team sports.

Through participation in team sports, children often develop life-long habits that contribute to a healthy lifestyle.

By participating in competitive sports, children benefit in many ways. These include the following:

- They learn teamwork skills.
- They learn to get along with their peers.
- They benefit from the exercise.
- The activities bring enjoyment.
- A pattern for a healthy lifestyle begins to form.

There are also drawbacks to participating in team sports. There is no safe sport. School-age children can be injured. Bumps, bruises, and scrapes are common injuries. The most serious injuries are head and neck injuries, which usually result from playing football. To reduce injuries, children need to be instructed on the safe use of equipment. They also need to be taught the importance of conditioning activities, such as stretching and warm-up exercises.

Critics of adult-organized sports teams claim they resemble more work than play for children. As the focus is often on winning, children feel pressure from their peers, parents, and coaches to win at all costs. Since adults often control the game, children may not be developing decision-making and leadership skills.

Moral Development

Moral development is the process of acquiring the standards of behavior considered acceptable by a society. **Morality** involves understanding and using accepted rules of conduct when interacting with others. Standards of behavior become internalized.

Children learn moral behavior by interacting with others, 7-13. Preschoolers begin to learn acceptable behavior through the use of rewards and punishment. Some behaviors bring rewards, such as praise or attention. They learn to repeat these behaviors. Other behaviors bring punishment. They have not yet internalized any standards of behavior, but they learn how to avoid punishment.

Children in middle childhood are more aware of the world around them and more sensitive to the feelings of others. As they become more concerned about others' needs, they want to help them. This desire influences their moral development. They begin to internalize rules of conduct.

7-13 Children during middle childhood internalize standards of behavior they learn from their parents and others.

Summary

Middle childhood refers to the span of years between ages six and twelve. Physical development during middle childhood slows down from the rapid pace of earlier years. Children grow about two to three inches per year during this time period and gain about five to seven pounds per year. Large motor skills are improving, including greater speed and accuracy of movement. Fine motor skills improve the neatness and accuracy of writing.

Though this is often one of the healthiest periods for children, several chronic illnesses may surface during middle childhood. Ulcers, asthma, and diabetes may develop. Vision and hearing need to be checked regularly so that any problems can be corrected. Obesity is becoming more common among school-age children.

Cognitive development continues as children begin to think mentally using logic and symbols. They no longer rely only on what they see or perceive. They can process and recall information more readily. Memory improves and their attention span is longer. Because they can now use logic in their mental operations, children learn several new concepts during the middle years. These include the concepts of conservation, seriation, and classification. Vocabulary and grammar skills also improve dramatically.

As children take a closer look at the world around them, they begin to make social comparisons. Their strengths and weaknesses become more apparent to them. Children's self-concept forms, which affects their self-esteem. They also begin to develop feelings of empathy and compassion towards others. Friendships and group activities take on greater importance during the school-age years. Most of these relationships are with friends of the same sex.

Morality begins to develop during middle childhood as standards of behavior become internalized.

Review and Reflect

1. True or false. By 12 years of age, most girls have surpassed boys in height and weight.

2. List the motor skills in which girls generally outperform boys.

3. True or false. A person who is nearsighted can see close objects better than distant objects.

4. List three factors that may lead to obesity in children.

5. Explain how the way children process information changes from the preschool years to the school-age years.

6. Describe a test that you could use to check a child's understanding of the concept of conservation.

7. How does language change during the school-age years.

8. Explain the relationship between self-concept and self-esteem.

9. School-age children begin to develop empathy. What does this mean?

10. Describe the gender differences in play areas and space.

11. Why are team sports important for children's development?

12. True or false. Morality involves the internalizing of accepted rules of behavior.

Apply and Explore

1. Visit a local elementary school during recess and observe the motor skills of school-age children.

2. Invite a teacher of school-age children to discuss their cognitive development.

3. Visit an after-school program. Observe the children's social interactions and peer groups.

4. Invite a panel of four parents to debate the advantages and disadvantages of adult-organized team sports for school-age children. Choose two parents who favor team sports for school-age children and two that oppose them. What conclusions did you draw from the debate?

5. Visit an after-school program. Bring along ten pennies and two balls of play dough. With six- and seven-year-olds, assess their ability to conserve number and mass.

Part 2

Creating a Safe and Healthy Environment

8 Preparing the Environment

9 Selecting Toys, Equipment, and Educational Materials

10 Promoting Children's Safety

11 Planning Nutritious Meals and Snacks

12 Guiding Children's Health

Your primary goal as a child care teacher is to keep children safe and healthy. Creating a safe, healthy environment requires careful planning and preparation.

As you read this part, you will discover how to arrange the space in a center to promote safety as well as learning and fun. You will also learn criteria for choosing toys and equipment that will safely help meet your program goals.

This part gives safety objectives to help you prevent accidents and illness. It also makes you aware of your responsibilities in detecting and reporting child abuse and neglect.

Guidelines for planning and serving nutritious meals and snacks are provided in this part. Also, procedures are given for handling such medical emergencies as wounds, burns, and fevers.

Teachers are responsible for preparing both indoor and outdoor areas for children.

Chapter 8

Preparing the Environment

After studying this chapter, you will be able to

- explain the value of planned indoor and outdoor space.
- name the basic activity areas in a center, along with the functions of each area.
- list criteria to consider when choosing playroom furniture and color schemes.
- summarize factors that affect the organization of space in a center.
- organize basic activity areas of the classroom and outdoor play yard.

Terms to Know

isolation area

staff room

audiovisual board

acoustic material

cubbies

cool colors

warm colors

traffic pattern

sensory table

stationary equipment

Michiko is running. Susie is hiding. No one saw Mary take the fish out of the bowl. There is no place for Jose to play with the blocks. The behavior of children in this classroom is affected by the way the space is arranged.

In another classroom, the space is carefully organized. All the children are involved in constructive play. The layout encourages independent learning and communication. There are few, if any, behavior problems. Heather is smiling. Fred is looking at books in a quiet corner of the classroom. At the same time, Wong and his friends are building a large block structure.

In a developmentally appropriate, well-organized environment, children grow and learn. The teacher is responsible for creating an environment that is shaped by the needs and interests of the children.

Classroom arrangement reflects program quality. It also provides clues about expected behavior. A well-planned setting usually promotes interesting play, provides children with choices, and reduces behavior problems. It should encourage interaction with other children and adults, as well as active exploration. Well-planned space is arranged based on the children's temperaments, developmental needs, interests, and program goals. The classroom should also be attractive and inviting.

A nurturing, safe environment is critical for children's social, emotional, physical, and cognitive development. Children need space to build, move, sort, create, pretend, spread out, work, and interact with friends. They need diverse materials in sufficient quantity to keep them actively involved. They need a place to be quiet, to be active, to talk, and to move. Space affects the activity level of children. The choices children make and the way they carry out their choices are also affected by space. Space can even affect the children's concentration and the length of time they will remain with one activity. Therefore, space should be arranged according to children's needs and interests. However, the space should also be convenient for the staff. See 8-1.

Value of Planned Space

The early years are crucial for the cognitive development of children. Before arranging a classroom, review the developmental objectives of the program. For example, two-year-old children do not have refined large motor skills. To promote safety and motor development, they need large, open spaces. The classroom should be planned with these goals in mind.

An attractive, well-arranged classroom conveys a sense of order. It encourages children to use materials and to do things for themselves. It also molds their behavior. Boundaries found in this type of classroom make the children more

responsible. They know where to find classroom materials. They also know where to return them when they are finished.

Safety is an important concern in planning space. When children feel safe, they feel free to learn. Open spaces must be provided so adults can supervise the entire room. The ratio of caregivers to children also affects safety. If the number of caregivers is low, the room arrangement should be simple to make supervision easier.

Studies have shown that the arrangement of space greatly affects teachers' behavior as well as children's. In centers with well-planned space, teachers were more friendly, sensitive, and warm to children. These teachers taught their children to respect others' rights and feelings. In centers with poorly-planned space, teachers were often more insensitive to their students.

The goals for a well-planned space include
- providing a physically safe environment for the children.
- providing children with areas that promote cognitive, emotional, social, and physical growth.
- providing adults with a space that is easy to supervise.

8-1 Quality early childhood programs have ample space for children and teachers.

- providing space that is pleasing to the eye for both adults and children.
- providing easy access to materials when needed so children are able to direct themselves, 8-2.
- encouraging children to take part in activities.

Physical Space

The physical space of a center may be divided into seven main areas. These basic areas include the following:

- entrance
- director's office
- isolation area
- kitchen or kitchenette
- staff room
- bathrooms
- classroom or playroom

8-2 Low shelving units in the small manipulative play area provide this child with the opportunity to choose her own activity.

Entrance

The entrance to the center should be attractive and appealing to children and adults, 8-3. Plants, the children's artwork attractively displayed, and a bulletin board for parents will enhance the appearance. If space permits, chairs and a sofa are welcome additions for parents who need to wait.

Director's Office

The director's office should be just inside the center's entrance. School records, children's records, and public relations material can be stored here. This office can also be used for parent interviews and conferences. Some directors also have a small table in their offices for teachers' meetings and planning sessions.

Isolation Area

Most states require centers to provide a special room or space for children who become ill or show signs of a communicable disease. This room, often called an **isolation area**, should contain a cot and a few toys. If the space

8-3 The entrance to this center helps children feel welcome.

is not available, a cot may be placed in the director's office when needed.

Kitchen

The size of a center's kitchen depends on the amount of daily food preparation. Even if meals are not served, most centers have a small area with a sink, refrigerator, and stove for preparing snacks. Regardless of the kitchen's use, the local health department personnel should inspect it. They can tell you if all legal requirements are being met.

Floor coverings in the kitchen should be easy to clean. Vinyl coverings and ceramic tile are recommended floor coverings for the kitchen.

Staff Room

Adults need an area for their own use. This area is called a **staff room.** It should contain a locked storage space for personal belongings. A coat rack, sofa, and tables or desks also should be available for the staff. Most staff members prefer having a telephone, professional journals, and curriculum guides available, too. A coffeepot or appliance that can boil water is also useful. Privacy is also important for the staff area. This area may be used for meeting with parents or other staff members.

Bathrooms

Most states have laws requiring a certain number of toilets and sinks for a group of young children. Some states require at least one toilet for every ten children. However, a higher ratio is more convenient. There are many times during the day that several children may have to use the bathroom at the same time.

The size of the toilet fixture will vary with the size and age of the children. A group of two-year-old children would be comfortable with toilet fixtures ten inches from the floor. Five-year-old children would find thirteen-inch toilet fixtures more comfortable.

If small toilets are unavailable, a sturdy wooden step can be used for smaller children. This same wooden step can be used in front of the sinks that are too high for children to reach.

For safety purposes, the water heater that supplies water to the children's bathroom should be set on low heat. Only tepid water should be available in this area.

Bathroom flooring should be easy to clean. Tile is recommended. Also, it should not be slippery. Avoid having wax applied to the flooring in this area.

Classroom or Playroom

The classroom or playroom should be on the ground floor close to an exit. A rectangular room is the best shape as it allows for optimal supervision. This shape also allows for many more space arrangements than other shapes.

Quality child care centers have enough space for children and for a variety of materials and equipment. The recommended amount of space varies from state to state. It can range from 35 to 100 square feet of indoor space per child. The National Association for the Education of Young Children recommends at least 35 square feet of free indoor space per child. This amount should not include hallways or space taken up by equipment and toilets.

Walls

All walls should be durable and washable. Many teachers like to attach bulletin boards to the walls. This provides space to hang artwork and papers, as well as absorb sound, 8-4.

8-4 A brightly decorated bulletin board is a welcome addition to any classroom.

Chalkboards can also be attached to walls. They should be installed at the children's eye level.

Instead of bulletin boards and chalkboards, some centers use audiovisual boards. An **audiovisual board** can serve as a bulletin board, chalkboard, and movie screen. It is usually white, off-white, or beige. The disadvantage of the audiovisual board is that magnetic strips must be used to hold up objects when used as a bulletin board. These strips can be costly.

Floors

A recent trend for playroom floor coverings has been carpeting. Carpeting is easy to maintain. It also provides a sound cushion.

Windows

Windows in the playroom should be placed so that children can see outside. Screens should be installed outside all windows. All windows should open in case of a fire.

Drapes or blinds may be used to help control light. They also add interest, softness, and color to a room. Drapes or blinds reduce glare, heating bills, and noise. One disadvantage of drapes is that they become soiled easily. This is caused by children brushing by them with dirty hands or art supplies.

For a different effect, you might wish to hang a valance above each window. This can be a nice addition to a classroom if the colors complement the decor. If you use valances instead of drapes, also use miniblinds or pleated shades to reduce glare.

Doors

Doors should be lightweight. To guard against injury, the doors should push out to open. Doorknobs should be low enough so children can reach them.

Acoustics

Studies show that noise affects children's behavior. For this reason, make an effort to use materials that will reduce or eliminate most noise.

Acoustic material is used to deaden or absorb sounds. Carpets, drapes, bulletin boards, pillows, stuffed toys, and sand are examples. Due to the physical makeup of these materials, noise can be reduced or eliminated. For instance, carpeting will absorb the sound of footsteps. Carpeting can also add visual appeal, comfort, warmth, and softness to a room.

If the classroom is still noisy after the addition of draperies, carpeting, and bulletin boards, acoustical tile may need to be installed on the classroom ceiling. Whenever possible, the ceiling should range from 10 to 12 feet high to reduce noise and provide a feeling of spaciousness.

Temperature

Temperature and humidity are important in planning a comfortable environment for young children. They cannot attend to or process information in an uncomfortable environment.

Usually a temperature range of 68 to 70 degrees Fahrenheit will be comfortable. When vigorous physical activities are planned, the temperature should be decreased. In order for children to be comfortable, adults may have to wear a sweater.

Humidity

Humidity, like temperature, influences the comfort of the environment. Usually a 40 to 60 percent relative humidity range is considered comfortable. Typically, a temperature of 68 degrees Fahrenheit with a relative humidity of 60 percent would be comfortable. If comfort is to be maintained, the relative humidity should be decreased as the temperature rises.

Electrical Outlets

For safety purposes, electrical outlets should be above the children's reach. When outlets are not being used, safety caps should be inserted for protection. Many times a room arrangement will be influenced by the location of electrical outlets. For example, the music area would be located near an outlet so a record or tape player could be used. For the safety of the children and staff, do not use long electrical cords. These can cause someone to trip or fall. Because of this danger, many states ban the use of long extension cords in the classroom.

Furniture

Classroom or playroom furniture should be durable, washable, and stackable. Tables and easels should be adjustable. Then they can be adjusted to fit each child who may use them. To check if an easel is the proper height, have the child stand next to it. Ask the child to touch the middle of the easel pad. If the child has to bend or reach to touch the middle of the pad, adjust the easel.

Chair and table heights are checked in a different manner. Ask the child to sit on a chair. Then push it under the table. If the table and chair are suited to the child, there will be room between the bottom of the table and the child's knees. The child should be able to place his or her feet flat on the floor.

Chairs

Children's chairs are often used in the art, dramatic play, and dining areas. Chairs should always be the proper height for the children. Plastic, stackable chairs are preferred by most teachers. Plastic chairs have other advantages. They are light enough for the children to move, and they do not require refinishing. An adult-sized rocking chair may be used by children in the library or dramatic play area. The chair may also be used by adults as a special place to hold or comfort a child.

Tables

Classroom tables should be hard, smooth, and washable. The tables should be light enough to move. Most preschool teachers prefer tables that are large enough to seat four to six children. Rectangular tables are often preferred over round tables. The rectangular shape allows children to have their own space. This reduces the chance for aggression. Low, round tables are sometimes used in the library and dramatic play area.

Storage Units

Storage units should be organized for easy access of equipment and supplies. Blocks, books, art supplies, games, and other classroom materials are kept in storage units, 8-5. These units should be arranged to encourage children to independently remove and return materials. For flexibility, all storage units should have casters so they can be moved easily. The casters should be equipped with locks so they do not move accidentally. For units without casters, hardware can be bought and easily installed. Keep in mind that pegboard or corkboard can be attached to exposed sides and backs of units. These can serve as bulletin boards.

8-5 Blocks and other toys are well-organized on this shelving unit.

Storage units should match the height of the children. They must be able to reach the materials. Therefore, choose small, lightweight sections of cabinets.

If doors are needed on the storage units, sliding doors are best. When opened, swinging doors can cause safety hazards. Children may be playing in front of the doors.

Lockers and Cubbies

Children can learn responsibility for their own belongings when they are provided personal storage space. Each child enrolled in the program should have a locker, 8-6. Most lockers for preschool children are 10 to 12 inches wide and 10 to 15 inches deep. Each locker should contain a hook for hanging a coat.

The primary purpose of lockers is to store children's clothing. Finished artwork, library books, parent letters, and other valuable items must also be stored. For storage of these items,

many lockers have a top section. These are often called **cubbies**. If the lockers do not have cubbies, containers can be stacked to store the children's belongings. See 8-7.

Lockers and cubbies should have a coat of varnish or paint. This coating will help prevent staining from muddy boots, wet paints, etc. If lockers are painted, use a washable enamel paint.

Lockers should be placed near the entrance. This will save parents time when picking up children. It will save the class from being disrupted when someone must go to his or her locker. It will also save clean-up time during bad weather.

Color Choices for Child Care Centers

Color affects how teachers and children feel about their classroom. Colors can either calm or stimulate young children. Too many vivid colors in an environment may overstimulate young

8-6 Use symbols on lockers to help young children identify their space.

8-7 Empty containers can be used to store children's small personal belongings.

children. Because of the emotional effects of color, select colors carefully. The goal should be to create a room that looks pleasant and feels spacious. This can be done using **cool colors**, such as blue, green, and purple. Cool colors make a room appear larger. They create a feeling of openness. **Warm colors** make a room seem smaller. These colors include red, yellow, and orange. Studies show that children prefer warm colors until about age six. After the age of six, they start to prefer cool colors.

Other factors affect color selection. These include the amount of available light in the room and the amount of time spent in the room. For example, if the room does not have much light available, a warm color will help the room appear brighter.

Since child care centers are active places and contain a lot of colorful materials, white is often used in classrooms. Children respond well to white. White rooms are perceived as clean and cool. White is an excellent color for the eating, isolation, administration, and reading areas. It is also a good color for the bathroom.

Light blue is often used in child care centers. Children respond to this color by feeling comfortable, soothed, and secure. Therefore, light blue is useful in the nap, reading, eating, and isolation areas.

Light green, like light blue and white, creates a positive response. It makes children feel calm, refreshed, peaceful, and restful. It is useful for isolation, nap, reading, and eating areas.

Yellow makes people feel happy and cheerful. It is a good color in art and music areas. Playground equipment is often painted yellow.

Orange is a welcoming, forceful, energetic color. Its use should be limited. Clearly, an orange room can be overwhelming. However, orange can be used effectively in small areas, such as an entrance.

As with orange, the use of red should be limited, 8-8. Overuse of red can be too stimulating for children. Children may become overactive. Red is best used on indoor gross motor equipment, outdoor equipment, and teaching aids designed to stimulate children.

The color purple can have a mournful effect. It is best used only as an accent color on equipment, bulletin boards, and teaching aids. When used as a wall color, limit its use to reading areas.

8-8 The use of red on this decoration creates interest without being overpowering.

Factors That Affect Space Organization

An organized classroom can inspire children to take part in the activities of the day. The space should be arranged to define the scope and limits of activities. Therefore, the space must provide for proper learning experiences.

When planning classroom space, many factors should be considered. These factors will greatly affect how the classroom is organized. They include licensing requirements, program goals, group size, scale, and traffic patterns.

Licensing Requirements

All states have their own licensing requirements for child care centers. You will need to know these your state's requirements before you begin planning classroom space. Requirements vary from state to state. However, some common requirements exist. For example, they all require a minimum number of fire extinguishers. Also, all exits must be clear, and entrance doors must open to the outside. In addition, a minimum number of square feet of space must be available for each child.

Program Goals

A program's goals should be based on the children's abilities, age, and skills. The goals a teacher selects should represent the major stages of development and growth. (These stages were discussed in Chapters 4, 5, 6, and 7.) The environment, as well as planned classroom activities, should stimulate growth and development.

Caregivers concerned with all developmental areas might select the following program goals:

- To promote a positive self-concept.
- To promote independence.
- To promote problem-solving skills.
- To promote small muscle coordination.
- To promote large muscle coordination.
- To promote self-control.
- To promote language skills.
- To promote prosocial behavior.
- To promote an appreciation of cultural diversity.

After the goals for the children are listed, review each goal. Decide how each goal will be supported by the classroom environment. For instance, most teachers set a goal to develop independence in children. The arrangement of the room can help children achieve this goal. Materials, locker hooks, and shelving units should all be within easy reach for the children. This will encourage children to act without help from adults in many cases. Chart 8-9 lists a number of ways to meet various program goals.

Program goals should also reflect state licensing requirements. Therefore, if the state requires that children receive one meal and two snacks each day, a program goal might state that children receive nutritious meals and snacks.

Group Size

Group size is an important factor to consider when arranging space. A large number of children crowded into a small area will cause problems. Children are likely to become upset and fight more when crowded. Likewise, a small number of children with too much space will also cause problems. Too much open space encourages children to run. You must strive to create an arrangement that will be the proper size for the group.

The more children, the more empty space is needed. A good rule of thumb is to plan between one-third and one-half of the classroom for open space. Also, the room arrangement needs to be fairly simple. Children will feel safe and secure in this arrangement.

Arrange shelving units and other furniture with group size in mind. A good arrangement allows teachers and children to move easily through the room. It also allows for teachers and children to see and be seen easily. This will promote a relaxed setting.

Scale

The classroom environment must be scaled to the size of its occupants. Child-sized furniture should be purchased or built. Bulletin boards, toilets, water fountains, sinks, pictures, and other items should all be at the children's level. One method to judge if the setting is scaled for children is for an adult to walk on his or her knees through the entire classroom. Anything positioned too high for the children should be noted and adjusted.

Traffic Patterns

The arrangement of a classroom centers around the **traffic pattern**. This is the way people move through the classroom area. Furniture should be arranged to create a useful traffic pattern. For instance, children should be able to walk from the art area to the block-building area without going through the middle of the library area.

Program activities will affect traffic patterns. For example, most child care centers provide breakfast and lunch. These meals may be prepared on site or contracted. Whichever plan is used, the food will likely be made in or delivered to a kitchen. For this reason, the kitchen should be near a delivery door and near the eating area of the classroom.

How Goals Are Supported by the Environment	
Goal	**How Goal is Supported by Environment**
To promote independence.	Similar materials are stored together. Drawers, shelves, and containers are labeled with outlines of contents. Materials and equipment are easily accessible to children. Coat hooks are low enough for children to hang their own clothing. Individual storage is provided for each child.
To promote a positive self-concept.	Equipment is correct for developmental stage. Children's work is displayed. Unstructured materials are available in each area. A variety of materials are available for children to choose.
To promote problem-solving skills.	Equipment is correct for developmental stage. Open-ended materials, such as blocks, are available. A variety of materials are available for children to choose. Materials are rotated to create interest.
To promote small muscle coordination.	A classroom area is devoted to manipulative equipment. Enough material to maintain children's interest is available. Materials are easily accessible to children. Materials are changed frequently to create interest.
To promote large muscle development.	A classroom area is devoted to large muscle development. An adequate amount of space is provided for play. The traffic flow does not interfere with the children's use of materials. The area is located away from quiet activities.
To promote self-control.	Enough space is provided for children to use materials in each classroom area. The classroom traffic flow permits children to work without interruption. Noisy areas are located away from quiet areas. Sufficient variety and quantity of materials are available in each area.
To promote language skills.	A book display space is placed at children's eye level. Classroom materials are labeled. A wide variety of materials, including books, puppets, and tapes are available.
To promote social skills.	Boundaries between areas are defined with low shelving units. A sufficient amount of materials are available to encourage cooperative play.
To promote an appreciation of cultural diversity.	Dolls, puppets, picture books, and bulletin board figures represent different racial and ethnic groups.

8-9 Defining program goals is the first step toward well-organized space.

Organizing Basic Activity Areas

Classrooms arranged according to activity areas allow children to make their own choices. Each activity area should clearly convey to the children what those choices are. For example, the art area should have an easel and art supplies. By displaying these materials in an inviting manner, the children will be aware of what is available to them. This gives them the chance to choose what they will do.

Each activity area is a space of its own, and each area supports the program goals. Each area should be defined, but the space should be flexible. Shelves placed in U or L shapes can create boundaries for classroom areas. The shelves can be moved when the shape of the space needs to be changed.

Arrange activity areas by function. Think carefully of each area as wet or dry, active or quiet, 8-10. Wet and dry activities should be placed far away from each other. Sensory and science activities are examples of wet/active activities. Art, eating, and cooking are types of wet/quiet activities.

Active activities should take place far from quiet activities. Woodworking, blockbuilding, music, and dramatic play are all active activities. Each of these could disrupt a quiet activity. Sleeping, reading, and small manipulative play are all examples of quiet/dry activities.

Most teachers prefer to map out two or three possible area arrangements. This helps them see what will work best and why. Some room arrangement principles are shown in 8-11.

Remember that rather than being static, room arrangements must be dynamic. Rearranging the classroom areas is necessary when the children's interests change. With changing interests, the addition and elimination of equipment and materials needs to be considered.

Introducing Activity Areas

Children require an introduction to the activity areas in the classroom. They need to learn what materials are in each area. They need to learn what activities take place in that area. They also need to learn the safety and cleanup rules of the area. In programs that operate for nine month sessions, the children can be introduced to the areas at the start of the session.

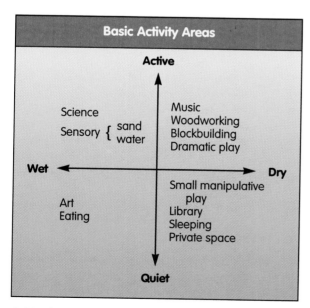

Basic Activity Areas

Active

Science
Sensory { sand
          water

Music
Woodworking
Blockbuilding
Dramatic play

Wet ← → Dry

Art
Eating

Small manipulative play
Library
Sleeping
Private space

Quiet

8-10 Planning space requires that you consider each activity as it relates to other activities that take place in the same area.

Principles of Room Arrangement

- Whenever possible, arrange areas around the edges of the room. This allows the center of the room to be used for traffic flow.
- Arrange shelving units so that the teacher can clearly view the entire room.
- Store objects together that are used for the same activities.
- Place the art area near a water source.
- Place quiet activities far away from active activities and traffic areas.
- Place dry activities far from wet activities.
- Provide open space for blockbuilding and group activities.
- Define areas by arranging storage units into U- or L-shapes.
- Provide a private space where children can be alone.

8-11 Keep these principles in mind when planning space. Would you add any guidelines to this list?

In programs that operate throughout the year, children can be introduced to each area when they first enroll in the program. Children who have been in the program for a time may help the teacher introduce the areas to new students.

Children need to learn the routine for using and replacing materials. Carefully arranging materials will enable the children to help maintain the learning environment. To help children feel comfortable in using and moving about the areas, use labels and signs, 8-12. Labels and signs direct children's attention. This then helps children become self-directed learners. Labels and signs also encourage children to return materials to storage areas. Tape pictures to the storage areas to serve as reminders.

Blockbuilding Area

Blocks give children practice sorting, grouping, comparing, arranging, making decisions, cooperating, and role-playing. Therefore, this area should be well-equipped and well-defined. See 8-13.

The best location for blockbuilding should be on a carpeted area. Carpeting helps by reducing the noise level. Define the area with low cabinets. Allow enough room for building. Children will need room to build structures that go around, up, and out.

8-13 Blockbuilding areas are very popular. Make sure this area is well-equipped and spacious.

In addition to blocks, provide other items in the blockbuilding area. Examples include plastic zoo and farm animals, people, traffic signs, wheeled toys, pulleys, and boxes.

Use the low cabinets that define the area for storage of materials. Make sure there are enough shelves to arrange the blocks according to shape. Place all blockbuilding materials at the children's eye level and within their reach.

Large, heavy blocks (and other heavy materials) should be placed on a bottom shelf or on the floor to avoid accidents. Save higher shelves for lightweight items. Label each shelf with the shape of the block that can be found there. You can use paint or contact paper to label the shelves. Labels help children return the blocks to the correct shelf. Labels also provide matching practice and reduces clean-up time. See 8-14.

Art Area

Place the art area near a water source. Arrange the space so either groups or individuals can use the area. Use tables, chairs, easels, drying racks, and shelving units that are easy to clean and maintain. See 8-15. Label the shelves with the materials found there.

8-12 With the help of labels and signs, children will learn to move around their environment easily.

8-14 Promote independence by labeling storage areas for children's health care products.

8-15 Make efficient use of space by placing a drying rack for artwork overhead.

Dramatic Play Area

The dramatic play area is also known as the home living or housekeeping area. This area needs to be arranged to look like a real home. A stove, refrigerator, table, chairs, sink, and doll bed are basic furniture you may wish to provide. Other props may be added. For instance, you may wish to provide dolls, kitchen utensils, cleaning tools, and dress-up clothes. Place the dramatic play area in the active area of the classroom.

Sensory Area

The key piece of equipment in the sensory area is the **sensory table**. It is also known as a water or sand table. The size of the table will depend on the amount of space available and depend on the age of the children. Two- and three-year-old children love the sensory appeal of water and sand. A sensory table can give the children practice in social situations.

Not all centers have sensory tables. Some centers use plastic wading pools or washtubs. Whatever container is used, it should be placed near a water source. Children and teachers enjoy adding water to the sand to change the feeling.

Other items are often used in the sensory table. Provide rustproof spoons, shovels, sand pails, measuring cups, funnels, strainers, old pots, and other kitchen items. Place shelving units near the table for storage. If shelves or other storage are not available, use plastic buckets or laundry baskets for storage.

Woodworking Area

After building wood sculptures, many children enjoy decorating them with paint. For that reason, locate the woodworking area near the art area, 8-16. For the children's safety, place this area outside the line of traffic.

Items you may wish to provide at the woodworking bench include tools, wood scraps, and styrofoam pieces. Hang a pegboard next to the wood bench, within children's reach. It can be used to hold tools. To encourage the return of tools, paint outlines of the tools on the pegboard. The children can replace tools by matching them with outlined shapes.

Sleeping Area

Most preschool children rest or nap after lunch. Not all programs, however, have separate sleeping areas. For those that do not, a flexible room arrangement is key. Such an arrangement can be quickly and quietly altered during or

8-16 The woodworking table can hold the attention of children for extended time periods.

language arts. For example, paper, pens, pencils, and felt-tip markers encourage writing skills. Shelving units, a table, and chairs are all useful in this area. See 8-17. For comfort, pillows may also be added. Many centers also carpet this area or add an area rug.

Music Area

Rhythm instruments, cassette players, and audiotapes are found in almost all music areas. When space permits, some centers have a piano. If a lack of money or space exists, an Autoharp® or guitar is an alternative to a piano.

Private Space

Provide a private area in the classroom where children can be alone. Children then have the option of limiting contact with others when they choose. This reduces the pressure of being around others when they wish to be alone. Set a classroom rule stating that children who go to the private space will not be disturbed by others.

immediately after lunchtime into a sleeping area. Allow sufficient space for sleeping. Some states require that two feet of open space exist between cots. Check your state's regulations.

Small Manipulative Area

The small manipulative, or small motor, area should be located in a dry, quiet area of the playroom. Table blocks, puzzles, plastic building pieces, parquetry blocks, stringing beads, lotto boards, sewing cards, and color cubes with pattern cards are some items you may wish to provide. Many teachers also include math materials and equipment in this area. A table, chairs, and shelving unit are also useful in this area.

Library Area

The library area should be located in the quietest part of the classroom. Often this is next to the manipulative area. In addition to providing books and magazines, you may want to promote

8-17 Display books at the children's eye level in the library area.

8-18 Children sometimes like to be alone. This loft provides a perfect setting.

A loft is one unique way to provide private space, 8-18. In programs where a wooden loft is not in the budget, large cardboard boxes and wooden crates can serve the same purpose.

The private space should be small, allowing room for only one or two children to use at a time. The children in the private space should not be visible to other children in the room. However, the teacher must be able to see into the private space.

Science Area

Place the science area in the wet, active area of the classroom. Most science areas contain at least one table. If needed, a shelving unit may also be placed in this area. For more information on guiding science experiences, refer to Chapter 23.

Eating Area

When space is available, provide a separate eating area. This area should be located near the kitchen. This allows for easy service and clean-up.

If space is limited, have children sit at tables in other areas of the classroom. The daily schedule will have to be arranged to allow for this.

Chart 8-19 summarizes each classroom area and the furniture, materials, and equipment you

Classroom Area	Furniture	Materials and Equipment
Blockbuilding	labeled shelving units	large hollow blocks; solid unit blocks; wheeled toys: cars, buses, trucks, fire engines, tractors, planes; small toy people of various ethnic backgrounds; small, colored wooden blocks; zoo animals; farm animals
Art	adjustable easels shelving unit(s) tables drying rack	clay, pencils, crayons, colored chalk, ink markers, paper, tempera paint, scrap paper and fabrics, tape, glue, paste, brushes, scissors, painting smocks
Dramatic Play	doll bed child-sized refrigerator, stove, sink, cupboard, and doll bed trunk or tree to hold clothes tables and chairs	child-sized cleaning equipment: broom, dustpan, and mops; doll clothes; telephones; mirror; dishes and cooking utensils: tubs, buckets, and pans; dress-up clothes, costumes; purses, backpacks, suitcases; dolls

8-19 Providing materials and equipment for activity areas is a thought-provoking process. Many everyday materials can be used for learning.

(Continued)

Classroom Area	Furniture	Materials and Equipment
Sensory	sensory table shelving unit (optional)	funnels, pitchers, spoons, sponges, containers, strainers, rotary beaters
Woodworking	woodworking bench	saw, screwdrivers, hammers, vice, nails, screws, scraps of wood and styrofoam, glue
Sleeping	cots mats	blankets, pillows
Small Manipulative	shelving units table (optional depending on space) chairs (optional depending on space) shelving unit	hand puppets, blocks, puzzles, plastic forms for joining, Lego® plastic building blocks, parquetry blocks, stringing beads, board games, sewing cards, colored cubes with pattern cards, bingo games, rods and blocks of different sizes, flannel board numerals, number puzzles, wooden numbers, magnetic numbers, measuring containers, scale, rulers, Tinkertoy® building blocks
Library	table chairs rug soft pillows (optional) bean bag (optional) shelving shelving unit flannel board chalkboard	picture books, children's magazines, child-authored books, charts, games, alphabet letters, pencils, felt-tip markers, paper, chalk, tape recorders
Music	piano (optional) shelving unit cassette player	rhythm instruments, tapes, silk scarves for dancing
Private Space	loft TV box wooden crates	pillows
Science	aquarium table shelving unit terrarium	magnets; scissors; prism; measuring instruments; jars and other empty containers; collections of related objects such as leaves, nuts, rocks, and insects; magnifying glasses; small pets; scales; mirrors
Eating	tables chairs	vases and centerpieces, placements, plates, eating utensils, cups
Writing Center	table chairs computer printer	photographs, different colors of lined and unlined paper, pens, pencils, felt-tip markers, alphabet letters, word lists, picture dictionary
Large Muscle	balance beam steps walking boards jungle gym	balls, ropes, hula hoops, fabric tunnels, tumbling mat

8-19 Continued.

may wish to supply in each. In each of the activity areas, include ethnic and cultural materials and artifacts whenever possible. Items such as artwork, fabric, jewelry, tools, utensils, toys, and children's books should be included.

Displaying Children's Work

The work of the children should be displayed throughout the activity areas. Bulletin boards, wall hangings, clothesline, or appliance boxes can all be used for display purposes. All display areas should be placed at the children's height, allowing them to mount and view their own work.

A wall hanging can be made from a 36- or 52-inch wide piece of felt, burlap, or sailcloth. The length of the hanging can vary. Hem each end of the hanging. Then insert a dowel through each hem.

Colored yarn or a piece of clothesline can also be used to display work. Colored plastic clothespins can be used to clasp work to the line.

A large appliance box can provide a free-standing display area. The advantage of this type of display is that it is portable. It can be used in any area of the center. Even after it is assembled, it can be moved.

Recognize the work of all the children when putting displays together. To keep displays interesting, set a time limit for each display. Change the work often.

Outdoor Play Area

Children need to take part in both indoor and outdoor activities. Many classrooms do not have the proper amount of space for large muscle activities. Other activities such as science, art, and music can also take place outdoors during pleasant weather. The outdoor play yard can fill these needs, 8-20.

In outdoor areas, the required number of square feet per child varies from state to state. Usually the requirement ranges from 75 to 200 square feet per child. A rectangular space is most functional. Such a play yard can be seen from end to end. U- or L-shaped play yards are more difficult to supervise and arrange, 8-21.

8-20 The play yard is an exciting and fun place for children.

Planning the Play Yard

The play yard, like indoor space, needs to be studied in terms of use and then broken into areas. A well-planned play yard usually has empty space and a wheeled vehicle path. These two items aid movement through the yard.

The wheeled vehicle path divides the activity areas of the play yard. This path creates space between areas and makes moving about easier. Without a path, children may constantly be bumping into each other.

To determine where a path should be laid, the teacher should kneel down to be at the children's eye level. The path should be wide enough and clear enough so children can see all areas of the play yard, even when outside school grounds.

Empty space should be located in the center of the yard. Activity areas can be placed around the outside of the yard, around the empty space. You may also need to leave empty space around some pieces of equipment. For instance, children may wish to use wooden planks and crates to extend their play at the jungle gym. Therefore, extra space will be needed around the equipment to allow for this.

8-21 This play yard is designed to be completely visible from this angle. This allows for better supervision.

When planning play yard space, consider the following guidelines:

- Equipment should be far enough apart so a child using one piece of equipment cannot touch a child using another piece of equipment.
- All equipment should be visible to the teacher from any spot in the yard or classroom.
- Children should not have to walk through one area to get to another.
- Between one-third and one-half of the yard should be used for play equipment and the remainder should be open space to allow for ease of movement.

In addition to paths and empty space, there are other factors to consider when planning an outdoor play yard. Among items to be considered are fences, the play yard surface, landscaping, storage, wheeled toy paths, stationary equipment, a water source, and animals and their shelter.

Fencing

Most states require play yards be fenced for safety of the children. Fences prevent children from wandering away from the play yard area. This makes outdoor supervision easier for teachers.

Selecting the proper fence requires careful thought. The goal is to purchase a fence that can keep children safe. The fence should fasten securely at the gate. There should be no sharp metal pieces or splintered wood to hurt children.

Two types of fences are commonly found in play yards: chain link and wood. Each type of fence has its good and bad points. For instance, because chain link is an open design, it is possible for the children to observe activities outside of the play yard. This gives the play yard an open feeling. However, some children are able to climb chain link fences. This can be dangerous. In addition, many people feel that chain link fences are unattractive.

Wood fences that complement the center design are very pleasing to the eye. However, the fence must also be designed with the children's safety in mind. Children should not be able to climb over or through a well-designed wood fence. The boards should be sanded to prevent children from getting splinters.

Surfaces

A portion of the play yard area should have grass. This is best for running and organized games. Under equipment, the best surface for safety is loose material such as bark nuggets, shredded bark, or sand. When children fall on such material, they receive fewer and less severe injuries than when they fall on hard surfaces. Nine to twelve inches of loose material provides a good cushion.

The drawback to loose materials is that they tend to pile up in one spot. They shift under weight placed on them. In high traffic areas they will thin out and pile up around the edges of the area. Therefore, the material must be raked or shoveled back into position fairly often.

Landscaping

A well-landscaped play yard makes for pleasant surroundings. In addition, landscaping can also be used as part of the science program by encouraging observation skills and promoting learning. Trees, shrubs, and flowers in a variety of sizes, colors, and growing cycles will interest children. Trees are also a good source of shade, beauty, and sound control. A well-landscaped yard gives children a place to be alone, as well as corners for play. Hills in the yard can be used to develop large muscle skills.

Before choosing flowers or shrubs, consult a landscape architect. Some plants are poisonous. Any landscape architect can tell you which plants to avoid. The architect can also recommend shrubs and flowers from a number of growing cycles. This will ensure children will always have a seasonal plant to study and view.

Storage Shed

Tricycles, wagons, scooters, shovels, rakes, balls, plastic wading pools, and gardening tools are just some of the items you may want to keep in a storage shed. See 8-22. The materials stored will vary with the climate of the area. For instance, in a warm climate, many indoor activities can be conducted outdoors throughout the year. If this is possible in your area, and the funds are available, you may wish to purchase duplicates of some equipment. Then you will not need to move classroom materials. Materials for construction, dramatic, and creative play may also be housed in the storage shed.

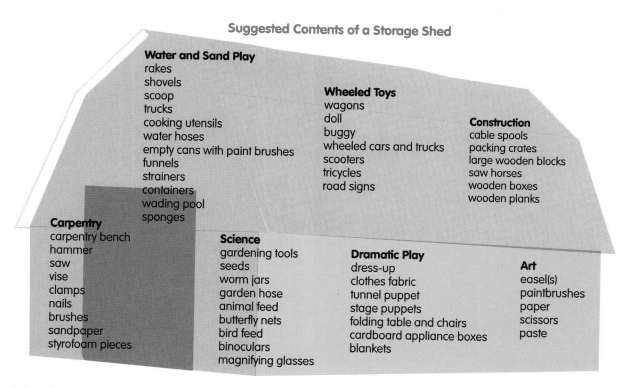

Suggested Contents of a Storage Shed

Water and Sand Play
rakes
shovels
scoop
trucks
cooking utensils
water hoses
empty cans with paint brushes
funnels
strainers
containers
wading pool
sponges

Wheeled Toys
wagons
doll
buggy
wheeled cars and trucks
scooters
tricycles
road signs

Construction
cable spools
packing crates
large wooden blocks
saw horses
wooden boxes
wooden planks

Carpentry
carpentry bench
hammer
saw
vise
clamps
nails
brushes
sandpaper
styrofoam pieces

Science
gardening tools
seeds
worm jars
garden hose
animal feed
butterfly nets
bird feed
binoculars
magnifying glasses

Dramatic Play
dress-up
clothes fabric
tunnel puppet
stage puppets
folding table and chairs
cardboard appliance boxes
blankets

Art
easel(s)
paintbrushes
paper
scissors
paste

8-22 The contents of storage sheds varies from center to center.

Storage space should be arranged so children can return materials themselves. Painted lines on the floor of the shed can be used to outline parking spaces for wheeled toys. Large barrels or baskets can be used to store many types of materials. Rakes and shovels can be hung on hooks from the wall.

Wheeled Toy Paths

A path that children can use to push or ride wheeled toys is key for two reasons. The first reason is safety. A path with one-way traffic will prevent children from riding into each other. The second reason is protection of the outdoor play area. A path gives children a place to ride so they do not destroy grassy areas, 8-23. Set limits regarding the use of wheeled toys and paths, and enforce these rules.

The path should be joined to the storage shed. Children can then drive their toys directly into or out of the shed. The path should be designed with curves instead of sharp right angles. This will allow children to make easy turns on curves, keeping them from tipping over on sharp turns.

Stationary Equipment

Jungle gyms, slides, and tree houses are all **stationary equipment** that are set permanently in the ground for stability, 8-24. For added appeal, place large pieces of stationary equipment in different corners of the play yard.

Sandbox

Children will play in sandboxes for long periods of time. If the sandbox is in a sunny area, children are at risk for sunburn. Therefore, place sandboxes in shady areas. If there is little or no shade in the play yard, build a roof over the sandbox for protection. Also, place the sandbox near a water source. By adding water to dry sand, children can build more detailed structures.

To prevent cats from using the sandbox as a litter box, build a cover for the sandbox. When the sandbox is not being used, place the cover over it, 8-25.

Water

Water play is a pleasant activity for children during warm weather. For this reason, some centers have built-in wading pools. Other centers use plastic, aboveground wading pools when licensing permits. Regardless of the type of pool,

8-23 Wheeled toy paths should have a hard surface.

8-24 These stepping logs are a type of stationary equipment. They are firmly secured in the ground.

constant supervision is necessary. For reasons of safety, pools need to be emptied at the end of each day.

A garden hose is also useful in the play yard. Attach it to a sprinkler so the children can play in the water during hot weather. The hose can also be used to water gardens and other plants.

Animal Shelter

Play yards for young children often have a number of animals. The type of animals may be determined by city zoning laws or state child care licensing rules.

To shelter animals, use cages. The cages should be large enough for the animal, have a mesh floor to keep the cage tidy between thorough cleanings, and have a quality padlock to protect against vandals. Place the cages where animals will be protected from wind, sun, and rain.

8-25 This sandbox can be covered with sheets of plywood when not in use.

Summary

Properly organized space is a key to promoting children's learning. It provides children with the option of working alone or cooperatively. It defines expected behavior for children. Properly organized space frees the children to play without interruption. They will stay with activities for longer periods of time, increasing their attention spans. Properly organized space also provides children with choices.

Space should reflect children's developmental needs and interests, as well as program goals. In such a space, children are more relaxed and positive. They feel good about themselves. As a direct result, teachers can spend more time nurturing and less time redirecting children's behavior.

Review and Reflect

1. Properly planned space is arranged based on _____.
   A. children's developmental needs
   B. children's interests
   C. program goals
   D. All of the above.

2. True or false. Teachers are affected by the arrangement of their classrooms.

3. List four goals for well-planned space.

4. What is the purpose of an isolation area?

5. A _____ room is the best shape for a classroom.

6. An audiovisual board can serve as a _____.
   A. movie screen
   B. chalkboard
   C. bulletin board
   D. All of the above.

7. Acoustic materials include _____.
   A. brick walls
   B. sand
   C. tile floors
   D. stone

8. Storage units should be selected based on the _____ of the children.

9. The top part of a locker is often called a _____.

10. Until about age six, children prefer _____.
    A. warm colors
    B. cool colors
    C. plaid
    D. All of the above.

11. What cool color can have a mournful effect?

12. Organized space should define the scope and _____ of activities.

13. List two ways to promote
    A. self-control through the classroom environment.
    B. social skills through the classroom environment.

14. Are problems created when a small group of children have too much space? Why or why not?

15. _____ are the paths people follow through an area.

16. Activity areas are best defined by arranging storage units into _____ or _____ shapes.

17. What activities should be placed in the active/dry area of the classroom?

18. True or false. Children do *not* need to spend time alone.

19. A _____ in the play yard divides activity areas and makes moving about easier.

20. What is the safest surface to use under play yard equipment?

Apply and Explore

1. Draw a room arrangement that includes each of the basic activity areas. Include a center of interest for each area.

2. Read your state's licensing requirements as they apply to classroom space. For instance, how many square feet of space is required per child? How many toilets are required for a group of 40 children?

3. Interview child care teachers about space arrangement. Ask them what they like best about their classroom space. Ask them what they would like to change.

4. Plan a color scheme for a classroom. Be prepared to explain the reasons you chose the colors you did.

Chapter 9

Selecting Toys, Equipment, and Educational Materials

After studying this chapter, you will be able to

- explain guidelines for selecting developmentally appropriate toys, equipment, and educational materials.
- describe safety factors to consider when purchasing toys and play yard equipment.
- explain how to report unsafe toys and equipment to the appropriate agencies.
- list sources and methods for purchasing toys and equipment.

Terms to Know

spectator toys
physical age
chronological age
developmental age
multicultural
co-op (cooperative)
consumable supplies

Children learn about their world by playing with toys, exploring materials, and interacting with other people. They learn best when provided with a wide range of toys and educational materials. This allows them to make choices. Toys play an important role in facilitating the learning process. For instance, children can learn speech and dressing skills while playing with toys. Children can learn about other people through the use of toys. When playing with toys, children often interact with others. They make choices, solve problems, and apply some control over their environment, 9-1.

Developmentally appropriate toys motivate and engage children as active learners. Simple toys like building blocks can promote cognitive growth. For example, if children do not build a strong foundation under their block building, the building will topple. Thus, they learn physics concepts. If they join two semicircular pieces, they make a circle. In this way, they learn math concepts.

Selection Criteria

In early childhood programs, selecting toys and equipment for children is often the teacher's responsibility. In preparation, you will need to determine what the children should learn. You will then need to decide what materials would best meet those needs. As you can see, this is an important job. Careful planning is required.

9-1 Toys help children build many skills.
By playing together, these children
learn important social skills.

Questions you will want to ask yourself include
the following:

- Does the toy support program goals?
- Does the toy add balance to existing
  toys and equipment?
- Can the toy be used in available classroom space?
- Does the toy require a great deal of
  supervision?

- Is the toy easy to maintain?
- Is the toy durable?
- Can the toy be purchased in needed
  quantities?
- Does the toy require the involvement of
  the child?
- Is the toy appropriate for the develop-
  mental stage of the children who will
  use it?
- Will the toy be of interest to the children?
- Is the toy nonviolent?
- Is the toy nonsexist?
- Is the toy multicultural?
- Is the toy safe?

Guidelines for answering these questions
are discussed in the following sections.

Program Goals

Classroom toys and equipment should
reflect program goals. If a program goal is to
have the children develop language skills, then
language materials should be placed in the classroom. Books, pictures, cassettes, CDs, alphabet
cards, puppets, pencils, and paper can all be used
to promote language skills.

Write your program goals on paper. Then
make a list of items that promote each goal.
Review the goals and lists. Take count of items
you already have in the classroom. Then decide
in which areas more toys and equipment are
required. You may find a planning sheet helpful
for this task, 9-2.

Toy Selection Planning Sheet		
Program Goals	**Available Toys**	**Toys Needed**
To encourage sensory exploration.	water table, shovel, cups, pitchers, scoops, clay, egg beaters, feely box, harmonica, kazoo, guitar	bells, drum, texture matching games, pumps, funnels
To promote large muscle development	low climber, wagon cart, large rubber balls, planks, boxes, jungle gym	low slide, balance boards, bicycle

9-2 Committing program goals to writing can make the
selection of proper toys an easier task.

Balance

Examining program goals helps you decide what toys and equipment might be purchased. Before buying, however, review each item to decide if it will add balance to the items already available. Ask yourself the following questions: Can the item be used with other toys? Will it help children reach goals that are not being met sufficiently with current toys? Will it promote interaction with peers? Will it help balance toys for all areas of development—physical, cognitive, emotional, and social?

Space

Keep in mind the space and storage needed for any new items you are thinking about buying or building. This is especially true for large pieces of equipment. For instance, an indoor jungle gym is a useful item in many centers. However, if the space for storing it is not available, it is a poor investment. It may end up being stored in another part of the building. If the location is inconvenient, the jungle gym will not be used very often.

Supervision

Consider the number of staff available for supervision when selecting toys and equipment. You must think about how each item will affect your ability to properly watch over children. You will have to consider each item individually, balancing safety and developmental needs. Safety is a primary concern. For example, you may want to buy swings for the play yard. The state may require one adult supervisor for every ten children. You can comply with state guidelines for ratios, but you might feel that more supervision is needed for safety. You may decide, in this case, that the swings would be an unwise purchase.

The developmental stages of children also need to be considered when choosing toys and equipment. This will affect the amount of supervision required. For instance, many five-year-old children can use blunt-nosed scissors with some guidance. However, four-year-old children require much more supervision for the same task.

Maintenance

All toys and equipment require maintenance. The care required varies with the type of toy or equipment and the amount of use. For example, an aluminum jungle gym needs less upkeep than a wooden one because aluminum is weatherproof. A wooden set might require a coat of paint each year, otherwise it could rot. Such upkeep can become costly.

Durability

Children's toys need to be durable. Children drop, stand on, sit on, and lie on toys. When angry, they may even throw toys. Broken toys can pose a danger to children. A broken hard plastic toy can have sharp edges that cut. A broken wood toy may splinter. In addition to the danger posed by broken toys, children can also feel guilty if a toy breaks in their hands. To avoid these problems, it is usually best to buy toys and equipment that are well built.

Wood and cloth are two materials that are durable, 9-3. Wood toys can withstand many years of use by many children. When buying wood toys,

9-3 Wooden equipment is durable and can withstand rough play from children.

look for those made of hardwoods such as maple. The toys should also be split-resistant. The corners of the toy should be rounded.

Quantity

The quantity of toys can be as important when purchasing materials as the quality. In most classrooms, it is common to find two or more children playing with the same toys. To promote this type of cooperation, supply an ample amount of toys and materials for children. If there is a shortage of play materials, undesirable behavior can result. Therefore, be certain that any toys you wish to add to the classroom can be purchased in the needed amounts.

Variety should also be considered along with quantity. Is the item you wish to add to the classroom similar to existing items? Studies show that children who have been exposed to a wide variety of toys are more imaginative and creative. In order to provide variety, rotate toys and equipment regularly.

The chart in 9-4 lists suggested toys and equipment for a class of 15 children. These items represent a varied group of toys and equipment.

Suggested Equipment and Supplies for a Class Unit of 15 Children	
Type of Materials and Equipment	**Select**
Indoor blockbuilding	• 400 hardwood unit blocks, including such shapes as units, half units, double units, quadruple units, pillars, large and small cylinders, curves, triangles, ramps, Y switches, X switches, floorboards, roof boards
Floor play materials	• 24 cars, airplanes, boats, fire engines, wagons, tractors, trains of assorted sizes • 30 rubber, plastic, or wooden figures of farm and domestic animals; community workers: policemen, firemen, postmen; family members: mother, father, boy, girl, baby, grandparents • 1 rocking boat
Family living and dramatic play	• 8-10 rubber dolls; doll clothes; baby boy, multicultural dolls; chest for doll clothes; baby bottles • 2 doll carriages • 1 doll bed, big and sturdy enough for a child to crawl into • 1 smaller doll bed or crib • Blankets, mattresses, pillows for doll beds • Furniture for household play: wooden stove, cupboard for dishes, sink, small table and chairs • Kitchenware: plastic dishes, tea set, small cooking utensils, silverware • Housekeeping equipment: broom, mop, dustpan, brush, iron, ironing board, clothesline, clothespins • Full-length mirror • Dress-up clothes: men's and women's shoes, pocketbooks, jewelry, hats, belts • Supplies for other dramatic play: office equipment, telephones, cash registers, firemen's hats, badges, play money, stethoscope, doctors' bags and white coats, nurses' hats
Table and perceptual activities	• Bingo and lotto games • 12 wooden inlay puzzles of varying degrees of difficulty • 1 puzzle rack • Pegs and peg boards • Matching games • Sets of small blocks (cubes, parquetry, interlocking, snap-in, number) • Large table dominoes: picture sets, number sets

9-4 The toys and equipment in this list comprise a well-stocked classroom. You may have ideas for further additions.   (Continued)

Chapter 9 Selecting Toys, Equipment, and Educational Materials 135

Suggested Equipment and Supplies for a Class Unit of 15 Children	
Table and perceptual activities (Continued)	• Nested blocks • Color cone • Pounding peg board • Cuisenaire rods, counting frames; abacus • Hammer and nail sets with fiber insulation boards • Cards: geometric shapes
Art activities	• 2 easels • Drying rack for art materials • 24 easel paint brushes with ½ in. and ¾ in. handles • 75-100 quarts liquid tempera paint of various colors* • 8000 sheets white manila paper, 4000 sheets newsprint 24 in. by 36 in. • Paste and paste brushes • 20 packages finger paint paper or glazed shelf paper • 24 packages construction paper of various colors* • 4 clay boards, 2 plastic covered pails for storing clay, and clay • 100 lb. flour and 40 lb. salt for dough • 18 blunt scissors, including some left-handed and training • 5 aprons or smocks • Miscellaneous supplies: orange juice cans, baby food jars, drying rack, florist wire, pipe cleaners, armature wire, colored toothpicks, macaroni pieces, transparent colored paper • 5 dozen crayons* • Rolling pins • Transparent tape • Stapler and staples
Music	• Phonograph and records • Autoharp® • Xylophone • Scarves, streamers • Rhythm instruments: kazoos, shakers, maracas, sticks • Drums, triangles, tambourines, cymbals, tom-toms • Sleighbells for hands and feet • Balls, hoops
Woodworking	• 1 sturdy, low workbench with 2 vises • Tools: four 7 oz. claw hammers, two 12" crosscut saws, 1 hand drill, 1 rasp, 1 file, 2 screwdrivers, assorted nails with large heads, screws, 2 large C clamps • Soft wood scraps, doweling • Sandpaper • Miscellaneous: buttons, washers, corks, wire, nuts, hooks and eyes, spools, bottle caps
Furniture	• 15 chairs, 8 in. to 12 in. in height • 3 tables, 18 in. to 22 in. in height, for snacks, meals, and tablework activities • 2 room dividers • 15 mats or throw rugs for resting in half-day programs • 15 lockers for hanging coats, hats, boots, extra change of clothes
Science and special projects	• Bar and horseshoe magnets • Children's cookbook • Magnifying glass • Large indoor and outdoor thermometers • Tubes • Seeds
	*Include colors and hues of art materials and supplies to reflect skin tones.

9-4 Continued.

(Continued)

Suggested Equipment and Supplies for a Class Unit of 15 Children	
Science and special projects (Continued)	• Animals: hamsters, mice, rabbits, fish, ducks, and gerbils (where permitted by law) • Magnets • Picture collection: machines, animals, plants, and geography • Books with science concepts • Tape measure, yardstick, rulers • Scales • Measuring cups and spoons • Dry cell batteries, flashlight bulbs, electric wire • Pulleys and gears • Hand mirrors • Hot plate and electric frying pan • Aquarium and terrarium • Cages for pets • 1 typewriter for the children to use
Water play (indoor and outdoor)	• Small pitchers, watering cans, measuring cups, bowls of various sizes, plastic bottles, medicine droppers • Funnels, strainers, egg beaters, ladles, straws, lengths of hose, brushes • Soap and soap flakes • Sponges
Outdoor equipment	• Sandbox, cans, buckets, spades, spoons, small dishes, colander • Jungle gym • Ladder box • Horizontal ladder • Sand box • 5 tricycles • 3 four-wheeled cars or "horses" manipulated by a child's feet • 2 sturdy doll carriages • 2 sturdy wooden packing cases (42 in. by 30 in. by 30 in.) • 2 sturdy wooden packing cases (35 in. by 23 in. by 16. in.) • 24 hollow wooden blocks (5½ in. by 11 in. by 11 in.) • 12 hollow wooden blocks (5½ in. by 11 in. by 22 in.) • 12 low sawhorses • 8 small wooden kegs • Wooden ladders • Walking boards (balance beam) and flexible jumping boards • Lengths of sturdy rope and garden hose • Automobile and airplane tires and rubber inner tubes • Rubber balls of different sizes; bean bags
Language arts	• 50 picture storybooks appropriate to the age, culture, and special interests of the children; books should include a range of poetry and prose, humor, fiction, and non-fiction • Alphabet books
Audiovisual aids	• Chalkboard, erasers, chart paper • Lotto and picture games • Typewriter, primary • Tape recorder • Slide projector • Video cassette recorder (VCR) • Computer • Video camera • Television • Felt board and felt figures

9-4 Continued.

Adapted from Project Headstart, Equipment and Supplies—
Guidelines for Administrators and Teachers in Child Development Centers.

Child Involvement

Choose toys that will actively involve children. Toys should move children to explore, manipulate, invent, and problem solve. In this way, children learn for themselves. They learn to use their imaginations.

Spectator toys such as battery-powered cars and talking dolls require little action on the child's part. Avoid purchasing these types of toys. Besides being costly, their appeal with children is quite often brief. Children will leave these toys for others that involve more imagination.

Choose simple toys, 9-5. Too much detail limits imagination. Open-ended materials free children to use their minds and express their creativity.

Blocks, play dough, paint, sand, and construction sets are open-ended toys. Using these items, children build structures, make designs, and play games. Children find endless ways to use such toys.

Use the checklist in 9-6 to define what skills can be learned from a specific toy. This task will help you see in what ways a toy will affect children. This knowledge can then be used when deciding on a purchase.

Developmentally Appropriate Toys

Children's physical age and developmental age are often quite different. **Physical age** is an

Checklist for Skills Learned from Toys		
Will the children learn or improve:	**Yes**	**No**
auditory discrimination?		
balance?		
color concepts?		
counting?		
eye-hand coordination?		
hearing-doing skills?		
language concepts?		
large muscle development?		
matching?		
number concepts?		
patterning?		
seeing-doing skills?		
self-esteem?		
sensory discrimination?		
sequencing?		
social skills?		
small muscle development?		
space perception?		
strength?		
throwing-catching skills?		
visual discrimination?		

9-6 What other skills might you add to this list?

9-5 These toys can be the source for a variety of unstructured play. What is done with them is limited only by a child's imagination.

age determined by a birth date. It is also known as **chronological age**. **Developmental age** refers to a child's skill and growth level compared to what is thought of as normal for that physical age group. For example, Kathy may be four years old physically, but only functions as an eighteen-month-old child. A child who functions as a four-year-old would be able to string beads. However, Kathy would only be able to do those tasks and activities that an eighteen-month-old child can do. She lacks the eye-hand coordination needed to string beads. As you choose toys, remember the difference between physical and developmental age, 9-7.

9-7 Toys that are appropriate for children's developmental ages are challenging for those children.

Toys that suit children's developmental ages help them build self-esteem. For instance, Leon will feel powerful as he learns to ride a scooter, or as he pushes a wagon up a hill. As he masters this skill, he gains a sense of control and builds an "I can do it" feeling.

Toys that do not match the child's development can cause frustration. This does little for a child's self-esteem. Lack of success with a toy can have a negative effect on a child. For instance, it is not likely that a two-year-old child would be able to put together an 18-piece puzzle. The child may make a number of attempts at the puzzle. Soon the child will become frustrated and move on to a toy that is more rewarding.

Chart 9-8 lists a number of toys and equipment pieces that are appropriate for various age groups. The ages on the chart refer to developmental ages.

Violence and Toys

Children should not be taught to handle conflict with aggression or violence. Instead, they need to find useful ways to vent their feelings. One way to prevent aggressive behavior is to avoid giving children monster toys, toy guns, and war games. Children learn very little from these toys. The play that revolves around such toys is most often aggressive and destructive. For instance, when a child plays with a toy gun, he or she does little more than pull the trigger and play in a threatening way. Research shows that violent behavior increases when children play with action toys and replicas of weapons. Children who played with toy guns were more likely to destroy other children's work.

Many parents and teachers are opposed to the presence of these toys in the classroom. Therefore, it is best to simply avoid buying these toys.

Nonsexist Toys and Materials

Nonsexist toys and materials provide children with the opportunity to explore nontraditional roles. Children are not locked into play that is common of their sex. For instance, boys can be nurses, preschool teachers, and stay-at-home fathers. Girls can be airplane pilots, truck drivers, and plumbers. This type of play will also help children form early ideas about careers.

As a teacher, it is important to set up an environment that is free of gender bias. Your attitude about toys will affect what children learn about sex roles. Make a conscious effort to use or suggest a variety of toys to all children. At the same time, however, be matter-of-fact. For instance, you might suggest to Omar that he try playing in the kitchen. You can explain to him that there are many fun things to do in the kitchen.

Developmentally Appropriate Toys and Equipment (Ages 6 months–5 years)							
Age Group	**Block and Dramatic Play**	**Large Muscle Equipment**	**Housekeeping**	**Sensory and Science**	**Creative Art and Books**	**Classroom Furnishings**	**Miscellaneous**
Six months–one year	grasping toys foam blocks soft animals bucket and blocks	beach balls push/pull toys stroller	soft dolls stuffed animals puppets acrylic plastic mirrors	tub toys sensory mat	wall hangings mobiles	infant seat crib changing counter adult rocking chair cubbie high chair	soft balls cradle gym standard crib and mattress music boxes mirrors rattles
One-year-old	Add: large trucks interlocking blocks	Add: toddler stairs driving bench large foam blocks toddler barrel tire swing	Add: doll bed doll blankets doll mattress unbreakable doll wooden telephone	Add: sponges buckets funnels pitchers measuring cups	Add: large crayons hard books cloth books tapes tape player play dough	Add: clothing lockers storage shelves book display cots	Add: stacking and nesting toys pull toys 3 to 5 piece puzzles pop beads stacking cones pegboards
Two-year-old	Add: unit blocks wooden figures	Add: doll wagon hollow blocks rocking boat small jungle gym simple climber and slide tricycle	Add: simple doll clothes doll carriage child-sized sink, stove, pots, pans, aprons	Add: sand table water table	Add: picture books blunt scissors paste finger paints	Add: bookcase block cart play table and chairs	Add: simple puzzles large wooden threading beads small cots rest mat rest mat cover sheet
Three-year-old	Add: dollhouse small dolls furniture	Add: walking board large wooden nesting boxes scooter wheelbarrow	Add: ironing board iron rocking chair broom, dustpan	Add: balance scales magnets ant farm prisms	Add: easels paints brushes glue scissors	Add: work and library tables and chairs	Add: wooden puzzles portable screens (room dividers) cots plants
Four-year-old	Add: puppets puppet theater more unit blocks	Add: planks swings slide shovel, pail, and rake triangle set coaster wagon large climber and slide	Add: chest of drawers washbasin clothesline and pins basket aprons, ties, etc. child-sized bed/cradle, carriage, wardrobe	Add: thermometer incubator	Add: clay modeling wax	Add: storage cart chalk/peg and bulletin boards

Add: woodworking bench | Add: aquarium pets |
| **Five-year-old** | Add: derrick | Add: balls roller skates | Add: tepee balance scale microphone | Add: microscopes tape measures motors | Add: sewing machine camera video camera | tool cabinet tools | Add: giant dominoes construction sets |

9-8 Plan toy selection well. In this case, the toys from one age group blend into the next age group.

Multicultural Toys and Materials

Multicultural toys and materials are those that represent a variety of racial and ethnic groups. When choosing hand puppets, puzzles, and dolls, include a wide range of racial and ethnic backgrounds. Pictures and books should also be chosen with this in mind, 9-9.

The early childhood environment needs to support a child's ethnic group and cultural heritage. This helps children to develop a sense of identity. Thus, it is important to choose toys and materials that reflect the ethnic diversity of the children in your classroom. By choosing multicultural toys, you are communicating respect for all cultures. A checklist for evaluating the multicultural materials in a classroom is given in Figure 9-10.

It is important that you use a variety of materials representing different cultural groups. When putting on a puppet show, use puppets representing many races and ethnic groups. Provide and read storybooks that include a wide variety of cultural groups.

Multicultural Checklist		
Does your classroom provide the following multicultural materials?	**Yes**	**No**
• A variety of books containing accurate information about many different cultures.		
• Puppets and dolls representing different ethnic and racial backgrounds.		
• Puzzles and small manipulatives representing people from around the world.		
• Colors of art materials and supplies reflecting a variety of skin tones.		
• Posters and pictures representing a diversity of people.		
• Instruments and music representing the children's cultural backgrounds.		
• Dress-up clothing and cooking utensils for the dramatic play area representing different cultures.		

9-10 Use this checklist to choose multicultural toys that reflect the diversity of the children.

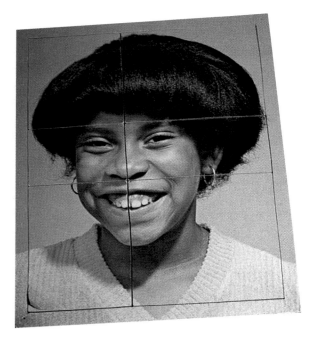

9-9 Include multicultural toys and materials in all areas of the classroom.

Selecting Safe Toys

To promote safety, choose toys carefully. Serious injuries can be the result of poor judgment when purchasing toys. The safest toys are not those that appeal most to adults. Rather, the safest toys are those that meet the standards outlined in this chapter. Perhaps the most important of these standards in terms of safety is that toys be developmentally appropriate. Small stringing beads can be a useful toy for many four-year-old children. In the hands of a two-year-old, however, they can be dangerous.

Many hazards cannot be seen at a glance or with normal use. Because of this, study each item thoroughly before buying. Keep in mind that young children often take toys apart. Small pieces of large toys can be dangerous.

To be certain that a toy is safe for the children in your care, ask these questions before buying:

- Can the toy be swallowed?
- Are there small parts that could be placed in ears or mouth?
- Is the toy easy to clean?
- Are there sharp points or edges on the toy?

To help consumers choose safe toys for children under age three, the U.S. Consumer Product Safety Commission has set part-size standards. Small parts on toys for this age group must be at least 1¼ inches in diameter or 2¼ inches long, 9-11. Any parts smaller than these sizes are potential choking hazards. Some toy stores assist customers in choosing safe toys for young children. They provide plastic forms that customers can use for measuring small parts on toys.

Remember that a toy can be safe in the hands of one child but a danger in the hands of another. To protect children, avoid buying the following:

- Hard plastic toys that break easily. Once broken, the sharp edges are a safety hazard.
- Metal toys that have sharp edges.
- Pull toys that have small, ball-like objects inside them. If these toys are broken, the objects can fall out. Placed

in the mouth, they can cause choking or may be swallowed.

- Toy vehicles with small parts. Once removed, these parts can be put in the mouth. As a result, a child may choke on or swallow them.
- Balloons. Children often place them in their mouths to suck or chew. If swallowed, they can cause choking.
- Stuffed animals or dolls with button eyes or sharp wires. The eyes can be pulled off and placed in the mouth. Choking and damage to the throat can result. Eyes are small enough to lodge in a child's windpipe, ears, or nostrils. Check ears, paws, and tails of all stuffed animals for sharp wires that are used to stiffen them.
- Electrical toys designed for children's use. Burns, fires, or electrocution are some hazards. Poor wiring can cause fires and electrocution. High heat produced by electrical toys can cause fires and burns.

In addition to the guidelines listed above, there are other hazards related to specific items. On a store shelf, a doll may appear safe. This may not be the case if a child changes its hairstyle, removes a leg or arm, changes its clothes, or holds it near a flame. Many times straight pins or small safety pins are used to attach clothing or to hold hair in place. Once removed, these pins can pose danger to a child. Sharp wires may be used to hold the doll's arms and legs together. These can also be hazardous. Danger also exists if the doll is made with flammable materials.

Before buying any doll, always read the label on the toy. Check that only nonflammable materials are used. Also make sure pins are not used to fasten hair. And finally, make sure the arms and legs are securely attached.

Colorful, plastic climbers are popular pieces of equipment in child care centers. However, many climbers are designed for only one or two children. They are unsafe when many children try to use them at the same time. According to the U.S. Consumer Product Safety Commission, the leading cause for significant injuries in child care settings is falls from climbers. The commission warns that plastic climbing equipment should not

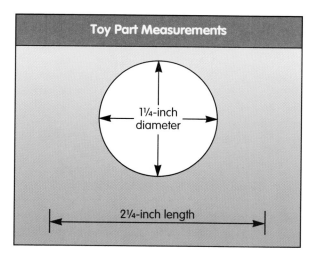

9-11 The safest toys for children under age three have small parts that meet these size standards.

be used indoors even if the floor has been carpeted. Carpeting does not provide adequate protection if a child falls. As a result, serious head injuries or even death can result.

Sources of Safety Information

There are several sources of safety information for toys. Consult these as you go through the list of toys and equipment you may wish to purchase.

Consumer Reports often contains results of tests they have conducted on toys and play equipment. Always consult the latest issue that contains the information you need. Older issues may have outdated information.

The Toy Manufacturers of America, the National Safety Council, and child protection laws have all set standards for choosing toys. These standards include the following guidelines:

- Fabric products such as puppets and doll clothes should have labels that state they are either *flame retardant* or *flame resistant.*
- Electrical equipment including tape recorders, CD players, and record players should have a seal from a safety testing organization, such as Underwriters Laboratories (UL).
- Stuffed toys should have labels stating they are *machine washable* or *surface washable.*
- All painted toys should be labeled as *nontoxic.*

Selecting Play Yard Equipment

It is important to have a wide variety of equipment for children to use in the play yard. Children need equipment on which they can push, pull, balance, and slide, 9-12. For instance, studies show that outdoor equipment that can be used only for climbing is not used very often. Children climb on this equipment for a short period of time, then become bored. At that point, they move on to something else.

When shopping for play yard equipment, keep in mind the children's height as compared to the piece of equipment. Equipment should not be more than two times their height. This can, however, be hard to apply with a mixed-age

9-12 Equipment such as this allows children to do a variety of activities.

group. A jungle gym that is a good size for most four-year-olds will be a hazard to many two-year-olds. You may need to purchase separate equipment designed for two size groups.

Many play yard mishaps occur on slides. To prevent such injuries, buy slides that are low, wide, and have a platform surrounded by guard rails. Several children can use this type of slide at one time. High, narrow slides, on the other hand, can be dangerous for many children. Some children do not realize how high the slide is until they reach the top. Then they may decide to crawl back down. The danger of falling exists. If other children are also on the ladder, this increases the chance for a mishap.

High slides can also be dangerous for confident children. Bored with just sliding down, children may decide to explore other ways of using the slide. They may even be bold enough to try sliding down while standing.

All ladders should be slanted. Rungs should be close together. This will help prevent children from slipping. Ladders made of steel are easier to maintain. Wooden ladders, after being weathered, may splinter. Steel ladders can get cold in winter climates. However, they do not require sanding and painting every few years.

Swings are not found often on playgrounds designed for young children. This is often because swings require a great deal of supervision. Without thinking, some children will walk in front or back of swings. They may get bumped, bruised, or even knocked over. Also, more confident children will try swinging too high.

Equipment Safety

Did you know that at age five, children are most likely to be hurt on playground equipment? Jungle gyms, merry-go-rounds, and swings cause most of these injuries. Therefore, be careful when buying outdoor equipment. Avoid buying on impulse. Supervise play, and repair broken equipment.

The most frequent play yard injuries are from falls off climbing equipment and slides. In fact, almost 70 percent of play yard accidents result from children falling from equipment. Children are also injured when they walk in front of or behind a moving swing. Injuries are also sustained from protruding bolts, rough edges, and from fingers and toes getting caught in equipment. Chart 9-13 contains a list to use for evaluating outdoor equipment.

The U.S. Consumer Safety Commission reports the following play yard equipment dangers:

- Pinch-crush parts on seesaws and gliders that are not covered. If this equipment is already on the play yard, check it for this hazard and remove the equipment.
- Rings between five and ten inches in diameter that can trap a child's head. Remove and discard rings of this size.
- Open end S-rings on swing sets that can catch clothing or skin. If this hardware is on swing sets in the play yard, pinch the rings shut with a pair of pliers.
- Wooden swing seats that can hit children who walk in the path of them. Replace any wooden swing seats with seats made of plastic or canvas.

Evaluating Outdoor Equipment	Yes	No
1. Is the construction durable?		
2. Is it an appropriate height?		
3. Does it complement existing equipment in function?		
4. Are the exercise rings less than 5 inches or more than 10 inches in diameter?		
5. Is it free of open "S" rings?		
6. Are the seats on swings made of plastic or canvas?		
7. Is it free of exposed nuts and bolts?		
8. Is it free of sharp edges?		
9. Can the equipment be properly anchored?		
10. Is the equipment easy to maintain?		

9-13 Evaluation of play equipment aids the teacher in locating problem areas and possible hazards.

- Inadequate spacing. To prevent injuries, place play equipment at least six feet away from other equipment, buildings, walkways, fences, or other play areas. Space for sandboxes, wheeled toy paths, fences, and sidewalks needs to be planned so they are not too close to play equipment.
- Exposed screws and bolts on outdoor equipment that can scratch or cut children. Most equipment comes with plastic protective caps. However, with use they can break and fall off. Check all the equipment from time to time. If caps are missing, apply tape to all the bolts and screws.
- Hard surfaces that can cause injuries. Play equipment should never be installed over blacktop, brick, or cement. The space under and around all

playground equipment must be covered with an impact-absorbing material. Examples of such materials include resilient tiles, wood mulch, fine sand, and fine gravel.

■ Sharp edges that can cause cuts and scratches. Using your hands, carefully wipe over all equipment edges. Cover all sharp edges with tape. After the tape has been applied, check often to see if the tape is still in good condition.

■ Play yard equipment that is not anchored properly. Equipment needs to be stable to avoid overturning, tipping, sliding, or moving in any way. The equipment needs to be anchored in concrete below ground level before it is used. The anchoring process needs to comply with the manufacturer's specifications.

■ Ladders and stairways on equipment that could cause a child's head to be entrapped. To prevent this, risers on ladders and stairs should be closed if the distance between steps is greater than 3.5 inches or less than 9 inches. There is a risk of strangulation even when openings are low enough for a child's feet to reach the ground. When panicked or scared, a young child may lack the cognitive ability and motor skills to free his or her head.

Reporting Unsafe Products

If you have a safety problem with a toy or piece of equipment, report the item. This will help keep other children safe from the same danger.

To report an unsafe toy or piece of equipment, write or call the United States Consumer Product Safety Commission (CPSC), Washington, DC, 20207. The CPSC Hotline number is 800-638-2772. This organization works to guard against items that can be harmful to children.

Legislation has been passed to protect young children. The Child Protection Act was passed in 1966. This law requires stickers or tags be placed on items that present possible danger. It permits seizure of items that do not conform to the standards set forth in this law. The law also allows *injunctions* to be placed on manufacturers who break this law. This means the manufacturer must refrain from making the item until a decision is reached. Criminal charges can be brought against manufacturers who do not comply with these standards.

Several years after the Child Protection Act was passed, the Child Protection and Toy Safety Act became law. This act expanded the federal government's authority to include all mechanical, electrical, and thermal items designed for children's use.

Sources for Toys and Equipment

Before you begin selecting new toys and equipment, take an inventory of materials that are on hand. After this is done, compare the inventory with program goals. For example, you may note that there are too few manipulative toys. These then should be at the top of the list for purchase. See 9-14.

9-14 The exhibit area at an early childhood conference is a good source for toys and equipment.

Using your list, browse through catalogs to find items you need. Take time to look through all the catalogs at the center. Catalog prices can vary a great deal. Consider all costs before ordering. For instance, does the shipping cost for an item make the purchase price too high? Some companies will not charge a shipping fee if the order is large.

Equipment can also be bought through a co-op. A **co-op** (cooperative) is a group of people or organizations who join together for the mutual benefit of more buying power. Co-ops are sometimes formed by directors of several small centers. One of the goals of the co-op is to purchase toys and equipment at the lowest cost. Companies will often give a discount on large orders. The directors share the savings with all those who are making purchases.

If time is available, you may wish to visit flea markets, garage sales, and discount stores. Materials can often be purchased at reduced prices.

Toys can also be designed and built at the center. Senior citizens, Girl Scout and Boy Scout troops, and others may volunteer to help. Many of these people are skilled in making puppets, doll clothes, dramatic play clothes, and wooden toys.

Buying Consumable Supplies

Clay, paper, paint, paste, glue, and other art materials are called **consumable supplies**. In most cases, once a consumable supply is used, it cannot be used again. In order to save money, some centers order these materials only once or twice a year. There are many ways to purchase these supplies.

If the order is large, the center may ask vendors to make bids on the sale. *Vendors* are the people who sell the supplies. Their bid is the price at which they will sell the items.

The center might also contact a vendor when placing a large order and ask for a 10 percent discount, plus free shipping. Many directors are surprised to learn that this can be done. This is very useful for stretching the center budget.

Another approach is to make a list of the supplies needed. Mark those items that could be donated, 9-15. Note who is in charge of securing what items. For example, the head teacher may be in charge of getting newsprint. Another teacher would be in charge of getting wallpaper. In some centers, the director is solely responsible for securing all donations.

Consumable Supplies					
Quantity	Item	Purchase	Solicit Donation	Source	Person Responsible
1 roll	Newsprint		X	Dunn County News	Anna
10 cans	Red tempera paint	X		ABC School Supply	Jodi
10 cans	Yellow tempera paint	X		ABC School Supply	Jodi
5 rolls	Wallpaper		X	Menomonie Paint Store	Anna
2 buckets	Sawdust		X	Peterson Lumber Co.	Anna
4 gallons	Dried corn		X	Hardy's Elevator	Jodi
4 yards	Fabric scraps		X	Northwest Fabrics	Anna
2 gallons	Paste	X		ABC School Supply	Jodi
1 box	Styrofoam® packing pieces		X	James Jewelers	Anna
24 boxes	Crayons	X		ABC School Supply	Jodi

9-15 Many groups are often eager to donate materials to worthy programs such as child care centers.

Summary

Selecting toys and equipment is an important task. There are several guidelines that should be followed before purchases are made. Key factors to be considered are program goals, balance, space, supervision, maintenance, durability, quantity, child involvement and developmental age. Toys should also be nonviolent, nonsexist, multicultural, and safe.

Safety is a key consideration when buying toys and play yard equipment. Guidelines have been developed that can help you choose safe products for the children in your care. If products prove to be defective or unsafe, report them to the U.S. Consumer Product Safety Commission.

Once guidelines are reviewed, purchases can be made. The teacher must know where and how to make these purchases. In this way, the teacher will be able to use the center budget wisely.

Review and Reflect

1. True or false. Toys can promote the development of specific skills.

2. List six questions to ask when selecting toys for young children.

3. Classroom toys and equipment should reflect the _____ that the center has developed.

4. How does available space affect toy and equipment selection?

5. True or false. Maintenance is not an important factor in choosing equipment.

6. Toys must be durable because _____.
   A. children will sit on, stand on, and drop them
   B. broken toys can be dangerous
   C. children may feel guilty if they break a toy
   D. All of the above.

7. Why is the quantity of toys an important consideration in toy selection?

8. _____ toys require little action on the part of children.

9. Explain the difference between physical and developmental age.

10. Why is it important to choose toys that are appropriate for a child's developmental age?

11. Play that revolves around violent toys is often _____.
    A. constructive
    B. aggressive and destructive
    C. a good learning experience
    D. None of the above.

12. What are multicultural toys?

13. True or false. The safest toys are those that appeal to adults.

14. List three safety guidelines to follow when purchasing toys.

15. Name the dangers of each of the following:
    A. Rings.
    B. Wooden swing seats.
    C. Screws and bolts.

16. Name three impact-absorbing materials that would be appropriate to use under outdoor play equipment.

17. What is a consumable supply?

Apply and Explore

1. In small groups, make a basic list of equipment for a classroom.

2. Discuss favorite childhood toys and the value of each.

3. Ask an early childhood program director to discuss toy and equipment maintenance.

4. Using equipment catalogs, make a list of toys and equipment that could be made with a minimum of time and money.

5. Cut pictures of toys from equipment catalogs that would be safe and appropriate for most two-year-old children.

6. Visit a child care center. Make a list of toys and equipment available to the children. Decide which items are open-ended. Make a list of other toys that may be added, including multicultural toys.

7. Compare the prices of slides, jungle gyms, and wagons from three catalogs. Discuss the reasons for the cost differences.

Chapter 10

Promoting Children's Safety

After studying this chapter, you will be able to

- list objectives for maintaining a safe environment for children.
- describe guidelines for promoting children's safety.
- name the types of fires and the fire extinguishers used to fight them.
- outline the procedures for treating poisonings.
- recognize the signs of child abuse.
- teach children how to resist child abuse.
- explain types of liability as a child care provider.

Terms to Know

class A fire	emotional abuse
class B fire	sexual abuse
class C fire	incest
emetic	molestation
nonaccidental physical injury	statute
	privacy law
neglect	

"Please give me that broken toy," Tina Goldstein said to the child. The teacher immediately saw the danger of the unsafe toy. At the same time, Gloria Hernandez, the center director, was checking the art supplies. In the kitchen, the cook was filling out the monthly safety and sanitation checklist. All these staff members were showing their concern for the children's safety by checking the safety of their surroundings.

Dangers can be found everywhere in a child care center, 10-1. Electrical outlets, cleaning

10-1 Young children are active and adventurous. They can get themselves into dangerous situations in seconds. Supervision is necessary at all times.

supplies, woodworking tools, outdoor climbing equipment, and cooking tools can all cause injuries. Staff members must closely watch for and remove these dangers. Failure to do so may result in accidents. Most of these accidents can be avoided.

Accidents are more likely to occur when the children's routine is disrupted. Accidents also occur more frequently when staff are absent, busy, or tired.

Children can also be put in danger through abuse. Teachers must be aware of the signs of physical and emotional abuse. By law, teachers must protect their pupils from abuse.

As an early childhood teacher, you will need to be alert to any dangers that threaten the safety of your pupils. In addition, your center must have safety rules and procedures. The staff must also be aware of their legal responsibilities for protection of children in their care.

Safety Objectives

The staff is responsible for providing a safe environment for children. The following are basic objectives toward this goal:

- Supervise the children at all times.
- Maintain the minimum staff/child ratios as required in your state.
- Develop safety rules.
- Provide a safe environment.
- Practice fire safety.
- Know emergency procedures for accidental poisoning.
- Develop plans for weather emergencies.
- Recognize signs of child abuse and report any suspected cases.
- Teach children how to protect themselves from sexual assault.

The following sections will summarize procedures for meeting each of these objectives.

Supervise the Children at All Times

"It happened so fast—I just left them for a moment or two," said the child care teacher. This teacher did not understand that children cannot be left alone, not even for a moment. A teacher who is responsible for a group of children should supervise constantly. Young children do not always understand the concept of danger. As a result, child care teachers must protect the children until they can protect themselves.

Young children are unpredictable. They are quick, fearless, and not able to care for themselves. As a result, they lack sound judgment. They may bite, throw, push, or shove. All of these actions are hazards to others as well as to themselves. Young children may not recognize that these behaviors or actions can cause injuries.

To properly supervise a group of children, keep your back to the classroom wall. Focus on the interior of the classroom. The entire room should be visible. Move closer to an area if you observe children who are confused over classroom rules or who need assistance. Likewise, constantly observe children who are not involved in an activity. Bored children can create potential safety problems.

Bumps and bruises can occur in overcrowded classrooms. Make sure there is enough space for furniture and equipment. Observe children as they play. Is there enough space for them to move from area to area without bumping into furniture or other children? If sufficient space does not exist, remove some of the furniture or rearrange the classroom.

Maintain Minimum Staff/Child Ratios

Staff/child ratios are important to safety. Usually, younger children are supervised in small groups. Therefore, younger children require more staff. Chart 10-2 outlines the staff/child ratio and maximum group size requirements of a midwestern state.

At least the minimum number of staff members set by your state's licensing rules must be present at all times. Failure to comply may result in the center's license being revoked or a citation indicating the center was not in compliance. Remember, too, if a child is injured, and staff/child ratios are not being met, center staff may be held liable.

Develop Safety Rules

Safety rules protect the children in the classroom. Make rules clear, simple, and easy to understand, 10-3.

	Maximum Number of Children in a Group	Minimum Number of Staff to Children
Infant to one year	8	1 to 4 children
One to 2 years	8	1 to 4 children
Two to 3 years	16	1 to 8 children
Three to 4 years	20	1 to 10 children
Four to 5 years	24	1 to 12 children
Five and over	28	1 to 14 children

10-2 These are the staff/child ratio requirements at a Midwestern state. The number of children in a group and ratios vary among states. Obtain your state's licensing regulations for local requirements.

10-3 Use bulletin boards to teach children about safety.

Some typical rules that will protect children include:

- Walk indoors. Do not run.
- Cover your mouth when you cough or sneeze.
- Use blocks for building, not for hitting.
- Wipe up spills right away.
- Wash your hands before eating and after toileting.
- Tell the teacher when equipment breaks.

Remind children about rules. Otherwise, they may ignore or forget them. For example, Eino may walk directly to the lunch table, forgetting to wash his hands. When this happens, say, "Eino, we wash our hands before eating." Usually, this reminder will redirect a child. If Eino still fails to comply, you may have to say, "Eino, you need to wash your hands." Do not allow Eino to eat lunch until his hands are washed.

Teach children to cover their mouths when coughing or sneezing. Always keep at least one box of tissues in the classroom. Place the tissues in a spot that the children can see and reach. When children forget to cover their mouths, remind them. Likewise, it is important to praise children who remember. Say, "Gerald, thank you for covering your mouth when you sneezed."

Provide a Safe Environment

Closely observing children and setting safety rules for them to obey helps create a safe center. This is only part of the process. You must also keep watch for hazardous situations. Toys, equipment, electrical appliances, hot water, and cleaning supplies can pose danger to children. Center vehicles and the building itself can also be hazardous to children.

Toys and Equipment

Equipment selection is important to the safety of young children. Refer to Chapter 9, *Selecting Toys, Equipment, and Educational Materials* for information about choosing safe materials for children.

There are a few general rules to remember. Beware of stuffed toys that may have button or glass eyes. These can be pulled off easily by some children. Once removed, children may place the small objects in their mouths and swallow them. This could cause choking. Stuffed toys can also be unsafe for children with allergies to certain fabrics or fillers.

Use of plastic rattles must be carefully observed. Many contain small pellets. Others are made from hard, brittle plastic. These rattles can break easily. If the rattles break, children may place the pellets or broken plastic pieces in their mouths. Choking can result.

Remember, a toy can be safe for one child, but dangerous for another. Accidents can occur when children use toys that are too advanced for them. For instance, five-year-old children love to play with large marbles. These same marbles can be dangerous for infants, one-year-olds, and even most two-year-old children. Younger children may place the marbles in their mouths, swallow them, and choke.

Check toys frequently for safety. To illustrate, check the seams of cloth toys for tearing and weak threads. Tug at the different parts of the toy to test its strength. If the toy lacks durability, remove it from the classroom. Depending upon the condition and value, it can either be repaired or discarded.

Plastic and wooden toys should be examined for sharp or splintered edges. Observe to see if any small pieces have broken off or splintered. If a plastic or wooden toy needs minor repairs, immediately remove it from the classroom.

Playground Equipment

If not used properly, even the safest playground equipment can cause accidents. Supervision by staff and playground rules are extremely important in preventing accidents. Teach children how to play safely. If developmentally appropriate, involve them in making playground rules. Consistently enforce rules. Remember to praise children when they practice playground safety.

Playground equipment needs to be checked often for dangers: slivers, sharp edges, unstable equipment, rusted parts, frayed or stressed ropes, etc. See 10-4. Some centers use safety checklists to promote the children's safety.

Contact the child welfare or social services department to learn your state's safety codes for equipment. Using the code, prepare a safety checklist. Make a habit of filling out the checklist weekly. Report any problems to the center director.

Most playground injuries are due to falls. To protect the children, playground surfaces should be soft. To illustrate, a child is less likely to be hurt falling on grass than on blacktop. To prevent injuries from falls, place sand, bark, grass, or a cushioned material under climbing devices, swings, and tree houses. The playground does

10-4 To protect children's safety, an impact-absorbing surface was installed under this playground equipment.

need to include a hard surface for wheeled toys. However, most of the playground can have a softer surface.

Center Vehicles

Motor vehicle accidents pose the greatest threats to children's lives. Vans, buses, and other vehicles owned by the center should have safety door locks and seat belts. For younger children, car seats that meet standards for the appropriate age should be installed. Train all staff and parent volunteers on the proper use of safety seats. While riding in any center vehicles, children should be fastened in a properly adjusted seat belt or safety seat. Do not allow children to put their arms or heads out of the vehicle's windows. When a number of children are riding in a vehicle, extra adult supervision may be required.

Center vehicles should be equipped for emergency situations. A first aid kit for treating minor injuries should be located in each vehicle. Moreover, a fire extinguisher and tools for changing tires should also be present in each vehicle.

Building Safety

Many accidents that occur in centers involve the building and building fixtures. Windows, floors, and stairs all may cause injuries.

Keep windows closed at all times, unless gates or sturdy screens are in place. Keep floors dry. If wax is used, use a nonslip type. Cover stairways with carpet or rubber treads. Make sure stairways are well-lighted and free of clutter. Install railings at the children's level on both sides of the stairs.

Sliding patio doors, doors with glass panels, and storm doors can all be dangerous. The Bureau of Product Safety estimates that over a quarter of a million people are injured by glass each year. To protect the children, use only safety glass. Decals applied to sliding glass doors at eye level warn children of glass they might not otherwise see.

Cover all unused electrical outlets in the building. Avoid using extension cords, particularly if they are placed under carpets or rugs. If the cord becomes worn, a fire may occur.

Practice Fire Safety

To promote fire safety, check the center regularly for fire hazards. The best protection against fires is to prevent them from happening. For instance, store matches where children cannot reach them. Then they cannot accidentally start fires. As a teacher, you need to find and correct fire hazards. A fire safety checklist is shown in 10-5. Study this list so you will be able to spot hazards and take action quickly.

Check smoke alarms at least once each month to make sure they are working. If smoke detectors are battery powered, change batteries when indicated.

Fire Safety Checklist		
	Yes	No
1. Exit passageways and exits are free from furniture and equipment.		
2. Locks on toilet doors can be opened from the outside, and can be opened easily by center staff.		
3. Protective covers are on all electrical outlets.		
4. Permanent wiring is used instead of lengthy extension cords.		
5. One wall outlet contains no more than two electrical appliances.		
6. A fire evacuation plan is posted.		
7. Fire drills are conducted monthly.		
8. Flammable, combustible, and other dangerous materials are marked and stored in areas accessible only to staff.		
9. Children are restricted to floors with grade level exits (no stairs).		
10. The basement door is kept closed.		
11. There is no storage under stairs.		
12. Fire extinguishers are in place and checked regularly.		
13. Smoke alarms and fire alarms are checked at least once a month.		
14. Matches are kept out of the reach of children.		
15. Toys, chairs, tables, and other equipment are made of flame-retardant materials.		
16. Carpets and rugs are treated with a flame-retardant material.		

10-5 A fire safety checklist may include many items. Would you add any items to this checklist?

Fire Extinguishers

Each child care center needs several fire extinguishers, 10-6. One fire extinguisher should be placed in or next to the kitchen. Place another extinguisher in or near each classroom. A third extinguisher is needed in the laundry area. Check your state's licensing regulations for the placement of fire extinguishers. Test fire extinguishers regularly to make sure they are in working order.

Not every fire extinguisher is useful for every fire. There are three classes of fires and four types of extinguishers. **Class A fires** involve ordinary combustible materials, such as plastics, fabrics, paper, and wood. **Class B fires** involve flammable liquids, including gases, grease, paints, and solvents. **Class C fires** are electrical fires.

Water-type extinguishers are designed for use on Class A fires. They should not be used on any other type of fires. In fact, they can make Class B and C fires worse.

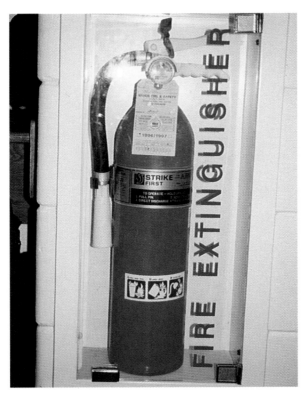

10-6 Check the maintenance information and instructions on your fire extinguisher.

Water-type extinguishers have three disadvantages. First, their usefulness is limited. Second, the water in the extinguisher may freeze unless it is treated with an antifreeze. Third, water-type extinguishers are heavy, usually weighing over 20 pounds.

Purple K dry chemical extinguishers are used to fight Class B and C fires. They are slightly more useful against Class B fires. *Standard dry chemical extinguishers* are also designed for Class B and C fires.

Multipurpose dry chemical extinguishers are the only type able to put out all three classes of fire.

Contact your local fire department before buying any fire extinguisher. The fire chief can recommend the extinguisher best suited for your needs. In addition, the fire chief can provide maintenance information and instructions for restoring a charge after an extinguisher has been used.

Schedule an in-service on fire extinguisher use prior to the opening of the center. Some directors prefer to have a local firefighter conduct this in-service. After this orientation, update all staff members yearly on fire extinguisher use.

Fire Drills and Evacuation Procedures

Most state licensing rules and regulations require fire and disaster drills. Most states also recommend drills be scheduled on a regular basis, such as once a month. These drills will prepare staff and children for a real fire or other emergency. During drills, use the daily class roster to take roll. It is an important tool for checking on the evacuation of all children and their safe return indoors.

Every center needs to have well-planned evacuation procedures. The procedures should include escape routes, staff assignments, and location of alarms. The evacuation procedures should be posted in every room where they can be easily seen. Emergency phone numbers should also be posted. In case of blocked routes, alternative evacuation routes should be planned. An example of procedures to be used is shown in 10-7.

If a fire is discovered in the center, sound the alarm immediately. Stay calm. If you panic, the children will panic as well. Evacuate children from the building at once, even if you do not see flames. Smoke, not fire, is responsible for more deaths. Leave the classroom lights on and close

Evacuation Procedures

1. Sound fire alarm.
2. Evacuate the building.
3. When leaving the building, leave lights on and close doors.
4. Call the fire department after leaving the building.
5. Call roll as soon as the children are together in a safe place.
6. When the firefighters arrive, report whether or not all children and staff are out of the building.

10-7 Review evacuation procedures with children. Post the procedures in a noticeable place.

the doors. Lights allow firefighters to see better in a smoke-filled structure.

Call roll as soon as the children and staff have cleared the building. When the firefighters arrive, inform the chief whether or not anyone is still in the building.

When making evacuation plans, remember that infants are more difficult to remove than older children. This is because infants cannot walk. Most adults cannot carry more than two infants at one time. Therefore, when ratios are higher than one caregiver to two infants, a careful plan needs to be made. Some centers practice by placing several babies in a crib and rolling it out of the building. Wagons can be used for evacuating older children.

Plan and introduce fire and burn prevention into the curriculum, if developmentally appropriate. Teach the children what to do if their clothing catches on fire. Chart 10-8 shows the stop, drop, and roll technique.

Weather or Disaster Emergencies

Blizzards, hurricanes, floods, electrical storms, tornadoes, and earthquakes are examples of weather or disaster emergencies. All of these conditions pose safety threats for the children and staff. Therefore, it is important to have an emergency plan for possible weather or disaster emergencies. The plans you formulate will depend upon the geographical area in which you are located.

In areas where natural disasters occur more often, evacuation drills should be practiced with

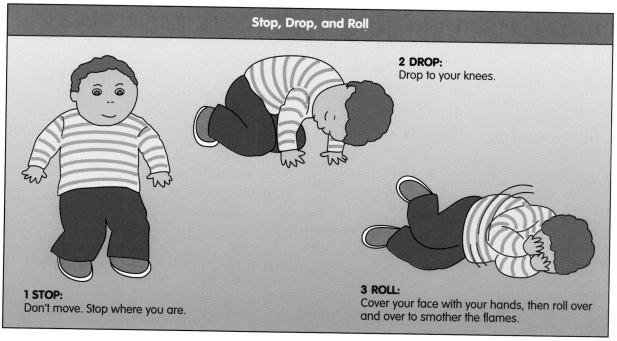

Stop, Drop, and Roll

2 DROP: Drop to your knees.

1 STOP: Don't move. Stop where you are.

3 ROLL: Cover your face with your hands, then roll over and over to smother the flames.

10-8 If clothing catches on fire, the stop, drop, and roll technique should be used.

the children on a monthly basis. Evacuation procedures need to become routine for the children.

In some weather emergencies, you may decide to close the school. You need to have a plan in place for notifying parents of such an emergency. Special arrangements may need to be made for transporting the children.

Be prepared for weather emergencies. Always keep battery-operated flashlights and a radio in a convenient spot. For some weather emergencies, blankets, water, food, and a first aid kit should also be available.

Poisonings

Studies show that children under five years of age account for almost two-thirds of poisonings that occur each year. Nearly any substance can, under certain conditions, be poisonous. The National Safety Council claims that the average residence contains over 40 poisonous products. Chart 10-9 lists many of these poisonous products.

Children eat many things adults would not think of placing in their mouths. There may be times when you are not sure whether a child has eaten something. For instance, you see a child playing with an empty aspirin bottle. The child has powder around the mouth. When in doubt, always assume the worst. If the child has eaten the aspirin, failing to act may result in great harm.

If you suspect that a child in your classroom has eaten something poisonous, remain calm. Telephone the nearest poison control center. If your area does not have a poison control center, call the nearest emergency room. Ask for instructions on treating the child.

Emergency Procedures for Poisonings

Poisoning emergencies often involve swallowing toxic substances. Other types of poisoning emergencies can occur, also. These include breathing toxic fumes and chemical injuries to the eyes or skin.

If any type of poisoning emergency occurs, follow the procedures given below. Do not rely on first aid information, antidote charts, or product information. Often this information is outdated or incorrect. The child may experience additional injury if the wrong action is taken.

Always contact your local poison control center for all cases of poisonings. When you call the center, be prepared to provide specific information. You will be asked to describe the child's symptoms. You will also be asked to identify any first aid procedures you have already administered. Report the time at which the substance was taken and the child's age and weight. Then provide the name of the poisonous substance. If the child removed the substance from a container, have the container with you when you call. Report the amount of substance the child consumed. Unless the exact amount is known, overestimating the amount consumed is better than underestimating it.

All first-aid stations at child care centers should have an emetic available for poisoning emergencies. An **emetic** is a substance that induces vomiting when swallowed. Syrup of

Poisonous Substances			
After-Shave Lotion	Drain Cleaner	Lemon Oil	Paint Thinner
Ammonia	Flowers and Plants	Matches, Safety	Perfume
Anacin™	(azalea, caladium,	Matches, Sulfur	Plant Food
Ant Poison	cherry, daffodils,	Medication, Contents	Reducing Pills
Battery Acid	hyacinth, hydrangea,	Unknown	Shampoo
Bleach	lily of the valley,	Moth Repellent	Shoe Polish
Candle Wax	mistletoe,	Mouthwash	Soap
Cold Pills	philodendron, rhubarb	Nail Polish	Spot Remover
Crayons	leaves, rubber vine,	Nail Polish Remover	Suntan Lotion
Dishwasher Detergent	tobacco, yew)	Nose Drops	Toilet Cleaner
Dishwashing Liquids	Glue	Paint, Liquid	Vitamin Pills

10-9 These common household items are all poisonous and should be kept out of the reach of children.

ipecac is an example of an emetic. Use extreme caution before giving a child syrup of ipecac. *Never give a child ipecac unless the physician at the poison control center advises this treatment.* Some poisons, such as drain cleaner or lye, can cause serious damage to the child's esophagus if vomiting is induced. These substances are called caustics. They burn going down the child's esophagus. If vomiting is induced, they will also burn coming up.

One of the leading causes of poisoning in young children is plants. When eaten, certain plants can cause skin rashes, upset stomachs, or even death. Many common household plants are poisonous. To prevent poisoning, check with your florist before purchasing a plant for the classroom. Finally, teach children never to put any leaves, flowers, or berries into their mouths without first asking a teacher.

Child Abuse

As a child care professional, you are very concerned about the health and safety of the children in your care. You do everything you can to see that the center is a safe place for them to be. However, the children are not in your care throughout the day and night. It is during this time that some children are abused. Because you are with the children for several hours a day, you may be the one to notice signs that a child is being abused or neglected. It is your responsibility to report suspected cases of child abuse.

There are four types of child abuse: nonaccidental physical injury, neglect, emotional abuse, and sexual abuse. Be aware of the signs of each type of abuse.

Nonaccidental Physical Injury

The most visible type of child abuse is **nonaccidental physical injury**. This is physical abuse inflicted on purpose. Children being abused in this way often come to school with bruises, bites, burns, or other injuries. They may have frequent complaints of pain.

Physically abused children often refuse to discuss their injuries. This may be because their abusers threaten them with further harm if they tell someone. Other children may talk about harsh punishment they have received.

Often these children come to the center wearing clothing to hide their injuries. Their clothing may be unsuitable for the weather.

As a result of being physically abused, some children may show an unusual fear of adults. Katrina is one example. She was abused by her father for two years before the center director contacted authorities with her suspicions. Katrina had an unusual fear of adults, especially her father. Whenever he came to pick her up, she backed away and avoided eye contact with him.

Child abuse was suspected for other reasons as well. Katrina often arrived at the center with visible bruises. She also wore clothing unsuitable for the weather, such as long-sleeve turtleneck tops in warm weather. One hot summer day, her teacher was concerned that Katrina might be too warm. When she removed Katrina's top, the teacher found many bruises. Katrina could not explain the injuries.

Neglect

When children are not given the basic needs of life, they suffer from **neglect**. Neglect takes many forms. A neglected child may be deprived of proper diet, medical care, shelter, and/or clothing. Children who have been unsupervised for long periods of time may be neglected. Neglect may or may not be intentional on the part of the abuser. However, the potential for harm is possible.

Children who wear clothing that is too small or dirty may be neglected. Neglected children may also wear clothes that are inappropriate for the weather. Children who are poorly groomed may also be neglected.

Other signs of neglect may appear in a child's health. Neglect may result in children who are too thin or malnourished. Constant fatigue, illness, or poor dental care may be other signs of neglect.

Alert teachers should observe for signs of neglect. They must be sensitive to different child-rearing practices as well as cultural expectations and values.

Derek is an example of a neglected child. His teacher observed that he appeared small for his age. After observing him for several more months, she noted he had developmental lags. He appeared to be lagging behind many of his same-age peers.

Often he would ask when snack or lunch would be served. During cooking activities, he would try to eat or take food. He also complained of being hungry. Derek lacked proper nutrition.

Observing these signs, Derek's teachers suspected neglect. They compared information and shared their concerns. As child care teachers, they knew they were required to report suspected child abuse. They knew Derek would never reach his full potential without proper nutrition.

Emotional Abuse

Emotional abuse is abuse of a child's self-concept through words or actions. Children have low self-esteem due to continual verbal abuse. Excessive or inappropriate demands may be made on the children by parents or guardians. This can cause emotional harm to children. Emotional abuse is the result of insufficient love, guidance, and/or support from parents or guardians.

Children who are emotionally abused may repeat certain behavior over several months. Look for the following signs:
- Refusal to talk.
- Unusual or unpredictable behavior.
- Excessive clinging or crying.
- Withdrawn behavior.
- Destructive behavior.
- Poor motor coordination for age.
- Fear of adults.

Sexual Abuse

Sexual abuse is forcing a child to engage in sexual activities with an adult. Rape, fondling, and indecent exposure are all forms of sexual abuse. Each of these acts involve adults using children for their own pleasure. **Incest** is sexual abuse by a relative. **Molestation** is sexual contact made by someone outside the family with a child.

There are many signs of sexual abuse. A child may have problems when walking or sitting. The child may complain of itching, pain, or swelling in the genital area. Some sexually abused children have bruises in the genitalia, vaginal, or anal areas. They may also have bruises in their mouths and throats. Some may complain of pain when urinating.

Sexually abused children commonly have poor peer behaviors. They may show extremely disruptive or aggressive behaviors. Often they will withdraw to infantile behaviors, such as baby talking, thumb sucking, or bed wetting. Some will show a lack of appetite. These children often express affection in improper ways.

Annabelle is an example of a sexually abused child. She would refuse help with clothing or toileting needs. She would not allow teachers to help her remove her outdoor clothing. Her teachers thought Annabelle's behavior was unusual. After observing another incident, they suspected she was sexually abused. Annabelle liked Richard, one of the children in her group. Several times she was seen rubbing his crotch with her hand during group time.

After observing Annabelle's behavior, the teachers reported the abuse. They realized if they continued waiting for more proof, there could be greater risk to the child.

Reporting Child Abuse

Doctors, social workers, school administrators, and teachers must report suspected cases of child abuse. This is the law. Information concerning your legal responsibility is contained in your state's **statute**, a formal document drawn up by elected officials. To receive a copy of the statute, contact the district attorney's office, state attorney general's office, social services department, city attorney's office, or a law enforcement office.

Teachers who suspect child abuse should contact the community agency responsible for handling these cases. It is important that you know what agency to contact in your state. The names of these agencies vary depending upon the area of the country and state. Examples include the Bureau of Children and Family Service, Department of Social Service, and Social Rehabilitation Service.

Report suspected child abuse cases immediately by telephone. The report should include the name, age, and address of the child and his or her parents. Report the facts that led you to your suspicion. Ask for advice as to how to proceed. After the telephone conversation, confirm your report in writing. Make a copy for your own files.

If a child abuse case results in a trial, you may be required to testify in court. This should not keep you from reporting suspected abuse. As a teacher, you are immune from liability if the report is made in good faith.

Protection Education

Planning for children's safety goes beyond the classroom. Children need to learn how to deal with dangers outside the classroom. They must learn about child abuse, especially sexual abuse. And they must learn how to protect themselves from it.

Warning children about strangers has been a common practice for some time. However, only 10 to 15 percent of child abusers are strangers to the children they abuse. The other 85 to 90 percent are people known to the children. These people may be neighbors, relatives, friends of the family, scout leaders, siblings, or parents. Most offenders are men. However, women are also reported.

Before age eight, 30 to 46 percent of all children are sexually assaulted. About 10 percent of these children are assaulted by the time they are five years old. Girls are abused more often than boys. Studies show that race, intelligence, family income, and social class do not appear to affect the occurrence of sexual assault.

Teach children to resist sexual attacks. Encourage them to "yell and tell." To do this, they must first resist the offender by saying no. Then they must tell a trusted friend or relative about the attack. Role-play this process with the children. Give them useful phrases to use if they find themselves in trouble. For example:

- If someone tries to give you a wet kiss, shake hands instead.
- If someone tries to get you to sit on his or her lap and you do not want to, say "No, not now."
- If someone wants to give you a hug and you do not want it, say "No thanks."
- If someone tries to touch your genitals, say "Stop. That is not okay."
- If someone rubs or pats your bottom, say "Do not do that."

Children can also learn by playing "What if" games. To play, ask such questions as:

- "What if a stranger asks to give you a ride?"
- "What if a stranger offers you candy?"
- "What can you do if a neighbor gives you a sloppy kiss?"
- "What can you do if a relative pats you on the bottom?"
- "What if someone places a hand under your clothes?"
- "What if someone tries to place you on his or her lap?"
- "What if the babysitter told you to take off your clothes and play with or look at your genitals?"
- "What if a neighbor invited you into his house to play a secret game?"

Children also need to learn how and who to tell if someone assaults them. Use puppets, charts, movies, or other materials to teach children this lesson. For instance, you might develop a "Who would you tell?" game using puppets.

Remember, as a teacher, it is important to believe comments made by children. Children do not lie about child abuse. If a child relates an attack to you, believe the child. Report the incident to your administrator and/or the proper law enforcement officials.

Liability

By law, young children are not expected to care for themselves. This is the primary role of the staff at the center. The staff must ensure their safety and health. Education is a secondary function.

Center directors are responsible for the acts of their employees. The extent of their liability may vary, however. As a result, only individuals who are safety and health conscious should be employed, 10-10. Once hired, the director needs to observe these people to ensure that they use good supervision techniques.

Types of Liability

Child care staff can be held responsible for failing to follow state licensing rules and regulations. Center staff can be liable for *not* doing the following:

- Obtaining a signed health form from a licensed physician for each child.
- Requiring a staff member to have an approved physical before working with children.
- Providing safe indoor and outdoor equipment.

10-10 Safety-conscious staff members watch for danger in all situations.

Operating a center with the required adult/child ratios.
- Providing proper supervision.
- Providing proper food storage.
- Maintaining fence and door locks in proper condition.
- Providing staff with information on children with special needs. This includes visual problems, hearing problems, allergies, epilepsy, emotional problems, or family problems.
- Refraining from corporal (physical) punishment.
- Providing a safe building.
- Removing children who lack self-control and are a hazard to themselves as well as others.
- Covering electrical outlets.

Center directors and staff must keep constant watch over the center environment. They must ensure that it is safe as well as healthy. New teachers will need constant support from the staff and director. As new teachers learn the importance of safe surroundings, support can decrease.

Forms

Every center should develop a number of forms related to the health and safety of the children. Many of these forms direct the staff in the care of the children and protect staff members from possible liability. Two forms commonly used by centers are injury report forms and various types of release or permission forms.

Every center should have a standard injury report form. Any information recorded on this form is useful if legal action is brought against the center. Parents also appreciate having the details of a child's accident. A sample form is shown in 10-11.

Various permission forms should also be on file. These forms should be filled out at the time of the child's enrollment. Permission is usually required for such items as special screening tests or walks around the neighborhood. To protect children from being picked up from the center by

---

Injury Report Form
Child and Family Study Center

Name of injured child_____ Age_____

Date_____ Time of injury _____ A.M./P.M.

Witness(es) _____

Location of injury_____

Person(s) notified of injury: Time of notification:

_____   _____

_____   _____

Staff member(s) supervising the child at the time of the

injury _____

Description of the incident: (Include specific information such as where the child was playing, with whom, with what, etc.)

Child's reaction to injury:

Description of injury:

10-11 The information in an accident report form is useful for parents and teachers.

a stranger, unauthorized person, or even a non-custodial parent, a transportation form should be used. This form should contain the names, relationship, and telephone numbers of people who have permission to transport the child to and from the center. In the event a parent wants to add or remove an individual from the list, a new form needs to be completed. Figure 10-12 shows a sample transportation form.

Privacy Law

The **privacy law** is designed to protect children. It states that a child's records cannot be given to anyone other than parents, without the parents' permission. Give a child's records only if the parents have made the request in writing. After receiving the request, the materials must be released within 45 days. A form that can be included in each child's file is shown in 10-13.

Parents are given unlimited access to all of their child's records kept by the center. Included may be screening information, developmental evaluations, and parent meeting planning sheets and summaries. Many teachers share all of this information during parent meetings. These meetings will be discussed more in Chapter 31, *Parent Involvement*.

The information contained in this file is confidential and is not to be circulated outside the center without the prior written consent of the child's parents.

Under Public Law 93-380: Parents have access to all educational records. According to this law:

(1) You are not allowed to provide the information contained in this file to anyone without the written consent of the child's parent or guardian.

(2) You must advise parents of their rights concerning their child's life

(3) Parents have the right to read and review the file. Moreover, they may request a revision of information in their child's file.

(4) Within forty-five (45) days, you are required to respond to a parent's request.

File reviewed by:

Name and Title	Address	Reason	Date

10-13 Use a form such as this to record reviews of children's files.

Transportation Permission Form
Hillsdale Child Care Center

The following people have permission to bring/pickup my child, _____:

Name	Relationship	Telephone Number

Parent's Signature

Date

If any of the above information changes, parents must file an updated form with the director.

10-12 A transportation form designates who may transport a child to and from the center.

Summary

Providing a safe environment for children requires a great deal of time and attention to details. Danger can be found in every corner of the center. These dangers can threaten both the physical and mental well-being of children. Protecting children from these dangers is the most important job of a teacher.

Child care professionals need to be prepared for any emergency. You should know how to use fire extinguishers and how to safely evacuate the children in case of a fire or other disaster. You should know how to handle accidental poisonings. Child care workers also need to recognize signs of possible child abuse and know how to report suspected cases.

Child care staff can be held responsible for failing to follow state licensing rules and regulations. It is important to know what those rules are and to know the extent of any possible liability.

Review and Reflect

1. Name four basic safety objectives.

2. What is the primary role of the staff at a center?

3. True or false. Most accidents in a child care center can be avoided.

4. Usually, younger children require _____ staff supervision than older children.

5. Name three ideal places to keep fire extinguishers in a child care center.

6. Classify the following fires. Name the type (or types) of fire extinguisher you would use to fight the fire.
   A. A burning toaster.
   B. A burning plastic milk carton.
   C. A burning pan of cooking oil.
   D. A burning painting done on paper.

7. True or false. Smoke, not fire, claims more lives.

8. Applying _____ at eye level to glass doors makes glass visible to children.

9. True or false. Nearly any substance, under certain conditions, can be poisonous.

10. What is an emetic?

11. Name the four types of child abuse.

12. List three behavior patterns exhibited by emotionally abused children.

13. List three unsafe situations for which a center is liable.

14. True or false. Parents are allowed limited access to records kept by the center concerning their child.

Apply and Explore

1. Design an evacuation chart for the classroom.

2. Using the poisonous substances chart in this chapter, conduct a safety check of your home. List the poisonous substances you found.

3. Arrange a visit to a center to learn about their safety objectives. Ask to view any safety checklists they might use.

4. Ask the local fire chief to address your group concerning the proper use of fire extinguishers.

5. Arrange a visit to the emergency room of a local hospital. Ask the doctor on duty to discuss emergency procedures used for poisonings.

6. Create a puppet play using phrases that children may use if ever faced with sexual abuse.

Chapter 11

Planning Nutritious Meals and Snacks

After studying this chapter, you will be able to

- list goals for a good nutrition program.
- explain the importance of a healthy diet.
- describe nutritional problems that can result from a poor diet.
- name the food groups in the Food Guide Pyramid and the main nutrients they supply.
- plan nutritious and appealing meals and snacks for children.

Terms to Know

nutrition

nutrients

undernutrition

malnutrition

Food Guide Pyramid

It was lunchtime at the New Horizons Child Care Center. Nidda asked for a second serving of spinach, a food being served for the first time. Maria said the potatoes were yummy. Geneva said her mother was sending oranges for her birthday treat. Throughout her meal, the teacher talked with the children and ate portions of the foods served.

The lunchroom was decorated with twelve large paper ice cream cones. Each cone represented one month of the year. The children's names and birthdays were written on paper scoops of ice cream. These scoops were placed in the cone that matched their birthday month.

On the other side of the lunchroom was a large carrot cut out of tagboard. A cloth measuring tape was pasted down the center. Each child's height was marked next to the tape.

In this classroom, children learn about nutrition. They learn both directly and indirectly. For instance, the variety of foods served and the teacher's comments about the food are direct learning experiences. Children learn about many types of food and that mealtime is a pleasant time. The positive attitudes and pleasing surroundings of the lunchroom are indirect learning experiences. By watching friends and teachers, children develop healthy habits and attitudes about food. Many of their food attitudes and behaviors will last into adulthood. Hopefully, they will be establishing a lifelong pattern of eating a healthy, well-balanced diet.

Teaching children about nutrition will be an important responsibility for you as a teacher. Proper nutrition is needed for children's health, growth, and development. Behavior and learning ability is related to proper diet. Some studies suggest that young children who have learned healthy food choices may experience lifelong health benefits. Thus, teaching nutrition concepts is a responsibility of the child care teacher.

Teaching nutrition concepts requires a good nutrition program. A good program centers on the needs of the children, including their ethnic backgrounds. These nutrition concepts should be integrated into all subject areas. Program goals should include the following:

- Providing nutritious meals and snacks.
- Introducing new foods that are nutritious.
- Encouraging healthy eating habits.
- Involving children in meal activities.
- Providing nutrition information to parents.

To meet these goals, you will need to understand how food is used by the body. In addition, you must know the various nutrients and their sources. Meal plans and food experiences for the children are also needed to meet program goals.

Nutrition

Nutrition is the science of food and how the body uses the foods taken in, 11-1. **Nutrients** are the chemical substances in food that help build and maintain the body. Certain nutrients are needed to build a strong body and mind. There are six groups of nutrients needed for growth and maintenance of health. These are proteins, carbohydrates, fats, vitamins, minerals, and water. Chart 11-2 contains a list of nutrients, their functions, and sources.

Food also provides the body with energy. Each type of food has its own energy value. This value is measured in calories. Energy from food maintains body functions such as breathing and blood circulation. It also maintains vital organs: the heart, lungs, liver, and kidneys. Energy from food maintains body temperature.

The amount of calories a person needs depends on age and activity level. Children need more energy than adults, in relation to body weight. For instance, a four-year-old boy weighing 42 pounds needs about 1800 calories per day. A 45-year-old man weighing 160 pounds needs about 2700 calories per day. Thus, the

11-1 Knowledge of nutrition is needed for planning healthy snacks.

child needs about 43 calories per pound while the man needs about 17 calories per pound. Children's physical growth is greater than adults' growth. Children are also very active. All their physical activities use a great deal of energy.

Nutritional Problems

Undernutrition and overeating are two problems that affect children's health and development. The effects of poor nutrition on cognitive abilities have been found in several studies. In order to plan balanced, nutritious meals and snacks, you need to know the effects of these problems.

Undernutrition is a lack of proper nutrients in the diet. It is caused by not eating enough food in an otherwise well-balanced diet. **Malnutrition** is a lack of nutrients. It is caused by the inability of the body to use the nutrients in the food. Malnutrition can occur even in children who eat the proper amounts of food.

Nutrient	Functions	Sources
Proteins	Build and repair tissues. Help build antibodies, enzymes, hormones, and some vitamins. Regulate fluid balance in the cells. Regulate many body processes. Supply energy, when needed.	Meat, poultry, fish, eggs, milk and other dairy products, peanuts, peanut butter, lentils.
Carbohydrates	Supply energy. Provide bulk in the form of cellose (needed for good digestion). Help the body efficiently digest fats.	Sugar: Honey, jam, jelly, sugar, molasses. Fiber: Fresh fruits and vegetables, whole grain cereals and breads. Starch: Breads, cereals, corn, peas, beans, potatoes, pasta.
Fats	Supply energy. Carry fat-soluble vitamins. Protect vital organs. Protect the body from shock and temperature changes. Add flavor to foods.	Butter, margarine, cream, cheese, marbling in meat. Nuts, whole milk, olives, chocolate, egg yolks, bacon. Salad oils and dressings.
Vitamins Vitamin A	Helps promote growth. Helps keep skin clear and smooth. Helps keep mucus membranes healthy. Helps prevent night blindness.	Liver, egg yolk, dark green and yellow fruits and vegetables, butter, whole milk, cream, fortified margarine, ice cream, cheddar-type cheese.
Thiamin (Vitamin B-1)	Helps promote normal appetite and digestion. Helps keep nervous system healthy. Helps body release energy from food.	Pork, other meats, poultry, fish, eggs, enriched or whole grain breads and cereals, dried beans, brewer's yeast.
Riboflavin (Vitamin B-2)	Helps cells use oxygen. Helps keep skin, tongue, and lips normal. Helps prevent scaly, greasy areas around the mouth and nose. Aids digestion.	Milk, all kinds of cheese, ice cream, liver, other meats, fish, poultry, eggs, dark leafy green vegetables.
Niacin (a B-vitamin)	Helps keep nervous system healthy. Helps keep skin, mouth, tongue, and digestive tract healthy. Helps cells use other nutrients.	Meat, fish, poultry, milk, enriched or whole grain breads and cereals, peanuts, peanut butter, dried beans and peas.
Vitamin C	Helps keep gums and tissues healthy. Helps heal wounds and broken bones. Helps body fight infection. Helps build cementing materials that hold body cells together.	Citrus fruits, strawberries, cantaloupe, broccoli, green peppers, raw cabbage, tomatoes, green leafy vegetables, potatoes and sweet potatoes cooked in the skin.
Vitamin D	Helps build strong bones and teeth in children. Helps keep adult bones healthy.	Fortified milk, butter and margarine, fish liver oils, liver, sardines, tuna, egg yolk, sunshine.
Vitamin E	Acts as an antioxidant although exact function is not known.	Liver and other variety meats, eggs, leafy green vegetables, whole grain cereals, salad oils, shortenings, and other fats and oils.
Vitamin K	Aids in blood clotting.	Organ meats, leafy green vegetables, cauliflower, other vegetables, egg yolk.

11-2 Each nutrient performs a specific function and can be found in several sources.   (Continued)

Nutrient	Functions	Sources
Minerals Calcium	Helps build bones and teeth. Helps blood clot. Helps muscles and nerves function properly. Helps regulate the use of other minerals in the body.	Milk, cheese, other dairy products, leafy green vegetables, fish without bones.
Phosphorus	Helps build strong bones and teeth. Helps regulate many body processes.	Protein and calcium food sources.
Iron	Combines with protein to make hemoglobin. Helps cells use oxygen.	Liver, lean meats, egg yolk, dried beans and peas, leafy green vegetables, dried fruits, enriched and whole grain breads and cereals.
Water	A basic part of blood and tissue fluid. Helps carry nutrients to cells. Helps carry waste products from cells. Helps control body temperature.	Water, beverages, soups, and most foods.

11-2 Continued.

Children with these problems often are shorter than their peers. Long-term deficiencies can slow, or even stop, growth. Other signs of poor nutrition include irritability, bowed legs, sunken eyes, decaying teeth, and fatigue.

Overeating is the intake of more food than is needed by the body to function properly. Many factors contribute to overeating. There is a larger and more available supply of food. There also is a trend toward more snacking. Unfortunately, overeating can cause many health and emotional problems. A major health problem caused by overeating is obesity.

Obesity can lead to many other health problems in adult life. These include hypertension (high blood pressure and related problems), diabetes, heart disease, hardening of the arteries, and many other diseases.

Obesity can also cause emotional problems. Many obese children have poor self-concepts. Some of these children become loners due to their low self-concepts.

Obesity is easier to prevent than to treat. First, note the activity level of any heavy children. Encourage them to join in large motor play. Second, discuss your concerns about a child's nutrition with staff and parents.

The Food Guide Pyramid

To ensure good nutrition, children need to eat a variety of foods. One easy way to plan a well-balanced diet is to use the **Food Guide Pyramid**,

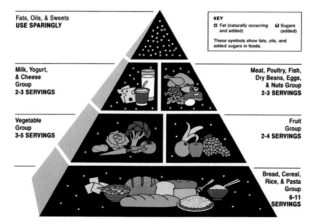

Food Guide Pyramid
A Guide to Daily Food Choices

11-3 The Food Guide Pyramid can help you see how the different food groups work together to form a balanced diet.

11-3. This guide is divided into the following six groups:

- breads, cereals, rice, and pasta
- vegetables
- fruits
- meat, poultry, fish, dry beans, eggs, and nuts
- milk, yogurt, and cheese
- fats, oils, and sweets

The first five food groups must be included in a child's daily diet. Foods in the sixth group should be limited. Chart 11-4 lists foods that are included in the Food Guide Pyramid, along with recommended serving sizes for children.

Milk, Yogurt, and Cheese

Children need a minimum of two to three servings from this group daily. The most important nutrient provided by this group is calcium, 11-5. Riboflavin, protein, and phosphorous are also provided. Fortified milk and milk products also provide vitamins A and D.

Milk is considered the best source of calcium in this group. Milk products such as cheese and yogurt are also good sources. Whole milk is preferred for most preschool children. Physicians sometimes recommend that overweight children be provided skim or lowfat milk. If you serve milk other than whole milk, be sure that it is fortified.

Food Groups, Sources, and Daily Needs			
Food Group	**Sources**	**Number of Servings Needed by Children**	**Child-Sized Servings***
Breads, cereal, rice, and pasta	Baked goods from enriched flour, cereals, crackers, flour, macaroni, noodles, rolled oats	6	½ slice of bread ¼ cup cereal, macaroni, noodles, rice, or spaghetti ½ cup ready-to-eat cereal 3 crackers ½ cup rolled oats
Vegetables	Vitamin C: tomatoes, cabbage, green pepper, potatoes, broccoli Vitamin A: brussel sprouts, broccoli, carrots, spinach, pumpkin, sweet potatoes	3 Serve one vitamin C rich vegetable every day. Serve one vitamin A rich vegetable several times a week.	½ cup juice ¼ cup cooked vegetable ½ potato
Fruits	Vitamin C: orange, grapefruit, strawberries, kiwifruit Vitamin A: cantaloupe, apricots	2 Serve one vitamin C rich fruit every day. Serve one vitamin A rich fruit several times a week.	¼ cup juice ¼ cup cooked fruit ½ apple or banana
Meat, poultry, fish, dry beans, eggs, and nuts	Beef, veal, lamb, pork, fish, shellfish; variety meats such as heart, kidneys, and liver	2 to 3 (5 ounces total)	1 egg 1 ounce lean meat, poultry, or fish 2 tablespoons of peanut butter 1 frankfurter ½ cup dried beans, peas, lentils ¼ cup canned fish
Milk, yogurt, and cheese	Milk: whole, 1%, 2%, skim, buttermilk, evaporated, and nonfat dry; cheese, yogurt	2 to 3 (2 cups total)	½ cup milk ½ cup yogurt ½ cup baked custard ½ ounce cheese ¾ cup cottage cheese

*Larger servings are needed as children grow older.

11-4 Nutritious meals can be planned using the Food Guide Pyramid.

11-5 The calcium found in milk helps build strong bones. This is very important for the body of a growing child.

Breads, Cereals, Rice, and Pasta

A child's diet should include six servings of breads and cereals daily. Carbohydrates, iron, and B-vitamins are the chief nutrients in these foods.

Foods in the breads and cereals group include whole grain and enriched breads. Also included are pancakes, pastas, crackers, and hot and cold cereals. Only whole grain and enriched products should be served to children. Most bread and cereal products are whole grain or enriched. However, check labels on products to be sure. Also, if you make bread products at the center, be sure to use whole grain or enriched flour.

Meat, Poultry, Fish, Dry Beans, Eggs, and Nuts

Two to three servings from this group should be included in a child's daily diet. Protein is the most important nutrient supplied by foods in this group. Meats are also good sources of B-vitamins, iron, and phosphorous.

Animal products in this group provide the highest quality of protein. These include beef, pork, veal, lamb, eggs, seafood, and poultry. Dried beans, dried peas, and nuts are also included in this group. The proteins in these foods are not as high-quality as the proteins in animal products. However, they are good sources, especially if they are served with milk, milk products, breads, or cereals.

Vegetables

Preschool children should receive three servings from this group daily. Foods in this group are major sources of vitamins C and A, 11-6.

Rich sources of vitamin C include green pepper, brussel sprouts, broccoli, and tomatoes. Rich sources of vitamin A are found in deep yellow and dark green vegetables. Carrots, pumpkin, and winter squash are examples of deep yellow vegetables. Spinach, broccoli, and asparagus are deep green vegetables.

11-6 Serving a fruit or vegetable at snack time gives children one of the servings they require.

When planning meals for children, be sure to include sources of vitamin A and vitamin C. At least one source of vitamin C should be served daily. A good source of vitamin A should be included several times a week. Vegetables should be served raw or cooked as little as possible. This is because cooking in water can lower the vitamin A and C content of foods.

Fruits

Preschool children should receive two servings from this group every day. Like vegetables, fruits are major sources of vitamins C and A. Serve fruits raw or slightly cooked to retain nutrients.

Rich sources of vitamin C include citrus fruits such as lemons, limes, oranges, and grapefruits. Strawberries and kiwifruit are other sources. Deep yellow fruits, such as apricots and cantaloupe, are rich sources of vitamin A. Serve at least one source of vitamin C each day and one source of vitamin A several times a week.

Fats, Oils, and Sweets

Foods in this group do not have very high nutritional value other than providing calories. Such foods as butter, margarine, jellies, syrups, and salad dressings are included. Pastries, candy bars, doughnuts, and many other sweets and snack items are included, too.

Eating large amounts of fats and sweets can lead to weight gain and obesity. If children fill up on fats and sweets while refusing other foods, they can be deprived of needed nutrients. That is why it is important to limit offering foods from this group. Instead, offer such items as fresh fruit or crackers with cheese for snacks. Of course, it is okay for children to have foods from this group from time to time. However, be sure that you offer enough servings from the first five food groups for that day.

Planning Meals and Snacks

Nutrition is the most important part of a well-planned menu. However, many other factors also contribute to a well-planned menu. For instance, scale serving sizes to the children's appetites. A usual child's serving is about one half of an adult's serving. Children manage best with small servings. Their appetites often vary from day to day. Suggested serving sizes for specific age groups are listed in 11-7.

Food	Ages		
	1	2-3	4-6
Milk	½-1 cup	½-1 cup	¾-1 cup
Bread	½ slice	½-1 slice	1-1½ slice
Cereal	¼ cup	⅓ cup	½ cup
Vegetable			
Vitamin A Source	2 tablespoons	3 tablespoons	4 tablespoons
Other	2 tablespoons	3 tablespoons	4 tablespoons
Fruit			
Vitamin C Source	¼ cup	⅓-½ cup	½ cup
Other	2 tablespoons	3 tablespoons	4 tablespoons
Meat, lean cooked without bone	½ ounce	1-½ ounce	1½-2 ounce
Egg	1	1	1
Dried Peas or Beans, cooked	1 tablespoon	2-3 tablespoons	3-4 tablespoons
Peanut butter	1 tablespoons	2-3 tablespoons	3-4 tablespoons
Cheddar cheese	½ ounce	1-1½ ounce	1½-2 ounce
Cottage cheese	1 tablespoon	2-3 tablespoons	3-4 tablespoons
Butter or Margarine	½ teaspoon	1 teaspoon	1 teaspoon

11-7 Consider the age of children as you plan meals and snacks.

Food Appeal

Children will eat more if the food appeals to them. Variety, texture, flavor, color, form, temperature, and food preferences all affect how much a child enjoys a meal.

Variety

Children like variety in the foods served to them. A meal with all the same texture or color could be boring for children. Children also enjoy trying new foods. A new food should be added with a meal of familiar and well-liked foods. This is because children may be overwhelmed if given too many new foods at once.

Texture

Soft, hard, chewy, mashed, chopped, crisp, creamy, and rough are all textures. It is wise to combine textures when planning meals and snacks for young children. This makes the meal more interesting for the children. For instance, at mealtime, serve one soft food, one crisp food, and one chewy food. See 11-8. Combine contrasting textures for a pleasing effect. This also provides you with an opportunity to include language concepts during meals and snacks.

11-8 Bananas covered with peanut butter combine the textures of soft, chewy, and creamy.

Dry foods are hard for children to eat. Serve dry food only in combination with two or more moist foods. Cream sauces or gravy poured over dry food makes the food more pleasing to young children.

Some meats are difficult for young children to chew. Their teeth cannot grind meat as easily as adults' teeth. Because of this, children usually prefer hamburgers. Chili, spaghetti, and casseroles are other ways of serving meat with varied textures.

Flavor

In general, children prefer mildly seasoned foods. One rule of thumb is to use only half as much salt as noted in a recipe. Whenever possible, enhance the natural flavor of the food. This means that only small amounts of sugar and spices should be added.

Color

Children enjoy color in their meals. If the foods you are serving are not very colorful, add color to one or more of the foods. For example, tint the applesauce pink. For St. Patrick's Day, you might color vanilla pudding green.

Food Forms

Serve most foods in bite-sized pieces no larger than ½ inch. Children have poorly developed fine motor coordination skills. They find it difficult to use spoons and forks well, 11-9. Therefore, slice cooked carrots and other vegetables in large pieces rather than dicing them. Try adding diced vegetables to another food. For instance, add diced carrots to mashed potatoes.

Soup is also difficult for many young children to eat. They become tired from spooning. Children may get frustrated if they spill on clothing or the table.

Two methods can be used to make soup easier to eat. One method is to thicken the soup. This can be done by adding solid ingredients or a thickener, such as flour. The second method is to let the children drink the soup from a cup.

Whenever possible, prepare foods so they can be eaten with the fingers. For example, serve chopped raw vegetables instead of a tossed salad.

11-9 The large pieces of fruit in this salad will be easy for children to pick up with forks or spoons.

Temperature

Children are more sensitive to hot and cold than adults. Therefore, they prefer foods close to room temperature. Serve hot dishes warm. Fruits, salads, and other cold foods should not be frozen or very cold. They should be cool.

Food Preferences

A child's home environment affects food preferences early in life. Family habits and culture strongly affect food preferences. For instance, Mexican-Americans may prefer more spicy foods than Americans of European background.

Consider the children's backgrounds as you plan meals. Offer foods that are familiar to them. Then add foods from other cultures from time to time for variety. See 11-10.

11-10 Children will accept new foods more readily when they are made occasionally.

Serving Meals

Licensing requirements exist that outline how often and how much food must be provided for young children in child care centers. These requirements vary from state to state. As a rule, the number of hours a child spends at a center governs the number of snacks and meals served. In most states, children who attend less than four hours a day must be served a fruit juice or milk and a snack item. Children who attend five to eight hours must be served both a meal and a snack.

The decision to serve breakfast is often based on two factors. These are the length of the school day and the distance the child travels to reach the center. Centers that have full-day programs or children who travel long distances often serve breakfast.

Breakfast

The purpose of breakfast is to break the 10 to 14 hour overnight fast. Breakfast provides energy for morning activities. Studies show that children who eat a nutritious breakfast perform better mentally and physically.

A good breakfast should include foods from at least four of the five required food groups. The United States Department of Agriculture (USDA) Child Care Food Program recommends:

- fruit or juice
- protein-rich food
- milk
- bread with butter or margarine

Fruit drinks or punches are not juice substitutes, even when fortified with vitamin C. Fruit juices have fewer additives and less sugar.

Self-Serve Breakfasts

Self-serve breakfasts are popular with center staffs. This is because children can eat their breakfasts as they arrive. They can choose what and how much to eat, based on their own appetites. The self-serve breakfast gives children the chance to prepare their own breakfasts.

Many prepackaged breakfast foods come in child-sized servings. These include dry cereals, yogurt packs, and muffins. Juice and milk are also available in child-sized servings.

Snacks

Most children eat small amounts of food at one sitting. They may not be properly nourished by just eating three meals a day. Therefore, provide snacks between meals. Snacks satisfy hunger and help meet daily food requirements.

In most centers, snacks are served mid-morning when there is no breakfast program, and again in mid-afternoon. Snacks should not interfere with a child's appetite for meals. Because of this, it is best to schedule snacks at least 1½ hours before meals.

Snacks should include one or more of the following: milk, fruit, vegetable, juice, or protein-rich food. In addition, a snack may include a bread or cereal product.

Choose snacks according to the Food Guide Pyramid. Plan a snack based on the menu for the day. Consider the nutrients, colors, and textures of the meals. Then choose snacks that complement the meals. Avoid fats, sweets, and highly salted foods such as potato chips, pretzels, and corn chips. Children usually enjoy simple snacks they can eat with their fingers. Suggestions for snack ideas are shown in 11-11.

Lunch

The USDA recommends the following pattern be used to ensure children receive the proper nutrients in their lunch:

- protein-rich food (main dish)
- vegetable and/or fruit (two different kinds)
- bread (whole grain or enriched rice or pasta)
- butter or margarine as needed
- milk
- dessert

Try including foods from different cultures. This will help the children develop an appreciation of other foods. The children will learn that people have different food preferences. Where rice is an important staple in some cultures, bread is in others.

Desserts are optional. They need not be served with every lunch. Plan desserts carefully. Many are high in fat and sugar and low in nutrients other than calories. For example, plain cookies and cakes have little nutritional value, but are high in calories. Instead, plan to use carrots or pumpkin in recipes to provide vitamin A. Custards and puddings are considered good desserts since they contain calcium and protein.

When included, desserts should be part of the meal, like the vegetable or bread. They should not be treated as a special part of the meal. Never tell children they must eat everything on their plates in order to get dessert. This will only make desserts appear special.

Chart 11-12 contains sample daily food plans for one meal and a snack. Note how the meals and snack complement each other.

Snack Ideas	
Breads, cereals, rice, and pasta Granola Rice cakes Dry cereal mixes (not presweetened) Seed mixes (pumpkin, sunflower, sesame, poppy, caraway) Roasted wheat berries, wheat germ, bran as roll-ins, toppers, or as finger food mix Variety of breads (tortillas, pocket breads, crepes, pancakes, English muffins, biscuits, bagels, popovers) and grains (whole wheat, cracked wheat, rye, cornmeal, oatmeal, buckwheat, rolled wheat, wheat germ, bran, grits) Toast (plain, buttered, with spreads, cinnamon) Homemade yeast and quick breads Waffle sandwiches Whole grain and spinach pastas Pasta with butter and poppy seeds Cold pasta salad	**Fruits** Fruits (use variety): pomegranates, cranberries, apricots, pineapples, tangerines, kiwifruit Kabobs and salads Fruit juices and juice blends Fruit muffins, yogurts, and milk blends Stuffed dates, prunes, etc. Dried fruits (raisins, currants, prunes, apples, dates, figs)
Vegetables Vegetables (with or without dips): sweet and white potatoes, cherry tomatoes, broccoli, cauliflower, radishes, peppers, mushrooms, zucchini, squashes, rutabagas, avocados, eggplant, okra, pea pods, turnips, pumpkin, sprouts, spinach Kabobs and salads Vegetable juices and juice blends Vegetable soups Stuffed celery, cucumbers, zucchini, spinach, lettuce, cabbage Vegetable spreads	**Meat, poultry, fish, dry beans, eggs, and nuts** Meat strips, chunks, cubes Meatballs, small kabobs Meat roll-ups (cheese spread, mashed potatoes, spinach as stuffing) Meat salads (tuna, chicken, turkey, etc.) Sardines Hard boiled eggs Deviled eggs Egg salad spread Red beet or pickled eggs Beans and peas mashed as dips or spreads Bean, pea, or lentil soup Roasted soybean and peanut mix 3-bean salad Chopped nut spreads Nut breads Peanut butter on, in, around, over, or with anything
	Milk, yogurt, and cheese Dips (yogurt, cottage cheese) Cheese (balls, wedges, cutouts, faces) Milk punches made with fruits or juices Yogurt Conventional cocoa Cottage cheese with vegetables or pancakes Cheese fondue (preheated, no open flame in classroom)

11-11 Plan snacks to coordinate with the Food Guide Pyramid.

Serving Safe Meals and Snacks

When planning nutritious meals and snacks, keep safety in mind. Remember that young children are learning how to chew and swallow. When they are in a hurry, they may gulp their food. Depending on the forms of foods they are eating, children risk choking. To prevent choking, avoid serving foods that, if swallowed whole, could block children's windpipes. Foods to be avoided include cherries with pits, hard candies, marshmallows, nuts, peanut butter by the spoonful, popcorn, pretzels, raw celery, whole raw carrots, whole grapes, and whole frankfurters (unless sliced lengthwise, then crosswise into bite-sized pieces).

Sample Daily Food Plans for One Meal and Snack (Other foods may be used to add nutrients and to meet the varied calorie needs of children.)					
Pattern	I	II	III	IV	V	VI
Snack	Orange juice Whole wheat bread Butter	Apple wedge Cheese	Milk Banana	Hard cooked egg Tomato juice	Celery stuffed with peanut butter Apple juice	Milk Peanut butter and cracker
Lunch	Ground beef patty Peas Carrot strips Enriched roll Milk	Roast turkey Broccoli Mashed potatoes Whole wheat bread Milk	Fish sticks Scalloped potatoes Stewed tomato Whole wheat bread Milk	Black-eyed peas with ham Mustard greens Purple plums Corn bread Milk	Scrambled eggs Spinach Fried apples Biscuit Milk	Oven fried drumsticks Corn-on-the-cob Sliced tomato/green pepper rings Whole wheat bread Milk
Pattern	VII	VIII	IX	X	XI	XII
Snack	Apple juice Cheese toast	Milk Raisins and peanuts	Grapefruit juice Finger-size pieces of leftover meat	Raw carrot strips, green pepper with cottage cheese dip	Tomato juice Flour tortilla with melted cheese	Fresh fruit in season (strawberries, melons, tangerines, etc.)
Lunch	Meatloaf Green beans Baked potato Carrot strips Enriched bread Milk	Tuna sandwich on whole wheat bread Tomato juice Raw cabbage (small pieces) Apricots Milk	Pinto beans with melted cheese Chili peppers, chopped Tomato, onion, lettuce Flour tortilla Milk	Meatballs in tomato sauce over spaghetti Zucchini Peaches French bread Milk	Lunchmeat roll-ups Sweet potato Apple, banana, and orange salad Rye bread Milk	Swiss steak cubes Cauliflower Cooked carrots Whole wheat roll Milk

11-12 Planning menus is the first step toward teaching nutrition concepts.

Summary

Teaching children about nutrition is an important responsibility. Children who learn healthy food choices can use the information their entire lives. Proper nutrition promotes children's growth and development.

In order to teach about nutrition, you must first understand how food is used by the body. You must also understand how nutrients and their sources fuel the body. You can then use this information to plan nutritious meals and snacks. The Food Guide Pyramid is a useful tool for planning menus. Food will appeal more to children if you consider the texture, flavor, color, form, and temperature of the foods you plan to serve.

Review and Reflect

1. True or false. Children who have learned healthy food choices may also experience lifelong good health.

2. List four goals of a good nutrition program.

3. Define nutrition.

4. What are nutrients?

5. Name the six groups of nutrients.

6. The energy value of food is measured in _____.

7. Describe the difference between undernutrition and malnutrition.

8. What are the six food groups in the Food Guide Pyramid?

9. Milk is a good source of
   A. calcium.
   B. riboflavin.
   C. phosphorus.
   D. All of the above.

10. What are the chief nutrients found in breads and cereals?

11. A good source of vitamin _____ should be served several times a week, and a good source of vitamin _____ every day.

12. Good sources of _____ include cream, olives, egg yolks, and nuts.

13. Why should food be served to children in bite-size pieces?

14. List the recommended foods for a nutritious breakfast outlined by the USDA.

15. True or false. It is a good idea to tell children to eat everything on their plates in order to get dessert.

16. Name four foods that should not be served to young children because they might cause choking.

Apply and Explore

1. Plan a breakfast, lunch, and snack menu for one week for a group of three-year-old children.

2. Ask a dietitian to discuss the importance of a well-balanced diet with your class.

3. Observe a group of children at lunchtime. Describe their food preferences. Make notes of what is or is not lacking in their lunch menu based on the USDA recommendations.

4. Prepare a list of desserts. List the nutritional information for each of these desserts. Are they nutritious? Why or why not?

5. Discuss reasons why obesity is easier to prevent than treat.

Young children enjoy setting the table using outlined placemats.

Chapter 12

Guiding Children's Health

After studying this chapter, you will be able to

- develop a workable health policy for a child care center.

- list steps for controlling the spread of food-borne illnesses.

- explain the importance of first aid training

- identify various injuries and outline procedures for treating them.

- explain how to care for children who become ill while in your care.

- describe your responsibility when caring for children with special illnesses.

Terms to Know

policy

communicable
   diseases

food-borne illness

bacteria

food poisoning

wound

closed wound

open wound

abrasion

rabies

burn

first-degree burn

second-degree burn

third-degree burn

anaphylactic shock

head lice

allergy

diabetes

insulin

epilepsy

HIV

AIDS

Tu-Ling's health affects his performance, ability to learn, and behavior. Tu-Ling has a constant inner ear infection, and he is having trouble hearing. This hearing loss may affect his development of language skills, contact with peers, and general behavior.

A child's health is a key concern when planning, preparing, and maintaining a classroom environment, 12-1.

A healthy environment for young children starts with sound health policies. To avoid the transmission of disease, stress personal hygiene

12-1 Contact parents on health issues when appropriate.

and safe food handling practices. Plan for emergencies such as control of head lice. Also plan for sudden illnesses. In addition, obtain the knowledge and skill to provide first aid treatment.

Objectives for Guiding Health

It is your responsibility to protect, maintain, and improve children's health. Thus, you will need to create a healthy environment. The following objectives should be considered:

- Develop center health policies.
- Review the children's health records to ensure that they receive immunizations.
- Recognize ill children when making daily health observations.
- Isolate children who may have an illness from the group.
- Contact parents on health issues when appropriate.
- Plan a safe environment to prevent accidents.
- Provide first aid treatment.
- Take part in health-related in-service training.
- Include health in the children's curriculum.

Health Policies

A **policy** is a course of action that controls future decisions. It is important for your center to have health policies. These policies will help you make consistent decisions regarding the health of the children in your care.

In most states, the health of children in child care is regulated by state licensing rules and regulations. Their purpose is to protect young children. These rules and regulations address only the basic health requirements. Your center may have additional health policies that are more specific.

Medical Examination

All children enrolled in your program should have a preadmission medical examination. This exam will help you learn

- whether the child is free from **communicable diseases**. (These are illnesses that can be passed on to other people.)

- if the child has had all needed immunizations.
- whether the child has any known allergies.
- if the child has any special health problems that would affect his or her enrollment.

To provide the best environment for children, the staff must also be in excellent physical, mental, and emotional health. They should have an examination prior to their first day of work. A record of these examinations should be maintained in the employees' files.

Immunizations

To protect all children, each child attending the center must have the proper immunizations. The only exception to this policy is when a child is exempted by your state laws for religious or medical reasons. Children who are not properly immunized must be excluded from the center. Partial immunizations do not provide protection against many diseases. Immunizations recommended for preschool children are oral polio, DTP (diphtheria, tetanus, and pertussis, or whooping cough), measles, mumps, rubella (German measles), and HbCV (*Haemophilus influenzae* type b conjugate vaccine). HbCV provides protection against bacterial infections. Chart 12-2 shows the immunizations required for each age. Figure 12-3 shows a typical immunization record form.

Immunizations for Preschool Children	
Age	**Immunization**
2 months	Oral Polio, DTP, and HbCV
4 months	Oral Polio, DTP, and HbCV
6 months	DTP and HbCV
12-15 months	Oral Polio, Measles, Mumps, Rubella, and HbCV
15-18 months	DTP (Booster)
4-6 years	Oral Polio and DTP (Booster)

12-2 Proper immunization is a health policy required by most state licensing agencies.

DEPARTMENT OF HEALTH & SOCIAL SERVICES
Division of Health
DOH 4192 (Rev. 02/94)

Day Care Immunization Record

STATE OF WISCONSIN
Wisconsin Statutes
ss. 140.05(16) & 120.12(16)

INSTRUCTIONS TO PARENT: COMPLETE AND RETURN TO DAY CARE CENTER WITHIN 30 DAYS AFTER ADMISSION.
State law requires all children in day care centers to present written evidence of immunization against certain diseases within **30 school days of admission**. These requirements can be waived only if a properly signed health, religious, or personal conviction waiver is filed with the day care center (see "Waivers" below).

PERSONAL DATA   PLEASE PRINT

STEP 1

| Name (Last, First, M.I.) | Birthdate | Mo/Day/Yr | Telephone Number |

| Parent/Guardian/Legal Custodian (Last, First, M.I.) | Address, Street, City, State, Zip |

IMMUNIZATION HISTORY

STEP 2

List the **MONTH, DAY AND YEAR** your child received each of the following immunizations. DO NOT USE A (✓) OR (X). If you do not have an immunization record for this child at home, contact your doctor or public health agency to obtain the dates.

TYPE OF VACCINE	Type	First Dose mo/day/yr	Type	Second Dose mo/day/yr	Type	Third Dose mo/day/yr	Type	Fourth Dose mo/day/yr	Type	Fifth Dose mo/day/yr
DIPHTHERIA-TETANUS-PERTUSSIS (Specify DTP or DT)										
POLIO										
Hib										
MEASLES-MUMPS-RUBELLA										
Hepatitis B										

REQUIREMENTS

STEP 3

The following are the minimum **required** immunizations for the child's age/grade **at entry**. It is not a **recommended** immunization schedule for infants and preschoolers. For this schedule, contact your doctor or local health department. Children who reach a new age/grade level while attending must have their record updated with dates of additional doses required. If your child received the third dose of DTP-DT-Td or polio after the fourth birthday further doses of these vaccines may be recommended, but are not required. Measles, mumps and rubella vaccines **must** have been received on or after the first birthday.

AGE/GRADE			NUMBER OF DOSES			
15 months through 23 months	3 DTP/DT	2 Polio	1 Measles	1 Rubella	1 Mumps
2 years to Kindergarten Entrance	4 DTP/DT	3 Polio	1 Measles	1 Rubella	1 Mumps
After Kindergarten Entrance	Refer to the Student Immunization Law Age/Grade Level Requirement.				

Note: Haemophilus influenzae b Vaccine (Hib) and Hepatitis B are recommended but not required at this time.

COMPLIANCE DATA AND WAIVERS

STEP 4

CHILD MEETS ALL REQUIREMENTS
Sign at Step 5 and return this form to day care center.

———— **Or** ————

CHILD DOES NOT MEET ALL REQUIREMENTS
Check the appropriate box below, sign and return this form to day care center.

☐ Although my child has not received all required doses of vaccine for his or her age group, at least the first dose of each vaccine (DTP/DT/Td, polio, measles, rubella and mumps) has been received. I understand that it is my responsibility to obtain the remaining required doses of DTP/DT/Td and polio vaccines for my child **WITHIN ONE YEAR** and to notify the day care center in writing as each dose is received.

NOTE: Failure to stay on schedule or report immunizations to the day care center may result in court action against the parents and a fine of up to $25.00 per day of violation.

☐ **For health reasons** this student should not receive the following immunizations: _____

(Please list in Step 2 any immunizations already received.)

Physician Signature _____

☐ **For religious reasons** this student should not be immunized. (Please list in Step 2 any immunizations already received.)

☐ **For personal conviction** reasons this student should not be immunized. (Please list in Step 2 any immunizations already received.)

SIGNATURE

STEP 5

This form is complete and accurate to the best of my knowledge.

X _____

Signature of Parent, Guardian or Legal Custodian   Date

12-3 This form supplies written proof that a child is properly immunized. Parents or legal guardians and the child's physician must sign the form.

Attendance Policy

For the safety of all the children, centers need a policy stating when an ill child should be kept at home. For example, your policy might state that a child should be kept at home if he or she shows any of the following symptoms:

- A temperature over 100 degrees, unless the child's normal temperature is above the average.
- Intestinal upset along with diarrhea or vomiting.
- Sore or discharging eyes.
- Profuse nasal discharge.
- Rash with a fever.

It is also advised that a child should be kept home for a period of 24 hours after a fever. Instruct parents to report all sickness to center personnel.

Administering Medications

To protect staff against lawsuits, most centers have policies for medication. These policies must adhere to, but can exceed, your state's licensing requirements. For instance, your state may require that only a doctor-prescribed medication may be given to a child. You must follow this rule. Likewise, if the state requires a record of the child's name, time, and date, and amount of medication given, you must keep these records.

Medicines should also be stored appropriately. Refrigerated medications should be stored in a secure, labeled container. Nonrefrigerated medicines should be stored in a locked place out of the children's reach. It is important that medications contain a label specifying the child's name, physician's name, name of medication, dosage, and how often to administer.

Napping

One health policy that is needed to help prevent the spread of illness is related to napping. Children should not share cots or beds. Rather, each child should be provided with a washable cot or bed and clean sheets. See 12-4. Clean sheets should be provided on a weekly basis. At times, it may be necessary to change sheets more frequently, such as when a child is ill, has perspired a great deal, or has soiled the sheets.

12-4 Surfaces should be cleaned daily with an antibacterial spray.

Daily Health Inspection

To protect children's health, conduct an informal health inspection each day. This inspection is best conducted as soon as each child arrives at school. Observe for rashes, sores, swelling or bruising, changes in appearance of eyes, runny noses, flushing of skin, coughing, sneezing, and a sweaty appearance.

Even after the health inspection at arrival time, observe the children from time to time for symptoms of illness. Throughout the day watch for irritability, frequent trips to the bathroom, sleepiness, vomiting, and uncommon aggressiveness. Also watch for symptoms of infection, 12-5. If a child appears sick, contact the parents.

Preschool children are prone to communicable diseases. These include chicken pox, conjunctivitis (pink eye), influenza, and measles among others. Observe for symptoms of each of these diseases. Make this information known to all staff. Post a communicable diseases chart in the staff room, 12-6.

Infection Symptoms
• A sensation of heat. • Pus, either draining from a wound or beneath the skin. • Fever. • Redness of affected area. • Red streaks leading from wound. • Swollen lymph glands. • Tenderness in affected area. • Throbbing pain.

12-5 Infections are very dangerous and sometimes even fatal. Be aware of the early signs of infection.

Contacting Parents

Children may arrive at the center in good health, but later show symptoms of illness or infection. When do you decide to contact a parent to pick up a sick child? The answer to this question varies from center to center. The need to contact parents mainly depends on program resources, along with instructions from the parents. Some programs have a sick bay and a flexible staff. When a child becomes ill, the child is moved to the sick bay and the parent is contacted. An adult stays with the child until the parent arrives.

Always contact parents when a child shows signs of illness. Describe the symptoms to the parent. If the child is very ill, the parents should be responsible for picking the child up within a reasonable amount of time. Programs need to have this clearly stated in their policies.

Each child's folder should contain emergency information. Record parents' or guardians' home and work telephone numbers. Also note phone numbers of the family doctor and dentist. An example of an emergency information sheet is shown in 12-7.

Communicable Diseases				
Disease	**Incubation Period (Time from Exposure to First Signs)**	**Signs and Symptoms**	**Period of Communicability Precautions and Restrictions**	**General Information**
Chicken pox (Varicella)	2 to 3 weeks, commonly 13 to 17 days	Sudden onset, slight fever, lesions often appear first on scalp, then on face and body. Successive crop of lesions remain 3 to 4 days, leaving crusts.	Keep patient home until all lesions are crusted over, usually 5 to 6 days after onset of rash.	Mild disease in children. May be more severe in adults and in children with cancer, leukemia and other high risk conditions.
Conjunctivitis (Pink Eye)	24-72 hours	Redness in the white of the eye. May or may not have pus discharge. Eye irritation.	The communicable period depends on the cause, but is usually while inflammation or drainage is present. Keep patient home during communicable period, and refer for medical diagnosis and treatment.	Most infections are viral by cause; some are bacterial. May spread person to person through hand to eye contact. Also an early symptom for measles. Some symptoms may be an allergy, and are noncommunicable.
Viral Hepatitis Type A (Formerly Infectious)	15-50 days. Average 25 days	Usually abrupt onset with fever, fatigue, loss of appetite, nausea, and abdominal pain. Jaundice is less common in children than in adults.	Most communicable during first week of illness and up to 1 week after jaundice. Keep patient home and no food handling or patient care while communicable.	Vaccine not available. May be confused with Hepatitis B. Differential diagnosis is important for prevention and control. Careful hand-washing is essential. Household contacts should be given immune serum globulin as soon as possible.
Influenza	24-72 hours	Rapid onset with fever, chills, headache lack of energy, muscle ache, sore throat, cough.	Communicable for 3 to 7 days after clinical onset. Keep home until symptoms disappear.	Vaccine is available and should be given to persons with greatest risk of serious complications from the disease: the chronically ill and the elderly.

12-6 Awareness of the symptoms and treatment for communicable diseases and illnesses is important in order to control the spread of sickness through the center.

(Continued)

Communicable Diseases				
Disease	**Incubation Period (Time from Exposure to First Signs)**	**Signs and Symptoms**	**Period of Communicability Precautions and Restrictions**	**General Information**
Measles (Rubeola)	8-13 days	High fever (101 F or more), with cough, runny nose and /or conjunctivitis. Blotchy rash appears 3 to 5 days after early signs, beginning on face and becoming generalized, lasting 4 or more days.	Communicable from onset or respiratory illness until 4 days after appearance of the rash. Keep patient home until 5 days after the appearance of rash.	A very serious, highly contagious but vaccine preventable disease.
Mononucleosis, Infectious	2-6 weeks	Characterized by fever, sore throat, and inflamed posterior lymph nodes.	Keep patient home, at the discretion of physician.	In children the disease is usually mild and difficult to recognize.
Mumps	12 to 26 days, commonly 18 days	Fever, pain and swelling about the jaws involving one or more salivary glands. Many infections occur without symptoms.	Keep patient home until salivary gland swelling has subsided, or other symptoms have cleared.	Infectious early. May cause complications in adults. Vaccine available.
Pediculosis (Lice)	Eggs hatch in a week; reach maturity in about 2 weeks	Excessive scratching on head or other parts of body. Light gray insets lay eggs nits in the hair, especially at the nape of the neck and around the ears.	Keep patient home until treated (should not need to miss more than 1 day of school.)	Avoid sharing personal belongings such as clothing, head gear, combs and brushes.
Ringworm (scalp, skin, feet)	Variable, 1-3 weeks	Scalp: Scaly patches of temporary baldness. Infected hairs are brittle and break easily. Skin: Flat, inflamed, ringlike sores that may itch or burn. Feet: Scaling or cracking of the skin, especially between the toes or blisters containing a thin watery fluid.	Communicable as long as active lesions are present. Keep patient home until adequate treatment is begun.	Preventive measures are largely hygienic. All household contacts, pets, and farm animals should be examined and treated if infected. Ringworm is spread directly by contact with articles and surfaces contaminated by such infected persons or animals.
Rubella (German Measles)	14-21 days	Mild symptoms, slight fever, rash lasting about 3 days, enlarged head and neck glands common (particularly in back part of neck, behind ears.)	Keep patient home until 4 days after appearance of rash.	Highly communicable, but vaccine preventable disease. Complications are mild except in pregnancy when fetal infection or damage may occur. If contacts include a pregnant woman, she should consult her physician immediately.
Pertussis (Whooping Cough)	5 to 10 days	Begins with upper respiratory symptoms. An increasingly irritating cough develops with a characteristic "Whoop" and frequently occurs in spasms accompanied by vomiting.	Keep patient home for 21 days from beginning of "Whoop," or 5 to 7 days after onset of appropriate therapy.	Most dangerous to preschool children. Immunization is not recommended for children over 6 years of age. Susceptible contacts should be treated and observed for respiratory disease.
Scabies	4-6 weeks with first infections several days with reinfection	Small raised reddened areas or lesions with connecting grayish-white lines. Marked itching. Most commonly found in the folds of the skin, finger webs, wrists, elbows, thighs, beltline, abdomen, nipples, buttocks.	Keep patient home until under adequate treatment and no open lesions can be observed.	All cases, family members, and other close physically contacts should be treated for scabies simultaneously.
Streptococcal Infections including Scarlet Fever (Strep throat)	1 to 3 days	Fever, sore throat; tender swollen glands with a fine, red rash present in Scarlet Fever.	Keep patient home for 7 days from onset if untreated; with adequate medical treatment, 24 hours.	Medication for symptomatic patients is recommended because of possibility of complications, including rheumatic fever. Culture survey rarely recommended.

12-6 Continued.

Emergency Information

Child and Family Study Center

Child's Name _____   Birthdate _____

Home Address_____   Home Phone _____

Mother

Home Address_____   Home Phone _____

_____

Work Address _____   Work Phone _____

_____

Father

Home Address_____   Home Phone _____

Work Address _____   Work Phone _____

_____

In Case of Emergency, Who Should Be Notified?

Name _____   Phone _____

Name _____   Phone _____

Family Doctor _____   Phone _____

Address _____

Family Dentist_____   Phone _____

Address _____

12-7 Always have the information needed to contact parents in an emergency.

Parents should also be notified if their children have been exposed to a communicable disease. Send notices home to all parents if even one child has been infected with head lice. An example of a notice is shown in 12-8. Provide space to include the child's name, illness exposed to, and the date.

Personal Hygiene

Personal hygiene is an important component of a healthy environment. When cleanliness is stressed, fewer children and staff become ill.

Stress the importance of cleanliness to all new employees, as well as volunteers. This can

Dear Parent:

This is to notify you that your child,

_____, was exposed to

_____ on _____

at the Child and Family Study Center.

Signed _____
                    (Head Teacher)

Date _____

12-8 It is important that you inform parents when their children have been exposed to head lice or any other communicable disease.

be done through an in-service training, employee handbook, or orientation. Each person should follow basic habits of cleanliness. They should bathe or shower daily and keep their hair clean. A hairnet should be worn while working in the kitchen. Refrain from smoking in the center. Use disposable tissues. Once used, tissues should be discarded. Cover the mouth when coughing or sneezing.

Emphasize to staff members the importance of proper hand washing while working with children. Hands should be washed at the beginning of the day, before eating or handling food, after using the toilet, and after diapering a child. Wash hands after coughing, sneezing, rubbing the nose, or handling handkerchiefs. Hand washing helps prevent the spread of contagious diseases in a child care center. Studies show that many illnesses, such as diarrhea, can be greatly reduced when proper hand washing policies are followed.

Controlling Diseases Transmitted by Foods

Food-borne illnesses are those caused by foods that are not stored or prepared in a clean or safe manner. Many food-borne illnesses can be traced back to the staff. Because of this, all new employees should be required to have a complete physical exam. A chest X ray or tuberculosis test should be included. Staff members should not prepare food when they are sick. The germs causing their illness could infect the food and pass the germs on to the children and other staff members.

Food Poisoning

Small living organisms, called **bacteria**, can cause food-borne illnesses. An infection may occur in the gastrointestinal tract from eating food containing harmful bacteria or other organisms. This is called **food poisoning**. Common symptoms are vomiting and diarrhea. Other symptoms include chills, cramps, fever, headache, muscular pain, nausea, and weakness.

The effect of the bacteria or the bacteria's toxin (poison) varies. The types and numbers of bacteria and the person's reaction to the bacteria affect the strength of the illness. Commonly, the larger the number of bacteria, the more severe and quick the onset of illness. Young children, the elderly, and the sick are most likely to have a severe reaction.

People can transmit bacteria to food in several indirect ways. Chief among these methods are unclean cooking equipment and utensils. To help prevent food poisoning, thoroughly wash all kitchen equipment, 12-9. Replace kitchen towels daily. Do not allow classroom pets to eat from dishes used by people. After playing with classroom animals, tell the children to wash their hands.

Foods need to be properly handled, prepared, stored, and served to prevent bacterial growth. Foods should be stored at temperatures below 40°F or above 140°F. Bacteria grow most rapidly at warm temperatures. At temperatures below 40°F, bacteria will remain inactive. At temperatures above 40°F, bacteria become active and start multiplying. Very high temperatures (140°F or more) will destroy most harmful types of bacteria.

12-9 A refrigerator that is clean and in good working condition helps control transmission of food-borne illness.

First Aid

In every preschool, injuries and illness occur. Sometimes, it may just be a scratch or bumped knee. At other times, it may be a sudden high temperature.

First aid training provides the knowledge and skill needed to handle emergency medical care. With the proper training, you will know how and when to treat illnesses and injuries. You will also know when professional medical help is required.

All employees in child care should be certified by the American Red Cross. This certification may have been acquired through prior course work or past employment. If an employee is not certified, he or she should be required to obtain certification in order to be employed.

Conduct a first aid in-service training session for all center personnel each year. Include secretaries, janitors, cooks, and bus drivers in the training session. Training should focus on updating personnel on first aid procedures of the American Red Cross.

First Aid Supplies

In order to administer first aid, you will need some basic supplies. Most drugstores, department stores, and school supply catalogs sell first aid kits that would include these basic supplies. You may also purchase your supplies separately and put them together in a kit.

Store all first aid items in one area. Keep them out of children's reach. However, do not keep first aid supplies in a locked cabinet. During an emergency you may not have time to search for a key.

Each month, check the contents of the first aid kit. Make sure all first aid kits have the necessary supplies. To do this, check the contents against a list, such as the one shown in 12-10. Many programs have one person responsible for this duty. Replace any supplies that have run out.

If some children have special health needs, you will need to add additional first aid supplies. An antihistamine or bee sting kit may have to be added for children with allergies. Children with diabetes may need sugar or honey. For emergency preparedness, always take a first aid kit on field trips.

Wounds and Their Treatment

A **wound** is damage to the surface of the skin or body tissue. Basically, there are two types of wounds. A **closed wound** is an injury to the tissue directly under the skin surface. It does not involve a break in the skin. An **open wound** is a break in the skin.

Closed Wounds

Children usually get closed wounds from falling, being struck, or running into some object. Most closed wounds involve the soft tissues under the skin. The most common type of closed wound is a bruise.

First Aid Kit Inventory

Date _____   Staff Signature _____

Quantity	Item	Complete	Replacement
1	Quick reference first aid manual.		
15	Individual adhesive bandages in ½-inch, ¾-inch, and round sizes.		
10	2 x 2 inch sterile first aid dressings, individually packaged for burns and open wounds.		
10	4 x 4 inch sterile first aid dressings.		
1 roll	Gauze bandage, 2 inches by 5 yards.		
2 rolls	Adhesive tape, 1 inch wide.		
20	Disposable paper tissues.		
1 bar	Mild soap, for cleaning scratches, wounds, etc.		
1 pair	Tweezers for removing splinters.		
1 pair	Blunt tipped scissors, for cutting tape and bandages.		
1 package	Safety pins.		
1 bottle	Calamine lotion, for insect bites.		
5	1 ounce bottles of syrup of ipecac.		
1	Flashlight.		
1	Synthetic ice pack.		
1	Thermometer, strip-type that can be used on the child's forehead.		
20	Alcohol wipes.		
1 package	Absorbent cotton balls.		
1 bottle	Antibacterial skin cleaner.		

12-10 Make sure the first aid kit is well-stocked at all times.

Common signs of a closed wound are tenderness and pain in the damaged area. To help control the pain, apply a cold cloth or pack to the injured area, 12-11.

Open Wounds

Cuts and scrapes that break the skin are called open wounds. Two first aid problems are caused by open wounds. First, there may be rapid blood loss. If this is the case, the injured child may go into shock. Second, exposed body tissue may become contaminated and infected.

Some open wounds bleed freely. This reduces the danger of infection. Other wounds bleed very little. These are more likely to become infected.

Open wounds on the top skin layer require simple treatment. To clean the wound, wash it with soap and water. If the wound is deep or does not stop bleeding in a short amount of time, seek medical attention.

Abrasions

An **abrasion** is a scrape that damages a portion of the skin. Children usually get abrasions from falling and handling rough objects. It is

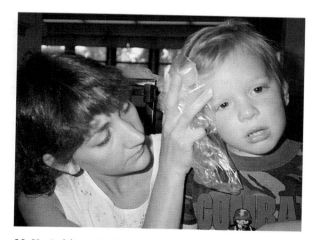

12-11 Cold packs help reduce swelling in closed wounds.

common to have several children in a classroom with skinned knees, scratched arms, or rope burns.

Bleeding from an abrasion is often limited to blood flow from broken capillaries (small veins). However, bacteria or dirt may still enter the wound and infection can still occur. Dirt particles may actually slow down the healing process. Sometimes, abrasions heal around the particles, forming a permanent scar.

Cuts

Cuts, or incised wounds, on body tissues are often caused by broken glass, metal, or sharp edges. Bleeding can be heavy if a blood vessel has been cut. Nerves, muscles, or tendons can also be damaged if the cut is deep enough.

Puncture Wounds

Puncture wounds are made by sharp objects such as nails, splinters, thumbtacks, and even sticks. In order to puncture the skin, the force at which the object meets the skin must be strong. Bleeding is often light. As a result, the wound is not flushed out. Infection may set in. Harmful bacteria such as tetanus organisms may grow in the presence of moisture and warmth. This can then be carried within the body.

Bites

Bites are a type of puncture wound. They can be inflicted by humans and animals. In the case of a mild human bite, you may need only to thoroughly wash the injured areas. However, if the skin is broken, consult a doctor at once. This is especially important if the bite was from an animal. This is because there is a danger of an infection such as rabies.

Rabies is a disease caused by a viral infection of the nervous system and brain. Humans who are infected are not able to swallow. This is a result of the tightening of throat muscles.

Rabies is transmitted through the saliva of a rabid animal. It can be contracted by a human when animal saliva enters an open cut. The infection is most often spread to humans when the rabid animal bites and breaks the skin.

Call a doctor at once if a child is bitten by an animal. Report the animal's size and color to the police. If the animal cannot be caught and tested for rabies, the child will need to undergo rabies immunization. This is a very painful series of shots. Without the immunization, the child can die.

All animal bites are dangerous. They carry great risk of infection. Most animals carry a wide variety of bacteria in their mouths, not the least of which is rabies. For that reason, it is important to take immediate action when a child is bit by an animal.

Open Wound Care

Some open wounds require medical attention. See 12-12. As the teacher, you can usually treat minor wounds such as abrasions and small

Open Wounds That Require Medical Attention

- An animal or human bite that has broken the skin.
- Bleeding that cannot be stopped despite all effort to control it.
- A cut on the face or some other part of the body where scar tissue will be noticeable.
- A wound that goes deeper than the outer layer of skin.
- Wounds with foreign objects such as dirt deep inside the tissue.
- A wound with foreign matter that cannot be removed.

12-12 Recognizing the severity of a wound can help a teacher determine if medical attention is necessary.

cuts. First, wash the area with warm water. Then, as you apply a bandage, bring the wound edges together. This will help prevent a scar from forming.

Assume that any loss of blood is harmful to the child. To control severe bleeding place a sterile gauze over the wound. Press on the wound with the palm of one hand. The object is to control the bleeding by pressing the blood vessels against something solid such as a bone or muscle.

If there is no sign of a fracture, elevate open wounds of the leg, arm, neck, or head. To elevate, raise the injured area above the level of the child's heart. The force of gravity will help reduce blood pressure in the injured area, thereby slowing blood loss.

Burns and Their Treatment

A **burn** is an injury caused by heat, radiation, or chemical agents. Burns vary in size, depth, and severity. Burns are generally classified by degree or depth. There are three classes: first-degree burns, second-degree burns, and third-degree burns. A burn victim can have more than one type of burn resulting from a single accident.

Children are commonly burned by hot liquids, cooking and electrical equipment, open fires, matches, chemicals such as strong detergents and acids, and overexposure to the sun. See 12-13. When developmentally appropriate, you should teach children to stop, drop and roll in case their clothes catch fire.

First-Degree Burns

First-degree burns are burns to the top layer of skin. They are the least severe of all burns. They may result from brief contact with hot objects, overexposure to the sun, or scalding by hot water or steam. Common signs include redness or mild discoloration, pain, and mild swelling. Healing is normally rapid because the burn does not go deep.

Special medical treatment is not needed for first-degree burns. Applying cold water to the burn will often help relieve some pain.

12-13 Care must be taken to keep children safe around items that cause burns.

Second-Degree Burns

Second-degree burns cause damage to underlying layers of skin. These burns are more serious than first-degree burns. They are caused by extreme overexposure to the sun, contact with hot liquids, and contact with flash fires from gasoline, kerosene, and other products.

Second-degree burns are marked by pain, blistering, swelling, and discoloration. Over several days, the burn is likely to swell a great deal. Due to the severity of these burns, they require medical treatment. Do not treat the burn by breaking blisters or by placing an ointment on the burn. This may cause infection. If infection arises in the wound, a second-degree burn can quickly become a third-degree burn.

Third-Degree Burns

Third-degree burns destroy the skin layer and nerve endings. They can be caused by open flames, burning clothing, immersion in hot water, contact with hot objects, and contact with live electrical wires.

Third-degree burns are very serious. They require prompt medical attention. An ambulance should be called at once.

Sunburn

Children can get first- or second-degree burns from exposure to the sun's ultraviolet rays. There is usually a 3- to 12-hour lapse in time between exposure and development of sunburn. Sunburn commonly does not require a hospital stay. However, sunburn can cause a child to be out of school several days due to swelling, pain, headache, and fever.

Protect children from sunburn when they are in your care. Apply a good sunscreen with a sun protection factor (SPF) of at least 15. Apply thoroughly to the ears, cheeks, nose, and shoulders. These are the areas that tend to burn. Schedule outdoor play periods to avoid exposure to the sun between 10:00 a.m. and 3:00 p.m. This is the time when the sun's rays are strongest.

Splinters

Children often get splinters. It will be your job to remove them. A pair of tweezers is the best tool for this process. First wash the area with soap and water. Then remove splinters at the same angle they entered the skin. Do not put any ointment or antiseptic on the wound. Cover with a sterile bandage until a doctor can see it. If you cannot remove a splinter, consult a doctor.

Insect Stings

Wasps, bees, hornets, yellow jackets, and fire ants are all stinging insects. The stings are painful to all children. For children who are allergic to insect stings, a sting can be fatal. React quickly when a child has been stung. Most deaths from insect stings occur within two hours of the incident.

A rash or swelling is usually the sign of a mild allergic reaction. A condition called **anaphylactic shock** results from an extremely allergic reaction. Shock symptoms develop quickly. These symptoms include weakness and collapse. Other signs include problems breathing,

a drop in blood pressure, and severe itching. Abdominal cramping, which may be followed by vomiting, can also occur. Watch the child closely. If you notice any of these signs, get prompt medical help.

Children who are allergic to stings and have been stung before may have their own medication and injection equipment. Make sure that it is available for emergencies. When you leave the school grounds, take the equipment.

Choking

Young children, especially those under four years of age, often put small objects in their mouths. Young children may also put too much food in their mouths at one time. In either of these cases, the object or food can get lodged in the windpipe, causing choking.

The best way for the child to get rid of the blockage is to cough it up. If the child can cry or talk, it may be best to wait and see if the child can dislodge the object on his or her own.

If, however, you see that the child is not able to breathe or speak, take immediate emergency steps. The procedure often used in choking emergencies is called the Heimlich maneuver (abdominal thrust), 12-14.

Dental Emergencies

Dental emergencies include cut or bit tongues, lips, or cheeks, knocked out permanent teeth, and broken teeth. With any of these problems, take quick action and remain calm.

If a child complains of a toothache, help the child rinse the affected area with water. Apply cold compresses if the face is swollen. Urge the parents to take the child to a dentist.

If a child has a cut or bit lip, tongue, or cheek, apply ice to the injured area. If you see blood, hold a clean gauze or cloth over the area. Gently apply pressure. Contact the child's parents if the bleeding does not stop in fifteen minutes. If the cut is severe, arrange to take the child to an emergency room for treatment.

To provide emergency care for a knocked out permanent tooth, first find the tooth. Pick it up by the crown, not the roots. If the tooth is dirty, rinse

First Aid for Children Who Are Choking

1. **Call for help!**
   - Do not slap the child on the back.
   - Do not hold the child upside down.
   - Do not probe the child's throat with your fingers.

2. **Recognize choking.**
   A child found unconscious, not breathing, and not showing signs of other injury is most likely choking. Bluish lips and fingernails also are signs of choking. DO NOTHING if the child is talking, breathing, or pink.

3. **Pick the child up from the rear around the waist.**
   Place fist of one hand above navel, but well below ribcage. Cover fist with other hand. For a very small child, use two fingers from each hand.

4. **Pull upward with both hands quickly, but gently three to four times.**
   Repeat if necessary to dislodge the object from the windpipe. For a very small child, lessen the force of thrusts.

5. **If the child is too big to pick up, kneel over the child.**
   Place hands above navel well below ribcage. Press upward into the stomach with three to four quick thrusts. Repeat if necessary.

6. **If all else fails, use back blows.**
   Drape a small child or infant over your arm or thigh so the child's head is down. The child's abdomen should be against your arm or thigh. Strike child sharply three to four times between the shoulder blades.

7. **Watch breathing and check pulse.**
   Be prepared to give mouth-to-mouth breathing and chest compressions.

12-14 The Heimlich maneuver can save the life of a choking child.

it gently under running water. However, avoid unnecessary handling. Keep the tooth moist. If the tooth is not broken, put it back in its socket and gently hold it in place. Some children may refuse to let you do this, or if there is swelling. In that case, place the tooth in a cup of cool, clean water or milk. Call the child's dentist and parents immediately. In order to save the tooth, the child must see a dentist at once.

If a child breaks or chips a tooth, report it to the parents. They can decide whether a dentist should be consulted. Gently clean the injured area with warm water. If there is swelling, use a cold compress to reduce the swelling.

Head Lice

To maintain a healthy environment, you will need to recognize head lice. **Head lice** are small insects that live on people's hair and scalp. They are small, about one-tenth to one-eighth of an inch in length. They have no wings and do not fly. They have six pairs of hooks in their mouths. With these hooks, they attach themselves to the hair shaft. Short legs and large claws help them keep their grip on hair. They produce small round eggs, called nits. These nits look like grains of sand.

It is difficult to see head lice with the naked eye. However, there are several signs you can recognize. Look for the following:

- A constant itch of the scalp, especially behind the ears and at the base of the scalp. Often the child will also have infected scratches or even a rash on the scalp.
- Small, silvery eggs attached to individual hairs. Usually a hand lens, or magnifying glass, will help reveal these.
- In severe cases, swollen lymph glands may appear in the neck or under the arm.

Head lice can spread from one infected person to another person through direct contact with the hair. Combs, brushes, hats, and bedding are key sources of transportation. Head lice can also crawl from person to person.

If one child in your classroom has head lice, most likely other children and staff members may get it, too. Send notices home to all parents if even one child has been infected with head lice. In some areas, a county or city nurse will conduct daily inspections at a center that has had an outbreak.

The best way to get rid of head lice is to seek medical help. Most physicians prescribe a medical shampoo. Doctors also suggest boiling or dry cleaning all personal items such as hats, combs, brushes, clothing, bedding, and furry toys. Items that cannot be washed or dry cleaned should be sealed in a plastic bag for 30 days, which is the life cycle of a louse. Rugs, upholstered furniture, and mattresses should be vacuumed. Combs and brushes should be boiled for 10 minutes or soaked for one hour in a bleach solution.

Caring for Children Who Become Ill

Whenever a child becomes ill, he or she should be moved into a separate area at once. An isolation area or room is needed in every early childhood center. Some states require that centers have isolation rooms.

Due to a lack of space, some centers do not have a special room for this purpose. Instead, a cot in the director's office is used for these emergencies.

When children become ill, they may vomit, develop diarrhea, or develop a fever. Child care workers need to know how to handle these signs of illness.

Children often vomit when ill. After the child has vomited, he or she will need a place to rest and keep warm. The child may request foods and drinks. However, only provide sips of water. Any other foods may prompt more vomiting.

Record the number of times the child vomits and the amount thrown up. At the same time, remove the child from the group. Always report any continued vomiting to parents.

Diarrhea may be caused by a virus, food contamination, or allergies. Many illnesses cause diarrhea, which typically lasts for two or three days. Chronic diarrhea may be a symptom of infection, inflammation of the intestines, or allergies. Chronic diarrhea may last for up to 10 days.

With diarrhea, a child will have an increased number of stools compared to the child's normal pattern. The stool may be loose, watery, and unformed.

Children who have diarrhea need to be isolated. Remove them from the classroom and contact their parents. They should be diarrhea-free for 24 hours before returning to the center.

Temperature Emergency

The human body normally maintains a constant internal temperature of 98.6°F. Normal temperatures range, from 97°F to just under 100°F. For this reason, it is important to have each child's normal temperature recorded on a health form.

A slight change in a child's temperature is a signal that the body is preparing against illness. A temperature at least two degrees above normal is significant. Most, but not all, young children will run a higher fever than adults.

A child may have a slight rise in temperature for several reasons. For example, the presence of infection raises a child's temperature. Too much physical activity will also raise a temperature. Temperature also may vary depending upon the time of the day. Temperatures are somewhat lower in the morning than the evening.

Call the parents right away if a child has a fever. Report any other unusual behavior.

Special Health Concerns

If a child with a special physical condition is enrolled in the program, you will need to make special plans for this child's health and well-being. Begin by discussing the child's condition with the parents. Be certain you understand what the condition is and what type of emergencies may arise. Find out what approach the center needs to take. Does the child require a special diet? Medication? Specific exercise? Also discuss with the parents how you can help the child feel comfortable.

Allergies

Since allergies are common in young children, you need to be aware of them. An **allergy** is a reaction of the body to a substance in the environment. Common reactions are sneezing, runny nose, coughing, itchy eyes, skin rashes, hives, diarrhea, or vomiting.

Allergies develop when a child is repeatedly put in contact with a substance in his or her environment. The body's immune system overreacts to the substance, causing an allergic reaction. These reactions may be caused by substances that can be swallowed, inhaled, or touched. Some reactions are caused by foods such as eggs and milk. Other common substances include dust, pollen, animal fur, or lotions and soaps that come in contact with the skin.

Treatment of allergies involves keeping the child away from the substance that triggers the allergic symptoms. Medications may be prescribed. Follow the parents' directions for treatment.

Diabetes

Diabetes is a disease in which the body cannot properly control the level of sugar in the blood. Having too much or too little blood sugar can cause serious health problems.

Children with diabetes cannot produce enough insulin. **Insulin** is a hormone that is needed to keep sugar in the blood at a proper level. As insulin is released, the blood sugar level drops. Healthy people produce insulin when the blood sugar level gets too high, but diabetic children do not. To correct this problem, diabetic children are given insulin injections. However, they must also balance food intake and exercise. If these are not balanced, an insulin reaction may occur.

Symptoms of an insulin reaction vary. Hunger, irritability, headaches, confusion, fatigue, crying, sweating, and drowsiness are all symptoms. With severe reactions, the child may pass out. If this happens, take the child to an emergency room or call a doctor at once. This condition is dangerous.

To avoid an insulin reaction, space the child's meals and snacks throughout the day. Glucose levels will remain constant when this is done. On days when the child exercises a great deal, food intake must be increased. This is because exercise decreases the amount of insulin needed and lowers glucose levels. Keep a supply of candy, soft drinks, and juice for the child to eat in case of an insulin reaction.

Epilepsy

Epilepsy is a condition in which a person has periodic seizures. There are two types of seizures. Grand mal seizures consist of repeated convulsions, or jerking, over the entire body. Petit mal seizures are milder than grand mal. The person may have a few muscles twitch briefly or may become confused with the surroundings.

Most seizures can be prevented with proper medical care. If a child in your program has epilepsy, discuss treatment with the parents. You may be required to give medication or take other action.

If a child has a grand mal seizure, you must make sure the child does not injure himself or herself. Clear the area around the child. Make sure the child stays lying down and keeps breathing. Do not place any object in the child's mouth during the seizure. Watch the child until the seizure is over. Then loosen any tight clothing around the child's neck. Take the child to a quiet place. Let the child rest on a cot or bed.

Contact the child's parents or doctor after any seizure, even a petit mal. The doctor may want to know what was happening before the seizure. This information may help the doctor find new ways to prevent further seizures. Therefore, try to record as many facts as you can about the time right before the seizure, as soon as you have a chance.

HIV Infection

HIV (human immunodeficiency virus) breaks down the body's immune system, eventually causing the disease **AIDS** (Acquired Immune Deficiency Syndrome). Most HIV-infected children acquired the virus from their mothers during pregnancy or delivery. The HIV virus can also be passed to an infant through breast milk from an HIV-infected mother. The incubation period for HIV-infected children is brief; most develop AIDS in less than two years.

HIV-infected children are at greater risk from common childhood infections that may occur in child care centers. These children often have immune systems that do not function properly to prevent infections. Exposure to diseases such as measles or chicken pox through other children at the center can cause serious illnesses. If HIV-infected children are exposed to any infectious diseases, contact their parents immediately. Prompt medical treatment is important for these children. The Center for Disease Control recommends that infected children only be excluded from group child care if they have open sores, uncontrollable nosebleeds, bloody diarrhea, or are at high risk for exposing others to blood-contaminated body fluids.

The center should maintain and protect all children's health. Center personnel should always use precautions whether or not HIV-infected children are attending the center. Some children at the center may have weakened immune systems resulting from other causes. Encourage frequent handwashing practices for the staff. Advise the staff to wear disposable gloves when handling children's stools, blood, or body fluids. Disposable gloves should also be worn when administering first aid. Use disposable towels, diapers, and tissues. Clean all solid surfaces with a disinfectant. Soiled items should be sealed in plastic bags.

Summary

Children's health can be protected, maintained, and improved in many ways during each day at the center. This is a very important part of the job of a teacher.

The best way to begin guiding children's health is by setting health policies. Policies might include requiring all children enrolled to have medical exams and immunizations. Contacting parents about health-related issues might also be addressed in your health policy.

The second step in guiding health is having knowledge of various illnesses and diseases. You will need to know how to control transmittable illnesses and diseases. You also will need to know what steps you should take in caring for children who are injured or become ill while at the center.

Protecting, maintaining, and even improving health is a major responsibility of a teacher. The teacher is trusted with the well-being of many children.

Review and Reflect

1. What will a preadmission medical exam help you learn about a child being enrolled?

2. List the immunization(s) needed for preschoolers at the following ages:
    A. 12-15 months
    B. 15-18 months
    C. 4-6 years

3. True or false. Each child should be provided with a washable cot or bed and clean sheets for napping.

4. Name four signs of illness you should watch for daily.

5. True or false. Parents should be contacted whenever a child shows symptoms of illness.

6. What is food poisoning?

7. In order to prevent the growth of bacteria, keep foods at a temperature above _____ or below _____°F.

8. A _____ is damage to the surface of the skin or body tissue.

9. The most common type of closed wound is a _____.

10. Skinned knees, scratched arms, and rope burns are examples of _____.

11. Why should a doctor be contacted immediately if a child is bit by an animal?

12. Which is the most serious burn, a first-degree burn or a third-degree burn?

13. How should you treat a burn caused by a child touching a hot object?

14. Most deaths from insect stings occur within how long of the incident?

15. What is the best way for a child to get rid of blockage in the windpipe?

16. List two symptoms of head lice.

17. _____ is a hormone that keeps sugar in the blood at a proper level.

18. What is epilepsy?

Apply and Explore

1. Invite a first aid instructor to give a demonstration on the Heimlich maneuver (abdominal thrust).

2. Prepare a handout listing the health policies of a center for preschool children.

3. Stage a panel discussion on ways of promoting a healthy environment for young children.

4. Write a research paper on a serious illness that can affect children. Explain the illness itself and dispel any commonly believed untruths about the illness. Explain various treatments for the illness.

Part 3
Guiding Children

As you work in child care, guidance will be a routine part of your experiences with children. Children need positive guidance to learn how to get along with others and to stay safe.

In this part, you will study and practice techniques for guiding children throughout the day. You will gain insight into methods for handling such guidance problems as negativism and fear.

You will learn guidelines for establishing and enforcing rules throughout the classroom. This part will also teach you ways to guide children through such daily routines as dressing, eating, and napping.

Understanding children's behavior is an important part of guidance.

Chapter 13

Developing Guidance Skills

After studying this chapter, you will be able to

■ identify goals of effective guidance.

■ list personality traits of effective early childhood teachers.

■ describe principles of direct and indirect guidance.

■ explain various techniques for effective guidance.

■ summarize ways to promote a positive self-concept in each child.

Terms to Know

guidance
prosocial behaviors
indirect guidance
direct guidance
positive reinforcement
consequence
natural consequences
artificial (logical) consequences
time out
I-messages
prompting
redirecting
modeling
active listening

Alicia sat in the corner looking at a library book. Slowly she ripped a page from the book. On the other side of the room, Wyatt knocked Hunter's block tower over. Then she sped to the art table and grabbed Ryder's play dough. At the same time, May entered the room, greeted another child, and threw her coat on the floor.

How will you, as a teacher, guide each of these children? Guiding children is a complex process. Understanding and guiding children's behavior requires knowledge of child growth and development. It also requires the ability to understand each child's behavior. This is a constant process that never ends. As a teacher, you will continually learn more about your role in guiding young children.

Goals of Guidance

Guidance consists of direct and indirect actions used by an adult to help children develop appropriate behavior patterns, 13-1. Effective guidance should maintain children's self-esteem and produce a desired change in behavior. Self-control is the long-term goal of guidance. That is, the children should learn to direct their own behavior without outside control.

Another goal of guidance is to promote prosocial behaviors among the children. **Prosocial behaviors** include acts of kindness toward others. They are behaviors that demonstrate cooperation and helpfulness. The following are examples of prosocial behaviors:

■ accepting others' feelings

■ verbally and physically comforting others

13-1 Younger children often require more guidance than older children.

- cooperating with others in play and cleanup time
- sharing toys and materials
- sharing affection
- showing concern

Guidance and You

As a teacher, your personality will affect the behavior of the children in your care. Many studies have been conducted to determine the effect that specific personality traits have on children's behavior. These studies show that effective early childhood teachers encourage and show interest in children. These teachers use more suggestions than commands. Children respond faster to suggestions than commands.

According to research, teachers should interact often with their children and ask *open-ended questions*. These questions require more than one-word answers. Children in this type of environment will show certain positive characteristics. These include independence, verbalization, cooperation, task persistence, and high self-esteem. See 13-2.

Studies also note that uncooperative teachers have more hyperactive, disruptive, and

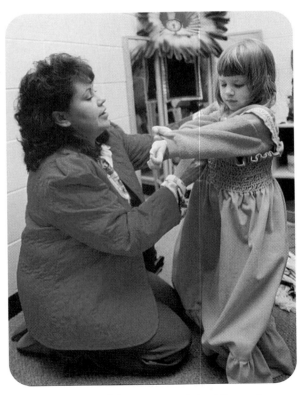

13-2 This child will learn a great deal through interaction with the teacher.

bored children. On the other hand, children in the classes of talkative teachers tend to be more shy. Nurturing teachers have children in their classes who interact easily with others.

Aggressive and attention-seeking behavior on the part of the children is also influenced by the teacher. This behavior occurs most often with permissive teachers. Such teachers often fail to get involved with or stop aggressive and attention-seeking behavior. The children who behave this way may see the teacher's lack of involvement as permission to engage in such behavior.

Studies also show that a teacher's behavior is affected by available space. When the ratio of space to children is low, teachers are more demanding. They tend to restrict play. For example, self-selected play may be limited to playing with toys at a table. Likewise, a greater ratio of space to children results in a more relaxed teacher.

Preparing for Guidance

There are some general guidelines for developing effective guidance skills. Study these guidelines. They will help you become an effective teacher.

One of the first steps toward effective guidance is observation of the children. Watch and note how individual children behave in certain situations. This will help you understand the children in your class. Review the observation techniques described in Chapter 3.

Ask yourself how you respond to each of the children in your class. Do you have any biases? Are you expecting certain behaviors from children based on race, sex, personality, or appearance? The stereotypes you hold may affect your perception of a child. For example, do you expect Clarice to be better behaved because both of her parents are doctors? Being honest about your own attitudes and how they may influence your interactions will allow you to be more objective.

Another important guideline is to plan with other teachers. Sharing observations, feelings, and suggestions will help you fully understand the children. One teacher may be able to add to your observations, 13-3. As a result, you will better understand why a child refuses to take part in art activities.

Next, do not talk to other adults when you are teaching, unless it is important. The children's needs should always come first. Being alert to these needs requires your full attention. Make a practice of talking with other teachers only if necessary. Save other comments for after program hours.

Finally, sit with the children whenever possible. You will be closer to the children's level.

13-3 With the help of other teachers, you can learn more about the children in your center.

As a result, they will find it easier to approach you and gain your attention. Do not interrupt an activity unless you can add to knowledge or safety. Let the children begin interaction with you. Remember that to develop independence and self-confidence, never do for the children what they can do for themselves.

Direct Guidance

Child guidance may be direct or indirect. **Indirect guidance** involves outside factors that influence behavior. The layout of the center is a form of indirect guidance. Indirect guidance will be discussed later in the chapter.

Direct guidance involves nonverbal (physical) and verbal actions. Nonverbal actions include facial gestures such as eye contact, a smile, or even a surprised look. Your words are also a form of direct guidance.

Facial expressions can communicate a variety of messages ranging from disapproval and sadness to approval and reassurance. Body gestures are another type of direct guidance. Putting your arm around a child is one form of direct guidance.

Young children gain much information from nonverbal actions. They might learn the caregiver's mood and expectations. Infants and toddlers focus most of their attention on what they see and feel rather than on verbal clues. Even as children begin to pay more attention to words, they still rely on nonverbal actions to help them understand messages.

Your nonverbal actions need to reinforce what you are communicating verbally. Watch that your words match your nonverbal signals. For example, if you are asking a child to stop a behavior, your facial expression should also convey disapproval. Children become confused when adults' words give one message and their actions another.

Direct guidance principles are shown in 13-4. Following these principles will help you develop direct guidance skills.

Use Simple Language

Using simple language is important. Young children have limited vocabularies. To communicate clearly, use language they can understand.

Direct Guidance Principles
• Use simple language.
• Speak in a relaxed voice.
• Be positive.
• Offer choices with care.
• Encourage independence and cooperation.
• Be firm.
• Be consistent.
• Provide time for change.
• Consider feelings.
• Intervene when necessary.

13-4 These direct guidance principles outline the verbal and nonverbal skills you will need for effective guidance.

Consider the ages of the children. Adjust your vocabulary to fit those ages. For instance, two-year-olds usually learn the word *big* before they learn *large*. Therefore, use the word *big* with these children. Working with three-year-olds, you might use the word *large*. This depends, however, on their level of development. With four- and five-year-olds, again adjust the level of your vocabulary. With these children, you might say *huge*.

Speak in a Relaxed Voice

Speak in a calm, quiet, relaxed tone of voice. Children will listen to this type of voice. Save loud voices for emergencies. At those times, you will gain the children's attention with a loud voice. If you raise your voice during the normal course of the day, children will become used to this level. When an emergency occurs, you may not be able to gain their attention. In addition, when you raise your voice, the children will also raise their voices. The classroom will become a very noisy place.

Be Positive

Guide the children by telling them what to do, as opposed to what not to do. Children will feel more comfortable with a positive comment. For example, instead of saying "Don't put that puzzle on the floor," say "Put the puzzle on the table." See 13-5. This will remind the children of the rule that puzzles are used on a table.

Using Positive Guidance	
Negative	**Positive**
"Do not put the puzzle on the floor."	"Put the puzzle on the table."
"Do not touch anything!"	"Place your hands in your pockets."
"Do not run."	"Please walk."
"Quit screaming."	"Use your indoor voice."
"Do not drip paint."	"Wipe your brush on the container."
"Do not get paint on your clothes."	"Put on a painting smock."
"Do not rip the pages."	"Turn the pages carefully."
"Do not walk in front of the swing."	"Walk around the swing, please."
"Do not use your fingers."	"Use your fork."

13-5 Be aware of negative comments you make and try to replace them with positive comments.

Offer Choices with Care

New, unskilled teachers sometimes confuse offering a choice with giving a direction. For example, when it is lunchtime, the teacher may say "Do you want to go in for lunch?" By asking this question, the child is given a choice. If the child is not interested in eating lunch then, he or she may answer by saying no.

Children should be offered a choice only when you want them to have a choice. In this case, a better direction would be "It is time for lunch now," or "We need to go inside for lunch now." Make sure that once you offer a choice you allow the child to carry through with his or her choice. For example, you might ask a child if she or he prefers watering the plants or feeding the fish. If the child chooses feeding the fish, accept the choice. Do not try to get children to change their minds. When you do this, you are telling them that there really was not a choice.

Encourage Independence and Cooperation

Give children the least amount of help they need. In this way, they will have opportunities to learn independence. For instance, encourage children to dress and feed themselves. Encourage them to share responsibility for keeping the classroom clean and orderly.

Some children begin school dependent on others. At home, these children have an adult or sibling to attend to their needs. As a result, they come to school expecting the teacher to dress them, pick up after them, and intercede for them. Encourage independence from the start in order to change this behavior. For instance, when Eugene reports that Tommy is teasing him, ask Eugene how he feels when this happens. If he says that he does not like it, tell him to share his feelings with Tommy. Likewise, if Talia does not want to share her clay, Eugene needs to tell Talia that he is mad because she will not share.

Children only become independent if allowed the opportunity. Many people are surprised at the competence of three-, four-, and five-year-old children who are provided the chance to do for themselves. See 13-6.

These children also must learn to help each other. Encourage children to work with each other. When Toby tells you he cannot zip his coat, say "Ask Joanne if she can help you." If Marlene cannot tie her shoe, say "Ask Luis to help you tie it." These experiences help the children to learn prosocial behaviors.

Be Firm

Be firm when disciplining children. At the same time, speak in a quiet voice. Some children are very demanding. When you tell them that

13-6 Even young children can do for themselves, if given a chance.

they cannot do something, they may cry. Some may even throw temper tantrums. If it is behavior that you cannot allow to continue, you must stand firm.

When a child throws a temper tantrum, you may feel like giving in. If you do, the child will likely use the same method again when he or she wants his or her own way. Effective guidance requires firmness.

Be Consistent

Children are good at testing adults. If they feel an adult is not firm in disciplining, they will repeat their unacceptable behavior. In fact, they may want to find out what will happen if they continue to repeat their unacceptable behavior. For this reason, discipline and approval should be given consistently. For instance, do not discipline children one day and praise them the next for running to the door at playtime.

Make sure that you are also consistent from child to child. Children quickly develop a sense of fairness. If you tell one child to pick up the

toys at cleanup time, all children should have to clean up. When you are not consistent, children will challenge your requests.

Provide Time for Change

Young children need time to change activities. It is important to provide them with ample time for change. Without this time, children can become confused. By allowing time, you will provide children with an adjustment period. For instance, when children are preparing to go outside during cold weather, allow them time to put on their coats, hats, and mittens. This time will allow them to prepare themselves for new activities and new surroundings.

Consider Feelings

Although it is not always included in daily lesson plans, learning about feelings and emotions is an important part of any day at the center. Children need to recognize, understand, and express their feelings.

Young children often have strong feelings. These feelings often center around control of their environment. Such feelings often relate to their bodies, siblings, eating, friendship, and toileting.

Feelings are best discussed in small group settings or alone with a child. For some children, talking about feelings and emotions is difficult. It is your responsibility to help them understand their feelings. See 13-7.

Facing someone else's pain is also difficult for young children. You will observe that children do not know how to deal with the pain of others. When a new child begins school and cries over separation from parents, the other children do not usually get involved. Some may pretend to not see or hear the child. Others may have a pained look on their faces. This shows sensitivity. Although they may feel sympathy, they tend not to get involved. Usually, if a child is bleeding, only then will they get involved. They will bring the child to you for a bandage. However, they will not usually console the child.

You can show them how to help these children. For instance, if Patrick is crying, put your arm around him. By doing this, you will teach the children a way to comfort each other. They will learn that crying can be mended with a hug.

13-7 Many children do not know how to handle their feelings. They may require your help in order to feel good about themselves.

13-8 Children need to be encouraged to help with cleanup.

Young children also need to learn how to handle mistakes. When a child spills milk or breaks a toy, do not overreact. Instead, show the child how to handle the mistake. The child will then know not to fear mistakes. See 13-8. For example, remind the child who spilled the milk that the milk must be cleaned up. Show the child how to do this. Depending on the situation, you may wish to help clean up.

Intervene When Necessary

To be an effective teacher, you will need to know when to intervene. Allow children to explore on their own. Interrupt only when you can add to their knowledge or promote their safety. For example, if a four-year-old says "Cows give eggnog at Christmas," clarify this statement. Unless you intervene, children who are listening may believe this comment.

Safety intervention will often require words and action. If James is not careful climbing up the slide, you will need to walk over and review the rules with him. Make clear the dangers of falling. Intervention would also be required if you were observing a group of children and noticed that a child was in danger of being hurt. It is important to intervene before this happens by redirecting the play or providing assistance.

You may also need to intervene for health purposes. Remind children to dress properly for outdoor play in the winter. Encourage children to cover their mouths when they cough. When cooking, remind children not to taste the food using the cooking utensils.

Children need to learn to be friends with all the children. Thus, do not allow children to be excluded from play because of age, race, or sex. When Erica says "Only girls can come into the playhouse," it is important for you to intervene. One way to handle this is to say "This school is for everyone." By doing so, you will give the children the words they need to defend their right to participate.

You must also intervene when children are impolite. Sometimes you will hear a child say "I do not like you," or "You are ugly." When this happens, you need to intervene. Point out to the child that such words can hurt another's feelings. With young children, that may be sufficient to end the behavior.

Property arguments may also require intervention. Center property does not belong to the children, but to the school. Therefore, the children must share it. During a property argument, remind the children to share. If this does not work, give the equipment to one child for a set time period. Then give it to the other child for another time period. For instance, tell Mandy that she may play with the truck in the morning and Mark may play with it in the afternoon. Then make sure each child has a turn.

It is important for children to learn that they cannot grab materials from others. No matter how strong the child's feelings, others have rights, too. Children need to take turns painting at the easel, participating in cooking activities, and watering plants, 13-9. While children learn and develop, you will need to intervene. That is why in many early childhood classrooms, you will hear a teacher saying many times a day "You can have a turn next," or "After she is finished, you can paint."

Indirect Guidance

You will recall that indirect guidance involves outside factors that influence behavior. The physical setup of a center is a form of indirect guidance. It can indirectly influence both the children's and teacher's behavior. For example, a well-planned facility makes supervision easier. The fact that you can supervise properly will help you to feel relaxed and in control. The children will feel safer knowing they are being protected.

In order to carefully supervise young children, an open classroom is best. Stand with your back toward the classroom wall. You should be able to view the entire room. Such an arrangement will allow you to observe and give help when needed. It will also reduce your own fatigue, since you will not have to run back and forth between areas.

A healthy, safe environment can be promoted through the physical setup of the facility. In one large room, you will be able to see everything that happens, 13-10. Therefore, you can step in when dangerous situations arise. For instance, the behavior of two-year-old children needs close monitoring. Many two-year-olds will hit another child instead of saying "I do not like that." With the proper physical arrangement, you

13-9 These children have learned that they must take turns as they participate in activities.

13-10 These teachers can see all the children as they sit in this large room.

can see such situations occurring and step in immediately.

Young children, and especially two-year-olds, often do not have well-developed large motor skills. They often stumble, trip, or fall. To reduce the number of these accidents, large, open areas are best. Shelving units should be placed around the outside walls of the room.

Children's independence can also be encouraged through the physical setup of the facility. Independence should be a learning objective of every early childhood program, no matter the ages or abilities of children in the program. For example, you should encourage toddlers to use the washroom if they have developed control of their bowels and bladders. For this reason, the washrooms should be easy to find and use. Sinks, toilets, and hand dryers should be set at the children's level.

Children can also be encouraged to hang up their own coats and assist with cleanup. To encourage this, provide low hooks for hanging coats and hats. Low shelf units and sinks will encourage children to help with cleanup. All toys and materials should have a designated place in the classroom. Placing a picture of the item on a shelf or container is one way of

assisting the children. When containers are marked, teachers are usually more successful in having the children replace toys and equipment to the proper storage place.

Through these arrangements, you will save time and energy assisting the children. This will allow you more time to observe and work with the children and plan meaningful activities.

Techniques for Effective Guidance

As an early childhood teacher, you will teach children acceptable behaviors. Likewise, the children in your classroom will also teach each other. Whatever effect you have on the children's behavior, the children, in turn, will affect others.

There are specific guidance techniques that can be useful in guiding children's behavior. These techniques include positive reinforcement and the use of consequences. In addition, you will want to include warning, time out, I-messages, praising, affirming, suggesting, prompting, persuading, redirecting, modeling, listening, ignoring, and encouraging.

Positive Reinforcement

Children's behavior can often be molded by rewarding positive behavior. This technique is called **positive reinforcement**. For instance, if you thank a child for holding the door, the child will most likely hold the door again. You have provided a positive reinforcement of the child's behavior. Positive messages will encourage the child to repeat the behavior. Repeated positive reinforcement will result in repeated behavior.

You must be careful when using positive reinforcement that you are rewarding behaviors you want the child to repeat. Teachers sometimes do not realize that they are rewarding children for unacceptable behavior. For instance, laughing at a child who is acting silly at group time is reinforcing the child's behavior. This reaction is seen by the child as a reward. It encourages the child to repeat the behavior.

Using Consequences

Consequences are important in molding children's behavior. A **consequence** is a result that follows an action or behavior. Consequences can be very effective in shaping behavior. There are two types of consequences: natural consequences and artificial (logical) consequences.

Natural consequences are those experiences that follow naturally as a result of a behavior. They do not require anyone's intervention. For example, the natural consequence of forgetting to put away an art project is that it might be thrown away during cleanup time. The natural consequence of forgetting to put on your gloves is that your hands will get cold. Natural consequences can be very effective in guiding children's behavior, but they cannot be used if a child's safety is at risk. For instance, if a child runs into the street without stopping to look for cars, the child could be hit by a car. In this case, an adult must intervene to make sure the child stops and looks before crossing a street.

When natural consequences cannot be used to guide behavior, artificial consequences may be established. **Artificial consequences** (also called logical consequences) are those that are deliberately set up by an adult to show what will happen if a rule is broken. The consequences should be related to the behavior as much as possible.

When using artificial consequences, the children must first be made aware of the rules. Then they need to know the consequences that you (or the center) have established if the rules are broken. For example, if Brad drives his scooter into Lawrence, tell him to stop. Remind him of the consequence if he does not stop. The consequence might be that he will have to give up his turn on the scooter. If Brad runs into Lawrence again, enforce the consequence. Thus, Brad will learn that driving into others is not acceptable behavior.

Warning

When children fail to follow a classroom rule, you must remind them that they are misbehaving and their behavior will have consequences. You are warning the children. Warn only once. If the behavior continues, proceed with the consequences. Effective warnings contain only two parts. First, state the misbehavior. Then state the consequences. Examples include:

- "Joel, sand needs to be kept in the sandbox. If you throw it again, you will lose your turn."
- "Tunde, either choose a place in the circle, or I will choose one for you."
- "Mandy, blocks are not to be used like guns. If you use the block as a gun again, you will need to leave the block area."

When warning children, use a firm voice. Your voice should reflect your displeasure with the child's behavior.

Time Out

Time out is a guidance technique that involves moving a child away from others for a short period of time. Time out is used when a child's disruptive behavior cannot be ignored. The child needs time to calm down. In some classrooms, this technique is used when a child is out of control with anger. To protect the other children, the teacher moves the angry child to a quiet place away from the group. This is one way of allowing the child to gain self-control. However, time out should never be used as a form of punishment.

Time out can be an effective guidance tool for some children. Four- and five-year-olds usually understand the purpose better than younger children. By this age, most children have the ability to understand their behavior can have negative consequences. Time out is an example of an artificial consequence.

To be effective, tell children in advance what behaviors will result in time out. If you decide to use time out, carry it out in an unemotional, direct way. Simply state the rule that has been broken and say "Time out." Promptly remove the child to an area away from the group, but within your vision. Nothing further should be said. You do not want to reward the child with added attention. Limit the time to three minutes. If the child returns to the group and the behavior continues, add another minute to the original time.

Not all teachers agree with the use of time out. These teachers feel the technique should seldom be used, if at all.

I-Messages

When a child misbehaves, use an "I-message" to communicate your feelings. An **I-message** tells the child how you feel about his or her behavior. It does not place blame with the child, which would cause the child to feel that he or she was a bad person. Rather, it helps the child learn how others view his or her actions.

Your I-message statement should include three parts: (1) the child's behavior, (2) your feelings about the behavior, and (3) the effects of the behavior. After you state the I-message, you should then say what you want done. For instance, you may say "When I see you hitting Yasser, I am unhappy because you are hurting him. I want you to stop hitting Yasser." Note that in this example, the behavior is hitting, it makes you feel unhappy, and the effects cause another child to be hurt. An I-message shows the child how his actions are perceived by others.

Praising and Affirming

Praising involves recognizing children's accomplishments. Young children thrive on praise. When you say "I like the way you helped, Cedric," you tell the child he is important. This is a form of verbal praise. See 13-11. Nonverbal praise can also be used successfully. A smile,

Ways to Say "Good for You!"

"Wonderful!"
"I love it!"
"Beautiful."
"You are a good listener."
"I like the way you listen."
"Good work!"
"I am proud of you."
"I am pleased."
"Congratulations!"
"Perfect!"
"Fantastic!"
"Terrific!"

"Marvelous."
"Thank you."
"Lovely."
"Super!"
"I like the way you work."
"I like the way you try."
"I like the way you help each other."
"You are a good worker."
"Let me show your work to others."
"You do that very well."
"I can tell you are trying."

13-11 Opportunities for praising young children are limitless.

wink, or pat on the back are all types of non-verbal praise. Displaying a child's work on a bulletin board is also a form of praise. Some teachers paste a star or sticker on paperwork or artwork that a child has done. This is also non-verbal praise.

When praising young children remember the following:

- Make praise age appropriate.
- Give praise immediately. It is most effective to praise children while they are still in the act.
- When praising, always establish eye contact.
- Do not overuse praise. If you do, it will not be as effective.

Affirming helps the children by identifying and labeling positive behavior. Like adults, children love to be acknowledged, and they repeat behaviors that are acknowledged. A teacher might use such affirmations as "You enjoy helping others" or "Raul likes having you share the toys with him." When behaviors are affirmed, they are likely to be repeated.

Suggesting

Suggesting means placing thoughts for consideration into children's minds. This, in turn, often leads to action. For instance, after Candy spills her milk at the table, you may have to suggest she clean it up. To do this, say "Candy, here is a sponge." This will likely be enough to encourage Candy to wipe the spill. If not, you may have to add, "You need to wipe up the milk." During snack time, you may suggest to the children that they try a new fruit. This can be done directly or indirectly. Simply stating "This fruit is delicious," is enough to encourage some children to try the food. A more direct approach may work for other children. For example, you may say "Tammy, try this fruit today. It is delicious."

Always make suggestions positive. Lead children's thoughts and feelings in a desirable direction. If you tell the children to listen carefully to the story, they will probably follow your advice, 13-12. However, if you tell the children that they are noisy and behaving poorly, they will probably continue to act this way. Negative suggestions usually produce negative behavior.

13-12 This boy's teacher suggested he sit on his carpet square and listen to a story.

Effective teachers use suggestions many times each day. You will have many daily opportunities to mold behavior through suggestion. For example, Darlene may forget to put the blocks back on the shelf. A suggestion may work here. Corinna may drop her coat on the floor as she enters the room. A suggestion may work here, also.

Prompting

Children often need **prompting** either to stop an unacceptable action or start an acceptable one. Prompting can also be used to prepare children for transitions. Prompting differs from suggesting because a response is required of a prompt. Examples of verbal prompting include:

- "Moses, do you remember where we keep the play dough?"
- "Glenda, what is our rule when riding bikes?"
- "Michelle, do you remember where you put your painting?"

Prompting can also be nonverbal. You may place a finger over your lip at group time to signal "Quiet, please!" Rules printed on a poster board (if age appropriate) are nonverbal prompts. Frowning can show your disapproval. Even turning a child around to attend to group activities is a form of prompting.

Generally, make prompting simple and noncritical. Prompt in a calm, impersonal manner. You may ask a child "What are you supposed to be doing?" or "What should we be doing before we have a snack?"

Prompting may need to be repeated often before acceptable behavior is developed. A child who is new to the center may need to be prompted for several days to hang his or her coat on the hook before this behavior is developed. Once the child complies, praise this behavior.

Persuading

By *persuading*, you encourage children to act or behave in a certain way by appealing to their basic wants and needs. Seeing things from their point of view will give you an idea on the best way to approach a situation.

Link behavior with the children's feelings. For instance, a child who hangs back from an activity might be persuaded to join by appealing to his or her need to belong. You might say, "We are having such fun, Elizabeth. Will you join us?"

A child who interferes with another child's activities also needs to be persuaded. You can persuade the interfering child by helping him or her understand the other child's feelings. For instance, you may say, "Kenny, Joanie is afraid that if you keep jumping, you will knock her building down."

Redirecting

Children often need **redirecting** to a substitute activity. When redirecting, you divert, or turn, their attention in a different direction. One way to redirect is through distraction. A child who cries when his or her parent leaves may need to be distracted. Choose an interesting toy or book to distract the child's interest away from the parent.

Redirection encourages children to express themselves in more socially acceptable ways. For example, an active child may constantly push around other children. To help this child release energy, provide activities that are physically demanding. Playing with a punching bag, carpentry tools, or play dough will provide an outlet for extra energy. The key to redirecting is providing an appealing substitute.

Modeling

Children learn by imitating others. Whenever you speak or move, you are **modeling** behavior. Modeling involves both verbal and nonverbal actions. It is a powerful tool when working with young children. At an early age, children become aware of the actions of the adults around them. Thus, it is important to set a good example. Social development is an important part of the early childhood curriculum. Much of what children learn is the result of watching others and imitating their behavior. Set an example by modeling prosocial behavior, 13-13.

Listening

Listening involves giving children your full attention. It is more effective when you are at eye level with the child. Nodding also conveys your attention. One type of listening is called active listening. Through **active listening**, you first listen to what the child is saying to you. Then you respond to the child by repeating what was just said. This lets the child know that you have heard what he or she said and that you accept it. It does not mean, however, that you solve the problem. See 13-14.

For instance, Jerome was playing in the housekeeping area. He wanted to use the broom that Sherry was using. He asked Sherry, "May I have the broom?" Sherry responded, "No, I am using it. Besides, I had it first." Jerome got angry. He ran over and shared the incident with the teacher's aide. The aide listened carefully to what Jerome was saying. Then the aide repeated what Jerome had just said to make certain she heard correctly. The aide said, "You are angry because Sherry will not let you use the broom." Jerome learned that people will listen to him and his feelings will be accepted. However, he will have to solve the problem himself.

13-13 Modeling can be used in many situations at the center.

13-14 Active listening is a nonverbal skill that helps children develop self-esteem.

Ignoring

Do not encourage inappropriate behavior. When a child is able to gain your attention by whining, crying, or throwing a temper tantrum, you have reinforced the child's behavior. The child will likely continue this behavior rather than control it.

If a child's inappropriate behavior is not dangerous, avoid giving the child attention. Do not look directly at the child. Avoid acknowledging the behavior. This is called *ignoring*. On the other hand, praise the child when he or she models acceptable behavior.

Ignoring is inappropriate when the child's behavior is harmful, either verbally or physically, to other children. Likewise, it is inappropriate to ignore a child who is damaging property. If you choose to ignore the behavior, you should tell the child what the behavior is that you are ignoring. Also, tell the child the behavior you desire. Then, do not look at the child. Be sure that you do not acknowledge the behavior in any way through either your actions or your words. When the child models acceptable behavior, praise him or her.

For example, Mrs. Garcia has noticed that whenever Miranda wants something she whines and uses baby talk. Mrs. Garcia tells Miranda that she will not pay attention to her until she uses her "big girl" voice. Mrs. Garcia also demonstrates for Miranda what she means. Miranda continues to whine and use baby talk, so Mrs. Garcia ignores Miranda's requests. Eventually Miranda uses the appropriate words, and Mrs. Garcia answers Miranda's request.

Changing a young child's behavior is usually not a quick process. In fact, the behavior may actually become worse before it improves! It is important to be patient. Unless you ignore unpleasant behavior 100 percent of the time, it is likely to reoccur.

Encouraging

Encouraging is a guidance technique that helps children believe in themselves. By encouraging children, you are recognizing their efforts and improvements. You may observe that successful teachers often use this technique. They want children to feel good about themselves. Examples of encouraging phrases you may use include:

- You can do it all by yourself!
- You know how it works.
- I know you can fix it.
- You were able to do it last week.
- You must be pleased.

Promoting a Positive Self-Concept

When guiding children's behavior, your actions should always promote a positive self-concept in each child. A child's self-concept is the qualities the child believes he or she possesses. It is a result of beliefs, feelings, and perceptions a child has of himself or herself, 13-15. Children's self-concepts reflect the feelings others have for them and the confidence they have in themselves.

Children's self-concepts are mirrored in their behavior, 13-16. A child who lacks confidence may reveal feelings of inadequacy. For instance, the child may not be willing to try new activities, may withdraw from an experience, show little curiosity, or appear overly anxious or overly dependent. This child may also be hostile, seek attention, or perform poorly.

13-15 A child with a healthy self-concept is not afraid to explore new and different types of play.

Children with positive self-concepts perceive themselves as able and important. They accept and respect themselves as well as others. These children are often able to judge their own skills and cope with problems they confront. Typically, they are more objective and understand other people's behaviors.

You can promote or undermine a child's self-concept by your words and actions. In many subtle ways, a teacher affects how children feel about themselves. Your reactions may give children the feeling that they are bad or annoying. For instance, you may need to ask children to be quiet. Consider the message the children will receive. If you ask them to be quiet because they are too noisy, they may feel that they are bad

Checklist for Evaluating a Child's Self-Concept	Yes	No
Does the child speak positively about himself/herself?		
Does the child appear to feel proud of his/her appearance?		
Is the child proud of accomplishments?		
Does the child accept failure?		
Is the child willing to try new experiences?		
Does the child make decisions on his/her own?		
Is the child independent?		
Does the child share his/her possessions?		
Is the child willing to vocalize thoughts?		
Is the child naturally curious?		
Does the child usually appear calm and controlled?		

13-16 Observation is an important tool in social studies. Not only is it used to determine skill level, it can also be used to evaluate a child's self-concept.

Teacher Checklist for Promoting a Positive Self-Concept

☑ Do I observe children carefully before speaking?
☑ Am I an open-minded person?
☑ Do I recognize and value differences in children?
☑ Do I constantly strive to gain more knowledge about the world and share it with the children?
☑ Do I provide the children with choices so that they may become independent decision makers?
☑ Am I constantly trying to increase my human relations skills?
☑ Do I state directions in a positive manner?
☑ Do I encourage parents to share their attitudes with me?
☑ Do I avoid showing favoritism?
☑ Do I listen to the children?
☑ Do I help children sort out their mixed emotions?
☑ Do I plan developmentally appropriate activities?
☑ Do I respect cultural differences in young children?
☑ Do I permit enough time to complete activities?
☑ Do I call attention to positive interactions between and among children?
☑ Do I make expectations clear?
☑ Do I acknowledge the child's attempts at tasks as well as accomplishments?
☑ Do I encourage children to use self-statements of confidence?

13-17 The teacher's behavior can promote or hinder development of a positive self-concept.

people because they make too much noise. If you ask them to make less noise because it is disturbing you, the children see that they can help you by being quiet. They do not feel that they are bad, noisy people.

If a child spills juice, do you call the child clumsy or react negatively by scowling? Instead, do you accept this as common behavior for a young child and help wipe up the spill? Caring adults are able to separate children's needs from their own. Clearly, they are able to see the difference between adult needs and children's.

Every day you provide subtle messages in the form of verbal and nonverbal feedback. These signals can either promote or decrease children's sense of self-worth. You can make children feel appreciated, worthy, loved, and secure by being accepting, concerned, and respectful. Helping young children grow to respect themselves, as well as others, is not easy. Listen carefully to what you say and how you say it. Consider the impact your words have on the children. Watch the subtle ways you interact with them. Your message should always convey that they are important. Review the checklist shown in Figure 13-17 to see if you are promoting positive self-concepts.

There are many ways you as a teacher can promote the development of positive self-concepts. You can plan activities that focus on making children feel good about themselves and their abilities. Several are described in Figure 13-18. You can also provide children with experiences with which they will have success.

Building Positive Self-Concepts

- After an outing, make an experience chart. Include children's names and their exact words.
- Provide a special chair and crown for each child on his or her birthday. Take an instant snap-shot of the child.
- Make a slide show of the children in action: on a field trip, at a party, at a play, or at the end of an ongoing project. Present the slide show to the children.
- Record children's stories from sharing and telling time on a large piece of posterboard titled Our News.
- Make charts of children's likes. For instance, you might chart children's favorite colors or animals.
- Make charts of hair and eye color to reinforce concepts of similarities and differences among people.
- Tape record children telling their own stories.
- Make height and weight charts.
- Add a full-length mirror to the room.
- Label children's lockers and artwork with their names.
- Make a mobile or bulletin board with the children's pictures or names.
- Provide children with family face puppets. Encourage children to act out imaginary family situations using the puppets.
- Outline children's bodies on large sheets of paper for the children to paint or color and display.
- Provide dramatic play kits to encourage children to try new roles and roles that they find interesting. For example, a carpenter kit could include a hat, an apron, a hammer, nails, and boxes or scraps of wood.
- Display pictures of the children at eye level.
- Use children's names frequently in songs and games.

13-18   These activities are quite useful for helping children build positive self-concepts.

Summary

Effective guidance skills are necessary for effective teaching. Effective guidance should maintain children's self-esteem and produce a desired change in behavior. Self-control is the long-term goal of guidance. That is, the children should learn to direct their own behavior without outside control. Another goal of guidance is to promote prosocial behaviors among the children.

Child guidance may be direct or indirect. Direct guidance involves physical and verbal actions. The direct guidance principles described in this chapter will help you to more effectively guide children's behavior. Indirect guidance involves outside factors that influence behavior. One important factor that indirectly affects guidance is the physical setup of the classroom.

Guidance techniques will help you put your guidance skills to work. Specific techniques you may wish to use include positive reinforcement, natural and artificial consequences, warning, time out, I-messages, praising, affirming, suggesting, prompting, persuading, redirecting, modeling, listening, ignoring, and encouraging.

When guiding children's behavior, your actions should always promote a positive self-concept in each child. A child's self-concept is the qualities the child believes he or she possesses.

Review and Reflect

1. What are prosocial behaviors?
2. Studies show that _____ teachers have more hyperactive, disruptive, and bored students.
3. Why do children of permissive teachers often exhibit aggressive and attention-seeking behavior?
4. Describe one of the general guidelines you should follow for effective guidance to occur.
5. Give three examples of actions useful in direct guidance.
6. Use positive guidance statements to rewrite the following:
    A. Do not scream!
    B. You are getting paint on your dress.
    C. Do not spill the milk.
    D. Quit running!
7. Name the direct guidance principle being used in each of the following examples.
    A. Penny was disciplined yesterday for running through the cooking area. When she ran through the cooking area today, she was again disciplined.
    B. The children are playing in the art area. It will be lunchtime in 10 minutes. Their teacher says to them, "Children, it is almost time for lunch. Please start cleaning up the area."
    C. Henry is running from one end of the teeter-totter to the other. His teacher comes over to him and says, "Henry, stop that. You might hurt yourself."
    D. A teacher says to her children, "On Friday, we will be eating lunch outdoors. You can choose to have either a hot dog or a hamburger for lunch."
8. Give an example of how the physical setup of the classroom can be used to encourage independence in the children.
9. Why would a teacher want to use positive reinforcement?
10. Explain the difference between natural consequences and artificial consequences.
11. True or false. Praise should be given at the end of the day for any positive behaviors observed during the day.
12. How does a prompt differ from a suggestion?
13. The key to _____ is supplying an appealing substitute.
14. Explain the process of active listening.
15. True or false. Ignoring is an appropriate guidance technique when the child's behavior is verbally harmful to other children.
16. List three ways that you can encourage the development of children's positive self-concepts.

Apply and Explore

1. Observe a teacher interacting with children for one hour. Record all incidences of verbal guidance.

2. Practice verbal guidance techniques by showing a friend how to use a puzzle.

3. Discuss situations in which a teacher may have to intervene in the classroom.

4. Conduct a self-observation. Using a tape recorder, record your interactions with children. Listen to your interactions. Were they positive? Did you help the children in identifying and labeling positive behavior? How would you change some of your interactions with the children to make them more positive?

5. Make a list of children's activities that promote a positive self-concept.

Teachers must help guide children through tension-causing events.

Chapter 14

Guidance Problems

After studying this chapter, you will be able to

- identify situations and feelings that cause tension in children.
- describe behavior problems that result from tension.
- guide children as they learn appropriate behavior.

Terms to Know

overstimulated

frustration

stress

Four-year-old Missy is tattling on the other children. After arriving at the center, she told the teacher that Toby had pushed her the day before. During snacktime, she announced loudly that Hunter did not take the muffin he touched. Later, during clean-up time, she told the teacher that Jafar did not put away his puzzle.

Hoa does not like to take a nap during naptime. He begins crying every day after lunch as naptime approaches. Yolanda, who is normally very cooperative, has been less so in the weeks following the birth of her new brother. Rather than taking turns, she has become bossy on the play yard. The teacher has also seen her hitting other children.

During your teaching career, you will likely have several children in your classes who will have similar behavior problems as Missy, Hoa, and Yolanda. Many times, behavior problems will be disruptive to the class. The behavior may be harmful or it might infringe on the rights of others. Mishandling of classroom pets, equipment, and materials may also occur.

Disruptive behavior often is caused by tension. Overstimulation, changes in routine, and loud noise are just a few causes of tension in children. Because children do not know how to handle tension, they often react with disruptive behavior such as pushing and disturbing other children, running, and yelling, 14-1.

Helping children to deal positively with tension-causing events is an important job of the teacher. You will need to understand situations and feelings that cause tension in children. Recognizing behavior patterns that result from tension is also important. Then you will need to

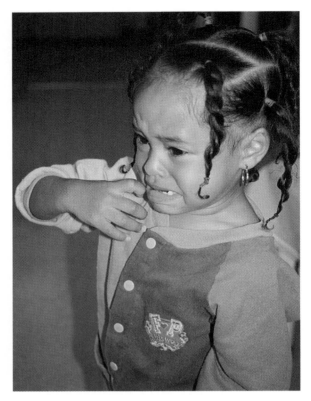

14-1 Some children yell and become disruptive when they feel tension.

of children, the greater the likelihood that overstimulation will occur. You may want to limit the number of children that can be in a certain area at any time. This will help prevent the chaos created when a large group of children play together. For example, post a sign in the blockbuilding area limiting the space to four children at any given time. For younger children who do not read, make a simple sign showing four stick people. It will serve the same purpose. Similar signs can be posted in other areas of the classroom.

Some children become overstimulated when there are program changes. Holidays, such as Christmas and Valentine's Day, can be overstimulating times for children. Avoid making holiday plans too early. When this happens, the children may get keyed up long before the event occurs.

Overstimulation can also result from having too many activities planned. When this happens, some children have a hard time making choices. Instead of staying with one activity, they run back and forth between several. Their activity and excitement, in turn, can affect others.

be able to help children deal with this tension. With this information, you will be able to effectively guide and help these children.

Causes of Tension

There are many causes of tension in children. These include certain situations and feelings children do not know how to handle. In addition, there are physical problems that can cause tension in children. Being aware of situations and emotions that produce tension is important. This knowledge will allow you to avoid, or at least lessen the effects of, these causes.

Overstimulation

Children can become overexcited, or **overstimulated**, by many things. For instance, simply playing with other children can overstimulate some children, 14-2. Usually, the larger group

14-2 The combination of being outside and climbing on a jungle gym can cause overstimulation in some children.

Breaks in Routines

Routines are important to children. They let children know what to expect and when. If routines are not followed, children become confused. Behavior problems can arise. For instance, Jimmy is put down for a nap at 12:30 p.m. on a regular basis. If this is not done, he may become overtired. This may result in disruptive behavior.

All children need consistent daily schedules. Quiet activities need to be followed by active activities. If children sit still too long, they may lose interest in the activity and become disruptive. Likewise, if children remain active too long, they may become overstimulated and disruptive. When changes in routine are necessary, such as a planned field trip, prepare the children ahead of time. Talk to them about what will happen. Also, explain to the children what your expectations are before, during, and after the trip.

Noise

Noise affects children differently. Children with very sensitive ears are particularly upset by noise. For example, these children will cover their ears when a smoke alarm goes off. Likewise, if an ambulance drives by with its siren wailing, some children will cringe. While some children may try only to escape the noise, others may react by pushing or hitting others.

To avoid the problems caused by noise, control the volume of tapes, records, and CDs. Also pay attention to the volume of your own voice. In frustration, you may yell. Unfortunately, this causes a chain reaction. As the volume of your voice increases, the children's voices also become louder. This, in turn, will affect children sensitive to noise. The result will be chaos.

Waiting Time

Children often behave poorly when they have to wait for long periods of time. By nature, they are usually in motion. Therefore, if they are kept waiting too long for a story, they may start pushing or hitting. This behavior is not the children's fault. However, it may gain the teacher's disapproval. If this occurs, it may contribute to the children's negative self-concepts.

Cut down on waiting time by being prepared, 14-3. If you are going to read a book for a

14-3 Preparing visual aids before the activity helps reduce children's waiting time.

large group, choose it in advance. Place it where it will be convenient. Likewise, prepare materials for all small and large group activities in advance. If the children are actively involved in self-selected activities, more preparation time may be available. Manage your time effectively. This will reduce waiting time and resulting guidance problems.

Frustration

Children sometimes feel they are not in control. They feel defeated or discouraged. These feelings are called **frustration**. They cause tension in children, 14-4. In order to control frustration, carefully plan each day's activities. The activities you choose should reflect the needs and interests of the children in the center.

Some children arrive at the center full of energy. These children need to be active. Provide wheeled toys, blockbuilding, and woodworking activities for these children. Other children enter the center in quiet moods. They prefer quiet activities such as looking at books, putting puzzles together, stringing beads, working with play dough, or watching others. By observing the children in your program, you can provide the proper materials, supplies, and equipment.

14-4 Being in control is important for young children. When they are not in control, they may become frustrated.

Forcing children into activities they are not prepared to join can result in frustration. A better approach is to allow the children to decide what is best.

Conflict over toys can also create frustration. Therefore, make certain that several kinds of toys are available to the children at all times. Conflicts often arise over toys. When possible, purchase several toys of the same kind. Wise teachers buy more than one wagon, scooter, fire engine, and car.

Select materials and equipment to match children's developmental level. This allows the children to feel success and develop an "I can do it" attitude. Working with mixed-aged groups presents special problems. Include open-ended materials such as blocks, play dough, and sand. Children of all ages will play with these, but in different ways. See 14-5. Provide puzzles and books for a range of abilities.

When necessary, redirect children to materials that match their abilities. Repeated failures will cause frustration, which may lead to anger. An angry child may pinch, hit, push, kick, or bite.

As an adult, you may become angry when the children are uncontrollable due to frustration. When this happens, try to relax. Carefully watch your words and actions. If the children sense you are upset, they, in turn, will become more upset. They need to feel that you are calm and in control.

Physical Problems

Poor health or other physical problems can cause tension and behavioral problems in children. One teacher, Mr. Peterson, had such a problem in his center. During Ethan's first day at the center, Mr. Peterson and several other teachers observed Ethan. They feared he would be a behavior problem. He ignored all directions and suggestions made by Mr. Peterson. Ethan also seemed to have a high anxiety level.

Ethan's behavior became a source of frustration for Mr. Peterson. More than once, he wondered whether Ethan should even be in the center. He feared that other children would copy Ethan's behavior. Mr. Peterson was also concerned about

14-5 A sensory table and paints are materials that appeal to children of many ages.

his ability to handle Ethan's behavior. This concern continued for several weeks.

Mr. Peterson finally decided to ask the center director to observe Ethan's behavior. After observing Ethan for less than half an hour, the director determined a possible cause for Ethan's problem. First, the director noted that Ethan did not respond to many of the verbal requests made by Mr. Peterson or other children. The director also noted that while interacting with others, Ethan closely watched their faces when they spoke. The director suspected that Ethan's hearing was poor. For added information, the director then picked up two wooden blocks, stood behind Ethan, and clapped them together as hard as she could. While several other children either jumped or turned to see what was happening, Ethan did not respond.

Before sharing these observations with Ethan's father, Mr. Peterson repeated the clapping incident. Ethan failed to respond. In addition, other staff members tried speaking to him when they were out of his field of vision. Again, each time he failed to respond. At this point, the center director shared these observations with Ethan's father. She encouraged Ethan's father to have his hearing tested.

Luckily for Ethan, his father, the staff, and other children in the center, the cause of Ethan's behavioral problems was pinpointed. After having his hearing tested, Ethan received a hearing aid. His behavior improved dramatically. At the same time, his speech also improved.

Children may be overly active or tense due to other health problems, 14-6. A child who is in constant pain due to lack of dental or medical assistance may act inappropriately.

Medications can affect some children's behavior. Observe for symptoms such as dilated pupils, drowsiness, slurred speech, poor coordination, and general irritability. In many states, parents are required to report to the staff when their children are on medication.

Prolonged or recurring illness can cause frequent absences from the center. When this occurs, some children are not able to maintain their friendships. Coming back to the center is difficult for them. Some of these children may become *onlookers*. This means they watch others, but do not get involved. Other children may become aggressive. By acting out, they hope

14-6 Pain from this child's head injury may cause him to be tense and uncooperative.

to gain the other children's attention. Onlookers and aggressive children need your help. Carefully observe them. Focus on their needs.

An onlooker needs to get involved. Encourage this child by suggesting activities he or she might try. If the child does not respond, gently take the child by the hand, and walk him or her to an appealing activity. You may have to play with the child for awhile or involve other children in the activity.

Aggressive children need a calming influence. Direct these children to activities in which they can release energy. For instance, direct the aggressive child to woodworking, sculpting, or water play activities.

Poor or inadequate nutrition can also affect behavior. Studies show that between one-fourth and one-third of preschool children do not receive the caloric intake recommended for them. Children who do not have the proper caloric intake or a proper breakfast may be inattentive and sluggish. Motor skills and motivation are also affected. To avoid this problem, meals are served at many centers.

Stress

Stress is the body's reaction to physical or emotional factors. The reaction often takes the form of tension. Occasional stress is not a problem. However, constant stress can cause many problems. This is because stress builds on itself. The stress created by one situation builds on the stress of another.

There are definite differences in how children bear up under stress. Some become illness prone. Some are slow to develop. Others become withdrawn and nervous, while others show more anger. Then there are children who are resilient. Nothing seems to touch them.

Causes of Stress

Stress can be caused by both negative and positive events. One negative event that can cause stress in children is the breakup of a family. Physical abuse, rejection, separation, and fights are also negative events that may cause stress. Positive events that cause stress include birthday parties, overnight visits to friends' houses, new pets, and births of new brothers or sisters.

Family events often are a source of stress for children. Events such as a parent losing a job or the death of a sibling, parent, or grandparent can create stress. The birth of a new brother or sister will have an effect on the child. Likewise, having a new babysitter can be stressful. Even daily occurrences have the potential of creating a stressful atmosphere at home. The family that is constantly active from morning to night creates its own tensions. In this family, a young child's needs may be overlooked as parents and siblings rush to meet their many obligations.

As a teacher, you need to be aware of what is happening in a child's home that could affect the child's behavior. It is especially important that you be informed of significant family events, such as births and deaths. When a child's behavior patterns change suddenly, the cause may be stress related. You should talk with the parents about what is taking place at home.

Signs of Stress

Common signs of stress are listed in 14-7. These signs might also signal problems other than stress. How do you determine, then, if children are suffering from stress?

First, observe children's behavior. Children who remain apart from other children may be feeling stress. Likewise, children who are easily irritated or excessively lazy or aggressive may also suffer from stress.

Second, watch closely for changes in habits or behavior. For example, Barry has always been a friendly, but quiet, child. You have noticed that recently Barry has been fighting with his friends. Barry may be suffering from stress. If you are aware of the normal behavior of each of the children in your class, you will also be aware of changes in their behavior.

Children can feel stress in the same way adults feel stress. Unlike adults, however, children lack the skills needed to understand and control these pressures. As their teacher, you are in a position to help these children.

What should you do when a child's normal behavior changes? First, accept the child's behavior. Scolding a child for thumbsucking will not stop the behavior. Likewise, forcing a child to eat will not make the child eat. When you notice unusual behavior, remain close to and comfort the child. Reassure the child that you care about him or her.

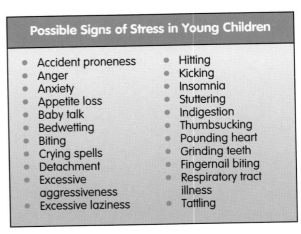

Possible Signs of Stress in Young Children

- Accident proneness
- Anger
- Anxiety
- Appetite loss
- Baby talk
- Bedwetting
- Biting
- Crying spells
- Detachment
- Excessive aggressiveness
- Excessive laziness
- Hitting
- Kicking
- Insomnia
- Stuttering
- Indigestion
- Thumbsucking
- Pounding heart
- Grinding teeth
- Fingernail biting
- Respiratory tract illness
- Tattling

14-7 The problems shown in this list may signal stress.

To help reduce stress, promote a positive environment. Praise children for the good things they do. Help them see themselves as positive, worthwhile people. Listen to them. Help them clarify their feelings. Correct any misconceptions they may have about themselves or their feelings.

Reactions to Tension

Young children often behave in a socially unacceptable way when they are tense. Negativism, theft, anger, biting, exploration of the body, thumbsucking, and fear are all possible reactions to tension. These reactions remind us children are people, too. You must deal with and guide their behavior, just as you would an adult.

Negativism

Preschool children can be negative, particularly between two and three years of age. See 14-8. It is not unusual for a child of this age to oppose every request you make. Children at this age are wanting to become more independent. A "no" in many cases is a child's attempt at independence. For instance, you may say "Pick up the block." The child might look at you and say "No."

Guiding Negative Behavior

Accept a young child's negative behavior. However, keep in mind all health and safety regulations. For example, children must wash their hands before eating. If a child refuses to do this, take the child's hands and wash them. Tell the child "You need to wash your hands." Let the child know, through your voice and body language, that you expect cooperation.

A negative child cannot be hurried. If he or she is hurried, opposition will be stronger. Given time, children outgrow this stage of development.

Stealing

Preschool children do not understand the difference between *mine* and *yours*. When children under three years of age take something, they are not stealing. At this age, children do not understand the concept of stealing. Before

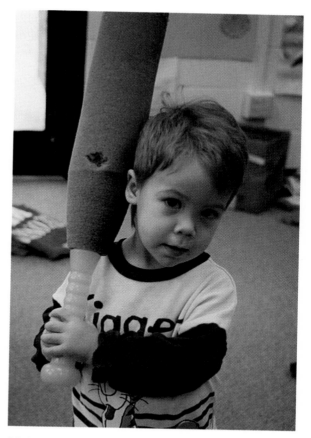

14-8 Young children may resist your requests for them to use materials appropriately.

considering the needs of others, preschoolers attempt to meet their own needs. The desire for something appealing may combine with a young child's natural impulsiveness. As a result, they may take items that do not belong to them.

Small objects, such as toy cars and puzzle pieces, may vanish from the classroom. When you notice these items missing, warn the other teachers. Ask them to closely observe the children.

Guiding

Help children learn to respect the possessions of others. If you see a child take something, do not ask the reason he or she stole it. Likewise, do not lecture about stealing. Instead, make the child return it. Otherwise, the child may keep taking things from others. Remember that preschoolers do not understand ownership.

A useful way to teach children about ownership is to respect their property rights. That is, before trying Jodi's new puzzle, ask her permission to use it. If you see another child looking at Jodi's toy, say "Why don't you ask Jodi if you can use it?"

You should also try to minimize opportunities for stealing. When children bring toys or other items from home, problems can occur. If toys are allowed to be brought to the center, there need to be clear rules. Toys are best left in the child's cubby and only taken out for naptime or show-and-tell. To avoid potential problems, many centers have a policy stating that toys should not be brought from home.

Anger

A child's anger can serve a useful purpose. Anger draws attention to something that annoys the child. You can then help that child learn to deal with anger. The greatest number of tantrums typically occur at about 18 months of age. After this age, there is a sharp decline. Age also affects how a child will project anger. Young children often use their whole bodies to express anger. By age two, children may hold their breath for as long as they can. Screaming, kicking, hitting, pounding, and hitting one's head against a wall are other ways these children express anger. By the time children turn three, verbal abuse is more common, while four-year-olds often engage in name-calling.

Handling Anger

Discourage hurting behavior. Young children should not be allowed to hit each other. However, they will try. When they do, stop them immediately. Say "I am sorry, but Jeff does not like that." At the same time, you might have to hold the child's hand. The child may try to hit you. Stop that action also. For older preschoolers, you may also use comments. For example, you may say, "You are usually kind. I'm surprised you did that."

Ignoring outbursts is also a successful technique when dealing with an angry child. Of course, ignore this behavior only if there is no threat to the health and safety of the children. If children are able to get attention or gain control through outbursts, they will keep using this behavior. For example, if Carrie cries and yells for another cookie and then receives one, she will cry and yell again. On the other hand, if she does not receive the cookie, she will learn that her outburst is unacceptable.

The children need to express their feelings and assert their rights in socially acceptable ways. You can redirect anger through activities such as finger painting, modeling with clay, punching a punching bag, hammering, and playing at the sensory table, 14-9. All these activities involve use of children's hands, arms, and legs. Their anger will be redirected into physical movements. Remember to have enough supplies and equipment for these activities. Use a minimum of rules.

Surprisingly, noise can also help relieve aggression. Yelling, beating drums, dancing to loud music, crying, and making animal noises can all relieve anger. Remember, however, that noise can be catching. If several children make

14-9 Children can release energy through physical activity.

too much noise, the rest of the group may also become noisy.

Whenever possible, catch children before they react angrily. For instance, if you see that Mattie is going to kick over Tommy's blocks, stop her. Then say, "Would you like Tommy to knock over your blocks?" Mattie will be forced to think about what she was going to do.

Biting

Young children often bite when they are upset. This is not unusual behavior, particularly with two-year-olds. For many of these children, biting is only a temporary problem. They may bite because they cannot express themselves using words. For them, biting is a form of body language.

Handling Biting

You need to help children who bite. Start by keeping playtime simple for these children. Limit the number of playmates they may have at any time. Large groups often create stressful situations. Therefore, biters become nervous and then bite.

You need to respond quickly to prevent children from hurting each other. Isolation of a biter sometimes helps to curb this habit. When the child bites another, say, "Paula does not like that." Then say, "I am sorry, but you must sit down over here." Make the child sit for a few minutes, but no longer than five. Then, allow the child to return to the play area.

Do not forget the child who is being bit. This child also needs to feel secure. To provide security, observe constantly. Never allow a child to bite back. Biting back does not prevent biting. It only creates more aggressive behavior.

Tattling

Tattling seems to occur in many classrooms and is a typical behavior for many young children. Frequently, the child who tattles is insecure and tattles to get your attention. As a teacher, you may find tattling irritating, but you need to listen to the children. You want the children to be aware that classroom rules are important. You do not need to be told, however, each time a rule is broken.

Guiding Tattling

To prevent tattling, try to build children's self-esteem. This, in turn, will make them feel more secure. For the child who is insecure, stay close while supervising. Knowing that a caring adult is nearby is helpful.

Try to have a daily one-to-one time for listening and talking with each child. This may be during free play or small group time. During this time, provide the child feedback by recognizing his or her positive qualities. To illustrate, you may say, "Sharice, I like the way you help Marco" or "Eileen, Brian enjoys having you help him with the puzzle." Positive reinforcement will help to prevent a child's need to tattle.

Try ignoring tattling behavior. If Jared tattles to you that Ronnie has taken his scissors, comment by saying "You need to tell Ronnie to return your scissors." This encourages Jared to speak to the child who has broken the rule. Likewise, if Christopher tattles that Julia has taken his bicycle, encourage problem solving. Say "Christopher has taken your bike. What should you do?" If Kelsi is always talking about other children, you need to set a limit by saying "I enjoy talking with you, but we shouldn't talk about others."

Exploring the Body

Children begin to explore their bodies early in life. It is common for one-year-olds to explore their genitals during diaper changing. As children begin to gain control of their body functions, interest in the genital area grows. By three years of age, children are aware of sex differences. Boys may, in fact, become concerned because girls do not have penises. By age four, children who have to use the bathroom may hold the genital area. When this occurs, remind the child that he or she needs to use the bathroom. By five years of age, children may begin to manipulate their genitals. They may do this by rubbing pillows between their legs, or even squeezing their thighs together tightly. Some children may begin to rub their genitals in an effort to reduce irritation caused by tight clothing.

Guiding

Exploration of the body is normal behavior in development. However, it is not considered proper to engage in such behavior in public. Therefore, it is important to guide children away from public display of body exploration.

During naptime, you might see children touching themselves. Children sometimes rub their genitals while trying to get to sleep. When this occurs, never shame or threaten the child. Remember, whenever possible, use a positive approach when guiding young children. This can be done by firmly telling a child that this behavior is impolite in public.

Thumbsucking

Like adults, children feel certain tensions. To relieve the tension, some children may suck their thumbs. Studies show that almost half of all infants suck their fingers or thumbs. By 18 months, thumbsucking usually reaches its peak. Then the behavior becomes less frequent, especially during the day. By four or five years of age, children who suck their thumbs usually only do so before they go to bed. Children of this age will sometimes engage in thumbsucking if they are tired.

Many parents are concerned about thumbsucking. Reassure them that usually there is no need to worry about this behavior. Encourage them to accept this behavior as a normal stage of growth. Most children outgrow thumbsucking by six or seven years of age.

Parents may be concerned that thumbsucking will affect children's facial appearance or damage teeth. Dentists state that there is no cause to worry if thumbsucking stops before permanent teeth erupt.

Guiding Thumbsucking

Children's urge to suck may be satisfied by supplying a pacifier. One advantage of a pacifier is that it does not place pressure on the roof of the mouth or the jaw. In addition, most children give pacifiers up between one and two years of age. In fact, some children may have an intense sucking need for only the first few months of life. When these children stop using their pacifiers, they can be taken away permanently. If, however, a child reverts to sucking fingers or thumbs, return the pacifier.

If you notice a child thumbsucking, do not pull the thumb out of his or her mouth. This

guidance may not be successful. In some cases, it might cause the child to increase thumbsucking. During the first three years, the harder you try to stop thumbsucking, the stronger it becomes. Instead, accept and ignore the behavior. In this way, children will usually stop thumbsucking between four and five years of age.

Attending a child care program may help curb thumbsucking for some children. At the center, the child will find many new interests and friends. As a result, you may not notice thumbsucking. Many times children will only suck their thumbs when they lie down for naps or are tired.

Fear

Every child experiences fear. By three years of age, most children have many kinds of fear. Some fears will be real while others will be imaginary. As the child grows, real fears will be kept. Imaginary fears will be outgrown.

Common childhood fears include falling from high places, putting faces in water, thunder, the dark, people in uniforms, fire engines, ambulances, and animals. Fear of the unknown is also common in young children. You may see this fear on the first day of school. Children may cry, cling, and refuse to leave their parents. As the teacher, be prepared for this fear. Inform parents in advance about this common fear.

Guiding

Understanding children's fear is important in guiding young children, 14-10. For example, fear of the dark is quite common among young children. You may notice this fear at naptime or when a videotape is being shown. Understand that this behavior is due to unfamiliar surroundings. These children cannot sleep or concentrate on videos. Instead, the children may focus on scary images formed by the shadows in the darkened room. Help these children by keeping a small light turned on during these times. Then the room will not be totally dark. Also, allow children to keep a familiar stuffed toy or blanket near them.

Accept children's fears. For young children, even the silliest fear is real. When a fire engine passes the play yard and a child cries, give the child immediate attention. You may wish to hold the child's hand, kneel down and put your arms

14-10 Teachers need to be prepared for fears on field trips that may be caused by unfamiliar sights or sounds.

around the child, or hold the child on your lap. When you do this, you are meeting the child's immediate needs. After the crisis, talk to the child about the fear.

Children may need to act out situations in order to conquer their fears. See 14-11. For instance, Toby's grandmother died in the hospital. When Toby came back to the center, he

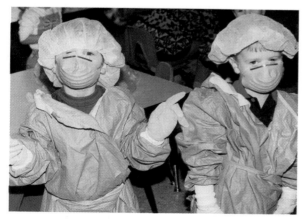

14-11 Playing hospital helps many children deal with their fears of hospitals and doctors.

asked two other children to play hospital with him. Toby played the role of a doctor while one of his friends played the nurse. This was Toby's way of handling the fear he felt when his grandmother died at the hospital.

Talking with children can also help them control fear. For example, Mark visited his cousin Chris. When he returned to school, Mark told his teachers that the house had ghosts. As a result, Mark said that he was never returning. Mark's teacher was observant. He talked to Mark about his visit with Chris. He explained that sleeping in strange places is often frightening because it is new.

Jennifer was afraid of the new bunny. Fortunately for Jennifer, her teacher was understanding. She helped Jennifer face her fear by introducing her to the bunny in gradual steps. First, she asked Jennifer to place a carrot in the cage. Then she encouraged Jennifer to watch the bunny eat. The next day she encouraged Jennifer to touch the bunny's fur. Jennifer continued this for about one week. Her teacher did not rush Jennifer. Finally, she asked Jennifer if she wanted to hold the bunny. Jennifer said yes. Jennifer's teacher carefully and slowly took the rabbit from the cage and placed it on Jennifer's lap.

When children feel unsafe or strange, they may reject a person or situation. For example, a child may greet a new aide with "Go away, I hate you." If this happens, do not scold the child. Telling the child that he or she likes the aide will not help either. Instead, accept the child's feelings. You may say "Miss Brown is our new teacher. When you get to know her, you will learn to like her."

Children sometimes will hit others when they are afraid. For instance, a resource person visited a group of four-year-olds. This person brought a large snake to show the children. When Janice saw the snake, she began to act aggressively. She hit Susan and Peggy. The teacher then stepped in. She explained to Janice that her friends might be frightened, too. She then explained to Janice that this type of snake was not dangerous. There was no need to fear the snake.

Summary

Disruptive behavior often is caused by tension. Overstimulation, changes in routine, and loud noise are just a few causes of tension in children. Frustration, physical problems, and stress can also cause tension. Stress is often caused by problems within the child's family, such as a divorce, job loss, or even death. Because children do not know how to handle tension, they often react with disruptive behavior. Some of the behaviors you will likely see are negativism, stealing, anger, biting, exploring the body, tattling, thumbsucking, and fear.

Helping children to deal positively with tension-causing events is an important job of the teacher. You will need to understand situations and feelings that cause tension in children. Recognizing behavior patterns that result from tension is also important. Then you will need to be able to help children deal with this tension. With this information, you will be able to effectively guide and help these children.

Review and Reflect

1. Why do children react disruptively when they experience tension?

2. Name four events that can cause tension in a child.

3. True or false. Usually, the larger the group of children, the greater the likelihood that overstimulation will occur.

4. _____ let children know what to expect and when to expect it.

5. True or false. Noise affects all children in the same way.

6. Name two ways to cut down on waiting time.

7. Describe frustration and list two causes of frustration in children.

8. Frustration can be prevented by _____.
   A. supplying the same materials to all children
   B. letting children choose which play activities they would like to do
   C. forcing children to play with certain materials, regardless of their abilities
   D. planning only one or two activities a day

9. Name four ways that medications can affect children's behavior.

10. _____ are children who watch others participate, but do not participate themselves.

11. What is stress?

12. Name two steps you can take to help a child deal with stress.

13. What will happen if you hurry a negative child?

14. Explain how you would effectively guide the children in the following situations.
   A. Philip gets angry whenever you announce clean-up time.
   B. Joanne bites a nearby child whenever George takes a toy from her.
   C. Amber runs to tell you every time another child breaks a classroom rule.
   D. Martin cries when a clown visits the class.

15. True or false. Exploration of the body is a natural stage in development.

Apply and Explore

1. Prepare a checklist of ways to avoid overstimulation of children.

2. Discuss teacher strategies for reducing waiting time.

3. Visit a child care center. Observe children for any signs of stress. Note what signs you see. Discuss your findings when you return to class.

4. Discuss the advantages of thumbsucking from the child's point of view.

5. Invite a child psychologist to talk to your class about children's fears.

6. Invite a panel of parents to discuss with your class problems they have guiding children.

Chapter 15

Establishing Classroom Rules

After studying this chapter, you will be able to

- explain the reasons for having classroom rules.
- list guidelines for establishing classroom rules.
- describe methods for enforcing rules.
- list useful rules for various classroom areas and activities.

Terms to Know

rules

consistency

flexible rules

Rules are often necessary for people to effectively work together in groups. In child care centers, effective rules serve as a kind of short-hand that state the goals of the center. As such, **rules** should focus on actions and behaviors that reflect goals. As a teacher, your input in suggesting rules for the center are important to the director and other staff members. Likewise, you will help determine what will happen when rules are broken.

Every area of the classroom will need to have rules. As the classroom teacher, it is your responsibility to explain and enforce rules. Rules need to be explained at the children's level of understanding. The staff and children should also know the reasons for the rules. In addition, you should make sure that each adult working in the classroom is given a copy of the rules. The rules should also be posted in the teachers' lounge and in the classrooms.

Establishing Rules

There are three reasons for establishing classroom rules. First, according to the law, children's health and safety must be protected. Rules help make the classroom a safe place for the children. Second, children feel free to explore when they know their teacher will stop them if they go too far, 15-1. Thus, they feel protected from mistakes. Rules, then, may set limits. Finally, rules also help children develop self-control. As children learn to accept and obey rules, they gradually come to learn that rules are part of life. One of the center's goals should be to develop socially

15-1 Setting rules helps children feel freer to explore.

responsible behavior in young children. Establishing rules will help the center reach this goal.

Guidelines for Setting Rules

When setting rules for children, make the rules short. Focus on one main point. Use familiar language and short, simple sentences that the children can understand. You and the children need to have the same understanding of what the rule means. Be sure that the words you use describe the exact behavior you desire. Children are often confused by such general words as *be nice, stop it,* or *behave.* These words can have many meanings and do not say precisely what you want. State the rules in terms of the positive behavior that you expect.

Set rules that are reasonable. This means that children have the ability to carry out the action. Rules should serve a useful purpose. Give children specific reasons for each rule. If you cannot think of a reason for having a rule, rethink the rule. Try to determine whether your expectations really are that important. Unreasonable rules can cause young children to feel angry.

Avoid making too many rules. Having a few well-established rules is better for the children and for you. If you have too many rules, the children will forget them. You, too, may have trouble remembering and enforcing them.

Define both acceptable and unacceptable behavior. Decide how to deal with unacceptable behavior. Normally, the best approach is to stop such action firmly and quickly. You may find, however, that the child will become angry, 15-2. This anger may show in several ways. The child may resist set limits, cry, yell, or simply stare at you.

Rules need to be re-examined by the entire staff on a regular basis. Children's behavior will change as they grow and develop. Therefore, rules should change as the children change. Any rule changes must be discussed with the entire staff. Discuss what changes need to be made and why. If you determine that a rule no longer fits the group's needs, discard it.

Rule changes also need to be discussed with the children. When an issue arises, invite the children to discuss the problem. Begin by stating the issue. Then ask the children to think of ways of solving it. During the discussion, encourage the children to state the rules in a positive way.

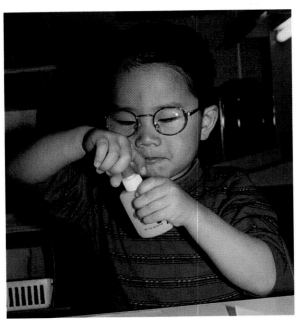

15-2 Undesirable behavior should be stopped, even if the child becomes upset.

Write out each new rule, calling attention to the printed words.

Enforcing Rules

Children follow rules best when the rules are enforced in a regular, unchanging manner. This is known as **consistency**. Children then know what is expected of them. However, children will often test these well-established rules. You should feel comfortable with this testing process. At the same time you should also maintain your position. Do not be afraid or back down. For example, if you said that each child may do only one painting, make sure that no child paints two. Friendly reminders may also be helpful, such as "When you are finished, Tommy wants a turn to paint a picture."

Enforcing rules also requires that rules be flexible at times. **Flexible rules** allow you to adapt to the needs of an individual or situation. For instance, your rule states that children are allowed thirty minutes to eat lunch. A sick child may need extra time to finish. Perhaps the children are required to eat at a table. On a field trip, however, tables may not be available. The children will have to sit on the ground in this instance. Your rules must be flexible enough to handle such situations, 15-3.

The way you react to children who break rules affects children's feelings of security. Children feel secure knowing that the rules protect them. However, when one child breaks a rule, another child's security may be threatened. For instance, a child may express his or her anger in a violent way, such as hitting. That child is breaking a rule. You must tell the child that hitting is wrong. The child who was hit is also affected. He or she has lost some security. You need to reassure and pay attention to this child. In fact, giving attention to the injured child shows the child who hit that hitting is not a good way to gain attention.

Rules for Specific Areas and Activities

The rules you set may be very different from the rules set at another center. This is because no two centers are alike. Equipment, facilities, and staff vary among centers. However, similar activities take place at many centers, regardless of location. For instance, cooking, blockbuilding, and reading occur at most centers. General rules

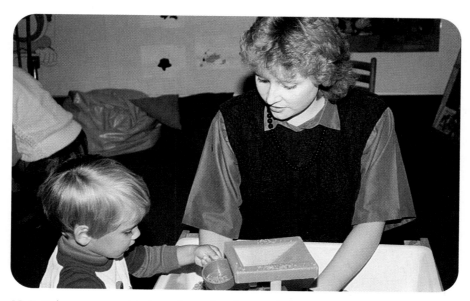

15-3 Rules may need to be adapted to the needs of an individual child or situation.

for some of these areas and activities can be used as guidelines for all centers.

Sensory Play

In some classrooms, sensory activity is provided each day. A water or sand table is often used for this activity. During a typical week, shaving cream, ice cubes, snow, colored water, or soapy water may be used in the water table. Dried beans, seed corn, oats, rice, or pebbles may be used in the sand table.

Depending on the material being used, the rules may change somewhat. For instance, a child would not need to wear a smock for protection when playing with dried seed corn. When using shaving cream, however, the smock may be required.

Rules for the children might include the following:

- Wear smocks for all wet or messy activities, 15-4.
- Wipe up splashes and spills immediately.
- Keep sand and water in the sandbox.

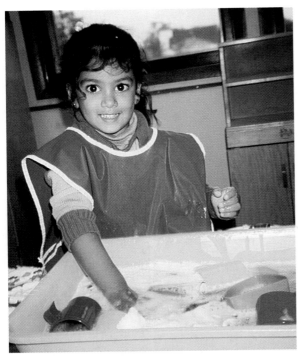

15-4 Wearing smocks during messy activities will keep children clean and dry.

Throwing sand and water is not allowed, but the rule should be stated in a positive manner as shown above. If a child does not follow the rule, direct the child to another area.

Dramatic Play

The dramatic play area might be called the home living or housekeeping area in some centers. Materials should be provided to help the children gain a better understanding of themselves and others around them. Dramatic play also allows children to work out their own feelings. Thus, to provide the children with the least restrictive environment, limit rules to the following:

- Wipe up all spilled water.
- Replace materials after they have been used.
- Respect the participation of other children.

Small Manipulative Activities

This area of the classroom contains games and small objects. With these materials, children learn to build, compare, sort, arrange, and match. Also, color, number, size, and shape concepts can be mastered. As children use these materials, they also develop small muscle coordination and hand-eye coordination.

Usually, rules in this area are limited. Suggested rules include the following:

- Return toys to the shelf after use.
- Keep games and puzzle pieces in this area of the classroom.

Cooking

Children learn about food by participating in cooking activities. Cooking allows the children to feel a sense of accomplishment. Tasting, smelling, touching, listening, and seeing help build language, number, sequence, and physics concepts.

Arrangements for health and safety must be included in the rules. Therefore, the following rules are needed:

- Wash hands before cooking.
- Wear an apron or smock.
- Wipe up spills immediately.
- Only teachers pick up hot kettles and pans.

- Eat prepared foods only during lunch or snack time.
- Everyone assists with cleanup, 15-5.

Supervision is required during all cooking activities. Whenever electrical appliances are being used, never leave the activity area! If more supplies are needed, signal for another teacher to get them for you. Always use pot holders and hot pads with cooking appliances.

Use recipe cards for all cooking activities. By following directions, children will learn sequencing. Recipes will also call attention to the importance of printed words. Chapter 25 contains many ideas for cooking activities.

Blockbuilding

Blockbuilding encourages children to be productive and creative. Blockbuilding also provides children with a way to release energy. The children's safety is important in this area. Rules must stress safety. Close supervision is always required in this area. Because of this need, building activities should be allowed only during a set time period.

Rules for blockbuilding activities might include the following:

- Use blocks for building only, 15-6.
- Keep blocks in the blockbuilding area.
- Return blocks to the storage shelves after use.
- Touch only your own building project unless you ask permission.

Music

All children enjoy music, 15-7. It is a universal language. By participating in music activities, children can develop self-expression, listening, language, and coordination skills. Music, like other activities, needs to have specific rules:

- Children select the instruments they want to use.
- Return instruments to their assigned places on the shelves after use.
- Use musical instruments only for creating sounds. (Hitting others is not allowed.)

15-5 After the self-selected play period, children must help with cleanup.

15-6 Blocks are to be used for building only.

15-7 Children enjoy listening to and creating music.

15-8 Children can learn valuable pre-reading and language skills in the book corner.

Art

For children, art is usually a pleasing activity. Therefore, they usually spend a lot of time playing in this area. Art is offered daily in most centers during the self-selected activity period.

Children in this area should be encouraged to explore materials. They should not be told what to make, nor should their artwork be compared. Most centers use only the following rules:

- Cover tables.
- Wear smocks for messy activities.
- Wipe up spills immediately.

Book Corner

In the book corner, children can develop language and pre-reading skills. Children should be encouraged to explore the books in this area, 15-8. In doing so, they will learn about their own family and community. They also will learn

about other cultures. Rules for the book corner might be the following:

- Turn one page at a time.
- Give torn books to the teacher.
- Return books to the shelf after use.

In order to encourage the children to explore, change books on a regular basis. Some teachers change books on a weekly basis, leaving several favorites to carry over. Control the number of books available at any given time. When too many books are in the area, it can become cluttered. Likewise, a child may have difficulty locating a favorite storybook.

Science

All children need science activities. These activities encourage them to discover their own environment. As they observe and question, they will see relationships and draw conclusions.

Teachers need to follow several rules when planning science activities. Include a variety of classroom and outdoor activities. Emphasize hands-on activities that allow children time to explore their surroundings, 15-9. During these activities, encourage the children to participate by observing, touching, holding, and questioning.

As a teacher, you will need to demonstrate some of the rules in this area. For example, you

15-9 Hands-on activities encourage children to become involved in the world around them.

will need to show the children how to hold a bunny, water a plant, or feed classroom pets. Equipment use will also need to be demonstrated for the children. You may even choose to have some children assist with cleaning the animal cages.

The science rules might include the following:

- Feed pets and water plants only with a teacher's supervision.
- Keep science equipment in the area.
- Handle pets with care.

Playground Activity

On the playground, children can express themselves in creative ways. They can build ships, houses, forts, and other objects with wooden crates and other materials. Through play, children develop motor coordination skills, social play skills, and a sense of cooperation.

The primary concern of the teacher is the children's safety. You will be responsible for helping the children develop safe play habits. Rules must be set and enforced if children are to play happily and safely on the playground. These rules will vary, depending upon the specific piece of equipment being used.

Swings

Swings are not found on all playgrounds because they require constant teacher supervision. If swings are available, specific rules must be followed. Included should be the following:

- Only one child on a swing at a time.
- Sit in the center of the swing.
- Use both hands for holding on.
- Stay on the swing until it has stopped.
- Only teachers push children on swings.

Slides

Slides are also a source of hazard for young children. Accidents happen when children bump into each other. Some children are injured when they stand up as they go down the slide, or when they slide head first. As a result, follow these rules:

- Use both hands when climbing up the steps.
- Stay one arm's length behind the child in front of you.
- Wait until the person in front of you has cleared the slide before you slide down.
- Slide down feet first and sitting up.
- Get off the slide as soon as you get to the bottom.

Jungle Gyms

Jungle gyms are very appealing to young children. Since children are adventurous, any activity on this piece of equipment has to be carefully supervised. Children must also be taught the correct and safe way to use the jungle gym. Include the following rules for jungle gym use:

- Only four or five children may use the jungle gym at one time.
- Use both hands to hold on, 15-10.
- Look down to see that you do not step on another child's hand when climbing.

Seesaws

Seesaws are another piece of equipment that require constant supervision when being used. Therefore, the rules you establish should stress safety. Include the following:

- Hang on to the handle with both hands.
- Keep feet out from under the board as it goes down.
- Stop before the board hits the ground.
- Tell you partner when you are getting off.

15-10 Children need to hold on with both hands when they play on the jungle gym.

Communicating Rules

What method can you use to clearly communicate rules to young children? As you have already read, rules need to be short, simple, and reasonable. Some teachers make this task easier by first dividing their rules into three categories. These categories include (1) be safe, (2) be kind, and (3) be neat. When reminding children about certain rules, the teachers begin by using one of the three categories. Figure 15-11 shows examples of this method.

Category	Examples
Be safe!	Use both hands to hang on to the swing. Sit at the table while using scissors.
Be neat!	Hang your jacket in the locker. Wear your smock while painting.
Be kind!	Say thank you when someone helps you. Hold the door for others.

15-11 Use clear, concise language when communicating rules to children.

Summary

Rules focus on actions and behaviors that reflect the goals of the center. Rules must be made for all classroom areas and for all activities. As the classroom teacher, it is your responsibility to explain and enforce rules. Rules need to be explained at the children's level of understanding. The staff and children should also know the reasons for the rules.

Rules that are consistently enforced and fair help create a relaxed atmosphere at the center. Rules may need to be flexible to adapt to the needs of an individual or situation. Rules will be different from one center to another. It is important that all staff members have input into setting rules. These rules should be reviewed on a regular basis and revised as needed.

Having rules teaches good citizenship. Children know what is expected of them. Adults know what to expect. Both groups find the center a pleasant place to be.

Review and Reflect

1. Explain the importance of having rules in a child care center.

2. List three reasons for establishing classroom rules.

3. Name three guidelines for setting rules for children.

4. Give an example of a rule that is stated negatively. Rewrite the rule so it is stated positively.

5. Should rules ever change? Explain your answer.

6. Why is it important that rules be enforced consistently?

7. _____ rules allow you to adapt to the needs of an individual or situation.

8. By following directions on a recipe card, children may learn _____.

9. List two ways teachers can encourage children to look at the books in the book corner.

10. Name one rule for each of the following pieces of playground equipment: swings, slides, jungle gyms, and seesaws.

Apply and Explore

1. Discuss ways in which rules may change as children grow. Give some specific examples.

2. Collect classroom rules from two centers. Discuss the similarities and differences between the two sets of rules.

3. Role-play the following scenes:
   A. Toby is in the book corner. While looking at a book, she accidentally tears a page.
   B. Tommy goes down the slide. When he reaches the bottom, he continues to sit there.
   C. Sarah and Frank are on the seesaw. Suddenly, Sarah jumps off.
   D. During a cooking activity, Mark accidentally spills his milk.

4. Cut pictures of two pieces of outdoor play equipment from a catalog. Write rules for each piece.

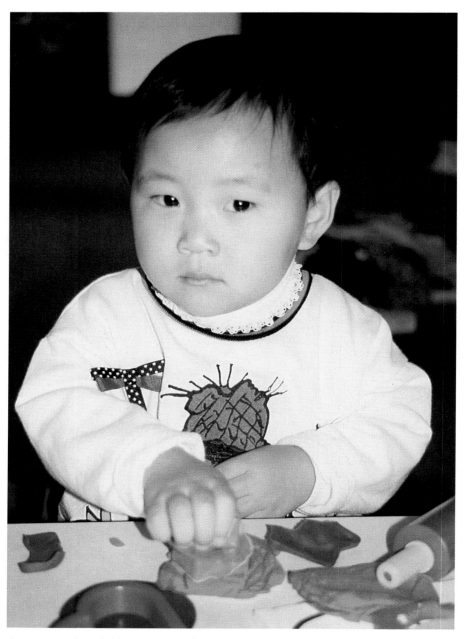

A routine helps children become familiar with daily events.

Chapter 16

Handling Daily Routines

After studying this chapter, you will be able to

- explain the importance of a daily schedule.

- guide children successfully through the daily routines of dressing and undressing, eating, napping, toileting, and cleanup.

- explain the use of transition techniques to move smoothly from one activity to another.

Terms to Know

routines
pica
dawdling
transitions
auditory signals

Routines, such as dressing, undressing, eating, napping, and toileting, are everyday experiences. Routines at child care centers reassure children by providing a pattern for each day. By following a daily schedule, children know the order of events throughout the day. They also know what to expect with each event.

Daily routines provide opportunities for children to develop independence. Young children feel great satisfaction in doing things for themselves. Remember to provide them with as little help as they need. This allows the children the opportunity for growth. See 16-1.

Daily routines will need your guidance. Without guidance, routine activities may become time consuming and frustrating. Learning to handle routines helps your classroom run smoothly, and the children will feel relaxed and happy.

The Daily Schedule

A well-planned schedule provides the framework for the day's activities. Schedules for early childhood programs vary by type of program. For instance, the sequence of events in an all-day program will not be the same as that for a half-day program. Factors such as the length of the program's day and the time children arrive will need to be considered.

The daily schedule must also be planned to meet the children's physical and psychological needs. Health and safety are important considerations. Very young children need to have time for meals and rest. Like adults, young children have

16-1 Teaching children how to buckle their shoes allows them to be more independent.

Scheduling Segments
I. Arrival
II. Indoor activities
III. Teacher-structured large group activity
IV. Outdoor self-selected activities
V. Mealtime
VI. Nap time
VII. Self-selected activities, indoors or outdoors
VIII. Snack
IX. Departure

16-2 A daily routine may give children a feeling of security.

psychological needs. For security, they need to have consistency and predictable routines.

The daily schedule should be designed to include basic routines. Figure 16-2 shows the segments of a typical schedule designating large blocks of time. Provisions need to be included for active play and quiet play. During the spring, summer, and fall in colder climates, longer outdoor play periods may be scheduled. When the weather becomes colder, you will need to shorten this outdoor play period. In addition, time needs to be allowed for nourishment and napping.

When planning the daily schedule, include large blocks of open time. At least half of the day should be set aside for free play (self-selected activities). Young children thrive on making choices. They enjoy selecting activities and deciding how long to remain with each activity. Many preschool children have short attention spans. Differences also exist in the speed at which they complete projects. By providing larger blocks of time, you will be meeting these children's individual needs.

There will be differences in each child's response to the schedule. For some children, the pace may be too fast, and they may feel stressed. Other children may become bored if the pace is too slow. Children's reactions often depend on the number of hours they spend at the center. Children attending full time may feel differently than those attending part time.

Arrival Routines

The arrival of children should follow a regular routine so children know what to expect at the start of each day. The children's arrival requires the teacher's full attention. Group activities should not be scheduled until later.

A typical arrival routine begins with the greeting of each child. Kneel down to the child's level and make each child feel welcome. Acknowledge any item the child might have brought from home. The children should then be directed to store their outer garments and other belongings in their cubbies. They then can move to a free-choice activity until all of the children have arrived.

Children react differently to separation from their parents. Some will remain silent while others cry. Some will refuse to enter the room, and others will bring favorite toys from home. Children vary in the duration of their separation anxieties. Some children will feel comfortable in a day or two. For other children, this may take a week or even several weeks. As a teacher, recognizing and responding to these anxieties is important. Your caring and understanding will be a key in helping the children make this transition.

Large Group Activities

In most programs, time is included in the schedule for large group activities. Teachers may refer to this segment as group time, story time, or circle time. Often this time is used for stories, songs, finger plays, and discussions. If developmentally appropriate, teachers also use it for discussions about the weather and calendar.

Schedule large group activities when the children are well-rested and nourished, such as mid-morning. Since not all of the children arrive at the same time, avoid scheduling group time at the beginning of the day. Scheduling it at this time would be inviting interruptions, making it difficult to promote good listening skills. Problems can also occur when large group time is scheduled just before lunch. Usually the children are under the most stress at this time of day. They are becoming tired and hungry, which could impact their behavior.

Group time should take place in an area where there are few distractions. The children should be seated away from books, puzzles, and other materials that they could pick up. Many programs have a carpeted area for group time. Some teachers prefer using individual carpet squares. A teacher or aide may prearrange the squares prior to large group activity to make sure the children are not sitting too close together. It will also ensure that the children are sitting near the teacher and not blocking other children's views.

A key to the success of group time is that you are organized and ready. Immediately capture the children's attention with a finger play, puppet, or song. This will encourage stragglers to pick up their pace and join the group.

Small Group Activities

Small group activity periods may be scheduled for 10 to 15 minutes. Typically, the four to six children in the group have similar interests or abilities. During this time, the children work with a teacher or aide. The purpose may be to teach specific concepts such as colors, numbers, shapes, or sizes.

Self-Selected Activities

The largest block of time in the schedule is for self-selected activities. This may also be referred to as center time or free play. The activities may be scheduled for indoors or outdoors. A variety of developmentally appropriate activities should be available. These activities usually support the curriculum or current theme being studied.

When longer play periods are available, children engage in more involved activities. Larger blocks of time help lengthen the children's attention spans. These longer time periods are also valuable to you. As a teacher, you can engage in conversations with the children, asking questions and assessing learning.

Meals and Snacks

A half-day or two-hour preschool program usually provides a 15-minute snack period. Lunch is usually provided in centers that operate full-day programs. Typically a half hour is allowed for lunch. The amount of time needed for snack or lunch will vary depending upon the age of the children and the number in the group.

Nap Time

Check your state's regulations on rest or nap time. Most states require children enrolled in a full-day program to have a nap time. Usually this is scheduled after lunch. Allow one to two hours for this activity. Nap time routines will be discussed later in this chapter.

Daily Routines

Throughout the day, many routines take place in the center. As an early childhood teacher, you will need to know how to handle these routines. You will want to encourage the children to become as independent as possible in carrying out these basic routines without any assistance from you. These routines include dressing and undressing, eating, napping, toileting, and cleanup.

Dressing and Undressing

As a teacher, you will want to encourage the children to dress and undress themselves as much as possible. Begin by telling the children what you expect of them. This is important. When four-year-old Frankie hands you his coat, refuse to help him put it on. Instead, tell Frankie he is able to dress himself. If needed, prompt him by providing verbal instruction. Once his coat is on, do not forget to praise him for his accomplishment. This will help him enjoy becoming independent. See 16-3.

Children should also be responsible for hanging up their own coats. You may notice that many of the children simply lay their coats in their lockers. Do not allow this to happen. For instance, if you see Eileen lay her coat in the locker, say "Eileen, you need to hang your coat on the hook." If she does not understand, show her how to hang it on the hook. Then take the coat off the hook and let Eileen hang it up herself.

Label lockers so children can find their own spaces. The labeling method you use will vary with the ages of the children. Names are usually written on the lockers for infants. This helps both teachers and parents. For two-year-olds, use a picture of the child. Names and symbols are helpful to three-year-olds. If children cannot recognize their own names, they can find the symbol they know is their own. Remember to give each child a different symbol. Most four- and five-year-olds can recognize their own names. If not, they can be taught.

Suggestions for Parents

Dressing can be time-consuming and frustrating for teachers and children. For this reason, some centers provide parents with a list of clothing suggestions for the children. The list usually includes the following:

- Send an extra set of clothing for your child to keep at school. These can be used in case of an emergency. For instance, a child might fall in mud, rip a pair of pants, or have a toileting accident.
- Attach labels to the inside of your child's clothing. It is common for several children to have the same style and size of clothes. Labeling helps prevent confusion.

16-3 Letting children know they are capable of dressing and undressing themselves helps children build independence.

- Select clothing for your child with large zippers, buttons, or snaps. This makes dressing easier for children who do not have well-developed small motor skills.
- Boots and shoes should fit properly and slide on and off easily.
- Shoelaces should not be too long because they can be a tripping hazard and are hard for children to tie. You may want to choose shoes with Velcro closings, which are easier for younger children to manage independently.
- Consider buying elastic-waist slacks and shorts instead of snap or button types. They are easier for children to handle during toileting.

Demonstrating

Buttoning, zipping, pulling on boots, tying shoes, and putting fingers in gloves are all actions that can be demonstrated. Demonstrating at the child's eye level is the most effective. Sometimes, verbal guidance is all that a child needs. At other times, you may need to start an action. Allow the child to finish the process. He or she will feel a sense of accomplishment. For example, Siri can put on his coat but cannot get the zipper started. You may help by starting the zipper and having Siri finish zipping it by himself.

Tying Shoes. Tying is a skill that requires advanced coordination. As a result, most children do not learn this task until five years of age.

There are several methods for teaching children how to tie shoes. One method is to place the child on your lap. From this angle, the child can observe the process. For most children, the easiest technique to learn is to loop each string like a bunny ear. Tie these loops into a double knot. Encourage the child to repeat this process.

Some children will have shoes that clasp with Velcro instead of tie with laces. Bring shoes with ties to the center to teach these children how to tie. Let them use these shoes to practice. This will help them learn tying skills, or you can let them practice on a shoelace box, 16-4.

Boots. Boots can be hard to put on when children are wearing boots that are too small.

16-4 A shoelace box is useful for teaching tying to children.

When this happens, place a plastic bag over the child's shoes or feet. This will help the boot slip on and off more easily.

Some centers keep a box of surplus boots. When a child is wearing boots that are too small, the teacher can make an exchange. Boots from this box are also handy if a child forgets to bring boots from home.

Children can practice putting on and taking off their own boots, or they may practice using the extras in the box.

Coats. To demonstrate putting on a coat, lay the child's coat, button or zipper side up, on the floor. Have the child kneel at the collar end. Tell the child to place his or her hands and arms into the sleeves. Then tell the child to put it over his or her head. Using your own sweater or jacket, demonstrate this technique for the children. See 16-5.

Eating

Nutritional services provided by centers vary. Some centers serve only lunch, while others may also serve breakfast. Snacks may be the only

1. The child kneels at the collar end of the coat.

2. The child puts his or her hands in the coat sleeves.

3. The child flips the coat over his or her head.

4. The child puts his or her arms all the way into the sleeves.

16-5 This technique can be used by children to help them learn how to put on a coat.

food served in centers that do not operate all day. Some centers require that children bring their own bag lunches. While most centers provide older children with meals, they require that parents provide infant formulas.

As a teacher, you will have many concerns during mealtime. A main concern is serving nutritious meals that children will like. This concern is addressed in Chapter 11, "Planning Nutritious Meals and Snacks."

Making mealtime pleasant and orderly is another concern of teachers, 16-6. This means making meals appropriate for the ages, abilities, and interests of children. It also means teaching rules of etiquette during meals.

16-6 Proper manners and order contribute to a pleasant meal.

You will notice that children's appetites change. Children's appetites are influenced by illness, stage of development, physical activity, and a body's individual chemical needs. Emotions can also affect appetite. For example, if Lila has cried since her parents dropped her off this morning, she may not be hungry at lunchtime. Appetite changes will require you to be flexible regarding the children during meals.

Infants

Infants have definite food likes and dislikes. It is not unusual for infants to spit out or refuse foods they do not like. On the other hand, they will eagerly eat foods they enjoy.

Cup feeding may begin as early as six to seven months of age. At first, children may take only a few swallows. Spilling will occur for several months. Later, children will enjoy using cups by themselves. To help these children, provide spill-proof cups.

Once children become mobile, their interest in food may decrease. During this stage, some children are too interested in moving to sit still very long. Even if placed in a high chair or feeding table, they may try to get out and continue with their play.

Provide finger foods to infants whenever possible. By picking up small bits of food, the child will develop fine motor skills and hand-eye coordination skills. It also gives them a sense of accomplishment and helps them in developing independence.

Interest in self-feeding using spoons may occur between 15 and 18 months of age. You will need to be patient with children who are learning to feed themselves. You may have to help them fill their spoons. Since spilling occurs often, the children should wear bibs. Also expect food to be spilled on the feeding tray, high chair, and floor. Wipe up the spills immediately so others do not slip on them.

Two-Year-Olds

Two-year-old children become increasingly skilled at handling cups and spoons. Provide these children with child-sized spoons and small, unbreakable cups. Fill the cups only halfway. Then if a drink is spilled, there is less to clean up.

Use small milk or juice pitchers (16 ounces) with two-year-olds. Encourage the children to fill their own cups. Watch carefully and provide support. See 16-7.

Three-Year-Olds

By the age of three, children have distinct food preferences, 16-8. They may refuse to eat certain foods because of their color, shape, or texture. Your attitude will help children accept these foods. In addition, family food attitudes and preferences can influence what children may eat. Other children can also influence food preferences. Some children who flatly refuse to eat vegetables at home may enjoy eating them with their peers.

Three-year-olds are old enough to assist with mealtime. Ask them to set the table. Make place mats containing outlines of the plate, glass, fork, and spoon. These patterns will help children set

16-7 Supervise two-year-olds as they pour their own drinks. They may need help handling the pitcher.

16-8 Pizza is a favorite food among children.

16-9 Children enjoy helping prepare
foods they will eat later.

the table properly with minimal adult assistance. Provide forks and spoons to help the children develop handling skills. Use glasses with weighted bottoms to help prevent spills. Use pitchers with lids and pour spouts. Shallow bowls allow the children to see what is in the bowls.

Have children serve themselves. As a rule, tell children to fill their milk glasses only halfway. Keep portions small. A simple guideline to follow is one tablespoon of food for each year of age. If children want more food, they may ask for second portions.

Keep a wet sponge on the table for spills. When children spill, accept this as a normal occurrence. Avoid scolding the child. Rather, guide the child in wiping up the spill.

Four- and Five-Year-Olds

Four- and five-year-olds like to help at mealtime. They may ask to set the table, serve, and assist with after-meal cleanup. They may also enjoy helping to prepare the meal. As the teacher, encourage them to do so. For a classroom activity, have them prepare pudding, rolls, or other simple foods, 16-9. Later, serve these foods for snack or lunch.

Older children enjoy talking at the table. You may wish to help them begin conversations. Mention activities they have seen, heard, or done.

They will begin talking with each other and naturally move on to other subjects.

Rules

Rules for eating depend on the ages of the children. However, general rules might include the following:

- Taste all foods before asking for seconds of food or milk.
- Remain at the table until everyone has finished.
- Wipe up your own spills.
- Eat food only from your own plate.

Eating Problems

Eating problems are common during the preschool years. These problems usually peak at three years of age. Eating will remain a problem for 25 percent of four- and five-year-olds. In most cases, problems will end somewhere around the sixth birthday. Food refusal, dawdling, pica, and vomiting are all eating problems that can become serious.

Food Refusal. Food refusal problems are related to a lack of interest in food. Food refusal often begins between one and two years of age. At this time, children's need for food decreases. Some children may need only one meal a day. Refusing food because it is not needed is not a problem. However, children who do not eat even when they need food have food refusal problems.

Lack of exercise or energy, excess energy (hyperactivity), and illness can all cause a lack of interest in food. These fairly common problems sometimes cure themselves. There are steps you can take, however, to help children with food refusal problems.

To encourage children to eat, serve small portions, 16-10. Avoid pushing the children to eat. Instead, talk with the parents of children having problems. Find out what these children eat at home. Despite mealtime refusal at the center, these children may be getting proper nourishment at home.

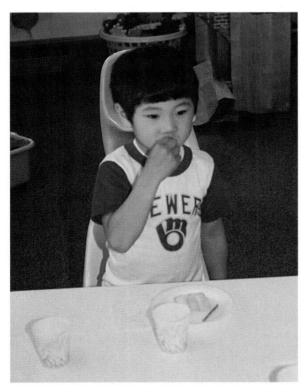

16-10 Children with small appetites are more likely to eat if they are given smaller portions.

Do not provide between-meal snacks to children who refuse to eat breakfast and lunch. If you provide these children with food throughout the day, they will not be hungry at mealtime.

Pica. **Pica** is a craving for unnatural foods. Cravings include paper, soap, rags, and even toys. This condition is fairly uncommon in most preschool children.

If you think that a child may have this problem, ask other staff members to observe the child. Compare your observations. Discuss the problem with the center director. You may want to schedule a conference with the parents to discuss the problem. A combined effort between parents, medical professionals, and teachers may solve the problem.

Dawdling. While one child eats only one or two teaspoons of food, the other children may have finished an entire meal. It is common to have several children who eat slowly in a group of preschoolers. This is called **dawdling**. Some may hold food in their mouth for a long time, failing to chew or swallow it. Others are so busy talking at the table that they fail to take the time to eat. Still others may push the food around their plates or play with it. These children lack interest in food.

Many times dawdling is an attempt to gain attention. Therefore, do not urge or threaten dawdling children. Instead, provide these children with small portions of food. After being given a reasonable amount of time to eat, clear the table without comment. Children will learn that if they want to eat, they must do so in a timely fashion.

Vomiting. Young children are able to induce (to produce on purpose) vomiting. If a child in your class vomits often, without other signs of illness, he or she is possibly inducing it.

If you are sure a child is not sick, ignore repeated vomiting. Clean up the mess quickly, without emotion. If the child notices any concern, he or she may begin vomiting to get your attention.

You should, however, share the child's behavior with the parents. Find out if this behavior also occurs at home during or right after a meal. If it does, you will need to work with the center director and parents to solve the problem.

Napping

"Will my child be required to take a nap?" This question is asked often by parents who are thinking of enrolling their child in a center. Some children may have outgrown napping at home. Your response will depend on your state's child care licensing regulations and center policies.

Most states require that preschool children nap at least one hour, 16-11. A center can expand that requirement if they wish. For instance, if a state requires all children under the age of five to have naps, a center may expand that rule to require all enrolled children to have naps. In any case, you should check your state's guidelines for requirements.

Most child care centers have a set nap time. At the end of this time, most children are awake. If not, they are gently woken. You may note that a certain child needs to be woken every day. If this happens, the child may not be getting enough rest at home. This needs to be discussed with the parents. Check with your center director to find out who is responsible for talking to the parents. If you are asked to contact the parents, use a positive approach. Share your observations with the parents. Try to arrive at a solution together.

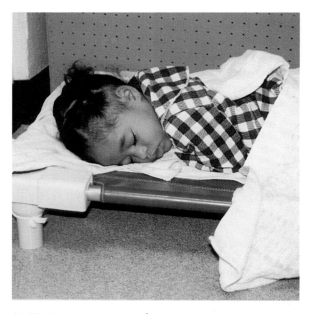

16-11 Naps are required in many states.

Nap Time Rituals

Schedule quiet activities prior to nap time. Children often enjoy hearing a story at this time. Select stories that will soothe the children. Four-year-olds may like to look at books until they fall asleep. You may want to play soft music.

Lack of rest can cause irritability in young children. Most preschool children, tired or not, can postpone sleep at nap time. Younger children may simply cry. Older children, however, may make repeated demands for your attention. They may request to go to the washroom or have a drink of water. In most cases, these are only pleas for attention.

Plan ahead to prevent children from making too many demands at nap time. First, have the children use the toilet, brush their teeth, wash their hands, and have a drink of water before they lie down. Ask if anyone needs a tissue or wants to look quietly at a book. Make sure they have their blankets and stuffed toys. After this, begin to cover them. Do not be surprised, however, if a child still asks for another drink of water or trip to the bathroom. These rituals seem natural to most two- and three-year-old children. They sincerely believe their needs are real. However, if you allow these children to meet these needs before nap time, they will have an easier time getting and staying settled. See 16-12.

Not all children will fall asleep at nap time. Their need for sleep varies. It is common for some of the five-year-olds to remain awake. Five-year-olds will cooperate, however, if nap time limits are stated clearly and enforced.

Children who do fall asleep may tell you they had bad dreams while sleeping. Others may cry out in their sleep. When this happens, calmly approach the child. Let the child know you are near. One way to do this is to hold the child's hand or straighten the covers.

As a teacher, it is important to respect the children's need for sleep. Because it is difficult for some children to fall asleep, try to remain as quiet as possible. Avoid talking to other teachers or walking in and out of the room during nap time.

Toileting

The toileting needs of infants are met through the use of diapers. Infants cannot control

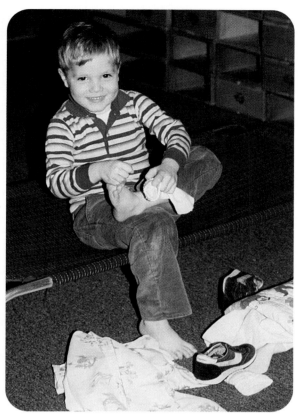

16-12 Allow children to remove shoes and socks at nap time. They will be more comfortable and relaxed.

elimination, bowel and bladder release. For them, elimination is a reflex action. The first few weeks after birth, infants eliminate many times each day. They may cry when it happens. The number of eliminations will decrease as the infant gets older. However, the volume increases. By 28 weeks, a child may remain dry from one to two hours. When they do eliminate, however, the diaper is usually soaking wet. It may leak unless it is changed immediately. Diapers need to be checked often and changed when wet to prevent diaper rash.

Children differ in their toilet training needs and schedule. Some children are toilet trained as early as eighteen months. Others may not have full bladder and bowel control until two and one-half to three years of age. For some children, toilet training will take just a few days. Other children may require several months.

Toilet Training Timetable

Children cannot be taught to perform toilet functions until their central nervous systems are ready. As a rule, this does not occur until after two years of age. At this age, most children will express their need to use the toilet. Some may pull down their pants and sit on the toilet. Others will tell you they have to use the bathroom.

Each child in the center will have his or her own toilet training timetable. Never force children to learn before they are ready. Instead, observe and praise them as they become better at keeping themselves dry. Controlling elimination is one step toward independence. It is a real accomplishment for young children.

Certain factors may affect a child's toilet training timetable. Illness, a new baby in the home, or weather changes are common factors. Remember, too, that toileting accidents are common during a child's first few weeks at the child care center. These accidents may indicate the emotional stress the child is feeling in a new environment. Another factor is the toilet training attitudes and practices at home. In some homes, adults may overreact to children's toileting accidents by showing their disapproval. These children may feel ashamed by their failure to control elimination. In the center, you need to be sensitive to children's feelings following an accident. Quietly help them change into clean clothes.

Guidance

As a teacher, maintain a matter-of-fact attitude in toilet training. Shaming and scolding have no place in helping a child develop control. Instead, provide children with the facilities and encouragement to stay dry.

Have toilet seats or potty chairs available. If you provide a seat for the toilet, also provide a step stool to help the children reach the toilet. Not all children like to sit on the toilet. Some are afraid they will fall in the toilet and be flushed down. These children will prefer the potty chair.

During toilet training, the child's clothing should be easy to manage. Pants that pull down easily work better than those that are hard to unfasten. Also during this time, it is a good idea to have several pairs of underwear and clothing at the center.

Children often provide clues when they have to use the toilet. Some start wiggling. Others cross their legs. When you notice these signs, provide reminders to the child. You can remind the child by saying, "It is toilet time again," or "Louis, do you need to use the toilet?" After children use the toilet, remind them to flush the toilet and wash their hands. At the same time, you may want to wash your own hands. See 16-13.

Cleanup

Cleanup is an important routine in early childhood classrooms. Children learn to be responsible for themselves, their belongings, and classroom materials and equipment. Cleanup time can be stressful for a new teacher. Consider Carlos, who recently began teaching in a preschool classroom. He has confided that frequently he finds himself raising his voice and either scolding or nagging the children to participate in cleanup. Carlos' frustration is not uncommon. The following suggestions may be helpful.

Guidance

Try to maintain a positive attitude toward cleanup. Scolding or nagging the children usually is ineffective. You will discover that some children are unresponsive and do not want to participate.

Begin by setting firm ground rules and then follow through. All children should be expected to participate in cleanup. You must deal on an individual basis with the child who refuses to participate. You may say "Tanya, you need to put the puzzle away." Observe Tanya closely. If she walks away from the table, take her hand. Then say "Tanya, come. You need to return the puzzle to the tray." If Tanya still refuses to put the puzzle away, she needs help in understanding the consequences. Explain that if she fails to put the puzzle away, she will not be able to play with the puzzles.

You will find that some children need encouragement or reminders. You might try saying the following:

- Help me put the blocks away.
- Show me where the puzzles are stored.
- Where do we hang these dress-up clothes?
- Timmy, you worked hard making your block structure. Now show Malcolm how to put the blocks away.

Foster independence by visually assisting the children in seeing where materials and equipment belong. For instance, in the woodworking area, paint a silhouette of each tool on a piece of tagboard. Hooks in the dramatic play area should be available for hanging dress-up clothes. To assist the children, attach an eight-inch loop of string to each item of clothing. On the block shelves, provide separate sections for each shape and size of blocks. The manipulative area needs to have separate, transparent containers for different types of pieces.

Young children enjoy pleasing others. They will work hard to win your approval. Thus, it is important that children's efforts at cleanup be praised. Praise their efforts by saying "Sally, I like the way you are helping Frankie put the blocks away" or "Ampario, I like the way you picked up all of the pieces of your puzzle."

Transitions

Transitions are changes from one activity to another or moves from one place to another. They occur many times during the day. Children may go from self-selected activities to using the bathroom to snack time to outdoor play in just a few hours. Transitions must be carefully planned to help children get through the daily routine without a fuss.

Provide a five-minute warning prior to making the transition to the next activity. This will allow children time to finish what they are

---

Tips for Guiding Toilet Training

- Each child has his or her own toilet training timetable. Never force children to learn before they are ready.
- Maintain a matter-of-fact attitude.
- Praise children as they become better at keeping dry.
- Do not shame or scold.
- Make toilet seats or potty chairs available.
- Watch for clues that children provide when they need to use the toilet.

16-13 Remember these rules for effective toileting guidance.

doing. You might play the piano for five minutes or use an egg timer.

There are four basic methods for making successful transitions. You may use concrete objects, visual signals, novelty, or auditory signals. You may use several types of transitions in one day. Remember to be consistent. Young children respond better if they know what to expect. Therefore, it is best to use the same transition for individual activities. For instance, play the same cleanup song on the piano every day to let the children know it is cleanup time.

Concrete Objects

Using concrete objects as a form of transition involves children moving items from one place to another. This technique directs a child's attention from one activity to another, 16-14. Examples include the following:

- "Leon, please put your picture in your cubby." This will direct Leon from an art activity to a new activity.

16-14 Putting away toys helps prepare children for the next activity.

- "Rose, hang up your coat." Rose will move from an outdoor activity to an indoor activity.
- "Ting, here is some play dough. Take it to the art table." Ting is directed toward starting an art activity.
- "Shilpa, put these washcloths on the bathroom hook." This signals the end of cleanup.

Visual Signals

Using visual signals is another transition method. This method involves informing children of a change through signals they can see. For instance, when you show the children a picture of lunchtime, the children move to the lunch table. After story time, you might hold up a picture of outdoor play. This will serve as a signal to the children that it is time to put on outdoor clothing and wait at the door for you. See 16-15 for other examples of visual transitions.

The first few times you use visual signals, you will need to explain them to the children. After you use them several times, the children will know what to expect.

Novelty

Novelty transitions involve the use of unusual, new actions or devices to move the children from one activity to another.

Locomotion is one type of transition. The children use motion to make their transition. For instance, ask the children to pretend they are elephants. Have them walk like heavy elephants to the snack table, or ask them to tiptoe lightly like tiny monkeys.

Using locomotion is limited only by imagination. Children can march, skip, or walk backwards. Before introducing a transition, however, consider the abilities of the children. For instance, do not ask a group of two- or three-year-olds to skip. They may not have developed this skill yet.

Transportation is another type of novelty transition. The children can move like freight trains, jets, buses, or cars. Each time you introduce a locomotion or transportation transition, get involved with the children. Model the movement you want them to make.

Using Visual Transition	
Visual Transition Method	**Application of Method**
Construction paper	Use to break children into small groups. Place a piece of blue, red, green, or yellow construction paper at each table. Divide children into four groups and assign each group one of these colors. Have groups find their tables.
Hand motions	Use on playground to motion children indoors or to a specific area.
Blinking lights	Use to gain children's attention or to warn children to complete an activity.
Clock	Use with older children by telling them "When the big hand is on the 12, it will be lunchtime."
Words	Use to dismiss children from a group. Make a name card for each child. Hold cards up one at a time. Children are dismissed when they see their names.

16-15 Visual signals can be used many ways for transition.

Identification games are also used for novelty transition. For instance, you may direct the children from one activity to another by asking "Who is wearing red today? You may go into the bathroom and wash your hands before we have our snacks." See 16-16. Continue using other colors that the children are wearing until every child has departed from the group.

16-16 Using a color identification game helps catch children's attention when making a transition.

Novelty transitions can also be made using single alphabet letters. Direct the children to another activity by asking "Whose name starts with the letter T? You may go outside." Continue calling out letters until all of the children are outdoors.

Auditory Signals

Auditory signals inform the children of a change through the use of sound. A bell, timer, Autoharp®, tambourine, or piano can all inform children of a transition. Some teachers use a simple song or chord of music as a transition signal. For example, when Mr. Andrews plays "Mary Had a Little Lamb" on the piano, the children know it is time to cleanup.

Auditory signals also need to be developed for individuals. There will be times when you may wish to signal only one child. For instance, you may quietly tell a child that he or she needs to cleanup or go to the snack table. This is called an *individual transition.*

Auditory signals are quite useful for providing warnings. For instance, a ringing bell tells the children that playtime will end in five minutes. At the end of the five minutes, they know it is time to cleanup.

Summary

A daily schedule and routines provide structure to each day. Within this structure, children have the opportunity to develop independence. Having a predictable schedule and helping children to handle daily routines allows the center to run smoothly.

A well-planned schedule provides the framework for the day's activities. Schedules for early childhood programs vary by type of program. Factors such as the length of the program's day and the time children arrive will need to be considered.

The daily schedule must also be planned to meet the children's physical and psychological needs. Health and safety are important considerations. Very young children need to have time for meals and rest. Like adults, young children have psychological needs. For security, they need to have consistency and predictable routines.

Dressing, undressing, eating, napping, toileting, and cleanup are all daily routines. Each of these presents its own particular challenges and problems during the course of a day. For instance, asking children to participate with cleanup seems like a predictable activity. However, without the proper guidance, this task may become frustrating for both the children and the teacher. Therefore, it is important that you learn positive guidance strategies to make children responsible.

Review and Reflect

1. How do routines and daily schedules benefit young children?

2. Why is it important to provide large blocks of open time in the daily schedule?

3. Describe a typical arrival routine.

4. Why do some centers ask that parents send a second set of clothing for children to keep at school?

5. Name five factors that may influence a child's appetite.

6. List three rules for eating that might be used with young children.

7. Give two suggestions for handling a child who refuses to eat.

8. What is pica?

9. Do child care centers have the right to decide if nap time should be included in the daily schedule? Explain your answer.

10. At what age are most children ready for toilet training?

11. Describe one way you could encourage children to participate in cleanup.

12. List four types of transitions and give an example of each.

Apply and Explore

1. Practice putting on your sweater or jacket using the technique outlined in the chapter.

2. From a sitting position, practice teaching tying, buttoning, and zipping to one of your peers.

3. Ask experienced teachers for their successful nap time techniques. Present this information as a report.

4. Observe children at cleanup. Record the techniques the teacher uses with the children to encourage them to participate. Discuss your findings with your classmates.

5. Ask parents what clues their children use when they need to use the washroom. Compare these to the clues you observe.

A variety of materials should be included in the curriculum.

Part 4

Learning Experiences for Children

Good learning experiences for children are based on careful planning that begins with the establishment of program goals for your early childhood program. Quality programs reflect children's developmental needs and interests. In this part, you will learn how to plan curriculum that is based on the development of the whole child. You will learn appropriate methods of developing and writing program curriculum.

Providing a variety of learning experiences helps children learn and grow in many ways. As you read this part, you will learn techniques for guiding the following types of experiences: art, storytelling, puppetry, manuscript writing, math, science, social studies, food and nutrition, music and movement, and field trips.

Each chapter will give you guidelines for planning and supervising activities. You will read many ideas for specific activities to try with children. You will also discover what types of supplies and resources you will need to conduct these activities.

Plan a variety of techniques to use in learning experiences.

Chapter 17

The Curriculum

After studying this chapter, you will be able to

- develop program goals.
- indicate who is involved in curriculum development.
- cite the importance of assessment in curriculum planning.
- explain the content and process-centered approach to curriculum development.
- describe factors to consider in curriculum planning.
- illustrate the use of themes as a basis for planning curriculum.
- write a block plan and lesson plan for one week of a program.

Terms to Know

program goals
content and
    process-centered
    approach
direct learning
    experience
indirect learning
    experience
field-sensitive
field-independent
visual learner

auditory learner
theme
spiral curriculum
flowchart
concept
block plan
lesson plan
learning objectives
motivation
closure

Reading a story, feeding a bunny, singing songs, and playing outdoors are all parts of the curriculum. Cooking applesauce, scribbling on paper, building with blocks, and playing in the dramatic play corner are also considered the curriculum. The curriculum includes a variety of materials and equipment, 17-1. Even room arrangements reflect the curriculum.

A good early childhood curriculum is based on how children develop and learn. It consists of a wide range of concepts, experiences, and materials designed to meet the developmental needs of a group of children. These needs include their

17-1 Children's physical needs are as important to the curriculum as their emotional, social, and cognitive needs.

social, emotional, physical, and cognitive needs. It involves determining what children need to be able to do and what they need to know. A good curriculum also focuses on children's learning styles and characteristics. It often organizes important concepts into themes.

A good curriculum is critical in supporting the children's learning and development. It requires detailed plans in addition to knowledge of child development. This chapter will describe the factors to consider when planning a curriculum.

Developing Program Goals

Before the curriculum can be planned, the goals of the center's program need to be determined. In an early childhood program, the program goals outline the philosophy of the center. **Program goals** are broad statements of purpose that state the desired end results—what is to be achieved. Some people describe goals as the "why" of the curriculum.

Program goals based on child development focus on the "whole child." Goals for children in an early childhood setting might include the following:

- To develop a positive self-concept and attitude toward learning.
- To develop independence.
- To think critically and develop problem-solving skills, 17-2.
- To respect and understand cultural diversity.
- To develop effective language skills, both listening and speaking.
- To develop fine motor coordination.
- To develop large motor coordination.
- To develop personal initiative.
- To develop a curiosity about the world.
- To develop positive social skills, including cooperation and interdependence.
- To develop respect for one's own rights as well as the rights of others.
- To develop an understanding of the relationship between people, events, and objects.

Each of these goals is broad. The goals include all four areas of development since a developmentally appropriate curriculum considers the whole child.

17-2 Bulletin board activities are a good method to teach problem-solving skills.

Meeting Goals

Teachers, available resources, activities, and the environment all influence whether goals will be met. For example, if one of the goals is to create independence, provide children with a minimum of help. This gives children many opportunities to grow in independence. Classroom activities should require little involvement on the part of the teacher. Children should be able to participate in most activities without an adult's help. The activities, then, will need to match children's skill levels.

The classroom environment, including room arrangement, can also foster the development of independence. Coat hooks, paper towels, tables, chairs, and equipment placed within children's reach is helpful. This allows the children to act on their own. They do not have to depend on teachers for help at all times.

Who Plans the Curriculum?

Curriculum development can involve one person or several staff members. In small centers, the head teacher is often the person in charge of planning the curriculum, 17-3. Teachers have first-hand knowledge of their children's interests, needs, learning styles, and prior experiences. In

17-3 Using a self-planned curriculum allows teachers to create their own games for the children.

some centers, a wide range of additional people are involved in the process. Directors, teachers, aides, parents, and in some cases even the center cook may all be included at some time. Each of these people can provide helpful information in planning the curriculum. In large organizations, a curriculum specialist may be hired to plan the curriculum.

The child care director usually plays a key role in curriculum development. In most centers, the director is in charge of supervising all center activities. Therefore, the director's position usually includes curriculum supervision.

Some child care chains provide the director with preplanned curriculum units. The director is responsible for introducing the curriculum to the teaching staff. After modifying it to fit the children's needs, the teachers are expected to use the curriculum.

A preplanned curriculum has both advantages and disadvantages. For a staff with little

training or experience, a preplanned curriculum can be helpful. Activities, procedures, and suggestions are often outlined in detail. Having these curriculum ideas at their fingertips saves teachers time and energy.

A preplanned curriculum has some disadvantages. It may not factor in the individual differences and learning styles of the children in your program. The curriculum needs to be based on the learners' abilities so it can build on what the children already know. Experienced teachers may feel stifled or limited by a preplanned curriculum. Because of their experience, they are more likely to observe a mismatch between children's needs and the curriculum. If this happens, experienced teachers are likely to feel frustrated.

Assessment: An Important Step in Curriculum Planning

Every child is unique, even though there are many similarities within age groups. For this reason, assessment is necessary in order to plan a curriculum that is both individualized and age appropriate for all areas of learning.

The assessment process should provide you with useful information for planning a curriculum. The first assessment supplies data on what the children already know and what skills they have achieved. This data can help you fit curriculum to individual children. It can also be helpful for informing parents of their children's progress over a period of time.

Assessment should be based on the children's activities at the center. It should highlight what the children know and what they can do. It should include collections of the children's work, such as artwork, stories, and projects. Teachers' observations and summaries may also be included.

The Content and Process-Centered Curriculum

Though there are a number of approaches to curriculum planning, the most popular method is the **content and process-centered approach**. Learning is seen as a constant process of exploring and questioning the environment. A hands-on curriculum is stressed. All four areas of child development—social, emotional, physical, and cognitive—are included. A wide range of age-appropriate materials, supplies, and experiences are used to enrich the environment, 17-4. Materials and equipment are matched to the children's abilities, cultural background, and development.

Basic learning materials are a key part of the content and process-centered curriculum. These materials are chosen and structured by the teacher. They may include puzzles, games, blocks, sand, water, books, records, and supplies for dramatic play and science study.

The physical environment is carefully planned and prepared with the content for learning. It should be based on an assessment of children's developmental needs and interests. Once established, the children assume responsibility by choosing most of their own activities. As a result, the use of time, space, and equipment is largely determined by the children.

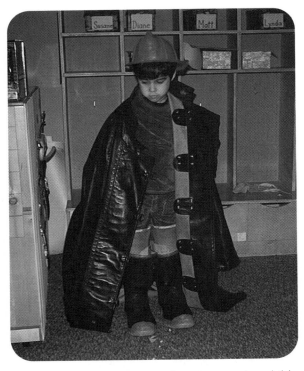

17-4 In this process-centered environment, a child learns more about firefighters by trying on a firefighter's outfit.

A good curriculum includes direct and indirect learning experiences. **Direct learning experiences** are planned with a specific goal in mind. For instance, a carpentry learning activity may be planned to develop fine motor skills and to teach the use of safety goggles. The room arrangement may be planned to foster the independence needed for this task and call attention to the activity.

Indirect learning experiences occur on the spur of the moment. For example, while watching Reina, Dwayne may learn how to button his coat. Shelly may learn how to paint by watching Mark. While mixing paint, Kelsie may learn that adding red paint to blue paint makes purple paint.

Factors to Consider in Curriculum Planning

As you begin planning a curriculum, there are a number of important factors to keep in mind. You must first decide what information should be covered. There are three important questions to ask as the content of the curriculum is determined. The learning activities selected need to be balanced. There are several factors to consider for a good balance of activities to be achieved. In addition, various learning styles and learning characteristics need to be considered.

Choose the Information to Cover

As you begin planning the curriculum, you must decide what information to cover. Three basic questions can help you with this process. First, consider the question: Is the information worth knowing? In order to answer this question, think about the cultural context. In some societies a certain learning outcome may be important. Ask yourself if the outcome will help the child better cope with his or her surroundings.

Children in the United States at some point must learn to read. Our culture places great importance on reading. As a result, children are read many stories in child care centers. Through listening, children learn to enjoy and appreciate literature. In an illiterate society, these skills would not be needed. Other skills important to that culture would be stressed.

A second question needs to be answered: Is the information testable? In other words, the child should be able to see firsthand that the information is true, 17-5. Many times, teachers choose activities based on personal appeal. They like the activity. For instance, activities related to dinosaurs have long been included in the curriculum of many child care centers. Think about the activity based on this question. Will children ever see a live dinosaur? This activity is not testable. Another activity would be more appropriate. Instead of reading a book about dinosaurs, choose one about an animal children know about or may have a chance to see at the zoo.

Here is another example. If you were going to do a unit on foods, making butter would be a testable activity. To begin this activity, tell the children that cream can be made into butter. Then show the children the consistency of cream. After this, give each child a container filled with whipping cream. Show them how to shake the container. Tell the children to keep shaking until the mixture becomes thick. After the cream has turned to butter, let each child taste the butter. This will help them test their knowledge.

The third basic question remains: Is the information developmentally appropriate? A learning activity that requires giving scissors and paper to three- and four-year-olds is appropriate. Children this age can use scissors properly. This activity would be inappropriate for children 18 to 24 months old.

Reading the book *Little Red Riding Hood* might also be inappropriate. You may find that even some five-year-olds may not be ready for this book. Many preschool children cannot separate fantasy from reality. As a result, this book could produce fear. It could also teach false concepts. For instance, wolves do not talk, although in the book they do.

Balance Learning Activities

An appropriate curriculum contains a balance of learning activities supporting all developmental domains. These activities must be chosen with care. Activities that keep children busy are not always the best activities. Likewise, just because children prefer a certain activity does not mean it must be kept included in the curriculum. You must evaluate each activity to be sure it is right for the children.

17-5 Information on cows is testable if children can see and touch a cow.

A good curriculum includes a balance of structured as well as unstructured learning activities. Examples of unstructured activities include blockbuilding, collages, water play, and sand play. Children should spend most of their time in self-initiated play with unstructured activities. This type of play allows them opportunities to practice newly developed skills.

Structured, or close-ended, learning activities also need to be included. These activities indirectly prescribe children's actions. Stringing beads, working puzzles, and cooking are all examples.

Whenever possible, also plan a balance of indoor and outdoor learning activities, 17-6. The climate in your area will determine whether this is possible. During extremely hot and cold weather, the children should remain indoors. When this happens, provide children with large motor activities appropriate for indoors.

In warmer climates, weather permitting, many indoor learning activities can be moved outdoors. Painting, water play, and story and music time can all be done outdoors.

Active and quiet learning activities must be balanced. Planning too many active learning activities in a row may overstimulate some children. The result can be chaotic. To prevent this, follow active learning activities with quiet ones. For example, outdoor activity followed by a story and small group would be a good balance.

Too many quiet learning activities in a row also have a drawback. Children will get restless. The results can be just as chaotic as too many active learning activities. Children may lose interest in the activities and begin to wiggle and talk out of turn.

Consider Learning Styles

When planning activities for young children, consider the diversity of individual learning styles. Basic learning styles include field-sensitive, field-independent, visual learner, and auditory learner.

Field-Sensitive

Field-sensitive children like to work with others, 17-7. In a group setting, they are helpful. They will volunteer and assist others in picking up blocks, setting the table, and finding a place for a puzzle piece. Field-sensitive children will also try to gain your attention.

17-6 Outdoor activities allow children to get fresh air and work off excess energy.

17-7 Field-sensitive children enjoy playing with others.

When introduced to a new activity, field-sensitive children want a model to follow. They may ask to be shown how to do the activity. If there is not a model or demonstration, they may wait. When someone else begins, they will observe. After this observation, they will begin their work.

Field-Independent

Field-independent children like to try new activities. They enjoy discovery. These children do not have to be urged to try new activities. In most cases, they will be the first to try new activities. Children who are field-independent will rarely contact the teacher for help. They enjoy engaging in new tasks without directions or assistance from the teacher.

Field-independent children prefer to work on their own, 17-8. However, they enjoy competition as well as individual recognition. Field-independent children are also task orientated. When engaged in an activity, they generally do not notice what is going on around them.

Visual Learners

Visual learners depend a great deal on the sense of sight. These children notice small changes in the environment. When a plant is added to the science table, they are the first to notice. Visual learners enjoy looking at books and other objects.

Auditory Learners

Auditory learners are those who learn best through hearing. These children are the first to hear a fly in the classroom or a snowplow outdoors. You will find that auditory learners enjoy listening. To meet their needs, tapes, stories, and poems need to be included in the curriculum.

You may find that learning styles vary from program to program. That is, last year more children might have been field-independent, while this year more children are field-sensitive. The number of children who are primarily visual learners may also vary from year to year. This information is important for planning a program that relates to the children's learning styles.

Most children use a combination of senses. That is, they use both visual and auditory input to learn. To provide for these children's needs, plan activities that involve several senses, 17-9. For example, while reading a book, also show the

17-8 Field-independent children enjoy working alone.

17-9 Showing and talking about a new activity appeals to a child's visual and auditory senses.

pictures. Using this method, children should retain more knowledge. They will also find activities more satisfying.

Consider Learning Characteristics

Each classroom has children with a wide range of learning characteristics. Some children work slowly, others quickly. Some children are attentive, and others are easily bored. Some are quick decision makers, while others are cautious.

Evaluate children's learning characteristics in relation to your own. If you work quickly, keep this in mind as you plan the curriculum. When demonstrating for children, slow down so

they can understand concepts. Avoid reading or talking too fast.

Use caution when planning group learning activities. If Joey works extremely slow and Tommy works quickly, being in the same group may be frustrating for both. It is better to place children with others who work at the same pace.

Some children have long attention spans. They are able to pay attention and sit still for long periods of time. Other children, however, are easily distracted. To hold the interests of these children, plan novel and interesting group activities. For instance, during story time use a variety of teaching methods. During one week, use at least three types of media. Flannel board

Activities for a Puppet Theme

Fine Motor Development
Handling puppets.
Making puppets.
- Paper bag puppets.
- Peanut puppets.
- Sock puppets.
- Paper plate puppets.
- Stick puppets.
- Milk carton puppets.
- Spoon puppets.

Art
Designing and making puppets.

Social Studies
Attending a marionette show.

Language, Storytelling, and Dramatic Play
Telling a story using a puppet.
Putting on a puppet show.
Telling a shadow puppet story.
Learning new vocabulary related to puppets.
Looking at pictures of puppets at group time.
Setting up a puppet stage with a variety of
   puppets.

Sensory Table
Provide a variety of puppets made from
   different materials.

17-10 A brainstorming session among several teachers yielded this list of activities for a puppet theme.

figures, flip charts, puppets, draw and tell charts, and videotapes could all be used to tell a story.

Children also make decisions in different ways. Some children are quick to make decisions. This type of decision making is called *impulsive*. When given the chance, impulsive decision makers act immediately.

Other children are slower to make decisions. This type of decision making is called *cautious*. These children approach a new activity carefully. They study the environment before they begin.

Remember that not all children complete activities in the same amount of time. Children move and learn at different rates. As a teacher, you will need to be aware of individual learning styles and characteristics when planning the curriculum.

Themes

As teachers plan their curriculum, they often use themes. A **theme** is one main topic or concept around which the classroom activities are planned. Successful themes take the children's age, abilities, and interests into consideration.

Other criteria to keep in mind when selecting a theme are the time of the year and the availability of supportive resources.

Once a theme is chosen, the activities can be developed, 17-10. This is best done through brainstorming as a group. The number and types of activities will vary with the theme. The environment and learning experiences are planned to complement the theme. For example, a theme on apples may include a trip to an apple orchard. A bulletin board with the three different colors of apples might also be planned. Books such as Johnny Appleseed could be read to the children at group time.

An apple theme lends itself to cooking. Applesauce, baked apples, apple muffins, apple bread, and apple butter could all be made. An art activity might involve making apple prints from sponges cut in the shape of apples. Lotto games could be made using three different colors of apples: red, yellow, and green. Apples of various sizes and colors could be placed on the science table. These can be cut apart and studied under a microscope. Chart 17-11 lists examples of themes.

Examples of Themes			
The Five Senses	Grandfather	Art	Travel
Zoo Animals	Aunts	Brushes and Brooms	The Circus
Pets	Uncles	How I Care for Myself	All About Measuring
All About Dogs	Sisters	Hats	Money
The Farm	Brothers	Scissors	Directions
Colors	Watches and Clocks	Our Town	Gestures
Music	Foods	Water Animals	Camping
Flowers	Vegetables	Wheels	Shapes
Health	Fruits	Transportation	Bugs
Weather	Breads	Land	Plants
Water	Meats	Water	Exercise
We Create	Dairy Products	Air	The Garden
We Dance	Seasons	Signs and Pictures	Hospitals
We Sing	Summer	Police Officers	Telephones
We Act	Fall	Firefighters	Safety Signs
Toys	Winter	Truck Drivers	Fairy Tales
Safety	Spring	Carpenters	Sounds
Emotions	Shadows	Doctors	The Newspaper
Fantasy and Reality	Homes	Nurses	Nature
The Family	Holidays	Mechanics	The Library
Mother	Clothes	Temperature	Computers
Father	Community Helpers	Friends	Machines
Grandmother	Puppets		

17-11 Themes can come from all segments of children's environments.

Very seldom do the majority of the activities that are planned relate to the theme. Some themes will have more related resources than others. Stories and bulletin board displays are the only two activities that nearly always relate to the theme.

Theme Ideas

As a rule, certain themes appeal to certain age groups, 17-12. Very young children's interests center on their immediate surroundings. As children grow, their circle of interests becomes larger, like a spiral. A curriculum based on this concept is called a **spiral curriculum**.

Two-year-old children are interested in their immediate world. Themes such as sight, sound, touch, taste, and smell are appealing to them. Families, colors, shapes, pets, farm animals, and foods are also good themes for two-year-olds. For each classroom area, plan a variety of activities that relate to the theme you choose. This will keep the young children interested.

Three-year-old children are interested in their families. However, they are becoming interested in their neighbors and their community. Themes based on the supermarket, bakery, library, post office, fire station, and police station are of special interest to these children. Their interests are growing in the spiral outside of their immediate surroundings.

Themes related to animals are also enjoyed by three- and four-year-olds. These themes can focus on groups of animals. Groups might include farm, forest, water, and zoo animals. Bugs, birds, dogs, and cats can also have appeal for these young children.

Four- and five-year-old children enjoy themes related to a wider variety of topics. Themes can be grouped into a few broad categories. For instance, broad themes might include *My World, Things I Like to Do, Things that Move,* and *Transportation.*

These categories could be broken down to contain a few sub-themes. *My School, My Home, My Feelings,* and *My Family* are just a few examples of sub-themes in *My World.*

Holiday Themes

Use caution when planning holiday themes for children. Preschool children lack a clear concept of time. If a holiday theme is introduced too early, children may become too excited. For instance, if Halloween is introduced the first week of October but does not actually happen until four weeks later, children will become confused. They will not know when to expect Halloween.

A Spiral Curriculum		
Themes for Two- and Three-Year-Olds		

All About Me	Concepts I'm Learning	
I'm Me, I'm Special	Big/Little	
My Family	Up/Down	
My Friends	Soft/Hard	
My Home	Wet/Dry	
My Toys	Things That Go	
My Senses	Cars	
Foods I Eat	Trucks	
Colors In My World	Boats	
Shapes I See	Airplanes	
Circles	Animals In My World	
Squares	Dogs	
Triangles	Cats	
Rectangles	Farm Animals	
Hearts	Zoo Animals	

17-12 Children's interests widen as they get older. Study this chart for evidence of the spiral curriculum concept.

(Continued)

A Spiral Curriculum

Themes for Three- and Four-Year-Olds

People in My World
  My Family
  My Friends
  Police Officers
  Firefighters
  Bakers
  Meat Cutters
  Librarians
  Printers
  Medical Doctors
  Nurses
  Pharmacists
  Ambulance Attendants
  Bankers
  Chefs
  Waiters and Waitresses
  Musicians
  Hair Stylists
  Photographers
  Secretaries
  Computer
    Programmers
  Clerks
  Sanitary Engineers
  Pilots and Flight
    Attendants
  Gas Station Attendants
  Auto Mechanics
  Painters
  Carpenters
  Plumbers
  Farmers
  Florists
All About Me
  My Senses
  My Feelings
  My Home
  My School

Themes for Four- and Five-Year-Olds

My Body
  Good Health
  Exercise
  Nutrition
Communication
  Speaking
  Listening
  Puppets
  Acting
  Writing
  Radio
  Television
My World
  Pets
  Plants
  Flowers
  Insects and Spiders
Transportation
  Air
  Land
  Water
Tools
  Garden
  Carpenter
  Mechanic
  Cosmetologist
  Dentist

17-12 Continued.

The activities planned around holiday themes are also often quite stimulating for children. If this excitement goes on for four weeks, behavior problems could arise. More guidance will be needed.

Theme Length

Children's attention spans and available resources are the two major factors affecting theme length. For example, if children are interested and resources are available, a Valentine's Day theme should be limited to a week.

Some themes can be carried out for a month or longer. A community helpers theme could go on for quite some time. Many community helpers could be used as bases for themes.

Developing Themes Using Flowcharts

An effective method for developing themes is to use resource books. To make this possible, many centers have a set of encyclopedias to use as references for background information. After using this resource, a flowchart can be drawn. A **flowchart** outlines major concepts related to a theme.

Drawing a flowchart is a simple method for listing concepts related to a theme. For example, when developing a theme on puppets, consult a resource. List all concepts you might include, 17-13. The major headings in a puppet flowchart could be vocabulary, movement, types, stages, materials, and characterization.

After drawing up a flowchart, writing objectives is the next step. Study the flowchart for objectives that can be developed. For instance, based on the flowchart in Chart 17-13, children might be expected to

- identify the six types of puppets.
- develop skill in moving puppets with rods, wires, strings, and hands.
- enjoy a puppet show.
- learn new vocabulary words: marionette, shadow, and dummy.

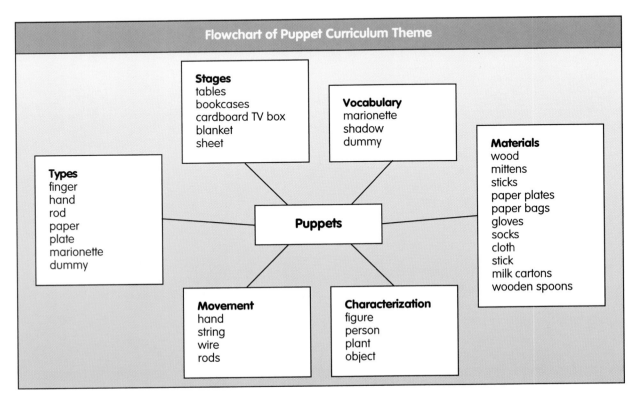

Flowchart of Puppet Curriculum Theme

Stages
tables
bookcases
cardboard TV box
blanket
sheet

Vocabulary
marionette
shadow
dummy

Materials
wood
mittens
sticks
paper plates
paper bags
gloves
socks
cloth
stick
milk cartons
wooden spoons

Types
finger
hand
rod
paper
plate
marionette
dummy

Puppets

Movement
hand
string
wire
rods

Characterization
figure
person
plant
object

17-13 Flowcharts can be developed using resources such as encyclopedias.

- construct puppets from a variety of materials.
- express their own thoughts and feelings using puppets.
- practice using a puppet behind a puppet stage.

Concepts Based on the Theme

Curriculum themes are an important vehicle for helping children form concepts. A **concept** is a generalized idea or notion. Learning basic concepts helps the children to understand their world. By forming concepts, children learn to group experiences in a meaningful way.

Concepts can be developed around a theme. To do this, review your flowchart, then write the concepts. For instance, if your theme is birds, concepts might include the following:

- There are many kinds of birds.
- Some birds are pets.
- Birds hatch from eggs.
- Most birds fly.
- Birds live in nests, trees, houses, and cages.
- Birds have a head, body, wings, a beak, and feathers.

Written Plans

After considering your curriculum approach, theme, concepts, and activities, written plans need to be developed. Many centers require two types of written plans. A **block plan** is an overall view of the curriculum. It outlines the general plans. A **lesson plan** is more detailed than a block plan. It outlines specific actions and activities that will be used to meet goals and objectives.

Block Plan

A block plan is key to planning a balanced curriculum. Without this written block plan, curriculum areas may be overlooked. You may think these areas were covered, but without a written record, you cannot be sure.

A block plan usually includes days of the week, time periods, and scheduled activities. Figure 17-14 shows a sample block plan.

Block plans should be kept on file. They can be used as a reference to review what has happened during the year. The plans also contain a variety of activities that may be used in future years, if appropriate.

To write a block plan, follow these steps:

1. Review your program goals.
2. Review your observations and assessment of the children.
3. Note the children's interests.
4. Consider the availability of your resources.
5. Select a theme.
6. Develop concepts.
7. Select activities and record them on the block plan.

Lesson Plans

Lesson plans are more detailed than block plans. While a block plan gives just the title of a book, a lesson plan provides step-by-step directions for sharing the book. Figure 17-15 contains a sample lesson plan. Lesson plans contain the following:

- Developmental goals
- Learning objectives
- Concepts
- Materials needed
- Motivation
- Procedures
- Closure/transition
- Evaluation

Developmental Goals

Developmental goals are statements that tell the "why" of the activity. They are more specific than program goals. Examples of goals for cooking applesauce with a group of four-year-olds are shown in the sample lesson plan in 17-15. To write developmental goals for a lesson plan, think carefully about each activity. Ask yourself, "What can the children learn from this experience?" Then write the lesson plan, as outlined above, including all the learning involved.

Learning Objectives

Learning objectives describe the expected outcomes of an activity. Objectives are used to plan teaching strategies. There are three parts to

Morning Session: 2-Year-Olds

Week August 27-31   **Theme** My School

	9:00-10:10 Free Play/Centers	10:10-10:25 Large Group	10:25-10:40 Snack	10:40-11:00 Small Groups #1	#2	#3	11:00-11:30 Outdoors
Monday	• water colors • water & toys in sensory table • tunnel • tennis shoes color match game	My Nursery School story cards / If You're Happy & You Know It	crackers & cheese spread milk	stringing beads	table blocks	stringing beads	• sand toys
Tuesday	• crayons and markers • goop in sensory table • driving wheel • tuff blocks	• Short walk around the neighborhood	Chex mix milk	table blocks	stringing beads	table blocks	• balls
Wednesday	• play dough • styrofoam pieces in sensory table • balance beam • color clowns	Little Red Wagon song / My Nursery School	honey nutters milk	book: Where Is It? by Tana Hoban	puzzles	feely box: exploring things around in the classroom	• painting with water
Thursday	• Ivory Snow finger painting • water in sensory table • rocking boat	Tour of school / "Little Red Wagon"	veggies & dip milk	feely box	Where Is It?- book	puzzles	• bubbles
Friday	• roller painting • sand in sensory table • crawling cubes	If You're Happy and You Know It / Tour of school	peanut butter cookies milk	puzzles	feely box	Where Is It?	• rocking boat

17-14   This block plan is for a group of two-year-olds. Notice the theme and the large group activities related to it.

A Sample Lesson Plan

Date: 9/21   **Time**: 10:00 A.M.
Group: 4-year-olds
Activity: Cooking Experience—Applesauce

Developmental Goals:
- To practice following directions.
- To practice using a knife as a tool.
- To develop cooking safety habits.
- To learn the parts of an apple: seed, core, flesh, skin, and stem.
- To observe the changes in texture and color when heat is applied to the apples.

- To practice personal hygiene by washing hands before the cooking experience.
- To taste the ingredients in applesauce.
- To taste cooked apples.
- To observe the beauty of an apple.

Learning objective:
Given apples, knives, measuring cup and spoons, a bowl, a mixing spoon, a microwave oven, sugar, cinnamon, and a recipe chart, the children will help peel apples and measure the ingredients to prepare applesauce.

Materials needed:

6	peelers	measuring cup and spoon
12	apples	kettle
	recipe chart	bowl
	water	mixing spoon
2	cups of sugar	microwave oven
3	tablespoons of cinnamon	

Motivation/introduction:
Set up the housekeeping area with recipe chart, cooking utensils, and tray with food. Ask "What can we make from apples?" Listen to responses. Tell the children "Today we are going to make applesauce."

Procedure:
1. Tell the children to wash their hands.
2. Review the recipe chart step by step.
3. Cut an apple in half. Show the children the parts of an apple: seed, core, flesh, skin, and stem.
4. Demonstrate how to use a peeler as a tool, stressing safety.
5. Pass out apples and peelers, again explaining safety.
6. Encourage children to observe and feel the apples.
7. Peel apples.
8. When apples are peeled, focus children's attention back to recipe chart. Proceed by following directions step by step until the mixture is ready for a heat source.
9. Discuss each of the ingredients, allowing children to taste them, if they wish.
10. Ask individuals to measure the sugar, cinnamon, and water.
11. Direct children's attention to the applesauce as it cooks. Clarify the process by asking questions such as How are apples different?
12. Serve the applesauce as a snack.

Closure/transition:
Assign cleanup tasks to the children. Tell the children the applesauce will be eaten at snack time. Then prepare the children for outdoor play.

Evaluation:

17-15 Lesson plans contain much more detail than block plans. Notice all the details needed to write a lesson plan for cooking applesauce.

Learning Objectives
Conditions of Performance: States the conditions under which the child will perform. 　Given a three-piece puzzle... 　Given crayons and a pencil... 　Given a set of blocks... 　Without the aid of a teacher... 　Given farm animals... 　Within a five minute time limit...
Behavior: States what the child will be able to do. 　...the child will cut... 　...the child will draw... 　...the child will construct... 　...the child will sing... 　...the child will match... 　...the child will climb... 　...the child will jump... 　...the child will skip... 　...the child will stack...
Level of Performance: States the minimum level of achievement. 　...four inches... 　...all... 　...at least three feet... 　...two out of three times... 　...within a five minute period...

17-16 Studying these parts of learning objectives will help you write effective objectives.

learning objectives. These parts are (1) the conditions of performance, (2) the behavior, and (3) the level of performance. Figure 17-16 includes examples of each part of the behavioral objective.

The *conditions of performance* list what materials, equipment, or tools the child will use. Included could be puzzles, paper, scissors, beads, or any other materials and equipment found in early childhood settings. The conditions of performance can also include what the child will be denied. For example, they may need to construct a puzzle without the aid of a teacher.

Behaviors refer to any visible activities done by the child. It tells what the child will be doing. When choosing behaviors, avoid words that are open to many interpretations. To *know, understand, enjoy, believe,* and *appreciate* are all words that can mean many things. For instance, how will you judge if a child understands? Useful words for writing learning objectives are listed in 17-17.

The *level of performance* states the minimum standard of achievement. It should note how well you want the child to do. The level of performance many times is understood. Therefore, it is not always included as part of the objective.

Behaviors for Objectives				
ask	explore	mark	replace	take
answer	find	mix	return	tap
attempt to	finish	move	roll	taste
blow	grab	nail	run	tell
button	group	name	say	touch
catch	hit	open	select	throw
choose	hold	paint	separate	tie
climb	hoop	paste	sequence	turn
close	feed	pick	show	use
collect	find	peel	sing	use two hands
comb	follow	place	solve	wait
comment	follow directions	point to	sponge off	wash
color	jump	pour	sit	weigh
contribute	lace	print	sing	wipe-off
clap	locate	put hand on	skip	write
cut	look at	put in order	solve	zip
dry	make motions	remove	stand	

17-17 Learn to use concrete terms such as these when stating learning objectives.

Materials

Under the materials section of the lesson plan, list everything that is needed for the activity. For example, if you are going to make instant pudding, include milk, pudding mix, bowl, wire whisk, spoon, scraper, and measuring cup. If you are going to do a finger painting activity, list paint, paper, aprons, and wet sponge.

Motivation

Motivation describes how you will gain the children's attention. The best devices are items that interest the children. A picture of a cat may be used as motivation before reading a story about cats. Motivation devices include pictures, puppets, alphabet letters, tapes, resource people, cards, artwork, photographs, animals, stuffed toys, clothing, and masks.

Procedures

The procedures section resembles a cookbook. Simple, step-by-step directions should be provided. The directions should be in order. If needed, number each step to remember the order. Each of the developmental goals should be included in the procedures. For example, if a goal is to have each child taste the ingredients, this should be a step in the procedures. An example of procedures for an activity is shown in 17-18. The sample lesson plan also contains procedures.

Closure/Transition

Closure refers to how an activity will end. It might include clean-up tasks or sampling of food items at snack time. Transition refers to the movement from one activity to another. In some cases, closure and transition are the same task. For example, at the end of a creative drama activity, you may ask the children to walk like heavy elephants to the snack table.

Evaluation

A staff who provides a quality early childhood program is continually evaluating the curriculum. In some centers, time is set aside every day for this purpose. Many child care centers, however, do not have the resources to do this with the entire staff. Instead, staff members will evaluate the activities they conducted on their

> ### Procedure Chart
>
> **Activity: Visual perception** (This type of activity encourages children to see fine differences between and among objects.)
>
> 1. Place individual cards face down on the table.
> 2. Provide each child with one game board.
> 3. Demonstrate how to play the game, stressing the importance of taking turns.
> 4. Ask one child to begin by choosing a card from the middle of the table.
> 5. After the child has drawn the card, ask "Do you have an object like that on your board?"
> 6. If the object does not match, instruct the child to return the card to the center of the table, face down.
> 7. Continue with the next player until one child has filled all of the game board spaces.

17-18 Using a procedure chart, you should cover each step of an activity.

own. This process involves three steps: (1) evaluating the learning experience, (2) evaluating the children and their responses, and (3) evaluating your own teaching strategies.

When evaluating the learning experiences, ask yourself whether the activity was proper for the age group. If, for example, children had trouble cutting paper there could be several reasons for the trouble. Were the scissors in good repair? Scissors with dried glue on the cutting edge will not cut properly. Left-handed children need left-handed scissors. Paper thickness could also be a problem. Children who are learning to cut need lightweight paper and proper tools.

Successful learning activities give children the chance to test their knowledge. For example, children will learn more about making applesauce by taking part in the activity than if they only watched an adult make it.

Your skills working with young children only have meaning if the children learn. Therefore, it is important to study the children and their responses to activities and to you. First, see that the children reach the objective. If they do not, think through the activity. Ask yourself what you could have done differently. Likewise, if there were behavior problems, try to find the cause.

Lack of organization, you will find, can affect the outcome of an activity. If you forget some of the ingredients for a cooking activity, leaving the group to gather them could affect outcomes. During your absence, some child may start to mix the ingredients. The product may not turn out if the ingredients were not measured properly.

Chart 17-19 includes a sample evaluation form for an activity. To help in the evaluation process, you may want to duplicate several copies of this form. After using it a few times, you will find that you can remember the three parts of the form, including the specific questions. At this point, you may want to start writing your evaluations on index cards. In time, you will be able to go through this process without paper and a pencil.

At first, you may find the evaluation process time consuming. You will learn, however, that it is a useful process. With constant evaluation you will improve your teaching skills as well as the curriculum.

A Sample Evaluation of an Activity

Activity: Story—"Never Talk to Strangers"
Group: Five-year-olds

I. The Activity: Selection and Development

A. Was the content (concept) worth knowing?
The content is valuable for five-year-old children since it deals with personal safety. With the increased incidence of child abuse, this is an important topic.

B. Was it developmentally appropriate?
Although fantasy was involved in the story, almost all the children were able to understand the content.

C. Was it interesting to the children?
All the children but Don listened and responded. During the repetitive sentences, the children repeated, "Never talk to strangers. "

D. Did the activity include opportunities for the children to use or "test" their knowledge?
After the story, the children were asked questions. These included:
- Is your grandmother a stranger?
- Is your neighbor a stranger?
- Is a man you never saw before a stranger?

E. What would you suggest as a follow-up experience?
Children's books related to child abuse will be read tomorrow. The game "Good Touch and Bad Touch" will also be introduced.

II. The Children: Responses

A. Did all the children reach the objective(s)? If not, why?
With the exception of Don, all the children reached the objective.

B. Were there behavior problems? If so, do you have any insight as to what caused them?
If Don and Ben were separated during the story, Don may have paid attention. Likewise, Ben found Don's behavior disturbing. He tried to move away from him, but another teacher made him sit down.

III. The Teacher: Strategies

A. Were you well organized?
Yes, the book was placed so I could easily find it. During the outdoor play period, an individual carpet square was laid out for each child. Approximately ten inches were left between each square. This spacing probably helped maintain group control.

B. Were you satisfied with the effectiveness of your teaching strategies in reaching the learning objective? If not, why?
I should have practiced the story beforehand. In addition, I should have held the book so that all the children could view the pictures.

C. Did you effectively guide or manage the group?
Yes, with the exception of Don, I managed the group effectively.

D. Did you introduce the concepts in a stimulating manner?
The cover of the book appealed to the children. After the story, two children asked to have it read again.

E. Did you involve the children in the closure of the activity?
Yes, I did. The children were involved through a series of questions. Concepts of strangers and safety were both discussed.

F. What strategies would you change if you were to repeat this activity?
First, I would separate Don and Ben. I would also practice reading the book to myself several times before sharing it. This would make me less dependent on the story lines. As a result, I would feel confident enough to share the pictures with the children.

17-19 Evaluation is the final step in the curriculum development process. It can be used to determine how well your curriculum worked

Summary

A good early childhood curriculum is based on how children develop and learn. It consists of a wide range of concepts, experiences, and materials designed to meet the developmental needs of a group of children. Before the curriculum can be planned, the goals of the center's program need to be determined. Program goals focus on the whole child. Assessment is also an important part of curriculum planning. It will identify what the children already know and can do.

The content and process-centered approach to curriculum planning is the method most often used. Learning is seen as a constant process of exploring and questioning the environment. As the curriculum is planned, several factors need to be considered. You first must decide what information you will cover in the curriculum. You will also want to balance the learning activities and consider individual learning styles and characteristics.

Activities are often selected based on a theme. Flowcharts may be used to develop ideas related to the theme. Concepts are formulated for the theme as well. Finally, written plans are developed which include activities for all the classroom activity areas. Both block plans and lesson plans are developed. The final step is evaluation. A staff who provides a quality early childhood program is continually evaluating the curriculum and finding ways to improve their teaching plans.

Review and Reflect

1. What are program goals?

2. True or false. Curriculum development involves only the teacher who is responsible for the group.

3. List two advantages of a preplanned curriculum.

4. Describe a process-centered approach to curriculum development. Explain how materials and environment relate to this approach.

5. How do direct and indirect learning experiences differ?

6. List three questions to ask when choosing the information to cover.

7. _____ children like to work with others and often volunteer to help.

8. _____ children like to try new activities and work on their own.

9. _____ learners enjoy looking at books and other objects.

10. _____ learners enjoy activities involving records, stories, and poems.

11. Explain the meaning of spiral curriculum.

12. What is a flowchart?

13. How does a block plan differ from a lesson plan?

14. How do developmental goals and program goals differ?

15. Name the three parts of learning objectives. Explain each of these parts.

16. The _____ section of the lesson plan gives step-by-step directions.

17. When evaluating the success of a specific learning activity, what three steps should you follow?

Apply and Explore

1. Ask a child care teacher to speak to your class about curriculum planning.

2. Invite a chain child care director who uses preplanned curriculum to speak to your class about the advantages and disadvantages of this type of a curriculum. Ask the director to bring sample materials.

3. Divide into four groups. Each group should prepare a flowchart on a different theme. Compare your flowcharts.

4. Write a lesson plan for preparing pancakes.

5. Write five learning objectives. Exchange papers with classmates and evaluate the learning objectives.

6. Discuss strategies for meeting the program goals given in the chapter.

Chapter 18

Guiding Art, Blockbuilding, and Sensory Experiences

After studying this chapter, you will be able to

- explain how art experiences promote physical, social, emotional, and cognitive growth.

- describe techniques for guiding art experiences.

- list the stages of art skill development.

- compile a list of art supplies needed for a well-stocked classroom.

- plan a variety of art, blockbuilding, sensory, and woodworking activities suitable for young children.

Terms to Know

string painting
mono painting
chalk painting
texture painting
salt painting
spice painting
vegetable printing
plasticene
collage
bridging

Preschool children are curious about their world. They thrive on hands-on experiences. For them, art activities can be learning opportunities. Using their imaginations, young children can think, plan, and create their own ideas. Their need for movement, self-expression, and achievement is fulfilled by working with modeling materials. While developing basic skills using art media, young children are expressing feelings and ideas.

The Importance of Art Experiences

Art promotes physical, social, emotional, and cognitive growth in children. Physical growth is promoted through the movements involved in painting, coloring, drawing, and even scribbling, 18-1. All these motions improve small muscle skills. When children mold clay, they gain control of their fingers and hand muscles. All art activities foster motor and hand-eye coordination. This in turn helps growth in other areas.

Social growth is promoted by art. Children learn responsibility. For example, they learn that they must put on their smocks before painting. They also learn that they must put their work in a safe storage space when they are finished. Learning to work and share with others is stressed, 18-2. In many programs, several children will share one container of paint or a box of crayons. They learn to respect the property of others. They also learn to value the work and ideas of others.

18-1 Children improve hand-eye coordination during art activities that use small muscles.

18-2 Cooperation is an important skill learned during art activities.

Art experiences also promote emotional growth. Through a creative activity, children are allowed to express emotions. For example, pounding at the woodworking bench, hitting play dough, or scribbling with crayons allows angry children to express their frustrations in an acceptable way. Children also have the chance to choose their own activity. For instance, during a painting session children decide what they will paint. Their choices—a pet, a friend, or a flower—are often expressions of their feelings. Through art, they learn to communicate feelings nonverbally.

Finally, the children's cognitive growth is promoted by exploring and experimenting with many materials and tools. Through this process they are using the skills of an investigative scientist. They are learning important concepts such as color, size, texture, and shape. By manipulating and controlling tools, skills such as drawing and cutting are learned. They learn that cutting takes things apart while taping and stringing helps put materials together. Visual and tactile senses are also developed. Rolling, smelling, rubbing, pounding, and tearing all use visual and tactile senses. Visual senses relate to sight and tactile senses are those that relate to touch.

Techniques for Guiding Art Experiences

As a caregiver, you must be creative in your approach to art. You must observe in order to find new ways to expand children's learning experiences. Creative growth is promoted through careful choice of various art materials and opportunities to create. A good art program allows children to express their ideas. It also provides them with time to experiment and explore new materials and techniques. These experiences should involve all five senses: sight, smell, taste, touch, and hearing.

Helping children during art sessions is an important task. If done properly, children will accept your help. If done improperly, however, children will come to think of you as an intruder. For instance, Rudy had just started cutting out paper shapes. Her teacher came by and finished cutting one of the shapes for her. Rudy walked away from the table. She did not need the teacher's help at that time. She preferred to do the cutting herself. Tasks done for or forced on children often cause tension and displeasure.

To foster independence, start each session by telling the children what supplies and tools are available that day. Encourage them to use the supplies, 18-3. For instance, if they have never worked with cotton balls, tell them "I think you will enjoy painting with cotton balls. They are very soft."

As you walk through the class, observe what the children are doing. However, it is best not to ask them what they are making. They might just be experimenting with different tools and supplies. In this case, they do not know what they are making. Keep in mind that some children lack the language skills needed to explain their artwork. Asking questions may make them uneasy.

Let children decide when their work is finished. Take them at their word. Do not urge them to fill up space or add to their work. This decreases their pride and confidence.

Always remember to praise the children's work. However, avoid singling out one child's work as being the best. Instead, use praise that invites everyone to respect everyone else's work. For instance, you might say "Mary loves red and blue," or "Mark's colors are happy colors." Hanging the children's work tells them that their work is valued.

In preschool children's artwork, color does not play an important part. Often there is no relationship between the colors chosen and the objects in the artwork. Children choose colors they like as opposed to colors that mirror real life. An apple may be painted bright pink or an elephant red. Studies show children do have color preferences. Beautiful colors, according to young children, include yellow, blue, orange, and green, 18-4. Brown, white, and black are labeled ugly. You may wish to keep a large supply of preferred colors on hand.

Stages of Art Skill Development

Children move through three distinct stages as they build art skills. These stages are scribbles, basic forms, and first drawings. Knowing these stages helps child care workers plan activities that reflect children's skill level.

18-3 Devise new supplies to use during sessions and show children how to use them.

18-4 Children prefer painting with bright colors such as yellow and green.

Scribbles

The first stage in art skills most often occurs between 15 months and three years of age. Children's motor control and hand-eye coordination are not well developed yet. However, they can make zigzags, whirls, and circles. In the scribble stage, children do not make the connection between the marks on the paper and their own movements. The scribbles that are made are by-products of the experience. They enjoy the physical sensation of making marks.

To help children in this stage, make them aware of their movements. Comment on how hard they press their pencils, how fast they move their arms back and forth, or how large they make their movements. Such remarks help children make the connection between their actions and the art they create.

Comments about the look of children's artwork are also helpful. For example, you may say "This is a long line," or "This line has a curve." As you speak, trace some of the lines with your finger. The children's attention will focus on the form they have created.

Basic Forms

The second stage in art skill development of children is basic forms. This often occurs between ages three and four. Children learn basic forms such as ovals, rectangles, and circles. They now have more control over their movements and better hand-eye coordination. As a result, they can control the size and shape of a line. During this stage, they are beginning to enjoy their ability to create forms.

At this stage, children also begin to see the connection between their movements and the marks they make. Before this time, children's scribbles were the result of the sheer pleasure of moving their arms and hands. Now children connect those motions to their artwork. Children may even begin to name their drawings at this stage.

As in the scribble stage, you can help the children understand and talk about their work by commenting on their movements. For example, say "You are moving your arm in big circles." You might describe the end product. Say "You have drawn a big picture."

First Drawings

The third stage of art development occurs during the fourth and fifth years, 18-5. During this stage, children produce their first real drawings. They attempt to mimic their own view of the world. Using their skill with basic forms, they begin to create symbols of objects and events that they know. The drawings are often large. Objects are randomly placed. Color is unrealistic. Crudely drawn human figures with straight lines for arms and legs are common. Later, children often add animals, trees, houses, cars, boats, and airplanes to their artwork.

Art Supplies and Tools

You have the option of buying or making many of your own art supplies and equipment. Most teachers need to purchase the basic tools: scissors, paintbrushes, cookie cutters, easels, and paper punches. Many of these items can be purchased at thrift stores or garage sales. Other places you might wish to look for supplies include school supply and stationery stores, hardware stores, paint stores, drugstores, and

18-5 First drawings represent a child's view of the world. Colors are often unrealistic. Notice the sun is blue.

grocery stores. You might also wish to secure donations of these items from parents or from the stores themselves.

Tempera Paint

Tempera paint is used in many child care centers. It has a slight odor and tastes chalky. When dry, painted surfaces tend to crack and peel. Tempera can be purchased in both liquid and powdered form. Many teachers prefer powdered paint over liquid because powdered is cheaper. Powdered tempera paint is water soluble (dissolves in water). Thickness of the mixed paint varies from a sticky paste to runny fluid. To avoid drips and runs, mix the paint to the consistency of thick cream. Consistency will also affect color.

To reduce costs, many teachers add bentonite, a thickening agent, to powdered tempera paint. Bentonite can be purchased through landscape and gardening stores. Adding bentonite to powdered paint can save about 80 percent of paint costs.

Some teachers mix enough paint to last for a week or two. Others mix the paint each day. Whichever you prefer, remember to put the powdered paint in the container before you add the liquid. To avoid paint that is too thin, add only a small amount of liquid to the tempera while stirring constantly. This will make a very thick paste. Then slowly add more liquid until you get the desired thickness.

To prepare a large quantity of tempera paint, use the recipe in 18-6. Some teachers prepare paint daily because they are unable to store it. Instead, they make a basic paint/bentonite mixture that can be mixed with any color. The recipe for this mixture is given in 18-7. You will notice that in this recipe, the powdered paint is added to the liquid. This method differs from mixing tempera with a plain liquid (either water or pure bentonite).

Brushes

Provide children with a number of paintbrushes. They should range in size from 1/2 to 1 inch wide. The youngest children should use the widest brushes. As their small muscle coordination improves, they can be given smaller brushes. Pieces of string, cotton swabs, and feathers may be used as paintbrushes by older children.

Tempera Paint

7 to 10 tablespoons bentonite
    A large bowl or jar
    One-pound can powdered tempera
   2 tablespoons soap flakes or detergent
   3 cups liquid starch
    Water

Place bentonite into large bowl or jar. Add to this entire contents of powdered tempera. Stir in soap flakes/detergent and liquid starch. Add water until desired consistency is obtained.

18-6 This recipe will yield a large amount of one color of tempera paint.

Basic Bentonite

¾ cup powdered detergent
1 cup powdered bentonite
2 quarts water

Mix all ingredients using a beater or wire whip. Place mixture into crock or plastic container. Let stand for two or three days. When you are ready to mix paint, remove some basic bentonite from container and add enough tempera to make desired color.

18-7 Use this recipe to make bentonite, a paint extender.

Easels

Sturdy, adjustable easels should be provided as a place to paint. Brushes and paint should be placed in an attached tray. Clamps or hooks at the top of the easels should be used to hold the paper in place, 18-8. The easel should be adjusted so that the painting surface is angled or slanted outward. This reduces the dripping and running of paint. Cleanup time is also reduced.

Crayons, Chalk, and Felt-Tip Markers

Children enjoy using crayons, chalk, and felt-tip markers. However, these items are harder to use than paint. As a rule, these tools need to be pushed hard with small muscles that are not

18-8 Easels are useful tools. They can be used to hold paper for painting or drawing activities.

well-developed in young children. Paint, however, flows easily.

Crayons come in regular and kindergarten sizes. Kindergarten-size crayons are round, large, and flat on one side. These crayons do not break easily, nor do they roll off tables or other surfaces. Crayons can be stored in bowls, baskets, or boxes.

Chalk is available in both an art and chalkboard form. Art chalk comes in a variety of sizes. As with crayons, chalk can be purchased in large, fat sticks. Choose basic colors that are clear and brilliant. Be careful that children do not use art chalk on a chalkboard. Marks from art chalk cannot be erased from a chalkboard. Store chalk in baskets, boxes, trays, or bowls.

Felt-tip markers come with washable or waterproof inks. Always buy washable felt-tip markers for use in child care centers, 18-9. Be sure that any markers you buy have tight caps. This prevents the markers from drying out. Remind children to replace the caps after use.

Paper

There are many types of paper that can be used successfully for art activities. Included are newsprint, manila paper, construction paper, wallpaper, cardboard, and old newspaper. Other alternative types of paper for art activities are listed in 18-10.

The least costly paper is newsprint. It is durable and easy to use. Roll ends of newsprint can be bought at little or no cost from local

18-9 Children enjoy using markers. This can be a messy activity; make sure the ink is washable.

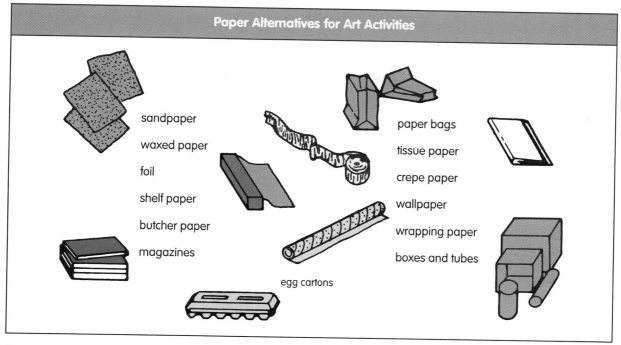

Paper Alternatives for Art Activities

sandpaper

waxed paper

foil

shelf paper

butcher paper

magazines

egg cartons

paper bags

tissue paper

crepe paper

wallpaper

wrapping paper

boxes and tubes

18-10 Paper for use in art activities comes in many forms. Some of these types of paper can be obtained for little or no cost.

newspaper printers. Cut the large sheets into the size sheets you want. To determine the size of the paper, remember younger children have poorer muscle control. As a result, they need large surfaces on which to paint or draw. A good size for easel painting is 18- by 24-inch sheets.

Coloring Books

Studies show that coloring books have a negative effect on children's creativity. The value of art as a form of expression is lost when children are limited to designs in a coloring book. Children become self-conscious and doubtful about their art talents. For example, Sara colors in the outline of a kitten in a coloring book. The next time she is asked to draw something, she recalls the perfect kitten from the coloring book page. She knows she could not draw that perfect kitten. She says, "I cannot draw very well." Lacking confidence in her own talents, Sara may not attempt to make many of her own drawings.

Some teachers see no harm in using coloring books and feel that their children enjoy working in them. Coloring books are also easy to buy and

keep on hand. However, for more enriching art experiences, rely on activities that allow children to explore interesting materials and experience cause and effect.

Paste

Library paste works well for adhering lightweight paper. Paste can be prepared or purchased. Many teachers prefer to buy paste by the gallon, which is more economical. Other teachers prefer to prepare their own paste, 18-11. To improve bonding strength, you may choose to add small quantities of glue to your paste. For young children, water-soluble adhesives are the best.

Glue

The best all-purpose adhesive is a white, liquid glue. It can be used on heavyweight paper, cardboard, fabric, plastic, and wood. Glue is more permanent than paste, and often more costly. If purchased by the gallon, it is a better bargain. Many building supply stores carry glue in gallon containers.

Paste
1 cup cold water 1 cup flour 2¼ cups boiling water 1 teaspoon powdered alum ¾ teaspoon oil of wintergreen (optional) Mix the cold water with the flour, stirring until smooth. Continue stirring while adding boiling water. Cook mixture on low heat in a double boiler until smooth. At this time, the mixture should look slightly bluish-gray and shiny. Remove from heat and add oil of wintergreen for an interesting smell. Store in a cool place.

18-11 Making paste is easy and can be a source of budget savings.

Take precautions when using white glue. Glue is difficult to remove from clothes, carpeting, and art tables. Therefore, wipe up spills immediately. Children should wear smocks. Table surfaces should be covered with newspapers. If used, you can provide small squeeze bottles of glue or pour small quantities into shallow pans or jar lids. Wipe the glue bottles immediately after the children are finished using them. Glue cleans up easily while it's still moist. Once it has dried, cleanup is difficult. Use with older preschoolers who are less likely to spill the glue.

Cleanup Tools

Keep cleanup tools in the art area so they are available when spills occur. Small buckets, sponge mops, and various sizes of sponges are useful. Keep supplies within children's reach. Cut mop handles down so they are child sized. This will encourage children to be responsible for cleaning up.

Space and Storage

Well-planned space is needed to encourage children to use art areas. Storage and display areas for artwork are part of a well-planned space. Bookshelves can be used to store staple supplies. These supplies include paper, scissors, paste, glue, collage materials, crayons, watercolor markers, chalk, tape, and paint.

Containers are needed to store paint, paste, scissors, and collage materials, 18-12. Baby food jars, plastic cups, and plastic bowls are often used to store tempera paint. Shallow dishes, including empty meat trays and frozen food containers, can be used in the art area to hold paint during painting activities. After use, the paint can be covered for storage.

Paste containers may be small enough for one child or large enough for a group to use. The size will depend on the activity. Empty catsup or mustard squeeze bottles and baby food jars are useful for individual activities. Foil or small plastic dishes are useful for several children to use at one time.

Scissors should be stored within easy reach. Special scissor holders may be bought. Scissor holders can also be made by the staff. Egg cartons, turned upside down, are often used to hold scissors.

Collage materials need to be well-organized to appeal to children. They should be sorted and placed in clear plastic boxes, shoe boxes, plastic dishpans, or baskets. Place these containers on a shelf within eye level of the children.

18-12 Store materials in individual containers.

Painting Activities

To learn what painting means to young children, listen and watch. You will note that most children find their work pleasing. The artwork of a two-year-old is different than that of a four-year-old. Children's paintings change from simple dots and strokes to crude figures as they move through art development. Some children enjoy moving the tools, 18-13. Other children enjoy the feelings and visual aspects.

Consider some of the children you might meet. Noah, a two-year-old, seems to be fascinated by the painting process. He dips his brush and paints, making large circles over his entire paper. His friend, Renee, delights in moving her brush back and forth. When she dips her brush into different colors, she ignores the cleaning process.

Mark, an active three-year-old, makes large dots and zigzags all over his paper. He pays little attention to the paint color but carefully watches his strokes. Heidi, another three-year-old, paints different colors on top of each other. As a result, her paper becomes soaked. At this point, she uses her hand to feel the paint. Then she proceeds to

18-13 Many children enjoy using different painting tools.

remove her painting from the easel. During this process, it tears. This does not bother Heidi. Like most three-year-olds, she is interested in the process, not the product. She paints one color on top of another and enjoys observing the changes in the layers of colors.

Jon, a highly verbal five-year-old, is comfortable handling the brush. He paints a man by making a circle face. Then he paints straight lines to represent legs. He uses a smaller circle for a mouth, two large round dots for eyes, and a V-shaped figure for a nose. As he paints, he keeps renaming his figure and inventing related stories. First, he tells the child standing next to him that the figure is a police officer. Later, he claims the same figure is a firefighter.

Children like Jon are not unusual. Some comment to themselves as they paint. They appear to be carrying on a conversation with their painting. These comments are useful. They tell you what the child feels and thinks. Sometimes children are eager to discuss their artwork; other times, they are not.

There are many types of painting activities that children will be eager to do. Included are easel, finger, string, texture, salt, mono, spice, and chalk painting. From these experiences, children learn to apply the correct amounts of paint and to recognize color and shapes.

Easel Painting

Easel painting should be a daily activity in all early childhood programs. Provide an easel, paper, brushes, and paint. Easels should be adjusted to the correct height for the children. Brushes with long handles (about twelve inches) in a variety of sizes should be provided on the easel tray. The size of the paper you give the children will depend on the activity and age of the children. For young children, provide large sheets of newsprint. Sheets of this size will encourage the use of large muscles. On special occasions, you may wish to provide colored paper and white tempera.

To ensure success in easel painting plan the session ahead of time. Provide only a small amount of paint since children often spill. Pour only enough paint to cover the bottom of the container. This will save cleanup time. Make only one color of paint available for early experiences.

When a second color is added, provide a brush for each container.

Permit only one child to use each easel. Encourage children to wear smocks. Push long sleeves above their elbows to prevent paint from getting on their clothing.

Teach young children how to use the paintbrush. Gently dip the brush into the paint container, 18-14. Then wipe the brush on the side of the container. This will rid the brush of extra paint. As children gain skill, give them smaller brushes and pieces of paper with which to work. Wash brushes after use. Until they are used again, place them with handles down in a storage container. This allows the bristles to dry.

Finger Painting

Finger painting is a sensory experience. It promotes expression and release of feelings. It is one of the most satisfying experiences for young children. Some may resist their first experience because they fear getting dirty. These same children, after having the chance to observe, may begin painting with one finger. Later, when they become comfortable, they will use their hands and arms as brushes.

Finger painting requires more supervision than most other painting activities. For this reason, work with no more than four children at a time. Children need to stay at the table until they are finished painting. Hands must be washed immediately after painting.

Finger paint recipes are given in 18-15. Finger paint may also be made from instant pudding, soap flakes whipped with water, partially-set flavored gelatin, and shaving cream. Children enjoy using a variety of paints.

String Painting

To prepare for **string painting**, cut several pieces of heavy yarn or string. Place a tray, or trays, of colored tempera paint and paper on the table. Show the children how to slide the yarn through the paint and across the piece of paper. Another technique is to place the string in a folded piece of paper and pull it out.

18-14 Recycle plastic food containers by using them as paint containers.

Finger Paints
Speedy finger paint
1 cup of laundry starch 3 cups of soap flakes 1 cup cold water
Mix all ingredients together. If colored finger paint is desired, add food coloring or colored tempera.
Blender finger paint
1 pound powdered tempera paint ¼ cup liquid starch ⅓ cup water 1 tablespoon of powdered laundry detergent
Place in blender. Mix until finger paint is blended well.
Cornstarch finger paint
1 cup of dry starch ½ cup water 1½ cups boiling water ¾ cup powdered laundry detergent
Mix starch and ½ cup water in heat-resistant bowl. Add 1½ cups boiling water while stirring rapidly. Blend in ¾ cup powdered laundry detergent until smooth.

18-15 Using recipes allows you to make the type and color of finger paint you need.

Mono Painting

A **mono painting** starts with a regular finger painting. After this, an 8 x 12 inch piece of paper is placed over the finger painting. The papers are patted together, then pulled apart.

Chalk Painting

To make a **chalk painting**, dip chalk into water and draw on construction paper. Use chalk at least one inch thick. Choose construction paper based on the color chalk being used. Add vinegar to the water to deepen the color of the chalk.

Texture Painting

Make paint for **texture painting** using liquid tempera or mixing powdered tempera with liquid starch. To this mixture, add sand, sawdust, or coffee grounds. For best results, the paint should be thick.

Salt Painting

Materials needed for **salt painting** include construction paper or cardboard, paste or glue, cotton swabs or tongue depressors, and salt mixed with colored tempera in shakers. Have the children spread paste or glue on the paper. Then have them shake the salt mixture onto the glue or paste. Shake off excess paint and set aside to dry.

Spice Painting

Spice painting results in a scented painting. Prepare the mixture by adding a small amount of water to liquid glue. Give each child enough glue to spread over their piece of paper. They can use their fingers to do this. Then have them shake spices onto the paper. When it dries it will look as interesting as it smells.

Cinnamon, onion powder, garlic powder, and oregano all make aromatic paintings. For texture, use bay leaves, cloves, or coffee grounds. The center budget may dictate which and how many spices you can use. In addition, consideration must be given to any policies toward the use of food. Some directors tend to discourage this type of food use.

Vegetable Printing

Vegetable printing involves dipping a mold into paint and then pressing the mold onto a surface. See 18-16. This makes a print. The molds in vegetable printing are made from vegetables. They are washed and dried, then cut in half. Place the cut vegetables on the table, along with trays of paint. Children dip the vegetables into the paint and then press them onto paper.

If school policy limits the use of food for art activities, common household items may also be used. Try using spools, clothespins, pieces of oddly shaped wood, pine cones, and jar lids.

Molding

Play dough, Plasticene, and clay are materials that can be molded and formed. Children enjoy the tactile appeal of these materials. Because they can be reshaped, they allow children the freedom to change their minds. You will observe them poking, rolling, stretching, pounding, squeezing, coiling, flattening, and tearing the clay or play dough. It can be turned

18-16 Children like to make prints using vegetables and other objects.

into a ball, snowman, cat, pancake, or snake. Often the children will use accessories such as pans, cookie cutters, and rolling pins to make pies, cookies, and other "baked goods" from these materials.

Children's play with molding materials reflects their level of development. Two-year-old children pull, beat, push, and squeeze. When children are about three years of age, they make balls and snake-like shapes. By age four, children can make complex forms, some of which they name. By age five, children will often announce what they are going to make before they begin.

Clay may be purchased at local art-supply stores and through school catalogs. It is available in two colors, white or red. When wet, the white clay appears grayish in color. Since red clay can stain clothing, most teachers prefer the white. Mixed properly, it should be stored in a plastic bag, diaper pail, or garbage pail to prevent drying. Clay can be used on large pieces of Formica, vinyl tablecloth, or tile to save on cleanup time.

Play dough is soft and pliable, and it has a softer texture than clay. It offers little resistance to pressure and responds easily when touched. Each type of play dough has different features. Provide the children with a number of types by using the recipes in 18-17. You can vary these play doughs even further by adding rice, cornmeal, pebbles, sand, oats, and coffee grounds. Scented oils such as peppermint and wintergreen add a fragrant smell.

Many teachers use plasticene for modeling. **Plasticene** is an oil-based, commercially manufactured modeling compound. It is available in many bright colors including blue, green, orange, red, and yellow.

Unlike play dough and clay, Plasticene does not dry out. It can be rolled up and used over and over again. It needs little care, even when used daily. However, one disadvantage of Plasticene is that it can leave an oily residue on the children's hands and table surfaces. For this reason, some teachers do not make it available to the children.

Cutting

Children need time, supplies, and space each day for cutting. Young children learn to cut because they enjoy working scissors. At first,

---

Play Doughs
Refrigerator play dough
1 cup salt 2 cups flour 1 tablespoon alum (optional, a preservative) 1 cup water 3 tablespoons oil   Food coloring or tempera Mix salt, flour, and alum. Add oil, water, and coloring, if desired, and mix. Check the consistency. If sticky, add more flour. Store in a tightly covered container in the refrigerator.
Sawdust dough
3 cups flour 3 cups sawdust 1 cup salt Mix the three ingredients together. Add water as needed to form a soft dough.
Cooked play dough
1 cup salt ½ cup flour 1 cup water Mix ingredients together in a pan. Cook over medium heat, stirring constantly. Remove the mixture from the heat when it becomes thick and rubbery. After cooling, the mixture will not be as sticky. Store in an airtight container.

18-17 Varying the types of play dough you make helps give children a variety of sensory experiences.

children just snip in a straight line. Provide strips of construction paper or wrapping paper. The paper should be long enough so the children may hold fast to one end of it. Avoid heavy wrapping paper, corrugated paper, or vinyl paper. Children do not have enough small muscle strength to cut through these materials. As children progress, they may wish to cut in curves. This requires good hand-eye coordination skills.

Have children work with one type of paper. This allows them to master handling one type of material and tool. To avoid failure, give children quality scissors. Provide left-handed children with proper scissors. Mark these scissors with colored tape. All scissors should have rounded tips.

Collages

The term **collage** means selecting and mounting materials on a flat surface. Collages are two-dimensional arrangements of many materials. Making collages gives children the chance to make choices. They can decide what material will be placed where. Two-year-olds may paste layers of materials on top of each other. Collages also introduce many materials of contrasting colors and textures to children. Materials that can be used in collages are listed in 18-18.

The base for a collage should be a heavyweight material. Construction paper or cardboard are ideal. Arrange collage materials in attractive containers. Children can browse through these containers choosing items for their collages. Remember to provide adhesives. Library paste is a good medium for children to use. It is inexpensive and easy to handle. As children gain skills in making collages, other adhesives can be used. Liquid starch, rubber cement, and white glue are examples. Liquid starch works well on tissue paper. Rubber cement or white glue is a better choice for holding heavier materials, such as buttons. To add interest, tint white glue with tempera paint.

Blockbuilding

Blocks are important learning tools for young children. They are probably the most popular materials in child care centers. While playing with blocks, children are in constant motion, reaching, stretching, and changing body positions. As they build with the blocks, they are improving their eye-hand coordination and strengthening their muscles. Through block play, children also learn many new concepts and skills. Figure 18-19 lists the many ways that block play promotes learning in the four developmental domains.

Stages of Blockbuilding

Children play with blocks in different ways as they grow older. The following stages of blockbuilding have been identified:

- Stage One. At two years of age, children carry the blocks around and do not engage in construction. They enjoy filling containers with blocks and dumping them out.
- Stage Two. From two to three years of age, building begins. The children will

Objects for Collages		
aluminum foil	gift wrap paper	plastic pieces
baking cups	greeting cards	sandpaper
bottle caps	lace	seeds
burlap	leather	shells
buttons	leaves	shoelaces
can labels	magazine pictures	small tiles
candy wrappers	netting	sponges
cardboard tubes	newspapers	straws
confetti	paper cups	suede
corks	paper plates	tissue paper
cotton balls	paper ribbons	tree bark
doilies	pebbles	twigs
egg cartons	plastic foam packing	wallpaper samples
fabrics	material	wood shavings
feathers	used gift boxes	plastic or wooden spools
flower petals	toilet tissue or paper	scrap yarn, string, and
seashells	towel tubes	ribbon
felt	plastic milk or juice cans	

18-18 The types of items used in collages are nearly limitless. Many types of items are listed here. What other interesting items could be used?

Learning Through Block Play	
Domain	**Learnings**
Physical Growth	• The development and coordination of large and small muscles • Eye-hand coordination skills • An understanding of object-space relationship • Motor coordination by lifting, carrying, and stacking
Cognitive Growth	• Understanding balance, weight, and measurement concepts • Exploration of shapes, sizes, and proportion • Understanding of mathematical concepts such as *larger than* or *smaller than* • Understanding language concepts such as *over, under, same, different,* and *besides* • Experimenting with balance, gravity, and cause and effect • Developing prediction and comparison skills • Developing skills in sorting and classifying
Emotional Growth	• A sense of accomplishment and success • The development of patience
Social Growth	• Cooperation skills • Practicing sharing and taking turns • Learning to respect the work of others

18-19 Children benefit in many ways from blockbuilding experiences.

either stack the blocks vertically or lay them in horizontal rows. They strive to build towers higher until they fall down, and their "roads" become longer and longer. They usually will continue building until they run out of blocks or space.

■ Stage Three. Simple bridging occurs. **Bridging** is a process of placing two blocks vertically a space apart. Then a third block is added. Children build these bridges and tunnels over and over again.

■ Stage Four. Children begin to construct enclosures. They enjoy building houses, apartments, barns, stores, caves for animals, and other types of buildings.

■ Stage Five. By three to four years of age, children begin to build more intricate buildings. These buildings are now higher and wider and more elaborate. They are beginning to choose blocks carefully in order to carry out their designs.

■ Stage Six. The children begin naming their structures and include dramatic play. They may build an airport for toy airplanes.

■ Stage Seven. By five years of age, children decide what they want to build prior to construction. Their structures becoming more symbolic and are used in dramatic play. They will build airports, garages, houses, and barns. Once built, their play becomes more creative by adding props and accessories. Often the children like to play with the same structure for several days.

Types of Blocks and Accessories

Blocks come in a variety of materials including wood, cardboard, plastic, rubber, and foam. Square and rectangular blocks made from lightweight materials are best for younger children. Children from three to six years of age prefer wooden blocks in a variety of shapes and sizes.

The children enjoy having accessories to use with block play. Usually they prefer simple figures such as animals and people. Often they will want to recreate a setting they have experienced. After a field trip to the farm, they may build a barn. Other settings may include airports, fire houses, parking garages, a zoo, racetracks, train stations, and bus stations. To maintain the children's interests, rotate the materials occasionally. To facilitate sharing and cooperative efforts, always purchase two of each item.

Sensory Experiences: Sand and Water Play

Sand and water play are often referred to as sensory experiences. They are provided in many programs with preschoolers. Both activities can occur indoors and outdoors. Children find pleasure in these materials. They are relaxing and tension is relieved as children interact with these materials. Water and sand play also encourage social interaction as children play side-by-side or with others.

Sand Play

A sandbox should have an 8- to 12-inch ledge. This ledge will provide the children a place to display their molded sand forms. When the sand is moist, it will also provide dry seating for the children.

Outdoors, the sandbox should be placed in a quiet area of the play yard, 18-20. If possible, it should be placed near a water source so the sand can be moistened. Moist sand can be used to pack molds and cans and to create castles. Moist sand is preferable to dry sand because it does not get into the eyes, shoes, or hair as easily. By placing the sandbox far from the building entrance, less sand will be brought into the center. As the children walk across the play yard, some of the sand should fall off.

The sandbox should also be placed near a water source indoors. It is usually located in or near the art area on flooring that is easily cleaned. Ceramic tile and linoleum are good choices.

A variety of containers should be provided for pouring, smoothing, and molding the sand. Cans, buckets, plastic cups, gelatin molds, cookie cutters, strainers, funnels, basters, muffin tins, bread pans, shovels and spoons are examples. With these items, the children can construct roads, caves, tunnels, and castles. They will also enjoy using trucks and cars in the sand. Plastic or rubber animals and people are other accessories children enjoy playing with in the sandbox.

18-20 This canopied sandbox helps protect children from the sun when they are playing outdoors.

Water Play

Water play is another activity that is developmentally appropriate for all children. Water play can take place indoors using a water table, plastic bins, laundry tubs, or wading pools. For variety, you can fill the tub with snow. Food coloring and soap can also be added for interest. Occasionally you may want to use shaving cream in the water table. The cream can be colored to correspond with different holidays.

A variety of nonbreakable kitchen utensils can be provided for use in the water table. Sponges, measuring cups, plastic squeeze bottles, egg beaters, and basters are examples. The children may also enjoy playing with boats and washing dolls and doll clothing.

Woodworking

Children enjoy woodworking activities. Hammering is usually their first interest. When provided the proper tools, they may pound nails for 20 minutes. Developmentally, woodworking can be a valuable experience. It promotes hand-eye coordination, small and large muscle development, and creative expression. In addition, it provides the children with an emotional release.

If properly used, tools are safe for children to use, 18-21. Teachers need to demonstrate how to use the tools safely. In some classrooms, teachers demonstrate hammering using golf tees and styrofoam. Some teachers have a large tree stump cut for their classroom. They place a can of nails and a hammer near the stump to encourage participation. Children using a hammer for the first time may want you to start the nail.

18-21 Proper safety equipment should be provided for woodworking activities.

Tools for the woodworking area need to be carefully chosen. They should be lightweight and have handles that are easy for the children to grip. Examples of woodworking tools include claw hammers, hand drills, pliers, sandpaper blocks, a vise, and saws. Thin nails with large heads are easiest for children to use. Wood glue should also be available.

Summary

For young children, art activities are important learning experiences. Through their own creativity, children express their ideas, as well as their emotions. Art promotes physical, social, emotional, and cognitive growth in children.

A good art program fosters independence. Let children decide when their work is finished. Always praise the children's work. Use praise that invites everyone to respect everyone else's work.

Children move through three distinct stages as they build art skills. Knowing these stages helps child care workers plan activities that reflect children's skills level.

The teacher has an important job in guiding art, blockbuilding, and sensory experiences. The teacher will decide what types of activities will be introduced. A variety of materials and techniques should be used. Knowing how to carry out this task so children benefit from the experience is important for the teacher.

Review and Reflect

1. How do art experiences promote social growth?

2. Why is it best not to ask children what they are making?

3. Name the stages of art skill development. Explain one stage in detail.

4. True or false. Children are careful to choose colors that mirror real life instead of choosing colors they like.

5. Explain how to mix tempera paint to get the desired consistency.

6. True or false. As children progress in art skills, paintbrushes should become more narrow.

7. Why are chalk, felt-tip markers, and crayons more difficult for children to use than paint?

8. Summarize the controversy concerning the use of coloring books.

9. _____ painting is a sensory experience that promotes the release of feelings and is very satisfying for children.

10. How does a two-year-old's play with clay differ from a five-year-old's?

11. Which molding material would you choose for children to use? Give the reasons for your selection.

12. Name three ways children benefit from blockbuilding experiences.

13. Name three woodworking tools that children might enjoy using.

Apply and Explore

1. Collect children's drawings. Determine what stage of development each drawing represents. Give reasons for your conclusions.

2. Make a list of materials that could be collected through donation for use in art activities. Indicate how each item could be used.

3. Make a list of objects that could be used as tools for printing activities.

4. Prepare and use each of the finger paint recipes. Discuss which has the best texture. Suggest methods for storing the paint.

5. Prepare each of the play dough recipes. Compute the cost to make each recipe. Compare these costs to the cost of purchasing commercial play dough products.

6. Review equipment catalogs and prepare a list of the different types of blocks and accessories for this area of the classroom.

Storytelling is often part of the daily routine.

Chapter 19

Guiding Storytelling Experiences

After studying this chapter, you will be able to

- explain the advantages of storytelling.
- list the four types of children's books.
- discuss the process of choosing children's books.
- outline the steps to follow when reading aloud to children.
- explain a variety of storytelling methods.

Terms to Know

storytelling
picture books
storybooks
family life stories
animal stories
fairy tales
reviews
props
draw and tell
flipcharts
flannel boards

The words "once upon a time" contain magic for young children. The art of storytelling has delighted millions of children throughout the ages. By inviting children to share in a make-believe world of adventure, the storyteller provides a strong educational tool.

Storytelling is an important task for child care teachers. It involves reciting a story or reading from a book. In most centers, storytelling is routine. It is included in the daily schedule, 19-1. Storytelling is a valuable experience for children. They develop a love for both stories and books as a result of daily storytelling sessions.

19-1 Storytelling is an enjoyable time for teachers and children.

This in turn enhances their language development. Moreover, children develop an understanding of customs and culture through traditional stories.

The Importance of Storytelling

Storytelling helps children develop many skills. Among these skills, storytelling helps young children

- understand other people
- develop a positive attitude toward books
- develop listening skills
- build correct concepts of objects and ideas
- form new ideas
- increase their vocabulary
- understand that printed words have meanings
- develop an appreciation of printed words
- develop a desire to read
- learn that people read from left to right across a page

Carefully chosen stories are a key part of the storytelling experience. Stories that draw on the children's backgrounds help them understand themselves better. Children learn the words that describe feelings and experiences they have. They learn to think about familiar situations in new ways. Stories invite children to explore and wonder about their world.

Stories also provide models of acceptable behavior and positive social relationships. When exposed to a variety of characters, children learn that other people often feel the same way they do. They learn how people express their feelings. They become more understanding of others' needs.

Storytelling helps children learn reading skills. As a teacher reads aloud from a book, children learn to follow the pages from left to right and top to bottom. By watching the storyteller read, children learn the relationship between spoken and printed words. They also learn to listen. Books help children learn alphabet letters, numerals, and language.

Storytelling is also a good form of relaxation, 19-2. Listening to a story is a quiet activity. Children are not moving about or interacting with other children.

19-2 Because storytelling requires children to sit and listen, it is a good form of relaxation for children.

Books as a Source of Stories

Children's books are an important source of stories. Most can be divided into two main groups: picture books and storybooks. **Picture books** have single words or simple sentences and simple plots. These are usually the first books shared with young children.

After picture books, **storybooks** are introduced. Storybooks are often categorized as family life stories, animal stories, and fairy tales. These books also contain pictures, but they have more words and more complex plots than picture books. Most of these books are built around themes of achievement, love, and reassurance. A book that uses all three themes is *Peter Rabbit*. In the story, Peter has an adventure but safely returns home (achievement). His mother tucks him into bed and gives him tea (love and reassurance). Examples of other such stories include *Little Bear, Mike Mulligan and His Steam Shovel,* and *Little Tim.*

Family life stories contain the theme of social understanding. The children in these stories usually have problems. Some problems may be funny; some serious. However, all problems are resolved with love and concern. The purpose of these stories is to help children develop social understanding by sharing the problems, troubles, and feelings of others. Examples include *Johnny Crow's Garden, My Dog Is Lost, My Grandpa, Timid Timothy,* and *Will I Have a Friend?*

Young children also enjoy **animal stories**. In these stories, animals are given some human qualities. Usually, the animal hero has some unusual success or ability. Examples include *Little Brown Bear; All About Dogs, Dogs, Dogs; Nothing But Cats, Cats, Cats;* and *Angus and the Cat.*

Fairy tales are another type of book enjoyed by older children. **Fairy tales** have a theme of achievement. The characters or heroes perform difficult tasks in order to succeed. They must confront giants, witches, and other obstacles. Kindness and goodness supported by courage and good judgment win out over evil. *Three Billy Goats Gruff, Three Little Pigs,* and *Cinderella* are popular examples of fairy tales.

Selecting Books for Children

Storytelling is an art that requires study and practice. The key to a good story is selection. Choose books that have dramatic elements. Children will enjoy "seeing" and "feeling" the events. Stories that mirror the children's emotional experiences will engage their hearts and minds. A story is only good if children enjoy it. If the story is to be an effective classroom activity, the teacher should also enjoy and value it. Otherwise, sharing it in an interesting way will be difficult.

Selecting storybooks is often hard for new child care teachers. Public libraries have many useful lists and descriptions of books. These are called **reviews**. Reviews will help you find titles, authors, and publishers of books. Reviews can also be ordered from the American Library Association Children's Service.

Fictional Content

Stories should match the children's developmental level and experiences. When choosing books for children, study the story content, illustrations, vocabulary, durability, and length. Familiar objects, people, and situations make stories more interesting to children. Stories about children with backgrounds and activities similar to their own are special favorites.

Most preschool children cannot separate fact from fiction. Therefore, it is important to look for realistic stories. Until children are about five years old, they are often not ready for fantasy, 19-3. Books in which animals or inanimate objects, such as trees and flowers, behave as humans should be avoided.

Illustrations

Illustrations are used to create interest and to arouse children's imagination. The pictures in a book for young children should almost tell the story by themselves. Children will be more interested if they can "read" the story by looking at the pictures.

19-3 Younger children may become confused or even frightened by fantasy stories.

Pictures should be easy to recognize. Too much detail and shading or lack of color will confuse young children. Instead, children respond best to brightly colored pictures with large, clearly defined objects. Illustrations should

- be large, colorful, and plentiful
- represent the written word
- reflect actions
- avoid unneeded detail
- be realistically and attractively colored

Vocabulary

A good children's book uses words that can be understood by most children of a certain age. Only a few new words should be introduced in a story. Repetition of some words will increase the children's enjoyment. This rhythm of word sounds is one major reason why children so enjoy stories such as Mother Goose tales.

Durability

Children should be allowed to hold and carry books as well as turn pages. Therefore, covers and pages must be sturdy. Covers made of strong, washable material are best. Pages should be easy to handle. The page surface should be dull to prevent glare. The book's binding should lay flat when the book is open.

Length

Appropriate book length varies with children's age. Infants and toddlers may stay with a book for just a few minutes. Their books are often only a few pages long. Two-year-olds will remain interested in a book for five to eight minutes; three-year-olds, from six to ten minutes; four-year-olds from eight to twelve minutes; five-year-olds from ten to fifteen minutes. This interest is reflected in the number of pages in the book.

Selecting Books Based on Age

Age plays an important part in choosing books for children. Chart 19-4 outlines some factors to consider for different ages.

Infants and toddlers need durable picture books. These books may be made of washable cloth or firm cardboard. Thick pages allow for easier handling. Pictures should be large and clearly outlined. Simple items in children's surroundings should be represented in the pictures. Toddlers may enjoy pointing at and touching objects in the pictures.

Two-year-olds prefer books about things they know, do, and enjoy. They respond enthusiastically when favorite activities, such as running, eating, and dressing, are mentioned. Animals and small children are the favored subjects. Books for two-year-olds should still be quite durable with plenty of large, clearly outlined drawings. Actions and sounds represented in the pictures should be familiar. The colors should be realistic. For example, goats should not be colored purple because some children may believe they really are that color.

Considerations for Children's Books				
Toddlers	**2-year-olds**	**3-year-olds**	**4-year-olds**	**5-year-olds**
Thick pages Pictures of simple objects Large, clearly outlined pictures	Imitate familiar sounds Repeat children's own experiences Contain large pages with big pictures Include the familiar	Include things and people outside of the home Explain the who's and why's Interpret the child's own experiences Contain repetitive sound words	Include humor in reality Contain new words Explain the how's and why's Include exaggeration	Add something to their knowledge Take them beyond the here and now Contain new information and relationships between familiar facts

19-4 Children of different ages each have their story preferences.

Three-year-old children may request stories by title. They show preference for stories about familiar subjects, 19-5. They also enjoy learning about people outside the home. They enjoy stories about community helpers such as police officers, mail carriers, and garbage collectors. Three-year-olds want to know what these people do and why. Pictures should be realistic, simple, and clear. The number of sentences on each page should be limited.

Four-year-old children are less self-centered than the younger group. These children are becoming more curious about the world around them. They want to know how and why things work. At this age, children enjoy short, simple stories that use exaggeration. Four-year-olds are often silly and enjoy pranks in books. Looking at the pictures can help them experience the story.

19-5 Children enjoy looking at books that contain familiar subjects.

Five-year-old children like stories that give them added knowledge. They will frequently memorize favorite stories word for word. They prefer stories that take them beyond here and now. These children want new information and relationships along with familiar facts. Fantasy trips beyond the confines of their world are now appreciated. Examples of these books include *Little Red Riding Hood, Peter Rabbit,* and *Goldilocks and the Three Bears.* Children of this age will clearly tell you their likes and dislikes.

Avoiding Stories That Reinforce Stereotypes

It is important to choose age-appropriate stories. It is also important to select stories that are not based on stereotypes. *Stereotypes* are preset ideas about people based on one characteristic, such as sex, nationality, religion, or age. Stereotypes are unfair and should be avoided. Read stories and study illustrations carefully before using them. Stereotyping is sometimes easier to find in pictures. Pictures should be examined closely since they have more impact on children than words.

Children's stories need to be free of sexism. *Sexism* is any action, attitude, or outlook used to judge a person based only on the sex of that person. In the past, many books did not show women who possess a full range of interests and skills. Most children's books showed women wearing aprons and doing housework. Girls were passive and helped their mothers around the house. Boys, on the other hand, were active and adventurous. Doctors, lawyers, and police tended to be men. Also, few men were shown in roles of teachers and nurses.

Study the ratio of men to women in the illustrations. As a rule, there should be as many men as women or girls as boys. Notice how characters are described and what kinds of activities the pictures show them doing, 19-6. Books that avoid sexism will describe women and girls as lively people who do interesting things. Likewise, men and boys will be shown as people who are interested in homes, families, and friends.

Through books, children can gain an understanding of people who have different skin coloring, food preferences, and languages. Knowledge of the differences among people can

19-6 Books that show men involved with their families and women in interesting jobs do not promote sexism.

promote acceptance. Both illustrations and text should depict all races and nationalities in a positive way.

Finally, search stories for stereotyping of older people. Children must be given a realistic and positive picture of seniors. Stories should describe warm, pleasing relationships between older people and children. In this way, children can learn to know and admire older members of their community.

Reading Stories to Children

Good oral reading takes time and effort. Three steps need to be taken before reading stories to young children. First, choose stories that both children and you will enjoy. Then become familiar with the story. Finally, decide how you will present the story. The success of the story lies in your ability to be interesting and enthusiastic.

Preparing to Read

Read the story several times so you know it well. Then a quick glance at the page will remind you of the text. This leaves your eyes free for contact with the children. No one way is best for learning stories. Each person has his or her own method.

Oral reading skills are important when storytelling. One way to build these skills is to practice reading in front of a mirror. Another method is to tape or video record yourself as you read. Using these methods, you can correct any problems you notice. For example, tape yourself and then ask the following:

- Did I convey enthusiasm about the story?
- Did I keep the tempo lively?
- Did I suggest different voices for different characters?

After you are familiar with the book, decide whether you want to read or tell the story. Reading the story has its advantages when working with young children. They can look at the drawings as they listen to the story. Reading stories may also get some children interested in reading. As they watch you, the children will learn the link between printed and spoken words. The advantage to telling a story is you are able to better dramatize action and characters.

A comfortable setting is required for a successful reading time. Children must be free from distractions. They should sit in a group to listen. Some teachers like to have children sit on carpet samples or pillows. A colorful quilt may also be used. Such seating arrangements prevent children from moving around and help them focus more on listening.

Story groups should be small, 19-7. You may wish to divide children into two or more groups, based on age and interest. This also allows the children more interaction.

Most children need a settling down time. To help children get ready to listen, some teachers recite a fingerplay. Another technique is to talk to the children using a puppet. Other teachers simply discuss the events of the day.

Introducing the Story

Begin stories by setting the mood. Ask questions, make personal comments, or show a book to get children involved in the story. Setting the mood should be brief. A few sentences or less is often enough.

A personal comment is one way to introduce a story. You may share where you learned about the story. For example, "This is a story that my grandmother told me as a child." You can set

19-7 In small groups, children are free to interact with the teacher.

a humorous mood by asking "How many of you like to laugh?" You might hold the book up and show the cover. The picture on the cover should suggest the story content.

Props are also good for introducing stories. **Props** are any items that relate to the story and would attract children's attention. To introduce *Peter Rabbit*, for example, you may bring in a live rabbit, a stuffed rabbit, or a picture of a rabbit. See 19-8.

Store props in a storytelling apron. As you introduce a story, pull props out of the apron pocket one at a time. A storytelling bag can be used in the same way. The bag is also useful for storing books in the reading area.

Explain any words the children do not know before you begin the story. For example, before reading *The Gigantic Elephant*, define the new word *gigantic*.

Before you start, create a feeling that something special is about to be shared. This feeling can be produced by the enthusiasm in your voice as you introduce the book. Your facial expression can also create excitement.

Props for Introducing Stories	
A red balloon	"The Red Balloon"
A red apple	"The Apple is Red"
A doll	"William's Doll"
A black cat	"The Tale of the Black Cat"
A purple crayon	"Harold and the Purple Crayon"

19-8 Well-chosen props will grab children's attention.

Reading the Story

Read stories with pleasure and feeling. Maintain eye contact with the children. Pause before introducing a new character or idea.

Read the story in a normal speaking voice. Speaking too softly or at a high pitch may cause the children to lose interest. Think of your voice as a tool. To add interest, you can whisper or shout when appropriate. You may mimic a sound, or speed up or slow down the pace. The pitch of your voice can also be changed. An example would be the story of *Goldilocks and the Three Bears.* Use a high pitch for the baby bear and a low pitch for the papa bear.

Handling Interruptions

Interruptions happen often when telling stories to young children, 19-9. The children will ask such questions as "Why is baby bear brown?" Accept these interruptions and answer

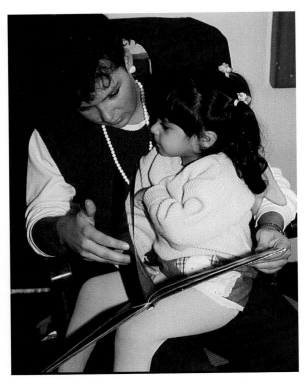

19-9 Do not be annoyed by interruptions. Young children like to ask questions and make comments on stories they are hearing.

questions patiently. There may be children who continue to ask many questions. If this happens, say "Mark, please save your questions until after the story."

Wiggling children can distract other children. Do not make an issue of this. It is best to ignore the wiggling and keep reading. A positive response is to praise children who sit still. For example, you may say "Joellen, I like how quietly you are sitting." This will strengthen Joellen's actions. It will also encourage wigglers to sit still.

Maintaining Interest

Children's interest in a story can be seen in their laughter, stillness, and expressions. If children do not appear to like a story, talk faster. You might use more emphasis or skip over some details. You can also restore interest by asking the children simple questions about the story. To quiet a bored or disruptive child, ask "Louis, what color is baby bear?" Sometimes, no matter what you do, a book does not have holding power. If this should happen, end the story. You may say, "Boys and girls, this is not the right story for today."

Ending Stories

Ending a story is as important as introducing it. The children need to know when you are finished. Therefore, the ending should be clear. You may ask a question about the story such as "What did you like best about the story?" You also may ask a question about the characters, the plot, or the setting.

At times, a simple "Thank you for listening" may be enough. You may also wish to give the children something to take home after some stories. This is done most often for special occasions. For example, when reading *Winnie the Pooh*, you may wish to give the children balloons.

Be prepared to read the same story over and over again. You will be pleased to hear "Please tell us that story again." This request tells you the children enjoyed the book.

Evaluating Your Performance

After reading a story, you will need to evaluate your methods. Children's reactions are good feedback. As a rule, the more children respond to a story, the better your methods. If children lose interest, you may have talked too fast or too slow. In other cases, you may have spoken so carefully that you forgot to add expression and vary tone.

Note your strengths as well as your weaknesses. When children smile, laugh, and watch closely, you have used methods that hold their interest. Build on your strengths as you read stories in the future. In addition, review the characteristics of effective storytelling listed in 19-10.

Achieving Variety in Storytelling

In addition to reading stories aloud, there are other methods of storytelling. Guidelines for these methods are like those for reading aloud. First, decide whether you will read from a book or make up your own story. Next, practice the story in front of a mirror using a tape recorder until you know it well. This will help you prepare to perform as a storyteller.

Characteristics of Effective Storytelling

- Choose a book that is developmentally appropriate for the children.
- Use a good introduction to establish the mood of the story.
- Explain unfamiliar words.
- Encourage child participation.
- Tell the story with a conversational tone.
- Use eye contact.
- Convey enthusiasm.
- Demonstrate good posture.
- Use different voices for particular characters to create interest.
- Pronounce words clearly.
- Use a lively tempo.
- Allow comments to be added to story.

19-10 Determining your strengths and weaknesses will help you improve your storytelling skills.

Younger children in particular will stay interested longer when several methods are used during storytime. As a child care teacher, you will need to learn a number of storytelling methods.

Draw and Tell

Draw and tell, or chalk talk, is one storytelling method. Drawings are made on chalkboard, tagboard, or an 18-by 24-inch newsprint pad as the story is told. Textbooks containing draw and tell stories can be purchased from school supply stores or catalogs. Some child care workers prefer to find a storybook and adapt it. Illustrations may be deleted, combined, and added. As a general rule, no more than five sheets of paper should be used.

If you do not have good drawing skills, you may want to use an opaque projector to prepare the stories. Find a book and place it on the projector. Tape a piece of cardboard or paper on the wall. Project drawings from the book onto this paper or cardboard. Lightly trace the drawings with a pencil. Then as you tell the story, use brightly colored markers to retrace the lines.

Draw and tell stories may be prepared so they can be used more than once. Cover original light tracings with clear laminate. Use grease pencils to draw in the outline and fill in the color. After the story is done, clean the clear laminate by wiping it with a piece of felt. Window cleaner may also be used for cleaning.

Tapes

Audio story tapes have appeal for young children. They contain sound effects and music. Story tape sets often include an illustrated booklet that children can use to follow along with the story. Tapes of many popular stories are available.

Videotapes can hold the interest of most children. One disadvantage is that children may already have seen them on television. Commercially purchased or teacher-made tapes may be used for storytelling. Audio and videotapes may be purchased through school supply stores, catalogs, or in the exhibit area at early childhood conferences.

To save money, some child care teachers prefer to make their own tapes. To do so, you will need a tape recorder, cassette tape, and story. As you make the tape, read the story clearly. Pause after each two-page spread. At this point, insert a signal. You may want to hit a spoon against a glass or play a piano key. This signal will tell children listening to the tape to turn the page in their book, 19-11.

Puppets

Puppets have always appealed to young children. Having puppets tell a story is a useful change of pace. Use a puppet as a listener who remarks and asks questions about the story. Puppets can be made from tin cans, tongue depressors, socks, and other inexpensive materials. A mitten also makes a good puppet. Cut eyes, a nose, and a mouth from construction paper and paste them onto the mitten. Use the mitten puppet with the story *The Lost Mitten*. Stuffed animals can be used in the same manner. For example, a brown teddy bear could be used to tell the story of *Little Brown Bear*.

After you tell the story, place the puppet in the library area. Puppets help children in constructing and expressing their understanding of stories, 19-12. (Refer to Chapter 20, Guiding Play and Puppetry Experiences, for more information.)

Individual or Group Stories

Given the chance, children can be clever storytellers. After a field trip, guest visit, or other special event, ask children to record a story about that special time. You might have the children work together in small groups. Write down the children's ideas as they tell you their story. Seeing their own words helps children understand the link between spoken and written words. You could write the ideas on a piece of tagboard paper or on the chalkboard. You can also record these stories with a camcorder and play them later for the children to enjoy.

19-11 Even young children who do not yet read can follow along in a book while listening to a tape.

19-12 Puppets help children express their understanding of stories.

Flipcharts

Flipcharts are stories drawn on large tag-board cards. If you lack drawing skills, you will find the opaque projector helpful. After you finish drawing, tracing, and coloring the cards, number the back of each card. This will help you keep the cards in correct order for storytelling. You may also wish to print the story for each drawing on the back of each flipchart. To protect the flipchart, cover it with a plastic film.

After telling the story, you may wish to place the flipchart in the book area. Then the children have an opportunity to use the flipchart themselves and retell the story. Some children also enjoy arranging the cards in order of the story.

Slide Stories

Slide stories usually center around pictures taken on field trips or during classroom events like holiday parties. You might start a slide story at the beginning of the year. Then at the end of the year the slide story can be told. Slide stories involving the children are also enjoyed by parents at special events.

Flannel Boards

A flannel board story is one of the most popular listening activities for young children. **Flannel board**, or *felt board*, storytelling uses characters and props cut out of felt and placed on a felt background, 19-13. Flannel boards may be purchased from school supply stores and catalogs or made by the teacher. To make a board, you will need a piece of foam insulation board, 27 by 17½ inches. This material can be bought at a lumber supply company. To prepare the board, cover it with two contrasting pieces of felt, 29 by 19½ inches. The two pieces provide different-colored backgrounds for felt figures.

Pieces of paper, cardboard, or felt are used to show major characters or objects. These may be hand drawn, bought, or cut out of storybooks. Flannel board books contain many stories. They also often contain patterns for characters and props. These can be bought from school supply stores.

A quick way to make figures is to use a non-woven interfacing fabric. Hold the fabric in place

19-13 Let children place the felt figures when using a flannel board.

and trace over the patterns with a black felt pen. Fill in the areas you wish to brighten.

Felt figures may also be made from a story-book pattern. Place a piece of carbon paper behind the paper and on top of a piece of card-board. Trace over the drawing with a paper clip. This transfers the image onto the cardboard. Cut out the cardboard figures to use as patterns. The patterns can be placed on felt and traced. If you need larger figures, use the opaque projector to enlarge the drawings.

Presenting a Flannel Board Story

Before you present a flannel board story, you will need to do some advance preparation. Practice reading the story script several times. Check your flannel board figures and place them in order of use. Keep the figures on your lap in a flat box or basket when you tell the story. Avoid placing the figures on the floor as a curious child may pick them up. This could interfere with the success of the story.

Place the figures on the flannel board one at a time. Like writing, the figures should follow a left to right sequence. Practice telling the story and placing the flannel figures on the board. For emphasis, look directly at the figure as you place it on the board.

After you finish telling a flannel board story, leave the assembled board in the book area. The children will enjoy using the flannel board figures to retell the story or create new tales. By observing and listening, you will be able to assess their understanding of the story. You may even want to encourage the children to create their own stories by providing them figures from a variety of stories.

Displaying Books

An important area of a classroom is the book area. Books, flannel boards, tapes, and other storytelling equipment are located in this area. The books should be arranged in an appealing manner. The book covers should be visible to attract the children's interest, 19-14. Books should be arranged so they will not fall after one is removed.

The book and reading areas should be located away from traffic. They should also be separated from the rest of the classroom by dividers. This provides a quiet atmosphere. Scissors, crayons, and painting should not be allowed here. These limits should prevent the books from being misused.

The books for the reading area should be carefully chosen. Each child's developmental needs should be considered. You may wish to include books on topics children in the group are facing, such as divorce, illness, and death. Some books, such as the children's favorites, can

19-14 Displays that show book covers encourage children to look at books on their own.

remain in the area for a long time. Other books can be rotated frequently. Fun books should always be available. Add new books often to stimulate children's interest and enthusiasm. You may want to borrow books from the public library, friends, and parents.

Summary

Storytelling can be a useful learning tool for children. Through storytelling, children can develop an enjoyment of books and learn many skills. Some of these skills include learning to form new ideas and increasing vocabulary.

Stories must be selected with care. Content must match the developmental levels and experiences of the audience. In addition, content must be free of stereotypes.

Illustrations should spark interest and be pleasant. The vocabulary and story length must match children's skills. Finally, the books must be durable.

Before reading to children, it is important to prepare ahead of time. There are several ways to present a story. Draw and tell, story tapes, and flannel boards are a few options.

Review and Reflect

1. Stories that draw on children's _____ help them understand themselves better.

2. True or false. Storytelling is a good form of relaxation.

3. Which types of books are usually the first books shared with young children?
   A. Picture.
   B. Fairy tales.
   C. Animal.
   D. Family life.

4. What theme is used in family stories?

5. In _____, kindness and goodness win over evil.

6. True or false. It is not important if a teacher likes a story as long as the children enjoy it.

7. What are the functions of illustrations?

8. The appropriate length of a book will vary with the _____ of the child.

9. What is sexism?

10. True or false. Teachers should choose books that show all races and nationalities in a positive way.

11. Name three ways to introduce a story.

12. The _____ of a story must be clear.

13. Name two ways to build oral reading skills.

14. Explain one storytelling method.

Apply and Explore

1. Using one of the storytelling methods explained in the chapter, prepare a children's story. Share it with the class.

2. Prepare a bibliography of children's books you might use in storytelling. Divide the books into groups based on age: toddlers, two-, three-, four-, and five-year-olds.

3. Create an introduction for a story. Use props when reading your introduction.

4. Select several multicultural children's books to add to the book area.

5. Listen to a children's story on an audio cassette. List the strategies used to hold the children's attention.

6. Video record yourself reading a book to a group of children. Evaluate your presentation.

Puppets are fun, effective teaching aids.

Chapter 20

Guiding Play and Puppetry Experiences

After studying this chapter, you will be able to

- describe the stages of play.
- explain the stages of material use in play.
- summarize the benefits of socio-dramatic play.
- prepare the classroom environment and guide socio-dramatic play activities.
- summarize the benefits of puppetry experiences.
- make and use three types of puppets.
- write and tell a puppet story.

Terms to Know

dramatic play

socio-dramatic play

projection

solitary play

parallel play

cooperative play

personification

manipulative stage of play

functional stage of play

imaginative stage of play

role-playing

coaching

modeling

prop box

puppetry

conflict

Play is an important part of a young child's day. Young children love to pretend and play make-believe. Such fantasy play provides opportunities for growth and development. Play also encourages experimentation and discovery. Young children are actors without stage fright. They say what they feel and feel what they say. By observing children at play, you will gain insight into their cognitive, social, and emotional development. Play is a window into their minds.

Dramatic play is a form of play in which a single child imitates another person or acts out a situation. **Socio-dramatic play** involves several children imitating others and acting out situations together, 20-1. It is the most complex form of play seen in child care settings. However, it is seldom observed before age three.

Puppetry is another type of play that allows a child to imitate others. A child's puppet may become a wolf, police officer, or even a witch. Through this play, a child may share his or her inner world. The child places feelings and emotions he or she feels onto the puppet. This is known as **projection**.

Stages of Play

Children go through several stages of play before they are able to take part in socio-dramatic play. First is solitary play, followed by parallel play. Finally, children learn to engage in cooperative play.

Infants most often play by themselves. This play is called **solitary play** or independent play. Their play is basically exploratory in nature.

20-1 Socio-dramatic play involves at least two children as they role-play. These children are role-playing workers in a farmer's market.

Solitary explorations involve the child gathering information. Until about nine months of age, infants explore single objects. After this, multiple objects.

Parallel play is typical of two-year-olds. In **parallel play**, children play beside each other, but not with each other. All the children may be involved in similar activities, but there is little interaction among the children. Children in this age group focus more on using play materials on their own.

Cooperative play is play between two or more children. As children grow socially and emotionally, they begin playing with their peers for short time periods. Gradually they learn to respect the property rights of others. This is a clue they are gaining social skills, 20-2. At the same time, they are learning that permission is needed to use some materials. They are more willing to share with others.

It is at this stage that socio-dramatic play begins. As children take part in cooperative play, they become more interested in social relationships. As this occurs, they learn how to develop and maintain peer relationships. From this grows socio-dramatic play.

20-2 Children learn social skills such as cooperation in socio-dramatic play.

Children who are aggressive and uncooperative may have problems with cooperative play. To be successful in cooperative play, they need to give affection, be friendly, and consider other children's wishes. They also need to understand the viewpoint of others.

As you observe children in these three stages of play, you will notice that many engage in personification. **Personification** means giving human traits to nonliving objects. For instance, children may talk to dolls or puppets. They act as if the toys can hear what they say. Many everyday situations are acted out. A child may say "Mommy is going to feed you now." While speaking to a puppet, a child may say "You're going to go for a walk now." They will use exaggerated movements and voices. This is typical behavior for most young children.

Stages of Material Use in Play

Children move through three stages of material use in their play. Not all young children, however, will reach the second or third stages.

The first stage of material use is called the **manipulative stage**. A child at this stage handles props. For instance, when given a baby bottle, children in the manipulative stage will screw and unscrew the cap.

The second stage is called the **functional stage**. During this stage, the child will use the prop as intended while playing with other children. Using a doll bottle, the child will pretend to feed a doll.

The third stage is called the **imaginative stage**. Children in this stage do not need real props, 20-3. They are able to think of substitutes. Instead of feeding the doll with a bottle, they may use their finger, a stick, a clothespin, or a pencil. Likewise, if a broom is needed to sweep the floor, a yardstick may be used.

Many times children at the imaginative level come up with unique ideas for their socio-dramatic play. They may use a toy to represent a dinosaur, a doll carriage for a grocery cart, or a paper bag as a chef's hat. When dramatizing a restaurant theme, they may make paper money to buy food.

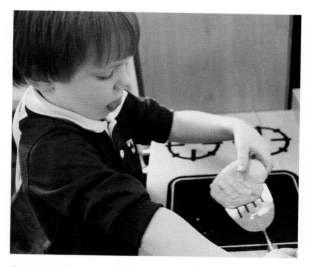

20-3 Making a hamburger out of play dough is a sign of imaginative play.

Some children find it difficult to get involved in a role if there are no real props. In a restaurant scene, for instance, some children will play the role of servers. Children at the manipulative or functional stage will say they cannot play the role without paper and pencil. Children who have reached the imaginative stage might use their hand for the paper and use a finger as a pencil. Not all young children are able to reach the imaginative level.

Socio-Dramatic Play

As children engage in socio-dramatic play, they mimic adult roles. They may play at being a wife, husband, mommy, daddy, doctor, or police officer. This is called role-playing. **Role-playing** allows children to try out a variety of roles, 20-4. As one child plays the role of a hairstylist, another plays the role of the customer. Each role follows social rules determined by the group of children. Children engaged in role-playing often give specific instructions for roles. A child might say "You be the doctor, and I'll be the little girl." Conditions are also common. For example, a child may say "I'll play, but I have to be the bus driver."

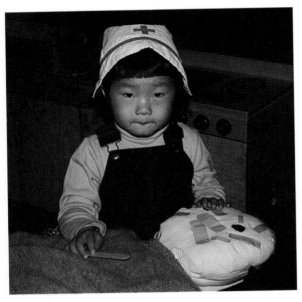

20-4 This child is role-playing a nurse.

Benefits of Socio-Dramatic Play

Children benefit in many ways from participating in socio-dramatic play. From this type of play, children grow physically, socially, emotionally, and cognitively.

Physical growth is promoted through the play actions of children: sweeping floors, dressing dolls, and pretending to paint furniture. Building structures that enhance socio-dramatic scenes also helps develop physical skills.

Social and emotional development are promoted through socio-dramatic play. Children try out different social roles. Sometimes negative feelings and situations that disturb children are acted out. Through these experiences, children learn about human relationships. They learn what kind of behavior upsets another child. They learn how to get along with others and discover important social skills. As a result, they gradually learn how to balance their play to satisfy and please others.

Cognitive development is also promoted through socio-dramatic play. Children's roles range from babies to parents to bears to astronauts. Their imaginations allow them to act out what they cannot yet be in real life. During this type of play, children make decisions and

choices. By doing so, they learn problem-solving skills, 20-5. Language concepts are also developed as children engage in play. They learn new names for equipment and gain new ideas from other children. As they generate plots and storylines, language skills, creativity, and imagination are fostered.

Play Themes

Themes for socio-dramatic play vary. The themes of play often focus on everyday situations children experience, 20-6. Children may imitate auto mechanics fixing cars, cooks making dinner, or painters working on a house. Teachers will often provide props that complement a unit of study, as well as the children's interests.

Themes change with age. Three-year-old children's play stresses process. There is no preplanned plot or theme. Real and pretend are still not firmly separated, so the child becomes what

20-5 Cognitive development occurs as this child uses a sewing machine in the dramatic play area.

Themes for Dramatic Play		
Occupational Roles	Scientist	
	Secretary	
Artist	Shoe salesperson	
Baker	Teacher	
Barber	Truck driver	
Builder	Waiter/waitress	
Bus driver	Veterinarian	
Computer operator		
Cook	**Other Themes**	
Dentist		
Disc jockey	Airport	
Doctor	Beach	
Farmer	Camping	
Fish catcher	Circus	
Florist	Costume shop	
Firefighter	Farm/ranch	
Garbage collector	Gardening	
Gas station attendant	Hat shop	
Grocer	Hospital	
Hairstylist	Pet show	
Librarian	Post office	
Mail carrier	Radio station	
Mechanic	Restaurant	
Pharmacist	Spa	
Pilot	Store	
Photographer	Television station	
Police officer	Theater	
Post office clerk	Zoo	
Sailor		

20-6 Many roles and situations can become the theme of play.

he or she imitates. Routines are important. Many three-year-old children always begin their day with the same activity.

Four-year-old children are more likely to take part in socio-dramatic play. Their play no longer centers primarily around the home. Play now involves more aggressive behaviors. Four-year-olds like to imitate ghosts, monsters, or action TV heroes. As you watch their socio-dramatic play, you will often notice feminine and masculine traits exaggerated. For example, to role-play a mother, children need all the props: gloves, hats, purses, high heels, and scarves.

Children's roles change frequently. One moment a child may be a career woman, and the next she may be a helpless baby. Children are included in or excluded from play based on sameness and difference. Sex, color, and kind of clothes worn may all be factors.

The socio-dramatic play of five-year-olds reflects games with rules, as well as fears and hostile feelings. At this age, the child usually can tell the difference between reality and fantasy. As a result, you may hear the child say "This is just pretend."

Real-life roles as well as folk heroes are part of five-year-olds' socio-dramatic play, 20-7. Queens, kings, nurses, teachers, brides, and characters such as Big Bird and Batman are all frequent themes. At the same time, children are quite interested in romance. Thus, they like to act out fairy tales such as *Cinderella*.

The Teacher's Role

The first role of the teacher is to act as a resource person who provides materials and space. Studies show that in classrooms where

20-7 Five-year-olds enjoy playing roles they see every day.

theme-related props were provided, children spent more time in socio-dramatic play. The quality of toys and activities in the classroom will also affect the time spent in socio-dramatic play. Provide interesting materials. Real materials will also enhance play. That is, instead of supplying small plastic firefighter hats, provide real hats from a local fire station. Change materials often to maintain interest.

The teacher's role also includes coaching, modeling, and reinforcing. **Coaching** requires that you provide children with ideas for difficult situations. For instance, a child may not want to be a baker because there is no baker's hat. You may then suggest that the child use a paper bag as a hat. Another child may be hitting a classmate. In this case, you should tell the child to stop because the other child does not like to be hit. You might also remind the child that others will stop playing if the experience is not pleasant.

In **modeling**, you show the children the appropriate behavior to use during their socio-dramatic play. In a shoe store scene, a child may not know how to sell shoes. You may say "Would you like to buy some shoes today?" Watching you, the child has a chance to model this behavior for the other children.

Verbal guidance is helpful. Remaining outside of the play, you may offer comments and suggestions, 20-8. For example, you may see a child unable to get involved in play. You may say to the child "Your son looks hungry. Shouldn't you go to the store and buy some food?" This statement may encourage the child to take the

20-8 Teachers sometimes need to encourage children to become involved in socio-dramatic play.

role of the parent. It should also get the child involved in dramatization with the children who have set up the grocery store.

Children's positive behaviors during socio-dramatic play should be reinforced. Comments may be made directly to the children who are using the desired behavior. If Sally just gave Sam a turn to use the cash register in their restaurant, say "Sally, I like the way you are giving Sam a turn."

Scheduling

Dramatic play is best scheduled during self-selected play periods. These periods must be long enough for the children to carry out their ideas. Many child care programs allow the first hour in the morning for this type of play.

Avoid scheduling too many activities. This affects the number of children who take part in and remain with socio-dramatic play. If few children are playing, too many activities may be scheduled. Reduce the number of activities. Schedule only activities that complement each other. Blocks, woodworking, puppets, and art activities all encourage dramatic play.

Equipment and Setup for Socio-Dramatic Play

The first decision in arranging for socio-dramatic play is to decide on the location of the play area. Children spend more time in socio-dramatic play when the area is in the center of the classroom. Small areas tend to promote quiet, solitary play. Large, open areas promote more socio-dramatic play.

The quality of socio-dramatic play is promoted through age-appropriate materials. To promote harmonious play, provide plenty of these materials and store them in accessible play areas.

Prop Boxes

Extend children's play by providing prop boxes. A **prop box** contains materials and equipment that encourage children to explore various roles. Boxes that are the same size, clearly marked, and made of lightweight cardboard can be stored and carried with ease.

Prop box themes might include a secretary, shoe shop owner, painter, hairstylist, post office

clerk, baker, or carpenter. Each prop box should contain materials for one role, 20-9. Whenever possible, integrate books which can be used to reinforce the theme. In addition, the materials should be nonsexist and multicultural. To illustrate, a prop box for a hairstylist should include styling tools and products for men as well as women.

Costume Corner

Every dramatic play area should have a costume corner. Rotate costumes to complement current studies. For instance, if the theme of the week is community service, provide clothing to reflect this. Clothing for firefighters, nurses, doctors, and post office clerks can all be included. If Halloween is the theme, provide a variety of Halloween costumes. Make sure that the costume corner contains clothing from a variety of cultures. For example, you might try to include wooden shoes, grass skirts, and kimonos.

Store these costumes after use. Lightweight, cardboard boxes are good for storage. Mark each box clearly so they are easy to locate.

Housekeeping Area

Every early childhood classroom should have a housekeeping area. Dramatic and socio-dramatic play often occurs in this area. Supply child-sized furniture and equipment. Kitchen utensils, furniture, and other household items that complement current themes should be included. To create interest, rotate this equipment often.

Beauty Salon Props	
brushes	towels
cordless curling iron	aprons
cordless hair dryer	emery boards
combs	newspapers and
empty shampoo,	magazines
conditioner, and	cosmetics
hair spray cans	play money
mirrors	cash register
rollers	

20-9 A prop box for a beauty salon might contain some of these items.

Outdoor Play Area

The outdoor play area needs equipment that promotes socio-dramatic play. Include a jungle gym, sandbox, housekeeping items, toy cars and trucks, sawhorses, wooden boxes, planks, and boards. Accessories such as tents, large blankets, and hats are also useful. With these materials, children can build forts, houses, and ships.

Puppetry

Puppetry involves the use of puppets in play. A puppet is a figure designed in likeness to an animal or human. Puppets come in a number of sizes and shapes. People make puppets move by using their fingers, hands, and wrists. Puppets can appear to express emotions if they have movable mouths, legs, and arms.

Puppets are powerful learning tools for young children. With a puppet, a self-conscious child can act out feelings and thoughts such as anger and love. While using the puppet, the child often becomes the character and loses himself or herself. All children can learn how to communicate feelings and thoughts using puppets, 20-10.

20-10 Children can use puppets to express their feelings.

They may say things to a puppet that they will not say to a person. By listening, teachers may learn what makes children angry, sad, happy, or joyful.

For the teacher, a puppet can be a teaching aid. Puppets can be used effectively in almost every area of the curriculum. Chart 20-11 points out some of the values of puppets. Often, puppets are used to motivate children, to encourage them to share their thoughts, and to spark ideas. Group time can begin with a puppet. The puppet can provide a greeting, share the day's weather, or explain any special activities for the day. The appearance of a puppet may be changed for special occasions. For instance, green can be worn for St. Patrick's Day.

Puppets can be used to help children solve problems. When children fail to cooperate at clean-up time, the puppet can say "I feel bad when all the boys and girls do not help pick up the toys." Puppets can also be used to provide suggestions, such as "Tell Ricardo that you want a turn."

Types of Puppets

Puppet types include hand, mascot, and "me" puppets. The value of each type depends upon the needs and interests of the children.

Hand Puppets

Hand puppets are the easiest to use since no strings or rods need to be worked. A hand puppet is worked by placing the second and third fingers in the puppet's head. In this position, the hand is more relaxed and the puppet's entire body can be spread open. The thumb should be placed in one of the puppet's arms and the fourth and fifth finger in the other arm.

Hand puppets can be held in front of the face or over the head. This allows the puppeteer to work the puppet from a sitting, standing, or kneeling position.

Mascot Puppets

Some teachers choose to have a mascot puppet in their classroom. A mascot puppet usually remains in the classroom all year. Therefore, it should be well made to withstand handling from the teacher and children.

| Puppets and Curriculum ||
Curriculum Area	Value of Puppets
Art	• Offers emotional release • Provides sensory stimulation • Promotes large and small muscle development • Encourages problem solving and decision making • Provides for exploration of materials
Math	• Encourages thinking through problems • Introduces concepts • Develops classification skills • Encourages measuring, ordering, and counting skills
Social studies	• Promotes communication skills • Models sharing and cooperation with others • Models critical thinking skills • Demonstrates concepts, such as friendship and self-esteem
Language arts	• Encourages development of language skills • Encourages listening and speaking skills • Promotes the development of abstract concepts such as *above, below, under, in front of,* and *behind*
Dramatic play	• Offers emotional release • Promotes listening skills • Encourages problem-solving skills • Promotes decision-making skills • Promotes self-expression and creativity • Provides opportunities to gain self-confidence as group members • Provides opportunities to express feelings
Science	• Classifies foods into food groups • Discovers the value of the five senses • Observes changes in texture, shape, and sizes • Evaluates ideas • Identifies food groups through the five senses

20-11 Puppets can be used as a learning tool in many areas of the classroom.

Mascot puppets can be used in many classroom routines. It can help introduce new activities and class members. The puppet can also be used as a teaching tool. It can model proper classroom manners. For this reason, the puppet should be given an expressive face and a strong personality. The mascot puppet can also be used to teach classroom rules. If a child neglects a rule, the teacher may have the mascot puppet provide a reminder.

"Me" Puppets

Children can also be taught how to make puppets using their own hands. These are sometimes called "me" puppets. To make "me" puppets, you will need nontoxic, washable marking pens, felt pieces, fake fur, construction paper, and double-stick tape. Demonstrate how to make a "me" puppet using your own hand. Line the inside opening between your index finger and thumb with a red marking pen. This line will be the puppet's lips. Using another colored marker, add the puppet's eyes. Use a piece of construction paper or fake fur for the hair. With double-stick tape, attach the hair to the top of your knuckle.

Show the children how the puppet can open and close its mouth and talk when you move your thumb. Urge the children to make a variety of puppets, including people and animals. School-age children may enjoy making "me" puppets on the first day of school. After making their puppets, each child can share something about himself or herself. They might tell their age, hobby, grade in school, favorite stories, or whatever else they feel like sharing.

Making Puppets

Many teachers make their own hand and mascot puppets using store-bought or self-designed patterns. Chart 20-12 contains a list of materials for making puppets. After cutting the fabric, the mouth, eyes, ears, nose, and other parts should be sewn on. It is quicker to attach these parts with glue. However, this method is not durable. In fact, many times the parts will fall off once the glue has dried. All seams should be

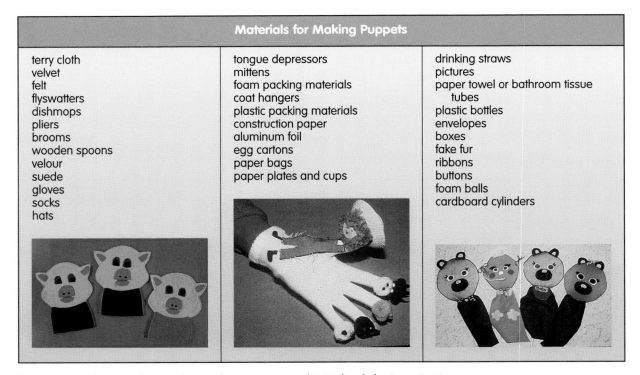

Materials for Making Puppets		
terry cloth	tongue depressors	drinking straws
velvet	mittens	pictures
felt	foam packing materials	paper towel or bathroom tissue
flyswatters	coat hangers	tubes
dishmops	plastic packing materials	plastic bottles
pliers	construction paper	envelopes
brooms	aluminum foil	boxes
wooden spoons	egg cartons	fake fur
velour	paper bags	ribbons
suede	paper plates and cups	buttons
gloves		foam balls
socks		cardboard cylinders
hats		

20-12 Items that can be used to make puppets are limited only by imagination.

sewn with a ¼ inch seam allowance. The seams on a hand puppet should be on the outside of the puppet.

Puppet Stage

A puppet stage is not always needed, 20-13. However, most classrooms have a lightweight, portable stage. The puppet stage should be easy to fold and store. In fact, a cardboard cutting board is an excellent puppet stage. These can be bought at fabric shops. If the board is too tall for children, it can be cut to the correct height. To make the stage more interesting, the cutting board can be painted or wallpapered. It can also be covered with contact paper or fabric.

A tension rod can also be used in creating a puppet stage. When covered with a gathered curtain, the rod can be placed across a door as a temporary stage. Use a simple curtain in a solid color that will not be distracting.

Puppet stages can be ordered through most equipment catalogs. Generally, they are made of wood. As a result, they are often quite heavy. Teacher-made puppet stages have the advantage of being more portable and less expensive.

Writing Puppet Stories

Not all puppet stories are found in books. In fact, most puppet stories are written by teachers.

These stories are often contemporary and designed to fit the children's needs and interests.

To begin writing a puppet story, select a theme. Using a theme will help you decide the order of the events in the story. Themes can be based on friends, relatives, or other people. Personal experiences are another useful theme, as are manners, safety, friendships, vacations, holidays, and center experiences. Some other theme ideas for puppet stories are listed in 20-14.

Developing a plot is the most challenging aspect of writing a puppet story. The children must be able to follow the action of the story. The

Theme Ideas for Puppet Stories
Odin's Broken Tooth
My Dog Heidi
Kelsi's Hamster
My Cousin Pilar
Hunter's Grandmother
Bobby's Friend Eric
Christmas at Aunt Sharese's
My Favorite Gift
A Trip to the Zoo

20-14 Children do not require complex themes for stories. Simple, familiar experiences are more interesting to them.

20-13 A low shelf can be used as a puppet stage.

events should occur in a logical manner. Begin with the theme and include the story events and problems. Remember, it is the problems that add interest and tension to the story.

End the story by resolving the conflict. In a story, **conflict** can be described as two or more forces that oppose each other. Conflict adds interest. When developing scenes of conflict, think in terms of synonyms and antonyms. Make a list of opposites. For example, opposite pairs might include: ugly—beautiful; poor—rich; weak—strong; soft—hard; kind—mean.

The ending of a puppet story finishes the picture for the children. The ending should make clear that the story is over. It should leave children with the story's most important point.

Working Puppets

When using a puppet in the classroom, the puppet should always model proper communication skills for the children. When the puppet speaks, it should move and face the children. When children or you speak, the puppet should be held still, facing the speaker.

Three basic types of movements can be modeled with hand puppets. The fingers, wrists, and arms may be moved. The fingers can create small movements in the puppet's arms and head. Waist movements can be made using the wrist. Arm movements can be used for locomotion movements. Chart 20-15 explains the various finger, wrist, and arm movements that can be used in puppetry.

Telling a Puppet Story

At this point, you have practiced the story and are comfortable working the puppets. You are now ready to tell the children a puppet story. Begin by creating the story setting and preparing the children.

The room should set the mood for a story. For a circus theme, you might place colorful balloons next to the storyteller. A Valentine's Day event might include a valentine box set next to the storyteller. Likewise, a Halloween story could be enhanced with dimmed lights. The purpose of this preparation is to put the children in the proper frame of mind for enjoying the presentation.

The first few minutes of a puppet story set the tone of the story. Make a special effort to gain the children's attention. This may be done using recorded music, slamming doors, or having the children sing a song. However, keep some surprises for later in the story.

Puppet Voices

To develop your puppet's character, use a special voice. Since puppets are not people, their voices should not be similar to human voices. Pitch is important. If there are two puppets being used, one should have a low-pitched voice and the other a high-pitched voice.

The children should be able to hear the puppet voices clearly. Voices should also be constant. The puppet should have the same voice throughout the story. If the puppet begins with a high-pitched voice, it should finish with one.

The voice should also match the puppet's size and character. A huge tiger should have a booming voice. On the other hand, a spider should have a tiny voice. A puppet of an elderly person may have a slower voice than that of a child.

Movements for Puppetry

Finger Movements

- The puppet's head can nod *yes* by moving the fingers up and down inside the puppet's head. This movement can also mean *I understand* or *I can do it.*
- The idea of *me* or *mine* can be expressed by pointing the fingers inside the puppet's hands toward the puppet.
- The puppet can gesture for someone to *come here* by waving one hand toward the body.
- Clapping and jumping up and down can express joy or enthusiasm.
- Pointing can convey such ideas as *you* or *over there.*
- Waving can be used to say *good-bye* or *hello.*
- Rubbing the puppet's hands together can mean the puppet is cold or thinking of doing something sneaky.
- Thinking can be expressed in a number of ways. The puppet can cross its hands or tap its head lightly.
- The fingers can be used to mimic sneezing, crying, and snoring (move the puppet's head up and down slightly).

Wrist Movements

- To show a **no** movement, rotate the puppet back and forth.
- To show a seated puppet, pivot the wrist, changing from a front to a side view. After this, the wrist needs to be bent, allowing the puppet to rest on a seat.
- To show a bow from the waist, bend the wrist down. At the same time, use the finger to make the puppet point toward itself.
- To show a puppet reading a book, model left to right progression skills by pivoting the wrist to mimic this action. At the same time, slowly move the fingers in the puppet's head to show reading action.
- To make a puppet appear to be looking for something, move the wrist back and forth. Using some arm movement, the puppeteer can make the puppet look to the sides of the stage and above and below it.

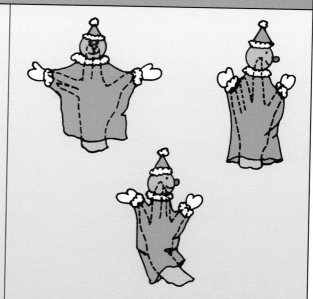

- To show a lifting movement, bend the wrist down as in bowing and grasp objects with the hands using hand and finger movements.

Arm Movements

- To mimic running, move the wrist up and down in a rapid, choppy motion. At the same time, move the puppet quickly across the stage.
- To mimic walking, hold the puppet upright and straight. As the puppet is moved across the stage, move its arms up and down.
- To mimic hopping, each hop needs to be deliberate. For variety, have the puppet hop in circles, returning to the ground as the last motion for each hop.
- To mimic flying, use broad arm movements. The puppet should always face the direction that it is flying.
- To mimic fainting or falling, use a broad arm movement and have the puppet land on its back. The speed at which the puppet lands depends on the desired effect. The best effect is acquired by freezing the puppet's movements for a few seconds before falling.

20-15 Simple finger, wrist, and arm movements can be used with puppets.

Summary

Play is an important part of a young child's day. Children go through several stages of play before they begin to take part in socio-dramatic play. These stages are solitary play, parallel play, and cooperative play. Children also move through three stages of material use in their play. These are the manipulative stage, the functional stage, and the imaginative stage. Socio-dramatic play and puppetry experiences are two types of make-believe in which children like to take part. Each offers its own benefits to children's growth.

Socio-dramatic play allows children the chance to try out many roles. Through this play, children grow physically, socially, emotionally, and cognitively. Themes for socio-dramatic play vary. With proper teacher guidance and age-appropriate materials, socio-dramatic play can be an excellent form of play for children.

Puppetry experiences provide children the chance to explore emotions, thoughts, and situations. Children can project their feelings onto puppets. Teachers can help children learn how to handle difficult emotions and situations in a constructive way through puppetry experiences.

Several types of puppets can be used with children, depending upon their needs. Puppets can be purchased or handmade. Most puppet stories are written by teachers.

Review and Reflect

1. Define socio-dramatic play.

2. Play in which children play by themselves but stay close by other children is called _____ play.
   A. cooperative
   B. solitary
   C. parallel
   D. dramatic

3. True or false. Socio-dramatic play is the simplest and first type of play used by children.

4. Children in the _____ stage of material use will screw and unscrew the cap on a baby bottle.

5. True or false. All children reach the imaginative stage of material use.

6. Indicate what age groups use the following play themes:
   A. Imitation of ghosts and monsters.
   B. No preplanned themes.
   C. Real life roles as well as folk heroes.
   D. Filling, emptying, and releasing objects.

7. In _____, the teacher shows correct behavior for children during their socio-dramatic play.

8. _____ requires that teachers provide children with ideas for difficult situations during socio-dramatic play.

9. State two recommendations for scheduling socio-dramatic play.

10. What is included in a prop box?

11. How can puppets help teachers to better understand children?

12. _____ puppets are made using the puppeteer's hand.

13. Why is conflict an effective element in a puppet story?

14. Explain how you would match a puppet's size and character with your voice for the puppet.

Apply and Explore

1. Brainstorm a list of prop box materials for a secretary, painter, baker, and carpenter.

2. Design a hand puppet.

3. Invite a puppeteer to speak to the class about his or her occupation.

4. Write a puppet story.

5. Create a portable puppet stage that is lightweight and easy to store.

6. Visit a local child care center and observe the socio-dramatic play area. What types of play did you notice? What stages were the children in?

7. Observe and compare a group of two-year-old and four-year-old children. Describe the differences in their play.

Chapter 21

Guiding Manuscript Writing

After studying this chapter, you will be able to

- define manuscript writing.
- list reasons for encouraging the development of writing skills in preschool settings.
- explain activities that help children develop writing skills.
- make letters following the Zaner-Bloser writing system.
- outline the sequence children follow in learning alphabet letters.
- discuss guidelines for helping children develop writing skills.

Terms to Know

manuscript writing

hand-eye coordination

skywriting

"Writing before starting kindergarten?" asked a concerned visitor. "Preschool children can't even read yet." This person is unaware that formal writing is developmentally inappropriate in preschool settings. Correct spelling, form, and style are given only minor attention during the preschool years. Instead, the emphasis is on a readiness to develop needed skills and attitudes for writing. As children explore, they learn how symbols and meaning combine. Art and play activities are critical in children's growth as symbol makers. Learning to write is an act of discovery.

When children begin to use symbols or drawings to represent ideas or words, they are beginning to write. When observing these children, you will note they use a combination of "sticks" and "circles" in their scribbling. Those children who are ready to create messages in print need encouragement. They should be immersed in a print-rich environment. Children who are not ready for writing must be introduced to the proper activities to help them prepare. Activities that promote small muscle and hand-eye coordination skills are needed. Eventually they will become interested in writing.

Manuscript writing, or print script, is a simple form of calligraphy. These simple strokes look like the printed words seen every day in the children's world in books, in newspapers, on street signs, and on computer screens. Print script does not require the sustained muscle control needed for cursive writing. It involves unconnected letters that are made of simple, separate strokes. Vertical lines (|), horizontal lines (—), diagonal lines (/), and circles (O) are used to compose the strokes. These basic strokes can be made easily by children who lack well-developed small-muscle coordination skills. Because of the separate strokes, this process is also slower to complete than cursive writing. However, manuscript writing is more legible. Children can learn their letters at a faster rate.

Manuscript writing is not taught formally in the preschool setting. Most young children are not developmentally ready for this task. It is included in this book only to introduce readiness activities and the sequence by which children should learn manuscript. It is also included to teach caregivers of young children correct letter formations. All teacher- made materials should be done using proper manuscript writing techniques, 21-1. Your work will then serve as a model for children. It may also stimulate some children, particularly four- and five-year-olds, to identify individual letters of the alphabet and to write.

Objectives for Writing

There are many reasons to encourage writing in the preschool, especially with children who are ready for the task. Children need to learn

- to note the differences in the formation of letters
- to write the alphabet letters and numerals
- that words are made up of letters
- that letters represent sounds
- that letters in the English language go from left to right, and top to bottom
- letter/sound associations
- that the spelling of words is related to their sound

Four elements are needed if children are to meet these objectives. Included are interest, enthusiasm, clear instructions, and support given by you to each child.

Prewriting Skills

Manuscript writing is mainly a perceptual and motor skill that requires the use of small and large muscles. Two skills are needed before children are able to communicate using manuscript writing. These include small muscle coordination and hand-eye coordination skills. Children need enough small muscle coordination to hold a pencil and make basic strokes. They also need

21-1 Teacher-made materials must be carefully prepared to serve as models for children. All letters must be accurately reproduced as shown on this game board. The attractive materials used on the board will also spark children's interest.

their hands and eyes to work together. Caregivers need to include activities that promote these skills in the daily routine. This will ensure that children learn the basic skills needed to learn manuscript writing.

Small Muscle Activities

Small muscle activities are those that encourage children to use the small muscles in their hands and fingers. Materials used in these activities are listed in 21-2. Observe the children's interest and success with these materials. Provide interesting developmental materials. Practice should provide the children with the small muscle coordination skills needed for manuscript writing.

Hand-Eye Coordination Activities

Hand-eye coordination is muscle control that allows the hand to do a task in the way the eye sees it done. Activities that promote this type of coordination are listed in 21-3. These activities will promote the development of writing skills. Therefore, they should be available for use at all times.

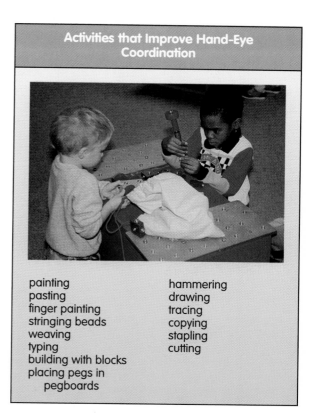

Activities that Improve Hand-Eye Coordination

painting
pasting
finger painting
stringing beads
weaving
typing
building with blocks
placing pegs in
    pegboards

hammering
drawing
tracing
copying
stapling
cutting

21-3 Eye-hand coordination activities help train the eye and hand to work together to accomplish a task.

Materials Used in Small Muscle Activities

play dough
clay
sand
building blocks
puzzles
finger paints
table blocks
small, wheeled toys
snap beads
threading beads
buttons and
    buttonholes
easel paints
rubber stamps
magnetic letters
wooden letters

21-2 Using these materials will require use of small muscles, thus promoting their growth.

Manuscript Writing Systems

There are a number of manuscript writing systems available for teachers to use. The differences in these systems are small. Included are the directions in which strokes are made and the shapes of the letters. Research does not support one system over another. Whatever system is used, you need to be a skilled and consistent model.

Zaner-Bloser is perhaps the most widely used system. It is the system introduced in this book, 21-4. It was selected because of its common use and the ease by which children can learn to print using it. D'Nealian is another manuscript system that is used in some kindergartens. Since the letter formation is more difficult, it is not popular for preschool children.

21-4 The Zaner-Bloser writing system is easy for children to use and for teachers to teach.

Materials

Preschool children lack the muscle control and hand-eye coordination to use lined paper. Use large, unlined pieces of paper such as newsprint instead. As children increase their muscle control and skill with writing tools, provide smaller sheets of paper. Writing tools for the children include chalk, crayons, watercolor markers, colored pencils, and lead pencils. Oversized lead pencils are not the best tools since they are hard for young children to handle. Provide regular-sized pencils instead.

Manuscript Sequence

There is a sequence in how children usually learn alphabet letters. First children recognize whether a line is curved or straight. Next they learn to distinguish round letters (*O, C*) and curved letters (*S, D*). Then they learn to recognize curved letters that have intersections, such as *B* and *R*. Finally, letters with diagonal lines (*K, X*) and horizontal lines (*L, H*) are recognized.

Certain letters are easier than others for children to form. The sequence recommended in the Zaner-Bloser method follows the similarities in lowercase letters. This is because lowercase letters are used more often. Zaner-Bloser's recommended sequence is as follows:

litoadcefgjqusbhprnmvywkxz
1, 2, 3, 4, 5, 6, 7, 8, 9, 10
LITOADCEFGJQUSBHPRNMVYWKXZ

The easiest letters are those made of straight lines or circles. You can follow this sequence as you design written materials.

Building Writing Skills

Proper writing skills are based on a few basic guidelines. With practice and maturity, children learn the importance of letter size, proportion, spacing, and line quality. You must be able to guide them through common problems, such as letter reversals. Also, you must be able to work through unique situations faced by left-handed children.

Size and Proportion

To provide useful models for children to imitate, you need to perfect your own writing skills. You must use the correct letter size and proportion. Lowercase letters are always half the size of uppercase, or capital, letters. This rule holds true no matter how small or how large the writing, and no matter where the writing appears (name tags, charts, chalkboard, games).

The size of the children's writing reflects development of their small muscle control and hand-eye coordination skills. First writings are typically large. The letters vary in size and proportion. As the children's coordination skills mature, their writing forms decrease in size. Within any given classroom, there will usually be a wide range of skill. Look at the writings in 21-5. Kathryn's writing is mature for a four-year-old child. Her letters are all of a similar size and proportion. Amy's writing does show some variation in both size and proportion. Given time, she will develop the skill to make letters of proper proportion and size. Jena's writing almost looks like a scribble. Even though she is the same age as Kathryn and Amy, she still lacks the skills needed to write her name so it can be read. Jena needs many more hand-eye coordination and small muscle activities.

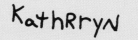

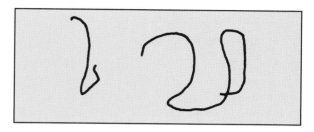

21-5 These writings show three levels of writing skill. Jena requires extra practice to bring her skills up to a higher level.

Spacing

Achieving proper spacing between letters and words is difficult for many beginning writers. Proper spacing requires more small muscle control than most preschool children have developed. There is one technique to help them gain control. Tell the children to write the letter *O* between words. However, this may still be too difficult for some preschool children. If so, direct them to place their index finger on the paper after the word. Then have them write the first letter of the next word to the right of their finger. Unless a child's fingers are unusually large, this technique should produce proper spacing.

Line Quality

Observe the line quality of children's writings. If a line wavers, this usually means immature coordination. Wavering lines can also result from writing too slowly or moving fingers but not the pencil. In this case, the writer is trying to draw rather than write. Most often, wavering lines are a sign that the child lacks enough muscular control to apply constant pressure to the writing tool. To remedy this, have children use more arm action and relax their grips. Illegible writing is another common problem. Pencil lead that is too fine or too hard may be the cause of illegible work.

Reversals

Young children have difficulty learning the direction in which letters face. In the early stages of writing, children often reverse letters. For instance, one letter becomes another letter. Children will print *b* when they intend to write *d.* Some letters are written backwards. A *J* may have the tail reversed. Children may also write the letters of a word in the reversed order. For instance, Mark may write his name *kraM.*

You can guide children with reversal problems by pointing out differences in direction. If the child confuses the letters *b* and *d,* say "*b*, line, then circle." This tells the child that a *b* contains a straight line first and then a circle. If the child is having a problem writing a d correctly, say, "*d*, circle, then line." After being given these directions, some children will repeat them aloud when writing *d* or *b.*

Practice

Children need many opportunities for practicing their writing. Be selective in what you provide for these times to promote this skill. Be careful that these practices do not become meaningless drills. For instance, when children are required to write a line of ten letters, they can become bored and tired. The result can be that the last letter is not formed as well as the first. Since children usually use the last letter they wrote as a model, any errors are repeated.

During practice with writing tools, show children how to hold the writing tool properly. First, ask children to watch the way you pick up a pencil. Place the pencil between your first finger and thumb. Lightly rest your index finger on the top of the pencil. Show the children how the index finger controls the heaviness of the letter. See 21-6.

Left-Handed Children

About 10 percent of all children are left-handed, 21-7. A series of activities can assist you

21-6 By holding this pencil properly, this child is successful in the practice activity.

21-7 Work with left-handed children to make sure they are comfortable with writing. This child has been correctly seated with her left arm toward the left end of the table.

in learning a child's preferred writing hand. Ask children to pick up a piece of paper, throw a ball, pick up a fork or spoon, and/or place pegs in a pegboard. To avoid stressing the use of one hand over the other, center objects in front of children. If a child repeatedly uses his or her left hand, he or she has shown a preference for that hand. Left-handed children should be placed so that their left arm is at the left end of a table for eating and work. Such placement prevents the problem of bumping arms with a right-handed child.

Early Experiences in Writing

Early experiences often determine whether children like or dislike an activity. For this reason, start slowly and provide activities children will not find frustrating. Since most children have an interest in the letters of their own names, begin by encouraging children to copy their first names, 21-8. Most children have had experience writing or watching adults write their names. Early childhood teachers should stress that children learn the proper letter forms. Do not capitalize all the letters. Children can become confused if they see their name written in different ways at school and at home. For instance,

the name *Tom* should be written using an uppercase *T* followed by lowercase *o* and *m*.

Techniques for Encouraging Writing

Your major role is to carefully prepare an environment that will encourage children to scribble and write. Children experience more success in developing print awareness in a print-rich environment. Some children will learn to recognize names and other words in their environment. To encourage this skill, you will need to use many teaching tools, 21-9.

Provide children with copies of their names. Then make a bulletin board containing the children's pictures. Under each picture, place the correct name.

21-9 Letter blocks provide an opportunity to trace and match letters. This helps children become familiar with all letters.

21-8 Introduce writing activities by helping children learn to recognize the letters in their names.

Other practices to encourage writing include using place mats at mealtime. Print the child's first name on the place mat. In addition, print names in the upper left corner of all papers. Writing can also be encouraged by printing labels for classroom materials and furniture. Label tables, windows, doors, clocks, sinks, shelves, and curtains, as well as other items.

Make children aware of printed names other than their own. Do this by printing all the children's names on tagboard cards. At transition times, place all the cards in a small basket. Then draw one name at a time, allowing the children to identify the name.

Encourage children who are ready to print their name on their artwork. To prepare them for the left to right progression required in reading, tell children to print their names in the upper left corner of their artwork. Gradually the children will learn to follow the left-to-right, top-to-bottom patterns of written English.

When working with children who are having trouble in writing a particular letter, try **skywriting**. Stand beside the child. Demonstrate the correct way to make the letter by writing it in the air in front of you. Have the child observe your motion, hold up his or her writing hand, and follow the strokes. Observe the child to be sure that he or she is making the correct letter.

Always use the correct terminology. For example, when writing capital letters call them capital, or uppercase, letters. Do the same for lowercase letters.

Provide children with letters cut out of sandpaper and mounted on tagboard. By feeling a letter, the children learn its form and shape. Another technique is to print the manuscript letters on paper and cover the paper with clear acetate sheets. Give children grease or china marking pencils to trace the letters. Their markings can be removed with a piece of felt or window cleaner spray. The acetate sheets are reusable. You might also develop puzzles that require children to match uppercase letters with the proper lowercase letters.

Group Experiences

There are many group situations in which writing can be encouraged, 21-10. Write in the children's presence. Have children dictate an invitation, letter, or thank-you note to you. As they dictate, record their message in print. Follow the correct manuscript format. Call attention to the use of an uppercase letter at the beginning of a sentence, a question mark or a period at the end, and an uppercase letter at the beginning of proper names.

Space for Writing

A writing center has particular appeal for four- and five-year-olds. This space should be separated from other areas of the classroom by bookshelves, screens, or mobile bulletin boards. This allows the privacy and quiet required for writing. Provide a variety of writing tools such as crayons, pens, pencils, chalk, and watercolor markers. Provide paper of many sizes, picture dictionaries, and models of the alphabet. See 21-11.

21-10 An oversized thank-you card from the entire class encourages these children to practice their writing skills.

21-11 A well-organized writing center provides a positive learning environment for children to develop their writing skills.

Teachers also need to display materials that encourage printing. These materials include alphabet models, sandpaper letters, and sandboxes. Using a sandbox, children can practice tracing various alphabet letters with their index fingers. A large chalkboard can also be a useful display. On chalkboards, children can make large, free movements that give writing a smooth quality. Charts and other label materials throughout the classroom can be useful displays for the children to copy.

Watching children's writing progress will be exciting as well as rewarding. Observe the appearance of simple letter shapes as they appear in a child's writing. Celebrate these accomplishments by hanging the child's work in a prominent place.

Summary

Learning to write is a complex process. In the preschool setting, children can observe and practice manuscript writing. This type of writing involves unconnected letters made of simple, separate strokes. These skills are an excellent basis for the more advanced writing done at later ages. Taught properly, children can also build basic reading skills.

Review and Reflect

1. Manuscript writing _____.
   A. is a complicated form of calligraphy
   B. is more difficult to learn than cursive writing
   C. does not require the sustained muscle control that cursive writing does
   D. All of the above.
2. True or false. Manuscript writing should be taught formally in the preschool setting.
3. List three objectives for encouraging writing in preschool.
4. In order to meet these objectives, what four things must the teacher provide to each child?
5. What two activities should be provided to encourage children to build skills in manuscript writing?
6. True or false. The differences in writing systems are small.
7. Why should lined paper be avoided for young children's writing activities?
8. Arrange the following letter groups in the order in which children learn to recognize them.
   A. Curved letters with intersections (B, R).
   B. Round letters (O, C).
   C. Straight and curved lines.
   D. Letters with diagonal lines (K, X).
9. True or false. Uppercase letters are always half the size of lowercase letters.
10. What is another name for uppercase letters?
11. A common writing problem in which children might confuse b and d is _____.
12. List three items that can be placed in the writing area to encourage printing.

Apply and Explore

1. Collect, compare, and discuss writing samples from a group of five-year-olds.
2. Practice making the letters following the Zaner-Bloser writing system.
3. Practice writing a letter using manuscript writing. When you finish, check your letter for line quality, spacing, and letter formation.
4. Prepare two sets of tracing alphabet cards that children can use. Make one set using uppercase letters. Use lowercase letters for the second set.
5. Brainstorm a list of all equipment and fixtures in the classroom that could have labels attached. Prepare the labels.
6. Create a writing suitcase. Include paper, colored felt tip markers, crayons, and grease pencils.

Chapter 22

Guiding Math Experiences

After studying this chapter, you will be able to

- list objectives of early math experiences.
- use two basic assessments to determine math skills of children.
- recognize a variety of items that can be used to promote math experiences.
- identify math experiences that promote the development of key math concepts.
- design math experiences that stress specific math concepts.

Terms to Know

specific task assessment

parquetry blocks

classification

matching

sorting

recognizing

set

empty set

one-to-one correspondence

rational counting

numerals

"One, three, five, two" and similar phrases can often be heard from young children. They are searching for meaning as they echo these words. Reciting numbers is a key step in learning math concepts. Math is sometimes defined as the science of shapes and numbers. For the young child, math is an active process of thinking about and organizing experiences to make sense of their world.

Children create math concepts by relating new experiences and information to what they already know. Meaningful learning requires the ability to see patterns. Classroom equipment, materials, and activities must provide opportunities for the children to understand patterns through play.

Early math experiences for children should focus on exploration, discovery, and understanding. Concepts are developed by the exploration of hands-on materials and the discovery of their relationships. Math concepts are usually taught informally in day-to-day activities in early childhood classrooms. The many activities that involve math concepts include art, cooking, games, dramatic play, stories, and storytelling, 22-1. Almost every activity area in the classroom promotes math exploration.

Children may learn shapes, color, and order (logic) concepts through art activities or by playing with blocks. Cooking activities teach how quantities are related and ordered. For instance, you might tell a child "Beat the eggs first, add the sugar second, and add the vanilla last." Classroom games can teach the concepts of first and last, as well as high and low numbers. If

22-1 Games help children learn many math concepts.

dice are used in games, addition concepts can be taught to the older children. Dramatic play offers many teaching opportunities. For example, as children play store, they can learn about money, 22-2. Songs, stories, and fingerplays can contain numbers and math words.

Other ways to include math concepts in the daily routine include asking "Are there enough chairs?" "Is everybody here today?" or "Is there a cookie for each child?" Math concepts can be used in any appropriate situation. For example, you may introduce counting concepts by remarking "Kelsie brought three kittens to school."

Transitions (time between scheduled activities) are a good opportunity to present new math concepts. For example, you might say "It's two o'clock and time to go to the library." At clean-up time, one-to-one relationships can be taught if there is one puzzle for Juan and one for Nikki to put back on the shelf. After group time, you may have the group of children wearing red use the bathroom first.

Goals of Early Math Experiences

Well-structured settings provide play experiences that also help promote math skills. These math experiences should help form concepts such as color and shape recognition, classification, measurement, counting, time, temperature, space, and volume concepts. The math experiences should stress the following:

- observing and describing concrete objects
- recognizing colors, patterns, and attributes

22-2 As children play store, they start to form concepts about money.

- comparing objects and using terms that describe quantity, such as "more than" and "lighter than"
- classifying sets of objects
- copying patterns
- recognizing shape concepts
- recognizing and writing numerals
- using logical words such as "all," "none," and "some"
- using one-to-one correspondence

Assessing Math Ability

Before planning math activities for children, first determine the children's skill levels. In order to do this properly, children need to be assessed individually. There are two common forms of assessment: observation and specific task assessment. The information obtained from these processes will help you increase your knowledge of the children's skills and needs. It will also help you plan developmentally appropriate math activities.

Assessment by Observation

Observation involves informal viewing of a child during self-selected activities, 22-3. Specific behaviors to watch for include the following:

22-3 Observation assessments are made by noting children's math-related actions as they play.

- identifying colors and shapes
- sorting and classifying objects
- counting objects
- setting a table correctly
- pouring liquids and carefully watching the amount poured
- constructing patterns
- writing numerals

Through observation, you will be able to determine a child's needs. If you notice a child cannot sort objects, you will need to provide sorting activities. Specific activities are outlined later in this chapter.

Specific Task Assessment

Specific task assessment involves giving children set activities to determine skill and/or needs. Examples include the following:

- Present a child with crayons and say "Tell me the colors." After the child has replied, say "Now count these for me."
- Show a child one group of four pennies and one group of seven pennies. Then ask the child "What group has more pennies?"
- Present a child with circle, diamond, square, and rectangle shapes. Say "Find the square." Then have the child identify each of the remaining shapes.
- Show a child four different-sized balls. Ask "Which is the smallest ball?" and "Which is the largest ball?"
- Lay 10 blocks in front of the child. Ask "How many blocks do I have here?"

As with observation, the information provides information for use in planning math activities.

Math Equipment

The physical environment needs to foster mathematical thinking. Provide the children with a variety of materials that promote physical and mental activity. Include collections of items. These items encourage counting, observing, creating, sorting, discussing, constructing, ordering, and comparing. From these activities, children can develop math concepts. Chart 22-4 lists many materials for learning math concepts. If these materials are available in the classroom, children can explore and discover many math concepts.

Supplies for Math Activities

flannel boards	thermometers: indoor, outdoor,	buttons for counting and sorting
felt-covered numerals	play	empty spools
felt cutouts of various sizes, colors,	alarm clock	puzzles with geometric inserts
numbers, and shapes	egg timer	jigsaw puzzles
scraps of cloth	giant wooden dominoes	sequencing puzzles
pegboards	giant counting rods	measuring spoons
magnetic shapes	scales: bathroom and balance	tactile numbers
calendars	light and heavy objects; rocks,	counting frame
lines numbered 0 through 20	pennies, corks	pattern blocks
rules, yardsticks, and tape	measuring containers of various	
measures	sizes and types	

22-4 Many items can be used to stress math experiences.

Mathematical Activities

Math activities for preschool children should promote the development of many skills. For example, children should learn to identify, classify, and understand the concept of a set. Children should also learn to count and recognize numbers and understand the concepts of space, size, volume, and time. The art of curriculum design is matching children's needs to their interests. This requires good observation skills and a good knowledge of child development.

Color Concepts

Color is considered a math concept since it helps children learn to discriminate among objects. Using color, children can classify, pattern, and sequence, 22-5. Identifying colors also seems to help language development. It requires the skill to recall a name and associate it with a visual image. Then, as the children's language skills grow, their skill at naming colors improves.

22-5 The color in this bulletin board helps children see differences between the circles, crayons, boy, and girl.

According to studies, children learn to identify colors before shapes. However, it is not uncommon for a preschool child to confuse color and shape. For example, you may ask a child to name a shape, and the child will answer with the name of a color.

Infants as young as four to six months old begin to distinguish color hues. Red, yellow, and blue (primary colors) are recognized more quickly than green, violet, and orange (secondary colors).

By age two, many children can match a color to a sample. However, some three-, four-, or five-year-old children may not be able to match colors. This problem may be caused by color blindness. Color blindness can be discovered through careful observation of children as they try to learn colors. Children who are color blind see shades of green and red as grayish brown. They may even see all colors as gray. If you notice that a child has a problem, report it to the center director. Often the director can discuss the problem with the child's parents. The parents can then decide if their child should be tested for color blindness.

Color concepts can be taught formally or informally. You can teach children to name colors using different-colored blocks. Hold up a red block and ask for the name of the color. Continue by asking the children to point out other red objects around the room. Repeat these steps using the rest of the blocks.

Color recognition can also be taught at transition times. For instance, at the end of story time you may say, "All the children who are wearing red may go to the bathroom." Repeat this, using different colors, until all the children have been excused.

Sorting objects by color can also be used to teach color concepts. Provide each child with a small bag containing several colors and shapes cut from tagboard. The children can be directed to sort by color and then by shape.

Charts are a good way to teach color concepts. Charts also teach children the usefulness of graphing. An example would be a chart labeled "eye colors." Divide a piece of tagboard into four even, vertical sections. Then divide the tagboard into enough horizontal sections for every child in the class. Have each child in the class look at the chart and determine their eye

color. If the children are able, encourage them to write their name under the color that matches their own eyes. See 22-6. If the children cannot write, give them pictures of themselves or round faces cut out of tagboard. After all the children are done, ask "Which eye color is the least common?" Then ask "What eye color is the most common?"

Colored shapes can also be graphed on charts. For example, cut basic shapes from colored tagboard. Using a felt tip marker or pencil, divide the tagboard into four equal horizontal sections. Next, divide the tagboard vertically into five or six sections. Glue different shapes in each box in the first vertical column. See 22-7. Then give the children shapes to match.

A feely box or bag is useful for teaching color. Place colored buttons, paper, felt strips, or blocks into the box or bag. Have children draw an object from the bag and identify its color.

Color hunts in the classroom are a fun way to teach color concepts. To conduct a color hunt, ask a child to choose a color. Then have other

Eye Color			
Brown	Blue	Green	Hazel
Pablo	Mark	Sandy	Cory
Sally	Chris	Reina	Rose
Shawnna	Pouneh		Ingrid
Tom			
Sung Jee			
Pedro			

22-6 This chart can be used to help children understand the concept of eye color.

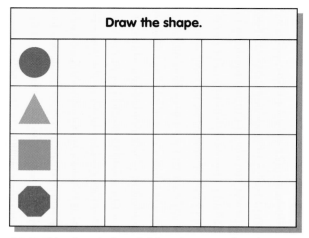

22-7 This chart helps children learn to identify shapes. Children need to focus on the outlines before they can identify the shape.

children point out objects of the same color found in the classroom.

Discussion helps children learn to recognize colors. Have a child choose a color. Then ask the child what thoughts the color brings to mind. One child may choose red and say, "Red makes me think of fire trucks and valentines." Another child may choose blue and say, "Blue makes me think of the sky."

Other activities you can conduct to teach color concepts include the following:

- Hold up a piece of green construction paper. Ask children wearing green to stand up. Repeat using different colors each time. To add interest for four- and five-year-old children, give more complex directions. For instance, say "If you are wearing blue, stand on one foot."
- Pour all your crayons into a basket or box. Then set out several empty baskets or boxes—one for each color of crayon. Encourage the children to sort the crayons by color.
- Display several identically colored shapes on a flannel board. Then add one that is the same shape, but a different color. Ask the children "Which one does not belong?" This activity can also be done using different shapes.

- Play "I Spy" with a group of children. First, note a brightly colored classroom object. Then say "I spy something red." Encourage the children to take turns guessing what object you are thinking about. If they cannot guess it, give them more clues. The next game is started by the child who guesses correctly.

Shape Concepts

Children are often confused by shape. At first they will say circles and squares are the same figures because both have closed boundaries. Over time they will become aware of the features of the boundaries themselves.

The skills needed to identify and draw shapes do not develop at the same time. Children can most often name shapes before they can draw them. When copying shapes, circles are easiest for children, followed by squares, then rectangles and triangles. Most children cannot copy shapes other than circles until they are about five years of age. Before this, their copies have round corners and distances of uneven length.

To learn basic shape concepts, use a variety of activities that stress touching, holding, and matching of shapes. Each activity should stress that shape. *Shape* is defined by what "goes around the outside," or the outline of the object, 22-8. To help the child grasp this concept of shape, have them trace around the outside of the shape.

Some teachers prefer to use **parquetry blocks** to teach shape concepts. These blocks are geometric pieces that vary in color and shape. When the children are familiar with the blocks, hold up a block and ask the children to find a block with a similar shape. Next, build a simple design with three or four blocks. Ask the children to copy it.

Other activities to encourage the identification of shape include the following:

- Cut geometric shapes out of one color of tagboard. Ask the children to name and sort the shapes.
- Place a circle on a flannel board. Ask the children to name an object in the classroom of that shape. Repeat this activity using squares, rectangles, and triangles.

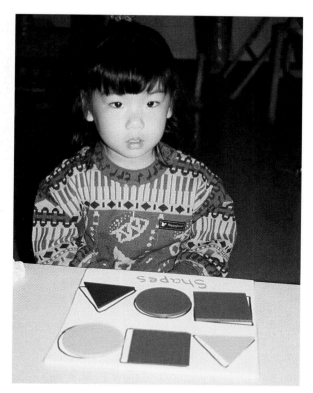

22-8 Children need to focus on the outlines of these shapes before they can identify them.

- Use jump ropes, masking tape, or chalk to make shapes on the floor. Ask children to name the shapes as they walk, march, or walk backwards on the figure.
- Give each child a shape cut out of tagboard. Then have the children move around the classroom to find another child with the identical shape. This activity is most useful with four- and five-year-old children.
- Introduce a game called "It's in the bag." The objective of this game is to help children name shapes by touch. Begin by placing a variety of tagboard shapes or blocks in a paper bag. Hold up one shape and ask a child to find its match by feeling in the bag.
- Plan a treasure hunt. Instruct children to find shapes around the room. For example, a round clock can be pointed out as a circle.

Do not attempt to teach shape and color concepts at the same time. Wait until color concepts are well understood. Otherwise, some children may confuse color names with shape names.

Shape concepts are harder to teach than color concepts. Since color descriptions are used more often in everyday conversation, they may be easier for children to understand. For example, children often hear phrases such as a black puppy, yellow socks, red shirt, and green room.

Classification

Classification is one of the first skills displayed by young children. **Classification** is the process of mentally grouping objects or ideas into categories or classes based on one attribute. Examples include size, color, shape, pattern or function. If the object belongs to a class, it has one or more features in common with another object. Classification allows people to cope with large numbers of objects.

Matching is a form of classification. It involves putting like objects together, 22-9. **Sorting** also involves classification. It is the process of physically separating objects based on unique features.

Children begin to learn classification skills in their first few weeks of life. By two months, children begin to classify experiences as pleasant or unpleasant. Eating applesauce may be pleasant. Sitting in an infant seat may be unpleasant.

22-9 The simplest matching activities involve putting two objects that are exactly alike together.

Infants gather information to make classifications by using their senses through repeated experiences. This gives them the ability to relate past and present experiences. This process is known as **recognizing**. Recognizing is a simple form of classification.

First classroom experiences with classification should involve only one feature. Often this feature is color, size, or shape, 22-10. Provide items with obvious differences. For young children, this might include size, length, height, shape, color, or thickness.

Some useful classification tasks for young children include the following:

- Provide children with a set of black and red buttons. Have them sort the buttons into piles by color.
- Give children toys with and without wheels. Have them sort the toys into two piles based on whether or not they have wheels.
- Give children pictures of known and unknown objects cut from old magazines. Ask them to sort the pictures into "I don't know the name of" and "I know the name of" piles.
- Provide children with a bucket of household items. Fill the water table. Have them put the items in the water, then sort them into "float" and "sink" piles.
- Give children kitchen and bathroom items. Have them sort the items based on use.

As children build classification skills, increase the number of common features in the activities, 22-11. This can be done in two ways. Either increase the number of items to be classified, or increase the number of groups into which items can be sorted.

Advanced activities include classifying classroom items according to function. For example, some items are used for listening, some for talking, and some for writing. As another activity, give children a set of fabric squares. Ask the children to sort the materials into piles of striped, plaid, polka-dotted, and solid fabrics.

22-10 These blocks are designed to be classified by shape or color.

22-11 This sorting game involves the use of a spinner and familiar classroom objects.

Notice that after children learn classification skills, they begin to watch and describe features of objects. First a child may say an apple is round and red. Later the child may classify it as good food. Finally the child may say the apple belongs to a group of foods known as "fruit."

Sets

Before children learn to add and subtract in elementary school, they need to understand sets. A **set** is a group of objects that are alike in some way and, therefore, belong together. Common features of a set may be color, shape, size, material, pattern, texture, name, and use.

A key objective of early math activities is to have children learn to organize objects. Objects belonging to a set are its members. A set can have a few or many members. A set of glasses is often a certain number, such as four or twelve. A set with no members is called an **empty set**.

In order to understand the concept of a set, children first need to learn about sets that have like members. This is best taught in small groups. Items needed are sets of objects having like members, such as puzzle pieces, blocks, crayons, and squares of colored paper. See 22-12. Introduce one set of objects at a time. Say "What are these? These are all blocks. We call them a set of blocks." Then introduce the remaining sets.

22-12 Many common items can be used to teach the concept of set.

Repeat the process. Stress the concept of set. To conclude the activity, ask "What are some other sets in the room?"

The concept of set can be strengthened by asking a small group of children to divide themselves into a set. First divide the children into sets of light- and dark-haired children. Encourage them to regroup themselves into different sets. They might divide by sex, age, color of eyes, or color of clothing.

Teach the concept of an empty set during snack time. Provide each child with a plate holding a banana sliced into five pieces. Tell the children to eat one piece of banana. Explain that they now have a set of four banana pieces. Tell the children to eat another piece. Ask the children how many pieces remain. Tell them that is the number of members still in the set. Keep going until all the pieces are eaten. Then explain that a set without any members is called an empty set. To strengthen this lesson, ask the children to name other empty sets in the room. For example, the set of tables without legs or the set of children with beards are empty sets.

Another way to explain the empty set is through experience. To do this, use five empty jars. Leave the first jar empty. Place a penny in the second jar. Place two pennies in the third jar, three pennies in the fourth jar, and four pennies in the fifth jar. Then ask the children to observe and compare the number of objects in each jar.

Counting

Counting is a basic math skill. It needs to be included in the curriculum because it is a key problem-solving tool. The foundation for understanding counting is called one-to-one correspondence. **One-to-one correspondence** is the understanding that one group has the same number as another. It is the most basic part of the concept of numbers.

Since counting is not always taught at home, it needs to be taught at school. Most children can count up to their age. For example, three-year-olds usually can count to three. Some children can count higher. Many four- and five-year-old children can count beyond their age.

Children are often first exposed to counting by an adult who counts the children's toes or fingers. After they hear this routine enough times, children will begin to count along. This same technique is used to count other objects, such as beads, puzzle pieces, and blocks. Only after children learn the spoken number do they learn the written numbers (two) and the numerals (2).

The ability to count occurs in two stages: rote and rational counting. Rote counting is learned before rational. Rote counting is recitation of numbers in order. This skill involves memory, not understanding. **Rational counting** involves attaching a number to a series of grouped objects, 22-13. For example, a child has a box of crayons sitting on the table. If you ask the child for some crayons, he or she may place them on the table one at a time. As the child places each crayon, he or she assigns it a number in sequence.

Many children you teach will be able to recite numbers in their correct order. However, they will often not understand the meaning the numbers represent.

Three-year-old Tammy has typical number skills. The following activities illustrate her understanding:

■ The teacher places seven pennies on the floor and asks Tammy to count them. She counts from one to nine before she fingers the last penny.

■ The teacher then arranges the pennies in a circle. Again she asks Tammy to count them. She becomes confused several times and has to begin again.

22-13 Rational counting involves attaching a number to a series of objects.

■ Next, the teacher places seven pennies in a pile and spreads out seven pennies more. When asked which pile has more pennies, Tammy points to the pennies that are spread out.

Children should always be exposed to rational counting using concrete objects. The simplest way to do this is through physical guidance. Use buttons, books, disks, table blocks, and crayons. Lay the objects in a straight line. Then take the child's hand as he or she counts, touching each object as it is counted. At first, you may have to help the child count aloud.

After children have had many counting experiences, test their understanding. Send a child to get four crayons, two pieces of paper, or three blocks.

Identifying Numerals

Number symbols are called **numerals**. Each numeral must represent a quantity. Numerals are shorthand for saying how many. In order to read and write, children must first recognize written numbers and their symbols. This skill develops as children are exposed to written numerals. Take advantage of opportunities for math experiences. Group time is a good time to emphasize numbers. Have children help you keep a record of daily attendance and daily temperature. Discuss the calendar.

A good activity for teaching number symbols is to have the children take part in a number walk. To do this, collect ten sheets of 9-by-12-inch paper. Number the sheets from 1 to 10. (To increase the durability of these sheets, cover them with clear adhesive sheets.) Then place the papers in a circle on the floor at random. Play some familiar music and ask the children to walk through the path of numbered pieces. When you stop the music, ask they children to tell the name of the number on which they are standing.

Another way to teach symbols is to set up a grocery store in a dramatic play area. Collect empty food containers and attach stickers with price tags from one to five cents. This activity can also include a toy store or drugstore. Look for numbers on measuring tools, calendars, books and puzzles.

A number line is yet another way to teach numbers. This teaching aid is based on units of length instead of objects. Make a calendar using a number line and refer to it daily during group time.

Children should have the opportunity to write numerals in their symbol form. Since children often find numerals hard to form, you may see many reversals. These problems are common and usually are self-correcting in time. You may be surprised to learn that children often prefer to write numbers over alphabet letters. Have children practice by writing in numerals on calendars or charts.

Space Concepts

Describing the positions of objects in space is an important part of early math experiences. Space concepts that should be introduced are listed in 22-14. You should be aware that prepositions are abstract—they represent a location in space. To best learn the meanings of prepositions, children should be shown concrete examples. Since children's awareness of location and space grows out of their own bodies, have them move physically.

Space concepts can be taught during cleanup time, art time, blockbuilding, and other activities. Some experiences for teaching space concepts include the following:

- Play the game "Simon Says" using the words listed in 22-14. Give directions to the children, such as "Place your finger on top of your head" and "Raise your right hand." Using simple concepts often works well, even with two-and-a-half and three-year-old children.

Space Concepts
before, after
high, low
up, down
here, there
far, near
above, below
in front of, in back of, between
inside, outside
top, center, bottom

22-14 These word groups stress space concepts.

When using a new concept, you may have to model it for the children. You can also use an animal puppet, stuffed toy, or doll to lead the game. To get the children more involved, allow them to take turns using the puppet and giving directions.

- Place several pictures of fruit on a flannel board. Then ask, "Which piece of fruit is below the orange?" "Which piece of fruit is above the apple?" "Which piece of fruit is below the grapes?"
- Give each child three different items, such as a block, a penny, and a button. Then give the children verbal directions using space words: "Place the penny on top of the block." "Place the button under the block." "Pick up the block with your right hand."
- Use familiar circle games such as "Hokey Pokey" to teach space concepts.
- Stack five familiar items, such as a penny, stick, rock, clothespin, and puzzle piece, on a table. Then ask the children questions about the items: "What item is at the top?" "What item is at the bottom?" "What item is in the middle?" A stack of colored blocks or puzzle pieces can also be used to teach the concepts of top, bottom, and middle.

Remember that children need frequent review to maintain any skill. Unlike adults, children do not tire easily from repetitive experiences. Your enthusiasm and support is important.

Size Concepts

Children develop size concepts only through experience. Introduce and stress the words listed in 22-15 to teach children about size. These words can be used throughout the day.

Volume Concepts

An early childhood program should offer many opportunities to explore volume. Sand tables and water tables are useful for this task. Provide many containers of varying volumes and shapes for measuring. During the children's play with these materials, introduce volume concepts

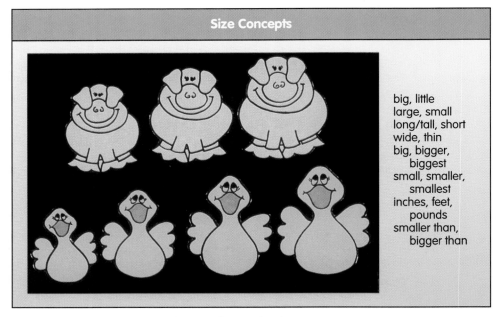

Size Concepts

big, little
large, small
long/tall, short
wide, thin
big, bigger,
    biggest
small, smaller,
    smallest
inches, feet,
    pounds
smaller than,
    bigger than

22-15 Use of proper terms, along with visual aids, will help children grasp the size concepts.

such as empty, full, little, much, a lot, and some. When children use these concepts, they think about their world in terms of quantity.

Time Concepts

"Is yesterday Christmas?" Molly, a four-year-old, asked one of the other children. Molly's question is common of a young child. Time is a difficult concept for children to understand, partly because "time" can stand for so many situations. Past, present, future, tomorrow, and soon are all examples of time concepts.

Studies suggest that young children have only a vague concept of time. In fact, the average five-year-old child knows only the difference between afternoon and morning, and night and day. Children usually cannot read the time on a watch or clock until about age seven.

You can use routines to teach time concepts to young children. For example, you might say the following: "After lunch, we take naps." "Your mother will come to pick you up after outdoor playtime." "Before large group time, we need to put our toys away." You can offer time experiences to children by using the correct time words. Include the words such as those listed in 22-16.

Children should also learn about the passing of time. For example, you may ask "Do you remember the clown that came to school?" or "How did we make the play dough last time?"

There are many activities for teaching children time concepts. Included are the following:

■   Provide children with a large, month-long calendar. Use the calendar each day during a large group activity.

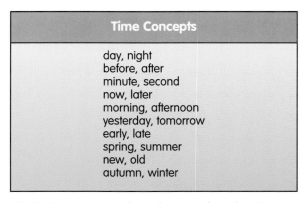

Time Concepts

day, night
before, after
minute, second
now, later
morning, afternoon
yesterday, tomorrow
early, late
spring, summer
new, old
autumn, winter

22-16 Use terms such as these to describe time. This reinforcement will help children understand time concepts.

Review the days of the week and use such words as yesterday, tomorrow, last week, and next week.

- Encourage children to play with a toy alarm clock.
- Hang a large classroom clock at the children's eye level.
- Use a cooking timer during cooking experiences. Some teachers also use a cooking timer to give children a warning before they change activities. For example, the teacher may set the timer and say "In five minutes, it will be time to clean up."
- Provide time recording equipment, such as a stopwatch, alarm clock, wristwatch, hourglass, etc. Place these items on a table where children will feel free to explore them.

Temperature Concepts

Cooking and outdoor activities help introduce temperature concepts. (Many ideas for cooking activities are given in Chapter 25.) To teach these concepts, include such words as thermometer, hot, cold, warm, and cool.

Integrating Computers in Child Care Centers

Computer technology is a part of our daily life. Computers are used at home, work, and school. As the result of technological advances, the role of computers in education has grown. Computers will increasingly be used for instructional purposes, starting with child care centers. To be computer literate, children need to learn the basic parts of a computer and gain experience using computer programs.

A classroom computer should be a tool that fosters the children's opportunity for discovery learning, imagination, and creativity. A computer cannot replace the value of playing with puzzles, blocks, and other manipulative materials. When used, a computer should complement these activities and provide opportunities for social interactions.

Selecting Computer Software Programs

Advances in computer technology have improved the quality of software programs used for instructional purposes. (A *software program* tells the computer what to do.) Knowledge of the keyboard is no longer necessary for young children to operate a computer. Directions have been simplified. To use the programs, children need only touch one or two keys, a touch pad, or a box on the screen.

Select developmentally appropriate software programs carefully. A variety of programs that focus on numerals, colors, sounds, and shapes are available for preschool children. Two characteristics are vital in making your selection. The program must be age appropriate, and it must be easy to operate. In addition, software programs should provide the following features:

- clear, user-friendly directions children can follow without adult help
- colorful, animated, realistic graphics that hold children's attention
- logical sequences
- interactions with the child
- promotion of problem solving by making choices
- exploration of alternatives
- feedback.

You will need to be selective in introducing the computer. The first interaction should be relatively simple. For two- and three-year-olds, choose simple "cause and effect" software programs. To make programs easier, provide touch screens. Otherwise, choose programs requiring only one or two character key presses.

Four- and five-year-olds enjoy using the computer alone and with their peers. They enjoy operating the machine, selecting software programs, and replacing disks by themselves. However, computers also stimulate verbal interaction. Studies show that children speak twice as many words per minute while using computers as they do when engaged in other activities.

By six years of age, most children are comfortable operating simple programs and following instructions from a picture menu. They enjoy showing others how to use the computer. They frequently have a favorite program they enjoy teaching or playing with others.

Summary

Math experiences in the early childhood setting should stress exploration, discovery, and understanding. Children of this age require these broad, basic experiences. With such a foundation, they can build more advanced math skills as they get older.

For younger children, math experiences can be informal in nature. Many daily events and routines lend themselves to informal math experiences. Play experiences can also be a setting for math experiences.

Review and Reflect

1. List four objectives of early math experiences.

2. Name and describe the two common forms of assessment used to determine math abilities.

3. True or false. Math materials and equipment should consist of only traditional items such as an abacus and flash cards.

4. Why is color considered a math concept?

5. _____ defines "what goes around the outside."

6. Is it a good idea to teach shape and color concepts at the same time? Why or why not?

7. _____ is the process of mentally grouping objects based on some unique feature.

8. What is the difference between sorting and matching?

9. A _____ is a group of objects that are alike in some way, and, therefore, belong together.

10. _____ is a difficult concept for children to develop because the word represents the past, present, and future.

11. List three vocabulary words that can be used to teach temperature concepts.

12. List two characteristics that are vital in selecting developmentally appropriate software programs.

13. The age at which most children can comfortably operate simple computer programs is _____.
   A. three
   B. four
   C. five
   D. six

Apply and Explore

1. Review a school equipment catalog and make a list of any equipment that can be used to teach space concepts.

2. Discuss methods to use to help young children understand size concepts.

3. Make a list of activities parents or guardians can use to teach counting.

4. Find a recipe that could be used for a cooking activity to teach temperature concepts.

5. Discuss activities that could be used to teach children the concept of set.

6. Invite an early childhood teacher to visit your class to share math experiences.

7. Research and compile a bibliography of children's storybooks that include mathematics.

Chapter 23

Guiding Science Experiences

After studying this chapter, you will be able to

- explain what is meant by the term science.
- discuss reasons for studying science.
- outline the procedure for planning science activities.
- list a variety of science activities and sources for supplies.
- explain the role of the teacher in guiding science experiences.
- identify methods for developing children's understanding of their senses.
- name and explain various ways to teach science concepts.

Terms to Know

science
science table
open-ended questions
close-ended questions
feely box

Two-year-old Ricardo's first contact with a butterfly was accidental. His study of the bug was brief but intense. It involved mainly his senses of sight and touch. Quickly he picked the butterfly up and said, "What's dat?" His mother replied, "It's a butterfly." This experience opened the world of natural science to Ricardo. Later, whenever he saw a butterfly or a moth, he repeated his new word, "butterfly."

Science is everywhere. Much of what children learn relates to science concepts. Their first learnings are often simple but meaningful. You can help form children's science concepts through science experiences. Teaching children science concepts will help them develop respect for their environment, too.

What Is Science?

Science is the study of natural processes and their products. It is a way of viewing the universe. In order for children to understand their world, they must explore and question. As children explore, they actively construct their own knowledge. For this reason, early childhood experiences should use the hands-on approach for both process and products. The hands-on approach allows children to be involved in and think about the sights, sounds, and smells of their environment. Your role as a teacher is to provide a rich and inviting environment filled with hands-on activities.

Science is a creative field of study. It requires the development of curiosity and imagination. As children watch, study, wonder, or question, they learn about science. Therefore, science activities should relate to the children's daily experiences.

Science is a way to gain understanding of why events happen the way they do. Studying science inspires children to be aware of, and involved with, their surroundings. The answers to such questions as How will it change? and What will happen if...? can be found.

Science involves observing, exploring, measuring, comparing, classifying, predicting, and discovering. The focus for young children should be on observing and exploring, 23-1. Young children are good observers and explorers because they see the world from a fresh point of view. They have no preset ideas of how the world and nature work.

All attempts to gain information about our surroundings begin with observation. Using the senses to observe is the start of discovery. By using their senses, children begin to see relationships between different events. They start to group their information and make generalizations.

Why Study Science?

Studies show science activities enhance the curiosity of children, 23-2. Children also build skill in picking out similarities and differences. Vocabulary improves. Children improve their language skills and general knowledge as concepts such as *round*, *triangular*, *big*, and *small* are discussed. This promotes reading readiness skills.

Small muscle development and hand-eye coordination improve as children measure items, collect samples, and handle objects. By weighing and counting items, math skills are also enhanced.

Planning Science Activities

Some of the most successful science experiences will be unplanned. For instance, you might bring in a small snake you found on the way to the center. This can be the starting point to a discussion of snakes. As a spider moves across the

23-1 This child is learning to observe and explore as he views the nature collection through the magnifying glass.

23-2 Developing a marble bulletin board that illustrates the concept of gravity enhances the curiosity of young children.

floor, you can watch, study, and discuss it. If the wind rises suddenly, blowing debris around the play yard, you can discuss the wind.

However, most science experiences need to be planned. Focusing on a theme helps children learn about their world by structuring and organizing information. You will need to schedule events, prepare materials, and arrange the science area. You will find that science activities mesh well with other daily activities. You may plan a water, food, or sensory activity that teaches a science concept. Fingerplays, stories, field trips, math activities, physical activity, and art projects can all be the basis of science concepts.

Give children time to play with, examine, and try the science materials and equipment, 23-3. Science activities should offer children the chance to

- observe
- note differences and likenesses

23-3 Having the chance to play with, examine, and use science equipment will promote children's growth in science knowledge.

- solve problems
- collect samples
- develop new interests and skills
- listen to sounds and tapes
- view filmstrips and videos
- look at books
- collect pictures

Science Area

The science area is often set apart from other classroom areas. Tables, shelves, and/or storage cabinets can be used. The science area is best located near a kitchen. This allows access to both heat and water sources, which are quite important for many science projects.

An outdoor science area may also be used. This area may contain a garden space and an area for conducting weather tests. Small animals, such as rabbits and birds, may be raised. Store garden tools, insect nets, and water tubes in an outdoor shed to encourage children to use the outdoor area.

Equipment and Materials

Equipment and materials for a science area need not be costly. Most items can be obtained for free or at little cost. Two factors must be given some thought during the selection process. First consider whether the item you are thinking about buying is safe. Then decide whether the children have the skills needed to use the item. See Chart 23-4.

Many child care centers have a **science table,** 23-5. This table is used to display science-related items. The teacher often obtains the items to be placed on the table. Whenever possible, the science table should have a focus. The collection of items should provide direction for advancing the children's learning. A group of plastic reptiles may be placed on the science table. Resource books showing pictures of the reptiles should also be placed on the table next to the reptile. This will allow the children to compare the model reptiles with those in the reference book. Finally, concept-related literature books should be included on the table. Children can also be encouraged to bring their own items for the table. Collections children often enjoy adding include leaves, nuts, rocks, insects, nests, cocoons, and seeds.

Science Supplies

School supplies

globes	chart paper
paints	scissors
clay	paste or glue
chalk	string
felt-tip markers	blocks
straws	measuring instruments
colored paper	magnifying glass
construction paper	

Scrap items

pocket mirrors	flashlights
large spoons	watering cans
discarded clocks	airplane and automobile
sawdust	parts
locks and keys	funnels

Classroom pets

hamsters	gerbils
snakes	spiders
frogs	fish
birds	mice
rabbits	guinea pigs

Nature items

stones	logs
snails	pinecones
rocks	leaves
shells	plant bulbs
soil	seeds
sand	birdfeeders

Construction tools

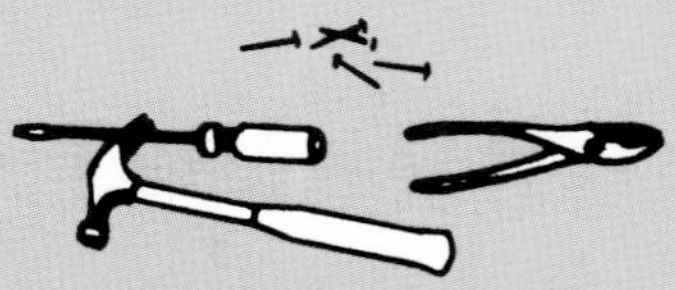

hammers	vice
nails	pliers
rulers	levers
saws	ramps
screwdriver	pulleys
screws	wheels
bolts	magnets

Household items

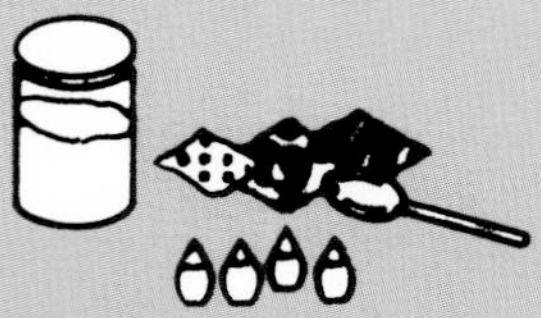

jars	empty containers
strainers	cloth pieces
food coloring	wood scraps
salt	plastic meat trays
sugar	cardboard tubes
metal scraps	flashlights
spoons	

23-4 Materials and equipment that can be used in science experiences are nearly endless.

23-5 This science table has many interesting items for children to explore.

Children should feel motivated to explore the science table on their own. Therefore, the material on the science table should be changed often. If collections remain on the table too long, children become bored and lose interest. It also helps to house collections in an appealing way. You might display items in a tent, store setting, cave setting, booth, trailer, push cart, or wagon.

The science table should sit away from walls. This allows children to move about the table freely. They will feel comfortable touching, smelling, hearing, and observing as they explore.

Centerpieces at the snack or lunch table also promote children's interest in nature. A bowl of pinecones or gourds or a bouquet of flowers brings the world of science indoors. They also promote discussion during mealtime.

Playground equipment can be used to teach science concepts. For example, pedaling a bike makes the energy needed to move a bike. Using a teeter-totter demonstrates the laws of balance.

Role of the Teacher

As the teacher, your role is to plan a wide variety of science activities and projects, 23-6. You must know when to let children work alone and when to step in. At times, a simple suggestion can help a child who is frustrated. On the other hand, unneeded input can sometimes stifle curiosity. This can destroy the desire to keep experimenting.

23-6 Teachers direct science experiences, but they must also know when to step back and let children do for themselves.

The activities you plan should include materials for all children. Children should have ample hands-on activities in which they work with materials. This process allows children to discuss relationships and concepts among themselves.

Activities should promote development of the following five basic process skills:

- observing objects using the five senses: seeing, feeling, tasting, smelling, and hearing
- drawing conclusions from observations based on knowledge gained in past experience
- classifying objects into sets based on one or more observable properties
- comparing sets of objects by measuring and counting
- communicating by describing objects, relationships, and occurrences

Provide many chances for children to practice being careful observers. Children enjoy watching and wondering. Going on field trips, viewing filmstrips, looking at pictures, and viewing objects on the science table are all good ways to help children build on powers of observation.

To encourage children to explore, use effective questioning techniques. Asking numerous questions is not always a useful technique. Instead, ask fewer questions that require more thought. **Open-ended questions** promote discussion and require decision-making skills. **Close-ended questions** (sometimes called single-answer questions) demand few decision-making skills and are most often answered with yes or no. See 23-7. Poor questioning techniques encourage children to guess.

Children need time to respond to open-ended questions. Positive response should be given to all answers. When a better answer is offered, the teacher can explain how it adds to other answers. Children also need to be heard. Listening on the teacher's part strengthens a child's wish to participate.

The caregiver or teacher generally sets the tone for learning science in the classroom. A simple rule is to base activities on children's questioning. Do not give answers to questions children have not asked. Let the children use process skills as well as listen, watch, or read about science. Teachers who control the learning activity do little to promote questions. To create the right climate, provide material for all children, study their interaction with the materials, and listen to them talk to each other. Finally, ask only those questions that add to the child's knowledge.

Developing the Child's Understanding of Senses

As children learn more about their senses, they become aware of how to explain their surroundings. Help children learn to focus on how they use their senses by peeling an orange. During the experience, children can see and smell the orange. After it is peeled, they can feel it and taste it. By peeling an orange, children can learn the following concepts: we see with our eyes; we smell with our noses; we feel with our skin; we taste with our tongues.

Feeling

Feeling is a fun and important sense to explore through science activities. Whenever time permits, provide opportunities to feel a number of objects in the classroom. A **feely box** can be made by cutting a circle in a box large enough for the children to put their hands in. (A *feely bag* can also be used. It should be opaque and easy to reach into without exposing the contents.) Put different objects and materials inside the box. Let each child reach in the box and try to identify an object. If they are unable to respond, provide clues. For example, if the item is a spoon, you may say "It is something we use to eat cereal with in the morning."

Open-Ended and Close-Ended Questions	
Open-Ended	**Closed-Ended**
What are you observing?	What color is it?
How could you classify these?	Can you classify these by shape?
What happens to hamburger when it is fried?	Has the hamburger changed color?

23-7 Can you think of other pairs of open-ended and close-ended questions?

Children can also build the sense of touch using fabric samples of varying textures. These may include velvet, leather, flannel, knit, burlap, felt, and cotton. Encourage the children to explain what each piece feels like. You might add other materials such as pinecones, leaves, fur, sandpaper, glazed paper, sponge, pebbles, and cork. To add variety, place the materials on the science table where the children can sort them based on like textures.

Smelling

Preschool children need to learn that objects can be named by their smells. One method for teaching this is to collect items in the classroom that have distinct odors, such as tempera paint, markers, crayons, play dough, bar soap, sawdust, and gerbil food. Place a small amount of each item in a container such as a small paper cup. Explain to the children that the game you will be playing involves naming items by smell.

Food can also be used in the smelling activity. For example, place ketchup, mustard, applesauce, chocolate syrup, orange juice, and other common foods in containers and repeat the same steps.

Seeing

Experience using sight is just as important as smelling. One game that has been used in early childhood centers is "I See Something." For example, you may say "I see something green. It is small and round. It is in the art area." After you speak, pause to allow the children to guess. If the children are not able to guess, provide more clues.

An activity that helps children build visual memory skills is naming what is missing from a group. Use this activity for one child or small groups of children. Collect common classroom objects such as crayons, blocks, puzzle pieces, paintbrushes, and toy cans. Gather the children, show them the objects, and explain that you will remove one object. Instruct the children to close or cover their eyes. Remove one object, then have them open their eyes and tell you what object is missing.

There are many variations to this game. You may increase the number of objects. You might place three or four objects in a sequence and ask which objects are out of sequence. You may remove two or three objects from the group and have the children name what is missing.

Hearing

Hearing is another sense that helps children understand and explain their environment. To help children become more aware of this sense, use a tape recorder.

Teach the concept that each person's voice sounds different from any other. Record the voice of each child. To encourage the children to talk, ask each child to tell you about a family member, a favorite person, or a story. After you have taped all the children in the classroom, play the tape to the group. Ask the children to identify each child's voice by name.

Tasting

Tasting skills can be built through the use of food. Plan a tasting party using a number of common foods. Blindfold a child and give him or her a small sample of some food. Ask the child to name the food. Repeat the activity with all the children in the group. Some teachers prefer to do this as a group activity, providing a sample of each food for all the children at the same time.

Using Color to Teach Science Concepts

Color is a part of science that children observe daily. Naming colors is one way children describe their world. Color also serves as a basis for grouping. The primary colors, red, blue, and yellow, can be introduced to the children in the science area. Encourage the children to match red, blue, and yellow toys, such as beads or blocks, with similarly colored boxes. The secondary colors, purple, green, and orange, can be introduced next. Again, using toys, have the children match the color of the toy to the container.

Some teachers have special color days. For example, Monday may be orange day. To prepare for this day, send a note or letter to parents or guardians. Ask that children wear the color of the day. This may be in the form of a hair ribbon, pin, barrette, or any article of clothing. You may also use a nature walk to observe colors. Snacks may be coordinated with the color of the day. For example, orange slices, carrots, or cantaloupe may be served on an orange day.

Mixing colors is another way to teach color concepts. By mixing primary colors to make secondary colors, the children learn how colors are made. Thus, as children learn color concepts, they become aware of their surroundings. One way to show mixing of colors is to overlap colored cellophane. Another way is to set up jars or clear plastic glasses in the science area. Have the children fill the jars with water. Using food coloring, have the children place drops in each container, 23-8. Stress color comparisons by using terms such as *lighter than*, *darker than*, or *same color as*.

Using Water to Teach Science Concepts

Water delights almost all children. As young children play with water and accessories, they learn about science concepts. Some concepts taught with water include the following:

- Water flows when poured.
- Water dissolves some foods.
- Water takes many forms.
- Water makes objects wet.
- Water can be held in a container.
- Some items float on water.
- Some materials absorb water.

Equipment and Accessories

In programs without water tables, large washtubs, sinks, photographic developing trays, or plastic swimming pools can be used. A table can also be made, 23-9. Supply water table accessories. Include funnels, spoons, sprinkling cans, nesting cups, plastic containers, egg beaters, measuring cups, strainers, corks, sponges, plastic tubing, soap, and food coloring.

23-8 Food coloring can be used to teach children the concept of color mixing.

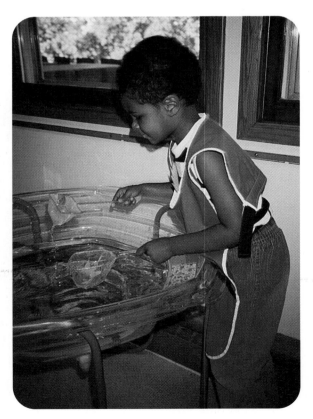

23-9 This water table is transparent allowing children to observe the contents.

To avoid excessive cleanup, put down a shower curtain or plastic tablecloth to protect the floor. Plastic aprons may be used to protect the children's clothes.

Fill the container with water based on the children's experience and age. (Younger children only need two or three inches.) Provide the children with accessories and allow them to experiment freely.

Activities

Freeze water for the children. From this, the children will learn that

- ice is frozen water
- ice can melt
- melted ice is water
- ice can be picked up
- ice melts in warm places

Teach the children that some materials absorb water. Use sponges, terry cloth, tissues, paper towels, cardboard, plastic wrap, waxed paper, newsprint, finger paint, and plastic. You may wish to make a chart listing the materials and noting whether they absorb water. From using these materials, children should learn that some materials soak up water.

Water can teach children about floating. Fill the water table half full of water. Provide items such as wooden blocks, pencils, paper, plastic alphabet letters, metal spoons, large nails, and aluminum foil. Record each item that floats on a chart. Children will learn that some items float on water.

Through observation and participation, children can also learn what materials dissolve in water. Fill several small pitchers with water. Then have each child fill several small baby food jars or plastic glasses. Provide each child with a material that dissolves in water, such as salt, sugar cubes, or baking soda. Also supply items that will not dissolve, such as cooking oil, rice, or margarine. Then let each child stir the mixture. Ask the children "What happens when you add (salt, rice, etc.) to water?" Encourage the children to discuss the results as each item is added to the water.

Painting with water is an activity best suited to the outdoors. Provide the children with cans of water and wide paint brushes. Have them paint surfaces such as a cement sidewalk. Then ask them what happens to the water. Try this in different types of weather. Children will see that on hot days the water evaporates and on cold days it freezes. Select a cement area that will not be used for walking to avoid accidents.

Using Foods to Teach Science Concepts

Science experiments that can be eaten are both fun and educational. By watching foods as they cook, children learn how solid materials can change. Some foods become softer and some firmer as they are heated. Heat may also change the color and blend the flavors of foods. Many guidelines for using foods in classroom experiences are given in Chapter 25.

Baking bread is a science project that involves both a process and a product. In order to have baked bread, a process must be followed. This process involves

- reading the recipe
- collecting all the ingredients, pans, and utensils
- mixing the correct amounts of ingredients
- setting the correct oven temperature
- checking when the bread should be removed

A number of other cooking projects can be used. Some teachers prefer to tie these experiences to weekly themes or units. For example, they may have a unit on fall, Halloween, and/or Thanksgiving. Cooking experiences can focus on pumpkins, squash, apples, or cranberries. Activities should include

- preparing food in different ways (boiling, baking, broiling)
- using many kitchen tools (mixers, food processors, blenders)
- examining the insides of foods (peeling a potato, slicing an apple)
- observing the way products change during preparation

Foods that can be prepared easily in the center are listed in 23-10.

Foods Children Can Prepare	
ice cream	scrambled eggs
cookies	cocoa
pumpkin bread	butter
applesauce	ice pops
bread	pudding

23-10 Making food items such as these will give children the chance to both proceed through a recipe and see the finished product.

Children can learn that food varies in size, shape, and color. Some foods are heavier than others. One way to teach these concepts is to supply children with carrots, celery, apples, bananas, oranges, and grapes for snacks. Have them discuss the differences among these foods.

Using the Child's Own Body to Teach Science Concepts

Children go through rapid physical changes during the preschool years. These growth changes are often more obvious to parents and teachers than to the children themselves. One way to help children understand their own bodies is through science experiences. Using photographs and drawings of the children is quite effective.

One science concept to introduce is that people can be recognized by the way they look. To teach this, take pictures of each child using an instant camera. After the picture is developed, show it to the child. Encourage the child to tell you about the picture. If he or she does not respond, ask specific questions about the photo, such as "What are you wearing in the picture? What color eyes do you have? What color hair do you have?"

Some children may find it hard to link a photo with themselves. For instance, one teacher had a very difficult time teaching this concept to twins. Each time the twins saw themselves in a mirror or a picture, they identified their sibling. Experiences like these are helpful for showing children they have special physical traits.

A growth chart can be used to teach the concept of measurement, 23-11. A chart can be made by outlining and cutting a shape such as a carrot from a piece of tagboard. Use orange for the carrot and green for the stem. Glue a tape measure vertically down the center of the carrot. Hang the carrot to a door, wall, or bulletin board. Have each child stand next to the tape. Record the children's heights on the tagboard.

The concept of weight can be taught in the same way. Create a chart to record each child's weight. You may want to record weight at the start of the year and again at midyear to show this concept to the children.

Measurements and the concept of growth can also be taught using body shapes. Have each child lie down on two large pieces of paper. Trace around the child's body and cut the shape from each piece of paper. Choose one piece for the front and one for the back. On the front piece,

23-11 Colorful growth charts are a fun way to teach children about measurement.

have the child draw his or her facial features, hair, and clothing. Color clothing and hair on the back piece. Place the two shapes back to back and staple together on one side. Stuff the figure with newspaper and staple the entire figure closed. Hang each child's figure in the room and use it as a frame of reference for the child's growth.

Using Gardening to Teach Science Concepts

The study of gardening and seeds helps children build an interest in growing things. By five or six years of age, most children can identify common seeds such as watermelon, apple, and peach seeds. However, not many children know they are eating seeds when they eat bananas. Not many children know walnuts, pecans, rice, and peas are also seeds.

Seeds and Food

Science experiments using seeds can be introduced during snack or lunchtime. Talk about only one type of seed at a time. For example, ask the children "What color is the orange? What is inside the orange?" Then give each child an orange that you have begun to peel. Show them how to peel the rest of the fruit. Show them how to pull the orange apart. Encourage the children to look for seeds. Ask questions about the orange seeds, such as "How many seeds are there in your orange? Are the seeds the same size? How do the seeds look? How do the seeds feel?" When they are through, have them place their seeds on the science table.

Introduce new seeds at snack times or lunchtimes. Use the same steps. Compare the seeds from different fruits in terms of size, color, and texture. Again, collect the seeds. Place them on the science table. Collect seeds from a number of fruits to display on the science table.

Seed Party

Have a seed party to teach children that some seeds must be shelled before they are eaten. Collect a number of nuts that can be eaten: peanuts, walnuts, pecans, and a coconut. Ask the children to help you crack the seeds and remove the meat. As they sample the meat from each seed, discuss the flavors and talk about which seeds are grown underground.

Pumpkin, sunflower, soybean seeds, and mixed nuts may also be used. You may want to roast and sauté some of the seeds. During the roasting period, ask questions such as "Which seeds are labeled nuts? How does cooking change the taste? How does cooking change the texture?"

Observing Seeds

A nature or seed walk is another way to teach children that seeds come from fruits of plants. Before leaving on the walk, give each child a paper bag with the child's name on it. You may prefer to wrap a piece of packing tape with the sticky side out on each child's wrist. The children can stick the seeds to the sticky tape as they are discovered. Walk to a park or other area where seeds are plentiful and encourage the children to collect seeds. When the group returns to the classroom, ask each child to choose three seeds to add to the science table. Save the rest of the seeds for an art display.

Place magnifying glasses on the science table next to the seeds, 23-12. Encourage the children to use the glasses to view the shapes,

23-12 This child is using a magnifying glass to study the shape, size, color, and texture of the seeds from a gourd.

sizes, colors, and textures of the seeds. This activity should help the children become aware of the seeds' differences and similarities.

Planting Seeds

Planting seeds is another way to teach children concepts about plants and their growth. Have children plant bean, corn, and radish seeds in individual containers. Use paper cups, tuna cans, milk cartons, or clay pots. If possible, use transparent recycled containers so the children can observe root growth below the surface. Write the children's names on the containers. Provide soil for the children to use for planting. The best mixture for growth is garden soil, or loam. It supplies nutrients for the plant and provides good moisture and drainage control. Have children fill the containers with soil. Then let the children choose seeds to plant. Show them how to use their fingers to make holes in the soil. Add the seeds and cover with soil. Label each container with the seed name. Then show the children how to lightly dampen the soil using a watering can.

Most seeds will grow when given proper moisture and temperature. When the seedlings emerge from the surface of the soil, place the containers where they will receive sunlight. Encourage the children to check the containers daily. Ask questions such as "What seeds sprouted first? Do all plants have similar leaves? How many leaves does each plant have?" From this experience the children should learn the following:

- Seeds planted in soil and given water, warmth, and sunshine grow.
- Some seeds germinate earlier than others.
- As plants grow, their size changes.

Dish Garden

Make a dish garden using pineapple, turnip, carrot, or beet tops. First, cut the tops off about one and one-quarter inch below the leaves. Then place the tops in clear, shallow dishes with water and sand. Put the dish on the science table where the children can observe the growth.

Vase Garden

Collect an onion, sweet potato, or avocado pit and a jar large enough to hold the vegetable. Suspend the vegetable on toothpicks, 23-13. You

23-13 Many vegetables grow with little care if suspended in this way.

may have to add small amounts of water from time to time. As the vegetable sprouts and evaporation takes place, the water level will decrease. Students can observe the roots and stems as they grow.

Using Air to Teach Science Concepts

Every day children have experiences with air. They watch airplanes and birds, fly kites, and blow up balloons. They feel the wind blow against their bodies and clothing.

Teaching About Air

To help children understand the concept that air takes up space, inflate some balloons. Do this activity in a group. Start by showing the children a deflated balloon. Then tell them to watch closely as you blow up the balloon. After the balloon is inflated, ask "What is inside the balloon?" Pass out balloons to all the children. Encourage them to fill the balloons with air. After the activity, collect the balloons.

Bubble solutions are another way to teach children that air takes up space. You can buy a prepared solution or use the recipe in 23-14. After you have mixed the solution, give each child a straw and a paper cup. Using a pencil

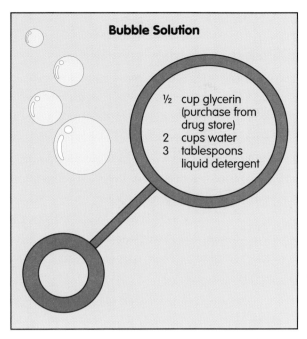

Bubble Solution

½ cup glycerin (purchase from drug store)
2 cups water
3 tablespoons liquid detergent

23-14 Bubble solutions are very easy to make.

23-15 As children blow bubbles they become aware that the bubbles, and therefore air, take up space.

point, make a hole about one inch from the bottom of the paper cup. Have the children place a straw in the hole. Then have them dip the open end of the cup in the bubble solution. Finally, ask them to remove the cup from the solution and, with the cup in an upside down position, blow into the straw.

Encourage the children to blow bubbles. Ask them "What is inside of the bubbles? How did you get air inside of the bubble? How can you make the bubble larger? How can you make the bubble smaller?"

Use a clear container, such as an aquarium or glass mixing bowl, to conduct another experiment. Fill the container with water and pass straws to each child. Tell the children to place their straws in the container and blow, 23-15. Ask "What happens when you blow air through the straw into the water?"

Teaching About Wind

To teach the concept that the wind makes things move, use thin strips of newsprint or crepe paper streamers. For this activity to work, you need to introduce it on a windy day. Take the children outside and hand out the streamers. Show them how to hold the streamers. Ask "What happens to the streamer when the wind blows? What direction is the wind moving in? What happens when you run fast?"

Using Weather

Develop environmental awareness by focusing on the weather—snow, wind, rain, thunderstorms, and rainbows all appeal to young children. Develop a weather felt board with accessories to use at group time. Include figures of children, clothing for all seasons, clouds, sun, snow, and raindrops. Each day a child can select the clothing and symbols to represent the weather.

Using Magnets to Teach Science Concepts

Children are intrigued by magnets. Concepts about magnets are best learned through a combination of teacher guidance and hands-on activities, 23-16. Therefore, teachers need to buy

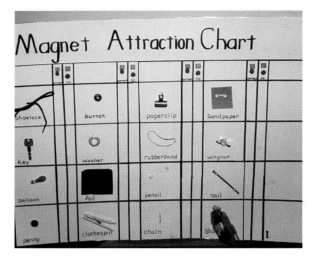

23-16 Charts are also useful for learning magnet concepts.

quality magnets. These can be bought through science equipment or school supply stores. Buy a variety of magnets, including horseshoe, ceramic, bar, disk, and rod-shaped magnets.

As children work and play with magnets they will observe the following:

- Magnets pull some things, but not others.
- Some magnets are big; others are small.
- Some magnets are stronger than others.
- Magnets pick up objects made of iron.

To aid in building these concepts, place several magnets on a table. Collect objects that magnets will pick up and others they will not. Types of objects magnets attract include metal screws, staples, nails, paper clips, and other small metal objects. A magnet will not pick up objects that do not have an iron content. Such objects include paper, cloth, wooden pencils, crayons, shoelaces, and aluminum dishes.

Place a variety of horseshoe and bar magnets in a small box. In a second box, place chalk, toothpicks, paper, nails, paper clips, plastic spoons, and other objects. Have the children name the objects and tell whether the magnets can lift each item.

Children also enjoy making magnet faces. To do this, draw a face on a piece of heavy tagboard. Place iron filings on the tagboard. Then cover it with a sheet of clear plastic and seal the tagboard and plastic with tape. Show the children how to move the magnet under the tagboard, making hair, eyebrows, and a mustache.

Using Wheels to Teach Science Concepts

Children see wheels every day. They may ride in a car or truck to their child care center or preschool. There they see wagons, tricycles, scooters, and other toys with wheels. At home they might see machines with wheels, such as vacuum cleaners and lawnmowers. Perhaps on a trip to the airport they have seen people pulling suitcases with wheels. All these experiences should help them learn about the uses of wheels.

Children can learn the following concepts about wheels:

- Wheels are round.
- Wheels roll.
- Wheels usually turn on an axis.
- Wheels make work easier for people.

To learn these concepts, children need to be exposed to many types of wheels. You might demonstrate these concepts using wagons and wheelbarrows.

To help children learn to identify a wheel, use a feely box or bag. Place cubes, balls, wooden blocks, and rubber wheels in the box. Ask one child at a time to feel in the box and find the wheel.

Another way to teach children about wheels is to cut out and hang pictures of wheels from magazines. Include fire engines, cars, trucks, tractors, wagons, airplanes, golf carts, scooters, and roller skates. Then cut out and hang pictures of other types of transportation. These might include motorboats, sailboats, skis, rafts, sleds, ice skates, donkeys, elephants, and horses. When you have finished, ask the children to point out the pictures with wheels.

Using Field Trips to Teach Science Concepts

Field trips promote curiosity, supply opportunities for discovery, and encourage interaction with the environment. During field trips, children can observe how machines make work more precise, easy, and orderly. For example, on a trip to the fire station point out the fire alarm system, ladder, ax, hose, and fire extinguisher. A "technology walk" is also a type of field trip. It can provide children with chances to see machinery, including computers and typewriters, being used. Chart 23-17 lists field trip locations and things to observe there.

Using Animals to Teach Science Concepts

Some animals can be used as classroom pets. Science concepts can be taught to young children using these pets. For example, children can learn how different animals look and feel, what they eat, how they should be handled, and how they respond to their environment. Pets can help teach respect for all kinds of life. After having the opportunity to observe and compare animals, children can draw conclusions from their experiences, 23-18.

23-18 Having classroom pets gives children a chance to observe, care for, and learn about pets as a part of their daily routine.

Science Field Trips	
Location	**Science Concepts Studied**
Lumber company	Nature of wood and sawdust
Automobile and bike shops	Workings of motors, gears, chains, wheels; use of tools
Grocery stores	Forms of foods
Vacant land	Insects, plant life, animal shelters
Print shop	Mechanics of the printing process
Commercial laundry	Effects of cleaners, heat, starch
Produce market	Nature of fresh fruits and vegetables
Interior decorating shop	Nature of fabrics, use of colors
Television and radio studios	Production and transmission of images and sounds
Fire department	Mechanics of trucks, engines, ladders
Animal hospital	Care of pets
Toy shop	Nature of toy materials, such as plastic, wood
Excavation site	Nature of soil, rocks, building materials
Zoo	Birds, insects, animals
Botanical gardens	Plant life
Museum	Rocks and other geological formations

23-17 Field trips can be used to teach a variety of science concepts. For instance, a trip to a fruit market can teach children about plants and seeds.

Care of Animals

All animals brought into the classroom should receive humane care and treatment. Children should always see animals being handled and cared for properly. Make every effort to provide for the basic needs of classroom animals. These needs include food, water, light, air, proper space for movement, and exercise.

Value of Animals

Experiences with animals should teach children the following concepts:

- Animals, especially pets, require care.
- Pets depend on humans for proper care.
- There are many kinds of animals; some are small and some are large.
- Animals need water, proper food, shelter, and exercise.
- Animals have different kinds of body coverings. Some have feathers, some scales, some hair, and some smooth skin.
- Animals move in different ways. Some fly, some swim, some walk, some run, some crawl or creep, and some hop.
- Animals are fun to watch.
- Animals have different numbers and kinds of legs. Some have two legs, some four, some six, some eight, and some have none.
- Animals make different sounds.
- Animals can be identified by their sounds.

Animals as Classroom Pets

Many animals can be used as classroom pets. Hamsters, snakes, toads, snails, frogs, rabbits, and guinea pigs have all been used in early childhood programs. Chart 23-19 lists the life span of some common classroom pets.

Hamsters

A healthy hamster is chubby and has a shiny coat and bright eyes. Buy hamsters only from pet stores that handle healthy animals. (One strain of hamster spreads a form of meningitis.)

Hamsters should be housed in a wire, rust-proof cage. The cage should have an exercise

Life Span of Classroom Pets	
Canary	11-15 years
Gerbil Hamster Mouse	6 years
Guinea pig	5-9 years
Rabbit	10-12 years

23-19 When cared for properly, classroom pets have long life spans.

wheel. Since hamsters are able to chew through many materials and escape through small holes, a wire cage prevents escape. Wood shavings or sawdust should be spread on the floor for cage litter. This litter should be replaced daily. Newspaper should also be placed in the cage for the hamster to shred for nesting. Because hamsters have two pairs of gnawing teeth, they enjoy having a piece of soft wood for gnawing. Gnawing also helps keep the hamster's teeth at a healthy length.

Provide hamsters with nutritious food. This includes one or two large dog pellets or one and one-half teaspoons of grain. Hamsters also enjoy almost all greens such as lettuce, clover, alfalfa, and grass. Provide them with fresh water in a special bottle purchased from a pet store. This bottle prevents spilling and ensures that the animal has a constant supply of water.

Generally, hamsters have been found to be quite friendly with children if they are treated gently and fed regularly, 23-20. When they are handled roughly or exposed to loud voices, they have been known to bite. For this reason, you need to make rules for handling the hamster. Supervise this activity closely.

Snakes

Harmless snakes make good classroom pets. They require little care and, when handled properly, rarely bite. Having a snake in the classroom can also prevent or dispel any fear the children might feel.

Aquariums are good housing for snakes. Spread newspaper on the bottom of the

23-20 Hamsters are popular with teachers and children.

aquarium. Then cover the newspaper with gravel and a small piece of wood. For privacy, build a cave in one corner with small rocks. Add a small dish of water. To prevent the snake from escaping, cover the top with a secure screen.

Different types of snakes require different foods. Your local pet shop salesperson or conservation authority worker can help you determine the snake's dietary needs. As a rule, small snakes can exist on insects, worms, and meat. Frogs and mice are required by the larger species. Some teachers prefer to arrange for their local pet store to feed large snakes.

Toads and Frogs

Toads and frogs are common classroom pets. They can be housed in an aquarium. To avoid odors, clean the housing often. Water should be changed at least twice a week. You will notice that frogs often sit in their water. They do this to moisten their bodies, which is necessary for their survival.

Toads and frogs enjoy eating small earthworms or insects. They will accept raw or chopped beef, or canned dog food. Children enjoy watching these animals use their sticky tongues to catch food such as bugs.

Fish

Fish are an ideal pet for some teachers because they can be left without attention longer than most other pets. If you would like fish as classroom pets, you will need to decide whether to buy tropical or freshwater fish. Freshwater fish are less costly and have easier care requirements.

Fish should be housed in an aquarium. Most teachers prefer 20-gallon aquariums. They are easier to maintain than smaller tanks. Also, children can see the fish more easily. Maintain a water temperature between 70°F and 80°F at all times. To ensure this range, purchase a thermometer and a self-regulating aquarium heater.

The pH balance of the water is important. It should be kept close to neutral. This is especially important if you wish to breed fish. If the pH is acidic, it can be corrected by adding sodium biphosphate or sodium bicarbonate. Either of these products can be purchased at a pet store. You might also buy a kit to test the water.

Fill the tank with water and allow it to settle. There should be a half gallon of water for every inch of fish in the aquarium. Wait one week for the water to reach the correct temperature and pH balance. Then add the fish.

Talk to the salesperson at your pet store to find out exactly what, how much, and how often to feed your fish. Chances are a prepared fish food and/or shrimp brine will be recommended.

Rabbits

Rabbits have always been a favorite pet of young children and their teachers. However, not all teachers enjoy having a rabbit indoors. This is because rabbits must be cleaned quite often.

Rabbits are often kept in large wire cages that allow plenty of room for movement. For shelter, place a wooden box at one end of the cage. Wood shavings or straw should also be placed in the bottom of the cage for bedding.

You may prefer to keep the rabbit outdoors to prevent classroom odor. Make sure that the cage is placed so it is sheltered from the wind and sun. If your play yard is enclosed, you may let the rabbit exercise outside the cage for short periods.

Because rabbits are hearty eaters, they require large amounts of food and water. Green or leafy vegetables, including lettuce, cabbage, and celery tops, are preferred. You may wish to omit cabbage and other strong-smelling vegetables from their diet. This will help control the unpleasant odor of strong-smelling urine.

Guinea Pigs

Most early childhood teachers agree that guinea pigs make good pets for young children. They are easy to handle and they do not bite. Also, guinea pigs are very gentle. They enjoy being held and cuddled by children. In addition, children can easily observe, care for, and handle them. These pets have heavy bodies and tight skins. They can be picked up easily by placing a hand under the pig's body.

Wire cages provide good housing for these animals. Recommended cage sizes are about two and one-half to three feet in length, one and one-half feet deep, and one and one-half feet wide. Doors on cages need to fit tightly to prevent the animals from escaping. Spaces to hide, exercise, and sleep should be included. A small cardboard box can be placed inside the cage for sleeping.

Food for a guinea pig is similar to that of rabbits. They enjoy pellets or grains including corn, wheat, and oats. Grass, alfalfa, clover, and carrots can be added to their diets for variety. Most teachers who have guinea pigs for classroom pets recommend pellets as the most convenient type of food.

Care of the Earth

The children need to learn to preserve the earth by keeping it clean, 23-21. Set the stage by recycling in your classroom. To do this, place four bins labeled *paper*, *glass*, *metal,* and *plastic* in a classroom area. Encourage the children to sort items.

23-21 Children should be encouraged to recycle whenever possible.

Summary

The nature of modern life makes studying science important. Young children can be introduced to science at the center through simple experiences.

In order to guide these experiences, teachers must know the objectives of studying science. They must also know how to help children reach these goals. This will require planning.

With a solid plan, teachers can then design a variety of activities to teach science concepts. Many methods and items can be used to teach these concepts, including colors, water, food, bodies, gardens, air, magnets, wheels, field trips, and pets.

Review and Reflect

1. What is the definition of *science*?

2. Because science is creative, it requires the development of children's _____ and _____.

3. List three reasons why science should be studied.

4. True or false. All science projects need to be planned in detail.

5. During their science experiences, children should have many opportunities to _____.
    A. observe
    B. solve problems
    C. collect samples and pictures
    D. All of the above.

6. Why should the science area be located near the kitchen?

7. What is a science table?

8. True or false. Unneeded teacher input can sometimes stifle children's curiosity, thereby limiting their desire to continue experimenting.

9. List the five basic process skills.

10. _____-ended questions promote discussion, but _____-ended questions tend to require only one word answers.

11. Name four ways to teach science concepts. Of these four methods, explain one in detail.

Apply and Explore

1. Develop a collection of items that could be placed on the science table. Explain how the collection would contribute to the science experiences of young children.

2. Brainstorm a list of centerpieces for the snack or lunch table that would help develop science concepts.

3. Draw a sketch of a science area as you would design it. Include placement of equipment.

4. Review a recipe book. List examples of cooking activities that would involve a process and product.

5. Develop a recipe file of foods that can be prepared by the children in an early childhood setting.

6. Make a dish garden using a pineapple, turnip, carrot, or beet top. Document the amount of time it takes for each to sprout.

Children enjoy preparing for holidays and special events.

Chapter 24

Guiding Social Studies Experiences

After studying this chapter, you will be able to

■ explain the importance of social studies experiences.

■ outline the role of the teacher in designing and guiding social studies experiences.

■ describe ways to include multicultural, intergenerational, government, ecology, geography, community living, holiday, and current events concepts in the curriculum.

Terms to Know

incidental learnings
perceptions
culture
omission
ecology

Young children approach classroom life eagerly and positively. They are interested in everything that goes on and are always full of questions. For instance, they might ask

■ Where is Africa?
■ How does the police officer help me?
■ Why doesn't she have a daddy?
■ What is Passover?

Many of these questions arise naturally during daily classroom activities. Children's questions might relate to social skills, cultures, careers, holidays, current events, history, or geography. These questions all revolve around social studies as a curriculum area.

The field of social studies includes many subjects that help children learn about themselves, as well as other people. Children learn about other families and people in the community. In addition, they learn positive group living skills, 24-1.

Young children build social studies concepts as they move through the world around them. For example, children learn key social studies concepts when they build an airport with blocks or walk around the neighborhood. Social studies concepts can also be developed by looking at many types of housing. Role-playing doctors, mail carriers, grocers, or mothers also promotes an understanding of social studies. So does the process of making and eating ethnic foods or hearing a story about community helpers. By taking part in tasks for maintaining the classroom, children learn social studies concepts. Watering flowers, feeding classroom pets, and putting blocks away teach children about getting along in their world.

24-1 Through social studies experiences, children learn to accept themselves and get along with others.

24-2 Learning to share ideas helps children build communication skills.

Importance of Social Studies

Children need to understand how other people live—their lifestyles, languages, and viewpoints. Social studies helps children acquire skills for living. By including social studies concepts in the curriculum, children will

- develop self-respect and a healthy self-concept.
- develop self-control and independence.
- learn to share ideas and materials, 24-2.
- develop healthy ways of relating to and working with others.
- gain the attitudes, knowledge, and skills needed for living in a democracy.
- develop respect for other people's feelings, ideas, and property.
- learn about the roles people have in real life.

- learn to appreciate the past and its relationship to the present.

The value of the social studies curriculum, then, is that it makes children better able to understand their world and their place in it.

The Teacher's Role in Social Studies

The key to a good social studies program is your skill as a teacher and the knowledge you bring to the classroom, 24-3. Your interests will determine the degree to which social studies will be included in the curriculum. Through your training, you will understand the need to use community resources, chance learnings, themes, group participation, observation, and evaluation to enrich the social studies program.

To provide quality learning experiences, you need to make daily observations. These routine checks should provide data related to the children's interests, abilities, developmental levels, attitudes, and knowledge. From this data, you can determine what children need to know and what behaviors need to be changed.

24-3 Teachers play a crucial role in quality social studies programs.

24-4 Children have many interests. To determine individuals' interests, playtime is an excellent time to observe.

Determine the Children's Interests, Abilities, and Characteristics

Every group of children brings a wide variety of interests to the classroom. Some children may be interested in airplanes, trains, or geography. Other children may prefer to study community helpers. To determine children's interests, you can

- observe them during play, noting the type of play and their use of materials and equipment, 24-4.
- interact with them in a casual way, asking them what they enjoy.
- ask the children's parents to share their children's interests with you.
- observe the children's choice of books.

Like interests, the skills of every group of children should influence the social studies program. In any given classroom, there will be many levels in cognitive, physical, social, and emotional development. As a teacher of young children, you will need to match materials and equipment with each child's ability level.

Determine children's ability levels by

- observing the children's social skills as they play with other children.

- reviewing the children's physical growth and health records.
- structuring a variety of tasks for each child to complete, noting their success.

There is no shortcut for gathering data to determine the children's skill levels. Gathering takes time. The information, however, is essential for planning a developmentally appropriate social studies curriculum.

Developmental characteristics are key to designing a social studies program. These traits can be observed and used as a starting point for planning social studies activities. Characteristics and their implementations are listed in 24-5.

Activities Related to Children's Characteristics	
Characteristics	**Implementations**
Interest centered on immediate environment.	Provide opportunities to explore the school, home, and neighborhood.
Enjoys opportunities for self-expression.	Provide small group opportunities whenever possible.
Shows interest in people with whom he or she is acquainted.	Share resource people with whom the children have indicated an interest.
Learns best through direct experiences.	Provide concrete materials and hands-on activities.
Enjoys pretending.	Provide many opportunities and props for dramatic play.
Tends to be egocentric (self-centered: I or me)	Provide consistent guidance in respecting other's rights.

24-5 Watch for children to show these characteristics. Social studies activities can be implemented to either enhance or discourage such traits.

Develop the Curriculum

Once the children's interests, abilities, and characteristics have been determined, you are ready to plan the curriculum. Encourage children to take part in the planning. This process will help them organize their thoughts, express their ideas, and experience the results.

During the planning process, allow children to make important choices. Involve all children in the group. You may find that some may be quite shy. These children may feel better if given a chance to plan individually in a small group.

Young children are able to plan the following aspects of their activities:
- Whom to play with.
- Materials needed for a project.
- Places to visit.
- People to invite to the classroom.
- How to celebrate birthdays and holidays.

Themes

Many teachers use themes when planning a social studies program, 24-6. One theme can be used to combine the learning opportunities of many different activities. Therefore, varied experiences help children learn concepts. (See Chapter 17 for additional information on themes.)

24-6 A pet theme can be the basis for teaching many social studies concepts.

Use Community Resources

Look closely at your community resources for a variety of learning opportunities. Record the names of stores, museums, art galleries, community services, community workers, and housing groups that may be of interest. The people providing these services might also have suggestions for curriculum objectives and goals.

Incidental Learnings

Structure the classroom to promote **incidental learnings**. These are learning experiences that happen during the course of a normal day. You might set up incidental learnings by keeping the cap off the paint container, letting a plant die, placing pictures on the library table, or adding dramatic play props to the housekeeping area. These situations cause children to question and learn on their own.

Every classroom makes its own incidental learning experiences. The following are examples:
- Classroom and playground repairs.
- Classroom rules.
- Roles of school center workers such as the janitor, bus driver, or secretary.
- Handling an argument.
- Happenings in the local community.

Evaluation

Evaluation is a key part of planning the social studies curriculum. The evaluation process will help you see if goals have been met, what new goals are needed, and whether any current goals need modification. This process can be done with the children. For example, you may ask the children the following questions:
- What did you like best?
- Why did you like it?
- What did you learn?
- What do you want to learn more about?
- What would you like to do again?

Building Social Studies Concepts

Young children want to find out about their world. They touch, taste, smell, see, and hear in an attempt to learn. They form perceptions from such activities. **Perceptions** are ideas formed about a relationship or object as a result of what a child learns through the senses. Repeated experiences form a set of perceptions. This gives rise to concept formation. For instance, a young child sees a black and white cow with four legs. Later, the child sees a black and white dog and calls it a cow. Given proper feedback, the child will learn to tell the difference between a dog and cow.

Concepts help children to organize, group, and order experiences. Concepts help them make sense out of the world. Once learned, they help children communicate with each other.

Personality, experiences, language skills, health, emotions, and social relationships all affect the formation of accurate concepts. Many varied experiences help form more concepts. Experiences are affected by feelings and emotions. Therefore, by having contact with others, children learn to view other ways of thinking. Children with well-formed language skills form useful concepts. Good physical and mental health help children form proper sensory concepts.

A number of concepts are formed through social studies activities. These include multicultural, intergenerational, government, ecology, geography, community living, current events, and holiday concepts.

Multicultural Concepts

Social scientists use the word culture to describe all the aspects of people's lives. This includes a group's ideas and ways of doing things. It includes traditions, language, beliefs, and customs. **Culture,** then, is learned patterns of social behavior.

A child's culture is a lens by which the child judges the world. Culture influences feelings, thoughts, and behavior. It imposes order and meaning on all experiences. Culture provides children with a lifestyle that often defines what foods are eaten and when. Culture becomes a vital part of people. As a result, they do not realize that their behavior might be different from behaviors learned in other cultures.

A multicultural perspective is very important in planning a social studies curriculum. Studies show that children's attitudes toward their own identity and other racial groups begin to form during preschool years. They are aware of race and color as early as three years of age.

When planning the multicultural curriculum, you will want to keep the following goals in mind. You will want each child to develop

- respect for oneself as a worthwhile and competent human being.
- acceptance and respect for others' similarities and differences.
- an appreciation of the child's own racial and ethnic background.
- the skill to interact positively with all children.
- an understanding that there are many ways to do things.

You can meet these goals by involving parents and selecting and preparing appropriate learning materials and activities. Your behavior will also influence the success of your social studies curriculum.

Parent Involvement

Parents can play a key role in meeting multicultural goals for children. As a teacher, study the cultural background of each child. Parents or other family members are the best resources for this task. They can provide you information on their culture's child rearing attitudes and techniques. Meeting and talking with parents can provide knowledge of the family and their needs, concerns, and hopes. Parents can also share their heritage by taking part in classroom activities, 24-7. They can share stories, games, songs, dances, foods, and holiday observances related to their culture.

Selecting and Preparing Materials

Select materials that reflect the ethnic heritage and background of all children. The following are items useful for reaching this goal: cooking utensils, flags, weavings, traditional games, ethnically diverse children's books, musical tapes and CDs, pictures, and videotapes.

Teachers should examine materials for their appropriateness in teaching social science concepts. If biases exist in any materials, they should be noted. Then teaching methods must be developed to overcome the bias.

Be sure to watch for stereotyping when selecting materials for classroom use. Stereo-

24-7 Encourage parents to become involved in promoting multicultural perspectives in their child's classroom.

typing ignores individual differences. Take care when choosing games, books, puzzles, videos, classroom decorations, and visual aids.

Omission is another bias found in some teaching materials. **Omission** implies that some groups have less value than other groups in our society. This is done by omitting a group's presence in the material. All groups must be included and respected in teaching materials, 24-8. To build self-esteem in children, show them positive role models from all cultural backgrounds.

24-8 Dolls should represent the racial make-up of society.

Activities to Encourage a Multicultural Perspective

Studies show children are more likely to focus on differences than on similarities among people. As a result, you need to focus on people's similarities whenever possible. In the curriculum, include activities that show all people have similar ways of living within a family or other social group. Emphasize that all people have similar needs including food, clothing, and shelter. Language, art, and music are ways of expressing various attitudes, feelings, ideas, and knowledge.

Special activities can be planned to focus on similarities. For example, schedule a "special day" for a particular child. During group time, the child may share his or her favorite toy, food, or color. Ask each child to bring in family photographs. They can use these photos to observe similarities. Cooking and eating a variety of cultural foods is another way of stressing multicultural concepts.

Intergenerational Concepts

Young children's concepts of the aged, or elderly, are not always positive. When a group of preschool children were asked about aged adults and growing older, their comments included:

"Well, they sure have a lot of extra skin."
"My grandpa fixes my bike."
"They walk slow and have to sit a lot."
"They're sick."
"You get bald if you are old."
"They help you make cookies."

Such responses show the need to include intergenerational concepts in the early childhood program.

The number of aged persons in American society is steadily increasing. With this growth, there is a need to inform all people about the benefits of aging, as well as the problems the elderly face. For many children today, their only contact with the aged is with their grandparents. This may lead to one-sided views and ideas of the aged. Therefore, young children need to learn from and about the aged.

Negative stereotyping is one of the greatest problems faced by the aged. These views about growing older have also been noted in children.

Studies have found that some young children have already formed some stereotypes of the aged.

Studies show attitudes are formed early in life. These feelings and thoughts remain a strong force in a person's life. Children's attitudes toward the aged are generally based on their families views. Negative stereotypes of the aged may be caused by lack of knowledge. Another reason may be little or no contact with older people. These attitudes can be changed, if need be, through contact with the aged. Early childhood teachers can invite the elderly to take part in the classroom. Intergenerational contacts can benefit both the young and old. Contact with the aged will affect the formation of positive concepts of aging persons. Education and information from the radio, television, and newspaper can also change these attitudes.

Include intergenerational concepts in the program to encourage children to view the aged more positively. The goals for such a program are listed in 24-9. The center's program must support these goals. Interacting with the aged should be included. Books, videos, and pictures used in the classroom should all portray the aged without bias. These materials should show the varied interests, abilities, mobility, and health of the aged.

Selecting and Preparing Materials

There are increasing numbers of resources for teaching gerontology to young children. (*Gerontology* is the study of the aged.) Use care when choosing them. Books and other materials should depict the aged positively. Pleasing relationships between the children and aged should be shown.

If materials are limited, use your imagination to design your own. Cut pictures from magazines or take photographs of active elders. Then combine several pictures and use them to tell stories.

Activities for Developing Intergenerational Concepts

The curriculum needs to contain concepts of the aged that will foster positive ideas of the aged. There are many themes where these concepts can be shared, 24-10. For instance, using the theme "Me, Myself," children could focus on

Goals for an Intergenerational Curriculum

- Encourage social integration of the young and old.
- Increase awareness that the aged vary in health, abilities, mobility, and interests.
- Challenge the stereotypes of the aged as being inactive, unhappy, incapable, etc.
- View the actions and traits of the aged in a wide variety of roles.
- Develop an appreciation of others' points of view.
- Promote growth of healthy, positive attitudes toward aging.
- Promote healthy development of their self-concepts to reduce the fear of growing older.
- Provide opportunities to learn how all people, including themselves, change as they move through the life cycle.

24-9 The goals of an intergenerational program should include these items.

Themes That Can Contain Concepts of the Aged	
Families	Grandparents
Friends	Neighbors
Helpers	Hobbies
Crafts	Holidays
Games	Homes
My Favorite Aged Person	Grandfather's Job
Clothes	Music
Nursery Rhymes	Our Town
	Me, Myself

24-10 Can you think of activities that would revolve around these themes?

their own aging. Pictures of the children as babies could be brought to school. These could serve as a basis for a talk about growth and development. You might also discuss other changes to come. Height and weight records could be compared. Children could then guess what other changes will occur as they continue to grow. If developmentally appropriate, the children could also make booklets telling of things they liked to do when they were younger, things they enjoy doing now, and the things they think they might like to do when they are older.

If daily contact is not possible, arrange opportunities for contact with the aged. Arrange field trips to visit elderly neighbors, a retirement home, or a senior citizens' center. You might arrange to do seasonal activities, such as singing Christmas carols or making May Day baskets. Other classroom activities include having the children use drawings or pictures cut from magazines to form a large collage or mural depicting the aged in positive, active roles (swimming, jogging, skiing, nurturing). A caption such as "It can be fun to be older" can be added to the collage.

Older Adults in the Classroom

Older adults can make useful contributions to the classroom. For example, they may help with projects, work with children who need special attention, or direct small groups of children. The roles taken by older adults depend on the needs of the teacher, children, and the older person.

Intergenerational programs that focus on developing positive concepts of the aged need to consider the needs of the older person. Like other programs using volunteers, careful planning is required for a successful program. Consider the following guidelines:

- Ensure that each aged person has a definite role to play in the classroom.
- View each aged person as an individual, using his or her special talents, interests, and training.

- Maintain close communications between the administration, teachers, and the volunteer.
- Design and provide training and sharing opportunities for the aged person.

Intergenerational programs benefit adults as well as children. Both often enjoy the growth of caring relationships. Adults have the chance to observe children's interest as they share their special talents with them. The children gain understanding of and appreciation for the elderly.

Government Concepts

Before age five, children's concepts of government are based on the information they receive from the media, home, and center. By this age, children can usually point out the flag and pictures of the president. They can also recognize the National Anthem and the Pledge of Allegiance.

To help children learn governmental concepts, design group activities based on the function of a democracy. Such activities will help children understand the purpose of rules and laws. The following list contains sample activities that help build governmental concepts:

- When your class gets a new pet, let the children vote on its name.
- During cooking experience, let the children vote on what type of food to make.
- When a new toy arrives, let the children outline rules for its use.
- Encourage the children to suggest field trips they would like to take.
- Let children plan the type of sandwiches they will have on a picnic, 24-11.

Ecology Concepts

Ecology is the study of the chain of life. It focuses on water, land, air, grass, trees, birds, and insects. In order to develop ecology concepts, children need good observation skills. Using these skills, they can build an appreciation of their environment. They can also learn about the interdependency of all life on the planet. As a result of these activities, children will develop a social concern for the environment.

24-11 Choosing the type of sandwich for an indoor picnic helps children learn about planning.

Sample activities that focus on ecology include the following:

- Take children on a trip around the block. As you walk, point out plants, trees, flowers, shrubs, and birds.
- Keep plants and animals in the classroom or the play yard, 24-12.

24-12 Giving children their own plants helps children learn the importance of caring for the environment

■ Provide magazines that children may use to cut out pictures they feel are beautiful. Let each child explain the beauty of a picture.

■ Give each child a paper bag and take a "trash hike" around the play yard. Encourage children to pick up trash and place it in their bags.

Change Concepts

Children need to learn that change affects their lives in many ways. Change is constant. To help the children learn this concept, use nature and the family. Taking part in these experiences will help children learn to accept change.

By observing nature, children learn to understand the concept of change. Plan a nature walk. During the walk, point out the cherry trees budding, the leaves turning colors, flowers blossoming, and fruit ripening. Each of these experiences should help the child understand that all things change.

People are always changing. To help children understand how they have changed, include concepts about changes they have experienced. You might try the following:

■ Show a videotape on babies.

■ Record children's height and weight at the beginning of the year, at mid-year, and at the end of the year. Discuss with the children how they have changed.

■ Collect a variety of baby clothes and toys. Place these items on a table where the children can explore them.

Geography Concepts

Young children are geographers as soon as they become mobile. They explore space, play in water and snow, and dig in dirt. They note differences in wet and dry sand and begin to form some concepts about the earth.

The earth is home to many people. The relationship of humans to the earth is important for children to understand. They need to learn that man's food, shelter, and raw materials are provided by the earth. Since these concepts are quite complex, formal lessons are most often first introduced in elementary school. There are,

however, some informal activities to use with younger children. For instance, allow children to dig in a sandbox or a garden area, and play in a sandbox with cars, trucks, pails, shovels, etc. You might also play readiness games that use symbols that can prepare children to read maps. Finally, design a bulletin board that maps out the neighborhood surrounding the center. Children can study this board and then help "navigate" a field trip through the neighborhood.

Community Living Concepts

During the preschool years, children are becoming more and more aware of the world outside their homes and families. They are ready to explore their communities and to learn about the people they will meet there. Explore with the children the neighborhood around the center. What buildings and businesses will they find? Who are the people they will meet? What do these people do? How can they help you? Answering these questions with the children will help them develop community living concepts.

Plan field trips to some of the places in your community that provide services for people. These might include the library, museum, police station, fire station, bus depot, post office, train station, radio or television station, or newspaper. Introduce the children to the people who work at these places. These people should be introduced as community helpers because they help people live together in the community. Police officers, fire fighters, postal workers, and librarians are some of the community helpers that might speak with the children.

Also plan visits to various workplaces in the community so the children can see how people work. There are probably many businesses in the local neighborhood that would interest the children. You might plan to have them visit a grocery store, restaurant, farm, pet store, beauty salon, or doctor's office.

You can also invite people in various careers to visit your class and tell about the work they do. They can bring samples of the materials or tools they use in their work. You might invite a dentist, doctor, nurse, teacher, secretary, banker, chef, or other worker to visit. These activities will develop career awareness concepts.

Current Events

Preschool children are usually unaware of events outside their own environment. Therefore, they need to be encouraged to share events affecting their own lives. Show-and-tell is one activity that helps children understand current events. Some of the events children may share include personal achievements, family events, and special celebrations.

Some classrooms develop a current events bulletin board titled "News." Children can display cards, pictures, invitations, newspaper pictures, drawings, and paintings. You may want to add items such as pictures of the children's classroom activities or field trips.

Holiday Concepts

Celebrate different holidays in your classroom. From these experiences, children will begin to learn about their rich cultural heritages. Age-appropriate experiences and activities will teach children the social importance of each holiday. They will also begin to learn concepts regarding the continuity of life.

When introducing holiday concepts, observe some precautions. Avoid introducing a holiday more than one week before it occurs, otherwise the children may get confused. They do not have a well-developed concept of time. Choose celebrations that are most relevant to the children. For instance, if you have several Jewish children in your classroom, you may want to celebrate more than one Jewish holiday. Consider celebrating Passover in the spring and Yom Kippur or Rosh Hashanah in the fall. Also, consider including a "Special People's Day." Invite grandparents, uncles, aunts, neighbors, and volunteers to join the celebration.

Involve the children in your planning for holidays and special events. You will be pleased by their input. They may suggest special foods, songs, books, or games. They may even suggest inviting special people. You may expand upon their ideas by introducing a new food, fingerplay, song, or story.

Summary

Social studies concepts help young children understand the world in which they live. They gain skills, attitudes, and knowledge for living in a democratic society. A well-planned social studies program teaches children about people different from themselves. Children learn to accept and appreciate these differences.

When planning the social studies curriculum, teachers need to determine the children's interests, abilities, and characteristics. This information can be used to develop the curriculum using various themes and taking advantage of community resources. Incidental learnings also provide an opportunity to teach social studies concepts.

Effective social studies programs introduce children to different cultures and generations of people. They learn basic principles of a democracy. Children also learn about ecology and geography. These are just some of the many social studies themes that can be included in early childhood programs.

Review and Reflect

1. List three skills children should learn in a social studies program.

2. Describe four ways to determine children's interests.

3. What aspects of their activities are children capable of planning?

4. Define incidental learnings and give an example.

5. The _____ process will help you see if goals have been met, what new goals are needed, and whether any current goals need modification.

6. Ideas formed about a relationship or object as a result of experiences are called _____.

7. List the goals of a multicultural curriculum.

8. Explain how omission is a bias that should be avoided when selecting teaching materials.

9. True or false. Children are more likely to focus on similarities than on differences among people.

10. True or false. Young children have not yet developed stereotypes concerning the aged.

11. Give your own example of how you could teach a governmental concept to young children.

12. Explain this statement: "Change is constant."

13. How do show-and-tell activities relate to the social studies curriculum?

Apply and Explore

1. As a class, choose a theme and brainstorm a list of activities that could be used in various social studies areas.

2. Brainstorm a list of community resources. Include museums, art galleries, stores, and services that are available.

3. Visit a toy store and prepare a list of toys that reflect cultural diversity.

4. Ask a group of preschoolers what they think about older people. Are their comments similar to those listed in this chapter, or are they different? Do they reveal any stereotypes?

5. Plan a lesson for preschoolers on recycling as a way to protect the environment.

Chapter 25

Guiding Food and Nutrition Experiences

After studying this chapter, you will be able to

- explain the value of food and nutrition experiences.

- conduct positive food and nutrition experiences for children that promote healthy eating habits.

- give examples of ways to work with parents to best serve children's nutritional needs.

- list nutritional concepts to teach in early childhood settings.

- outline the procedure for conducting cooking experiences.

- select and prepare simple recipes for children to use in early cooking experiences.

- identify various eating problems encountered in young children.

- teach children to set a table.

Terms to Know

nutrition concepts

portable kitchen

Food and nutrition experiences involve many activities: preparing foods, setting the table, eating snacks and meals, and cleaning up. These activities help provide learning experiences that prepare children for an independent lifetime. Participating in food and nutrition experiences also builds feelings of independence, responsibility, and worthiness. These activities provide opportunities for teaching nutrition concepts. **Nutrition concepts** are basic concepts that will help children develop good lifetime healthy eating habits.

Experiences with food and nutrition promote the development of the whole child. This is done cognitively, physically, socially, and emotionally.

Cognitively, children learn observation and critical thinking skills by participating in food and nutrition experiences. By measuring, comparing, analyzing, observing the change in ingredients, and predicting outcomes, children learn science and math concepts. By learning cooking vocabulary and the names of food preparation tools, children develop emergent-literacy skills. By following a sequence of directions provided on recipe charts, children develop left-to-right progression skills that are necessary for reading and writing.

Physically, food and nutrition experiences promote the development of large and small muscles. Young children develop muscular control by rolling, pounding, peeling, and stirring. They also develop eye-hand coordination skills by measuring, spooning, and cutting.

Socially and emotionally, food and nutrition experiences promote self-esteem. Children take pride in being able to take part in an "adult" activity. By sharing utensils, ingredients, and taking turns, young children learn cooperation skills. By participating in food and nutrition experiences with their peers, they also learn about foods from their own and other cultures. Finally, by taking part in cooking activities, children learn independent living skills that they can use throughout their lives.

The key to an effective food and nutrition program is presenting cooking activities in a positive way, 25-1. It is quite easy for food experiences to become tense and unproductive. There may be children who refuse to eat. Other children refuse to help with the tasks. Still other children may eat too much or help to a point where others cannot take part. Follow several simple rules to promote happy, relaxed food and nutrition experiences:

- Schedule quiet, relaxing activities just before mealtimes.
- Provide child-sized tables, chairs, and serving tools.
- Eat with the children.
- Encourage children to serve themselves.
- Expect some accidents. Children will spill drinks and drop food. Be prepared by keeping damp sponges handy in all food areas. Encourage children to clean up their own messes.

Working with Parents

Parents need to be aware of how they can and do influence their children's eating habits. These influences can be direct or indirect. For instance, the snacks they provide their children are a direct influence. The atmosphere of the home at mealtime is an indirect influence. Several methods are useful for working with parents in this key area of child development.

Many centers have lending libraries. These libraries are a good way to share nutrition information with adults. Parents and guardians may check out pamphlets, magazines, and books to learn or update their nutrition knowledge. Recipes may also be shared in such a setting.

Parents' meetings, workshops, and discussion groups are also useful methods for interacting with parents. Here, parents, guardians, and teachers can discuss reliable information on nutritional needs of children, suggestions for dealing with common mealtime problems, and resources in the community for food.

Some centers find that a weekly or monthly newsletter is a good way to keep parents and guardians informed and involved. Such a newsletter can contain a great deal of useful information: home food activities that reinforce concepts learned at the center, suggestions for menu planning, serving, and stressing good nutrition. A center menu is also a useful addition. Parents can use this to coordinate home meals with those served in the center.

25-1 Food activities tend to go well when you have a positive attitude about them.

Nutrition Concepts

Nutrition knowledge is useful throughout life. Teaching nutrition, then, is an important part of guiding food experiences. For instance, children learn that a wide variety of foods are available to meet the needs of their bodies. This concept can be taught by introducing children to many foods during snack and mealtime. These experiences can also teach children that foods can be eaten in a number of ways. For example, apples can be eaten raw or cooked. They can be made into applesauce, apple bread, apple pancakes, apple pie, apple juice, and apple dumplings. Chart 25-2 highlights other nutrition concepts to include in an early childhood setting.

Cooking Experiences

Children enjoy cooking experiences. These experiences promote language, math, and science concepts and skills. Children learn the vocabulary of cooking. Words such as stirring, measuring, and pouring are added to their vocabularies. Basic math concepts such as shape, size, number, and temperature change are learned. By "reading" recipe charts, children learn to follow directions. By exploring similarities and differences in food they develop critical thinking skills. By finding new ways to combine ingredients, they also learn creative thinking skills.

By taking part in food and nutrition experiences, children learn how to use cooking utensils and work as a team. See 25-3. They learn how to use can openers, vegetable peelers, and egg beaters. Children learn left-to-right progression skills as the teacher helps them read recipes. Cooking is also a natural way to learn how to follow directions.

Nutrition Concepts for Young Children

- Nutrition is how our bodies use the foods we eat to produce energy, growth, and health.
- There is a wide variety of food available. Foods come from both plants and animals. In addition, the same food can be used to make many different dishes.
- Foods vary in color, flavor, texture, odor, size, and shape.
- Foods are classified into basic food groups:
  ✓ Bread, cereal, rice, and pasta group.
  ✓ Vegetable group.
  ✓ Fruit group.
  ✓ Milk, yogurt and cheese group.
  ✓ Meat, poultry, fish, dry beans, eggs, and nuts group.
  ✓ Fats, oils and sweets group.
- A good diet includes foods from each of the food groups.
- There are many factors that enhance the eating experience:
  ✓ Aesthetics of food.
  ✓ Method of preparation.
  ✓ Cleanliness, manners.
  ✓ Environment/atmosphere.
  ✓ Celebrations.
- We choose foods we eat for many reasons:
  ✓ Availability.
  ✓ Family and personal habit.
  ✓ Aesthetics of food.
  ✓ Social and cultural customs.
  ✓ Mass media.

25-2 Young children need to learn simple nutrition concepts.

25-3 Food and nutrition experiences help children learn how to use such items as wooden mixing spoons.

The "Cook's Corner"

Most teachers know the value of cooking experiences. To increase learning and decrease safety and health hazards, follow these actions:

- Have all cooks wash their hands in warm, soapy water and wear aprons.
- Clean and disinfect all work surfaces.
- When using recipe cards, write short, clear, instructions in order. Food labels, picture symbols, numerals, short phrases, and single words make recipes easy for young children to "read," 25-4.
- Place the recipe, ingredients, clean-up supplies, and utensils on a tray before the activity begins.
- Use large, stable, unbreakable bowls for mixing ingredients.
- Have the children sit when using sharp utensils such as knives and peelers.
- Limit the number of children taking part in an activity. Four to six children is usually best.

First Experiences

First cooking experiences should revolve around simple recipes that can be served at snack time. Have the children shake cream to make butter or prepare instant pudding. Measure the ingredients before the experience. This will help ensure a successful experience. Success is important. Then children will want to take part in future activities.

Planning

Plan a series of cooking experiences that gradually become more complex. Prepare the same food in a number of different forms. Each time, add something new. For example, add berries to instant vanilla pudding. Later you can add other types of fruit.

As you select recipes, be aware of any food allergies children may have. Common culprits include milk, milk products, and orange juice.

Limit the number of children who will take part in any activity. Usually no more than four to six children should be involved, 25-5. Therefore, children may have to take turns. Some teachers schedule cooking during small group activity times. In that way, the number of children is naturally limited and the children can be encouraged to take turns.

Collect enough tools and unbreakable equipment for all children involved. Plastic bowls and blunt tools are best. Each child should have a tool when activities such as peeling apples are scheduled. For cutting, provide strong plastic knives.

25-4 Even young children can follow recipes that are written using picture symbols.

25-5 Small groups work best for cooking activities.

Cooking

Some teachers create a **portable kitchen** in their classrooms. Create a portable kitchen by placing the ingredients, tools, and other equipment on a low table so all children can watch. Find an area near an electrical outlet so that you can use portable appliances such as an electric skillet or a hot plate rather than a stove. To prevent accidents, turn pan handles away from children. Remind children of safety rules.

Start the activity by telling the children what you are going to make. Then have all cooks (including you) wash their hands with soapy water. After this, explain the sequence of steps you will use. Discuss the different sizes of measuring cups and spoons. Ask simple questions such as which holds the most? If you have not prepared a recipe chart, write the steps on a chalkboard or large piece of paper. The children will enjoy following directions.

As the children move through the preparation steps, encourage them to talk about what is happening. Point out the changes in food form(s) due to blending, cooking, or freezing. Ask them to predict what will happen. Whenever possible, science, math, language arts, and social studies concepts should all be included if they mesh with the lesson. Name any new foods, processes, and equipment.

Cleanup is an important part of the experience. Children should be involved in the process. Dishes and ingredients will have to be returned to the kitchen. The table and dishes will have to be washed.

Tasting Experiences

After cooking, tasting helps children learn about new foods. New foods can be compared with familiar foods. For example, a lime can be compared with a lemon, or a sweet potato can be compared with a white potato. Food temperature and texture can be discussed. Many teachers use these activities as part of an interest center. This limits the number of children who can be involved at any given time.

Eating Habits

No doubt you will find that some children have poor eating habits. Often, these habits are learned from others. If parents, relatives, and peers have poor eating habits, chances are that the young children will have them, too.

You can use food and nutrition experiences to model and encourage good eating habits. By tasting all foods in front of children, you will encourage them to do the same. You also can model appropriate attitudes toward eating. Offering constructive comments is another way to improve eating habits. For instance, you might say, "Seth, I'm glad you tried the peas today. You probably found out how good they taste."

Changing Appetites

Children do not always eat the same amount of food every day, 25-6. If a child is very active

25-6 Earlier meals, activity level, weather, and health all affect a child's appetite.

on a certain day or has a light breakfast, the child will likely have a big appetite. If the weather is hot or a child has just eaten before coming to the center, he or she probably will not be very hungry. Fatigue and illness can also cause a change in children's appetites. When children do not feel like eating, do not force them.

If a child's lack of appetite at mealtime continues for a length of time, observe the child. Ask these questions:

- Is the child getting enough nutrients?
- Is the child eating too much at snack time?
- Is the child paying attention at mealtime?
- Is the child being properly reinforced at mealtime?
- Is the child always tired at mealtime?

After observing the child, you may notice one of these problem areas. For instance, if the child is eating too much at snack time, limit the amount of snacks the child is allowed to eat. If the child is always tired at mealtime, provide him or her with a quiet period before eating. Then at the table reinforce the child when he or she accepts food. You may do this with praise.

If the problem continues after these observations, you may wish to contact the child's parents.

Refusing Foods

There will be times when some children refuse to eat certain foods. They may do this for a number of reasons. They may have seen other adults and peers refuse to eat these foods. The food may not be prepared in a familiar manner.

Serve these children small portions of the food. Also, be certain you eat all of the food you have on your plate.

Setting the Table

Children should be expected to set the table. This routine provides experiences in counting and in space relationships. Have children take turns performing this routine. Teachers often list this task on a chart, along with other tasks to be done around the classroom.

Begin teaching children to set the table by explaining rules. Before the table is set, the children must wash their hands. Then they must wash the table with a sponge or cloth and soapy water. After this, they may participate in setting the table.

Place mats that show the positions of eating utensils, plates, and glasses are quite helpful for beginners. These mats also help children learn the space relationships of eating utensils.

Teach children to place the plate on the middle of the place mat. Then have them place the fork on the left side of the plate. Place the napkin next to the fork. After this, the knife is placed on the right side of the plate (if you are using knives). The spoon is placed next to the knife. Finally, the glass is placed at the tip of the knife.

25-7 Children can pour their own drinks from small pitchers.

Small centerpieces are a nice addition to the dining table. Those made of unusual materials can become the focal point of conversations. Centerpieces may be something a child has brought from home or something the class has made.

Serving and Eating

To foster independence, children should serve themselves and others. Place serving dishes on each table. They should be the proper weight and size for young children to handle. To encourage independence, provide small pitchers, allowing the children to pour their own milk, juice, or water, 25-7.

Begin a meal encouraging children to try a small amount of each food. This will be about one or two serving spoons. If a child eats all the food on his or her plate, allow the child to have another serving.

The meal should begin with a glass of milk. Some children prefer liquids to solid food. They will often drink their milk right away and then ask for more. Remind these children that more milk will not be provided until all other foods are tasted.

Cleaning Up

Cleaning up is also part of the eating routine. Children should learn how to clean up after themselves.

Place a utility cart or small table next to the eating area. After the main meal is completed, have the children take their plates to the cart. If dessert is being served, they may keep their eating utensils and glasses. When they have finished dessert, the children should then take all their dinnerware and eating utensils to the cart.

Summary

Food and nutrition experiences are of great value to children. Food and nutrition experiences promote cognitive, physical, social, and emotional development in children.

Guiding food and nutrition experiences includes many tasks. It requires planning cooking experiences, teaching basic nutrition concepts, setting tables, and eating. The skills children learn in this area will be used throughout their lives.

Food and nutrition experiences also involve movement and activity. The children may become excited and require extra supervision. For this reason, the experiences must be well planned and limited to small groups of children.

Guiding food and nutrition experiences will require extra effort from you as a teacher. Carefully structured and supervised, these experiences can be very useful and enjoyable for you and the children.

Review and Reflect

1. List three activities involved in food and nutrition experiences.

2. True or false. Experiences with food promote the development of the whole child.

3. List four rules that promote relaxed food and nutrition experiences.

4. Name three methods for working with parents regarding their children's nutrition. Explain one method.

5. When using _____, write short, clear instructions using food labels, picture symbols, and simple phrases.

6. True or false. Allowing 10 to 12 children to participate in a cooking experience at one time is a good idea.

7. As children move through the food preparation steps _____.
   A. plan the next activity
   B. remain with the experience, encouraging them to talk about what is happening
   C. clean up the work area
   D. None of the above.

8. Where do many children learn poor eating habits?

9. If a child constantly refuses to eat a certain food, _____.
   A. ignore the behavior
   B. scold the child
   C. give the child small portions of the food
   D. force the child to eat the food

10. True or false. To promote independence, have children serve themselves and others.

Apply and Explore

1. Design a newsletter to be sent out to parents. Determine columns and special features you would include.

2. Choose one nutrition concept. Design a brief lesson for teaching this concept.

3. Choose a simple recipe to use with young children. Write the recipe out in chart form, making it understandable to the users.

4. Select a simple recipe for children to use in a cooking experience. Prepare a teaching aid with picture symbols that teaches the children how to follow this recipe.

5. Watch a Saturday morning television program designed for young children. Compile a list of the food advertisements shown during the program. Determine whether or not the ads conveyed positive messages about good nutrition. In a written report, summarize your findings. Briefly describe how these ads may affect young children's food choices.

6. Develop a collection of simple recipes that are suitable for preschool cooking experiences.

Chapter 26

Guiding Music and Movement Experiences

After studying this chapter, you will be able to

- explain the benefits of music experiences.
- design a music center.
- outline the teacher's role in music experiences.
- name a variety of rhythm instruments.
- demonstrate the use and purpose of rhythm instruments in the program.
- list considerations for scheduling music activities.
- plan a variety of music activities.
- explain how to teach various movement activities.
- describe movement activities that promote children's development.

Terms to Know

phrase method

whole song method

phrase/whole combination method

Autoharp®

chant

body percussion

auditory discrimination skills

pantomiming

On a rainy afternoon, Mrs. Kohler noticed the children in her classroom were restless. They needed some activity. She decided to guide them in a movement activity using a piece of music designed to promote movement.

The children were told to listen closely. Then Mrs. Kohler told them to move the way the music made them feel. Watching the children, she saw that fast music made them quickly hop up and down. Slow music made them tiptoe, taking tiny steps.

After the activity, Mrs. Kohler felt she had met her goal. The children gained practice in listening. They also released pent-up energy and played cooperatively with each other. The activity Mrs. Kohler planned included both music and movement.

Music is a form of communication, 26-1. It is an important form of communication between adults and children. Adults often rock babies to sleep with lullabies. Adults play musical games with children, such as ring-around-the-rosy, London Bridge, and pat-a-cake. As adults play with children, adults convey messages. They communicate feelings to children. They pass on culture. They teach an appreciation for music. They also teach language skills and music basics.

Teachers use music with young children for many reasons. Music

- builds a sense of community
- provides an opportunity to learn and use language concepts and vocabulary
- provides an opportunity to practice counting skills
- provides a pleasant background for playing, eating, and sleeping

26-1 Music can be used many ways as a form of communication.

- releases tension and energy, and calms angry feelings
- can be used to express feelings through movement and dance
- can be used to manage behavior
- makes learning fun
- teaches listening skills
- helps build an understanding of musical concepts, including loud/soft, high/low, fast/slow, up/down
- helps build an appreciation of different cultural backgrounds (Encourage the children and their families to share their songs.)

Benefits of Music Experiences

Music experiences can build creativity when children are urged to experiment, explore, and express themselves. Music can also enhance the expression of feelings and thoughts. Also, music helps children build an awareness of the feelings of others. For young children, music can be a natural form of expression.

Language skills build as children take part in activities. As children listen and sing, they learn new words and sounds, and develop new concepts.

Music activities help children grow cognitively. They memorize words to songs. They learn to sing musical notes. They also learn to compare concepts: loud/soft, fast/slow, etc.

Children grow physically as they move in rhythmic activities and play instruments. Music experiences also can help children build positive self-concepts. As children learn about their culture and learn new skills, they learn to like themselves. Children also learn to respond to moods expressed by music. They become more at ease with their emotions.

Music should be a natural part of the daily routine in every early childhood classroom. Music experiences should be spontaneous and casual. Likewise, music time should not be at a set time every day.

Children respond to and enjoy many forms of music experiences. They delight in listening to music and stories about music. They enjoy singing and moving to music. They enjoy making simple rhythm instruments. With their instruments, children enjoy making sounds, 26-2. Four- and five-year-old children at times might even create their own songs.

26-2 Children enjoy listening to the sounds of a drum.

A Music Center

Design and decorate a music center to encourage use by children. Place it in an open section of the classroom to allow room for freedom of movement. The active section of the room is best. Creative play will be encouraged if housekeeping and block-building areas are nearby. Provide beanbag chairs and pillows so that children can sit and listen to music.

Display instruments on a table or open shelf, 26-3. The children should feel free to use these. Include drums, clackers, maracas, rhythm sticks, guitars, tonettes, and recorders on the shelf or table.

When buying instruments look for quality. Quality instruments produce the best sounds. Instruments and other supplies can be bought through local music stores, school supply stores, or catalogs. Consult the Yellow Pages for names, addresses, and telephone numbers. These businesses are listed under such headings as school supplies, music instruments, music, piano, or music dealers.

Parents are a good source for instruments. Often they are happy to lend or give instruments to the schools. Instruments of different cultures many times are supplied by parents.

The music center should also contain pictures of dancers, instruments, and singers. Local music stores may be happy to supply you with these. See 26-4.

The Teacher's Role

The teacher's role is to encourage musical expression. To do this, children need surroundings in which they feel free to explore, sing, and move to music. The extent of their participation and time they will spend in musical activities will vary. Children may be nonparticipants, distant observers, close observers, limited participants, or eager participants. The approximate time they spend in musical activities will depend upon their age, interest, and abilities.

Singing with young children is fun. However, you will find that it is not uncommon for novice teachers to be shy about singing before a group of children. This fear is needless. Young children are not critics. They enjoy hearing their teachers sing.

Enthusiasm is the key factor in conducting a positive experience, 26-5. Your delight in music will be catching. Share an expressive face. Remember to smile and enjoy yourself. If you do, you will see children smiling and enjoying themselves, too.

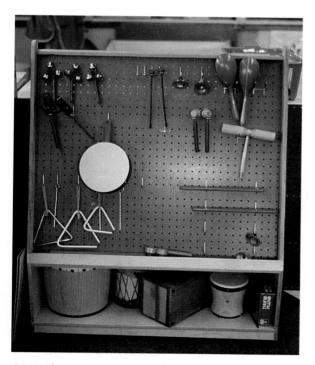

26-3 This inviting display of instruments encourages the involvement of children.

Contents of a Music Center
Autoharp® CD player Variety of CDs Tape recorder and cassettes Pictures of dancers, instruments, and singers Rhythm instruments Sound-producing objects (clocks, containers   filled with pebbles) Songbooks Scarves, crepe paper streamers Piano, guitar (optional)

26-4 The contents listed here are part of a useful music center. What other items might you add?

26-5 This teacher's enthusiasm is more important to the children than the instrument she is playing.

When singing with or to children, use a light, pleasant singing voice. Children find it easier to match the tones of human voices rather than pianos or instruments. Therefore, with children through age three, use instruments as little as possible.

Avoid forcing children to participate. Singing is a learned behavior, whether singing alone or in a group, it takes some courage. Generally, preschool children will participate in group singing. By age five, most children will be comfortable singing alone. When children feel ready to take part, they will. Meanwhile, try to make music an enjoyable experience for them. As a result, the children's natural creativity will blossom.

Music does not have to be introduced at a set time and place. It should occur throughout the day. For instance, children respond better to musical directions than spoken directions. For this reason, many teachers use music to make announcements, provide transitions, and direct cleanup activities. Teachers also may use music to welcome and say good-bye to the children. It is also important that the surroundings promote and support music. Cassette recorders, cassettes, CDs, rhythm instruments, and singing all invite children to share music.

Encouraging Discovery

Another role of the teacher is to promote children's interest in instruments and their sounds. This helps children grow in awareness. To promote children's interest, you must also show interest. For example, during a group play activity, you may ask one of these questions:

- How can you make a different sound?
- How was this sound different?
- Can you make a faster sound?
- Can you make a slower sound?
- Can you make a louder sound?
- Can you make a softer sound?

You may also increase music awareness by asking children to listen to each other play instruments. Place four or five instruments on a table during free choice play periods. Otherwise, introduce the instruments at group time. A comment like, "Here are some instruments that you may wish to play," may be all that is needed to arouse children's curiosity.

To encourage the children, comment on their efforts. Such statements as "You are making some interesting sounds," "Your sounds are beautiful," or "You found a new way," build positive self-concepts. You may also encourage children by prompting. For example, you may say "Show me how you did that."

Encouraging Nonparticipants

In every group of young children there are some children who prefer to observe. These children prefer to listen and watch the group. Nonparticipating children generally need more time to take part in music activities. Such children should be handled with patience, 26-6. Try to stand next to such children during movement activities. With a smile on your face, slowly take their hands and swing to the rhythm. Then continue to encourage participation by nodding and smiling at them, showing your approval and enthusiasm. A skilled aide can also help encourage children who do not want to take part.

26-6 Children who avoid taking part in music activities can be helped through individual contact with the teacher.

Selecting Songs

When choosing songs for young children, respect the children's age, abilities, and interests. Simplicity is the key. The best songs for young children

- tell a story
- have frequent repetition
- have a developmentally appropriate vocabulary
- have a strongly defined mood or rhythm
- have a range of no more than one octave. Most children are comfortable with the range from C to A or D to B
- have moods that children know or can mimic
- relate to children's level of development

Selecting appropriate songs is the key to involving the children. Begin by choosing songs that you enjoy. To arouse children's interest, you must convey enthusiasm for a song. For instance, you may ask children to clap the words of favorite songs. Children will not tire of a well-loved song. They will repeat it over and over again once they know it.

Most children enjoy many types of songs. Songs about familiar objects, families, lullabies, holiday songs, and songs with actions are all enjoyed by children. Some songs are best for older children. Others, because of their content, are best for younger children, such as *Twinkle, Twinkle, Little Star*.

Children's songbooks are available at music stores, professional conference exhibits, and from early childhood catalogs. These books can be used to find new songs. The books also may be used along with the piano, guitar, or Autoharp®. If possible, keep several of these books on hand.

Creating Songs

The best way to create a song is to use a known melody with new words. For example, *Baa, Baa, Black Sheep; Twinkle, Twinkle, Little Star;* and *A, B, C, D* are all tunes that can be used for other songs. You will find that changing words to these tunes is a good way to teach language skills.

Teaching Songs

The teacher's attitude about music influences children's responses. If you, as a teacher, are thrilled by and enjoy music, the children will likely also enjoy music. Know the song well. Try to sing clearly, using expression, proper pitch, and rhythm. If necessary, use a audio cassette to learn it. Sing with vitality and zest. When you do, the children will learn by imitating your voice. There are three methods for teaching songs; the phrase method, the whole song method, and the phrase/whole combination method.

The **phrase method** of teaching is used with longer songs and younger children.

First, prepare the children by telling them what to listen for. For example, say "I'm going to sing you a song about a dog named Wags. I want you to listen carefully and tell me what Wags does."

After this introduction, sing the entire song. Then stop and talk about the song. Next, sing short sections and have the children repeat these sections after you. Keep singing, increasing the length of the sections until the children know the song. After the children appear comfortable, drop out. This will prevent them from depending on you to lead songs.

The **whole song method** is used to teach songs that are short and simple. Tell the children to listen to you. After they have listened to you sing the song once, ask them to sing with you. Repeat the song a few times, to be sure the children know the words.

The **phrase/whole combination method** is done by teaching key phrases. Sing a key phrase and have the children repeat it. Continue until you have introduced a few key phrases in the song. Then sing the whole song and have children join in when they can. Repeat the song until children have learned all of the words. Stress key phrases with rhythmic movement or visual props to make them more meaningful, 26-7. An example would be "Johnny Pounds with One Hammer." As the song is sung, both you and the children can mimic a pounding action.

Accompanying Singing

Many early childhood teachers like to play the piano, Autoharp®, or guitar while children

26-7 This prop for *Five Green Speckled Frogs* helps children learn and remember the song.

sing. Instruments' availability and your playing skills will affect the choice. Remember, though, your enjoyment of the music is much more important than flawless playing.

Some teachers do not use instruments even if they are skilled. They believe that playing instruments detracts from the total experience. Children's attention tends to wander. To avoid this pitfall, use the Autoharp® or guitar. With these instruments, facial expressions and lip movements can be seen by the children. They will feel your involvement in the activity.

Piano

A piano has a clear sound and can be used to play melodies as well as to accompany singing. Advanced playing skills are not needed for successful music experiences. Children seldom notice missed chords or bad notes. Instead, they notice enthusiasm and delight.

Autoharp®

An **Autoharp®** is a simple chording instrument that can be used to accompany singing. The Autoharp® is more useful than a piano for several reasons. It is not as costly as a piano, and it is portable. It can be taken to class picnics, on field trips, and out on the play yard.

Learning to play an Autoharp® is quite simple. Begin by positioning the instrument so you can read the identification bars. Use your left hand to press the chord bars. Strum the strings with your right hand. For each beat, strum one cord. Many teachers have learned to play within a few hours by using a self-instruction book.

Guitar

The guitar is a string instrument. It is more difficult to learn to play than the Autoharp®. Like the Autoharp®, it is portable. It can be moved to the play yard or taken on a field trip. For this reason, it is often a favorite of many early childhood teachers.

Rhythm Instruments

Rhythm instruments can be used by children participating in music activities. By playing rhythm instruments, children can express their feelings. Children who have expressed little interest or skill in singing may respond to musical instruments, 26-8.

26-8 Children can have fun with rhythm instruments without worrying about their musical talents.

Rhythm instruments can be used to
- build listening skills
- accompany the beat of a sound or recording
- classify sounds
- discriminate between sounds
- project music or mood
- experiment with sounds
- organize sound to communicate feelings and ideas
- develop classification skills by learning the difference between quiet and loud, hard and soft, and other sounds

Your role should be to purchase instruments and create objects that can be used for music. Rhythm instruments can be store-bought or made by teachers, parents, volunteers, and sometimes even children. Handmade instruments often will not have the same quality as store-bought instruments. However, handmade instruments serve a purpose by exposing children to many sounds.

Introducing Rhythm Instruments

Rhythm instruments can be used during individual or group experiences. Before giving children instruments to play, set rules. The following guidelines are suggested for using rhythm instruments in a group:
- Quietly hand out the instruments. This prevents children from getting too excited and becoming disruptive. One method that works well is to choose one child to hand out the instruments. This prevents children from struggling with each other in an attempt to get their favorite instruments. Some teachers prefer setting the instruments in a circle to prevent crowding.
- If you have a variety of instruments, introduce only one at a time. The number of different instrument types should be limited to two, three, or four to keep the volume lower.
- Explain to the children that the instruments must be handled with care. The instruments will be taken away from children who abuse them.
- After the children have instruments in their hands, allow them a few minutes to experiment. Most children will want

to play their instrument right away. Use a signal such as beating a drum, raising your hand, or playing the Autoharp® to have the children stop.

- Rotate instruments after children have had time to experiment. This gives each child a chance to play all of the instruments.
- After the activity, have the children return their instruments to the box, table, or shelf where they belong.

Building Rhythm Instruments

Some teachers have the time and resources to make rhythm instruments. Directions are included for making sandpaper blocks and sticks, bongo and tom-tom drums, rattlers and shakers, rhythm sticks and bells, and coconut cymbals.

Sandpaper Blocks

Sandpaper blocks can be used by children of all ages. For this reason, they are often the first rhythm instruments used in the classroom. Some classrooms contain one pair of sandpaper blocks for each child.

Sandpaper blocks can be used for sound effects. They make a soft, swishing sound and are played by rubbing the two sandpaper blocks together. See 26-9 for instructions on making sandpaper blocks.

Sandpaper Sticks

Purchase rough sandpaper and wooden doweling 1 inch wide and 12 inches long for each stick. To construct the sticks, wrap and glue sandpaper around each of the dowels. Leave a small section for use as a handle. Then sand the end of the sticks smooth. Direct the children to scrape the dowels back and forth across each other to make a sound. These sticks, like the sandpaper blocks, will need to have the sandpaper replaced from time to time.

Bongo Drums

Bongo drums are a favorite of many preschool children. With a drum, they can create many tones by hitting the drumhead near the rim, in the center, and elsewhere.

Sandpaper Blocks
Materials
2 blocks of soft pine, 4 by 3 by 1 inches in size Several sheets of coarse sandpaper Colored enamel paint Thumbtacks or staples Strong glue (epoxy based) 2 straps of leather or flexible plastic, 4 to 4½ inches long Scissors Hammer
Procedure
1. Sand the wood to remove all rough edges. 2. Paint the blocks a bright color to make them attractive and to prevent the wood from becoming soiled. 3. Glue the handles to each block: 4. Cut the sandpaper to fit the bottom and sides of each block:  5. Attach the sandpaper to the blocks with thumbtacks or staples. (As sand is rubbed off the paper, replace with new sandpaper.)

26-9 It takes just a little effort to make these inexpensive sandpaper blocks.

To construct bongo drums, collect a pair of scissors, string, a piece of rubber, an empty coffee can with both ends removed, a hammer, and a large nail.

Use the plastic lid from the coffee can to trace two circles on the rubber. Allow an additional inch to pull over the edges. Cut the circles out. Take the hammer and large nail, and punch holes around the outside edge of the circle. After the holes have been punched, place each of the rubber circles over an end of the can. Then lace the rubber circles to each other using string.

Tom-Tom Drums

Making tom-toms can be a group project for the children. You will need oatmeal boxes (with lids) and tempera paint, watercolor markers, or construction paper. One way to get all the empty oatmeal boxes needed is to ask parents to send them from home. To make the tom-toms, tell the children to tape the lid on the box. After this, give them tempera paint, watercolor markers, or colored construction paper and paste to decorate their tom-toms. A rhythm stick can be used for a drum stick.

Tin can tom-toms can be made with large empty coffee cans. Use the plastic top to cut three sheets of wrapping paper 2 inches larger than the top of the tin for each tom-tom. Glue the three sheets together. Stretch the glued paper over one end of the coffee can. Secure the paper with a large rubber band or string.

Rattlers

Making rattlers is a simple activity in which the children can take part. To collect supplies for making instruments, ask parents to send a round salt box to school with their children.

To make the rattlers, give each child a handful of dry beans, corn kernels, or rice. Show the children how to pour them into the box. Then give each child a strip of tape to seal off the pour spout on the box.

After the box has been filled and the spout taped closed, the children can decorate their rattlers. Give the children tempera paint, washable markers, crayons, colored construction paper, and paste. After the rattlers have been decorated, put them on display. Encourage the children to explore the variety of sounds made by the different materials.

Shakers

Collect empty toilet tissue and paper towel tubes. Tape one end of the tube shut with paper fastened by masking tape. Pour small pebbles, dried corn, dried beans, or rice into each tube. Tape the open end shut. If desired, cover each shaker with construction paper, gift wrap paper, or enamel paint.

Shakers are most useful with light, fast music. Show the children how to hold the shakers at face level. Then demonstrate how to shake them briskly. You will discover that the children delight in using shakers.

Rhythm Sticks

Rhythm sticks are always made in matching pairs. Wooden doweling from ¾ to 1 inch in diameter is needed. Cut the doweling into 12-inch lengths. Sand each end of the doweling. Add a protective coat of shellac or enamel paint.

Rhythm sticks can also be made from bamboo. This type of wood will produce a hollow sound. A good source for bamboo is a local carpet dealer. To make the rhythm sticks, cut the bamboo into 10- to 12-inch pieces. Tape each end of the stick with tape to prevent splinters.

Teach the children to play rhythm sticks holding one stick in each hand. One stick should be held steady while it is struck near the top with a second stick. See 26-10.

26-10 Children quickly learn to play rhythm sticks properly.

Jingle sticks are rhythm sticks with bells attached to each end. The bells can be attached with a small cup hook. After placing the bell on the hook, use a pliers to force the cup hook closed. You may wish to paint the sticks bright colors. This may make them appealing to children.

Rhythm Bells

Materials needed to make rhythm bells include strips of elastic, ½ to ¾ of an inch wide and 5 inches in length. Five to six bells are needed for each strip of elastic. A needle and thread are needed to sew the bells to the elastic.

Sew the ends of the elastic together by overlapping the ends. This can be done by hand or on a machine. On one side of the loop, sew on five or six small bells. Vary the size of the bells on the loops for a variety of sound. The children will then learn that the sounds made by bells of different sizes vary.

Coconut Cymbals

Cymbals made of coconut halves offer many sounds. They can sound like horses galloping when clapped together. They can also be hit with a rhythm stick to make fast, light music.

To make coconut cymbals, buy several large coconuts at the supermarket. Each coconut will make a pair of cymbals. Cut each coconut in half with a sharp saw. Drain the milk and remove all the meat. Sand the outside and inside edges of the shell until smooth. After this, shellac or paint both sides of the shell.

Buying Rhythm Instruments

Many teachers do not have time to make all the instruments needed for their programs. As a result, some instruments will have to be bought.

Buy instruments that are sturdy, 26-11. For instance, buy maracas that are constructed in one piece. Otherwise the handles may come loose. Triangles should hang from sturdy holders. If the holder is not strong, the instrument may twirl around when a child is trying to strike it. Jingle bells should always be attached to elastic. This makes them flexible enough to use as either wrist or ankle bracelets. Check drum and tambourine heads to make sure they are durable and fastened firmly. The skins should be free from cuts or holes.

26-11 Center instruments get much use, so they need to be durable.

Try to buy instruments in a number of sizes. This allows for a good mix of tones. Usually, smaller instruments have higher tones. Larger instruments have deeper tones.

Scheduling Music

Music should be scheduled throughout the day. It fits in well after a story, at the start of the day, after a snack, and during free playtime. It can be used during waiting times, such as the end of the day, a bus ride on a field trip, or before and after lunch. Music can be used to remind children of rules they may have forgotten. For instance, if Sam and Gail did not hang up their coats, you may sing "At school we hang up our coats, hang up our coats."

In addition to these impromptu uses, music should also be scheduled as a group activity for four- and five-year-old children. This should occur at the same time every day since children thrive on consistent schedules.

Using Group Music

Group music activities are useful in building group feelings and pride. A group setting is a good way to introduce new songs and new instruments. These activities should focus on the group, not the individual.

Group time should be fairly brief. Schedule seven to ten minutes for two- and three-year-olds. You may later extend the period up to 15 minutes for four- and five-year-old children. Some centers schedule two short music periods. Child care centers may have to adjust their music time to meet the attention spans and developmental levels of the children.

Suggestions for Group Music

You will need to be well-organized for a successful music period. The following suggestions may help:

- Always be prepared. Make sure you have collected all the instruments, music, and other accessories needed.
- Use the same signal for calling the children together for group music time. This signal may be a song, an Autoharp® chord, a beat on a drum, or a piano tune.
- Have the children sit in a circle or semi-circle. Then the children can see you and you can see them. To help children sit in the proper places, mark the floor with chalk, tape, or carpet squares.
- Require all adults in the classroom to take part. Their support encourages children to obey. These adults can also sit on the floor by the children and help them learn words and responses to the music.
- Switch between active and quiet music activities. Children may become bored if they are always required to listen to music. Likewise, they may tire quickly from, or become too excited by, activities that involve a great deal of movement.
- Reward children for positive behavior. Tell them what type of behavior you expect: sitting quietly, waiting for their turns, holding instruments correctly, singing clearly at the proper volume. Ignore disruptive behavior if it is being modeled by only one child. If the child continues, despite being ignored, ask another adult in the group to remove the child. Children who act up when they sit together should also be separated during group time.
- Use familiar songs that include fingerplays every day. Such songs are favorites because children find it easy to take part.

Using Individual Music

Group music activities tend to stress conformity. Children are not as free during these times to express their creativity. For this reason, individual music activities are also an important part of the music experience.

During individual activities, encourage children to interact with the music. Play music during this period. Make rhythm instruments, the piano, and a tape recorder available throughout the day, 26-12. It is also a good idea to station a teacher or other adult in the music area. An adult's presence will encourage children to enter the area and engage in musical experiences.

Music Activities

Listening, singing, playing rhythm instruments, and moving to rhythm are all music activities. A good program contains all of these activities.

Listening

All music activities involve listening. The ability to listen is important for learning. Good listening skills help children build proper speech habits, an extended attention span, and reading readiness skills.

Listening to music can enrich the imaginations of young children. It also can help them relax and release pent-up feelings. Listening can take place when singing or when playing rhythm instruments, the piano, the CD player, or a tape player.

Children need to be taught how to listen. You, as a teacher, need to give them reasons for listening. For example, you may say, "Listen to this music and tell me how it makes you feel." After playing the music, let the children express their feelings. The games in 26-13 can help young children develop listening skills.

26-12 Many children love to spend time listening to taped music.

Listening Games	
What's the Sound?	**Body Sounds**
Tape sounds from different parts of the home. These may include running water, flushing toilets, ringing telephones, closing doors, or sounds made by scissors, egg beaters, doorbells, electric washing machines, radios, and electric garage door openers. Play each sound back to the children and ask them to name the object making the noise.	Tell the children that you are going to play a body sound game. Tell them to close their eyes or cover them with their hands and listen carefully. Then stomp your feet, snap your fingers, slap your thigh, smack your lips, and clap your hands. Have the children guess how you are making the sounds.
Instrument Sounds	**Guess the Instruments**
Provide the children with a box or basket of rhythm instruments to explore. Then ask the following questions: • What instrument sounds like jingle bells? • What instrument sounds like a church bell? • What instrument sounds like the tick of a clock? • What instrument sounds like thunder? • What instrument has a loud sound? • What instrument has a quiet sound?	Let the children become familiar with the classroom instruments. Then, based on developmental level or age of the child, choose a few instruments to use in a game called "Guess the Instrument." With two-year-old children, choose only two instruments. These should have very different sounds. As the children progress, add more instruments. To play the game, tell the children to cover their eyes and listen to the sound made by the instrument you are playing. Then they can guess what instrument you are playing. After children are familiar with the game, older children may want to play the teacher's role. In this event, you, too, should cover your eyes and take part.

26-13 Children have fun and develop their listening skills while playing these games.

Fingerplays

Fingerplays are another useful method for teaching listening skills. Choose fingerplays based on developmental levels. For example, a fingerplay for two-year-olds should be short and contain simple words.

Teachers who enjoy fingerplays may wish to order their own fingerplay books. These books can be ordered through a local bookstore. Also, they can be bought in the exhibit area at a professional conference or from a local school supply store.

Some teachers prefer to file fingerplays under certain themes. For example, "Two Little Apples" could be filed with units on apples, fall, or nutrition. "Roll Them" could be filed under transitions, movements, or body concepts. Size concepts or numbers would be good themes for using "Here's a Ball." "Lickety-Lick," a childhood favorite, is often filed under science concepts. It is used for teaching these concepts during cooking experiences. See 26-14.

Singing

Children's best musical instrument is their voices. Their voices are always with them. Children learn to sing at birth. Cooing and crying sounds are musical. These tones vary in strength and pitch. Voice control is learned as children grow.

After children babble, tonal patterns emerge. By age two most children can sing. They often sing as they dress, eat, and play. By this time, singing is a meaningful activity.

Children's singing skills vary a great deal. In a group of two-year-olds, there may be children able to sing in tune and make up tunes. Other children may not be able to master these skills until they are three or four years old.

You may notice that children who stutter often sing clearly. Speech skills can be improved through singing, 26-15.

Mouthing

Children's mouths can be used to make coughing, gurgling, sipping, kissing, and hissing sounds. Animal, train, plane, machinery, and traffic sounds can also be made with the mouth. As children compare these sounds, they will learn that some are fast, others are slow, some are

---

Fingerplays

Two Little Apples

Two little apples hanging high in the tree. (Place arms above head.)
Two little apples smiling at me. (Look up at hands and smile.)
I shook that tree as hard as I could. (Make a shaking motion.)
Down came the apples. Mmmmmmm, so good. (Make a falling motion with arms. Hold hands to mouth pretending to eat.)

Roll Them

Roll them and roll them. (Roll hands.)
And give your hands a clap. (Clap hands.)
Roll them and roll them. (Roll hands.)
And place them in your lap. (Place hands in lap.)

Here's a Ball

Here's a ball (Make a small circle with thumb and index finger.)
And here's a ball (Make a large circle by using both thumbs and index fingers.)
A great big ball I see. (Make a huge circle with arms.)
Shall we count them? Are you ready? One, two, three.

Lickety-Lick

Lickety-lick, lickety-lick. (Make a big circle with the left arm by placing hand on hip. Place the right hand inside the circle.)
The batter is getting all thickety-thick. (Stir with the right hand.)
What should we bake? What shall we bake? (Gesture by opening hands.)
A great big beautiful cake. (Extend arms to show a big cake.)

26-14   How would you file these fingerplays?

---

loud, and some are quiet. Thus, exploring mouth sounds can add to knowledge. As children explore these sounds, they learn others. Joining a variety of sounds can produce unique music.

To encourage children to make sounds, bring pictures to a group activity. For instance, collect pictures of large, medium, and small dogs in a number of poses. The dogs might be barking, showing their teeth, or playing with their owners. Show the children each picture. Ask them to

26-15 Singing along to music helps many children correct speech problems.

mimic the sounds a dog would make in each instance. You can use pictures of other animals, people, machines, cars, trucks, and other objects. These activities will help children become sensitive to sounds.

Chants

A **chant** is a group of words spoken with a lively beat. It is a song that has word patterns, rhymes, and nonsense syllables in one to three tones repeated in a sequence. "Teddy Bear, Teddy Bear, Turn Around" is a chant. Mother Goose rhymes are also chants. Chants are an important form of early childhood song. Children learn to speak together in unison by chanting.

Chanting is a beneficial activity for all children. They learn to share the joy of language. They also learn to cooperate. The rhythmic response to chants are useful for children who are learning English as a second language. Chanting is also an important activity for children who speak non-standard English. Shy children can develop self-confidence and self-expression by chanting.

Like singing, you will need to model chanting for the children. Begin by repeating it aloud several times. When the children feel comfortable, encourage them to join you.

Movement Experiences

For learning, movement is an important nonverbal tool. It provides opportunities to pretend. Children can walk like elephants, crawl like worms, or pilot an airplane. Children almost always enjoy these experiences, 26-16.

26-16 Children like to discover what their bodies can do through movement activities.

Movement activities should provide children with the chance to

- explore the many ways their bodies can move
- practice combining movement with rhythm
- discover that many concepts and ideas can be expressed to others through movement
- learn how movement is related to space

Some children will take naturally to movement activities. Other children may feel self-conscious or embarrassed. To help these children, begin with some short, simple movement activities. Knowing what type of responses to expect can help you prepare.

Children's Responses

Studies show that two- and three-year-old children's responses to movement vary. Most two-year-old children actively respond to rhythm, but at their own tempo. Their response may be to repeat the same basic movement through the entire activity. For example, a two-year-old may simply jump up and down during an entire song.

By age three, children have gained greater motor coordination. As a result, they have more control of rhythmic responses. Three-year-old children will likely use many responses. That is, they may circle with their arms, run, and jump up-and-down during the same recording.

Between ages four and six, muscular coordination keeps improving. At the same time, their interest in movement and space increases. If you watch children at this stage, you will notice they skip, run, climb, and dance to music. These movements are now done to the beat of the music. If the beat is fast, their movements are fast. If the beat is slow, their movements are slow.

Teacher Preparation

To prepare for movement activities, first select your activity. Chart 26-17 lists many movements. Then stand in front of a full-length mirror and practice the movements. Do each movement in the activity. If possible, repeat the movements several times.

Body Movements		
Finger Movements	**Hand and Arm Movements**	**Whole Body Movement**
Cutting	Carrying	Bending
Folding	Circling	Bouncing
Holding	Clapping	Climbing
Patting	Dropping	Crawling
Petting	Grabbing	Creeping
Pinching	Lifting	Dancing
Pointing	Punching	Galloping
Poking	Pulling	Hopping
Pulling	Reaching	Jumping
Rolling	Slapping	Rocking
Rubbing	Stretching	Rolling Over
Smoothing	Sweeping	Running
Snapping	Waving	Scooting
Tickling		Shaking
Touching		Shuffling
Typing		Skipping
		Sliding
		Swaying

26-17 These movements can be included in a variety of movement activities.

In the classroom, children learn best when they can see and hear. Rather than simply explain, you may have to act out certain movements. In the fingerplay, "Two Little Apples," for instance, during the line, "way up high in the sky," place your hands high above your head. Reinforcing the words with actions also adds interest.

Teaching Movements

In most movement activities, children should be encouraged to explore and express their own way of moving. A tambourine can be used to capture children's interest before and during the activities. Tambourines are very useful. They can be played loud or soft, slow or fast. They can represent a galloping horse or a frightened kitten.

For successful movement activities, you will need to follow certain guidelines:

- Choose a time when the children are calm and well rested.
- Define space limits. There needs to be enough open, clear space. If space is

limited, move chairs and furniture to the side.

- Tell children they need to stop when the music stops.
- For variety in movement experiences, provide props such as paper streamers, balloons, balls, and scarves, 26-18.
- Use movement activities involving cassette tapes, rhythm instruments, and verbal instructions.
- Allow children to get to know activities by repeating many of the experiences.
- Stop before signs of fatigue appear.

You may want children to be involved in planning some movement activities. Ask the children to suggest movement activities and to bring in their favorite cassette tapes. After the group experience, cassettes can be placed in the music center. This will give children the chance to listen to the music again.

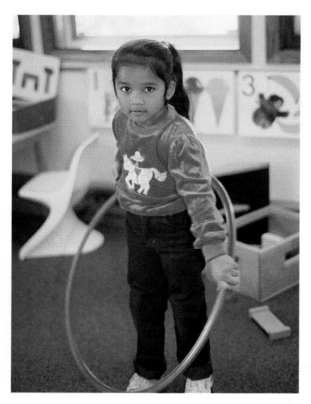

26-18 Using props adds a new dimension to movement activities.

Body Percussion Activities

Early movement activities should be simple. Stomping feet, clapping hands, patting thighs, and snapping fingers are all simple movements. These are called **body percussion**. All of these movements involve using the body to make rhythm. Body percussion can be used to learn to do more than one movement at a time. Body percussion also helps children build **auditory discrimination skills**—the ability to detect different sounds by listening.

Stomping feet to music has always been a favorite action of young children. To stomp correctly, children should bring their legs back and stomp down and forward.

Children should be taught to clap with one palm held up steadily. You should refer to this palm as the instrument. The other hand serves as the mallet. Children should clap with arms and wrists relaxed and elbows out.

The thigh slap is easy to teach. Relax your wrist for modeling the thigh slap. With arms relaxed, move your hands to slap your thigh.

When teaching children to snap their fingers, hold your hands high. Tell the children to follow you. Snap once. Have the children repeat this action. After they have mimicked your action, have them do two snaps, and then three snaps. Keep this up as long as they are able to repeat your action.

After children have learned to stomp, clap, slap, and snap, you can have them combine two actions. They might "snap, snap, snap," and then "clap, clap, clap." Depending on the skills of the children, you may gradually introduce all four levels of body percussion during one experience.

Movement Activities

Children learn to explore and express their imaginations through movement activities. One of the first movement activities should focus on listening to a drum beat. A drum is the only instrument needed for the activity. First, tell the children to listen to the drum and see how it makes them feel. For two-year-old children, provide one steady beat. With older children you may vary the rhythm: fast, slow, heavy, soft, big, small. Then ask them to respond. Encourage them to run, crawl, roll, walk, hop, skip, and gallop. After experiences using the drum, many more movement activities can be used with or without music. The key is to encourage the children to use their bodies to express themselves.

Partners

This activity is best for four- or five-year-olds. Instruct the children to choose partners. You will also need a partner to demonstrate. With your partner, move under, over, and around each other. Then have the other children mimic your movements.

Time Awareness

Use a drum to provide a beat that tells the children to run very fast. After they have done this well, tell them to run very slowly. Then tell them to jump on the floor quickly. Again, follow this request by having them jump slowly.

Space Awareness

Have the children stand in front of you. Make sure that there is enough space between each child so movements can be made freely. Stress your instructions with actions as you tell them to do the following:

- Lift your leg in front of you.
- Lift your leg backwards.
- Lift your leg sideways.
- Lift your leg and step forward.
- Lift your leg and step backwards.
- Lift your leg and step sideways.
- Reach up to the ceiling.
- Reach down to the floor.
- Stretch to touch the walls, 26-19.
- Move your arm in front of you.
- Move your arm behind you.

Weight Awareness

Children can learn differences between light and heavy using their own body force. To begin this activity, give verbal directions and demonstrate the actions. Tell the children to focus on the weight of their bodies as they make the movements. Give the following instructions:

- Push down hard on the floor with your hands.
- Push down softly on the floor with your hands.

26-19 Reaching helps make children more aware of the space around them.

- Lift your arms slowly into the air.
- Lift your arms quickly into the air.
- Walk on your tiptoes.
- Stomp on the floor with your feet.
- Kick your leg as slowly as you can.
- Kick your leg as hard as you can.

Organizing Movement into Dance

Combining time, space, and weight movements, children can learn to form their movements into dance. To teach this concept have the children do the following:

- Walk around quickly in a circle on the floor.
- Walk around slowly in a circle on the floor.
- Tiptoe slowly around the circle.
- Tiptoe quickly around the circle.
- Jump hard around the circle.
- Move your arms in a circle above your head.
- Move your arms in circles everywhere.

Word games

Word games can help children move in ways that express feelings. To play word games, tell the children to move the way the words you say might feel. Use such words as happy, sad, angry, sleepy, and lazy. After they have moved to these words, remind them to use their bodies and faces. Keep repeating the words.

Moving shapes

Four- and five-year-old children enjoy the moving shapes game. As with other movement activities, children will need ample space. Give children the following instructions:

- Try to move like something big and heavy: an elephant, tugboat, bulldozer, airplane.
- Try to move like something small and heavy: a fat frog, bowling ball, brick.
- Try to move like something big and light: a cloud, beach ball, parachute.
- Try to move like something small and light: a snowflake, flea, feather, butterfly, bumblebee.

Pantomiming

Pantomiming involves telling a story with body movements rather than words. It is best for use with four-, five-, and six-year-olds. Begin by telling the children they are going to get presents. Tell them to show you the size of their box. The children should show you a shape made by outlining with their hands and arms. Continue with the following statements:

- Feel the box.
- Hold the box.
- Unwrap the present.
- Take it out of the box.
- Put it back into the box.
- Rewrap the present.

Another pantomime children enjoy is acting out an occupation. Tell the children to think about an occupation. Then have them show how the worker acts. Sometimes this is fun to do one by one. Have one child act out his or her occupation while the rest of the class tries to guess it.

Pretending

Pretending is an activity best used with older children. Tell the children to pretend they are crying, singing, boxing, driving, cooking, laughing, typing, scrubbing, painting, playing an instrument, flying, playing cards, or building a house. See 26-20. There are many songs that children can act out as they sing. Classics include "Here We Go Around the Mulberry Bush" or "This is What I Can Do." The music to "Peter and the Wolf" provides the same opportunity for drama.

Another pretending activity involves telling the children to imagine there is a box in front of them. Then tell them they are outside the box and they should crawl into it. After they have crawled into the box, tell the children to crawl out of it. Continue by telling them to crawl under and beside the box.

26-20 Older children can pretend to show such expressions as laughter.

Summary

Music is a form of communication. It can be used to teach many skills. Through music experiences, children develop listening skills. They also learn about emotions and feelings, their culture, and sound. For these reasons, teaching music is an important part of an early childhood program.

The music center in the classroom should be designed to encourage participation in music and movement activities. A variety of instruments can be made or purchased.

Music and movement activities should be planned with the age, ability level, and interest of the children in mind. Enthusiasm is the key factor in constructing a positive experience.

Movement provides children with opportunities to pretend and exercise. Movement activities can be easily combined with music activities for meaningful experiences.

Review and Reflect

1. List four reasons teachers use music with young children.

2. True or false. Music experiences help children grow cognitively.

3. A music center should _____.
   A. be in a congested section of the classroom
   B. have instruments stored on high shelves or in a closet
   C. contain pictures of dancers, instruments, and singers
   D. None of the above.

4. Why is enthusiasm a key factor in conducting useful music experiences?

5. True or false. Nonparticipants should be pushed into taking part in music activities.

6. The best songs for young children should _____.
   A. have little or no repetition
   B. tell a story
   C. have a vocal range of two or three octaves
   D. All of the above.

7. Name three methods for teaching songs. Explain one method.

8. Why are the Autoharp® or guitar good instruments to use to accompany singing?

9. List four uses of rhythm instruments.

10. True or false. Music should be scheduled throughout the day.

11. _____ music activities are useful in building feelings of togetherness.

12. State five useful suggestions for conducting group music experiences.

13. True or false. All music activities involve singing.

14. _____ are songs that have word patterns, rhymes, and nonsense syllables used in sequence with one to three repeated tones.

15. List four objectives for movement experiences.

16. List three guidelines for successful movement activities.

17. _____ activities involve stomping feet and clapping hands.

18. What is auditory discrimination skill?

19. Combining time, space, and weight movements, children can learn to form their movements into _____.

20. _____ involves having children act out a story as it is told.

Apply and Explore

1. Observe a teacher during a music experience. Note the methods used to teach songs. Share these methods with the class.

2. Design a music center. Start by reviewing equipment catalogs. Develop a budget for this center. Make a list of instruments and equipment to include.

3. Select a movement activity and demonstrate it to your class.

4. Select a song and teach it to your class.

5. Construct two or three types of rhythm instruments. Plan a music activity using these instruments.

6. Visit a music store. Ask the manager to name the most popular children's artists. Compile a bibliography of these musical recordings.

Chapter 27

Guiding Field Trip Experiences

After studying this chapter, you will be able to

- describe the importance of field trips.
- explain points of consideration for first field trip experiences.
- list ways to promote safety on field trips.
- outline the process for selecting a field trip.
- explain the types and purposes of theme walks.
- plan a field trip from pretrip planning to follow-up activities.

Terms to Know

theme walks

resource people

behavioral expectations

"Apples grow on trees," announced Karla after a recent field trip. Alberto replied, "I know that, and I know something else. Apples are grown in special places called orchards." Hearing the conversation, Robbie added, "Orchards can have red, green, or yellow apples." By going on a field trip, these children have expanded their concept of an apple.

Mr. Smith, after hearing the children's comments, promoted further learning by saying, "It sounds like you know a lot about apples." All the children agreed. Mr. Smith then suggested that they write a story about the trip.

From the field trip, the children learned many concepts related to apples. They learned about color, size, shape, and plant growth. When planning the field trip for the children, Mr. Smith had two main goals. The first was to expand the children's concepts of apples. The second was to introduce orchard as a new vocabulary word.

The Importance of Field Trips

Young children have limited experience in understanding their world. Much of what they understand comes from books, pictures, television, and movies. Although these media help children learn about their world, they do not replace real experiences. To fully understand their world, young children need to use all their senses. They need to see, hear, feel, taste, and smell, 27-1. The more senses children use, the more they are likely to learn.

Children gain firsthand experiences during field trips. They are able to look at, listen to,

27-1 While children often learn about animals through books and videos, contact with live animals further enhances their learning.

touch, and feel their world. As children connect words and concepts with real objects and places, vague concepts become clearer to them. Field trips also help children

- build keener observation skills
- build vocabularies
- clarify concepts as new information is learned

- learn about their community
- take part in multisensory experiences
- gain new insights for dramatic play
- learn about their environment
- practice following directions in a group

First Field Trips

For young children, first field trips can be a very new experience. They may be unfamiliar with such activity. As a result, they may be anxious about what will occur. For this reason, first field trips should be short, nonthreatening, neighborhood events. For instance, a first trip could be a simple walk around the block, 27-2. Some children may be hesitant to leave the building. They may fear their parents will come for them while they are gone. Relieve them of their fears by reassuring them that this will not happen.

To provide security, remind children of their daily routine. Say, "First we are going to walk around the block. When we return, we will have a story. Then it will be snack time. After that we will play outside, and then it will be time to go home." Knowing a familiar routine will help prevent some fears.

After taking a few trips around the neighborhood, field trips may be taken to familiar places. A visit to a local grocery store is often a

27-2 First field trips should involve familiar surroundings.

rewarding trip. Here, children can see and talk about things that are well known to them.

First field trips can build or hinder children's confidence. Therefore, first trips need to match children's developmental needs. Generally, two-year-olds do best with short trips. Three-year-olds can take longer trips that may extend to an hour or so in duration. With longer field trips, allow plenty of time for walking slower and resting. Trips for four- and five-year-olds may be lengthened in time. Often these children can take trips that last several hours. Plan trips in which children will meet with success.

Selecting Trips

The trips you select will depend on the location of the site and the budget available. Centers located within walking distance of many potential sites will take more trips than those centers located in more isolated areas. Centers located in large cities have the option of using public transportation. Other centers may have their own vans to provide transportation.

Field trips are sometimes selected based on the season or weather. A trip to a pumpkin patch or an orchard can be taken in the fall. Trips that require walking, such as a trip to a zoo, should be taken during warm weather. Substitute days should be scheduled in case of bad weather.

Field trips are sometimes chosen based on the curriculum themes being studied. For instance, a trip to a farm may be chosen while children are studying about farms, food, or machinery. While learning about health, a trip to a dentist's office, doctor's office, or hospital may be chosen. Chart 27-3 lists many field trip suggestions based on themes.

Theme Walks

Simple field trips involving walks near the center based on a theme are called **theme walks**. The center neighborhood contains many interesting and meaningful opportunities for children to learn about the world. Most children enjoy walking, and the exercise is good for their bodies. Theme walks also provide an opportunity to sharpen their observation skills.

Field Trip Suggestions	
Field Trip	**Related Themes**
Airport	Air transportation or airplanes
Baker	Foods, community helpers
Bird sanctuary	Birds
Bookstore	Reading
Butcher	Foods, careers, tools
Cafeteria	Nutrition
Car dealer	Transportation, car, truck, wheels
Car wash	Cars, trucks, water
Carpenter's shop	Careers, construction
Children's homes	"My Friends" "Our Neighborhood"
Construction site	Buildings, construction, tools
Dairy farm	Food, farm animals, machinery
Dentist's office	Health, careers, teeth
Doctor's office	Health, careers, "My Body"
Fire station	Community helper, fire safety
Garage	Tools, careers, machines
Greenhouse	Plants, spring, flowers, food
Grocery store	Food, community helpers
Hair salon	Health, "I'm Me—I'm Special"
Hatchery	Animals
Hospital	Health, careers, people and places
Laundry	Health, careers, clothing
Library	Community helper, books
Newspaper office	Books, careers, communication
Orchard	Nature
Pet shop	Pets, animals, careers
Photography studio	Communication, careers, art
Planetarium	The universe, planets
Police station	Community helper, safety
Potter's studio	Careers, art
Poultry farm	Food, farm animals, eggs
Print shop	Books, careers, communication
Radio station	Communication, careers, listening
Train station	Transportation careers
Veterinarian's clinic	Pets, animals, health, careers
Zoo	Animals, homes

27-3 In your community, there are probably even more field trip sites that can be related to a theme.

Theme walks may center on many topics: numbers, colors, people, occupations, buildings, flowers, trees, or cars. For best results, focus on only one theme during each walk.

Before starting a theme walk, talk about what children might observe. For instance, if the theme is buildings, tell the children to observe types of buildings they see. They may see houses, apartments, offices, stores, and service stations.

Color is a good concept for a theme walk. Choose one or more colors the children should watch for throughout the walk. Two- and three-year-old children should be asked to look for only one color. Older children, especially five-year-olds, may enjoy looking for many colors. In fact, a fun walk for these children would be to record as many colors as they observe.

A shape walk is a way to teach children about shapes. Before leaving the classroom, review with the children what shape(s) they are to observe. As with colors, the number of shapes children are to observe depends on their ages.

Shapes are everywhere. Tires are round; most sidewalk slabs are square; doorknobs may be oval or round. Children encouraged to use their eyes to recognize shapes will also be busy using their minds.

Theme walks based on numbers and letters may also be useful learning experiences. As children walk, they will see numbers and/or letters everywhere. Numbers are seen on license plates, street signs, store windows, billboards, passing trucks, and houses. Determine the number of numbers or letters to observe based on children's ages, skills, and abilities.

People walks can teach many social concepts. The children will see that people may be tall or short and have different-colored hair and eyes. Children will also notice that some people wear glasses, some have beards, and some have long hair.

Two-year-olds may be able to identify a baby, man, lady, boy, or girl. Three-year-olds may be able to distinguish differences among these people based upon dress, hair color, and height. Four- and five-year-olds may be able to describe the actions of people they have observed.

During occupational walks, children observe what people are doing. They may see a bus driver, truck driver, bank teller, street sweeper, or house painter.

A building or architectural walk may be of special interest to older children. As you approach buildings, note their purposes. When children see a gas station-garage combination, discuss why large windows and large doors are part of the architecture. (Large windows are needed to see customers; large doors are needed for cars and trucks.) You may also encourage children to imagine what is inside the building.

To gain the most on these theme walks, carry a note pad and pencil, camera, or even a video recorder. Record observations that can be discussed when the children return to the classroom. These observations make good discussion topics for lunch, snack, or group time. Listening to the children's discussions, you will be able to note their interests.

Resource People

To promote further learning, invite interesting people to class. Another option is take the children on field trips to visit the people. These guests or field trip hosts are called **resource people**, 27-4.

27-4 Firefighters are nearly always at the top of the list of interesting resource people.

Parents, grandparents, great grandparents, aunts, uncles, neighbors, siblings, and friends are some of the best resource people. Ask them what interests and hobbies, photos, crafts, clothing, and foods they would be willing to share. This can be done personally or through a questionnaire. Select only people who enjoy children. They should represent many cultural groups, both sexes, and people of different ages. Compile a list of these people, along with their interests and hobbies. Place the list on file. During the year, select people from the list who complement your curriculum.

To be the most useful, resource people need an orientation before meeting the children. This is a necessary step for making the experience a success for both the children and resource people. Tell the resource people the number of children in your group, their interests, ages, and length of their attention spans. Suggest questions that they may ask the children. Let them know their presentation and words must be kept simple.

Warn the resource people that children often become very excited when they visit. They are proud of their guests, their classroom, and their classroom friends. Because of the stimulation, they may exhibit overly active behavior.

If possible, suggest to resource people that the children be allowed to have a "hands-on activity," 27-5. For example, if a grandmother is willing to demonstrate how she paints, encourage her to let the children try painting, too. If a person demonstrates playing the drums, ask that each child have the chance to hit the drum.

After a resource person has visited the classroom or hosted a field trip, always send a thank-you note or some other form of appreciation, 27-6. You may write a personal note, or children who can write may wish to express their own thanks. Younger children may choose to dictate thank-you notes to you. Other forms of thanking people include sending children's artwork or freshly baked cookies.

Appreciation may also take other forms. During the holidays, the children may go caroling at the fire station or home for the elderly. In February, handmade valentines may be mailed to all resource people who took part in the program during the year. Taped thank-you notes, songs on a cassette, and photographs of the children at the site are other thoughtful ways to thank resource people.

27-5 Hands-on experiences help make vague concepts more concrete for children. After holding this goat, the children will have a real experience to remember when they see goats in a book or hear about them in the classroom.

Dear Firefighter:

Thank you for showing us your fire truck. We enjoyed sitting in the truck. Thank you for showing us the truck's parts. Thank you for sounding the siren. Thank you for showing us a firefighter's clothing. We enjoyed trying it on, too.

Love,

Ron Smith's Class

27-6 Build a positive image of the center in your community with a thank-you note to resource people.

Planning a Field Trip

Successful field trips for young children need to be carefully planned. Consideration should be given to appropriateness, costs, scheduling, adult-child ratio, behavioral expectations, educational goals, and the children's preparation. As a teacher, you need to think about all of these factors. A good way to do this is to take a pretrip to the site to prepare for the field trip.

Pretrip

The success of any trip depends upon preparation. After setting goals, always make a pretrip if you have never been to the site. This visit will give you a chance to

- describe the purpose of the trip to the tour guide
- explain the children's interests and their need to use a number of senses
- prepare the tour guide for the types of questions the children may ask
- locate bathrooms
- check for any potential dangers
- ask about parking (if necessary)
- observe for teaching opportunities
- revise trip goals, if necessary

Keep a field trip file. In some centers, teachers maintain their own files, 27-7. In other centers, the director maintains a file for use by all personnel. This file may be a notebook, a folder, or an index card file box. As a rule, information to note for each trip includes

- name of site
- telephone number
- address
- contact person (tour guide)
- costs
- distance from center in blocks or miles
- dangers
- special learning opportunities
- location of bathrooms and water sources

Permission slips signed by parents or guardians must be on file for each child before a trip, 27-8. For convenience, many center directors use one form for all trips and walks. This form is filled in and signed at enrollment time. This saves the staff's time in obtaining permission slips for each trip. Busy parents will also benefit from this timesaving method.

27-7 A field trip file provides at a glance information about community field trip sites.

Before the trip, plan your "trip bag." It should include the essential supplies that you will need to take along. Paper tissues, a first-aid kit, premoistened towelettes, a garbage bag, emergency telephone numbers, and coins for phone calls are a must. Many centers also require that you take a folder with copies of emergency forms and signed permission slips. Depending on the length of the trip and the weather, you may want to take snacks and refreshments for the children. For young children, extra clothing might be a consideration in case of toileting accidents, spills, etc.

In hot weather, children often become thirsty. Make sure water or some other nutritious drink is on hand. Insulated jugs are a good way to transport liquids.

Field trips involve added safety risks and responsibilities for child care centers. Before taking field trips, teach the children pedestrian safety. Teachable moments may include short walks near the center. Before leaving the center for a walk, explain the rules the children must follow when crossing streets. When approaching a crosswalk, review these rules with the children. Be sure to observe traffic signals when crossing intersections. Make sure that you consistently

**Brown's Child Care
Field Trip Permission Form**

Child's Name _____ Date _____

Parent(s) Name _____ Business Phone _____

_____ Business Phone _____

Home Address _____ Home Phone _____

In consideration of _____ s

(child's name)

acceptance as an enrollee in Brown's Child Care Center, I hereby give permission for my child to participate in any walks or field trips planned and supervised by the staff. I understand that various modes of transportation may be used for these trips.

_____   _____
(Parent's Signature)   (Date)

27-8 Permission slips from parents, such as this one, are a necessity when planning a field trip.

enforce and follow the rules yourself. This is important since children learn by experience and imitation.

Suitability

Before choosing a trip, ask yourself "How appropriate is this trip for the children?" Consider the developmental level of the children. For five-year-olds, a trip to a television studio may be both fun and educational. This same trip would not be appropriate for two-year-olds. Two-year-olds are more interested in those things closer to their immediate surroundings. For example, pets, animals, babies, mothers, daddies, and grandparents are topics that capture the interest of two-year-olds.

Field trips for children from birth to 24 months are often simple walks around the neighborhood. For safety purposes, use strollers for these children. Many centers purchase special strollers that hold up to six children. This allows one teacher to handle several children at one time.

When planning field trips for young children, avoid crowds. Crowds may be overwhelming to some children. It is also difficult to watch children in a crowded setting. Trips to the zoo and the circus usually involve large groups of people. In these cases, during your pretrip ask what days are least crowded. When crowds cannot be avoided, ask for help from parents and other volunteers.

Choose trips that provide learning through participation. Children enjoy touching and doing things. When planning a trip to a farm, ask if the children can pet the animals, assist in milking the cows, and help collect the eggs, 27-9. Likewise, a trip to a apple orchard could provide children with opportunities to pick and taste apples.

Cost

When planning a field trip, always figure the costs. This helps you decide if the trip is the best use of your resources. You may feel that the cost of chartering a bus to the zoo is more than your budget allows. You may decide that the money needed for chartering a bus could be more wisely spent on classroom materials. If most of the children have already had this experience, you may want to use the money for some less costly trips. This would give the children new experiences.

Most field trips involve little or no expense, particularly if the site is within walking distance. In some cases, the only costs are admission

and/or transportation. If there is an admission fee, call in advance and ask if group rates are available for child care centers. At times, you may get a generous discount or free admission.

Transportation

Costs for transportation vary greatly, depending on the type used, 27-10. For centers that own their own vans, the costs of most field trips are minimal. To cut costs, some centers ask parents and teachers to drive their own cars. This type of arrangement is not recommended. In case of an accident, legal problems could arise, and the driver and/or center could be sued for damages.

Public transportation, such as the city bus or subway, is often less costly than a chartered bus. However, there are disadvantages to public transportation. Trains can be crowded and noisy. This can be stressful for children. There is also the danger of children being hurt or lost during the course of the trip. Accidents often happen as children enter or exit buses or trains. This is why some teachers elect not to use public transportation for their children.

If you decide to use a chartered bus, call several reputable companies. Check to see that the company meets any state safety inspection

27-9 Petting farm animals can be an enjoyable experience for children who are developmentally ready.

27-10 Children can travel to nearby field trip sites in wagons.

guidelines. Explain where you intend to go, the length of your stay, the number of passengers, and request prices. Ask them to send you the price quote in writing. After you receive all the quotes, compare to find the company that will provide the best service for the least amount of money. By thoroughly checking costs for a field trip, you can get the most for your resources.

Scheduling

Midmornings are the best time to schedule field trips. This time of day works best for several reasons. First, children are usually well rested. They often find it easier to listen, observe, and follow instructions. Second, children arrive at different times during the morning. Some parents may bring their children to the center at 7 a.m. Others may not bring their children until 8 or 9 a.m. If you schedule the trip too early, some children would be deprived of the experience. Also in colder climates, early morning temperatures can be too cool for children. This is a key consideration for trips that require walking.

Afternoon field trips are also difficult to plan. Most preschool children need to take a nap at this time. Also, children may be deprived of the trip if their parents pick them up early in the afternoon.

Field trips should begin after a quiet activity. This helps children avoid excess excitement or overstimulation during the trip. Over-stimulated children are very active and difficult to manage.

One question often asked is, "What is the best day for a field trip?" The answer to this question depends on the group and attendance. First, study the behavior and routine of the group. Some groups are always tired and restless by Friday. You may want to choose a day early in the week for such a group. Monday may not be a good day, depending on the program. The children may be tired as a result of weekend activities. Second, consider the days children attend. Some children may be deprived of trips if they are always scheduled for a day they do not attend.

The right day for a field trip may also depend on the site. If the trip requires formal arrangements to be made, ask the contact person to suggest a day. Many resource people prefer a midweek day. This allows time to prepare for the visit.

Carefully plan around the children's needs, children's schedules, and resource person's schedules. This takes time. However, a well-planned field trip produces the greatest amount of learning and pleasure for the children.

Adult-Child Ratio

To ensure safety and the success of the trip, provide enough chaperons. The best adult-child ratio is based on the number of children in the group, the nature of the field trip, and the dangers involved, 27-11. Walks around the neighborhood can often be handled by the center staff. More adults may be needed for trips using public transportation or for visits to places with potential dangers.

For most field trips, a ratio of one teacher for every four to six children is sufficient. This allows for close supervision and communication. Whenever possible, provide the lowest adult/child ratio as possible to promote safety. For two-year-olds, it is recommended that there be one adult for every two children. An adult should be assigned to every four three-year-olds, five four-year-olds, and six five-year-olds for optimal safety. However, if some children need to be closely watched, this ratio should be adjusted. Many times, children are grouped based on their temperaments. For instance, if Sam and Frank

27-11 Field trips can have many hidden dangers. For this reason, extra adult supervision is required.

behave badly when together, they should be separated. Place them in different groups. If there is a child who has a difficult time following rules, you may assign the child to one adult. Often, an "extra" adult is recruited who is not assigned any specific children. This adult is used when a teacher needs to handle emergencies or children who need a one-to-one contact.

When more adults are needed for field trips, parents may be contacted. Many programs maintain lists of parents and other volunteers interested in helping on field trips. When the need arises, give these people from one to several week's notice. Some parent volunteers may have to make special arrangements at work. Prior to the trip, provide the volunteers with information regarding the trip. Time of departure, arrival at the site, length of stay at the site, planned events at the site, and arrival time back at the center should be included. In addition, volunteers should be told the behavioral expectations.

Behavioral Expectations

Behavioral expectations need to be planned and discussed with children before the trip. Trip rules that the children are expected to follow will vary with the children and nature of the trip.

Some rules may apply to all trips. Regardless of the type of trip, rules are most often the same in most early childhood programs.

For best results, state all rules in a positive way. Tell the children exactly what they are expected to do. For example, tell the children to place their hands at their sides when they are in a store.

The first rule for field trips is that the children must wear their name tag at all times. Name tags should be durable so that they can be reused. They should be worn on all field trips. The child's name, school name, and school telephone number should be on the tag. This information is helpful in case a child wanders from the group. Some centers only print the school's name and telephone number on the children's name tag. This is often used as a measure of protection against abduction.

The second rule for field trips is that children speak softly. To ensure this, teachers need to set a good example. Speak in a low-key voice to avoid overstimulation.

The third rule is that the children must remain with their assigned group and adult supervisor on field trips. Then each adult will know the names of the children they are responsible for supervising, 27-12.

27-12 Correct trip behavior includes staying with adult supervisors.

Many teachers prefer to have children follow the "hold-your-partner's-hand" rule. However, this rule is not always useful. It is unfair to interested children to have partners whose attention is not focused on the learning experience. Also, constant physical contact can result in stress for some children.

Instead of holding hands children can hold on to a rope to keep them together as a group. To make this rope, purchase several 20-foot pieces of rope. With each piece of rope, loop and tie handles at 2-foot intervals. Show the children how to hold on to the handles and explain expectations during the trip.

Educational Goals

For the most benefit on a field trip, educational goals must be carefully planned. For example, a trip to a local service station may have a number of goals:

- to observe mechanics at work
- to learn about the care of cars
- to see how machinery works
- to learn vocabulary words: technicians, gas pump, nozzle, and hoist

During the pretrip visit, these goals need to be discussed with the resource person.

Children's Preparation

Preparation for children may begin a few days before the trip. Introduce the trip by putting up displays, reading a book, sharing a video, looking at the pictures, or simply talking about the trip.

On the day of the trip, tell children what to observe (educational goals) and how to behave (behavioral expectations). Give a name tag to each child. Assign children to their adult guides. After this, encourage children to use the bathroom. Explain that a bathroom is not always available on walks or some field trips.

Parent Preparation

Parents should always be informed in advance of field trips. A newsletter, calendar, or notice posted on a bulletin board or classroom door are all useful methods, 27-13. Inform the parents of the date, location, address, and exact times you will be leaving and returning. This will help parents plan their schedules for dropping off and picking up the children.

Before leaving, post a sign on the classroom door. Note where you have gone and when you will return. This will also serve as a trip reminder for the parents and center staff.

Field trip
to
Perkin's Pumpkin Farm
23 Half-day Road
Streamwood

Tuesday, September 23
We will leave the center at 10:00 am.
We will return to the center at noon.

27-13 Placing this notice on a center bulletin board helps remind parents of an upcoming field trip.

Share trip goals with children's parents. This information may help them plan related home experiences such as discussions and books that compliment the trip.

Follow-Up Activities

To help children clarify their learning, plan follow-up activities, 27-14. Once you return to the center, talk about what they saw and did. Plan an activity that reinforces the learning that occurred on the trip.

Recall the classroom scene after the trip to the apple orchard. Apples were discussed at lunch. Then the experience was used as a basis for writing a story. After a trip to a bakery, children could bake bread or cookies. Ice cream or butter could be made after a trip to a local dairy. See 27-15.

27-14 After a trip to an ice cream parlor, the children signed this thank-you note.

Follow-Up Activities	
Trip	**Activities**
Apple orchard	• Taste a variety of apples. • Make applesauce or apple muffins. • Read stories about apple orchards. • Serve apple butter, baked apples, or some other form of apple.
Fire station	• Place puzzles and stories related to the role of firefighters in the classroom. • Read stories about firefighters. • Place firefighters clothing in the dramatic play area. • Act out fire safety procedures.
Print shop	• Provide rubber stamps, ink pads, and paper on which to print. • Place a typewriter or computer in the classroom. • Make games using alphabet letters.
Hair salon	• Provide a prop box containing hair rollers, combs, brushes, towels, and a hair dryer with the cord removed. • Place dolls with hair and combs in the dramatic play area. • Hang up a mirror and have children compare the ways they wear their hair.

27-15 Follow-up activities based on field trips can be simple or complex.

Summary

Field trips can be a useful learning experience for children. Through field trips, children gain firsthand knowledge of the world around them. This learning can involve new experiences or enhance previous knowledge.

Field trips require planning. Children must be prepared for the experience. Their preparation includes pretrip talks and activities, rules to follow, and discussions.

The teacher must also be prepared. This preparation includes selecting a trip, taking a pretrip, setting goals, obtaining permission from parents, and arranging transportation. After the trip, thank-you notes should be sent to helpful individuals. Follow-up activities will also reinforce the value of the experience.

Review and Reflect

1. List four benefits children experience from field trips.

2. For young children, first field trips should be _____.
   A. long and unique
   B. short and nonthreatening
   C. at unfamiliar places
   D. None of the above.

3. True or false. The location of the site and the budget are two factors that affect what field trips you will select.

4. True or false. For best results, focus on many topics during a theme walk.

5. How should resource people be selected?

6. List four opportunities a teacher is given by conducting a pretrip.

7. When planning field trips for young children, avoid _____.
   A. crowds
   B. hands-on activities
   C. age-appropriate activities
   D. All of the above.

8. What are the disadvantages of using public transportation to reach your field trip site?

9. Explain how to determine what the best day for a field trip would be.

10. True or false. More adults may be needed for field trips using public transportation or for visits to places with potential dangers.

11. List three basic rules for field trips involving young children.

12. What is the purpose of follow-up activities?

Apply and Explore

1. Start a file of ideas for field trips that could be taken by young children in your community.

2. Compile a list of safety guidelines that should be followed on all field trips.

3. Make a list of follow-up activities for a field trip to a hair salon.

4. Invite a center director to speak to your group about successful field trips he or she has conducted.

5. Plan a field trip for your class. Go through the same steps that you would for a group of young children.

Infants and toddlers learn new skills quickly.

Part 5

Other People You Will Meet

Most early childhood programs are geared toward preschoolers. However, you may choose to work with younger children (infants and toddlers), school-age children, or children with special needs. In this part, you will discover what special qualities are needed by teachers in infant-toddler programs and school-age programs. You will learn special techniques for providing care and learning experiences for these children. This part also introduces you to the teaching concerns of children with special needs. You will understand how such needs as speech disorders, health disorders, and giftedness may affect your role as a teacher.

Parents are very much involved with the care and guidance of their young children. You will want to keep them informed of everything that is happening at the center. Parent involvement can be the key factor in the success of a program.

A world of career possibilities is open to early childhood teachers. It's up to you to choose a career path that fits your goals and to find a job that will start you on your path. This part will help prepare you for your job hunt. You will read about how to prepare a resume and find available positions. You will also discover ways to make the best impression possible in an interview and land the job you really want.

The infancy and toddler stages are a time of exploration and discovery.

Chapter 28

Programs for Infants and Toddlers

After studying this chapter, you will be able to

- list the characteristics of a nurturing infant-toddler caregiver.
- state guidelines for proper infant-toddler care.
- design functional and developmentally appropriate infant and toddler environments.
- handle the routines of infants and toddlers.
- select toys that are safe and developmentally appropriate for infants and toddlers.
- plan the curriculum for infants and toddlers.
- maintain the environment to prevent illness.

Term to Know

overfamiliarity

Ian is learning to walk. Hector has just said his first words and Ponueh has just begun exploring books. Working with infants and toddlers can be exciting and rewarding, 28-1. This is a unique and challenging stage in the life cycle.

28-1 Infants and toddlers depend a great deal on adults as they learn about the world around them.

The development of children from birth to age three is more rapid than any other period in life. For young children, it is a time of wonder and discovery.

As an infant or toddler caregiver, you will take pride in these children's achievements. You will marvel with them as they learn to crawl or take a few steps. You will be delighted when they learn to play peek-a-boo with you. All events are major accomplishments for very young children. They learn so fast and are so eager to learn new skills.

Characteristics of Infant and Toddler Caregivers

As an infant-toddler caregiver, your behavior will influence the behavior of the children. Children will react based on the ways you treat them. If you are warm and loving, the children will be warm and loving. Touch, smile, make eye contact, and speak affectionately to the children. Cuddle them, rock them, sing to them, and play with them. Likewise, be patient and accepting while working with them. Infants and toddlers need responsive caregivers. Trust, confidence, and self-esteem are promoted through caregiver responsiveness.

Young children are dependent on consistent relationships with their caregivers. You must have energy, be healthy, and enjoy children. You must always be readily available to comfort and protect the children. You must also be able to handle many situations and understand feelings. Part of your responsibility includes helping children express feelings such as joy, love, anger, satisfaction, and sadness.

Infants and toddlers need caregivers who provide consistent guidance. To provide this consistent environment, all center staff must agree on what is accepted behavior. In most cases, having only a few rules for children increases the chances that rules will be consistently followed.

Finally, you need to be aware of new research in the infant-toddler field. Read professional journals, books, and articles. Attend professional workshops and conferences. Another way to stay informed is to discuss your observations and needs with other infant-toddler caregivers.

Guidelines for Infant-Toddler Care

In order to provide a quality infant-toddler program, consider the following general guidelines:

- Provide the children with a safe and healthy environment, 28-2.
- Develop trusting relationships with the children and their families.
- Respect the cultures represented by the children and their families.
- Design a curriculum to meet the unique needs of each child.
- Care for each child affectionately.
- Respond to children's distress or discomfort signals immediately.
- Follow a consistent routine in providing for children's needs.
- Encourage curiosity by providing opportunities for the children to explore.
- Help children develop trust, respect, and a positive regard for their world.
- Avoid overstimulation. Too many new experiences at one time can overwhelm young children, particularly infants.
- Plan experiences so young children learn to master new skills.

28-2 Toddlers can be very curious. For their safety, keep all poisonous materials well out of their reach in a locked cabinet.

Infant Environments

Providing a quality infant environment cannot be left to chance. Such an environment should be attractive and comfortable for infants as well as caregivers. Environments for infants should address their daily routines. Areas for feeding, diapering, cuddling with a caregiver, sleeping, and playing should all be included.

The most convenient feeding area is near the entrance to the center. Parents arriving with baby food and bottles can place these items in the refrigerator at once. This area should be equipped with high chairs, feeding tables, a heat source, and comfortable, adult-sized chairs. A bulletin board can be placed in this area to post feeding charts and records. The floor surface must be washable.

The diapering area should be located next to a sink. As in the feeding area, the floor surface needs to be washable. This allows for easy cleaning and disinfecting. To prevent back strain for adults, changing surfaces and storage areas should be waist high. Place a mirror on the wall next to the changing surface so children can look at themselves. A bulletin board hung nearby can be used to post records of children's elimination patterns.

The sleeping area usually uses the most space because cribs take a large amount of floor space. The ideal location for this area is joining the diapering area. Do not worry about light. Infants do not need a dark room in which to sleep. However, a dimmer switch can be installed in this area to control lights used in the diapering area.

Crawling babies need their own play area. They need to be safely out of the way of older children. To ensure safety, use low dividers to make a crawling area. A short pile carpeting should be on the floor for comfort and warmth.

Toddler Environments

Balancing safety and health concerns is important in designing spaces for toddlers. Toddlers need more open areas than infants. When they are not sleeping, they are usually moving. Toddlers' needs can be met in several areas. Included are receiving, playing, napping, diapering, and eating areas. (Napping, diapering, and eating areas for infants can be shared by toddlers.)

The receiving area should be located near the main entrance. This area should contain a bulletin board for parent information and lockers or hooks to hold children's clothing. When standing in the receiving area, you should be able to have a clear view of all other areas, especially the play area. Provide interesting equipment in the room to encourage children to play and help prevent separation anxiety.

Toddlers need a play area that allows them to move freely, 28-3. To provide this, leave one-third to one-half of the total space open. In crowded areas, some children may find it hard to play. As a result, they are more inclined to cry and fight. If adequate space is not provided, the children will bump into each other.

Although a tile floor is easier to maintain, some teachers prefer a carpeted floor in the play

28-3 As children become mobile, their need for play space increases.

area. Carpeting has two advantages. First, it provides a cushion for falls. Second, it is warmer for crawling children. If carpeting is used, it should have a tight weave and be washable.

In a section of the play area, there should be equipment that encourages toddlers' rapidly changing physical skills. Open areas and equipment for crawling, walking, and climbing should be available. Scaled slides and tunnels are two types of equipment that invite exploration and climbing, as well as·carpeted platforms and low shelves. Cardboard boxes can also be fun for toddlers. Equipment should be arranged so all areas can be seen by the caregiver.

The outdoor play area should connect to the indoor play area. This outdoor area should have a large, grassy area for running and crawling. Grass, like carpeting, helps cushion falls.

Caring for Infants and Toddlers

As you work with infants and toddlers, you will notice each child has his or her own rhythm. Some will go about their routines quickly. Others move slowly. As a caregiver, you must adjust your own rhythm to each child's rhythm.

All infants and toddlers, regardless of their differences, require their needs to be met promptly if they are to learn trust. A child who has been promptly and properly cared for is likely to be happy. To provide this attention to needs, you must provide consistent care. Through this care, children learn that they are special persons and develop trust.

Crying As a Means of Communication

Infants often communicate by crying. They may cry to express needs, cope with frustration, or get attention. They may also cry when they feel lonely, uncomfortable, or neglected. Regardless of the reason, you should never ignore crying. Always remember that the crying has some meaning for the child.

Studies support the theory that an infant's crying should always be given prompt attention. According to these studies, when cries are answered promptly, the frequency of the crying will be reduced.

You will observe that babies have individual differences in their crying behaviors. Some babies cry more often and with greater strength. Other babies may seldom cry. All babies have various reasons for crying.

As a caregiver, you will have to learn the meaning of each child's cries. By listening to how a baby cries, you will soon learn his or her needs. A short and low-pitched cry usually means the baby is hungry. A loud and sudden high-pitched shriek followed by a flat wail is a distress cry. Sometimes the types of cries overlap. For instance, a baby may wake up hungry and will cry for food. If you do not quickly respond to this need, the baby may then cry with rage. You will also learn which cries indicate fussiness, soiled diapers, boredom, or discomfort related to being too cool or warm.

Always respond to a child's crying by first trying to solve the problem. If the baby is wet, change him or her. Likewise, if the child is hungry, feed him or her. If you cannot find an obvious reason for the child's crying, check the baby's daily care record. (This record is described later in the chapter.) Perhaps the baby is sleepy, teething, reacting to medication, or catching a cold.

Tired, crying babies can be comforted in a number of ways. Some enjoy being held; others love to be rocked. Often a child can be quieted simply by speaking or singing softly to him or her.

Separation Anxiety

Between nine to twelve months of age, some children will have difficulty separating from their parents. You may find that children experiencing this anxiety will cry each day when their parents leave them at the center. This is called separation anxiety. It is a sign that a child is learning and developing a special relationship with an individual, 28-4.

Parents may also have difficulty leaving children who feel separation anxiety. They do not enjoy seeing their children in distress. Some parents may even feel guilty for leaving their children. Other parents may unfavorably compare their children to those who are not crying.

28-4 Between the ages of nine and twelve months, many infants become aware of their parents and their need for parents. At this time, separation anxiety can occur.

When a child shows anxiety over separation, reassure the parent that this is normal behavior. Explain that the behavior may go on for several days or, in some cases, several weeks. During this time, it is important to relay any progress to the parents on a daily basis. This information may make the parents feel more comfortable and less guilty about leaving the child.

Whenever possible, allow infants and toddlers to visit the center with their parents before they enroll. This may help reduce some distress.

If time permits, children can stay a short time at the center the first day, perhaps an hour or two. Gradually the stay can be increased. It takes children about three to five weeks of regular attendance to adjust to the new setting.

Until the child adjusts, your support, patience, and understanding are required. You

will notice that the infant or toddler may react to strangers, sudden movements, noise, and strange objects. To help support the child, let him or her explore at his or her own pace. Meanwhile, gradually expose the child to new objects in the center.

Handling Routines

With infants and toddlers, routines make up much more of the day than routines do with preschoolers. It is important that daily routines be predictable. This will help the children gain a sense of security. It will also help them know what to expect and the sequence of activities. Much of your day will be spent feeding, taking care of diapering and toileting needs, and preparing for nap time. See 28-5.

It is important to coordinate home and center schedules for infants. To do this, parents

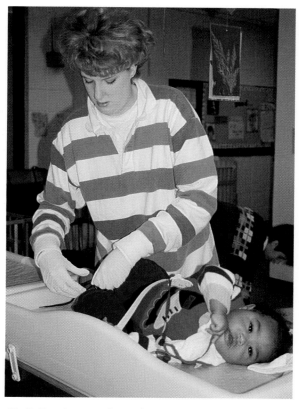

28-5 Routines such as diapering are an important part of caring for infants.

need to provide you with information daily. One effective method is to provide parents with a daily record to complete when they arrive each morning with their infants. Likewise, the caregiver also needs to record the infants' eating and elimination patterns during the day. Nap information and activities for the day can also be included. See Chart 28-6 for an example of an infant daily record.

Feeding Infants

The life of an infant consists of little more than sleeping and eating. Nutrition is very important at this stage of development. To provide properly for the infant, talk to the parents. Ask them to provide you information on their child's diet, diet changes, and feeding schedule. Many infants are on special diets. You may also find that some mothers may wish to come to the

---

New Horizon Infant Daily Record

Infant's name: _____

Day/Date: _____

Parent's signature: _____

Parent's name: _____

Time of arrival: _____

Time of departure: _____

(filled in by parent)

(filled in by staff member)

Baby seems: ❑ Fine (acting as usual)
             ❑ Bit fussy
             ❑ Not well (not acting as usual)

Baby slept: ❑ Soundly
             ❑ Woke up several times
             ❑ Did not sleep well

Baby ate: Amount   Time
❑ Ate breakfast before coming   _____   _____
❑ Took bottle before coming   _____   _____
❑ Took food before coming   _____   _____
❑ Took nothing this morning

Bowel movement: _____ Frequency
                _____ Consistency

Diet change for today: _____
_____

Special instructions: _____
_____

Prescribed medication: _____
_____

Medication last given at: _____
_____

Bottles: _____
         _____
         _____

Breakfast: _____
Time: _____
_____ _____

Lunch: _____
Time: _____
_____ _____

Snack: _____
Time: _____
_____ _____

Bowel movement number: _____
❑ Regular   ❑ Irregular

Number of wet diapers: _____

Nap time   _____ _____
                _____ _____

Medication given at: _____
_____

Look what I did today: _____
_____
_____

28-6 An infant daily record can help to coordinate home and center schedules.

center to breast-feed their infants. If this request is made at your center, provide the mothers with a quiet and comfortable place.

Just as important as the type of food is how the infant is fed. Most infants will need to be bottle-fed. In a good infant-toddler program, each infant is constantly cared for by one caregiver. This allows for one-on-one attention and physical closeness. The assigned caregiver should feed infants leisurely while holding and cuddling the infant. This will help form a bond between child and caregiver.

Infants vary in the amount and frequency of feedings. Some infants will drink only four ounces of milk at a feeding, while others will drink eight ounces. Some infants will need to drink every four hours, while others will demand food every two hours. Each of these infants' needs should be met. Infants should be fed when hungry, not when it is convenient for the caregiver.

Feeding Toddlers

Children's hand washing is important before and after eating. Many toddlers crawl on the floor and later use their hands to feed themselves. Before eating, always wash toddlers' hands, 28-7. If child-sized sinks are not available, use a small pan of water at the table. In the beginning, you

28-7 Older toddlers can sometimes wash their hands themselves.

may have to assist the children in swishing their hands as well as wiping them on a paper towel or cloth. You may want to apply a small amount of liquid soap to a dampened towel and wipe the child's hands. Rinse the hands with a clean towel moistened with water. Finally, wipe the child's hands with a dry paper towel.

Whenever possible, toddlers should be served finger foods. These are easy for children to handle. Always provide many sizes and shapes so children can practice picking them up. Examples include cubes of raw apple, cooked green peas, raisins, chopped cooked eggs, banana pieces, and soft cheese.

For feeding, toddlers can be seated in high chairs, at eating tables, or on low chairs placed in front of a low table. They will need some table space on which to move their food. Children of this age love to explore their food. Before eating, toddlers may smell, touch, and push around their food. This behavior should be encouraged. Exploring food can give children important sensory experiences that foster cognitive growth.

Diapering and Toileting

Changing diapers is a routine that a caregiver of infants and toddlers will repeat many times each day. For this reason, it should be a pleasant experience. Give the child all your attention. Look into his or her eyes. Smile, sing, and talk softly to the child. Stroke the child's hair. Diapering can be a time for personal interaction.

A diaper-checking routine is a useful policy to follow. To protect against serious rashes, and possibly infections, infants need frequent changes. Most newborns use about 10 diapers a day. A chart to record diaper changes should be hung in the changing area. If infants are sleeping, do not waken them. In addition to half-hour checks, infants should always be checked just before eating and sleeping.

Do not be shocked if, as a child grows older, he or she objects to having a diaper changed. Many times this objection occurs because the child is having fun playing and does not want to be interrupted. When this occurs, there is no harm in waiting a few minutes. Wait until the child finishes with an activity, and then gently guide him or her to the changing area. Many times this transition is easier if the child is allowed to carry a toy into the changing area.

If a child has a diaper rash, it is important to change the diaper right away when it is soiled. Always report any noticeable rash to the parents on the day it is noticed. Ask them if there is any ointment they prefer. If they prefer a certain brand, ask them to supply you with a tube. In some cases, parents may ask for your advice.

When diapering a child, certain steps should always be followed by all staff. First, always wash your hands with soap and water before and after diapering. Proper hand washing before and after diapering helps prevent the spread of disease. Therefore, all new staff should learn the proper procedures, 28-8. Included should be the choice of soap as well as step-by-step directions for cleaning the hands.

Liquid soap should be used because bar soaps, when wet and jellylike, harbor microorganisms. You will probably find that a soap dispenser is most convenient. Remember, though, that microorganisms may also grow in liquid soap. Therefore, clean the dispenser each time it is refilled.

If you have cracks in the skin of your hands, wear lightweight, disposable rubber gloves when changing diapers to avoid infection. Medical experts agree that it is nearly impossible to prevent microorganisms from growing in cracks within the skin.

After each change, spray the diapering table or changing mat with a disinfectant solution.

Sanitation Procedures for Diapering

1. Dispense enough liquid soap to provide a good lather.
2. Add a small amount of water and rub back and forth, providing friction.
3. Work up a good lather.
4. Rinse hands.
5. Use paper towels or an elbow to turn off the faucet and dry hands.
6. Diaper baby.
7. Examine the area under your nails for dirt. Remove any dirt with an orange stick.
8. Wash hands again using steps 1 through 5.
9. Apply lotion to hands to prevent chapping.

28-8 Proper hand washing is vital to preventing the spread of disease from diapering.

Wash your hands. Then record information on the diapering chart located near the changing table. The time of the change and whether the child urinated and/or had a bowel movement all need to be noted. If the child had diarrhea, this should be noted along with the amount, color, and consistency. Any evidence of a diaper rash also needs to be recorded. At pick-up time, each parent should be given their child's daily chart.

Some toddlers may be in the process of or showing an interest in toilet training. For these children, it is important that the home and center coordinate their efforts. Discuss with the parents the toilet-training process. Explain that it will be an easier process for the child if the home and center routines are consistent.

Like diapering, toileting policies must be used for health purposes. After each use, the seat of the potty chair needs to be sprayed with a disinfectant solution and wiped. The container under the chair must be emptied and rinsed with the solution. Finally, you will need to wash your hands with warm water and soap.

Nap Time

All children need a certain amount of sleep. This amount varies from one child to another. Newborns sleep 16 to 17 hours a day. Most infants need at least two naps a day ranging from one to three hours. Without adequate sleep, a child can become cranky and difficult to handle. When this happens, other children in the center can become disruptive.

One consideration for planning a nap time schedule is to check parents' preferences. Some parents keep their infants up late and wake them early in the morning. They want their child to sleep at the center so he or she is awake and alert at the end of the day. Other parents, who may have to travel some distance to get home, prefer to have a sleepy baby at the end of the day. Their goal is to have the baby sleep on the way home.

Nap times may have to be staggered to meet the individual needs of the children. This type of scheduling will allow you time to feed and rock each child to sleep. Often this will require meshing individual needs with group needs. Once a schedule has been developed that fits individual needs, it is necessary to be consistent.

Toys for Infants and Toddlers

To meet the special needs of infants and toddlers, appropriate equipment is needed. Toys serve as sensory stimuli for young children, 28-9. For instance, by positioning an infant's toys, you can create an incentive for the child to use his or her memory or locomotive abilities. Even during the first few weeks of life, an infant can touch, see, and hear. As the child exercises these abilities, physical and mental development are fostered.

Toddlers need a range of equipment from soft blocks to puzzles. To promote language skills, include picture books, story books, audiotapes, dramatic play props, and puppets. The audiotapes can be used to promote music and movement. Sensory materials, including nontoxic crayons, markers, and play dough, should also be available.

When planning environments for toddlers, balance is important. You need to provide a sufficient quantity and variety of toys to encourage exploration. However, you must guard against overstimulation. Too many choices can overwhelm the children.

28-9 Children's senses of sight, touch, and hearing are stimulated by many toys.

Many infant-toddler centers maintain a toy inventory that lists all the equipment available in the center. The inventory is subdivided into developmental sequences. See 28-10 for a sample toy inventory. This list is quite helpful when planning activities for children. Since it is important to frequently change toys, the list will help you keep a record of the toys already used and toys that are available. Another advantage of keeping a toy inventory is that it is helpful when ordering new toys.

Safety Issues

When choosing toys for the infant or toddler, safety is the number one consideration. Check each piece carefully for sharp edges or points. To avoid splinters, all wooden toys should be sanded smoothly. Small toys or toys with small parts should be avoided. Objects smaller than 2½ inches in depth and 2 inches in diameter could be swallowed or cause choking.

Each year many infants and toddlers accidentally swallow small toys or parts. This can cause suffocation from choking on the object. Also, a child may develop intestinal or respiratory problems as a result of swallowing a small toy. Unfortunately, most plastic toys do not show up on X rays. Toy companies, therefore, are now adding a special plastic to children's toys. This plastic is known as *nontoxic radiopaque plastic*. Toys made with this material will show up clearly on an X ray. When you choose toys, check to see if this material is included on the label or package.

Appropriate Toys for Infants

Mobiles make excellent first toys for infants. They provide visual appeal and require a minimum of physical interaction. Select mobiles carefully. Avoid mobiles that are not sturdy. If your center has such mobiles, hang them out of reach. For the young infant, place toys 7 to 24 inches from the eyes.

Between 1½ and 3½ months of age, infants will discover their hands. The hands then become a toy for the child. Infants will study their hands as they move them back and forth. Infants between three and six months of age will continue to watch their hands. Even when infants

Infant-Toddler Center Toy Inventory

Looking
- dog mobile
- farm animal mobile
- shape mobile
- metal mirror
- books

Reaching and Grasping
- ring cradle gym
- musical cradle gym
- colored cradle gym
- colored rattles
- frog rattle
- car rattle

Cuddling Toys
- monkey
- black bear
- baby lamb (with chime)
- pink pig
- brown pony
- black puppy
- dolls

Squeezing/Manipulation
- fish squeaker
- pretzel squeaker

- mouse squeaker
- bunny squeaker
- pig squeaker
- busy box
- plastic rings
- plastic rattles (various colors)
- snap beads
- chain of plastic discs

Kicking and Hitting
- large rubber beach balls
- colored foam balls
- bouncing clowns

Pull/Push
- popper
- wooden train (makes a noise)
- wooden dog
- lawnmower
- wooden car
- wooden wagon

Sound
- music box
- drum
- jingle bells
- tape player and tapes

- xylophone
- squeaky animals

Large Motor
- rubber balls
- push toys
- animals on wheels
- small, light wagon
- wheeled train
- wheeled lamb
- climbing tunnel
- small gym
- toy trucks big enough to ride
- plastic blocks

Small Motor
- geometric form board
- blocks
- snap beads
- small cards
- nesting cups and boxes
- shape sorting box
- strings of large beads
- sand toys
- stacking rings
- puzzles

28-10 A toy inventory is useful for planning and buying.

move objects to their mouths, they will continue watching.

Smiles begin to appear at about two months of age. Infants at this age also want to touch what they see. To provide stimulation for the child, place a mirror over the changing table. You will find it fun to watch the child smile at his or her reflections in the mirror.

Soon, infants begin touching objects within their reach. This behavior usually occurs between three and six months of age. As they do this, they gain information about the world and develop intelligence. Provide a variety of toys for the children to touch. These may include soft rattles and stuffed, furry animals.

To provide grasping exercise, infants need a variety of toys within reach, whether in the playpen, in the crib, or on the floor. Since the child is likely to place these toys in his or her mouth, choose only safe toys, 28-11. By placing objects in the mouth, babies learn about objects.

28-11 Large, thick books are best for infants because they like to explore with their mouths.

Studies show that between six and ten months of age, nerve endings in an infant's mouth are very sensitive.

Rattles are important for the infant's development. When a rattle is handed to an infant, he or she goes through a specific process. The first step is to locate the toy with the eyes. After this is done, the child will move his or her hand toward the rattle. Just before contact, the infant's hand will open. In this process the child will be persistent. He or she will repeatedly try to pick up a small toy.

Observations have shown that infants follow a progression of hand movement skills. First, there are raking motions which appear to be somewhat random. Next, scissor motions are made. The child uses the whole hand to pick up an object. Finally, the child develops the pincer pick-up. Using this method, the infant is able to pick up objects using only the forefinger and thumb. A child using this method will usually shape the hand into the grasp before reaching for the intended object.

Toys will encourage the development of all these hand movement skills. A variety of toys such as cradle gyms can be used to encourage raking motions. Scissor motions can be encouraged by providing small balls or figures that will fit into the hand. Finger foods, such as dry, ready-to-eat cereal, can be used to practice the pincer pick-up.

As the child develops, he or she begins to experiment with cause and effect. Up to this time, the infant has been more interested in watching the hands than the objects that were touched. By five to eight months, the child is more intent on watching the effects of his or her actions.

Around this age, the child will enjoy dropping objects. He or she will often drop objects, including silverware and toys, from the high chair or feeding table. As the child does this, he or she will watch for the consequences of the actions. As the toy hits the floor, the infant may wince at the sound it makes.

At about the same time the child begins to enjoy dropping objects, he or she will become interested in simple gadgets in the environment. Electrical receptacles appear to be appealing. For safety purposes, it is important that these all be capped. Other appealing objects include light switches, cupboard knobs, door knobs, television knobs, fringe on rugs, locks, and any other small objects within their reach, 28-12. The manipulation of these objects gives the child a sense of magic.

Appropriate Toys for Toddlers

Once the child begins to crawl or walk, he or she will want to continually explore the environment. To encourage this curiosity, make the environment safe. Maintain large, open areas where the child can pull or push toys, straddle large trucks, or roll large balls.

Toddlers love to climb. To meet their large muscle needs, provide them with small slides, jungle gyms, and sets of stairs. Make sure that you closely watch toddlers when they use the large muscle equipment. Some children may try to walk up the slide. When this happens, you need to take their hand and direct them back to the stairs. Once they learn how to use the equipment, it is not uncommon for children of this age to use the equipment over and over again. As they explore, they are growing physically and cognitively.

Small wagons, wheelbarrows, doll buggies, and strollers also appeal to toddlers. If you lack indoor space, limit the use of these toys to an outdoor area.

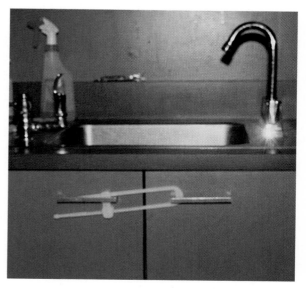

28-12 All accessible cabinet doors need to be equipped with a safety lock when toddlers are near.

Toddlers love to play with water. Encourage this play by providing floating toys, spoons, sponges, and cups in a water play area. Demonstrate how to pour water, sail a floating toy, and squeeze a sponge. For interest, add color to the water.

Books are also of interest to toddlers. They enjoy stories about families, people, animals, and objects. Objects in the books should be recognizable. Toddlers love the surprise of flipping the pages in a book. Since they enjoy turning pages, select books with large pictures, thick pages that are easy to turn, and contain only a few words. Book bindings should be strong and sturdy.

Puppets also appeal to young children. Children enjoy puppets that are soft and recognizable. Puppets made of fabric, instead of plastic or rubber, are the easiest for the children to work. Before buying puppets, ask if they are washable. It is not uncommon to find a puppet floating in the water table.

The most time-consuming activity of toddlers is staring. Approximately one-fifth of their time is spent either sitting or standing and staring. They may stare at a picture, another child, a toy, or even at you. Therefore, keep the room visually stimulating.

Some children will lack interest in a particular toy. This is a sign of **overfamiliarity**. Children who are given the same toy day after day may become bored. Once they are comfortable with a particular toy, they repeat the same actions over and over again. When this happens, new skills do not develop. It is time to provide a different toy that offers new challenges.

Young children like to have a variety of toys and need opportunities to make choices. Care must be taken, however, not to include too many choices. Toddlers need to feel a sense of control. As the teacher, you should change some toys every other day.

Curriculum

A balanced curriculum is based on the needs of the children attending the center. It is also based on child growth and development principles.

Curriculum for infants or toddlers differs from that planned for older preschool children. Babies set their own goals. As the teacher, you support this growth. The curriculum consists of

simple, basic activities. It includes physical activities: being fed, cuddled, held, bathed, rocked, diapered, and taken on walks. It involves both verbal and nonverbal communication: being sung to, talked to, and listened to.

Curriculum for toddlers requires more planning. Much of their day will involve activities that promote physical, emotional, cognitive, and social growth. Most of these activities can take place in various activity areas within the center.

Activity Areas for Toddlers

A developmentally appropriate environment promotes child-directed, age-appropriate learning. It supports the children's emotional well-being and challenges their motor skills. It also stimulates their social development. Toddlers need opportunities for seeing, touching, moving, and feeling.

The layout of the classroom needs to encourage play. The middle of the room should be open since motor development is critical to toddlers' development. This area can contain portable equipment such as tunnels, bolsters, and gyms. Toddlers also need some private space where they can rest and observe. This space may be included by introducing a small loft, a tunnel, a cabinet with a door removed, or even an enclosed corner of the room. The activity areas should be placed around the outer walls of the room.

Similar activities can be grouped into centers around the room. Each center should contain equipment and materials that offer the child a choice of activities. An interesting, well-equipped room invites children to take part. Areas that can be included in a toddler program include art, sensory, small muscle, large muscle, music, and language.

When planning the activity centers, ask yourself the following questions:

- Does the center encourage active exploration?
- Are the toys developmentally appropriate?
- Is there enough room for the children to play?
- Are the materials at the children's eye level and within their reach?
- Are the heavy toys stored on the bottom shelves?

- Are the children provided choices so they can pursue their own interests?
- Are a variety of toys presented including those for solitary play and those that support cooperative play?
- Are the toys safe and checked frequently for sharp edges, loose pieces, and small parts that could be swallowed?
- Are toys rotated so the children are exposed to new toys from time to time?

Art

A center for art activities can be fun for toddlers. Plan the area to encourage freedom and creativity. Art activities provide good opportunities for promoting small muscle development. Chart 28-13 lists tips for art activities.

Finger-painting experiences are quite appealing and soothing to young toddlers. Tempera paint, shaving cream, and colored liquid soap can all be used for finger painting. As the children use these materials, they enjoy squeezing them through their fingers. During the process, they learn to sense the different feel of each one.

Older toddlers also enjoy painting. Provide a variety of brushes for this type of experience. Regular art brushes, toothbrushes, small household brushes, and sponge staining brushes may all be used. You will need to mix paint with a thickener to help prevent dripping. Bentonite, starch, or a powdered laundry detergent usually work very well.

Toddlers also enjoy scribbling. Provide a variety of marking tools. Large crayons, chalk, and nontoxic watercolor markers can be used. To help children feel some control over their movements, give younger children larger tools. As their control improves, smaller tools can be used.

According to developmental principles, large muscle development precedes small muscle development. To accommodate large muscle movements, provide large sheets of paper for children to scribble or paint on. If paper is too small, drawings or paintings will run off the paper and onto the table or floor.

Sensory

Sensory activities should stimulate many of the children's senses. Most activities involve at least seeing, hearing, and touching. Many teachers often add the sense of smell. Food flavorings and extracts that have unique scents may be added to some of the activities at the sensory table.

Chart 28-14 lists sensory materials that can be used with toddlers. Small objects that can be inhaled or swallowed should be avoided. Likewise, discourage toddlers from chewing or eating any of the sensory materials.

Small Muscle

Most small muscle activities will revolve around toys. Stacking toys, building blocks,

---

Tips for Art Activities

- Provide only nontoxic materials. Young children tend to put materials in their mouths.
- Allow plenty of space to prevent children from putting paint, chalk, or markers on each other.
- Cover the table and/or floor with a plastic cloth or newspapers to catch spills.
- Provide large plastic bibs to use as art smocks.
- Keep cloth or paper towels handy to clean children's hands as soon as they finish activities.
- Wipe spills as they occur to prevent children from slipping or getting soiled.

28-13 Plan safe, healthy art activities. Then toddlers will not need to remember a large number of rules.

Sensory Materials

- Colored and/or scented water.
- Soap bubbles.
- Small plastic boats.
- Shaving cream, plain or with drops of food coloring.
- Dry or wet sand. Shovels, strainers, and/or small wheeled trucks.
- Wet or dry oatmeal.
- Snow.
- Ice cubes.
- Musical instruments such as drums, tambourines, bells on wrist bands, and cymbals.
- Common foods with strong smells such as peanut butter, oranges, etc.

28-14 You will find that toddlers are most interested in simple, everyday objects.

sorting boxes, puzzles, stringing beads, and play dough are all safe toys that promote small muscle development in toddlers. Most of these toys will also provide toddlers with problem-solving opportunities. These toys may also provide for eye-hand coordination and visual discrimination opportunities.

Large Muscle

Large muscle activities can take many forms. These may involve indoor equipment, outdoor equipment, or simple movement. As children crawl, walk, and run, they are developing their large muscle skills.

Much space is needed for large muscle equipment, both indoors and outdoors. Plenty of free space is needed around it. Allow enough space for active use by several children.

Balls, slides, tumbling mats, pull toys, small wagons, and large blocks can all be used to promote large muscle development. The development of the children's large muscles can also be promoted by having them run, crawl, or even chase bubbles outdoors.

Music

Young children love music. Background music from a tape or CD player is quite enjoyable and soothing for many toddlers. Some toddlers will even move to the music. If they do not, you may want to dance with them. The toddlers may also enjoy hitting drums with their hands or clapping their hands.

Language

Although planned activities are not required, you should be encouraging language growth at all times. During play, speak to the children. Encourage them to respond. Avoid using baby talk with toddlers. Young children will often mimic your speech patterns. If they hear baby talk, chances are they will imitate it. It is also important to use complete sentences and introduce new words. Use adverbs and adjectives to create colorful descriptions.

Puppets, unbreakable mirrors, books, pictures, posters, and dolls can all be placed on shelves in the language area. These materials should be placed so the children can safely remove them from the shelves. See 28-15.

28-15 Encouraging children to play with dolls is one way to promote language development.

Activity Files and Picture Collections

Many teachers maintain a file listing activities that have met with success. This will help you remember the best activities. Ask other infant-toddler caregivers to share their favorite activities. Observe other caregivers in your center. Make notes of useful interactions and activities.

You will also want to start your own picture collection. The best source for obtaining pictures is from calendars, children's books, magazines, and travel posters. Infants and toddlers enjoy large, simple pictures. People, animals, vehicles, and toys have the most appeal.

Before displaying a picture, mount it on a piece of colorful poster board. To frame each picture, leave at least a ½-inch border around the entire picture. Since young children enjoy touching pictures, protect the pictures by covering with clear contact paper or laminate.

Parent Involvement

Communication with the families of infants and toddlers is very important. Keep the parents informed of how their child's day went. Also, encourage parents to provide you with the significant happenings in their home. When children are first enrolled, always find out their routines at home, food preferences, and favorite toys. You can use a form at enrollment time to record the

information, 28-16. This information will help coordinate center and home activities.

To help you provide a quality experience for children, parents' goals and concerns need to be shared. It will also be helpful if any change in the home environment is shared. These changes such

---

Infant-Toddler Center

Child's Name _____   Birth Date _____

Home Address_____   Home Phone _____

_____

Mother's Name _____   Father's Name _____

Place of Employment_____   Place of Employment_____

Phone Number _____   Phone Number _____

If there are any special family circumstances such as divorce, separation, remarriage, parental death, adoption, etc., please indicate them.

_____

_____

In case of emergency, who should be notified?

Name _____   Phone_____

Name _____   Phone_____

Doctor or Clinic_____   Phone_____

Environment and Experiences

Names of brothers and sisters	Birth Date(s)	School(s) attending
_____	_____	_____
_____	_____	_____
_____	_____	_____

How does your child react when you leave him or her with someone other than a parent?_____

_____

List the name(s) of any previous child care center that your child attended. _____

_____

What was your child's response?

_____

_____

28-16 Stress to parents the importance of the information on this form.   (Continued)

Physical Development

Toilet Training:
Is your child completely toilet trained now?_____

Does he/she usually stay dry all day? _____

Eating Habits:
In general, describe your child's attitude toward eating.

What are his/her special food likes?

What are his/her special food dislikes?

Does your child have any food allergies?

Are there any special characteristics or problems which the school should know about in order to be of most help to your child and your family? Include any vision, hearing, physical difficulties, and unusual abilities or disabilities of which you are aware.

Favorite Toys
Describe your child's favorite toys.

Favorite Activities
Describe your child's favorite activities.

28-16 Continued.

as a death in the extended family, can cause stress for children. Other changes may cause pleasure. Examples include a new family pet or a grandparent visiting. Parents should also let the teacher know about such home routines as toilet training.

From time to time you may wish to share reading materials with parents. Information on topics such as toilet training, separation anxiety, language development, and toy selection can be quite useful for parents. Parents also enjoy receiving information on developmental stages. Knowing and watching for stages of normal development can be reassuring to parents.

Record Keeping

Record keeping is an important part of an infant-toddler program. Such records should track children's eating, sleeping, and eliminating routines. Also, keep track of new behaviors and skills as they occur and change over time.

Good records provide valuable information. Parents will be especially interested in their child's daily eating, sleeping, and eliminating patterns. Unusual patterns may signal illness or a need to change the child's diet.

By maintaining a record of the child's skills and behaviors, you will be able to note the child's progress and the start of any problems. Early detection is important for the child's development.

When reporting the child's daily routines to the parents, be objective and factual. Do not be negative or judgmental. Try to state comments in a positive manner. For instance, avoid remarks such as "Mark was very crabby and difficult to be with today." Rather, say "Mark's new tooth was causing him some pain today." Whenever possible, provide the parent with comments in writing.

Maintaining the Environment to Prevent Illness

As a staff member in a child care center, you will need to take steps to prevent illness. Disease-causing microorganisms grow in a damp, dirty environment. Play equipment, cribs, changing tables, strollers, floors, tables, high chairs, and feeding tables—as well as the children's hands—all need to be cleaned.

Since infants and toddlers explore with their mouths, it is important that all toys be routinely cleaned. Saliva forms a film on the surface of toys. Microorganisms grow on this film. As a result, any toys such as rattles and teething rings that go into the infant's mouth must be cleaned on a daily basis. If your center has a dishwasher, use it. Most small toys are dishwasher safe.

Clean by hand the toys that cannot be washed in the dishwasher. First, wash the toys in a hot, sudsy detergent and rinse well. Then mix a disinfecting solution of one gallon of water with one tablespoon of chlorine bleach. Wipe or spray each piece of equipment with the solution. Air dry.

Depending on the frequency of use, cribs and strollers need to be cleaned daily or twice weekly. Likewise, floors, tables, high chairs, and feeding tables also need cleaning each day. Food left on any of these can grow microorganisms. This process should be similar to cleaning toys. Begin by washing each piece with warm, sudsy water. Rinse well. Wipe or spray with a solution of disinfectant. Air or sun dry.

Contaminated hands are a common cause of the spread of illness in child care centers. To prevent illnesses, it is most important that you follow the hand washing procedures discussed under diapering.

Illness Policies

Sick children cannot be cared for in a center without endangering the health of other children. An environment for infants and toddlers needs to be healthy. As the teacher, it is your responsibility to maintain the best health conditions. In order to do this properly, you will need to have a center illness policy. This policy will help staff and parents decide whether a child is too sick to be brought to or remain in the center.

Prior to enrollment, every parent should be given a copy of the center's illness policies. At this time, it should be stressed that a primary objective of the program is to protect the children's health. Thus, center illness policies are always adhered to. An example of a center illness policy is shown in 28-17.

Infant-Toddler Center Illness Policy

To protect all the children's health, you must keep your child home when he/she has:
- An oral temperature of 101°F or above or a rectal temperature of 102°F or above.
- Diarrhea.
- Vomiting that extends beyond the usual spitting up.
- Bronchitis symptoms, including hoarseness and/or cough.
- A severe cold that is accompanied with a fever and nose drainage.
- A rash that has not been diagnosed by a doctor.
- Impetigo, chicken pox, mumps, measles, scarlet fever, or whooping cough.

28-17 An illness policy helps avoid misunderstandings when infants and toddlers are ill.

Summary

Infants and toddlers are at a special stage in their lives. They are just learning about their world and yet they learn and grow quickly. The care they receive at this stage is quite important for later development.

Caring for infants and toddlers requires skill in areas unique to the age group. Emphasis is shifted toward care of daily routines such as eating, diapering, and sleeping. However, infants and toddlers also require a developmentally supportive environment. The environment should balance safety and health concerns with developmental needs.

Infants often communicate by crying. As a caregiver, you will have to learn the meaning of each child's cries and respond promptly. Separation anxiety is also common between nine to twelve months of age.

To meet the special needs of infants and toddlers, appropriate equipment is needed. Safety is again the number one consideration. Curriculum for infants and toddlers differs from that planned for older preschool children. Though the curriculum for infants consists of simple, basic activities, the curriculum for toddlers requires more planning. Activity areas should be provided to meet toddlers' needs.

Review and Reflect

1. List three characteristics of a successful infant-toddler teacher.

2. What is the reasoning behind locating the feeding area near the entrance to the center?

3. Name the five major areas in the toddler space.

4. What portion of the play area should be left open for toddlers to move about freely?

5. All infants and toddlers require their needs to be met promptly if they are to learn to _____.

6. Always respond to a baby's crying by _____.
   A. ignoring the baby
   B. feeding the baby
   C. trying to solve the problem
   D. None of the above.

7. What is separation anxiety?

8. Describe how to feed an infant.

9. Should toddlers be encouraged to smell, touch, and push around their food before eating? Why or why not?

10. Why should liquid soap be used in the diapering area?

11. Name two advantages of keeping a toy inventory.

12. Why do infants seem to enjoy dropping objects from their high chairs?

13. In terms of curriculum, babies should set their own _____.

14. List five questions to ask yourself when planning activity centers for toddlers.

15. What should be your attitude when reporting the child's daily routines to his or her parents?

16. What is the purpose of a center illness policy?

Apply and Explore

1. Collect and compare illness policies from three child care centers.

2. Add 10 activities for toddlers to an activity file.

3. Practice directing the proper handwashing procedures using classmates or large, plastic dolls.

4. Design an infant space on a large piece of tagboard.

5. Visit a hospital. Ask about specialized care provided to hospitalized infants. Report your findings back to your classmates.

6. Invite a pediatrician to talk to your class about preventing illnesses in infants and toddlers.

7. Collect daily care records from several centers. Discuss the contents of each.

8. Interview several parents. Ask them the type of characteristics they desire in an infant or toddler caregiver. Share your findings with the class.

9. For a toddler environment, design three private spaces.

Chapter 29

Programs for School-Age Children

After studying this chapter, you will be able to

- describe the three basic program models used in school-age child care.

- identify the characteristics of an effective teacher in a school-age program.

- discuss how to arrange indoor and outdoor space in a school-age child care environment.

- explain ways to assess children's interests for curriculum planning.

- list the components of a typical daily schedule in a school-age child care program.

Terms to Know

child-centered program model

adult-centered program model

unit-based program model

There is a growing demand for school-age child care. Two main factors account for this trend. First, the number of working mothers with children between the ages of six and twelve has grown. Second, there are more single-parent families.

Due to cost or lack of quality programs, many school-age children are left to care for themselves. Felix, an eight-year-old, is an example. He returns home from school at about 3:40 in the afternoon. Felix carries a house key. When he arrives home, he unlocks the front door. Then he enters and locks the door behind him. Felix watches television until 6:00 p.m., when his mother returns home from work.

Felix's mother, like many others, cannot find affordable after-school care. Children like Felix are sometimes called *latchkey children.* This term refers to children left in self-care or in the care of a sibling under age 15. Many children are left in self-care for several hours each day.

Yolanda is another eight-year-old child. Unlike Felix who goes home to an empty apartment, Yolanda is fortunate. She attends a school-age child care program after school. Ricardo, her cousin who lives in the same community, also attends the program. Since Yolanda's school does not have a program, a bus takes her to a program at Ricardo's school.

Parents need to make decisions on an individual basis about how old children should be before leaving them in self-care. A general guideline is that parents should not regularly leave children alone until the children are in fifth grade. However, parents may feel comfortable occasionally leaving some responsible, self-disciplined children alone at a younger age. On the other hand, parents may not feel comfortable leaving some immature 13- or 14-year-old children in self-care.

Even mature children can benefit from attending a school-age child care program. Studies show children who lack adult supervision tend to have a variety of problems. They are more likely to experience loneliness and unhealthy fears. They are also more likely to lack physical exercise and have poor nutritional habits. Attending a quality school-age program can help children avoid these problems.

Quality School-Age Programs

School-age children have special needs. They need challenges. They need to be independent. They need others to accept them for who they are.

A quality school-age program will meet these needs. It will also provide companionship, supervision, a safe environment, and activities to promote children's development. A good school-age program has

- low adult-child ratios
- warm, caring, well-trained staff members
- well-organized space with room for active play, quiet play, and interest centers
- curriculum based on the children's emerging interests and needs
- parent involvement to achieve shared goals for the children
- flexible scheduling to allow for a balance of individual, small group, and large group activities

Types of Programs

Parents have a variety of options when choosing after-school child care. See 29-1. A nanny, an au pair, or a housekeeper can provide care in a child's home. Family child care homes and child care centers provide care outside the child's home.

Many for-profit child care centers provide school-age child care and transportation. These centers offer programs during the school year.

29-1 A variety of child care options is available for school-age children.

Many have special summer programs, too. Parents who can afford the tuition often select this type of program. Often, children participating in these programs have attended preschool in the same facility.

Nonprofit organizations such as United Way, YMCA, and the Salvation Army offer school-age child care programs in some communities. Churches and synagogues may also provide school-age child care for their members.

Program Models

There are three different program models used as curriculum formats in school-age child care programs. These are the child-centered model, the adult-centered model, and the unit-based model. A good program uses parts of all three models to complement children's school and home experiences.

Several factors may influence the program model used in a given program. These factors include the age, interests, and abilities of the children. Staff preferences and the amount of time children spend in the program can have an influence, too.

Child-Centered Program Model

The **child-centered program model** is a curriculum format that allows children an opportunity to self-select activities. Staff members encourage children's involvement by serving as facilitators and resource persons. Together the staff and children plan the daily activities. Available resources and the children's interests help determine the activities. See 29-2.

Adult-Centered Program Model

The **adult-centered program model** is a more structured curriculum format that includes a high level of adult direction. The curriculum includes recreation and tutoring programs. Children may also have opportunities to take music and dance lessons.

Unit-Based Program Model

The **unit-based program model** is a curriculum format that revolves around curriculum themes that reflect the children's interests. Frequently, these themes focus on special events and holidays. Staff members offer a variety of cooking, science, music, and art activities that relate to the theme. They choose children's literature and plan field trips, creative dramatics, and games to support the theme, too. Children can then choose many of the specific theme-related activities in which they will participate.

Regardless of the model used, school-age programs should focus on developing competence and self-confidence. Self-confidence contributes to an "I-can-do-it" attitude. It will help

children master reading and writing skills. Self-confidence will also help children develop positive social relationships with their peers.

Adult-Child Ratios

Program quality is enhanced when there are enough staff to respond to the individual needs of children. Studies show that low adult-child ratios and small group size improve program quality.

Children in school-age child care programs must be able to get adult help when they need it. Children will need assistance with their school work. They will also need adults to serve as role models and to provide emotional support and encouragement.

An appropriate adult-child ratio benefits staff as well as children. With a low ratio, adults can provide the constant supervision needed to create a safe environment. While supervising, adults can use observation to gain information about the interests, needs, and abilities of each child.

Most states have laws addressing adult-child ratios for children's programs. These ratios vary from state to state. However, for children through six years of age, a 1:10 ratio is usually recommended. For children seven years of age and older, a 1:12 ratio is usually recommended.

29-2 Children in a child-centered program model may select activities that interest them.

Characteristics of Staff

Who should care for school-age children? High-quality programs are staffed by well-trained personnel. These individuals understand child growth and development. They have age-appropriate expectations of the children's behavior and abilities. They are continuously seeking new ideas and learning new teaching techniques. These teachers also respect the cultural diversity of the children they teach.

Staff in school-age programs need to be understanding, patient, and warm. Moreover, they need to respond positively to each child's uniqueness and changing needs.

Act as Facilitators

Staff in school-age programs act as facilitators. They ask the children to share thoughts and listen to the view of others. They assist the children in developing skills and abilities. They help by offering suggestions, providing encouragement, and recommending activities. See 29-3.

29-3 Teachers can use bulletin boards to promote prosocial behavior.

They use demonstrations, explanations, and coaching as strategies to help children learn. Staff also ask thought-provoking questions that require the children to use their mental reasoning skills.

Use Positive Guidance

School-age children are learning social expectations. They are learning to recognize the impact of their behavior on others. By experiencing consequences, children begin to understand what is acceptable and unacceptable behavior.

Skilled staff use positive guidance to help children achieve self-control. They encourage prosocial behaviors, such as taking turns, helping, cooperating, negotiating, and talking through interpersonal problems. Staff work with children to develop clear limits and rules for social living. When needed, staff remind children of the rules. After this, they redirect the children to more acceptable behavior.

Involve Children

School-age children are learning to be independent. They want to solve problems.

Staff of school-age child care programs need to involve children in daily problem-solving activities. While developing rules, staff should involve the children in a discussion of expectations. This information will help children make decisions related to their actions. Staff should also involve children by allowing them to help plan curriculum and make choices about activities.

Promote Respect for Cultural Diversity

As school-age children become more aware of the world around them, they begin to make social comparisons. Through this process, children not only define themselves, they also identify qualities in others.

Conscientious teachers help children appreciate cultural diversity. Children need to learn how others express beauty through art, literature, and music, 29-4. Teachers use toys, games, foods, and holiday celebrations to teach children

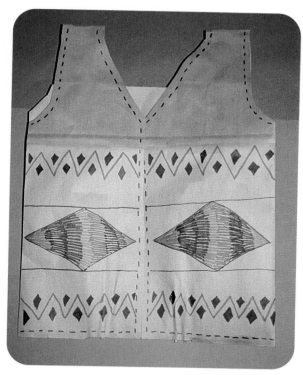

29-4 Teachers can plan activities to help children appreciate cultural diversity.

about different cultures. They use storybooks, videotapes, posters, and puzzles to show people from all cultures in a variety of positive roles.

Seeing images of people who look like them helps children develop a sense of pride in their culture. Seeing images of people from other cultures helps children respect and value people's differences.

Enjoy Physical Activities

School-age children thrive on physical activity. During a typical school day, they spend much time sitting in classrooms. When they arrive at after-school programs, they have pent-up energy to release. They want to move around, play games, run, and jump.

Teachers who are well suited for school-age programs enjoy physical activity. They do not have to be athletic. However, they need the energy and desire to join children in active play.

The Environment

Throughout middle childhood, children need room to practice their emerging skills. A quality school-age child care environment should provide appropriate space, materials, and equipment. The environment needs to reflect the children's interests, ages, abilities, and needs. This environment will allow children to have fun, learn, and thrive as they move at their own pace.

The ideal environment is designed specifically for school-age programs. However, any facility with a large activity room and an outdoor play area can serve as a school-age program environment. Many programs are housed in libraries, cafeterias, gyms, and church basements.

When facilities are designed for other purposes, restrictions may apply. Providing an appropriate environment may be difficult. Teachers in these spaces often have only a limited time to prepare the environment. They must develop creative strategies for getting the room ready each day. They may use moveable carts to store games, art supplies, books, and other program materials, 29-5. They may have the children help by including setup and cleanup in the children's daily schedule.

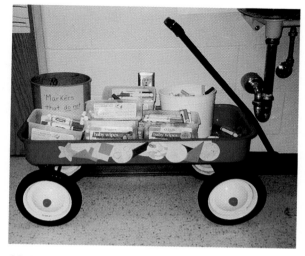

29-5 In a shared environment, staff can use wagons to store and transport art supplies.

Indoor Space

The indoor space for a school-age program should be adequate for the number of children enrolled. Children need room for individual, small group, and large group activities. At least 35 square feet of space should be available for each child.

Children need a secure and safe environment. For them, a child care center is a home away from home. A quality school-age child care environment is informal and provides a homelike atmosphere. In this setting, the children can explore interests and develop one-on-one relationships.

Indoor space should be well designed and pleasing to the eye. Provide storage units for children's personal belongings that are separate from those used to hold classroom materials and supplies. Use pillows, pictures, posters, bean bag chairs, carpeting, couches, and curtains to help create a warm and inviting environment.

As a teacher in a school-age program, you will need to carefully plan how to use the space in your room. As in programs for preschool children, the room needs to include interest centers. You will also need to provide space for quiet activities. Create some open areas for group activities, too.

Interest Centers

Interest centers are a focus of quality school-age child care programs. Whenever possible, set up centers for hobbies, blocks, cooking, science, math, games, music, dramatic play, and arts and crafts. Try to provide bulletin boards or display areas near each center to show children's work.

Arrange interest centers to encourage independent use by the children. Place labeled open shelving units in the centers. These units will help children know where to acquire and return materials and equipment.

Quiet Areas

Your room needs to include quiet areas. Children should be able to do homework, use computers, read, and relax in these areas. See 29-6. They should feel protected from the intrusion of others. Children often enjoy flexible quiet spaces that they can rearrange with movable furniture and privacy screens.

Open Areas

Your room needs to include large, open areas. Children can use these areas for group planning times and special projects. They can enjoy movement activities, creative dramatics, and indoor games in open areas, too.

29-6 A wide variety of literature should be available in the classroom.

Outdoor Space

Outdoor space is just as important in a school-age program environment as indoor space. Children need room for physical activity. At the end of the day, they need to make noise, play, and enjoy their friends.

These activities require at least 75 square feet of outdoor space per child. Make sure this space is protected from unwanted visitors and traffic. Create separate areas for running, climbing, swinging, and organized sports. Also provide quiet play space away from active play areas.

Planning Curriculum

Good planning allows you to offer an inviting and challenging school-age program. When you provide an appealing curriculum, everybody wins. You win because the children will enjoy participating. The children win because they have choices as well as opportunities to develop new skills and interests.

The question is, "Who should plan?" The answer is everybody—the children, the parents, and the staff. You need to listen to them all. Begin by finding out what is important to each of these groups.

Parents and staff are likely to have general goals for your program. They want you to provide a safe environment for school-age children during nonschool hours. They expect you to offer a variety of developmentally appropriate activities that allow children to develop new skills.

These goals will help guide your overall planning. However, your specific day-by-day activity plans will be guided more by the interests of the children.

Assessing Interests

No two school-age children are exactly alike. As a teacher in a school-age program, you must consider children's individual abilities and needs. You must also be aware of family backgrounds and special situations. This will help you plan personally meaningful curriculum built on what the children already know.

To plan a developmentally appropriate school-age program, you need to begin by assessing the children's interests. Children's interests are always changing. Therefore, you need to conduct assessment exercises on a continuing basis to improve teaching and learning, 29-7.

Informally, you can assess children by observing their play and interacting with them individually and in small groups. You can also

29-7 Teachers in school-age child care review and compare assessment information in planning a developmentally appropriate curriculum.

assess interests through get-acquainted interviews, group discussions, self-reports, and surveys.

Get-Acquainted Interviews

Get-acquainted interviews can help you assess interests at the beginning of the year or when new children enroll. This assessment technique involves having a child ask a peer questions about himself or herself. Questions can focus on favorite hobbies, sports, foods, holidays, music, books, television programs, and vacation activities.

Because school-age children enjoy using technology, you may want to record the interviews on videotape or an audio cassette. You can share the tapes during group time to help all the children learn more about their classmates.

Group Discussions

Group discussion is a useful method of determining individual interests of school-age children. Using this method on a regular basis can also help you keep up with changes in children's interests.

Group discussions are particularly effective with nonreaders. Begin the process by asking the following questions:

- What are your hobbies?
- What new hobbies would you like to learn?
- What are your favorite sports?
- Are there any new sports you would like to learn?
- What are your favorite activities at school?
- What are your favorite program activities?
- What do you like least about the program?
- What else would you like to do in the program?

Self-Reports

Another way to learn about children is through self-reports. These reports can take the form of either stories or pictures. Ask children to focus on a theme as they write or draw. Possible themes include "All About Me," "My Family," and "When I Grow Up." Invite children to share their stories and pictures with the class. Cele-brate the children's diversity. Then display stories and pictures on a bulletin board or wall.

Surveys

You can design a survey to assess children's interests. Children who are readers can complete the survey on their own. A staff member can ask questions and record the responses of nonreaders. When designing the survey, keep it brief.

Group Planning Sessions

After you have gathered information about children's interests, you are ready to begin making some specific plans. Group planning sessions are especially effective for planning themes, holidays, special events, and field trips. Begin by asking the children to brainstorm a list of ideas. Be sure to acknowledge each suggestion. You may want to record the ideas on a chalkboard or flip chart.

After children have presented all their suggestions, discuss each one. Explain your reasons for eliminating any ideas due to expense, location, safety, or lack of staff. When you have reviewed all the ideas, encourage the children to prioritize them.

Scheduling

Most school-age child care programs are open before and after school hours. Children may participate in these programs for up to five hours a day while attending kindergarten or elementary school. Some programs are available all day during vacation periods, holidays, and summer months.

As a school-age program teacher, you must carefully plan a daily schedule that meets children's needs for predictability. At the same time, your schedule should be flexible enough to allow for children's individual differences.

You will set up your daily program schedule between arrival and departure times. Your schedule will include times for children to eat and rest. It will include periods for children to participate in a variety of activities. It will also allow time for children to clean up. Figure 29-8 shows a typical schedule for a school-age child care program.

School-Age Child Care Program Daily Schedule	
6:00–8:30 a.m. • Arrival of children (Children will arrive at different times dependent on their parents' work schedule) • Breakfast • Self-selected indoor activities, such as games, blocks, sewing, crafts, pegboards, art materials, books, stories, discussions, hobbies, conversation, computers, card games, puzzles, and homework **8:30–12:00 p.m.** • Children attend kindergarten, primary, and area elementary schools **12:00–12:30 p.m.** • Lunch (half day kindergarten children return) **12:30–1:00 p.m.** • Group Time: Story, discussion, show and tell **1:00–2:00 p.m.** • Rest time	**2:00–3:00 p.m.** • Self-selected activities, such as dramatic play, crafts, sand, water, checkers, card games, cooking, science, books, tapes, hobbies **3:15–3:30 p.m.** • Group Snack (primary and elementary children return to program) **3:30–5:30 p.m.** • Outdoor Play: Field trips, organized sports, team games, mud, water, sand play, and gardening. Jumping, skipping, hopping, climbing and other physical activities involving balls and jump ropes. Music lessons and dance lessons **5:30–6:00 p.m.** • Group Time: Discussion, program planning **6:00–6:30 p.m.** • Indoor individual and small group activities, outside and indoor cleanup in preparation for going home

29-8 A comprehensive school-age child care program provides care 12 hours a day.

Arrival and Departure Times

Arrival and departure times represent more than just the beginning and end of the daily schedule in a school-age program. These are valuable times to share information with children and parents. They serve as a bridge between home and the child care center. Use these moments to update parents about their children and to solicit parents' support for program activities. Also use these interaction times to gain insight about family values, roles, and events that may be affecting children.

When the children enter and leave your room, be available. Identify children by name. Give them warm greetings. Listen to their parting comments. Be sincere. Remember that the tone of your voice tells children how you feel about seeing them.

Mealtimes

As you begin to plan your program schedule, think of your childhood. How did you feel when you arrived home from school?

Chances are you were hungry. Like you, the children in your program will probably want something to eat when they arrive.

Mealtimes should be a learning experience. Mealtimes should also provide children with a sense of responsibility and community. Children can learn how to measure and prepare foods. They can assist with planning the menus, setting and decorating the tables, serving, and cleaning up. They can use the time when they are gathered around the table to share the events of their day, too.

You can use mealtime as an opportunity to introduce multicultural foods. Invite children to share favorite family recipes. Ask them to help plan special meals for holidays, birthdays, and other events. For special events, you may want to have children invite a guest, such as a parent or grandparent. See 29-9.

Rest Time

Many school-age programs include a daily rest time. The amount of time you schedule for rest will depend on the children in your program.

29-9 School-age children enjoy holiday preparations and parties.

Before-school programs should focus on quiet activities. Some children may need to spend the time before school finishing their homework. See 29-10. Other children may enjoy looking at books, constructing puzzles, or playing quiet games. They may also enjoy talking with friends.

After-school programs are generally longer than before-school programs, and they offer a wider variety of activities. After sitting in a classroom all day, many children enjoy physical activities that help release energy. They enjoy outdoor play, competitive sports, preparing snacks, and working on projects. They may want to participate in clubs, such as Cub Scouts, Boy Scouts, Brownies, and Girl Scouts. They may want to join book clubs and special interest clubs.

Other children need to find space to be by themselves after school to recharge their energy. For them, being with a group of people, following directions, and completing tasks all day may be stressful. They may simply want to listen to music, page through a book, enjoy quiet games, do homework, or rest.

Age, health, and activity level will affect a child's need for rest.

Some children, especially those who are younger, will want to sleep during rest time. Others, especially older children, may simply enjoy low-key activities. You might encourage these children to play quiet games, listen to music on a headset, or look at books. The activities they choose should not disturb other children.

Soft music may help some children relax during rest time. Other children find pleasure in having a teacher read to them.

Activity Time

You are likely to devote the largest part of your daily school-age program schedule to activity time. You will notice fewer conflicts among children when they are all engaged in activity. Providing a variety of familiar and unfamiliar activities will ensure that all children can find something interesting to do. The specific types of activities you offer will depend on the length and time of your program.

29-10 Children often finish their homework during the program.

Balance of Activities

A good school-age program does not duplicate activities that take place during the school day. Rather, it complements the child's home and school experiences. The emphasis should be on recreational activities as opposed to academic ones, 29-11. The activities should be developmentally appropriate and provide opportunities for skill development.

The schedule for a school-age child care program needs to include a balance of activities. Schedule separate times for child-directed and teacher-directed activities. Allow time for small group, large group, and individual activities. Plan for large motor activities, such as team sports and outdoor play. Also plan for fine motor activities, such as writing and drawing.

29-11 Good programs provide children with recreational activities.

Group Activities

Some school-age program activities will involve all the children. However, children in the middle childhood years also need opportunities to participate in small, self-selected peer group activities. Listening to a story, taking a field trip, and planning a project can all be group activities. Such activities give children a chance to communicate, develop friendships, and learn social skills.

Use different ways of dividing children into groups. You may group children according to age, interests, and needs. However, you may also group children according to such factors as favorite sports, recording artists, cars, foods, pets, and hobbies.

Mixed groups representing different developmental stages benefit children at all levels. Such groups reduce competition. These groups give older children an opportunity to develop leadership skills. Older children can help younger children with such activities as board games and crafts. The younger children learn by observing and interacting with the older children.

Groups may undertake special activities. For example, publishing a newsletter is a special activity for a group of children. The children can write, edit, and print it using a computer. They can decide who will be the editors, reporters, and production staff. Once the newsletter is published, children can share it with parents.

Cleanup

Your school-age program needs to include scheduled time for cleanup. All children need to participate in cleanup activities. They have a responsibility for maintaining their environment.

Let children know your expectations for cleanup time. Tell them that they should return games and equipment to the proper storage units. Instruct them to place their personal belongings, projects, and art work in their lockers. Completing these tasks will help children develop a sense of pride.

Summary

There is a growing demand for school-age child care. Too many children are left alone to care for themselves. Parents should not regularly leave children alone until the children are in the fifth grade.

Parents have a variety of options when choosing after-school child care. These include in-home care, family child care homes, and child care centers. School-age child care programs generally follow one of three models: child-centered programs, adult-centered programs, or unit-based programs. High-quality programs are staffed by well-trained personnel. These individuals understand child growth and development. They have age-appropriate expectations of the children's behavior and abilities. They are continuously seeking new ideas and learning new teaching techniques.

A quality school-age child care environment should provide appropriate space, materials, and equipment. The environment needs to reflect the children's interests, ages, abilities, and needs. This environment will allow children to have fun, learn, and thrive as they move at their own pace.

Parents and staff are likely to have general goals for the school-age program. They want a safe environment for school-age children during nonschool hours. They expect a variety of developmentally appropriate activities that allow children to develop new skills. Specific day-by-day activity plans will be guided more by the interests of the children.

Most school-age child care programs are open before and after school hours. Children may participate in these programs for up to five hours a day while attending kindergarten or elementary school. Some programs also operate all day during vacation periods and summer months.

Review and Reflect

1. _____ is a term sometimes used to describe children left in self-care.

2. List four common problems of children who lack adult supervision.

3. Name and describe the three program models for school-age child care programs.

4. How do low adult-child ratios benefit both the children and the adults?

5. Name five characteristics of staff members in high-quality school-age programs.

6. Describe a quality school-age child care environment.

7. In order to plan a developmentally appropriate school-age program, what must you do first?

8. Name four techniques you can use to assess children's interests.

9. In planning activities for school-age programs, the emphasis should be on _____ activities as opposed to _____ ones.

10. How do mixed groups representing different developmental stages benefit children at all levels?

Apply and Explore

1. Visit two school-age child care programs that each use a different program model. Write a report explaining how the programs are alike and different.

2. Interview a school-age child care provider about the characteristics that are important in his or her work. Share your findings in a brief oral report.

3. Measure the indoor and outdoor square footage at a school-age child care facility. Calculate how much space is available for each child enrolled in the program.

4. Discuss methods for including school-age children in curriculum planning.

Chapter 30

Guiding Children with Special Needs

After studying this chapter, you will be able to

- contribute to the development of an Individualized Educational Plan for a child with special needs.
- develop individualized learning objectives and teaching strategies for a child.
- explain the role of the teacher in working with children who have special needs.
- describe methods for identifying and working with special needs that may be encountered in the early childhood program: hearing, speech, language, vision, physical, health, cognitive, and behavioral disorders.
- describe methods of integrating children with special needs into a typical program.
- explain the special needs of children who are gifted and how these needs can be met.

Terms to Know

Individuals with Disabilities Education Act (IDEA)

mainstreaming

inclusion

Individualized Educational Plan (IEP)

Individualized Family Service Plan (IFSP)

referral

articulation problems

chronic health needs

giftedness

acceleration

enrichment

learning disability

Miguel, a lively four-year-old, has a hearing impairment. He can speak and understand only a few simple words. Rosie, an active five-year-old, is color deficient. She cannot identify the primary colors. Stephen has cerebral palsy. He needs special help to develop fine motor skills. Toby is a two-year-old who has taught herself to read. These are children who have special needs.

By federal law, children with special needs must be provided with free, appropriate public education when they reach three years of age. The **Individuals with Disabilities Education Act (IDEA),** passed by Congress, requires that all states provide education for children who are developmentally delayed. Under this law, all three- to five-year-old children with disabilities that require special educational services must be provided with individual education programs. The same programs are available for children from birth to three years of age who are high risk or have significant developmental problems. Infants, toddlers, and preschoolers who might have a physical, sensory, cognitive, or emotional disability are guaranteed the right to a professional assessment under the Federal Education of Handicapped Children Act.

Mainstreaming is the term used for placing children with special needs in a regular classroom. This process allows children to learn in a *less restrictive environment.* All the children gain skills by interacting with each other. In this type of environment, children with special needs have "nondisabled" children as role models. This interaction can lead to developmental imitation. **Inclusion** is the term used to refer to a regular education setting in which children with and without special needs are integrated. Inclusionary classrooms are frequently team-taught by regular and special education teachers.

There are many types of special needs. Communication needs are the most common. These usually fall into three categories: hearing, speech, and language problems. Visual, orthopedic, and crippling, chronic health problems are other types of special needs. Culturally distinct, gifted, and talented children also have special needs, 30-1.

Assistants and volunteers can be most useful in mainstreaming. Instruct all staff members on the nature of the child's condition and how they are to help. Encourage adults to meet the special needs of the children in group settings if possible. To do this, the staff may have to adapt classroom materials, change expectations, and/or give extra help when needed.

Nondisabled children can also assist in mainstreaming by helping a child who has a disability adjust to the environment. The nondis-

abled child might introduce the other child to the classroom setting. At times, the nondisabled child can help the child organize his or her materials or practice a new skill. Nondisabled children also benefit from inclusionary classrooms. Children with disabilities frequently model unique adaptive skills and problem-solving abilities.

A word of caution is necessary when working with children with special needs. Sometimes the other children in the classroom will want to do too much for children with special needs. They try to "help" these children by doing the children's work for them or by helping them with their self-help skills. Remind the children that assistance should be provided only when needed. Encourage staff, volunteers, and the other children to be patient and give extra encouragement to children with special needs.

Individualized Educational Plans

Federal law requires that an **Individualized Educational Plan (IEP)** be written for each child with a diagnosed disability. The purpose of an Individualized Educational Plan is to ensure that each child who has a special need has his or her own plan. By law, parents are allowed to take part in designing their child's program. This plan is jointly developed by the teacher, the parents or guardians, and experts on the particular disability. A copy of the plan is given to the parent(s). Some children with special needs will come to your center already identified. These children will already have an IEP. Usually an IEP is written for a 12-month period extending from October 1st to September 30th. Children with a correctable disability or one that requires no special accommodations will not need an Individualized Educational Plan.

Each IEP requires six components. These components are
- a description containing an assessment of the child's current level of performance and skill development
- annual goals for the child
- short-term educational objectives
- a statement outlining the involvement of the child in the regular educational program

30-1 Children who are constantly curious and trying to figure out how objects work may be gifted.

- specific services that will be provided with a time line noting the dates services will begin and end
- evaluation criteria that will be used to decide if educational objectives are met

When a preschool age child is diagnosed as having a disability, an **Individualized Family Service Plan (IFSP)** is developed. The IFSP includes

- the family's needs in regard to enhancing the child's development
- goals for the child
- services to be provided to the child and/or family, by whom and when
- a plan for transitioning the child to other services and regular education

Teachers' Roles

Teachers' roles have expanded since federal law first mandated including children with special needs in classrooms. Now teachers need to

- take part in identifying children with special needs.
- work with speech clinicians, school psychologists, health professionals, and other resource persons to design individual programs.
- deal with children who have special needs and nondisabled children in the same classroom.
- share information with parents and make suggestions for referrals.
- base program decisions on input from several resources including parents, other professionals, and personal observations.
- encourage parents to participate in their child's education. This is their right. Find out what they are feeling as well as thinking. Be an equal partner with parents; keep them informed.

First, as a teacher, you will need to learn how to identify children with special needs. Then you will need to develop a basic understanding of the learning needs of children with hearing, visual, speech, physical, learning, behavioral, and health disabilities. With this knowledge, you can then adapt the curriculum and classroom environment to meet their special needs.

Identification

Early identification of special needs is the key to a child's successful development, 30-2. Children who are not identified early may go through years of failure. This failure, in turn, can create a poor self-concept that can compound the disability.

Many young children's special needs are identified after they enter an early childhood program. Often, identification is made by an adult who is not part of the family. You, as a teacher, may be the first to detect a speech, visual, or hearing problem. You also may be the first to note a cognitive, emotional, or physical disability.

To learn to identify special needs, you need to understand average development. When a problem is suspected, observe the child closely. Informal observation may be used for assessing a child's needs. These observations may be noted on cards or paper. When recording observations, mention those signs of behaviors that suggest a special need. Any unusual social, cognitive, emotional, or physical development could signal a possible special need.

For instance, you may suspect a certain child has a special need. Developmentally, there

30-2 Annual hearing tests are a vital tool for identifying hearing problems early.

appears to be something not quite normal. In this case, you observe the child closely. Make notes about any unusual behavior. If Terry cannot identify primary colors after studying color concepts a number of times, observe him closely. Ask yourself "Could Terry be color deficient?" Consider a child's behavior in comparison to his or her usual behavior and in comparison to his or her peers.

A number of techniques can be used to collect data. You might study a child's work, 30-3. Photographs and video tapes are also useful. Scales or checklists that name skills children of certain ages should be able to perform can be helpful.

After you have made and confirmed your findings, alert the center director. The director may wish to confirm your observations. He or she may give other tests to measure the child's abilities. After this, a conference will likely be scheduled with the child's parent(s).

Begin the conference by introducing the suspected problem. Share your observations. Provide parents with examples from your observations. Ask the parents if they have noticed any of these behaviors at home. If their observations confirm yours, suggest a formal diagnosis.

Some parents may not share your concern. If this is the case, keep making your observations and schedule more conferences. It sometimes helps to ask the parents to take part in structured observations in the home and school. Remember, any delay in diagnosis can hinder the child's development.

Referrals

When the parent(s) agree a problem may exist, direct them to the needed service. Your role as a teacher is to help them see a need for their child's treatment. Once this has been done, obtain a diagnosis. Public schools are responsible for planning and paying the costs associated with the diagnosis of a disability unless parents choose to have their own assessment conducted. In that case, school staff are obligated to consider the results. You may be able to suggest a professional parents can take their child to see. This is called a **referral**. Vision or physical problems may first be referred to a county or school health nurse. Hearing, language, or speech problems may be referred to a speech clinician. Learning and behavioral problems are most often referred to a school psychologist or local agency. Depending on the state, a referral may be made to the Department of Social Services.

Hearing Disorders

A child who is *hearing impaired* can often be identified by his or her lack of vocabulary and

30-3 If a child's work is quite different from work of other children that age, this may indicate a special need.

overall delays in language development compared to nondisabled children. This child may only speak a few simple words. Before you begin to alter your program, learn the extent of the child's hearing loss. This information can only be learned through a professional.

The child's hearing loss may range from mild to profound. With a mild hearing loss, the child's vocabulary will not be as large as that of his or her peers who have normal hearing. This child might also have difficulty during large group activities, stories, and field trips. He or she may appear inattentive and distracted. The child may miss as much as half of what is being communicated.

A child with a moderate hearing loss will also have trouble in large group situations. This child has a limited vocabulary. To understand the child's speech, you should stand face-to-face. This will allow you to read the child's lips.

Children with severe, or profound, hearing loss often have little understandable speech. These children must rely largely on their vision, body language, and contextual clues to communicate.

To make up for alleviate hearing losses, many children will wear either a hearing aid in their ear or a Y-shaped hearing aid over their chests. The advantage of the ear hearing aid is that it can be adjusted to compensate for the hearing loss in each ear. The Y-shaped aid is the most popular. It has one hearing aid with tubes going to both ears.

It is important that you understand the type of hearing aid used by a child. Ask the parents to tell you about it. If it falls out of the child's ear during program hours, you will need to replace it. You should also know how to check batteries. Keep a ready supply on hand.

The purpose of the hearing aid is to amplify and magnify all sounds. It will not perfect a child's hearing. In fact, most hearing aids are only useful within a 10-foot radius. Seat children who use hearing aids away from distracting noises. Hearing aids amplify close sounds.

Teaching Suggestions

When approaching a child who is hearing impaired, get down to the child's eye level, 30-4. Then get the child's attention before speaking. Sometimes this can be done by lightly

30-4 The key to working with hearing impaired children is to modify your teaching methods to meet the needs of the child.

touching the child's hand or arm. With practice, you will learn how close you must stand in order to be understood. You should also follow these suggestions:

- Speak in a normal volume and speed.
- Use the same sentence structure as you would for other children.
- Pause and wait for a response after you speak.
- If the child does not understand you, repeat, rephrase, or demonstrate.
- Encourage other children to imitate you when they communicate with the child. That is, they need to get the child's attention, look into his or her eyes, and speak at a normal volume and speed.
- Whenever needed, use gestures and facial expressions to reinforce the spoken word.
- In a group situation, let the child sit in front of you. This will encourage him or her to watch your body language and lips as you speak.

In addition to using these teaching strategies, adapt the curriculum for the hearing impaired child. Before you begin making these changes, however, you may wish to consult a language and speech clinician.

Visual skills are important for children who are hearing impaired. Finely tuned visual skills help compensate for their lack of hearing. However, hearing impaired children do not automatically acquire acute visual skills. To provide for their needs, stress visual activities.

- Use concrete materials to demonstrate abstract concepts. For example, if you are talking about pumpkins, use a real pumpkin or a picture of a pumpkin. (Avoid drawing on the chalkboard as you are talking. These children need to see your face as you communicate with them.)
- Provide a variety of classification games and puzzles for the children to practice visual perception skills.
- Label classroom furniture and materials.
- Select books with simple, large, and uncluttered illustrations. These children will rely more on vision than hearing during story time.
- Teach safety by using traffic signals with the wheeled toys in the play yard.
- Teach daily routines and transitions using a light switch. Flash the light to get the children's attention.
- Use a picture poster to point to the upcoming activity.

Some children with hearing impairments are taught to communicate manually through finger spelling and sign language. An oral approach, emphasizing lip reading and speaking, is used with other children. Some parents feel very strongly about using one approach over the other even though most professionals today recommend a combined or eclectic approach with children who have hearing impairments.

Speech and Language Disorders

A child may come to school who refuses to talk. Another child may speak but may be inarticulate (cannot be understood by teachers or peers). Still another child may not be able to recall sentences correctly. These children have speech and language disorders.

Identification

Before programs can be altered, you must identify the problem. Informal observations are the most common method used to identify

speech and language problems. Chart 30-5 contains a checklist to use when observing for these problems. You will need to listen carefully as the child speaks. Listen to both sounds and content.

When a child is having trouble pronouncing words, record those sounds causing the difficulty. Young children find the consonants *p, b, m, w,* and vowels the easiest to pronounce. *Cr, bl, sh, ch, th, j, r, l,* and *z* are more difficult sounds to pronounce and take longer to learn. Chart 30-6 contains the approximate ages at which most children use certain sounds.

Observe and listen to children in a variety of settings: on the play yard, in the housekeeping area, during lunchtime, and as they converse with others. As you identify the problem, make notes and continue observing to collect information.

Speech Observation Checklist
• Do the sounds the child makes match those listed for his or her age group on a developmental chart?
• Is the rate and fluency of the child's speech appropriate for his or her age group?
• Is the child's speech understandable?
• Does the amount of talking done appear to be normal?
• Does the child recall and repeat sentences correctly?

30-5 If you suspect a speech disorder, observe the child, paying close attention to the items listed.

Developmental Order for Speech Sounds						
Age	**Sounds**					
1½-3½	p	m	h	n	w	b
2-4	k	d	t	n	g	
2½-5½	f	y				
3-6	r	l	s			
3½-7	ch	sh	z			
4½-8	j	r				

30-6 Keep these parameters in mind when observing a child you believe may have a speech disorder.

Based on repeated observations, you may conclude that a child most likely does have a speech problem. Share your observations with your director. The director will determine whether a parent conference should be scheduled. The child may then be referred to a speech and language therapist for assessment.

Articulation Disorders

The terms "lazy tongue" and "baby talk" are frequently used to describe articulation problems. These terms imply that the child's tongue or developmental level is the problem. Neither is true. **Articulation problems** are most often omissions, distortions, or substitutions of vowels or consonants or both. It is possible for a child to have one or more of these problems.

Certain speech sounds are left out in an omission error. This results in only a part of a word being said. For example, a child may say "oat" for "boat." The child may say "had" for the name "Thad."

A child with a distortion problem sometimes has trouble identifying and producing the intended sound. For example, instead of pronouncing an *s*, a child may suck air in between his or her teeth.

Substitutions involve speech patterns such as "thome" for "some" or "tate" for "cake." The most common sound substitutions include *f* for *th*, *t* for *k*, *b* for *v*, *th* for *s*, *k* for *t*, and *w* for *i* or *r*. A common substitution problem is referred to as a *lisp*. It involves substituting *th* sound for the letter *s*.

After a child has been diagnosed as having an articulation problem, a speech clinician should be consulted. A speech and language clinician will provide direct therapy and/or advise you. Ask for advice on how to help the child.

As a teacher, your reaction to the child with articulation problems has a great effect. To help a child feel secure, always react positively. Ensure that the other children do, too. If the child does not respond verbally, do not demand a response. Instead, provide the correct answer for him or her.

Model good listening skills and speaking skills with all the children. Give the children your total attention. Look directly into their faces as they speak. Verbally respond with interest to what the children are saying. If you do not understand, ask the children to repeat what they have said.

Children with articulation problems need to be encouraged to talk. Set an example by feeding in language as they take part in activities. To illustrate, you may say to a child "You are placing a large red block in the square hole" as he or she plays with a sorting box.

Use language that is proper for the child's developmental level. For example, the child may point to a large red car and say "far." You should then say "That is a large, red car." This technique is called *expansion*. It involves taking the child's mispronounced words and correctly expanding them into sentences.

Some children are more comfortable talking about things that are special to them. One technique you can use is to have the child bring something special from home. Then have him or her tell everyone about the item.

Always provide a variety of activities in your classroom. The wider the variety, the more the children will have to talk about. Try to relate classroom activities to children's home experiences and cultural backgrounds.

Demand communication from all children, including those with articulation problems. Do this by asking open-ended questions. Instead of asking "Did you like the book?" ask "What did you like about the book?"

Voice (Phonation) Disorders

Voice characteristics include pitch, loudness, flexibility, and quality. The lowness or highness of the voice is the *pitch*. It is not uncommon for some children to use a pitch that is too low or too high.

Loudness is related to the amount of energy or volume used when speaking. The voice may be strong or weak. A strong voice will be loud and can be disturbing. A weak voice may be hard to hear and can also hinder communication.

A good speaking voice during routine conversation uses a variety of pitches and loudness levels. This is referred to as *voice flexibility*. Changes in pitch and loudness often reflect the emotions of the speaker.

Harshness, hoarseness, breathiness, and nasality are all *voice-quality disorders*. The harsh voice is often louder than normal. Hoarseness may indicate a problem in the throat. A breathy voice sounds like a whisper. It is weak and not clearly phonated. Nasality is a condition in which sound passes through the nasal cavities instead of the throat.

To help prevent or correct voice disorders, promote voice control:

- Encourage children to use the correct voice volume during indoor play. You may need to say "Teddy, you need to use your indoor voice in the building."
- Discourage children from screaming or yelling too much during outdoor play.
- Model good voice characteristics. Your own voice should be the proper pitch, loudness, quality, and flexibility.

Stuttering

Stuttering in young children is often characterized by repetition, hesitation, and prolongation. Few young children stutter all the time. It is often only under certain conditions that some children stutter.

In the early stages of language development, many children experience stuttering. This most often occurs when they feel pressured, 30-7.

Children function best in a warm, noncritical classroom. This type of environment helps all children speak with confidence.

If you have a stuttering child in your classroom, focus on creating good speaking conditions.

- Plan activities so all children will experience success. Praise the children.
- Provide children with enough time to say what they have to say.
- Listen closely to what the children are saying, as opposed to focusing on the stuttering.
- Avoid rushing children through a task. Do not complete a word or sentence for them.

Unfortunately, many well-meaning people try to provide directions to a stuttering child. "Stop and think," "Start over," and "Speak slower" are common examples. These suggestions often make the child feel even more fearful. A child's difficulty could continue as a result of this fear. An environment free of pressure is

30-7 Children who feel pressured are more likely to stutter than children who are relaxed.

important. When stuttering is severe, speech therapy may be necessary.

Vision Disorders

One of the smallest groups of children with special needs is the visually impaired. Common vision problems include amblyopia, nearsightedness, farsightedness, and/or a color deficiency. Physically, children with visual impairments are similar to children with normal vision. However, this disability can limit the motor abilities of these children as they take part in some physical activities. See 30-8.

To understand visual impairments, you need to understand how a healthy visual system works. Despite young children's thinking, the eye does not actually see. The purpose of the eye

30-8 Children with visual impairments often lack small muscle coordination. They need to experiment with an art medium to build these skills.

is to take in light. After it has taken in light, the eye transmits impulses to the brain through the optic nerve. The brain then decodes the visual stimuli, and "seeing" takes place. Most defects of the eye itself are correctable. If the brain or the optic nerve is damaged, however, the impairment is not correctable.

Early Identification

Early identification of a visual impairment is important. Many child care centers have a volunteer from the National Society for the Prevention of Blindness, a county health nurse, or some other professional conduct a visual screening each year. Children who appear to have problems are given a referral for a complete exam by an eye specialist.

Classroom staff need to observe children closely to identify vision problems. Certain symptoms may suggest problems:

- excessive rubbing of the eyes
- clumsiness and trouble moving around the classroom
- adjusting the head in an awkward position to view materials
- moving materials so they are close to the eyes
- squinting
- crossed eyes
- crust on eye
- swollen, red eyelids

Types of Visual Disabilities

There are several common visual impairments that young children may have. Amblyopia is a disorder you might note in your classroom. You may also find children with glaucoma, nearsightedness, farsightedness, a color deficiency, and some uncorrectable conditions.

Amblyopia

Amblyopia is often called lazy eye. This disorder is the result of a muscle imbalance caused by disuse of an eye. It is one of several visual conditions that can be corrected if found during early childhood. To force the use of the weaker eye, a patch is placed over the stronger eye. If this does not work, surgery may be required. If treatment of amblyopia is not done by age six or seven, the child's vision may always be poor.

Glaucoma

Glaucoma is a condition caused by failure of the eye fluid to circulate in the proper way. This results in increased pressure on the eye. Over time, this pressure can destroy the optic nerve. This problem can be treated with eye drops if diagnosed early. This can prevent loss of vision.

Nearsightedness

Some children may be unable to see things that are far away. These children suffer from *nearsightedness*. The medical term for this visual disorder is *myopia*. It results when the eye focuses in front of the retina.

Farsightedness

Children who have a difficult time seeing objects that are close to them suffer from *farsightedness*. The medical term for this visual disorder is *hyperopia*. It is caused by having the visual image focus behind the retina.

Color Deficiency

Color deficiency, or color blindness as it is sometimes called, is the inability to see a color. This problem is hereditary. It mostly affects males and is caused by a recessive gene. You should be able to quickly identify children with color deficiencies. They are not able to recognize one or more primary colors.

Uncorrectable Conditions

There are several visual disorders that cannot be corrected by glasses, surgery, or other means of treatment. Any damage to the optic nerve by disease or trauma is an example. After damage, signals do not get to the brain to provide the child with sight.

Teaching Suggestions

You may need to make changes in your classroom depending on the visual needs of the children. The following teaching suggestions may be helpful:

- Always create a need to see. For instance, if farsighted children refuse to wear their glasses, provide them with materials that have fine detail and print. The children will then realize the importance of wearing their glasses.
- Include a study unit on sight to help all the children understand vision.
- When ordering chalkboards, purchase those with a dull finish. Use yellow chalk on chalkboards. Use colored, rather than black, markers on white boards. Glare can be very tiring for partially-sighted children.
- Hang all the children's work at their eye level.
- Safety is always important. To ensure a safe environment, blocks, cars, and other items should be picked up right after play.
- Auditory clues are important for children with visual impairments. Provide a comfortable environment by keeping the noise level low.
- In the reading area, always have a number of large print books with clear, simple pictures.

- Provide many tactile (touch), olfactory (smell), and auditory (sound) clues to structure the environment for the child, 30-9. For instance, use a piece of shag carpeting in the story area and a bubbling aquarium or fragrant flowers in the science area.
- Use auditory reminders for transition times. These may include singing a song, beating a drum, playing a piano, or hitting tone bells.
- During activities, always encourage children to describe what they remember using their senses.

Remember that children with visual impairments may need to learn some skills children with normal vision already have. For instance, children with normal vision acquire eating, toileting, and dressing skills by watching others. A visually impaired child, however, may not possess these skills when he or she comes to the center. You will need to teach these skills. You

30-9 Activities involving touch are especially important for children with vision disorders.

will also need to teach the child the classroom areas. Do this by repeatedly guiding the child from one area to another.

Physical Disabilities

Most preschool children can crawl, walk, run, climb, and move their bodies in different ways. A child with a physical impairment may have a limited range of motion. Due to this limitation, his or her experiences may vary from those of his or her peers.

Types of Physical Disabilities

Like other children with special needs, children who are physically impaired are grouped based on their ability to function. Disabilities are classified as severe, moderate, or mild. Children with severe impairments usually cannot move independently. Typically, they have to be carried, pushed, or moved about using a wheelchair. Children with moderate impairments can do more for themselves, but they still require much help from staff members. Due to their need for accessible facilities and adaptations, children with severe or moderate physical impairment may not be enrolled in a nonadapted child care center.

Children with mild physical impairments can often do what most other children do. These children may need to use walking aids or other devices to help them move about. As can be expected, they will need more time to move about or to do tasks.

The children you will meet in the typical child care center will be *ambulatory*. They will be able to move from place to place. You may elect, however, to work in a center that caters to children with special needs. In these centers, you will observe a higher staff-to-child ratio. This is necessary to meet the special needs of these children.

Cerebral Palsy

Cerebral palsy results from damage to the brain. This damage can be caused by an infection or improper nutrition during pregnancy, physical injury to the brain during birth, or lack of oxygen during birth. It can also be acquired during the developmental years as a result of a tumor, head injury, or brain infection. Cerebral palsy is characterized by lack of control of voluntary movements.

Speech problems are often found in children with cerebral palsy. These problems are caused by the inability to control the muscles used to make speech sounds. If a child in your group has a speech disorder, consult with the parents and a speech clinician. A child with severe cerebral palsy may benefit from use of an *augmentative communication device* such as a board containing pictures of commonly referred to objects. Thus, the child can point to a picture of a glass of milk when he or she is thirsty.

Children with cerebral palsy also often lack fine motor skills. Many of their self-help skills are impaired. Eating utensils and other equipment may be difficult for them to use. An occupational therapist and the child's parents can best advise what type of eating utensils, crayons, and other items are most useful. Modifications may be needed on equipment. For example, you may want to glue large wooden knobs on puzzles so the child with cerebral palsy can remove and insert the pieces. A wide range of adapted toys, personal care, and independent living devices are available. Consult your nearest rehabilitation technology center for suggested adaptive aids.

Spina Bifida

Spina bifida is a condition in which the bones of the spine fail to grow together. The nerves are left exposed. This results in paralysis. This is a *congenital defect* (caused before birth, but not hereditary). The cause of spina bifida is unknown. Children with this problem often lack bowel and bladder control. They often cannot tell when they are wet because of lower body paralysis.

In order for a child with spina bifida to focus on learning activities, he or she needs to feel comfortable. You may need to ask such questions as "Are you comfortable?" or "Do you want to sit another way?" To provide the best environment for this child, discuss positions with the parents and physical therapist. They may suggest positions that will provide the child with a sense of balance. Specific questions you may want to ask them include "Should learning activities be on the floor or table?" and "Should the classroom tables be modified?"

Amputation

At some point, you may have a child in your classroom who is missing a hand, arm, or leg. Perhaps the severed limb resulted from an accident or cancer. Sometimes the limb is missing from birth. A child who is missing a limb is often fitted with an artificial limb called a *prosthesis.* Research has shown that young children adjust to an artificial limb quite easily, 30-10.

In order to use a prosthesis, it must fit and be cared for properly. To avoid frustrating the child, you, as a teacher, will need to know how the artificial limb works. Parents usually welcome a teacher's questions related to the device. In fact, these questions assure them of your interest in providing the best care for their child. Other children will model their teachers matter-of-fact acceptance of a prosthesis.

Teaching Suggestions

Although it is difficult for some, movement is important for all children. Children with physical disabilities may have to crawl or move with special equipment such as wheelchairs and walking aids. As a result, they need more time and energy to do small and large motor tasks. It takes them longer to go to the bathroom or to finish a project. To allow for this, you will need

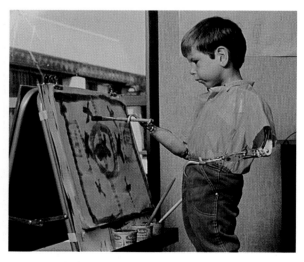

30-10 With the help of artificial limbs, this child can take part in many of the same activities as other children.

to provide time in your schedule. You may also have to make some adjustments in the facility.

- Modify chairs to accommodate the child.
- Provide space for a child's wheelchair, crutches, cane, walker, or cart.
- Provide ramps so the child has access to the classroom.
- Raise tables so wheelchairs fit under them.
- Glue knobs on puzzle pieces so the pieces are easy to remove and replace.
- Secure all carpeting or area rugs to the floor so the child does not slip or trip on them.
- Provide double handled mugs and deepsided bowls rather than plates.
- Serve finger foods as often as possible at snack time.

Health Disorders

Some children have more illness than others. These are often the children with chronic health needs. A **chronic health need** can be defined as an illness that persists over a period of time. For some children, a problem may last a lifetime, while for others, it may last a few months.

Children with health problems often have cycles of good and poor health. Since health needs are the most common type of special needs, it is vital that you be aware of a variety of these disorders.

Allergies

The most common health problem of young children is allergies. Studies note that up to 50 percent of all people have mild or severe allergies. An allergy may begin at any age. Studies also note that only a small percentage of children with allergies have been diagnosed.

An *allergy* is a sensitivity to something. This sensitivity may cause rashes, swelling, sneezing, or other reactions, 30-11. There are four categories of allergenic substances: inhalants, ingestants, contactants, and injectables. *Inhalants* are airborne substances that are inhaled. *Ingestants* are foods, drugs, or anything taken through the mouth. *Contactants* are things that make contact with the body through touch. *Injectables* are chemicals or drugs injected into the body.

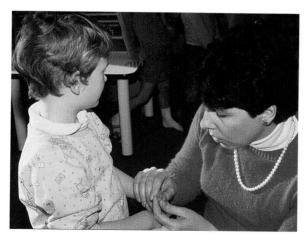

30-11 An allergic reaction to an insect bite may cause swelling and skin irritation.

Animal dandruff, dust, feathers, fungi spores, molds, and plant pollens are all types of airborne allergenic substances. If a child in your classroom has a severe allergy to animal dandruff, you may have to remove any hamsters, gerbils, or guinea pigs.

Beans, berries, chocolate, cinnamon, citrus fruits, corn products, cola drinks, eggs, fish, shellfish, milk, tomatoes, and wheat are typical foods to which the body reacts. Fabric dyes and fragrances or colorings added to soaps and shampoos are contactants that may also cause reactions. Aspirin, penicillin, and sulfa drugs are common drugs that are offenders. It is important that you ask parents at the time of enrollment whether their children have any known allergies.

If a child has food allergies, you will need to plan accordingly. Try to plan menus that avoid foods to which the child is allergic. At times, you may have to offer the allergic child food substitutes. For instance, if a child has an allergy to milk, you will have to supply another type of milk or substitute. Many times parents will provide the substitute to make sure their child is not tempted to have cow's milk.

Cosmetics, some detergents, wool, and starch are all substances that may cause an allergic reaction when they come in contact with the skin. Common reactions include a red rash and itching. These symptoms are a warning that the child is to avoid contact with whatever substance caused the problem.

Some substances cause a reaction when they enter the body through the skin. Examples include the drug penicillin and the venom from bee or wasp stings. You need to be keenly aware of insect bites. For some children, these bites can be fatal.

Bee or wasp stings usually result in redness and swelling around the wound. This indicates only a mild allergy. With a severe allergy, the child may swell all over the body and have trouble breathing. If this should occur, promptly seek medical attention. Death can result if treatment is not received immediately.

Some symptoms of allergies may be related to the season. For example, a child who is allergic to tree pollens may sneeze often in the spring. There are three major pollen seasons: early spring with tree pollens, late spring or early summer with grass pollens, and late summer and fall with weed pollens.

You may be the first to suspect allergies in a young child. Allergy symptoms are listed in 30-12. If you suspect that a child has an allergy, discuss it with his or her parent(s).

Allergy Symptoms	
Eyes • pink and puffy • red from being constantly rubbed • dark circles underneath • burning feeling and much tearing • lids may appear glued together by dry mucus	**Nose** • running nose • inability to smell • nasal discharge • frequent sneezing • itchy nose
	Skin • frequent rashes • lesions
Mouth • constant dry hacking cough • mouth breathing more common than nose breathing • wheezing • canker sores	**Throat** • tickling • enlargement of lymph nodes
	Body • chills • fever • sweating • abdominal cramps • vomiting

30-12 Allergies are quite common in young children. As a result it is vital that you recognize symptoms of more common allergies.

You may be responsible for following through on some aspects of treatment for children with allergies. There are three basic treatment methods for people with allergies. The sensitive person may avoid the offending item. For instance, if a child is allergic to chocolate, foods with chocolate should be taken out of the diet.

If the person cannot avoid the irritant, he or she may be *desensitized*. In this process, a doctor injects small amounts of the allergen into the body over a period of time. This builds immunities so the person is eventually able to withstand the irritant.

Finally, medication may be used to treat the symptom. For example, a person who has nasal congestion and blockage could use a medication to control this symptom.

Arthritis

Arthritis is a condition brought on by inflammation that produces swelling of the joints and surrounding tissues. The most common form of juvenile arthritis is called *rheumatoid arthritis*. General fatigue, loss of appetite, fever, aching joints, and a stiffness of joints as they become tender from swelling are the first signs of the disease.

After 10 years, 60 to 70 percent of affected children are free from juvenile arthritis. Adults who acquire the condition have a much smaller chance of recovery.

Arthritic children often find it difficult to remain in one position for long periods of time. They also may require more time to move from one place to another. They may need adapted toys, utensils, and clothing. Activities requiring fine finger dexterity such as cutting paper or stringing beads are particularly troublesome. Rheumatoid arthritis is typically most acute in the morning and subsides somewhat during the day. Regular, but moderate, activity is best. When the disease is in its active stage, the child will need more rest.

Asthma

Asthma is a disease characterized by a recurrent shortness of breath. An annoying cough, wheezing, and whistling breathing also often occur with asthma. An attack may last for weeks or for just a few hours. Some people are never free from asthma.

Asthma is often caused by allergies. In some cases, an attack may be caused by overextension and excitement. An attack may be relieved using medication. The medication is most often either a pill or inhaler.

Many children with asthma are allergic to dust. To prevent their attacks, you may have to make some changes in the physical environment. You may have to remove stuffed toys, pillows, rugs, or curtains. If this is not possible, make sure that the room is cleaned well each day. It is best to have the center vacuumed each evening. This will allow the dust to settle by morning when the children return.

Attention Deficit Disorder

What makes Carla so excitable and Chase so impulsive? Why is Bruce so destructive? Five to ten percent of school-age children have trouble focusing and staying on task. They are easily distracted. These children have an *attention deficit disorder (ADD)*. Many children with this disorder are also overactive, restless, and impulsive. This condition is called *attention deficit hyperactivity disorder (ADHD)*. Often such children become hostile and fail to follow classroom rules.

Attention deficit hyperactivity disorder affects more boys than girls. For every girl, there are five boys affected. The cause of ADHD is not known. However, children identified as having ADHD are usually treated with drugs that have a calming effect. Many of these children also receive behavior therapy.

Cystic Fibrosis

Cystic fibrosis (CF) is a hereditary disease that occurs almost from birth. This chronic condition involves persistent and serious lung infections, failure to gain weight, and loose, foul-smelling stools. Some of these symptoms are caused by a thick mucus produced by the sweat glands. This mucus interferes with the digestive and respiratory systems.

Seldom do children with cystic fibrosis enroll in early childhood programs. This is because they cannot risk developing lung infections such as pneumonia. Moreover, these children must be treated under the close supervision of a doctor. If children with cystic fibrosis are enrolled, they need frequent rest and a lot of fluids. They may also need to urinate frequently. The teacher should consult with the child's doctor and parents for specific care plans.

Diabetes

Diabetes is a hereditary disease. Common symptoms of diabetes include frequent urination, loss of weight, constant hunger, itching (especially around the groin), and slow healing cuts and bruises. However, it is also possible that some affected children will not show any obvious symptoms.

With diabetes, the body cannot make full use of the foods eaten, particularly carbohydrates. As a result, proper levels of the hormone insulin are not produced by the pancreas to burn or store foods as energy. This causes the body's sugar content to increase which, in turn, increases the sugar level of the blood. When the blood passes through the kidneys, the sugar is excreted in urine. This loss of carbohydrates leads to the disease. If diabetes is not controlled, it can be fatal.

A special diet is extremely important. A balance of proteins, fats, carbohydrates, vitamins, and minerals is necessary. The diet must also be constant in food value. In other words, the diet should not be high in carbohydrates one day and low the next.

Exercise, insulin, and proper diet are also necessary to manage the disease. Insulin is vital in the treatment of most cases of juvenile diabetes. The type and exact dosage for each is determined by a doctor. Most diabetic preschoolers receive insulin injections from their parent(s). If the amount of insulin is not properly adjusted to the child's food intake and activity level, an *insulin reaction* may occur. A late meal or excessive exercise may cause a reaction. A child who has an insulin reaction becomes uneasy, nervous, weak, and hungry. The child becomes pale and sweaty. Trembling, dizziness, and headaches may occur. If left untreated, the insulin reaction will lead to shock and coma. Feeding the child simple sugar sources such as orange juice or candy bars will help counteract the reaction.

Several teaching suggestions are important when a diabetic child or children are enrolled in the program. These are given in 30-13.

Epilepsy

Epilepsy is a convulsive disorder caused by damage to the brain. It affects about one percent of the population. As a result of this disorder, the electrical rhythms of the central nervous system are disturbed. Epilepsy is not a disease.

Epilepsy can cause varying degrees of reactions or seizures. Two major types are petit mal and grand mal. *Petit mal seizures* result in reactions that many times go unnoticed. Often, the only visible signs are the fluttering of the eyelids, frozen postures, staring, and a temporary stop in activity. This type of seizure may only last five to ten seconds.

As a teacher, you may not always notice a petit mal seizure. What you may notice is that the child's behavior is strange or that he or she may not be paying attention. During the seizure, the child may have only a brief lapse of consciousness. Most of these seizures do not require medical attention.

Grand mal seizures are much more pronounced. During a *grand mal seizure*, a child will lose consciousness. He or she may also jerk,

---

Suggestions for Teachers of Diabetic Children

- Ask the parents how to handle emergencies. Ask them to put these recommendations in writing. File this information in the child's file.
- Schedule snack and lunch at the same time each day.
- Make sure that diabetic children have the same food values each day.
- Keep quick sugar sources such as chocolate candy bars, soda, or orange juice on hand in case an insulin reaction occurs.
- Take the child immediately to a hospital emergency room if she/he becomes unconscious.

30-13 Follow these suggestions to assure that a diabetic child receives proper care in your program.

thrash, or become stiff. The child may also be injured by hitting objects or biting the tongue.

When the child regains consciousness, he or she may be confused. In fact, the seizure will not be remembered. Instead, the child may get up and continue with classroom activities.

Epilepsy is treated primarily with drugs. These drugs will either prevent or reduce the frequency of the seizures. Unfortunately, many drugs for epilepsy cause serious side effects, such as restlessness and lethargic behavior.

There may be times when you, as a teacher, may have to control a seizure. If a child falls, you should

1. let the child remain on the floor, clearing the area to provide him or her with ample room to thrash
2. remain calm
3. cradle the child's head in your lap. Avoid restraining movement. If possible, turn the child's body to the side, allowing saliva to drain from the mouth. This should help keep the child from choking. Never place your finger or other object in the child's mouth.
4. If the convulsion does not stop within two minutes, call for emergency medical help.
5. After the child has regained consciousness, allow him or her to remain lying down. Place a blanket over the child and allow him or her to sleep.

Hemophilia

Hemophilia is a genetic blood disease in which the blood cannot clot normally. Extreme *internal* (under the skin) bleeding may result from simply bumping against something. This causes joint problems and extreme pain that may require a stay in the hospital. The real threat, however, is death caused by internal bleeding of vital organs or by blood flowing into air passages.

With the help of the parent(s), decide what equipment is safe for the child to use. You should also

- tag the outdoor and indoor equipment the child can use
- ask the parent(s) what to do if the child is injured
- carefully watch the child's play to prevent accidents

Leukemia

Leukemia is a form of cancer that affects the blood-forming organs and the blood. There is a sharp increase in the number of white blood cells in the bloodstream.

Leukemia can be fatal. It is unlikely that a child with leukemia would enroll in a child care center. You may find, however, that a child currently enrolled may develop the disease. This child will have to be treated in the hospital. When the disease is in remission, the child may want to come back and visit friends at the center. If the parents elect to have a child with leukemia attend the center while the child is in remission, you will need to discuss the disease with them. Find out what goals the parents have for the child as well as implications of the disease.

Integrating Children with Special Needs

The number of children with special needs who can be accommodated in a center classroom varies. Several factors must be considered: the teachers' training and experience, the ratio of adults to children, and the specific needs of the children.

Regardless of a child's needs, he or she should be grouped with others based on developmental level, not age. This requires careful observation of the child before grouping.

It is important for children with special needs to enjoy the center, 30-14. Some of these children have not had a full range of home and neighborhood experiences. Others receive painful medical treatment. For these children, the center will provide a chance for companionship and education.

At times, to meet the individual needs of the children and to feel confident, you must ask for help from a specialist. For example, if a child has a speech problem, a speech therapist can be most valuable. The therapist can also help you plan helpful activities for the child.

If the parent does not remain with a child on a first visit, provide the parent(s) with feedback on the progress of that time. Parents will be most interested in their child's adjustment to the school setting. Some teachers make a habit of

30-14 Encouraging a child with special needs to try new experiences may help the child enjoy being at the center.

30-15 Puppets that represent people with disabilities may help prepare children for classmates with special needs.

either verbally sharing some positive experiences or writing a short note each day during the child's first week or two.

The children in your classroom should be prepared for a child with special needs. Explain any changes that will need to be made in the classroom. As you talk to the children, be positive and focus on strengths. This will help your group of children focus on positive expectations.

Inform the other children about this child. Some children are afraid of children with special needs. They fear the disorder or illness may be contagious. Create an open climate in which children are free to ask questions and discuss differences, 30-15. The older preschool-age child should be encouraged to educate classmates about his or her disability. Sometimes children's parents influence their attitude toward a classmate who has a disability. Respond to parent's concerns or fears while maintaining the right to privacy of the child with special needs.

Develop a few simple rules for classroom behavior. Stress to the children that the child with special needs should be encouraged to be independent. Young children may want to be overly helpful. This type of behavior can cause dependence and prevent a child from developing to his or her fullest potential. As children become more independent, they feel better about themselves.

As a teacher, your attitude toward the child with special needs will set the classroom tone. To make yourself feel comfortable, study the disorder or illness before the child begins at the center, 30-16. If the child is already enrolled and the condition has just become known, learn as much as you can about the condition. This process will help lessen any fears that you may have.

After you have learned about the disorder, arrange to have the child visit the classroom for a short period of time. This visit will reduce the fears of the child, the other children in the classroom, and perhaps the parents.

Parents of the child with special needs may wish to remain with the child for the first, brief

30-16 You will feel more comfortable working with a child with special needs if you study the need in advance.

visit. This practice usually reduces the separation anxiety the child and parents may feel.

Remember that parents are the primary teachers of their children. Therefore, it is vital that parents take part in planning useful, proper learning experiences. Parents should always be involved in planning for the child's individual needs, as well as planning for complementary opportunities in the home.

Gifted Children

No one had prepared Yvonne Libby, an early childhood teacher, for all the children she would meet in her first teaching position. Thad, a two-year-old child enrolled in the program, had taught himself to read. By 10 months of age, this same child had spoken in complete sentences. Thad is a minority in Ms. Libby's classroom. He is a child who is gifted, and he needs help.

Often, gifted children's unique educational needs are neglected in traditional education. They often spend time doing things they already

know. Only a small number receive instruction at the appropriate level for their needs or abilities. These children need programs and services different from those provided in the "normal" classroom. This is vital since gifted children's skills vary more than other groups with special needs.

Giftedness

Giftedness can be defined in many ways. Traditionally, giftedness was based only on intelligence quotient scores (IQ). Today scholars argue that there are many forms of giftedness.

People who are gifted can be defined as having exceptional skill in one or more of six areas:

- creative or productive thinking
- general intellectual ability
- leadership ability
- psychomotor ability
- specific academic aptitude
- visual or performing arts

About three to five percent of young children could be gifted. These children may become political leaders, artists, dancers, and scientists. These children need to be identified so they can receive the education they require.

Identification

Identifying children who are gifted is difficult. No single test, checklist, or observation will point out all types of giftedness. During the preschool years, observations are commonly made by parents and teachers.

A child's parents are often most familiar with his or her development, interests, and abilities. Because of this, they may be better able to identify their children as gifted.

Teachers are more aware of how the child's behavior compares with that of his or her peers. However, identification of children who are gifted by the teacher is not always the best method. Studies found that teachers who identified giftedness chose about one-third of the children incorrectly. In addition, over half the children who are actually gifted were not identified by their teachers.

There are certain characteristics that can be used to identify the gifted. Many children who are gifted have a constant curiosity about many subjects. Their social and emotional behavior equals or exceeds that of children the same age. They also are more independent and motivated. Chart 30-17 lists other characteristics of children who are gifted.

Teaching Suggestions

The needs of a preschool child who is gifted can be met by including acceleration and enrichment in the program. **Acceleration** is a process in which a gifted child is assigned to a class with older children. The objective is to move the child through activities at a faster pace than children with average ability. After spending a year with older children, the child who is gifted may be ready for even older children.

In **enrichment** the range and depth of experiences is broadened to provide the child with a special curriculum. This process will help the child identify areas of interests.

Children who are gifted often receive enrichment through individual or small group instruction. You or a volunteer may use audiovisual materials, games, and field trips to promote learning. The key to a useful program for these children is to build educational experiences around student interests.

Provide open-ended learning activities for creative children. They prefer loosely structured activities that give them the chance to express their own ideas and inquire and discover on their own.

Children who are gifted in a certain area, such as reading, should have instruction designed to match their skills. They should be provided with a variety of books related to their special interests. It also helps to have an adult who will take the time to listen to the child read and tell the child about the story.

Many small group activities should be planned to build leadership skills. These activities provide children with opportunities to learn to plan, organize, and make decisions.

As a teacher of children who are gifted, you need to understand the problems these children face. These children tend to be self-critical. As a result, they tend to be too hard on themselves. To help them, you will need to provide guidance so they learn to accept failure.

Sometimes, because of a critical nature, a child who is gifted will not involve himself or herself with other children. You will need to help the child learn to be considerate of others. This will help improve his or her social skills.

Learning Disabilities

Although children who have learning disabilities are in almost every classroom, their disabilities can be hard to define. Generally, a **learning disability** means having a problem with one or more basic skills of learning.

Children with learning disabilities model some common traits. They may have trouble following directions or have poor memory skills. After listening to a story, some children cannot remember it. They may have problems storing, processing, and producing information. Others have problems identifying or making numbers and letters. Poor eye-hand coordination skills is another trait.

These learning disability traits may occur in varying patterns. As a teacher, you will need to carefully observe all children for signs of possible learning disabilities. Remember, there are marked differences in young children.

Likewise, there are marked differences within a normal range of development. You may find that children who have disabilities in one area of development are developing normally in other areas.

Characteristics of Children Who Are Gifted
• Early speech
• Advanced vocabulary for age
• Keen observation skills: see more on field trips, in films, or pictures than other children
• Attention span is unusually long for age
• Inquisitive nature: constantly asking questions
• Flexible: adapt easily to new situations
• Persistent
• Responsible for age
• Self-critical
• Strive toward perfection
• Good memory
• Aware of other's feelings

30-17 Early identification of children who are gifted will promote further growth.

Summary

Children with special needs are, by law, entitled to a full, proper education. These children enter the average program through mainstreaming. As a result, children who have special needs may be encountered at any time in your career.

Despite their presence in a typical center, children with special needs still require Individualized Educational Plans. As a teacher, you will need to know how to identify a child with special needs. You then must work with the child so he or she receives the most effective education possible. Teachers must be able to accommodate special needs of children with hearing, speaking, language, vision, physical, health, cognitive, and behavioral disorders. These children must be integrated into a typical program. Teachers must also be able to identify and meet the needs of children who are gifted.

Review and Reflect

1. _____ needs are the most common special needs.

2. _____ is the term used to refer to a regular educational setting in which children with and without special needs are integrated.

3. Each individual educational plan needs six components. Name them.

4. A child who is _____ impaired can often be identified by his or her lack of vocabulary and overall delays in language development compared to nondisabled children.

5. True or false. A hearing aid will perfect a child's hearing.

6. What four consonants are easiest for children to pronounce?

7. Articulation problems usually take the form of _____, _____, and _____ of vowels or consonants or both.

8. The communication problem of _____ may increase when a child feels pressure.

9. One of the smallest groups of children with special needs is the _____ impaired.

10. _____ is the result of a muscle imbalance caused by disuse of the eye.

11. What is the difference between nearsightedness and farsightedness?

12. What actions might you need to take if a child with cerebral palsy is enrolled in your program?

13. _____ is a condition in which the bones of the spine fail to grow together.

14. List four teaching suggestions for working with children who are physically disabled.

15. The most common health problem of young children is _____.
    A. allergies
    B. attention deficit disorder
    C. diabetes
    D. spina bifida

16. True or false. Epilepsy is a disease.

17. _____ is a genetic blood disease.

18. List six characteristics of a child who is gifted.

19. List four signs of a possible learning disability.

20. True or false. Children who have disabilities in one area of development are likely to develop normally in other areas.

Apply and Explore

1. Observe the activities in a child care center that works with children who have special needs.

2. Invite a speech therapist to your class to discuss stuttering.

3. Discuss the disadvantages of labeling children's special needs.

4. Interview an ophthalmologist (eye doctor) to learn how visual impairments are detected and treated.

5. Make a list of items found in a child care center that may cause an allergic reaction in children.

6. Contact your state's Department of Education. Request information on early childhood programs for children with special needs.

7. If possible, visit a rehabilitation center and discuss adaptive aids.

Chapter 31

Parent Involvement

After studying this chapter, you will be able to

■ list objectives for parent involvement.

■ cite advantages and disadvantages of various methods for involving parents in the center.

■ describe the importance of a positive caregiver/family alliance.

■ design a center newsletter.

■ write a letter to parents.

■ plan, conduct, and follow up on a parent-teacher conference.

■ explain how to conduct a discussion group.

■ describe the process of recruiting and orientating parent volunteers.

Terms to Know

parent involvement

newsletters

letters

daily news flash

traveling backpack

problem-solving file

sunshine calls

theme bags

reinforcement

Regular communication is needed to establish and maintain an alliance between parents and caregivers. Parents need caregivers for reassurance and emotional support. Caregivers need to learn from family members to create an environment that reflects the children's home experience. To do this, they need to learn the child-rearing beliefs and culture of the family. This can only occur through mutual support and parent involvement.

Parent involvement refers to patterns of participation in educational programs by parents. There is no one model of parent-program interaction. Parent involvement activities may include assisting in the classroom, helping with fundraising activities, home teaching, supplying classroom resources, and attending parent education classes. Parent involvement can be the key factor in the success of a program, 31-1.

It is unfortunate, then, that little information has been written about the parent-teacher relationship. At times, staff and parents fail to view each other positively. Historically, teachers have neglected to contact parents to praise the child's efforts and accomplishments. Likewise, parents have neglected to express their appreciation of the teachers' roles.

The relationship between parents and teachers needs to be one of mutual support and learning. Often, teachers are surprised to learn that parents want unhurried time to experience relating with them. Parents want to learn more about their children's experiences, interests, and development. To provide this support, teachers and parents need to become partners in teaching young children.

As a teacher, you will need to build positive relationships with parents. To do this, set aside time to communicate with parents, particularly at the beginning or end of the day. During these causal conversations, share your observations and knowledge of early development behaviors. Parents also enjoy learning of their children's preferences and ways of responding to people and things. Begin by noting the child's strengths. Then communicate these strengths to the parents. Parents will then be more accepting when you have to share a child's weaknesses.

Always welcome parents to the center. Whenever possible, include them in program functions. Parents may be observers, resource people, volunteers, or guests at special celebrations. They can share a hobby or interest, as well as ethnic traditions. There should be open communication between parents and teachers. Studies show that teachers who are confident of their skills and abilities are more inclined to include parents in program functions. Likewise, studies show that good relationships with parents affect a teacher's feelings of self-esteem and competence as a teacher.

Objectives

The purpose of parent involvement is to help parents in

- developing an understanding of child growth and development
- gaining confidence in their parenting roles
- learning about their children's experiences at the center
- understanding their children by observing other children
- learning new ways of positively interacting with their children, 31-2
- becoming informed about community resources
- fostering the children's and parent's ability to interact with each other
- extending learning from the center into the home
- understanding how a center-home partnership can promote the children's development

31-1 A parent's involvement in a child's school program reaps many benefits for both child and parent.

31-2 Being exposed to other parents and children means adults can find new ways to work with children.

Parent involvement can be encouraged using several methods. These include written communication, parent-teacher conferences, and discussion groups. When parents see how their involvement can benefit their children, they are more likely to participate.

Written Communication

Three popular forms of written communication are newsletters, letters, and daily news flashes. **Newsletters** most often include information concerning a variety of subjects. They are shared on a regular basis. **Letters** most often address only one subject and are sent out on an as needed basis. A **daily news flash** contains bits of news that parents can discuss with their children. These forms of communication are often written or printed on paper. However, e-mail is also an option that parents and teachers can use for effective communication.

Written communications are popular for one important reason. These forms of communication require less time and energy for the teacher than meetings or multiple telephone calls. If a letter is sent out regarding an upcoming event, the teacher need only type one letter and then send copies of that letter to all parents.

Parents also like written communication for the same reason. A newsletter can be read over a weekend, during lunch hour, or while commuting. This saves parents time and energy, also.

The first step in developing a newsletter or letter is to choose a format. There are some important points to remember. Use the active, not passive, voice. Active verbs provide more enjoyable reading. The active voice states the subject did something. The passive voice says the subject was acted upon. For example, the active voice would say "Reza read books and painted pictures." The passive voice would say "Reading books and painting pictures were Reza's main activities."

Another factor to keep in mind is the educational level of the parents. Your writing style should match this level. A good rule of thumb is to keep your communications short, clear, and simple for all parents. Short messages are appreciated by busy parents. Simple, clear writing prevents misinterpretation of the message.

Newsletters

A newsletter serves as a link between home and school. In most centers, the newsletter is produced and sent out on a regular basis, 31-3. A center might send out newsletters on the first Monday of each month. Other centers, depending on budgets and resources, might send out newsletters on a biweekly basis.

A newsletter may include a variety of information:

- review of special activities
- special activities for children to do in the home
- guidance tips
- upcoming special events at the center
- short articles of interest
- summaries of books or articles related to parenting

31-3 A newsletter can be written quickly using a word processor.

- nutritious recipes
- child development information
- a want-ad section
- a help-wanted section asking for parent volunteers
- upcoming community events of interest to young children and their families
- a "meet the staff" section
- recognition for parent contributions
- suggestions for helping children at home
- a parent exchange section
- reminders of center policies
- helpful hints on parenting

Dear Parents,

Our curricular emphasis next week is "Eating Well: Foods for Good Health." This will be a continuation of our Self-Awareness unit. We have previously explored how our bodies work and the importance of exercise.

Next week the children will be involved in a wide variety of experiences. We will play "fruit basket upset," make collages of healthy foods that are good for us, play "grocery store," participate in having a "pickle party," paint with onions and potatoes, and enjoy tasting a variety of fruits. Thursday will be a very special day—our trip to Connell's Orchard! The children will watch apples being washed, dried, sorted, bagged, and boxed. We will taste "Connell Reds" and drink some delicious apple cider. After the trip, we will write a language experience chart.

Center Activities
Our learning experiences will focus on "Foods for Good Health." Activities will include
- making, preparing, and eating mini-pizzas (with jack o' lantern faces of pepperoni and green peppers)
- creating mosaics of eggshells
- having a play restaurant in our dramatic play area
- acting out a "Good Breakfast" version of the Three Bears (we heard it last week)
- making applesauce
- mixing colors with eyedroppers
- reading "Bread and Jam for Frances"

At-Home Activities
Activities you can do at home to reinforce the concepts learned at the center include
- visiting a grocery store, identifying foods in the Food Guide Pyramid: breads, cereals, rice, and pasta; vegetables; fruits; meat, poultry, fish, and alternates; and milk, yogurt, and cheese
- looking through old magazines, cutting out pictures, and making a collage of "Good Foods" for the whole family
- reading labels with your child, especially focusing on sugar (in its many forms) content within certain foods
- encouraging your child to try new foods (you can, too)
- allowing your child to help in the kitchen
- involving your child in planning what to eat for a meal

Here's to healthy eating!

Smiles,

Judy Gifford

31-4 Use detailed, descriptive language when writing a parent letter. It is an inexpensive way to keep all parents informed.

The design of a newsletter can also allow for a blank section. This section can be used by the teacher to write a brief, personal note. This should be a positive note about the child. For instance, a teacher may write, "I'm so pleased with James; he has learned how to tie his shoes."

Another section could also be provided for parents. After reading the newsletter, the parents might write their comments and/or thoughts. Perhaps they could respond to the newsletter or submit ideas or information for future issues. This way, the newsletter can be a two-way communication tool.

Letters

Letters are another useful written communication tool. Letters can be used to touch base with one parent or an entire group of parents. Letters are often one page long and sent on a weekly basis. Thus, parent letters can supplement parent newsletters.

The first letter sent to parents should introduce the teachers and staff to parents. This letter can also address classroom goals, rules, and expectations. The first letter should also welcome parents to observe and/or take part in center activities.

After the first letter, subsequent letters should include the theme of the week. Special center activities should be noted, along with the goals for the week. New songs and fingerplays should be written out with the accompanying music or actions that go with the play. Field trip sites, dates, and times should be included. Parents should also be thanked for any favors. Home learning activities for the parents to do with their child should be shared. Include with these activities a rationale for their use. This will make parents feel involved in their child's education. An example of a parent letter is shown in 31-4.

Families always enjoy reading about their children. On some occasions, you might wish to mention the children in a parent letter. When doing so, be sure to include each child in the classroom. For example, if the class has vegetables for its theme, ask each child to share his or her favorite vegetable. Report this information in a parent letter.

At times, you may choose to send home a special letter during the week. This letter should outline something special the children did on a special day. It may be an event, such as a field trip, or an activity within the classroom, 31-5. This letter can promote a learning experience between parents and children.

Daily News Flash

Parents and teachers may be too busy for daily in-depth, face-to-face communication. A daily news flash can be an effective tool for

We went to the apple orchard today.
We rode in a big yellow bus.
We saw many trees with apples on them.
We observed the beauty of apples on the trees.
The guide showed us four parts of an apple—
    stem, skin, meat, and core.
We tasted green, yellow, and red apples.
Tomorrow we will make applesauce.

To: Parents
From: Miss Libby
Activity: Field Trip to the
        Apple Orchard

31-5 This letter is intended to promote discussion between parents and children.

communicating with parents. The flash may contain news about special occasions or interesting events such as the following:

- We made blueberry muffins today.
- Erica lost her tooth today during lunch.
- Mrs. Huth is the new center cook.
- Henry is the name of the center's pet gerbil.
- Toby has a new brother named Ivan.

The daily news flash may be posted at the center's main entrance, on a classroom door, or on a bulletin board. Some teachers even use a computer screen to share this information on a daily basis. Others have been successful in videotaping classroom experiences and sharing them using a television monitor.

Class Videos

Prepare videos of the children involved in activities that can be checked out and shared with families. You may want to tape special days such as birthdays, Halloween, Valentine's Day, and other holiday celebrations. Tapes of favorite fingerplays and stories can also be interesting. Parents enjoy tapes of children participating in theme-related activities. Tape them in the dramatic play area acting out stories, building with blocks, preparing foods, and experimenting with creative media.

Parent-Teacher Conferences

Parent-teacher conferences are one way to involve parents in their children's center program. Conferences help parents and teachers understand the children. Parents will share what children are like at home. Teachers will share what children are like at the center. When these two viewpoints are shared, everyone gains, especially the children, 31-6. Plans can then be made to meet the needs of the children.

There are three phases to parent-teacher conferences. The first phase is planning. The second phase is the individual conference. The final phase is the follow-up.

31-6 Through parent-teacher conferences, the parent can gain insight into how best to work with a child.

Planning

Planning includes setting basic rules that will help you work successfully with the parents. Before the conference, spend time planning. A good conference does not just happen. It needs to be carefully planned if you are to win the respect of the parents. The responsibility for the success of the conference lies largely on you as the teacher.

Conferences provide an opportunity to review each child's progress. This time should provide an objective review of the child's total development. Begin the planning phase by gathering developmental data on the child. Gather records on the child's emotional, social, cognitive, and physical development. This information can most often be obtained from developmental checklists and from anecdotal records.

Some teachers use planning sheets to prepare for conferences. After reviewing all anecdotal records and developmental records, this information is recorded on the planning sheet. Included are the following:

- daily routines
- types of play
- activity preferences

- fine muscle skills
- large muscle skills
- social-emotional development
- relationships with children and adults
- cognitive development
- eating habits
- sleeping habits

The planning sheet is divided into sections. For instance, one section might cover these routines: dressing, rest patterns, eating, and cleanup, 31-7.

Be prepared to share children's portfolios with their parents. Begin by collecting notes, developmental assessments, and observations. Then continue by collecting some of the children's artwork to share with the parents. Make sure that the child's name and date are on each piece. Photographs, tape recordings, and notes can also be useful. If developmentally appropriate, ask each child to tell you a story about a picture. Record the story as the child speaks.

Video recordings are also becoming popular for use in parent-teacher conferences. A week or two before a conference, videotape each child engaging in classroom activities. Allow three to five minutes per child. Review the tape before the conference, and note the start and stop numbers for each child.

Preparing the Parent

A brief newsletter can be sent home explaining the purpose of the parent-teacher conference. Include in the newsletter the date(s) the conferences will be held and the length of the conferences. Generally, a half hour is adequate. In addition, tell parents they should feel free to use part of the time for questions they may have.

First Impressions

The first impression you make with children's parents is important. Be prepared. Have your notes outlined, including what you would like to discuss. Use your notes during the conference. This will show the parents that you are well prepared.

As you think through the conference, keep in mind that you will set the tone for it. If you are nervous and anxious, parents will likely feel the same way. If you are calm, parents will likely be calm, too. Your goal is to set the proper tone for a successful meeting.

Questions

You may ask parents questions during the conference to help them think. For instance, invite them to share how their children act at home and what their children's interests are. It is best to plan your questions before the meeting.

Ask open-ended questions if you want more than a yes or no answer. The "w" questions are many times the most successful. These include why, what, how, when, and where. Make sure to provide parents opportunities to share and ask questions.

The Setting

The conference setting can greatly influence success. Find an area in the center that is private. No interruptions should occur during the conference. To ensure this, place a sign on the door that states a parent-teacher conference is in session and must not be interrupted. If the conference is scheduled in an office, take the telephone off the hook or arrange for messages to be taken.

When an office is used, set chairs in a grouping that will help create a feeling of a partnership. Likewise, avoid sitting behind a desk. This places you in the position of authority. This will decrease the feeling of a partnership.

Scheduling

Scheduling parent-teacher conferences can be a problem. Working parents are only available certain hours of the day. Before you begin

Routines

Dressing:
_____ needs   _____ some   _____ much help
      no help

Cleanup:
_____ accepts   _____ helpful   _____ needs
                                       encouragement

Nap time:
_____ accepts   _____ resists

Eating:
_____ good   _____ fair   _____ finicky eater

Toileting needs:
_____ needs   _____ some   _____ much help
      no help

31-7 If you use a planning sheet, you may wish to divide notes into sections.

making plans, ask parents what time is convenient. Some teachers place a sign-up sheet outside the classroom door, 31-8. Parents desiring a conference can sign up for a time that is best for them. You might find some parents who are not willing to sign up for a conference. However, you may still feel a conference with them would be helpful. When this occurs, call the parents to set up an appointment.

Your schedule may also make scheduling conferences difficult. Time may be taken up by administrative duties. You might try scheduling conferences

- during nap time (one teacher may use this time for conferences)
- before or after program hours
- by hiring a substitute for one day each month
- by hiring a substitute over the noon hour, providing parents can come at this time

31-8 Many parents are at the center every day dropping off or picking up their children. A sign-up sheet posted near the main entrance is a convenient method for scheduling conferences with these parents.

- by dismissing center activities for a day every two or three months (this may not be an option if parents cannot find other care)

Parents' time must also be considered. If families have more than one child at the center, schedule successive conferences. This will prevent the parent from making several trips back to the center.

Plan a 10-minute break after each conference. This will provide you with a chance to record any important information. It will also provide time if the conference runs longer than planned.

Home conferences may also be scheduled when a center conference is difficult to arrange. Dual-career or dual-worker families may find this very convenient. This type of scheduling, however, is costly. It requires more time for travel. Transportation costs are also involved. As a result, not many centers offer this alternative.

A scheduled home visit can be valuable for the teacher. Seeing the child's home environment can provide a better understanding of the child. For instance, the teacher can observe parent-child interactions as well as the home environment.

The Conference

Always begin and end the conference with a positive comment. Parents always enjoy hearing something positive about their child. As you share the comment, try to be relaxed. If you are tense, the parents will be aware of it.

Avoid making general statements. "Tommy is doing fine" or "Jodi is doing well in school" does not give parents much information. Rather, be specific. For instance, you might say, "Travis has really improved in the area of routines. He no longer needs assistance with his clothing when preparing to go outside. At transition time, he takes care of his personal needs in the bathroom. At nap time, he accepts the center's rest pattern. Likewise, he no longer needs encouragement to help during cleanup. In fact, I am so pleased, for he is even encouraging other children to assist."

Watch how you word your comments. As you speak, put yourself in the parents' place. Try to imagine the effects of your remarks. You must evaluate the child's progress without being critical. To do this, always try to use a positive expression. See 31-9.

Language Expressions	
Negative Expressions	**Positive Expressions**
troublemaker	disturbs others at story time
below age	performs at his own level
lazy	is capable of doing more
stubborn	insistent in having his own way
mean	finds it difficult to get along with others
clumsy	is not physically well coordinated
selfish	needs to learn to share with others
show-off	tries to get others' attention

31-9 Practice using positive phrases when talking to others. Such phrases are much more acceptable than negative phrases.

During the meeting, watch for signs of emotion. These signs may include gestures, changes in tone of voice, or expression. If the parent appears uncomfortable, provide reassurance that all information will be kept confidential.

Questions Parents Ask

"How is Divina doing?" "Does Kelly behave at the center?" "Is Kris ready for kindergarten?" All these questions are common for parents to ask. Each question can have several answers. When planning for the conference, be prepared for these questions. Questions may be phrased differently, but they basically include

- Is my child happy in child care?
- How can I help at home?
- Does he or she get along with others?
- Does he or she respect others' property rights?
- How long does he or she nap?
- Does he or she eat a balanced diet?
- Is he or she making progress in all developmental areas?
- Who does he or she play with?
- Does he or she have any special abilities?

Be prepared to answer these questions with positive comments. Instead of labeling a child based on behavior, explain actions using positive expressions.

Listening

Most people can listen to 400 words per minute but only speak 131 words. Based on this difference, a good listener does not jump ahead of the speaker. Give parents time to finish their stories or thoughts.

While a parent is talking, show interest and alertness. Avoid preparing an answer while listening. The parent's last sentence may be a source of new information. This may put an entirely different slant on what was previously shared.

Never interrupt a parent. Also, avoid quibbling over words. Instead, focus intently on what the parent is trying to say. Also focus on areas of agreement. This will encourage more friendly, open communication from the parent.

Working with Parents

Some parents are more difficult to work with than others. For example, a timid parent may be speechless at the start of a meeting. To reassure this parent, be friendly. As you speak, provide this parent with several sincere compliments. Second meetings are often much easier for timid parents.

The worried parent always needs reassurance. This parent can often be identified by hand twirling, handkerchief twisting, or finger drumming. If the parent expresses concern regarding the child's developmental progress, provide reassurance. Often parents are unaware of unevenness of a child's development. They may also be unaware of the "spurts" that can occur in a short period of time.

A parent who is egotistical often enters feeling self-confident and smiling. The parent will want to talk about what a wonderful child he or she has and what a wonderful parent he or she is. With this parent, it is very important to remember that the ego is a precious possession and to comment on the parent's skills.

The critical parent can be hard to work with if not handled properly. This parent has expert opinions on teaching the children in the center. Be accepting. That is, do not show disapproval or surprise as the parent talks. Never argue with this parent or any other. Arguing only arouses resistance and bad feelings. Arguments will not benefit the child. Successful conferences depend on your relationship with parents.

Professional Behavior

Always model professional behavior. If a parent makes a negative comment about another teacher, ignore it. Your attitude should always be positive toward your colleagues. Do not bring up or respond to negative comments about other children or parents.

Ending a Conference

Just as a conference should begin on a positive note, it should also end on one. Summarize major areas that have been discussed. Begin by repeating positive comments made at the beginning of the conference. Note areas that may need attention, including the agreed upon goals and action. Then restate your goals at the center as well as what the parent(s) should do at home. End the conference by again making a constructive, pleasant comment. Let the parents know how appreciative you are of having an opportunity to share their children's progress with them.

Invite the parents to visit the center any time. Thank them for sharing. Stress the importance of shared information and common goals. Then walk them to the door. Leave them with a statement of encouragement or reassurance.

Follow-Up

The follow-up involves touching base again with the parents to make sure actions agreed on in the conference are being followed. It should also include a report of the progress made since the conference. A parent-teacher conference should allow for sharing of information. Just as parents will learn, so will you, the teacher. Specifically, you may learn answers to the following:

- the child's reaction to the center, including likes and dislikes
- how the child spends time outside the center
- what home responsibilities the child has
- special interests the child has shown at home
- the status of the child's health
- who the child prefers to play with in the home as well as in school

Record conference notes in the child's folder. Make a point of calling or sending a note to parents, sharing any progress the child has made. Some teachers schedule time each week to contact parents. Each week they contact a few parents by phone or with a brief note. Over the course of a month, each parent hears from the teacher regarding each child.

Discussion Groups

Another method for involving parents in their children's education is group discussion. Through discussion, parents become familiar with child growth and development concepts. They also learn to notice some crisis points in the family cycle and learn to understand their own roles better.

When conducting discussions, remember that adults

- need to integrate new information with what they already know
- tend to take errors personally
- prefer self-designed learning experiences
- like straightforward "how-to" approaches
- must be physically comfortable
- learn a great deal from interacting with others
- enjoy learning when many senses are used

Group discussions are useful for studying new ideas. Discussions allow several people to take part. Through discussion, individual thinking is challenged. As the group exchanges experiences during discussion, individuals have the chance to study and review their own experiences. They are made to think through their positions. Chart 31-10 lists techniques for helping parents relax in a discussion group.

Group discussion also has disadvantages. First, it most often takes a long time. Other methods, such as a film or lecture, are generally faster. If the group is not handled properly, the discussion may wander. See 31-11.

Preparation

Arrange the room so parents can easily talk face to face. A circle or horseshoe arrangement is usually best. Coffee, tea, punch, and/or water

Techniques to Help Parents Relax
• Place items of interest on the walls for parents to look at.
• Provide refreshments for parents to eat and drink.
• Play soft background music.
• Provide name tags on which parents can write their name as well as their child's name.
• Arrange the chairs in a circle.
• Greet parents individually as they enter.
• Introduce parents to each other.

31-10 Parents are not immune to being nervous when visiting the school. Listed here are several methods for helping parents relax prior to a group discussion.

Advantages and Disadvantages of Discussion
Advantages
• Ideas can be carefully studied.
• Many people can take part.
• Parent educators can note if parents understand the discussion.
• People are forced to think through their problems.
• Disagreement is clarified or agreement is reached.
Disadvantages
• It is time-consuming.
• Parents may pool misinformation.
• Parents expecting to be told what to do may dislike this method.
• Parents can come to the wrong conclusion.
• Tension and emotions may be aroused.

31-11 Before you decide to schedule a group discussion, study the advantages and disadvantages. Will your concerns be best addressed by such a discussion?

should be available for parents when they arrive. If all the parents do not know each other, hand out name tags. These tags should include the child's name under the parent's name. This will allow parents to identify parents of their children's friends. You may also ask parents to introduce themselves before the discussion begins. To encourage the parents to talk, you may want to begin with a short filmstrip or cassette tape addressing the subject to be discussed.

Several problems may arise. Some parents may not feel comfortable taking part. When this happens, ask a question that requires a response. For example, you may ask, "John, how do you feel?" Also, you can build on a previous comment by saying, "John, earlier you said you were opposed to physical punishment. Why do you think you feel this way?"

Another problem that occurs quite often is that small groups begin debating among themselves. If this happens, you will need to redirect the group's attention by asking them to share their comments with the whole group.

Other Methods of Involvement

There are many other ways to involve parents in their children's educations. These other methods are not as detailed as meetings and discussion groups. However, they are useful in their own way. These methods include a lending library, traveling backpack, problem-solving file, bulletin boards, sunshine calls, and theme bags.

Lending Library

A lending library is one way to share parenting information. If space is not available for a parent library, a few shelves in the director's office can be used. Current books and magazines that relate to parenting should be included in the library. Available reading materials can be mentioned during daily parent contacts, at conferences, in newsletters, and/or on the parent bulletin board.

Traveling Backpack

Another method for involving parents in their children's education is the **traveling backpack.** On a rotating basis, the children can choose their favorite books, music cassettes, puzzles, or games. Some teachers even encourage them to include paper and writing tools. When the children take home the backpack, they can share these items with their parents.

Problem-Solving File

Some child care directors use a **problem-solving file** to help parents. This file contains information on problems parents may face. Reading materials such as journal articles and newspaper clippings related to each problem are filed in folders. Topics you may wish to include in a problem-solving file are listed in 31-12. The file can be publicized through newsletters and at parent meetings.

Bulletin Board

Making a parent bulletin board is a convenient way to communicate with parents. Post meeting dates, newspaper clippings, and other center information, 31-13. Inform parents of local events, library resources, and educational television programs. Offer suggestions for choosing toys, books, and nutritious snacks. Handouts on childhood diseases, immunization needs, and child growth and development are also helpful to parents.

Hang the bulletin board in the most visible and well-traveled area of the center. Cover it with

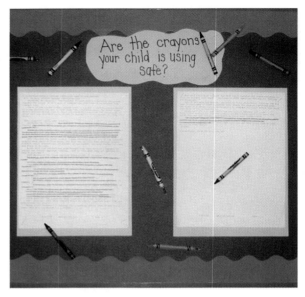

31-13 A parent bulletin board can be set up outside the classroom door to announce topics of interest and messages to parents.

Topics for a Problem-Solving File	
Allowances	Large muscle
Bedwetting	development
Blended families	Lying
Childhood diseases	Mental retardation
Child abuse	Nightmares
Children's clothing	Play
Crying	Personality
Emotional	development
development	Reading readiness
Death	Selecting toys
Divorce	Self-esteem
Food	Separation anxiety
Friendships	Small muscle
Gifted children	development
Handedness	Social development
Identity	Stealing
Cognitive	Speech problems
development	Teething
Language	Television
development	Thumbsucking

31-12 Today, parents are concerned about many topics that affect their children. A problem-solving file is a useful resource for these parents.

paper or attractive fabric. Change the background color often. This alerts parents to updated information on the board.

Sunshine Calls

Sunshine calls create positive parent-teacher relationships and foster two-way communication. A **sunshine call** is a telephone call made by a teacher to a parent to communicate praise and support for the child. The purpose of this call is to share with parents something outstanding or interesting the child has done recently. It also informs the parents of the teacher's interest in and knowledge of their child. For instance, Mrs. Barr may call Mr. Ross to let him know his child has just learned to ride a tricycle, jump rope, or even tie shoelaces.

Some parents have had poor school experiences. When these parents were in school, a call from the teacher usually meant they had done something wrong. Such calls often focused on a social or learning problem. As a result, these parents may be alienated.

Done well, sunshine calls can help dispel some of these negative attitudes and help build good feelings toward the teacher and center. The goal of sunshine calls should be to build feelings of cooperation.

Sunshine calls are valuable for the parent, teacher, and child. For the teacher and parent, the value of sunshine calls lies in the two-way communication that occurs. For the child, the call is a pleasant event. The teacher has taken a personal interest in him or her. A sunshine call, however, should not replace regularly scheduled parent-teacher conferences.

There are several guidelines that must be followed when using the telephone.

- Plan the conversation by carefully choosing what to say.
- Keep the call to about five minutes in length.
- Begin the conversation by asking the parent if it is a convenient time to talk. If it is not, arrange a time to call back.
- Put the parent at ease immediately by telling the reason for the call.
- Share positive statements about the child.
- Whenever possible, also give the parent a word of praise or thanks.

Some adults are at ease with a telephone conversation. They are used to using the phone. Thus, the conversation may be quite relaxed. Also, many teachers and parents are more relaxed when they do not need to talk face-to-face.

Theme Bags

For teaching parents how to promote children's learning at home, some teachers use **theme bags** to involve parents. These bags are in the form of a child's backpack. Included for the parent is a letter of introduction that includes the purpose of the backpack along with the contents. The specific value of the activities are described in terms of the child's development. The letter also includes specific suggestions for successfully involving their children in the activities.

Games, puppets, story books, songs, and charts can all be included. You may even send home a tape recorder to have the parents record their children's favorite stories. Be creative. Study your theme and brainstorm a list of related activities that can be shared at home. Then determine which ones would be the most successful for parents to introduce.

Volunteers

Parents want to be involved in their children's education. Many parents feel a need to improve their relationship with their child's center. A large majority of parents also note they would like to take part in center committees. This is why teachers and directors need to make an effort to involve parents. One way to do this is through volunteer programs.

Some teachers hesitate to include parents in their program plans. Their objections include:

- Parents may not have the time needed to devote to volunteer efforts.
- Parents may criticize the program.
- Parents may not have effective child guidance skills.
- Parents may want to take over classroom responsibilities.
- Children may act up when their parents are present.
- Parents may discuss confidential information outside of school.

These concerns are all worthwhile. However, most can be addressed by carefully recruiting and then training volunteers. These volunteers, in turn, will gain a great deal, including

- personal satisfaction
- a better understanding of child development and child guidance
- an understanding of how children learn
- an understanding of what activities are appropriate for young children
- an understanding of his or her own child by observing him or her playing with other children
- an experience of being part of a teaching team

Recruiting

The best volunteers are those who have an interest in working with young children. Perhaps they would have enjoyed teaching as a profession. Still others are interested in presenting the best experiences to their children. These people are interested in supporting the center and learning more about young children. Many parents have talents or interests that could be useful to your program. A letter that can be used to recruit parents is shown in 31-14. Parent

To: Parents
From: Cindy Mirro, Director

To help us provide a quality early childhood program, volunteers are needed from time to time. If you are interested, please check those tasks with which you would like to assist.

_____ Repairing books

_____ Repairing toys and equipment

_____ Coordinating and assisting with field trips

_____ Assisting with holiday celebrations

_____ Assisting with public relations activities

_____ Supervising art experiences

_____ Cooking with the children

_____ Newsletter editor

_____ Reading stories to children

_____ Sharing a musical instrument

_____ Organizing the fall family picnic

_____ Organizing the spring family picnic

_____ Making puppets, doll clothes, and/or dramatic play costumes

_____ Librarian

_____ Secretarial aide

_____ Other (specify):_____

_____

Please return this note to the basket in front of my office. If you have any questions, please contact me.

_____ _____
Parental Signature   Date

31-14 Written communication is effective when recruiting volunteers for the center.

volunteers are usually interested in what the job entails and what they need to know. Finally, they are interested in the day or dates they are needed, the time, and for how long.

Parent volunteers must be dependable, fond of children, and healthy. In order to take part in a program, parents need some type of orientation.

Orientation

To get the most from volunteers, plan a training session. During this session, share staff expectations of them, including classroom limits and state licensing rules. As you discuss these duties, make the parents feel welcome. In addition, prepare a list of guidelines for parent volunteers as shown in 31-15.

If you have not met parents before the orientation session, be prepared to make a good impression. Studies show that first impressions are lasting impressions. The tone for an entire relationship is often set in the first four minutes.

First, begin by making the parents feel comfortable. Welcome them. Offer them chairs. Begin the orientation by explaining how important volunteers are in a center.

Parents feel good when you remember their names. As you meet each parent, pay attention to his or her name. If you do not hear it, ask the person to repeat it. Say the name to yourself. Memory experts claim that by repeating the name to yourself, you will improve recall by 30 percent. See 31-16.

Whenever possible, use the parent's name in conversation. This process is called **reinforcement**. Through repetition, you will engrave the parent's name in your memory. Studies show people recall faces better than names. Another way to recall parents' names is to observe their

---

Suggestions for Parent Volunteers

General participation. Remember the children always come first. Share your interest in the children in the following ways:
- Provide praise with such statements as "I like your painting," "Thanks for hanging your coat on the hanger," or "You are good at helping with cleanup."
- State your suggestions positively by telling what the child should do. For example, instead of saying "Don't put the puzzle on the floor," tell the child where to place the puzzle. Say "Place the puzzle on the table."
- When talking with the children, get down at their level by squatting or sitting. As the child speaks, give him or her your full attention.
- Speak with other adults only when necessary.
- Never do for a child what he or she can do for himself or herself. That is, always stress independence. Let children put on their own coats, boots, etc. Assist only when absolutely needed, so the children gain independence.
- Avoid discussing the children outside the center.

At story time
- Sit in the circle with the children.
- Allow interested children to crawl on your lap.
- Show your interest in the story by listening attentively.
- If you are asked to read, hold the book so all the children can see.

At the easel
- Children need to wear a smock while painting.
- Only one child should use each side of the easel at a time.
- Encourage the children to replace the brushes in the proper container. (There is one brush for each container of paint.)
- Show an interest in the children's work, but do not interpret it for them. Do not ask children what they have made.
- After children finish painting, print their names in the upper left-hand corners of their work. Capitalize only the first letter of each name.
- Hang finished paintings on the drying rack.
- At the end of the day, encourage the children to take their artwork home.

At music time
- Participate with the children.
- Reinforce the head teacher's actions.
- Show your enjoyment of the music.

31-15 Parent volunteers need guidance when they begin their work at the center.

31-16 Parents and teachers both benefit by wearing name tags. These help everyone learn names more quickly.

faces. Concentrate on one trait such as the nose, eyes, or cheekbones. Then associate the names to their faces. By remembering the parents' names, you will make them feel important.

Schedule

Parents will only return to the classroom if they feel needed. Post a parent helper schedule such as the one shown in 31-17. This will help detail your expectations. You will also need to ask volunteers if there are any questions you can answer.

Thank-You Notes

Send each parent a thank-you note after he or she has volunteered. This gesture will show your appreciation. It will also encourage parents to volunteer again.

Parent Volunteer Schedule				
Time	**Teacher—Judy Tenario**	**Teacher—Lisa Sung**	**Parent—Rita Ulesich**	**Parent—Georgia Suski**
Before class	Set up equipment for special free play activities. Welcome volunteers.	Set up equipment for activities other than dirt-and-water play; special, and paint activities.	Place paper on easels. Put out paint.	Fill water table.
9:00	Welcome children. Supervise free choice of activities.	Welcome children. Supervise free choice of play activities.	Supervise painting.	Supervise water table.
10:00	Serve snack.	Supervise handwashing.	Put away easels and join snack table.	Put away dirt-and-water play equipment and help with handwashing. Assist with snack.
10:30	Help with equipment or story as needed.	Read story.	Assist Judy in putting away equipment.	Assist with story and quiet time.
10:45	Help with special activity, or on alternate days, introduce it.	Introduce special activity, or on alternate days, help with it.	Assist with cooking activity.	Help with special activity.
11:00	Supervise movement activity.	Put away equipment from cooking activity.	Assist with movement activity.	Assist with movement activity.
11:15–11:45	Do dishes and pick up classroom.	Supervise play yard.	Supervise play yard.	Supervise play yard.

31-17 Have duties outlined for parent volunteers for the days they work.

Summary

An alliance between teachers and parents is important. Parents play the key role in the physical, emotional, cognitive, and social development of their children. They are the children's primary teachers, as well as partners with the center staff. Involving them in the school program, then, makes sense.

Involve parents in their children's school program by keeping in touch with the parents. Set aside time to communicate with them, particularly at the beginning and end of the day. Conduct parent-teacher conferences during which you can get to know parents one-on-one. Hold discussion groups so all parents can share ideas and get to know one another. Communicate often using these methods: telephone, newsletters, letters, informal contacts, and even e-mail if it is available.

Parents can assume many roles in the classroom as volunteers. With their help, new activities that are impossible without adult assistance can be introduced.

Review and Reflect

1. What is needed to establish and maintain an alliance between parents and caregivers?

2. List four objectives for involving parents in the center program.

3. Name two points to consider when developing a writing style.

4. Newsletters should _____.
   A. include a review of special classroom activities and upcoming events
   B. be negative in nature
   C. be long and detailed
   D. All of the above.

5. What are the three phases of the parent-teacher conference?

6. True or false. About five minutes should be allowed for each parent-teacher conference.

7. The "w" questions are often the most successful for getting information from parents. What are these questions?

8. What is the purpose of scheduling a 10-minute break after each parent-teacher conference?

9. True or false. Always begin a parent-teacher conference with a positive comment.

10. Rewrite the following negative expressions as more positive expressions.
    A. Selfish.
    B. Show-off.
    C. Lazy.
    D. Clumsy.

11. When talking with a parent, avoid preparing a(n) _____ while listening.

12. During a conference, worried parents always need _____.
    A. to be ignored
    B. refreshments
    C. reassurance
    D. None of the above.

13. True or false. Adults tend to take errors personally.

14. List two advantages of group discussions.

15. Disadvantages of group discussions include _____.
    A. too many people can take part
    B. the discussion may wander
    C. parents will take over the discussion
    D. All of the above.

16. What is the purpose of a lending library?

17. A _____ file contains information on difficulties parents with children may face.

18. A sunshine call _____.
    A. is made by a teacher to a parent
    B. is made to share with parents something positive about their children
    C. can help dispel some negative feelings parents may have about school
    D. All of the above.

19. Who makes the best volunteer?

20. Send each parent a _____ after her or she has volunteered.

Apply and Explore

1. Interview several early childhood teachers and find out the strategies they use for developing alliances with parents.

2. Make a list of questions that parents most often ask teachers. Design answers for these questions based on the contents of this chapter.

3. Discuss ways you might build a positive relationship with
   A. a shy parent
   B. a worried parent
   C. an angry parent
   D. an unconcerned parent

4. Write a parent letter about an upcoming field trip to an ice cream factory. Use the active voice.

5. Collect parent newsletters from several centers. Analyze their design and content. Then, based on your analysis, design a newsletter for the A-B-C Learning Center.

6. Invite a child care teacher to your class to discuss parent-teacher conferences. Be prepared with questions to ask the teacher.

7. Brainstorm a list of discussion topics for a parents' group.

8. Identify two advantages for child care teachers who work as partners with parents.

9. Develop a list of materials that could be included in a portfolio for a four-year-old child.

Chapter 32

A Career for You in Child Care

After studying this chapter, you will be able to

- rank your job preferences.
- compile your resume.
- write a letter of application.
- list various methods for seeking employment.
- compute a salary range on which you could live.
- list questions to ask during an interview.
- prepare a teaching portfolio.
- explain the basic interviewing process.
- discuss illegal questions and how to respond to them.

Terms to Know

net income
resume
hidden job market
networking
teaching portfolio

Preparing for your future is both rewarding and exciting. Job hunting is an important, challenging task. To be successful, it must be approached in a thoughtful manner. Successful candidates often treat job hunting as a full time job. They commit themselves to the process 100 percent. They approach the hunt with a plan.

Many child care teachers have been successful using several types of job searching techniques. One method has been to apply directly to the employer or center director. This contact may be in the form of a request for an application, a visit to the center, or a telephone call. Usually these contacts are made just before their courses to meet state licensing guidelines or early childhood certification are completed.

Answering newspaper ads is one more way to seek employment, 32-1. Check the want ads on a daily basis. If you notice an appealing position, contact the center director at once. If a telephone number is listed, a call can be made. Many times, positions need to be filled immediately. Therefore, do not waste any time in making a contact.

Ranking Job Preferences

There are many types of jobs in child care. Before you begin hunting, make a list of the types of jobs you would enjoy most. This will help you find the right job. While going through this process, consider your skills.

If you are good with infants and enjoy them, think about working in an infant center or as a home child care specialist who is responsible for an infant.

32-1 Many new child care teachers find their first jobs through newspaper ads.

Job Preference List

12	parent education coordinator
11	infant teacher
4	toddler teacher
1	preschool teacher
2	child care teacher
5	Montessori teacher
6	parent cooperative teacher
8	teacher's aide
9	center director
10	assistant director
3	kindergarten teacher
7	kindergarten aide
13	Head Start teacher
14	school-age child care teacher

(Number one denotes most desirable)

32-2 How would you rank this list in terms of job preference?

Chart 32-2 lists several child care positions. Rank them in order, number one being your first choice. This process can help you determine your ideal job.

Salaries

Salaries for early childhood workers vary. As a part of your job search, you need to determine your minimum net income requirements. Your **net income** is the amount of pay you have to spend after taxes and other deductions are taken from your salary. For some people, this is easy. They simply add up essentials such as food, housing, clothing, and car expenses. For others, this process is more complex. If you are one of these people, you will need to prepare a second budget. The second budget could be labeled the "I wish budget." See 32-3. Figures in this budget should reflect an ideal salary.

After you have finished figuring your budget, add all the categories in each column and enter a subtotal. Most people tend to underestimate their needs. Therefore, add 20 percent to the budget. This can account for miscellaneous expenses. Finally, make an allowance for pay deductions such as federal and state income taxes, health insurance, and social security. You now should have a salary range on which you can live in a reasonably comfortable style.

Resumes

To prepare for your job search, first prepare a resume. A **resume** is a brief summary of your qualifications, skills, and experience. The purpose of a resume is to secure an interview and/or inform a potential employer of your qualifications and experience. If your resume is effective, you will receive invitations to interview from potential employers.

Resumes also serve many other purposes. First, a resume may serve as your own self-inventory. Having an objective list of your background and skills can be quite helpful when

A Monthly Budget		
	"Rock Bottom" $ Spent per Month	"I Wish" $ Spent per Month
I. Necessities		
food	_____	_____
housing	_____	_____
transportation	_____	_____
personal care	_____	_____
health care	_____	_____
clothing	_____	_____
insurance	_____	_____
other: _____	_____	_____
Subtotal I:	_____	_____
II. Extras		
entertainment	_____	_____
recreation	_____	_____
gifts and contributions	_____	_____
savings	_____	_____
education (optional)	_____	_____
other: _____	_____	_____
Subtotal II:	_____	_____
III. Taxes and Social Security		
Add 30 percent of Subtotal I + Subtotal II Subtotal III:	_____	_____
IV. Miscellaneous		
Add 20 percent of Subtotal I + Subtotal II Subtotal IV:	_____	_____
V. Total		
Subtotal I	_____	_____
Subtotal II	_____	_____
Subtotal III	_____	_____
Subtotal IV	_____	_____
Total:	_____	_____

32-3 It is important to know your salary needs before applying or interviewing for jobs.

looking for a job. It can also serve as a starting point in an interview. A well-written resume will give the employer information on which to base the interview. After the interview, your resume will help the employer recall your experiences as well as the interview.

Preparing a Resume

A well-prepared resume plays an important role in your job search. First, it instantly creates a favorable impression of you. Second, it creates a desire on the part of the employer to meet you. In many cases, it is your ticket to a job interview.

All resumes contain key information about the applicant: name, current address, and telephone number are always included. If you are applying for jobs outside your hometown, include the area code with your telephone number.

Remember, your resume represents you. Be accurate and neat. Use simple words and write in a clear, concise manner. Include your educational background, paid and volunteer work experience, professional activities, and other qualifications. Organize the experience section so your strongest experience comes first even if it was not the most recent. Always be explicit. For instance, if you want to share that you are a hard worker, create a statement that will deliver that message: "Worked 20 hours per week during the past two semesters."

Using a resume as a tool, your goal should be to present yourself as an active, well-rounded person. When mailed, your resume should be accompanied by a cover letter. The resume and cover letter should have an easy-to-read format. An example of a resume is shown in 32-4.

Helpful Hints

Directors will quickly look at a resume to find out if you have enough educational background and experience to qualify for the position. If your experience appears to meet the requirements of the job description, the resume is read more closely. At this time, most employers will look for gaps in your employment dates, the amount of space given to earlier jobs, and the emphasis on education.

Are there gaps in your job history? These gaps may make directors wary of problems in your job history. They may signal that you were unemployed between jobs. You may choose to leave out a job on your resume because it does not apply to the position you seek. Perhaps you were unemployed for a legitimate reason, such as returning to school. Be sure to explain such gaps in your cover letter.

When you give the time of your employment, be sure to specify the month and year of the starting and ending date of each job. Listing only years can be confusing to directors. Such a listing can also give the impression that gaps in employment are being concealed. Be honest in

your cover letter and resume. Center directors are experienced at dissecting resumes and cover letters. Avoid omitting facts.

A good resume should reflect progress in a career over the years. Also, directors are more interested in an applicant's most recent accomplishments. Therefore, the most recent job experience should be emphasized. Some resume writers devote more space to an earlier teaching position. This usually means one of two things. It may simply be due to poor judgment. It could mean the applicant has updated an old resume by simply adding a few lines about the new job. Overall, these errors convey a lack of ambition and/or poor planning on the part of the applicant. These errors may not always rule out an applicant from an interview. However, they do signal that the applicant needs to be closely reviewed during this process.

The director will also review a resume to see if there is too much stress on education and non-job factors. When an applicant has been out of school for several years, the resume should stress work experience. Applicants who stress post-secondary honors may be focusing too much on the past. If the applicant stresses more non-job factors, this may indicate where his or her real interests lie.

Students who are recent graduates have a special challenge. How can you stress work experience if you have little or none? Do not overlook any previous unpaid work experience. Any practice teaching or volunteer work in your field of study can be included on your resume. Any involvement in professional organizations related to your field of study such as an affiliate of the National Association for the Education of Young Children may also be included. You may wish to explain any leadership roles you assumed, or any skills you developed that will help you on the job.

Poor typing or writing skills and grammatical errors will always reflect badly on the applicant. Basic mistakes may cripple your job search. In fact, some highly qualified applicants have failed to obtain interviews because of poor writing skills. It is always wise to ask a friend who has outstanding writing skills to proofread any cover letters and resumes before you send them to an employer.

Sharon Kaminski

University Address:
University of Wisconsin-Stout
Tainter Hall
Menomonie, WI 54751
(715) 555-1111

Home Address:
109 Liberty Street
Valders, WI 54362
(414) 555-4422

Education

University of Wisconsin-Stout
- Graduating June, 1998 with a Bachelor of Science in Early Childhood Education.
- 3.83 (out of 4.0) cumulative grade point average.
- Dean's List: 1996-present.

Valders High School
- Graduated June, 1993.
- Activities: member of National Honor Society and school band, and president of women's volleyball team.

Experiences

Wee Care Child Care Center, Atlanta, Georgia, June, 1997-September, 1997
- Assisted head teacher with all program activities during the summer session.
- Created new teaching aids for art, science, music, and social studies activities.
- Supervised adult volunteers.

Course Assistant, Early Childhood Department at University of Wisconsin-Stout, September, 1996-June, 1997
- Coordinated teacher education resource room: maintained files, ordered materials, and designed room layout.

Valders Public Schools, September, 1993-June, 1994
- Assisted kindergarten teacher with special activities: coordinated and supervised holiday parties, prepared teaching aids, and maintained classroom centers.

Activities

International Relations Council, University of Wisconsin-Stout
- Delegate to State Model United Nations.

Dean's Student Advisory Council, University of Wisconsin-Stout
- Advised Dean on students' activities. Coordinated special school events including Parents Weekend.

Student Ambassador, University of Wisconsin-Stout.
- Visited community high schools to recruit students for the University of Wisconsin-Stout.

Interests

Alpine and cross-country skiing, reading, gourmet cooking.

References available upon request.

32-4 This in one example of a resume.

Avenues for Seeking Employment

Early childhood job seekers may use a number of methods to find employment. These methods include mailing cover letters with resumes and placing or answering ads in the newspaper. Career fairs and networking provide other opportunities to search for positions. Successful applicants also do not overlook the hidden job market.

Make sure your cover letter and resume are forwarded to the proper person. Find out the name of the individual who is responsible for hiring and address your letter to that person.

Newspaper Ads and the Internet

Answering newspaper ads and responding to announcements on the Internet can be helpful when looking for work. As a job seeker, make a habit of reading the ads every day. Newspaper ads are alphabetized from A to Z. Ads for child care center staff may be listed under different areas. Therefore, study the entire section. Examples of titles related to child care include child care teacher, infant teacher, toddler teacher, preschool teacher, child care teacher, early childhood teacher, school-aged child care teacher, program coordinator, curriculum specialist, and activities director. If you are looking for an administrative position, look closely for descriptions such as director, administrator, or coordinator.

If an ad appeals to you, respond according to the instructions given in the ad. Some ads contain telephone numbers. In this case, do not wait; call or e-mail right away, 32-5. Telephone numbers are most often included when a position must be filled as soon as possible.

If a phone number is not given, send your resume with a cover letter to the address or post office box listed. Attach a cover letter noting the date you are able to begin work and your interest in the position. Successful candidates tailor their letters to fit the specifications given in the ad. An example of a cover letter is given in 32-6.

If an advertisement does not ask for your salary requirements, do not mention them in your letter. By including a salary figure, you could be screened out and not have the chance to interview. Some ads state the exact salary or range

32-5 Quick action is needed if a phone number is included with a newspaper ad.

they will pay. For instance, an ad might note the exact dollar figure per hour or a range of several thousand dollars. Many times when a range is provided, the ad might state that salary is open "based on experience" or "based on educational background." See 32-7.

Internet Job Search

Have you ever thought about knocking on doors using the Internet? By using an Internet browser, you can search for a job. Job hunting on the information superhighway can be fun and rewarding. Although you may begin with a goal in mind, chances are you may encounter better contacts than you expected. On the Internet, there are thousands of home pages that will offer you assistance. A home page will provide you addresses.

Joining a chat room (discussion group) in your field is another way to find a job. Some professional associations sponsor list servers, message boards, and use net news groups.

August 1, 1998

Alex Briones
Director
Child Development Center
1318 Hillcrest Road
Springfield, MA 56789

Dear Mr. Briones:

While searching for job positions on the Internet, I read your advertisement for a teacher. I am interested in obtaining a position in the child care field and in relocating to Springfield, Massachusetts.

I hold a certificate in early childhood education. My interest in early childhood education as a profession started while I was in middle school. Since then, I have baby-sat, assisted with the preschool program at my church, and worked in an after-school program in a local center. These experiences convinced me of my interests, skills, and enthusiasm for working with young children.

My resume is enclosed for your consideration. You will see that both my experience and education match the qualifications outlined in your advertisement.

Thank you for considering me for a position in your center. This is exactly the type of opportunity I am seeking. If I can provide you with any additional information, please call me at 789-555-5748 or e-mail me at chak@uwstout.edu.

Sincerely,

Kim Cha

Kim Cha

32-6 Include a cover letter with your resume when responding to newspaper ads.

Head Teacher at the Sheboygan Early Childhood Center. Applicant must hold a two-year certificate from an accredited institution of higher learning. Salary range from $1,400 - $2,000 per month.
Call 1-414-555-4598 or e-mail: eccenter@sheboygan.edu

32-7 Newspaper ads give a short summary of the open position.

Placing Ads

Newspaper ads, ads in professional journals, or ads on the Internet can help you make your availability known. They are quite helpful if you are moving to another area. For example, you may want to work as a child care teacher in New York City after graduation, but you live in Chicago. You could place an ad in the New York Times in the positions wanted section of the paper.

Before placing an ad, write, e-mail, or call to find out the cost. The cost of placing an ad varies depending on the city, circulation of the paper, size of the ad, and the number of days it will run. Often, charges are either on a per word or per line basis. Depending on your budget and the costs of advertising, you may have to limit the length of your ad.

Placing a position wanted ad is a "passive" job search technique. It requires employers to seek you out. However, most employers will actively pursue only the most qualified candidates. Therefore, this method works best for those people who are experienced. It is best to also use "active" job search techniques.

College or School Placement Offices

Most early childhood certificate and degree programs provide a placement service. The purpose of this service is to find positions for graduates. Placement offices are usually located on campus. Employers are encouraged to call or electronically transfer information for the office to post job opportunities, 32-8. Likewise, employers are given help finding qualified graduates when they contact the office.

As a student, you will be asked to prepare a file concerning yourself. This file may be on paper or on a computer disk. Regardless of the format used, this file will usually include a standard form prepared by the college or school placement service. The form lists your current address, schools attended, degree earned, and past work experiences. In addition, your file will contain your resume and letters of recommendation from faculty and/or previous employers.

The Hidden Job Market

Many job candidates are most successful when they focus their efforts on the **hidden job market**. These are jobs advertised informally

---

Position:
Head Teacher, Child Care Program
Full-Time Position
Yearly contract renewal for a maximum of three years.

Date Available:
August, 1998

Job Responsibilities:
Head Teacher in child care center. Plan and implement a developmentally appropriate curriculum for three- and four-year-old children. Supervise a teacher's aide and volunteers from a local community college. Assist Director in applying for accreditation. Plan and implement parent meetings, conferences, and related activities.

Qualifications:
- B.S. degree in Early Childhood Education is required, graduate work preferred.
- Must be certified to teach preschool in Texas.
- Experience in assessment, curriculum development, and program evaluation.
- Demonstrated excellence in teaching young children for a minimum of three years.
- Demonstrated ability to interact positively with people and work cooperatively with other staff members, parents, students, volunteers, and children.
- Must be able to organize and coordinate activities with volunteers.
- Must be able to motivate children in a creative environment.
- Must be able to demonstrate initiative and continuous professional development.

32-8 Notices posted in school placement offices often give a comprehensive summary of the open position.

through word of mouth. Many child care positions are never listed in help wanted ads, in early childhood journals, or with placement offices. Rather, these jobs are filled through word of mouth. To find out about such openings, you as a job seeker should contact center directors personally. This can be done through a letter, a telephone call, or e-mail. Some candidates have met with success by arranging a visit to the center and then asking about job openings. Even if no position is open at the time of the visit, some applicants have been called later when jobs become available.

Get to know early childhood staff workers in the community. One way to do this is to join the local chapter of the National Association for the Education of Young Children. When you attend meetings, try to meet as many people as possible. Always let them know of your job search and when you will be available. In addition, become active in the organization. Volunteer for committees. Show the membership you are willing to work and are professionally motivated.

Networking

Networking is a process of building relationships with people who can help you. It is an important skill to develop for becoming connected with others. Networking is the jobseeker's most powerful tool. Almost 80 percent of positions are found through some type of networking. One way to have your resume on the top of a file is to have recommendations from people respected in the field. To find these people, you need to go where they are. Attend meetings of early childhood organizations, workshops, conferences, seminars, open houses, job fairs, and center tours. Since networking is a process, it usually takes several contacts to build a relationship. These contacts may be person-to-person meetings, phone conversations, e-mail contacts, voice mail, letters, and notes.

Maintaining a Filing System

Keep a file of all the centers or schools you have contacted. Make a photocopy of each cover letter you send or maintain copies on a computer disk. You may also prepare index cards or a file on your computer for each contact, 32-9. If you

32-9 A card file is one method of keeping your job search information organized.

get a call from a director, you should quickly be able to retrieve the information and refresh your memory on the open position. To assist in this process, always keep a record of the school's name, address, telephone number, contact person, and date the contact letter was mailed.

If you have answered an ad, you may want to attach a copy of the ad to your cover letter or index card. When you receive a response (whether negative or positive), record this on your cover letter or index card. Make notes of interviews, thank-you notes, and other contacts on each letter or card as well.

Preparing for an Interview

Job offers only happen during or after an interview. Interviews are the single most important aspect of a job search. When preparing for an interview, think positively. Picture yourself walking into the interview confident and relaxed. Get in the habit of being enthusiastic. Remember, enthusiasm is catching. It indicates appreciation and interest. Often, if you are enthusiastic, the interviewer will also share this feeling.

Employers want to hire self-directed people who have a range of skills. They want people who are dependable, enthusiastic, and committed to the child care profession. They also want people who work hard and learn fast. They want people who manage their time well and who look for extra work when their work is done. In order to run a quality center, directors need to hire people who are resourceful.

Chart 32-10 outlines traits for which employers look when hiring people to work in early childhood centers. In preparation for an interview, read the statements and check those that match qualities you would be able to bring to a position. Completing this task will bolster your own self-image. The exercise will help you get a clear picture of your skills. It will also prepare you to make a persuasive presentation that is needed during an interview.

Preparing Your Questions

In nearly all interviews, applicants are given the opportunity to ask questions. Thus, smart applicants always prepare questions for an interview. Learn everything you can about the center. You might form questions by talking to teachers who have taught at the center or asking questions of parents who have children attending the center. You can get general information about the center from the local Chamber of Commerce. Some questions you may wish to ask during an interview include

- What is the educational philosophy of your center?
- To what extent may I implement my own ideas?
- Is the staff encouraged to attend conferences? If so, how often may a staff member attend, and who pays the fees?
- What audio-visual equipment is provided by the school?
- How often are parent conferences scheduled?
- Does the center send home a weekly parent letter or monthly newsletter? If so, who is responsible for writing and editing them?

Asking questions tells the interviewer that you are serious about a job. You want the job to be right for you. Take time to practice everything from your questions to your eye contact and posture.

The Interview

When you go to a job interview, take a copy of your resume, arrive on time, and look professional. If you are female, wear an attractive dress or skirt and blouse. If you are male, wear a nice pair of slacks (no blue jeans) and a shirt or shirt and sweater, depending on the weather. Avoid overdressing. Instead, try to wear clothes that an early childhood professional would wear on the job. A simple rule is that you should always dress for the job for which you are applying. Have a good haircut, shined shoes, and clean clothing. Do not chew gum during the interview. This may offend the interviewer(s). Remember, you want to come out a winner.

Make eye contact, smile, and greet the employer with a firm handshake. Many interviewers begin an interview simply by introducing themselves and welcoming you to the center. This is usually followed by small talk that might include the weather or a center activity. After this, you will probably be told information about the job. The interviewer may then ask you structured questions concerning your education

Positive Traits of Early Childhood Workers

- Flexible
- Energetic
- Self-confident
- Enthusiastic
- Mature
- Willing to do extra work
- Patient
- Cooperative
- Easy to get along with
- A fast learner
- A good time manager
- Creative
- Cheerful
- Resourceful
- Dependable
- A good planner
- Committed to teaching
- Open to new ideas
- Self-disciplined
- Dedicated to hard work
- Motivated
- Self-reliant
- Thorough
- Self-directed
- Friendly

32-10 Deciding which of these traits fit you will help you focus on your best traits and skills during an interview.

or experience. Provide full, focused answers. Avoid answering a question with "no" or "yes." Instead say "no, but" and "yes, and." After all questions have been answered, the interviewer will ask you if you have any questions. At this point, you can ask those questions you prepared beforehand. Avoid asking questions about vacation time and breaks. The interviewer may think your main concern is with nonwork functions.

Follow the lead of the interviewer. Throughout the interview, listen with an intelligent, intent look on your face. When necessary, ask questions that will help you better understand the job. Other tips for successful interviewing are listed in 32-11.

Be careful not to volunteer negative information about your former employer or yourself. Employers are seeking positive people to work for them. If you were not happy in a previous job or jobs, you may not be happy with this job either. Thus, it is vital not to mention anything negative. Focus on the position.

Throughout the interviewing process, you will need to sell your positive qualities. When asked what you did during your practicum, student teaching, or last job, do not recite the daily schedule or curriculum. Instead, state specific things you did to improve the center or classroom. For example, you might tell about how you made protective education part of the curriculum. Perhaps you revised the format for parent letters and reorganized the children's library in addition to teaching a group of three-year-olds.

Interview Questions

Prospective employers usually decide before the interview what information they need to share with you about a job. Job expectations, duties, and benefits are often included. Specific questions that you may be asked are also recorded, 32-12. The following questions are often included:

■ Will you please share your educational background?

Tips for a Successful Interview

- Be on time.
- Present your best appearance.
- Extend your hand to greet the interviewer with a firm handshake.
- Use the interviewer's name and smile as you speak.
- Bring a resume and your teaching portfolio with you.
- Remain relaxed and friendly.
- Listen carefully.
- Convey a positive attitude.
- Show your enthusiasm.
- Stress your strengths.
- Use active verbs while speaking.
- Personalize your questions.
- Respond to questions carefully.
- Be truthful; if you do not know an answer, say so.
- Provide more than a "yes" or "no" response to questions, but be concise.
- Thank the interviewer for his or her consideration at the end of the interview.
- Send a thank-you note.

32-11 The interview is your chance to make a good impression. Following these tips will help you.

32-12 Interviewers often prepare questions for the applicant ahead of time. They may record the applicant's answers during the interview.

- What philosophy of education did that center have?
- What type of course work did you have?
- Do you have previous job experience? If so, describe your positions.
- Why are you looking for a new job?
- What are the most important characteristics of a teacher of young children?
- How would you describe your teaching style?
- Where do you see yourself professionally 10 years from today? Describe that job.
- Why are you interested in this job?

In addition, any of the following questions may also be asked:

- What is the value of children's play?
- How would you handle a child that is always hitting others?
- How would you plan a developmentally appropriate curriculum?
- How do you think your references described you when they were contacted?
- How would you handle transitions?
- How would you relate to parents?
- What is most annoying about children?
- On what basis do you plan curriculum for young children?
- What would you do if a child kicked you and said "I don't like you"?

Employers who have had training in interviewing techniques may ask the following questions to find out more about your performance in your previous position:

- What disappointments did you face in your last teaching position?
- In what areas did your supervisor criticize you?
- In what areas did your supervisor compliment you?
- For what things did you need guidance or help from your supervisor?

Questions will also be asked to determine your level of motivation.

- Why did you select teaching young children as a career?
- Why did you apply for this job?
- What is your long-term career objective?

- What are you looking for in this position that you have not had in past positions?
- What type of position would you like to hold in three years? Ten years?

It is not unusual for an interviewer to ask "What are your weaknesses?" If this happens, sit quietly for a moment. It is always a mistake to quickly answer a question off the top of your head. Give each question some thought, then form a response in your mind. Then respond carefully and positively. Do not put yourself down while answering this question. Rather, share your growth by saying something like "I have really developed skills in classroom control" or "My parent interaction skills really grew during the last few weeks of my student teaching." Or express your weaknesses in a positive way: I care too much about the children, I take my work too seriously, I try too many new ideas, etc.

Teaching Portfolio

Bring along your teaching portfolio to demonstrate your growth and success. Your **teaching portfolio** tells a story about your efforts, progress, and achievements. Your portfolio should contain evidence of your competence. Chart 32-13 contains the contents of a teaching portfolio.

Offer to share your teaching portfolio. You may say "I brought along my teaching portfolio. I would like to share the contents with you." While sharing the contents, use descriptions to support your materials. Explain why you chose each piece to include in the portfolio.

Exercise care so that your portfolio does not take the form of a scrapbook. This type of portfolio should include your philosophy of teaching. One way to organize a portfolio is to have a table of contents with two major subheadings. The first subheading could be labeled "Background Information." Your resume and background information on your teaching experience could be included. Also include information on your teaching goals, letters of recommendation, and teachers' evaluations of your work.

The second subheading could be labeled "Teaching Artifacts." This section of the portfolio

Teaching Portfolio

Table of Contents
Anecdotal records
Critical incident journals
Photographs of bulletin boards and room
    arrangement
Parent letters
Lesson plans
Curriculum units and themes
Resume
Teachers' evaluations
Videotapes of teaching
Teacher-made materials
Letters of recommendation
Educational philosophy and teaching goals
Extracurricular activities

32-13 Keep the contents of your portfolio updated to reflect the progress of your career.

should focus on the actual process and outcomes of teaching. Lesson plans, unit and theme plans, videotapes, parent letters, and examples of teacher-made materials could be included.

Legal Problems in Interviewing

At both the state and federal level, it is illegal to discriminate on the basis of age, sex, national origin, race, or religion. Most employers do not intend to use information obtained from an interview in order to discriminate. However, such information could affect the hiring decision. Therefore, it is illegal for an employer to ask questions about an applicant's race, national origin, or religion.

Interviewers are limited in the questions that can be asked. For example, a parent of small children cannot be asked how the children will be cared for while he or she is working. Likewise a parent cannot be asked about a spouse's employment or salary.

Women cannot be asked if they are planning to have a family or are currently pregnant. Inter-

viewers are also forbidden to ask applicants their marital status or the number of children they have. Chart 32-14 lists questions that may be asked. To prevent discrimination, all applicants for a job should be asked the same questions during an interview.

Despite the fact that they are illegal, you may still find yourself being asked some of these questions. Some prospective employers may purposely ask such questions to discriminate. Others, however, may simply ask them in an effort to get to know you better or make you feel at ease. These interviewers may not even know that the questions they ask are illegal.

If you are ever asked an illegal question, it is up to you to decide what the intent of the interviewer was. Based on your judgment, use discretion and tact to handle the situation. You may decide to simply answer the question. If you believe the person's intent was to discriminate, and then you are offered the job, you may ask why the question was asked. If the person's answer concerns you, you may decide to decline the job offer.

You may also choose to not answer the question. Do not accuse the person of discrimination. Instead, you may say simply and calmly "I am sorry, but I am not required to answer that question."

Ending the Interview

An interview can be ended with words and/or through actions. Verbally, the interviewer may thank you for coming to signal the end of the interview. Nonverbally, the interviewer may sit up straight or stand up. This gesture means the interview is over. At this point, the interviewer has obtained all the information from you that is needed. Respond by thanking the interviewer for his or her time. See 32-15.

Many people are disappointed when they learn they were not successful in getting the position. If you feel this way, do not think something is wrong with you. It is not unusual to feel depressed or feel a slip in your self-esteem. These feelings will pass.

Legal Questions	
Subject	**Interviewer**
Age	Only a question to determine if you meet state licensing requirements related to age. Date of birth
Arrest record	Nothing
Marital status	Nothing
Convictions	Only on convictions that would affect the job position.
Education	Only questions related to training and experience related to the position.
Family	Only questions related to meeting work schedule.
Disabilities	Only questions about disabilities that would affect job performance.
National origin	Only questions about ability to read, speak, and write the language the job requires.
Organizations	Only questions about participation in professional organizations related to your ability to perform the job.
Pregnancy	Only questions about anticipated absences from the center.
Religion	Only questions about anticipated absences.

32-14 Interviewers are not allowed to ask questions that may result in discrimination.

32-15 Be sure to leave the interviewer with a positive impression of you.

Thank-You Notes

Always write a brief note thanking the people who interviewed you. Sending a thank-you note will make you stand out. This simple courtesy is observed by as few as 10 percent of job seekers. In the letter, mention the secretaries, if appropriate. Also, your letter will serve as a reminder to those you met. Even if you are not hired for that position, these people may remember you for future openings. They may even pass your name on to someone else who is searching for a child care employee.

On the Job

Positive human relations are key for success in any position. As a new employee, make every effort to get along with the staff, 32-16. The best way to do this is to observe, listen, and gently question.

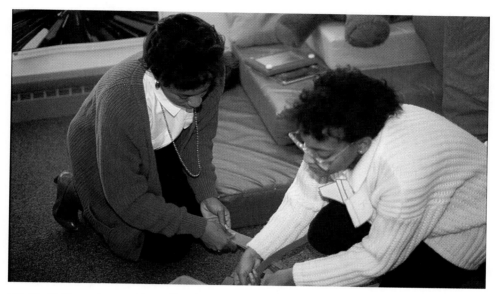

32-16 Getting along with staff members is as important to job success as working well with children.

Make a list of questions to show you are interested in knowing more about your job and improving your skills. As you think of each question, write it down. When there is time, ask your supervisor. If this person does not know the answer, he or she will likely direct you to someone who knows. Show respect for the knowledge and experience of your fellow employees. This attitude will promote good working relationships on the job and mutual respect in the future.

Summary

Searching for an early childhood position is a rewarding, but sometimes frustrating, experience. During your search for a position you can learn a great deal about yourself: likes, dislikes, strengths, weaknesses. A well-organized search is never boring!

While every person's search is different, there are some generally accepted guidelines for conducting your hunt. Start with a resume. Use your resume when you meet with or talk to potential employers.

When you secure an interview, be prepared. Bring your teaching portfolio along to share. Be prepared to answer the interviewer's questions. Also have questions of your own to ask the interviewer. Conduct yourself in a professional manner and show your enthusiasm for the child care field.

Once you have a job, observe, listen, and question. Make every effort to promote a good working relationship.

Review and Reflect

1. If you notice an ad for an appealing position, _____.
   A. wait a few weeks and then contact the center director
   B. contact the center director at once
   C. place your own ad in hopes that the center director will contact you
   D. None of the above.

2. A _____ should include a list of your qualifications, skills, and job experience.

3. True or false. Some highly qualified job applicants may not obtain job interviews because of poor writing skills.

4. How can a recent graduate stress job experience on his or her resume?

5. What is the major disadvantage of placing a position wanted ad?

6. What is the hidden job market?

7. What steps might you take to learn about job openings through the hidden job market?

8. When preparing for an interview, _____.
   A. think positively
   B. put the interview out of your mind until the time it is scheduled
   C. it's best if you are nervous
   D. None of the above.

9. Asking questions about a job shows the interviewer you are _____ about the position.
   A. desperate
   B. serious
   C. undecided
   D. None of the above.

10. True or false. For a job interview, you should always dress for the job for which you are applying.

11. If an interviewer asks you what your weaknesses are, you should _____.
   A. answer quickly
   B. think for a moment before answering
   C. refuse to answer
   D. None of the above.

12. Your teaching _____ tells a story about your efforts, progress, and achievements.

13. True or false. It is illegal to discriminate on the basis of an applicant's religion.

14. Why should you write a thank-you note to your interviewer following a job interview?

Apply and Explore

1. Prepare a resume. When you finish, ask your teacher for suggestions on how you might improve it.

2. Prepare a teaching portfolio. Practice describing the contents to a friend.

3. Clip ads for child care positions from the newspaper. Rank these positions according to your preference.

4. Attend a meeting of a local chapter of the National Association for the Education of Young Children. Talk with a variety of the members to learn about their work.

5. Conduct a survey of the salaries paid to teachers and assistant teachers in your area.

6. Role-play a job interview with a classmate.

7. Write a cover letter to accompany your resume.

Appendix

Developmental Traits of Children from Birth to Age Twelve*	
Birth to Two Years of Age	
Motor Skills	
1 Month	Does not control arm and leg movements since movements are still reflexive. Needs support for head. Without support, head will flop backward and forward. Lifts head briefly from the surface in order to turn head from side to side when lying on tummy. Twitches whole body when crying. Keeps hands fisted or slightly open. May hold object if placed in hand, but drops it quickly. Follows moving object briefly if the object is within the line of vision.
2 Months	Can keep head in midposition of body when lying on tummy. Can hold head up for a few minutes. Can turn head when lying on back. Cycles arms and legs smoothly. Movements are mainly reflexive, but may become voluntary. Grasps objects in reflex movements, but grasps are becoming voluntary. May hold object longer, but drops object after a few minutes. Uses improved vision to look at objects more closely and for a longer time.
3 Months	Can move arms and legs together. Turns head vigorously. Can lift head for several minutes. Can sit briefly, with support.
4 Months	On tummy, can lift head and chest from surface, using arms for support. On tummy, may roll from side to side. Can maintain a sitting position for several minutes if given proper support. Uses hands more skillfully. Begins to use mitten grasp for grabbing objects. Looks from object to hands to object. Swipes at objects, gradually improving aim.
5 Months	On back, can lift head and shoulders off surface. Can roll from tummy to back. When supported under arms, stands and moves body up and down, stamping feet alternately. Helps when being pulled to a sitting position. Can sit supported for 15 to 30 minutes with a firm back. Reaches for objects such as a cradle gym with good coordination and aim. Begins to grasp objects with thumb and fingers. Grabs objects with either hand. Transfers objects from one hand to the other, dropping objects often.
6 Months	Rolls from back to tummy. On tummy, moves by pushing with legs and reaching with arms. Gets up on hands and knees in a crouching position, but then may fall forward. Is able to stand while supported.

*The items listed are based on average ages when various traits emerge. Many children may develop certain traits at an earlier or later age.

Motor Skills (Continued)	
6 Months (continued)	May be able to sit for short periods of time. Reaches with one arm and grasps object with hand, then transfers the object to other hand, then reaches for another object. Holds an object in both hands. Learns to drop an object at will.
7 Months	Crawls awkwardly, combining movements of tummy and knees. Likes to bounce when in standing position. May be able to pull self up to a standing position. Can lean over and reach while in sitting position. Has mastered grasping by using thumb in opposition to fingers. Holds an object in each hand. Brings objects together with banging noises. Keeps objects in hands most of the time. Fingers, manipulates, and rattles objects repeatedly.
8 Months	Sits alone, steadily, for longer periods of time. Crawls. Achieves sitting position by pushing up with arms. Learns pincer grip, using just the thumb and forefinger. Is able to pick up small objects and string.
9 Months	Sits alone. May try to crawl up stairs. May be able to move along furniture, touching it for support. Uses index finger to point, to lead, and to poke. Waves "bye-bye."
10 Months	Likes to walk holding on to caregiver's hands. Climbs up on chairs and other furniture. Stands with little support. Can release grasped object instead of dropping it.
11 Months	Stands alone. Is able to stand and pick up objects. Likes to grasp feeding utensils and cup. May carry spoon to mouth in feeding attempt. Takes off shoes and socks.
12 Months	Climbs up and down stairs. May show preference for one hand. May be able to take off clothes. Walks with one hand held.
13 to 15 Months	Builds a tower consisting of 2 one-inch cubes. Turns pages in a book 2 or 3 at a time. Walks without assistance. While walking, cannot maneuver around corners or stop suddenly.
16 to 18 Months	Walks up steps. Walks well while carrying a toy or pulling a pull toy. Hurls a ball.

Motor Skills (Continued)	
19 to 22 Months	Draws with spontaneous scribbling. Completes a 3-piece formboard. Places 4 rings on post in random order. Rolls, pounds, squeezes, and pulls clay. Kicks backward and forward.
22 to 24 Months	Attempts to stand on balance beam. Builds tower of 6 cubes. Runs without falling. Pedals a tricycle. Kicks a large ball.

Cognitive Skills	
1 Month	Prefers to look at human faces and patterned objects. Listens attentively to sounds and voices. Cries deliberately for assistance. Is comforted by the human voice and music.
2 Months	Coordinates eye movements. Shows obvious preference for faces to objects. Makes some sounds, but most vocalizing is still crying. Shows some interest in sounds and will stop sucking to listen.
3 Months	Is able to suck and look at the same time, thus doing two controlled actions at once. Discovers hands and feet as an extension of self. Searches with eyes for sounds. Begins cooing one syllable, vowel-like sounds—ooh, ah, aw.
4 Months	Likes to repeat enjoyable acts like shaking a rattle. Enjoys watching hands and feet. Looks at an object, reaches for it, and makes contact with it. Makes first consonant sounds—*p, b, m, l.* Smiles and coos when caregiver talks to him or her.
5 Months	Recognizes and responds to own name. Smiles at self in mirror. Can recognize people by their voices.
6 Months	Grabs at any and all objects in reach. Studies objects intently, turning them to see all sides. Varies volume, pitch, and rate while babbling.
7 Months	Enjoys looking through books with familiar pictures. May begin to imitate an act. May say *mama* or *dada* but does not connect words with parents.
8 Months	Likes to empty and fill containers. Begins jargoning by putting together a long series of syllables. May label object in imitation of its sounds, such as *choo-choo* for train.
9 Months	Responds appropriately to a few specific words. Likes to look for content in a container.

	Cognitive Skills (Continued)
10 to 12 Months	Links specific acts or events to other events. Can point to body parts. Likes to look at pictures in a book. Puts nesting toys together correctly. Begins to find familiar objects which are not in view but have permanent locations (looks for cookies after being told he or she can have one).
13 to 15 Months	Identifies family members in photographs. Gives mechanical toy to caregiver to activate toy. Has an expressive vocabulary of four to ten words; most nouns in vocabulary refer to animals, food, and toys.
16 to 18 Months	Demonstrates knowledge of absence of familiar person (points to door, says "gone"). Enjoys cause-effect relationships (banging on drum, splashing water, turning on the television set). Has expressive vocabulary of 10 to 20 words.
19 to 24 Months	Mimics adult behaviors. Points to and names objects in a book. Plays identification games using body parts (points to ears, nose, eyes, teeth, etc., upon request). Has expressive vocabulary of 20 to 50 words.
	Social-Emotional Skills
1 Month	Reacts to discomfort and pain. Recognizes a parent's voice. Is comforted by the human face.
2 Months	Smiles. Is able to show distress, excitement, contentment, and delight. Can quiet self by sucking. Looks at a person alertly and directly. Quiets in response to being held. Shows affection by looking at person while kicking, waving arms, and smiling. May perform to get attention.
3 Months	Shows feelings of security when held or talked to. Senses that the hands and feet are extensions of self. Whimpers when hungry, chortles when content. Communicates with different sounds and facial expressions. Responds with total body to a familiar face. Tries to attract attention of caregiver.
4 Months	Expresses delight and laughs. May form an attachment to one special object. Responds to continued warmth and affection. Shows increased pleasure in social interactions. Enjoys social aspects of feeding time. Becomes unresponsive if left alone most of waking hours.
5 Months	May begin to show fearful behavior as separateness is felt. Distinguishes between familiar and unfamiliar adults. Builds trust when cries are answered; becomes anxious and demanding when cries are unanswered. May be able to play the peek-a-boo game.

Social-Emotional Skills (Continued)	
6 Months	Enjoys playing with children. Responds to affection and may imitate signs of affection. Likes attention and may cry to get it. May begin clinging to a primary caregiver. Laughs when socializing. Smiles at familiar faces and stares solemnly at strangers. Desires constant attention from caregiver.
7 Months	May show more dependence on caregiver for security. Has increased drive for independence but senses frightening situations. Shows desire for social contacts. Thoroughly enjoys company of siblings. Begins to have a sense of humor.
8 Months	Exhibits fear of strangers. May anticipate being left and becomes disturbed. Values quick display of love and support from caregiver. Likes to explore new places, but wants to be able to return to caregiver. Enjoys playing with own image in a mirror. Definitely prefers caregiver to strangers. Is more aware of social approval or disapproval.
9 Months	May show fear of heights; may be afraid to crawl down from a chair. May show a fear of new sounds, such as a vacuum cleaner. Shows interest in play activities of others. Likes to play games like pat-a-cake. Recognizes the social nature of mealtimes.
10 Months	Cries less often. Expresses delight, happiness, sadness, discomfort, and anger. May be able to show symbolic thought by giving love to a stuffed toy. Is more aware of and sensitive to other children. Enjoys music and may mimic movements others make to music.
11 Months	May not always want to be cooperative. Recognizes the difference between being good and being naughty. May say no while shaking head, but will continue to do the forbidden thing. Seeks approval and tries to avoid disapproval. Imitates movements of other adults and children. Likes to say no and shake head to get response from a caregiver. Tests caregivers to determine limits. Objects to having his or her enjoyable play stopped.
12 Months	May reveal an inner determination to walk. Begins to develop self-identity and independence. Shows increased negativism. Enjoys playing with siblings. Likes to practice communication with adults. Continues to test caregiver's limits.
13 to 15 Months	Shows pride in personal accomplishment. Likes to exhibit affection to humans and to objects. Prefers to keep caregiver in sight while exploring environment. Demands personal attention. May show fear of strangers.

Social-Emotional Skills (Continued)		
13 to 15 Months (Continued)	Shows negativism. Enjoys solitary play. Shows preference for family members over others. Recognizes self in mirror and may communicate with sounds.	
16 to 18 Months	Is emotionally unpredictable and may respond differently at different times. Is unable to tolerate frustration. May reveal negativism and stubbornness. May exhibit fear of thunder, lightning, large animals, etc. Is very socially responsive to parents and caregivers. Responds to simple requests. May punch and poke peers as if they were objects. Will perform for an audience. Is unable to share.	
19 to 21 Months	May become possessive about toys, hiding them from others. Likes to claim things as "mine." Gives up items that belong to others upon request. Begins to show sympathy to another child or adult. Continues to desire personal attention. Indicates awareness of a person's absence by saying "bye-bye." May enjoy removing clothing and is not embarrassed about being naked. Reveals a sense of trust in adults. Plays contentedly alone if near adults. Likes to play next to other children, but does not interact with them. Is able to play some simple interacting games for short periods of time.	
22 to 24 Months	Displays signs of love for parents and other favorite people. Is easily hurt by criticism. Becomes frustrated easily. May show some aggressive tendencies, such as slapping, biting, hitting. May assume an increasingly self-sufficient attitude. Wants own way in everything. May dawdle but desires to please adults. Is more responsive to and demanding of adults. Still prefers to play alone, but likes to be near others. Engages in imaginative play related to parents' actions. Uses own name in reference to self when talking to others. Is continually testing limits set by parents and caregivers. Likes to control others and give them orders.	
Two- and Three-Year-Olds		
Gross Motor Skills		
24 to 29 Months	Runs without falling. Pedals a tricycle. Kicks a large ball. Jumps in place. Plays on swings, ladders, and other playground equipment with fair amount of ease. Throws ball without falling. Bends at waist to pick up object from floor. Walks up and down stairs, both feet on step, while holding on to railings. Stands with both feet on balance beam.	
30 to 36 Months	Walks on tip toes. Performs a standing broad jump 8½ inches.	

Gross Motor Skills (Continued)	
30 to 36 Months (Continued)	Attempts to balance on one foot. Walks to and picks up a large ball. Balances on one foot for 5 seconds. Catches a large ball with arms. Walks up stairs with alternating feet. Rides a tricycle. Performs 1 to 3 hops with both feet together.
37 to 48 Months	Walks toe-to-heel for four steps. Balances on one foot for 8 seconds. Catches a beanbag while standing. Performs 1 to 3 hops on one foot. Catches a bounced ball with hands.
Fine Motor Skills	
24 to 29 Months	Inserts key into lock. Turns pages in a book singly. Strings large beads. Copies a circle. Copies a vertical line. Copies a horizontal line. Builds a tower consisting of 6 to 7 cubes. Uses two or more cubes to make a train. Uses one hand consistently for most activities. Holds scissors correctly. Opens and closes scissors.
30 to 36 Months	Builds a tower consisting of 8 cubes. Copies an *H*. Copies a *V*. Copies a circle. Imitates building a three-block bridge. Snips paper with scissors.
37 to 48 Months	Pours liquid from a pitcher. Copies a cross. Builds a tower of 9 to 10 cubes. Completes simple puzzles. Wiggles thumb. Folds paper twice (in imitation). Draws a person with three parts. Cuts a 5-inch piece of paper in two. Traces a diamond. Cuts along a 5-inch line within ½ inch of the line.
Self-Help Skills	
24 to 29 Months	Cooperates in dressing. Removes shoes, socks, and pants. Pulls on simple garments. Unzips zipper. Unsnaps snap. Verbalizes toilet needs. Usually remains dry during the day.

Self-Help Skills (Continued)	
30 to 36 Months	Seldom has bowel accidents. Unbuttons large buttons. Closes snaps. Sits on toilet without assistance. Puts on shoes. Pours well from a pitcher. Uses a knife for spreading.
37 to 48 Months	Washes and dries face and hands. Unbuckles belt. Usually remains dry at night. Turns faucet on and off.
Expressive Language Skills	
24 to 29 Months	Combines two or more words (boy hit). Developing three term relations such as, "I kick ball," "You go home," "See my daddy." Yes/no questions marked only by intonation (Mommy go? You see me?). *No* and *not* used to negate entire sentence (No eat; Mommy no; No sit down). Preposition *in* used (Go in house; Ball in box). Plural used (More cookies; cats).
30 to 36 Months	Negative elements *no, can't,* and *don't* used after subject (I can't eat; Mommy, don't go). Use of different modifiers: qualifiers (some, a lot, all); possessives (mine, his, hers); adjectives (pretty, new, blue). Overgeneralization of regular past with an *ed* (He eated it; I woked up).
37 to 48 Months	Preposition *on* used (book on table; sit on chair). Possessive ('s) used (mommy's coat; daddy's car). *When* questions appear. Negatives *cannot* and *do not* appear. Double negatives appear when using negative pronoun (*nobody, nothing*) or negative adverb (*never, nowhere*). Examples include "I can't do nothing" or "I don't never get to go." Sentences with two clauses are joined (then it broke and we didn't have it anymore).
Language Comprehension Skills	
24 to 29 Months	Child answers routine questions (What is that? What is your name? What is he doing?). Points to six body parts on doll or self. Provides appropriate answers to yes/no questions that deal with the child's environment (Is mommy sleeping? Is daddy cooking?). Comprehends pronouns: *I, my, mine, me.*
30 to 36 Months	Follows two-step directions. Provides appropriate answers for *where* (place) questions that deal with familiar information (Where does daddy work? Where do you sleep?). Comprehends pronouns: *she, he, his, him,* and *her.*
37 to 48 Months	Provides appropriate answers for *whose* questions (Whose doll is this?). Provides appropriate answers for *why* (cause or reason) questions (Why is the girl crying?).

	Language Comprehension Skills (Continued)
37 to 48 Months (Continued)	Provides appropriate answers for *who* (person or animal) questions (Who lives at the North Pole?). Understands the pronouns *you* and *they*. Provides appropriate answers for *how* questions (How will mother bake the pie?).
	Math Readiness Skills
30 to 36 Months	Gives "just one" upon request. Comprehends concepts light and heavy in object manipulation tasks. Comprehends size concepts *big* and *tall* in object manipulation tasks. Comprehends spatial concepts *on, under, out of, together,* and *away from* in object manipulation tasks.
37 to 48 Months	Gives "just two" upon request. Distinguishes between *one* and *many.* Understands the quantity concept *empty* in object manipulation tasks. Understands *smaller;* points to smaller objects. Eighty percent understand *largest.* Counts while correctly pointing to 3 objects. Understands quantity concepts *full, more,* and *less* in object manipulation tasks. Comprehends spatial concepts *up, top, apart,* and *toward* in object manipulation tasks. Comprehends spatial concepts *around, in front of, in back of, high,* and *next to* in object manipulation tasks.
	Social Skills
24 to 29 Months	Likes to play near other children, but is unable to play cooperatively. Becomes a grabber, and may grab desired toys away from other children. Does not like to share toys. Has not learned to say please but often desires the toys of other children. Likes to give affection to parents. May pull hair or bite before giving up a desired possession.
30 to 36 Months	Continues to have a strong sense of ownership but may give up a toy if offered a substitute. May learn to say "please" if prompted. Has increased desire to play near and with other children. May begin cooperative play. Distinguishes between boys and girls. Likes to be accepted by others. Enjoys hiding from others. Likes to play with adults on a one-to-one basis. Enjoys tumble play with other children and caregivers.
37 to 48 Months	Is learning to share and take turns. Follows directions and takes pride in doing things for others. May act in a certain way just to please caregivers. Makes friends easily. Seeks status among peers. May attempt to comfort and remove cause of distress of playmates. Seeks friends on own initiative. Begins to be choosy about companions, preferring one over another. Uses language to make friends and to alienate others.

Emotional Development	
24 to 29 Months	Continues to be self-centered. May exhibit increasing independence one minute and then run back to security of parents the next. Likes immediate gratification of desires and finds it difficult to wait. May exhibit negativism. Continues to seek caregiver approval for behaviors and accomplishments. Displays jealousy. May develop fear of dark; needs reassurance.
30 to 36 Months	May display negative feelings and occasional bad temper. May exhibit aggressiveness. May dawdle but insists on doing things for self. Likes to dress self and needs praise and encouragement when correct. Feels bad when reprimanded for mistakes. Desires caregiver approval. Wants independence but shows fear of new experiences. May reveal need for clinging to security object. Needs an understanding, orderly environment. May have trouble sleeping if the day's events have been emotional.
37 to 48 Months	Is usually cooperative, happy, and agreeable. Feels less frustrated because motor skills have been improved. May still seek comfort from caregivers when tired or hungry. Learns more socially acceptable ways of displaying feelings. May substitute language for primitive emotional feelings. May show fear of dark, animals, stories, and the "bogeyman."
Four- and Five-Year-Olds	
Gross Motor Skills	
4 Years	Catches beanbag with hands. Hops on one foot. Walks down stairs with alternating feet. Throws ball overhand. Carries a cup of liquid without spilling. Rides bicycle with training wheels. Balances on one foot ten seconds. Skips with alternating feet. Walks backward toe-to-heel for four consecutive steps.
5 Years	Marches to music. Jumps from table height. Climbs fences. Attempts to jump rope. Attempts to roller skate. Walks forward, backward, and sideways on balance beam. Catches ball with hands.
Fine Motor Skills	
4 Years	Builds a three block bridge from a model. Completes a six to eight piece puzzle. Folds paper diagonally (three folds). Copies a square.

Fine Motor Skills (Continued)	
5 Years	Copies a triangle. Prints first name. Prints simple words. Dials telephone numbers correctly. Models objects with clay. Colors within lines.

Self-Help Skills	
4 Years	Laces shoes. Buckles belt. Cuts with knife. Dresses and undresses with supervision. Distinguishes front and back of clothing. Zips separating zipper.
5 Years	Dresses and undresses without assistance. Washes self. Puts shoes on correct feet. Unbuttons back buttons.

Language Skills	
4 Years	Understands *has/doesn't have* and *is/is not*. Identifies penny, nickel, and dime. Follows three commands in proper order (clear the table, wash the table, and get ready to go outdoors). Understands the pronoun *we*. Uses irregular verb forms (ate, ran, went). Uses regular tense (ed) verbs. Uses third person present tense verbs (runs, shops).
5 Years	Uses third person irregular verbs (He has a ball.) Uses compound sentences. (I went to the grocery store and I went to my grandmother's.) Uses descriptions in telling a story. Uses some pronouns correctly. Uses words to describe sizes, distances, weather, time, and location. Asks the meaning of words. Recalls the main details of a story. Recognizes some verbal absurdities. Tells original stories.

Math Readiness Skills	
4 Years	Understands the concepts *beside, bottom, backward,* and *forward* in object manipulation tasks. Understands size concepts *short, fat,* and *thin* in object manipulation tasks. Counts 1 to 4 chips and correctly answers questions such as "How many altogether?" with cardinal number. Says correct number when shown 2 to 6 objects and asked "How many?" Can rote count 1 through 9. Understands the concepts of *triangle* and *circle*. Understands the concepts *tallest* and *same size*.
5 Years	Understands *square* and *rectangle*. Understands the concept of *same shape*.

Math Readiness Skills (Continued)	
5 Years (Continued)	Understands the position concepts *first* and *last* in object manipulation tasks. Understands position concept *middle*. Rote counts 1 through 20. Recognizes the numerals 1 through 10. Writes the numerals 1 through 5. May count 1 to 20 objects correctly.
Social-Emotional Development	
4 Years	May not be as pleasant and cooperative as at age three. May be more moody. Strives for independence; resents being treated like a baby. May be stubborn and quarrelsome. Resents directions; thinks he or she knows it all and can do it all. Learns to ask for things instead of snatching things from others. Is increasingly aware of attitudes and asks for approval. Needs and seeks parental approval often. Has strong sense of family and home. May quote parents and boast about parents to friends. Becomes more interested in friends than in adults. Shares possessions and toys, especially with special friends. Suggests taking turns but may be unable to wait for his or her own turn. Likes to play with friends in cooperative play activities.
5 Years	Shows increased willingness to cooperate. Is more patient, generous, and conscientious. Expresses anger verbally rather than physically. Is more reasonable when in a quarrel. Develops a sense of fairness. Likes supervision, accepts instructions, and asks permission. Has a strong desire to please parents and other adults. Still depends on parents for emotional support and approval. Is proud of mother and father. Delights in helping parents. May act protective of younger siblings. Shapes ideas of sex roles by watching parents' behavior. Is increasingly social and talkative. Is eager to make friends and develop strong friendships. May pick a best friend. Prefers cooperative play in small groups. Prefers friends of same age and most often of same sex. Stays with play groups as long as interests hold. Learns to respect the property of friends.
Six to Twelve Years of Age	
Physical Development	
6 Years	Becomes more slender with longer arms and legs; babyhood physique continues to disappear. Loses baby teeth, which are replaced by the first permanent teeth. Is constantly active. Prefers running over walking. May have frequent minor tumbles and scrapes.
7 to 8 Years	May look lanky due to thin body and long arms and legs. Becomes better coordinated; movements become more fluid and graceful.

Physical Development (Continued)	
7 to 8 Years (Continued)	Develops improved sense of balance and timing. Enjoys sports, especially boisterous games. Enjoys skating, skipping, and jumping rope. Girls are developing faster than boys. Able to handle simple tools.
9 to 10 Years	Continues to improve coordination. Improves sense of balance and timing. May develop particular physical skills. Enjoys organized games. Can run, kick, throw, catch, and hit. Improves small muscle skills. Is able to use hands skillfully in building models, learning handcrafts, or using tools. Enjoys drawing. Spends a lot of time and energy playing physical games. Girls may develop adolescent growth spurt.
11 to 12 Years	Boys may grow little in height. Girls may experience growth spurt. Girls may begin menstruation. Likes to test strength and daring. Becomes very conscious of overall appearance.
Cognitive Development	
6 Years	Asks more complex questions than just "Why?" and wants detailed answers. Concentrates on doing one activity for longer period of time. Has improved memory. Has better understanding of the concept of time. Is inquisitive and eager to learn in school. May begin to understand concepts of seriation, conservation, reversibility, and multiple classification. Usually can distinguish between fantasy and reality. Can understand and follow rules.
7 to 8 Years	Accepts idea of rules and that harm might result if rules are not followed. Understands concept of time. Has longer attention span. Understands value of money and may be ready for an allowance. Favors reality; is less interested in fairy tales. Beings to show interest in the collection of certain objects. Likes to help teachers. Enjoys reading animal stories and science fiction stories. May show interest in stories about children of other countries. Refines concepts of seriation; conservation, reversibility, and multiple classification. Beginning to understand cause and effect.
9 to 10 Years	Is able to consider more than one conclusion to problems or choices. Understands more about truth and honesty. Likes to act in a more adult manner. Is still enthusiastic about learning. Likes games that involve mental competition. Enjoys quizzing parents and impressing them with new facts. Shows increasing capacity for self-evaluation. Enjoys mysteries and secrets. May show less interest in TV programs. May continue to show interest in the collection of certain objects.

Cognitive Development (Continued)	
9 to 10 Years (Continued)	Has vocabulary of about 5400 words. Has better use of language and is able to converse with adults. Uses more abstract words.
11 to 12 Years	Is able to detect problems in daily situations and work out solutions. Grasps math concepts and applies them to daily activities. May like group projects and classes based on cooperative effort. Likes active learning, reading aloud, reciting, and science projects. May allow peer relationships to affect schoolwork. Has vocabulary of about 7200 words. May enjoy lengthy conversations with teachers. May enjoy long periods of solitude to think or to work on projects like building models. May show interest in reading; mysteries, adventure stories, and biographies are favorites. Understands concepts of seriation, conservation, reversibility, and multiple classification. Applies logic to problem solving. Uses language to discuss feelings.
Emotional and Social Development	
6 Years	Becomes more socially independent; chooses own friends. May feel less jealous of siblings as outside interests become more important. Is still egocentric, but is becoming interested in group activities. May still have a hard time waiting and taking turns. Wants desperately to be right and to win. Tattles often to check sense of right and wrong. Wants all of everything, making choices difficult. May have nightmares. Sense of humor often expressed in practical jokes and riddles. Beginning to see other's point of view. Learning to share and take turns.
7 Years	May seem withdrawn and moody. Likes to spend time alone or in the background. May feel that everyone is against him or her. Wants and needs approval of adults and peers. Is very conscientious; strives hard to please. Is sensitive and hurt by criticism.
8 Years	Shows more spirit; is willing to try just about anything. May turn to tears and self-criticism upon failure, but recovers quickly. Is able to get along well with others. Chooses companions of same sex and same age. Is very sensitive to what others think. Shows intense interest in groups. Wants to look and act like peers. Enjoys group activities in organizations and in own secret clubs. Chooses a best friend, but may change best friends often.
9 Years	Is relatively quiet. Worries about everything. Sensitive to criticism. Groups of same gender formed. Complains a lot. Has definite likes and dislikes.

Emotional and Social Development (Continued)	
9 Years (Continued)	Begins a new drive for independence; resents being "bossed" by parents. Knows right from wrong; will accept blame when necessary, but offers excuses. Shows increased interest in friends and decreased interest in family. Is interested in group activities and concerns. Competition is common.
10 Years	Is happy with life in general. Likes people and is liked by others. Is dependable and cooperative. Obeys adults easily and naturally. Likes to accept responsibility and tries to do things well. Likes praise and encouragement. Still has strong group spirit, but it may be diminishing. May begin to show more loyalty to a best friend than to the group, especially girls. May enjoy being part of a team. Likes teacher attention and approval.
11 to 12 Years	Is less self-centered. May express great enthusiasm. Likes to plan and carry out activities with a group. Is willing to reach out to others for friendship. Has improved social skills. May show more tact, especially with friends. Is patient and friendly with youngsters. If puberty has begun, may become moody and show signs of emotional turmoil Has strong desire to conform to peers in dress and behavior. Likes team games. Becoming interested in opposite sex; girls more interested than boys.

Adapted from *Parents and Their Children* by Verdene Ryder, Goodheart-Willcox Company, Inc., 1995.

Acknowledgments

Through the long months of revising this manuscript, there were many individuals whose encouragement, support, and expertise helped me immeasurably. My sincere thanks to all of them.

First, I would like to dedicate this book to my sons, John and Mark, who by their development and accomplishments have reinforced the value of the book's content and the importance of nurturing young children. They have more than earned all the credit and appreciation that I can give them; both have become independent, productive, and fascinating young adults.

To my husband, Dr. James Herr, who has supported and nurtured me throughout this process.

To Carolee Samuels, my editor, who has provided stimulating insights and ideas as well as continuous support and encouragement throughout the development of the manuscript and supplements.

To Dr. Judy Jax, who saw a need for this textbook.

To Vicki Weber, Shirley Gebhart, and Betsy Hartford, my secretaries, who so ably transcribed my writing.

To Deanna Applehans, Sandy Duncan, Karen Maggio, and Sue Unger for their professional support and friendship.

To Mary Hopkins-Best, who provided editorial assistance on the Special Needs chapter.

To Sue Dunkley, who allowed me to photograph in her centers.

To Donna Dixon, Eileen Zenk, Margaret Brunn, Judy Gifford, Paula Noll, Peg Saienga, Lori Register, Patti Herman, Janet Massa, Teresa Mitchell, Rita Devery, Dr. Priscilla Huffman, Candy Jordon, Carla Ahmann, Dianne Carriveau, Linda DeMore, Dr. Karen Zimmerman, Dr. Joan Herwig, Elaine Staaland, Janet Mafet, Cari Parent, Betty Misselt, Joanne Fruit, Kari Merritt, Dr. Penny Warnert, Nancy Graese, Nan Olson, Angela La Bonne Kaiser, Paulette Fontaine, Paula Iverson, Jeannette Daines, Sharon Kaminski, Sally Olm, Phyllis Barilla, Irene Larson, Florence Burke, Lori Pioske, Elizabeth Kaster, Jill Behnke, and my parents, Melba and Herb Knutsen, for their support and encouragement throughout this process.

To Yvonne Libby, a former colleague and coauthor on other publications.

To Chancellor Charles Sorensen, Vice Chancellor George DePuy, Associate Vice Chancellors Esther Fahm and Bob Sedlak, and Ed Biggerstaff, Dean of the College of Human Development, for their continuous support of the early childhood program.

To Martin Springer and Kathy Rucker Schaffer for assistance with contributing pictures.

To Gladys Earl, Assistant Professor in the Food and Nutrition Department, who contributed recipes for use in the text.

Finally, to all of the early childhood majors at the University of Wisconsin-Stout and the children in the Child and Family Study Center who have facilitated my thinking for this book.

Judy Herr

Photo Credits

American Red Cross, Washington, DC (by permission), 12-14.

Angeles Group, Inc., 9-12.

Children's World Learning Center, 4-13, 19-9, 19-10, 21-3, 22-3.

Gerber Leisure Products, Madison, Wisconsin, 11-5.

Holbrook 1992 Early Learning Years Catalog, 18-8, 22-3.

Images ©1996 PhotoDisc, Inc., page 12, 1-2, 4-10, page 80, 7-1, 7-2, 7-8, 7-10, 7-12, 7-13, 23-21, 31-6.

Landscape Structures, page 108.

Little Tykes, 4-4, 18-4.

Macander, Jo Ann, Thornridge High School, 22-1.

March of Dimes, 30-10.

New Horizon Child Care, 8-20, 8-21.

Springer, Martin, University of Wisconsin-Stout photographer, 11-10.

The Kids on the Block, Columbia, Maryland, 30-15.

The ServiceMaster Company, 2-2.

Glossary

A

abrasion. A scrape that damages a portion of the skin, such as a skinned knee, scratched arm, or rope burn. (12)

acceleration. Process in which a gifted child is assigned to a class with older children. (30)

accreditation. Certification that a set of standards has been met. (2)

acoustic material. Material used to deaden or absorb sounds. Carpets, drapes, bulletin boards, pillows, stuffed toys, and sand are examples. (8)

active listening. Listening to what is said, then repeating it. (13)

activity patterns. Levels of movements in infants.

adult-centered program model. A structured curriculum format for school-age child care that includes a high level of adult direction. (29)

advocacy group. Individuals who band together to work for a cause. The National Association for the Education of Young Children (NAEYC) is one example of a professional organization whose cause is young children.

AIDS (Acquired Immune Deficiency Syndrome). A disease caused by the human immune deficiency virus. The virus breaks down the body's immune system, leaving the body vulnerable to disease. (12)

allergy. A reaction to a substance, possibly causing rashes, swelling, sneezing, or other reactions. (12)

amblyopia. The result of a muscle imbalance caused by disuse of an eye. Often called lazy eye.

ambulatory. Being able to move from place to place.

anecdotal records. Notes kept by the teacher concerning children's play. (3)

animal stories. Books giving animals some human qualities. Usually, the animal hero has some unusual success or ability. (19)

anaphylactic shock. Extreme allergic reaction to insect stings causing shock symptoms and possibly death. (12)

arthritis. Condition brought on by inflammation that produces swelling of joints and surrounding tissues.

articulation. The ability to speak in clearly pronounced sounds. (6)

articulation problems. Omissions, distortions, or substitutions of vowels or consonants or both. (30)

artificial consequences. Those that are deliberately set up by an adult to show what will happen if a rule is broken. (13)

assessment. A process that involves observing, recording, and documenting children's individual capabilities. This information is the basis for curriculum decisions when planning for one child or groups. (3)

asthma. A respiratory disease that causes labored breathing, gasping, coughing, and wheezing. (7)

attachment. The strong emotional tie felt between people. (4)

audible. Making clear, easily heard sounds.

audio-visual board. A smooth wall board that serves as a bulletin board, chalkboard, and movie screen. (8)

auditory discrimination skills. The ability to detect different sounds by listening. (26)

auditory learner. A child who learns best through hearing. This child is the first to hear a fly in the classroom or a snow plow outdoors. (17)

auditory signals. Informing children of a change through the use of sound, such as a bell, timer, Autoharp®, tambourine, or piano. (16)

au pair. A person from a foreign country who lives with a family and provides child care in exchange for room, board, and transportation. (1)

Autoharp®. A simple chording instrument used to accompany singing. (26)

B

Babinski reflex. Reflex that occurs when stroking the sole of the foot, causing the infant to fan the toes upward.

Note: Numbers indicate the chapter in which the term is defined.

bacteria. Small living organisms causing food-borne illnesses. (12)

behavioral expectations. Rules that children are expected to follow. (27)

behaviors. Refers to any visible activities done by the child. It tells what the child will be doing.

bentonite. A clay product used as a thickening agent for powdered tempera paint.

block plan. A written overall view of the curriculum. (17)

body percussion. Musical movement activities such as stomping feet, clapping hands, patting thighs, and snapping fingers. (26)

bridging. A process of placing two blocks vertically a space apart, then adding a third block. (18)

burn. An injury caused by heat, radiation, or chemical agents, generally classified by degree or depth. (12)

C

capillaries. Small veins in the body.

cautious. Slower to make decisions.

cephalocaudal principle. Principle of development stating that development tends to proceed from the head downward. According to this principle, the child first gains control of the head, then the arms, then the legs.

cerebral palsy. Condition resulting from damage to the brain and characterized by lack of control of voluntary movements.

chalk painting. Art activity in which chalk is dipped into water and used to draw on construction paper. (18)

chalk talk. Storytelling method using drawings made on chalkboard, tagboard, or newsprint. Also called draw and tell.

chant. Song that has word patterns, rhymes, and nonsense syllables in one to three tones repeated in a sequence. (26)

checking-in services. Program assigning caregivers to children in self-care. These caregivers call the children to make sure there are no problems. (2)

checklist. Form of assessment designed to record the presence or absence of specific traits or behaviors. (3)

child care centers. Full-day child care facilities that focus on the child's basic nutritional, social, emotional, intellectual, and physical needs. (2)

child-centered program model. A curriculum format for school-age child care that allows children an opportunity to self-select activities. (29)

Child Development Associate (CDA) Credential. A national credential that requires post-secondary courses in child care education and a minimum number of hours of child care experience. To be eligible for this credential, a person must be eighteen years of age and have a high school diploma. (1)

chronic health needs. Needs for special care caused by an illness that persists over a period of time. (30)

chronological age. Age determined by a birth date. (9)

class A fire. Fire involving ordinary combustible materials, such as common plastics, fabrics, paper, and wood. (10)

class B fire. Fire involving flammable liquids, including gases, grease, paints, and solvents. (10)

class C fire. Electrical fire. (10)

classification. The process of mentally grouping objects or ideas into categories or classes based on some unique feature. (7)

closed wound. An injury to the tissue directly under the skin surface but not involving a break in the skin, such as a bruise. (12)

close-ended questions. Questions requiring few decision-making skills and most often answered with yes or no. Also referred to as *single-answer questions*. (23)

closure. How an activity will end. (17)

coaching. Teaching skill that provides children with ideas for difficult situations. (20)

cognitive development. Growth in the mental processes used to gain knowledge, such as thought, reasoning, and imagination. (4)

collage. Selecting and mounting materials on a flat surface. (18)

color blindness. The inability to see a color. This problem, also referred to as color deficiency, is hereditary.

color deficiency. The inability to see a color. This problem, also referred to as color blindness, is hereditary.

communicable diseases. Illnesses that can be passed on to other people. (12)

compassion. Being aware of others' distress and wanting to help them (7)

concept. A generalized idea or notion. (17)

concrete operations. The use of logic based on what has been experienced or seen. (7)

conditions of performance. List of tools a child will use, including puzzles, paper, scissors, beads, or any other materials and/or equipment found in early childhood settings. This list can also include what the child will be denied.

conflict. Two or more forces that oppose each other. (20)

congenital defect. A condition caused before birth but not hereditary.

consequence. A result that follows an action or behavior. (13)

conservation. Concept that change in position or shape of substances does not change the quantity. (7)

consistency. Enforcing rules in a regular, unchanging manner. (15)

consumable supplies. Supplies that, in most cases, cannot be used again. (9)

contactants. Objects that make contact with the body through touch.

content and process-centered approach. A teaching philosophy in which learning is seen as a constant process of exploring and questioning the environment with hands-on curriculum stressed. (17)

cool colors. Colors, such as blue and green, that make a room appear larger and create a feeling of openness. (8)

co-op. Group of people or groups who join together so they have more buying power. (9)

cooperative play. Type of play in which two or more children interact with one another. At this stage socio-dramatic play begins. (20)

crawling. A skill in the motor sequence occurring shortly after the infant learns to roll onto the stomach.

creeping. Movement in which infants support their weight on their hands and knees, moving their arms and legs to go forward.

cubbies. Top sections of lockers used to store finished artwork, library books, parent letters, and other valuable items. (8)

culture. A group's ideas and ways of doing things—such as traditions, language, beliefs, and customs—that become a learned pattern of social behavior. (24)

custodial care. Type of family day care where emphasis is on a safe and healthy environment, and in which meals are provided. (2)

cystic fibrosis. A chronic hereditary disease that involves persistent and serious lung infections, failure to gain weight, and loose, foul smelling stools.

D

daily news flash. A written communication tool used by centers to inform parents about program or center news. Parents can use this news to bring about verbal interaction with their children. (31)

dawdling. Eating slowly or having a lack of interest in food; sometimes used as an attempt to gain attention. (16)

deferred imitation. Watching another person's behavior, then acting out that behavior. This occurs between eighteen and twenty-four months. (4)

demonstrating. Showing children how to do a task, such as buttoning, zipping, pulling on boots, tying shoes, and putting fingers in gloves.

desensitized. A process in which a doctor injects small amounts of an allergen into the body over a period of time building immunities to an irritant.

development. Change or growth in a human being. Development is usually measured in terms of physical, intellectual, social, and emotional growth. (4)

developmental age. A child's skill and growth level compared to what is thought of as normal for that age group. (9)

developmental norms. Characteristics and behaviors considered normal for children in certain age groups. (3)

diabetes. A disease in which the body cannot properly control the level of sugar in the blood. (12)

direct guidance. Physical and verbal actions, such as facial and body gestures, that influence behavior. (13)

direct learning experiences. Learning experiences planned with a specific goal in mind. (17)

dramatic play. A form of play in which a child imitates others. (20)

draw and tell. Storytelling method using drawings made on chalkboard, tagboard, or newsprint. Also called *chalk talk*. (19)

E

early childhood. The period of life from birth up to nine years of age. (1)

ecology. Study of the chain of life, focusing on water, land, air, grass, trees, birds, and insects. (24)

egocentrism. Quality of people believing everyone thinks as they do. (5)

elimination. Bowel and bladder release.

emetic. A substance used for emergency poisonings. When swallowed, it will induce vomiting. (10)

emotional abuse. Abuse of a child's self-concept by parents or guardians through such acts as providing insufficient love, guidance, and/or support. (10)

empathy. The ability to understand the feelings of others. (7)

employer sponsored programs. Child care provided by an employer.

empty set. A set without any members, such as a set of tables without legs or a set of children with beards. (22)

encouragement. A guidance strategy teachers use to recognize a child's efforts and improvements.

enrichment. A process to broaden the range of experiences with special curriculum. (30)

entrepreneur. A person who starts his or her own business. (1)

epilepsy. A convulsive disorder caused by damage to the brain causing a person to have periodic seizures. (12)

expansion. Technique that involves taking a child's mispronounced words and correctly expanding them into sentences.

expressive language. The ability to produce language forms; used to express a person's thoughts to others. (5)

extended preschool centers. Full-day child care facilities that focus on the child's basic nutritional, social, emotional, intellectual, and physical needs.

F

fairy tales. Books having a theme of achievement. The characters or heroes of these stories must perform difficult tasks in order to succeed. (19)

family child care. Child care that is provided in a private home. (2)

family life stories. Books containing the theme of social understanding. (19)

farsighted. Able to see objects in the distance more clearly than those that are close. (7)

feely box. A box with a circle cut in it large enough for children to put their hands into and identify different objects and materials placed inside by touch. (23)

felt board. A board covered with felt or flannel that is used as a background for placing felt characters and props to tell a story.

field-independent. Children who are more independent and prefer to work on their own. They enjoy competition as well as individual recognition. (17)

field-sensitive. Children who are more interactive with others; volunteering, assisting, and helpful, they also try to gain attention. (17)

fine motor development. Improvement of skills using the small muscles, such as grasping, holding, cutting, and drawing. (4)

first-degree burns. Burns to the top layer of skin. They are the least severe of all burns. Signs include redness or mild discoloration, pain, and mild swelling. (12)

flannel board. A board covered with felt or flannel that is used as a background for placing felt characters and props to tell a story. (19)

flexible rules. Rules that can be adapted to the needs of an individual or a situation. (15)

flipcharts. Stories drawn on large tagboard cards used for storytelling. (19)

flowchart. Drawn chart that outlines major concepts related to a theme. (17)

food-borne illness. Illness caused by foods that are not stored or prepared in a clean or safe manner. (12)

Food Guide Pyramid. A model used for making daily food choices. Made up of six groups, the pyramid shows how food groups work together to form a balanced diet. It also shows the recommended number of daily servings for each group. (11)

food poisoning. An infection occurring in the gastrointestinal tract from eating food with a high bacterial count. Common symptoms are vomiting and diarrhea. (12)

franchised centers. Centers associated with a company. They may be owned by the company or a local owner may have purchased the right to be in the company's franchise.

frustration. Feelings of defeat or discouragement causing tension. (14)

functional stage. Second stage of material use. During this stage, a child will use a prop as intended while playing with other children. (20)

G

gender roles. Behaviors expected of girls or boys. (5)

gerontology. Study of the aged.

giftedness. Having exceptional skills in one or more of six areas: creative or productive thinking, general intellectual ability, leadership ability, psychomotor ability, specific academic aptitude, and/or visual or performing arts. (30)

glaucoma. Condition caused by failure of the eye fluid to circulate in the proper way, resulting in increased pressure on the eye. Over time, this pressure can destroy the optic nerve.

grand mal seizure. A reaction, or seizure, caused by epilepsy. During a grand mal seizure, a person will lose consciousness, jerk, thrash, or become stiff.

grasping reflex. Reflex that occurs when touching the infant's palms. This reflex disappears after the first three or four months after birth.

gross motor development. Improvement of skills using the large muscles, such as running, skipping, and lifting weights. (4)

guidance. Direct and indirect actions used by an adult to help children develop socially acceptable behavior. (13)

guidance problems. Difficulty in controlling or teaching a child or children.

H

hand-eye coordination. Muscle control that allows the hand to do a task in the way the eye sees it done. (21)

head lice. Small bugs that make their homes on the hair and scalp and feed on human blood. (12)

Head Start. A program developed by the federal government to strengthen the academic skills of children from low-income homes, and designed for the social, emotional, physical, and intellectual needs of four- and five-year-olds. (2)

hemophilia. Genetic blood disease in which the blood cannot clot normally.

hidden job market. Jobs advertised informally through word of mouth. (32)

hitching. Movement that occurs after an infant is able to sit without support. From this position, infants move their arms and legs, sliding their buttocks across the floor.

HIV (human immune deficiency virus). A virus that breaks down the body's immune system, eventually causing the disease AIDS. (12)

hyperopia. Difficulty in seeing things that are close. Also referred to as farsightedness.

I

ignoring. Avoiding an acknowledgment to a child's inappropriate behavior if the behavior is not dangerous.

imaginative stage. The third and final stage of material use. Children in this stage do not need real props; they are able to think of substitutes. (20)

I-message. A verbal statement that explains the effect of a child's behavior on others without placing blame. (13)

impulsive. Quick to make decisions.

incest. Sexual abuse by a relative. (10).

incidental learnings. Learning experiences that happen during the course of a normal day. (24)

inclusion. Term used to refer to a regular education setting in which children with and without special needs are integrated. (30)

indirect guidance. Outside factors influencing behavior, such as the layout of the center. (13)

indirect learning experiences. Learning experiences that occur on the spur of the moment. (17)

individual transition. Quietly informing a particular child of a change, such as cleaning up or going to the snack table.

Individualized Educational Plan (IEP). A written strategy for learning designed to ensure that each child with special needs is educated in the most appropriate manner for him or her. (30)

Individualized Family Service Plan (IFSP). Strategy developed when a preschool age child is diagnosed as having a disability. It includes the family's needs in regard to enhancing the child's development, goals for the child, services to be provided to the child and/or family, and a plan for transitioning the child to other services and regular education. (30)

Individuals with Disabilities Education Act (IDEA). Federal law requiring all states to provide education for children who are developmentally delayed. (30)

induce. To produce on purpose.

infant. Term used to refer to a child for the first year after birth. (4)

ingestants. Foods, drugs, or anything taken through the mouth.

inhalants. Airborne substances that are inhaled.

injectables. Chemicals or drugs injected into the body.

insulin. A hormone that is needed to keep sugar in the blood at a proper level. As insulin is released, the blood sugar level drops. (12)

insulin reaction. Occurs in a person with diabetes when the amount of insulin is not properly adjusted.

internal. Under the skin.

irritability. Tendency to feel distressed.

isolation area. Special room or space in the center for children who become ill or show signs of a communicable disease. (8)

K

kindergarten. School for children who are at least four years old. Some kindergartens stress preacademics, while others focus more on social development. Many kindergartens are part of public school systems.

L

laboratory schools. Schools located on a post-secondary or college campus with a primary purpose of training future teachers and serving as a study group for research. (2)

language comprehension. An understanding of language. Sometimes referred to as receptive or inner language. (5)

latch-key. Term used to describe children left in self-care; also refers to children left in the care of a sibling under age 15. (29)

lazy eye. An eye disorder that is the result of a muscle imbalance caused by disuse of the eye. Also referred to as amblyopia.

learning disability. Problems with one or more basic skills of learning. Poor memory skills, trouble following directions, or poor coordination may be signs. (30)

learning objective. Outcomes of an activity that are used to plan teaching strategies. (17)

lesson plan. A written plan outlining specific actions and activities that will be used to meet goals. (17)

letters. Written communication most often addressing only one subject and sent out on an "as needed" basis. (31)

leukemia. A form of cancer that affects the blood-forming organs and the blood. This cancer can cause a sharp increase in the number of white blood cells in the bloodstream.

level of performance. States the minimum standard of achievement and how well one might want the child to do.

licensing specialist. A person employed by a state to ensure that the state's child care rules and regulations are followed. (1)

limits. Classroom rules that protect the health and safety of the children, helping them feel freer to explore. (15)

listening. Giving full attention to another person or people.

M

mainstreaming. Term used for placing children with special needs in a regular classroom, allowing children to learn in a less restrictive environment. (30)

malnutrition. Lack of nutrients in the diet or the inability of the body to use the nutrients in the food. (11)

manipulative stage. First stage of material use. Children in the manipulative stage will screw and unscrew a baby bottle cap. (20)

manuscript writing. A simple form of calligraphy not requiring the sustained muscle control that cursive writing does. This writing involves unconnected letters made of simple, separate strokes. (21)

matching. A form of classification involving putting like objects together. (22)

maturation. Sequence of biological changes in a child giving the child new abilities. (4)

middle childhood. The span of years between ages six and twelve. (7)

modeling. Verbal and nonverbal actions by one person, setting an example for others. (13) Showing the children the appropriate behavior to use during their socio-dramatic play. (20)

molestation. Sexual contact made by someone outside the family with a child. (10)

mono painting. Art activity in which a piece of paper is placed over a finger painting. The papers are patted together, then pulled apart. (18)

Montessori approach. Schools provide children freedom within limits by a rather structured approach, and a fixed method in which materials are presented. (2)

moral development. Process of acquiring the standards of behavior considered acceptable by a society. (7)

morality. Understanding and using accepted rules of conduct when interacting with others. (7)

moro reflex. Reflex that occurs when a baby is startled by a noise or a sudden movement. The infant will fling the arms outward and quickly draw the arms into the chest. Lasts from birth to about three months of age.

motivation. In a lesson plan, a method of gaining children's attention. (17)

motor sequence. Order in which a child is able to perform new movements. Motor sequence depends on the development of the brain and nerves. (4)

multicultural toys. Toys that represent a variety of racial and ethnic groups. (9)

multipurpose dry chemical extinguishers. Only type of fire extinguisher designed to put out Class A, Class B, and Class C fires.

myopia. Difficulty in seeing things that are far away. Also referred to as nearsightedness.

N

nanny. A child care worker who usually provides care in the child's home. (1)

National Association for the Education of Young Children (NAEYC). A professional organization for people working with young children.

natural consequences. Experiences that follow naturally as a result of a behavior. (13)

nearsightedness. The ability to see close objects more clearly than those at a distance. (7)

neglect. Form of child abuse in which the child is not given the basic needs of life. Neglected children may be deprived of proper diet, medical care, shelter, and/or clothing. (10)

net income. The amount of pay a person has after taxes and other deductions are taken from his or her salary. (32)

networking. A process of building relationships with people who can help you. (32)

newsletter. Written communication most often including information concerning a variety of subjects. (31)

nonaccidental physical injury. Physical abuse inflicted on the child on purpose; the most visible type of child abuse. (10)

nontoxic radiopaque plastic. Special plastic added to children's toys making it possible for this plastic to clearly show up on X rays in the event the toy has been swallowed by the child.

normative scales. Lists of characteristics considered normal for children in certain age groups. Sometimes referred to as developmental scales.

novelty transitions. Unusual, new actions or devices to move children from one activity to another.

numerals. Number symbols, each of which represents an amount. (22)

nurture. To educate and nourish.

nutrients. Chemical substances found in foods that are needed for growth and maintenance of health. (11)

nutrition. The science of food and how the body uses it. (11)

nutrition concepts. Basic concepts that will help children develop good lifetime healthy eating habits. (25)

O

obesity. A major health problem caused by overeating. A condition in which the body weight is 20 percent above the normal weight for a given height. (7)

object permanence. An understanding that objects continue to exist even if a person cannot see them. (4)

observation. Informal viewing of a child during self-selected activities, watching for specific behaviors.

omission. Implication that some groups have less value than other groups in our society caused by not mentioning or including a group in teaching. (24)

one-to-one correspondence. The understanding that one group has the same number as another. (22)

open wound. An injury involving a break in the skin, such as a cut or scrape. (12)

open-ended questions. Questions promoting discussion and requiring decision-making skills. (23)

operation. The manipulation of ideas based on logic rather than perception. (7)

overeating. The intake of more food than is needed by the body to function properly, often causing health and emotional problems.

overfamiliarity. Lack of interest in a particular toy shown by children who are given the same toy day after day. (28)

overstimulate. To cause to become overexcited. (14)

P

pantomiming. Telling a story with body movements rather than words. (26)

parallel play. A type of play in which children play by themselves but stay close by other children. All the children may be involved in similar activities, but play between and among the children does not exist. (20)

parent cooperatives. Child care programs that are formed and run by parents who wish to take part in their children's preschool experience. (2)

parent involvement. Patterns of program participation by parents in early childhood settings that are related to their parenting roles. Volunteering in programs, home teaching, and helping with fundraising are examples. (31)

parquetry blocks. Geometric pieces that vary in color and shape used to teach shape concepts. (22)

participation chart. A tool used to gather information on specific aspects of children's behavior. (3)

passivity. Term for describing the level of involvement with a child's surroundings, such as withdrawing from a new person or event.

perceptions. Ideas formed about a relationship or object as a result of what is learned through the senses. (24)

personification. Giving human traits to nonliving objects, such as dolls or puppets. (20)

persuading. Encouraging children to act or behave in a certain way by appealing to their basic wants and needs.

petit mal seizure. An epileptic condition in which the person may have a few muscles twitch briefly or may become confused with the surroundings. These seizures are milder than grand mal seizures.

phrase method. Method of teaching songs using short sections of a long song, having children repeat these sections. These sections are increased until the children know the entire song. (26)

phrase/whole combination method. Method of teaching a song stressing key phrases with rhythmic movement or visual props. (26)

physical age. Age determined by a birth date. (9)

physical development. Physical body changes in a growing individual, such as changes in bone thickness, size, weight, vision, and coordination. (4)

pica. A craving for unnatural foods such as paper, soap, rags, and toys. (16)

picture books. Books having single words or simple sentences and simple plots. (19)

plasticene. An oil-based, commercially manufactured modeling compound available in many bright colors. (18)

policy. A course of action that controls future decisions, such as a center's health policy. (12)

portable kitchen. Kitchen created in the classrooms by placing the ingredients, tools, and other equipment on a low table so all children can watch. Also, portable appliances such as an electric skillet or a hot plate are used rather than a stove. (25)

portfolio. A collection of materials that shows a person's abilities, accomplishments, and progress over a period of time. (3)

positive reinforcement. Molding children's behavior by rewarding positive behavior. (13)

practical life experiences. Experiences in the Montessori curriculum that stress independence for children.

praising. Giving children recognition for their accomplishments.

preschooler. Term referring to children ages three to six. (4)

principle of proximodistal development. Principle noting that development of the body occurs in an outward direction. The spinal cord develops before outer parts of the body; arms develop before hands; hands develop before fingers.

privacy law. A law designed to protect children. It states that a child's records cannot be given to anyone other than parents without the parents' permission. (10)

privately sponsored programs. Child care programs sponsored by a church, hospital, charitable organization, or an individual.

problem-solving file. File containing helpful information on problems parents may face. (31)

program goals. Broad statements of purpose that reflect the end result of education. They state what is important. (17)

projection. A type of play allowing children to place feelings and emotions they feel onto another person or an object, such as a puppet. Through this play, a child may share his or her inner world. (20)

prompting. Making a verbal or nonverbal suggestion that requires a response; used either to stop an unacceptable action or start an acceptable one. (13)

props. Items that relate to the story and would attract children's attention. (19)

prop box. Box containing materials and equipment needed for certain roles in sociodramatic play. (20)

prosocial behaviors. Behaviors that demonstrate cooperation and helpfulness. (12)

prosthesis. An artificial limb, such as an arm, a hand, or a leg.

publicly sponsored programs. Child care programs funded by the government, school district, and/or division of social services.

puppetry. Using puppets in play. (20)

puppets. Figures designed in likeness to an animal or a human, used to enact stories, actions, or thoughts.

purple K dry chemical extinguisher. Extinguisher used to fight Class B and Class C fires. It is slightly more effective against Class B fires.

R

rabies. A disease caused by a viral infection of the nervous system and brain. Rabies is transmitted through the saliva of a rabid animal. (12)

racism. Any action, attitude, or outlook used to judge a person based only on the race of that person.

rating scale. Tool used to record the degree to which a quality or trait is present. (3)

rational counting. Attaching a number to a series of grouped objects. (22)

recognizing. The ability to relate past and present experiences and classify items. Recognizing is made possible by using the senses to learn from repeated experiences. (22)

redirecting. Diverting or turning a child's attention in a different direction. (13)

referral. Directing a parent to obtain a diagnosis from a professional when a problem exists with a child. (30)

reflex. An automatic body response to a stimulus. At birth, an infant's physical abilities are limited to reflexes. (4)

rehearsal. The repetition of information after it is used. (7)

reinforcement. The process of using a parent's name in conversation. Through repetition, a teacher will engrave the parent's name in his or her memory. (31)

resource people. Center guests or field trip hosts. (27)

resume. Brief summary of a person's qualifications, skills, and job experience. The purpose of a resume is to secure an interview and/or inform a potential employer of a person's qualifications and experience. (32)

reviews. Lists and descriptions of books, which can be found in public libraries. (19)

rheumatoid arthritis. Common form of juvenile arthritis that can also strike adults. General fatigue, loss of appetite, aching joints, and a stiffness of joints are the first signs of the disease.

role-playing. A type of play allowing children to mimic the actions of others, such as wife, husband, mommy, daddy, doctor, or police officer. (20)

rote counting. Reciting numbers in their proper order. (6)

routines. Everyday experiences such as dressing, undressing, eating, napping, toileting, and changing activities. (16)

rules. Guides to actions and behaviors that reflect the goals of the center. (15)

S

salt painting. Art activity using salt mixed with colored tempera in shakers. (18)

school-aged child care programs. Programs often sponsored by schools, churches, or child care centers that provide care for children before and/or after school. (2)

science. The study of natural processes and their products. (23)

science table. A table used to display items related to the science area. (23)

second-degree burns. Burns causing damage to underlying layers of skin, requiring medical treatment. These burns are marked by pain, blistering, swelling, and discoloration. (12)

self-concept. Qualities a child believes he or she possesses. A result of beliefs, feelings, and perceptions a child has of himself or herself as part of the world. (5)

self-esteem. The belief that you are worthwhile as a person. (7)

sensory table. Table in the sensory area that gives children practice in social situations. Also known as a water or sand table. (8)

separation anxiety. A child's difficulty in separating from parents, often occurring between nine and twelve months of age. (4)

separation distress. Attachment behavior shown when a child is unhappy because a familiar caregiver is leaving.

seriation. The ability to arrange items in an increasing or decreasing order based on weight, volume, or size. (7)

set. A group of objects that are alike in some way and, therefore, belong together. (22)

sexism. Any action, attitude, or outlook used to judge a person based only on the sex of that person.

sexual abuse. Abuse that involves adults using children for their own pleasure, including rape, fondling, incest, and indecent exposure. (10)

single-answer questions. Questions requiring few decision-making skills and most often answered with yes or no. Also referred to as close-ended questions.

skywriting. Demonstrating the correct way to make a letter by writing it in the air. (21)

social comparison. Process where people define themselves in terms of the qualities, skills, and attributes they see in others. (7)

social-emotional development. Growth in the two related areas of social and emotional skills. Social development involves learning to relate to others. Emotional development involves refining feelings and expressions of feelings. (4)

socio-dramatic play. Social play in which several children play together as they imitate others. 20)

solitary play. Independent play. (20)

sorting. A form of classification involving the process of physically separating objects based on unique features. (22)

specific task assessment. Giving children set activities to determine skill and/or needs. (22)

spectator toys. Toys requiring little action on the child's part, such as battery-powered cars and talking dolls. (9)

spice painting. Art activity in which children spread glue on a piece of paper, then shake spices onto the paper. (18)

spina bifida. A condition in which the bones of the spine fail to grow together, resulting in paralysis.

spiral curriculum. A curriculum based on the fact that as children grow, their circle of interests becomes larger. (17)

staff room. Room provided for staff to spend work-related time away from the classroom. (8)

standard dry chemical extinguishers. Extinguishers used to fight Class B and Class C fires.

staple supplies. Art supplies, such as paper, scissors, paste, glue, collage materials, crayons, watercolor markers, chalk, tape, and paint, that are used in the center on a frequent, regular basis.

stationary equipment. Permanently installed equipment in the play yard, such as jungle gyms, slides, and tree houses. (8)

statute. Formal document drawn up by elected officials outlining a teacher's legal responsibilities in a case of child abuse. (10)

stepping reflex. Reflex that occurs while holding the infant so that the feet are flat on a surface. The infant will move the legs in a walking motion.

stereotypes. Preset ideas about people based on one characteristic such as sex, nationality, or religion.

stereotyping. Showing people in a rigid, traditional way ignoring individual differences.

storybooks. Books that contain pictures but have more words and more complex plots than picture books. (19)

storytelling. Reciting a story or reading aloud from a book. (19)

stress. The body's reaction to physical or emotional factors, often taking the form of tension. (14)

string painting. Type of art activity in which heavy yarn or string is dipped in paint and pulled across a piece of paper. (18)

stuttering. Speech disorder that is often characterized by repetition, hesitation, and prolongation. (6)

suggesting. Placing thoughts for consideration into children's minds.

sunshine calls. Telephone calls made by teachers to parents to communicate praise and support for children. (31)

swimming reflex. Reflex that occurs when holding the infant horizontally, face down. The infant will stretch out the arms and legs in a swimming motion.

T

tactile senses. Senses related to touch, which are stimulated by such activities as cutting and drawing.

teaching portfolio. A collection of materials that tell a story about your efforts, progress and achievements. (32)

telegraphic speech. Two-word phrases used by toddlers when they first learn to combine words. (4)

temperament. Quality and intensity of children's emotional reactions to their environment, such as passivity, irritability, and activity patterns. (4)

texture painting. Using liquid tempera paints mixed with sand, sawdust, or coffee grounds. (18)

theme. One main topic or concept around which the classroom activities are planned. (17)

theme bags. A child's backpack filled with games, puppets, story books, songs, and charts and including a letter of introduction for the parents. (31)

theme walks. Simple field trips taken in and around the center based on a theme. (27)

third-degree burns. Burns that destroy the skin layer and nerve endings, requiring prompt medical attention. (12)

time out. A guidance technique used when a child's behavior cannot be ignored. It involves excusing the child from interacting with others so he or she can calm down and gain self-control. (13)

toddler. Term used to refer to a child from the first year until the third birthday. The term is used because of the awkward walking style of children in this age group. (4)

traffic pattern. The way in which people move through the classroom area, affecting its arrangement. (8)

transition. Changing from one activity to another and/or moving from one place to another. (16)

traveling backpack. A backpack in which children take home their favorite books, music cassettes, puzzles, or games to share with their parents. (31)

U

undernutrition. Lack of proper nutrients in the diet caused by not eating enough food in an otherwise well-balanced diet. (11)

unit-based program model. A curriculum format for school-age child care that revolves around curriculum themes that reflect the children's interests. (29)

V

vegetable printing. Art technique that involves dipping shapes made from vegetables into paint and then pressing the shapes onto surfaces to make prints. (19)

visual learner. A child who depends a great deal on the sense of sight. This child will notice small visual changes in the environment. (17)

voice flexibility. Good speaking voice during routine conversation using a variety of pitches and loudness levels.

W

warm colors. Colors including red, yellow, and orange that make a room appear smaller. (8)

warning. Reminding children to follow classroom rules, stating the misbehavior and the consequences.

water soluble. A substance that can be dissolved in water, such as powdered tempera paint.

water-type extinguishers. Extinguishers designed for use strictly on Class A fires that should not be used on any other type of fire.

whole song method. Method used to teach short, simple songs by having the children listen and then sing along. (26)

wound. Damage to the surface of the skin or body tissue. (12)

Index